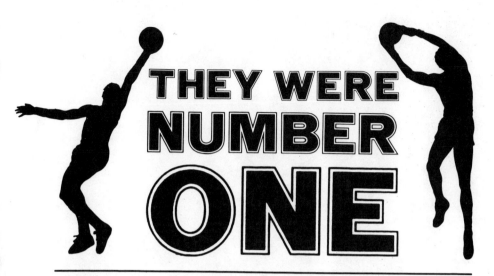

THEY WERE NUMBER ONE

A History of the NCAA Basketball Tournament

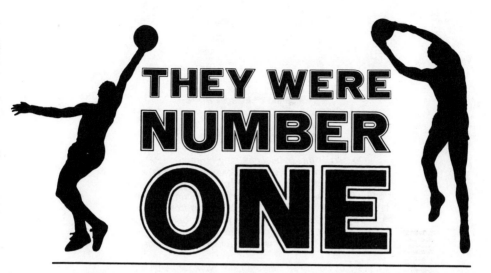

THEY WERE NUMBER ONE

A History of the NCAA Basketball Tournament

ROBERT STERN

LEISURE PRESS
NEW YORK

A publication of Leisure Press.
597 Fifth Avenue, New York, N.Y. 10017

Library of Congress Catalog Card Number 81-85622

ISBN 0-88011-122-4 (cloth)
ISBN 0-88011-219-0 (paper)

To Margaret, who is Number One!

CONTENTS

INTRODUCTION

The 1977-1978 college basketball season was about to start and with the anticipation of a dedicated fan I pored over the pre-season predictions, culled tables of statistics and charted television schedules of weekend games. The past season had finished on a highly emotional note as Al McGuire ended his coaching career with a national champion at Marquette. It was only the latest in a chain of championship tournaments that went back as far as I could remember. To me, the tournament was an annual spectacle resembling a medieval play with its pageantry, confrontations, appeals to loyalty and a cast of hundreds. Yet each year was a different experience with its own unique course, structure, plot and main characters. I wanted to learn more about the NCAA tournament but when I checked in the library I found out that nobody had yet chronicled the history of this unique event.

It was a challenge I rashly accepted, not realizing the scope of the task. But I have not regretted the assignment I took on, an assignment that took three years to complete and which included analyzing and recording every single game ever played in the NCAA tournament, interviewing hundreds of coaches and players, and plowing through stacks of statistics. The best part was talking to the coaches, a breed apart. They loved talking about the game, sharing their feelings and anecdotes with someone who appreciated the sport as much as they did. And their recall even after twenty or more years and hundreds of games was phenomenal. I loved every minute of it. In the process I became a member of the U.S. Basketball Writers Association with the satisfaction of having a vote in selecting the annual All American team.

Until I started the book I had actually attended only one tournament event.

That was a first round triple header in New York's Madison Square Garden in 1958. I cheered myself hoarse as Manhattan upset number one ranked West Virginia with their brilliant sophomore by the name of Jerry West. But I had also seen countless tournament games on television. There did not seem to be another event like it on the sports calendar. This was not a playoff series, like baseball, hockey or professional basketball. One loss and you were on your way home. Major college football had to settle for a mythical title voted on by the coaches or the media but rarely decided on the field. Only college basketball brought together a sizable field of contenders from every corner of the country, displaying a spectum of playing styles. Most had not faced each other before. The resulting team matchups and the absence of a second chance translated into drama and suspense.

Over the years the tournament field increased from eight to sixteen to twenty four to thirty-two and finally to forty-eight. Statistics grow as tournament follows tournament and records are broken by ever more dazzling performances. March is the time for the gathering of local champions. Night after night the field is reduced until only one remains. Number One! Usually as the field shrinks the cream at the top remains, and then the creme de la creme. But in almost every tournament some unheralded band of youths, playing with drive and dedication beyond expectation, score an upset or two or even three, to send some basketball power toppling. The tension and excitement build until that last night when only two teams remain to battle for the national championship.

But it is not only the format that attracted me. I have also been fascinated by this singular sport which can showcase the talents of a brilliant individual star such as a Bill Walton or a Magic Johnson and at the same time, place that performance within the context of a winning team effort. It is as if Nureyev or Baryshnikov are simply members of the corps de ballet, albeit outstanding ones. This combination of individual achievement within the scope and flow of team discipline is what makes basketball such an absorbing sport to watch. There is no I in TEAM, yet each player contributes individually, some more than others, and none can be overlooked.

Success on the court has spread to colleges in every corner of the country. Almost every major conference has had a national champion come from its ranks. The exception is the Southwest Conference. Almost every conference in existence for more than ten years has had a school in the Final Four, with the exception of the Big Sky and the Mid American. Almost every major university in the country has played in the tournament at least once. The exceptions are mostly in the South where Kentucky has dominated the Southeastern Conference for more than half a century. Georgia, Florida, Auburn and Tulane are still waiting for their first appearances as are Army, Nebraska, Northwestern and Seton Hall. Several of these universities emphasize football at the expense of the roundball sport. Auburn won the SEC one year but was barred from the tournament because they were on probation. Seton Hall was a basketball power in the forties and early fifties but chose the NIT over the NCAA tournament.

There have been some great teams that for one reason or another did not play in the tournament. Illinois' Whiz Kids in 1943 and undefeated Army in 1944 declined invitations because of World War II. Kentucky was undefeated in 1954 but had several ineligible, five-year players, and decided to stay home. Some thought it was the best team the Wildcats ever fielded. In 1969 LaSalle won 23 of 24 but was on probation as was undefeated North Carolina State in 1974. Several excellent teams chose the NIT over the NCAA tournament, the latest example being Marquette in 1970.

It is sometimes hard to remember, even among those who follow the sport closely, that schools like Maryland and Brigham Young with their highly developed basketball programs have never won a regional, while Wisconsin was once a national champion and Washington State and Baylor were runners up.

* * * * * * * * * *

Most of the statistics appearing in this book were compiled and distributed by the NCAA. I have listed the records of the teams as they were prior to the start of each year's tournament. I have given a player the title of All American if his name appeared either on the first or second team of the wire services or he was a consensus All American based on the various media that were selecting prior to 1950. Clock time given in the narrative refers to time left unless otherwise specified. Names of teams and players are given as they were at the time of the event. For instance, Oklahoma A and M later became Oklahoma State and Lew Alcindor changed his name to Kareem Abdul-Jabbar.

It has been a struggle to decide how many statistics to include without capsizing the narrative under the weight of numbers. I have tried to keep a balance between informing and entertaining.

Robert Stern
Seattle, Washington

FOREWORD

I remember once saying that the NCAA is so exciting, no coach should be allowed to win more than once. Of course, that was after I had retired from coaching. But the sentiment is true - there is nothing that can touch the electricity generated during NCAA Tournament games.

I remember my first NCAA game. In 1968, my fourth team at Marquette had gotten past a first round thriller (72-71) over Bowling Green. We then moved to the Mideast Regional against Kentucky and we played at their homecourt. In those days I was anti-establishment and Adoph Rupp was the fountainhead of establishment in basketball. I respected his record, but I wanted to aggravate him. I wasn't used to the large press conferences or the media blitz and I didn't know Kentuckians bled blue. So I made the mistake of taking on the Baron in his own territory. We got blown out, 107-89.

I learned a lot at that NCAA game, though, and the following year we were matched again in the Mideast Regionals with Kentucky - only this time the site was Madison, Wisconsin and I was on my own turf. I knew we could win that game and I had my team psyched for it. But after we did win (81-74), I found myself back in my hotel room alone, crying in frustration. I had realized midway through the game that I had keyed my team too high and they were out of control. It could have easily turned into a riot and there was nothing I could do to stop it. I also hit me later that because both teams had fought so fiercely in this game - neither one of us could have been ready to play the next day against Purdue. I learned the fallacy of playing too hard simply to get even.

I said earlier that there is nothing that can touch the electricity during an NCAA Tournament and this is something I still look forward to, even in broadcasting the games. Although the NIT is the oldest basketball tournament, the NCAA has eclipsed it and has really emerged as *THE* tournament. I think there is even more interest in the college playoffs than in pro playoffs because pro players are so proficient and talented that your eyes get tired of their ability. Amateur players are not as habitually perfect, but an audience can appreciate the constant maximum effort and get involved in the spirit of the game and this is what creates tournament fever.

The whole town or city is wrapped up in the games, the medias present a daily barrage of stories on every conceivable aspect of the teams and the tourist-related businesses are deluged. The Russian roulette principle of elimination also makes the tournament very suspenseful. You have to win every game; one slip and it's curtains. But perhaps the most exciting aspect of NCAA Tournament play is that on any given day, any team can win. The tournament favorites don't always play up to form and the possibility of a Cinderella team or a dark horse is very real. (The Marquette team that won the 1977 NCAA Championship for me was certainly a good example. We were the last team to be given an NCAA bid and had had many season losses.)

All of these variables make it next to impossible to predict a clear winner and also create an atmosphere that grows to fever pitch by the Final Four.

As far as the future goes, I can only see the NCAA Tournament growing bigger and better. We have seen players over the years grow bigger, more mobile and more agile. They are also technically better than the first players of NCAA Tournaments because they are specialists - they don't play in other sports in college. They have attended basketball camps and played in summer leagues since they were kids.

Even the coaches are more professional than those early competitors. They attend instructional clinics, they have larger staffs, and they use the best and most modern equipment to train players.

I think that today the tournament games receive more media exposure than even before - but even this will grow. In the future, I think multiple networks will handle the preliminary games and alternate the Final Four. I also feel that eventually the NCAA will reorganize the tournament so that all Division I teams can participate in preliminary games, both physically and monetarily and there will be a more equal sharing of the pot of gold.

Personally, as a coach, I always considered the NCAA Tournament to be the Mount Everest of basketball. Just to be asked to climb it was a compliment. Even though I'm the only coach who ever turned down an NCAA bid (which I don't regret since Marquette won the NIT that year), I've got to admit that one of the greatest and most humbling moments of my life was in Atlanta in 1977 when we took it all. And in all of the other tournaments Marquette played in, I had the same sensation, coming out of the locker room, walking to the court, hearing the noise, and seeing the fans. I felt like a gladiator. At that moment I was at the pinnacle of my profession. And there is no finer thrill than that.

Al McGuire
Former coach of the
1977 NCAA Champions,
Marquette University

1

A History of the NCAA Basketball Tournament

1940 NCAA Champions, Indiana University. 1st row: Jim Gridley, Herm Schaefer, Bob Dro, Marv Huffman, Jay McCreary, Curley Armstrong, Ralph Dorsey. 2nd row: Coach Branch McCracken, Chet Francis, Bill Menke, Andy Zimmer, Bob Menke, Ralph Graham.
(Indiana University Photo)

1

THE BEGINNING *1939-1941*

1939

On Tuesday evening, March 17, 1939, in Philadelphia's Palestra, the National Collegiate Athletic Association opened its first postseason basketball tournament. Three days later, in San Francisco, the western half of the tournament got underway in the city's Coliseum. The following week, the first NCAA basketball champion was crowned in Evanston, Illinois.

The eight teams that competed represented different sections of the country and exhibited varying styles of play. Some depended on ball control, a deliberate offense and a stingy, center-clogging defense, producing low scoring games. Others favored a fast breaking style featuring small, speedy players hurtling up and down the court like human polo ponies. There was one team that relied on height and strength, the ability to rebound effectively and to intimidate its opponents. That team was to win this first tournament.

It may not be entirely accurate to say that the NCAA established its postseason basketball tournament as a reaction to the National Invitation Tournament which had been inaugurated the previous year in New York but certainly the success of that tourney must have had a lot to do with it. College basketball in New York's Madison Square Garden had become enormously popular ever since the first game held there—a contest between New York University and Notre Dame in 1934. The idea of taking basketball out of the narrow confines of the college gymnasium and putting it into a big arena, where much larger crowds would appreciate the excitement of the sport, belonged to Ned Irish. It was he, too, who thought of the idea of a tournament to be played in New York, at the conclusion of the regular season, to determine a national basketball champion. It may have originated from the recent development of postseason football bowl games. The Orange Bowl, Sugar Bowl and Cotton Bowl had been inaugurated during the previous two years and had proven very successful. Americans, only slowly recovering from the Depression, were turning to sports to escape from the frustrations of the daily struggle to make ends meet.

In March 1938 six schools had been invited to the first NIT and its winner, the University of Colorado, considered itself the country's top college team. The NIT in 1939 had an imposing field. Three of the six schools selected, Long Island University, New Mexico A&M and Loyola (Ill.), were undefeated. Two others, Bradley and St. Johns of New York, each had identical 18-2 records. Roanoke College, the sixth school, came into the tourney with a 20 game winning streak. The final was a confrontation between unbeaten LIU and Loyola with the victory going to the New York school.

The NCAA, rather than choose colleges at random, decided to make its tournament nationally representative. It divided the country into eight regions and asked that a selection committee, composed largely of coaches, choose the best school in its region to play in the tournament. Since most of the selection committee coaches came from schools belonging to conferences, the NCAA tourney was composed largely of conference champions while the NIT maintained a more non-conference, or independent school, flavor. But winning one's conference did not automatically qualify one for the tournament. It was the selection committee which decided and they occasionally bypassed the league champion to pick a school with an inferior record but supposedly superior ability. This means of selection inevitably led to squabbling, jealousy, vindictiveness and occasionally unfair decisions. But, in general, the selectees were the best team in the region. It was a durable system and lasted twelve years.

Originally, the NCAA wanted to spread the tournament game around the country, as opposed to the NIT which was held only in New York. This would give more people a chance to see the schools play and cut down on travelling time, which in those days was mostly by train and bus and could be exhausting, as well as expensive. Thus the first regionals (the opening rounds) were held in Philadelphia and San Francisco and the finals in Evanston, Illinois.

The Region 1 representative in 1939 was Brown, a small school from the smallest state but one whose team had the best record (17-3) of any in the tournament. In the years following, the Region 1 bid usually went to the winner of the Ivy League, which was not officially organized until nearly 20 years later. However, in 1939 Brown was not even a member of this unofficial conference though very definitely an Ivy League school. They had a strong team and on two occasions scored more than 80 points, an astronomical figure for that time.

Region 2, consisting of the Mid Atlantic states, sent Villanova, an independent with a 19-4 record. Villanova's team was not considered especially strong, having played a rather easy schedule losing to nationally ranked DePaul and Illinois. But the regionals were going to be played in Philadelphia and Villanova was a local school, so consideration may have been given to the number of fans the Wildcats could attract. In any case, other Region 2 schools such as LIU and St. Johns, which had much better records, were going to the NIT.

Region 3, the southeastern part of the country, produced Wake Forest, the Southern Conference champion, with an 18-5 record. The Region 4 representative was Ohio State, the Big 10 champion. Ohio State's record was an unimpressive 14-6. They were weak offensively, having scored 50 points or more only four times in 20 outings.

Region 5 selected Oklahoma, the Big Six winner (later Big Seven after the admission of Colorado and Big Eight after the admission of Oklahoma State). They had earned the right to play in the tournament after turning back Oklahoma A and M, the Missouri Valley Conference champion, 30-21. For the next eleven years the Region 5 representative would be determined by a playoff between the two conference champions. Actually, Oklahoma's record was an inferior 11-8 and they were forced to share the conference championship with Missouri.

Region 6 was represented by Texas, the Southwest Conference champion with a 19-4 record. Texas had a strange penchant for scoring exactly 41 points during a game. They had done so five times during the season and would again in their first round game. Over the years the Southwest Conference champion would automatically receive a bid to play as its region's representative.

Utah State of the Skyline Conference was selected to play from Region 7. Except for one year during World War II, the tournament always included a team from the Skyline and its successor conference.

The final school to be chosen was Pacific Coast Conference champion Oregon, a school that played a backbreaking 31-game schedule which resulted in a 26-5 record. The PCC was then, and for many years thereafter, split into two divisions, North and South. The California schools made up the South Division and the Washington, Oregon and Idaho schools made up the North Division. They rarely scheduled each other, but the conference champion was determined by the winner of a best-of-three series between division leaders. In 1939 Oregon beat California, the South Division leader, by almost identical scores of 54-49 and 53-47.

Oregon and the other schools in its division played each other four times during the season, a total of 20 games. In addition, Oregon spent considerable time on the road playing in the East and Midwest against such teams as City College of New York, St. Johns, Canisius, St. Joseph (Pa.), Buffalo, Bradley and Western Illinois. Thus they came into contact with different styles of basketball as played in other regions and they learned how to adjust to unfamiliar offensive and defensive patterns. To keep themselves occupied, they also scheduled some non-college opponents such as the

Multnomah AC and Signal Oil, an industry-sponsored amateur team. Oregon was the only school in the tournament which boasted a certified All American. Actually, they had two of them—Urgel (Slim) Wintermute and Robert Anet.

Brown, despite having rolled up some impressive scores, had been trounced twice during the regular season, by Army 50-21 and by Dartmouth 52-30. Some felt the Bruins were overrated. The opening round did nothing to change these critics' minds. In a game that had about as much excitement as a long distance turtle race, Villanova overcame Brown 42-30. Certainly the Bruins showed none of the scoring ability of their earlier games. In the other contest Ohio State beat Wake Forest 64-52, smashing the Palestra record of 53 points by one team. Dick Baker of the Buckeyes also broke the existing individual record by scoring 25 points. This record lasted only one day. Jimmy Hull, Baker's teammate, poured in 28 points as Ohio State rolled to an easy 53-36 victory over Villanova after a 25-10 half time lead.

In San Francisco a disappointing, and disappointed, "crowd" of 3,000 spectators saw two more one-sided games. Oklahoma checked Utah State 50-39 and Oregon was just too tall and strong for Texas, ousting the Longhorns by a decisive 56-41 margin. The first half of the game was fairly even, Oregon leaving the court at intermission with a slim three point lead, 19-16. The second half was a different story as Oregon quickly established dominance over overmatched Texas. They stretched their advantage to 19 points and coasted the rest of the way. In contrast to the games in Philadelphia the scoring was evenly distributed. No player on the Texas team scored more than seven points!

The following evening Oregon again started slowly but picked up momentum after leading Oklahoma by only 21-14 at the half. The Ducks, known as a strong second half team, broke out of their lethargy and won going away, 55-37. Oregon, tall and strong defensively, would not let Oklahoma near the basket and so the Sooners had to shoot from long range; they rarely hit their target.

At Evanston the following Friday night Oregon got off to an untypical fast start and led 6-0 before Ohio State could connect. The rest of the half was fairly even but Ohio State, like Oklahoma, could not penetrate Oregon's defense. Having scored considerably more than their average in Philadelphia, Ohio State, now closer to home, reverted to a more characteristic offensive famine. Hull, despite leading the Buckeyes, was held to 12 points and Baker was shutout completely. Scoring persistently if not spectacularly, Oregon became the first NCAA basketball champion, winning 46-33. Coach Howard Hobson's strategy of exposing his players to a national rather than just a regional schedule during the season had paid off.

1940

Eight different schools were selected for the 1940 tournament. Three non-conference teams and a conference runner up competed in the eastern regionals. Although Dartmouth won the unofficial Ivy crown, they were overlooked in favor of small Springfield College. The Massachusetts school had a nifty 16-2 record but this was mostly against New England and New York teams. The death on February 28 of Dr. James Naismith, who organized the first basketball game at the Springfield YMCA training school which became Springfield College, may have had something to do with this choice, but such a sentimental decision is unlikely. The Region 2 selection of Duquesne was more understandable. The Dukes had lost only to Indiana while establishing a 17-1 record. They had then swept to the NIT final before losing to Colorado.

Region 3 sent Western Kentucky, 24-5, coached by one of basketball's early greats, Ed Diddle. Diddle, who had been at Western Kentucky since 1923 and would continue there for more than 40 years, was one of the most successful coaches in the history of the game. His Hilltoppers, over the years, won nearly three out of every four games they played.

No Southern or Southeastern Conference schools were represented in the tournament, the only time that they were overlooked by the selection committee. Western Kentucky was a defense minded team; in almost 30 games they gave up as many as 45 points only once.

Indiana was selected by the Region 4 committee when Purdue, the Big 10 champion, declined to participate. Indiana may have been the better team since they had beaten Purdue twice. The Hoosier's 17-3 record was attributable to a well-balanced attack in which no single player had to assume the scoring burden.

In the western part of the country Rice represented the SWC with a 21-2 record. Colorado, almost as successful at 17-2, was the Skyline champion. They had lost only to Utah State and to Duquesne in overtime during the season and had avenged one of those by beating the Dukes in the final of the NIT, 50-41. Another Colorado-Duquesne final became a possibility when both schools were invited to the NCAA tourney. This was the first time that a bid to play in both postseason tournaments had been extended and was made possible by the completion of the NIT prior to NCAA play. However, neither team survived the preliminary rounds. Only once, and that ten years later, would the NIT finalists meet in a NCAA tournament final.

Region 5 was represented by Kansas, coached by another basketball legend, Forrest "Phog" Allen, the man who had an opinion on every aspect of the game and needed no encouragement to express them all. His squad had tied Oklahoma and Missouri for the lead in the Big Six standings but Kansas' overall record, 17-5, was superior. Another defense-minded team, they had held seven opponents to fewer than 30 points.

The University of Southern California became the Region 8 choice when they beat Oregon State, the Pacific Coast Conference Northern Division champion, in the PCC playoff. The first game, won by USC 54-41, was fairly close. The next night the Californians blasted their way into the tournament by humbling Oregon State 62-26. USC was considered by many the best team in the country. (In the days before wire service ratings and limited intersectional contests, more than one outstanding regional team could, and did, lay claim to being "Number One.") On their way to a 19-2 season they had broken LIU's 34-game unbeaten streak.

Taken together the eight teams in the 1940 tourney had a combined 148-22 record or .871 compared to the previous year's 132-39 or .776. It looked like this year's field, featuring several All Americans and sporting better records, would provide a more exciting brand of basketball than last year's one-sided contests in which the closest game had been decided by 11 points. Indeed it proved to be so.

In the opening rounds in Kansas City not only were the games closer but the crowds, a near capacity 9,000 each evening, more enthusiastic. The first game pitted Colorado, fresh from its NIT triumph, against USC. These were potentially the best teams in the tournament, and there was some regret that one of them had to be eliminated in such an early round. The game was to have featured a battle between two All Americans, Jack Harvey of Colorado and Ralph Vaughn of the Trojans. Actually it was Joe Reising, USC's 6′5″ center, who made the difference as the Trojans won, 38-32, in a cautiously played, tactical confrontation. In the other first round game Kansas took Rice 50-44. Howard Engleman of Kansas had been bothered by a bad knee all season. Coach Allen did not know how effective he would be, but he found out soon enough. Breaking an 11-11 tie Engleman put in three quick buckets and Kansas was ahead to stay. Engleman went on to score 21 points, playing better on one good knee than his teammates on two. Ralph Miller, who was to coach teams at Wichita, Iowa and Oregon State to more than 500 victories, contributed 10 points.

The following night 9,000 partisan spectators were treated to the most exciting basketball game in the short history of the tournament. USC, leading 21-20 at the half, was still ahead by a single point with 17 seconds left to play. Then Engleman, taking matters in his own hands again, swished in a basket and the fans went wild as Kansas held on for a 43-42 win. Miller was high scorer with 15. The victory was attributable to Kansas' tight defense which held Vaughn to a mere two baskets and six points, considerably below his average.

In Indianapolis, meanwhile, Indiana completely outclassed Springfield, which was playing a school outside its region for the first time that season. The 48-24 score reflected the one sidedness of the contest. The co-feature was much closer as Duquesne beat Western Kentucky 30-29.

This set up a rematch between the Hoosiers and the Dukes. Earlier in the year Duquesne had suffered its only defeat of the regular season at the hands of Indiana 51-49. Led by All American Paul Widowitz, Duquesne was motivated not only by a desire to avenge its only defeat but also for another chance at a postseason tournament championship, something that had eluded them in New York. Indiana was the "home" team since they, like Kansas, were playing almost in their back yard. Proving their first victory no fluke, Indiana had little trouble beating Duquesne again, 39-30.

The final, in Kansas City a week later, saw Indiana get off to a slow start. The Hoosiers did not connect with their first field goal until the eight minute mark but then came on with a rush as they took a 32-19 half time lead. Another capacity crowd, most of them rooting for Kansas, were disappointed as Indiana, relentlessly extending its lead, went on to win 60-42.

Jay McCreary, coming off the bench, clinched the victory for Indiana by scoring 10 of his 12 points in the second half. Marv Huffman of the winners was voted the Most Valuable Player.

1941

March 1941 saw eight new schools enter the tournament. Dartmouth, which had been a dominant force in the unofficial Ivy League over the past four years, was selected as the Region 1 representative. Led by Gus Broberg, an All American, they finished the season with an 18-4 record. The city of Pittsburgh sent a school to each postseason tournament. Duquesne, 17-2, accepted a bid to play in New York while the University of Pittsburgh, with an inferior 12-5 record, was the NCAA's Region 2 choice. Pittsburgh had lost to a couple of Big 10 schools as well as to smaller Westminster and Waynesburg—hardly outstanding credentials for selection.

North Carolina, the Southern Conference champion with a 19-7 record, represented Region 3. Their All American, George Glamack, could put the ball in the hoop from anywhere on the court. He had scored 45 points in one game, only five short of the national record. Not all of North Carolina's victories had come against other colleges. Their schedule had been padded with games against teams such as the Greensboro YMCA, Hanes Hosiery and the McCrary Eagles, not an uncommon practice for college teams up until the mid 1940's.

A real surprise was Wisconsin which had finished ninth in the Big 10 the previous season. This year with All American Gene Englund at center dominating the action they had won 17 of 20.

In the West, Arkansas won the SWC, losing only to the Phillips Oilers (an Amateur Athletic Union team) twice while compiling a 19-2 record.* In Region 5 the Missouri Valley Conference sent its first representative to the

*AAU teams were composed mostly of former college players.

tourney when Creighton, 17-6, beat Iowa State of the Big Six 57-48 in a confrontation of conference champions. Creighton could on occasion be awesome. In one game they had given Marquette a fearsome 57-12 drubbing.

Another defensive team, Wyoming, 13-4, was the Skyline Conference champion and Washington State was the PCC representative after beating Stanford for the right to play in the tournament. It was to be their only NCAA appearance for 39 years and they came close to winning it all.

The field was not as imposing as in 1940. Several independents had stronger teams than conference schools, and these tended to gravitate to the NIT. Faced with a choice between playing in Madison Square Garden in New York before 18,000 people or playing in Madison, Wisconsin or Kansas City before 9,000, most schools chose the bigger arena with its higher receipts and national exposure. Certainly Duquesne would have been a greater attraction than Pittsburgh at the NCAA tournament, but the big city won out. The NIT was still the bigger attraction and the more prestigious of the two tournaments. On the other hand, the NIT field was not geographically representative. Three of the eight schools came from the New York metropolitan area and all except one, Ohio University, were situated within 300 miles of the city.

The tournament opened simultaneously in Madison, Wisconsin, and Kansas City. Wisconsin, playing on its home court, had to struggle against Dartmouth. The Indians from Hanover, N.H. led at half time, 24-22, and most of the second half until Wisconsin tied the game 44-44. Gene Englund then spun in a two pointer for the Badgers. With the Indians snapping at their heels the rest of the way, Wisconsin nevertheless pulled out a narrow 51-50 victory. Broberg contributed 20 points for the losers. In the other contest the fans were treated to the lowest scoring game ever played in the tournament. At the intermission only twenty points had been scored by both sides. The tempo picked up just slightly in the second half which ended with Pittsburgh on top of North Carolina 26-20, a score more appropriate to a football game. High scoring George Glamack managed only nine points in the game.

The next evening the gymnasium was packed with 14,000 spectators, nearly every one of them rooting for the Badgers. They were not disappointed as the local team ran away with a 36-30 victory. It wasn't easy. Pittsburgh, with a maddening, deliberate offense and tenacious defense so successful the previous evening, held a 14-8 lead at the half. For a time it looked doubtful that Wisconsin would even score in double figures. Somehow, though, they found the solution in the second half, and sparked by Englund and sophomore John Kotz, qualified for the final. In the consolation game Glamack rediscovered his scoring touch and poured in 31 points, an NCAA playoff record that would stand for the next nine years until broken by another North Carolina athlete.

Meanwhile in Kansas City, Arkansas beat Wyoming in a close match 42-40 and Washington State led by 6′7″ center Paul Lindeman, who scored 26 points, eliminated Creighton 48-39. The next night a disappointing crowd of only 7,000 saw Arkansas set up an impenetrable shield on defense. Undismayed, Washington State shot right over it. Their accuracy with medium and long range one handed sets was deadly and they went on to win 64-53, handing Arkansas its first loss to a college team that year.

The final was again scheduled for Kansas City. The Cougars were favored on the basis of their greater experience, height and shooting accuracy. On the other hand, Wisconsin was on a 14 game winning streak and had proved they could come back from early deficits. It was an exciting game. The Badgers in striped socks and leather knee pads looked almost quaint, a throwback to an earlier era. For once Wisconsin left the court with a first half lead. In the battle of centers Englund completely dominated Lindeman, outrebounding and outscoring his taller opponent who failed to hit on a single field goal. Wisconsin set up a strong defense and this time Washington State was unable to score from outside as they had against Arkansas. They suffered two long scoring droughts—a nine minute stretch in the first half and five minutes in the second. On the other end of the court, the Badgers repeatedly got behind their defenders to score from inside. At the buzzer it was Wisconsin on top 39-34. With that the Big 10 avenged a loss to the Pacific Coast Conference in the first tournament two years earlier. The Big 10 could claim to be the best conference in intercollegiate basketball. Three different schools had played in the finals in as many years and the last two had become national champions.

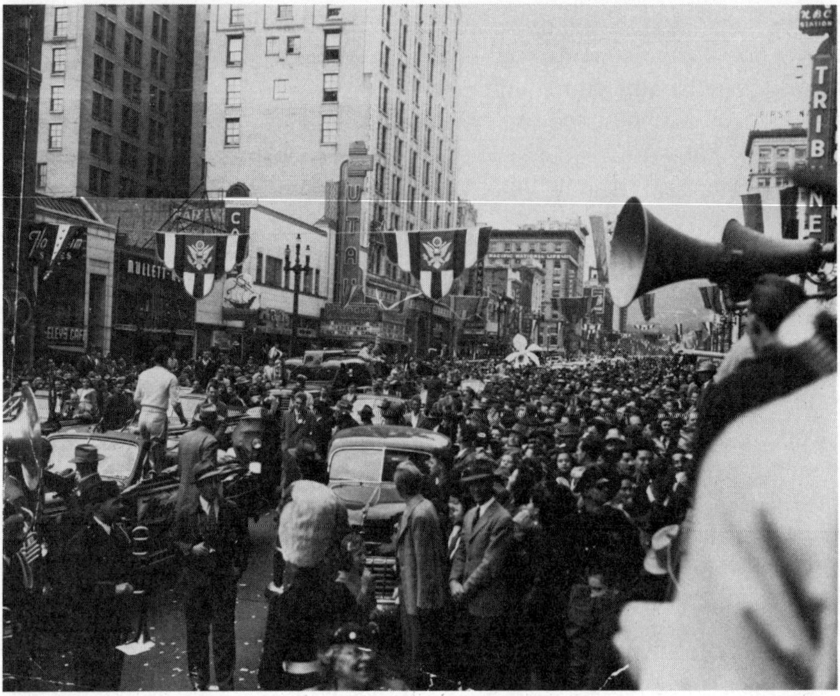

Victory celebration in downtown Salt Lake City after the University of Utah returned from New York with the 1944 NCAA championship. Arnie Ferrier, the only freshman to win the MVP award, is at left of center in the overcoat with the boutonniere.

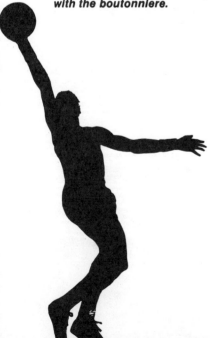

2

THE WAR YEARS 1942-1944

1942

World War II broke out just as the 1941-42 season got underway. It did not affect intercollegiate basketball immediately though a few players did enlist. In general, schedules were completed and schools honored their commitments. Since few colleges played intersectional games, travel restrictions had little effect. Later some universities dropped sports for the duration of the war, and a few conferences abandoned league games.

In 1942 Dartmouth won the Ivy League title for the fifth consecutive year and was again invited to play in the tournament. Despite winning 20 while losing only three, the Indians were an erratic team, rising to great heights one night but seeming to lose interest on others. For instance, they beat Pennsylvania by 44 points and Harvard by 26, but lost to both schools in return matches. The home court was, of course, an important factor. Broberg, their All American, was gone but they found another in George Munroe. They were given an excellent chance of winning the national championship.

Penn State, a stingy team which yielded an average of just 30.5 points a game, accepted a bid to represent Region 2. Kentucky, the SEC champion, which was to appear 26 more times over the next 40 years—more than any other school—made its NCAA tournament debut. The Wildcats had an 18-5 record but had lost their last game to Tennessee in the postseason conference playoff. Nevertheless, the selection committee picked them as the best team in Region 3. Illinois was the Big 10 champion with an overall mark of 18-3. Each year the conference had produced a different leader, proof of its depth and balance. Illinois' Whiz Kids, led by Andy Phillip, already an All American though only a sophomore, were the talk of the Midwest.

In the West, Rice and Arkansas shared the SWC title but Rice was chosen. Bob Kinney, their All American, was the dominant force on the team. Colorado with Bob Doll and Leson McCloud, leader and runner up in scoring in the Skyline, was the Region 7 representative. Colorado had the best record of any team in the tourney, coming within one point of a perfect season. Their only loss was to Wyoming, 40-39. They had started the season on the road playing against some excellent teams in the East and Midwest, among them St. Josephs, St. Johns, St. Bonaventure and Loyola (Ill.), and beating them rather easily. Their margin of victory averaged 16 points, a rather awesome statistic considering the level of their opponents and the depressed scoring of the era. Kansas, the co-champion of the Big 6 with Oklahoma, was picked in Region 5 after beating Oklahoma A and M, the MVC champion. Rice, Colorado and Kansas, along with Dartmouth, were all making their second appearance in the playoffs, the first schools to repeat.

Stanford won the PCC championship and ended with a 24-4 record. However, they were extended to the limit before eliminating Oregon State in three games in the interdivision playoff.

The East regionals, held in New Orleans, opened on March 20 before a slim crowd of 3,000. Dartmouth took the initial lead against twice beaten Penn State and never trailed as they won, 44-39. The losers could not cope with Dartmouth's 6-5 center Jim Olsen, who accounted for 19 points. Showing more fizz than whiz the kids from Illinois succumbed to Kentucky 46-44 in a mild upset. It was the first time that a Big 10 team had been ousted before the final round.

1943

The war had a restrictive effect on the 1942-43 intercollegiate basketball season. Players were drafted or enlisted; schools cancelled games or entire schedules. To make up for the lack of college opponents, many schools scheduled matches against service bases, industrial league teams or YMCAs. Travel restrictions cut down on the number of interregional contests and some schools declined to send teams to the postseason tournaments. Others allowed freshmen to play, one of whom, George Mikan of DePaul, too tall to be drafted, was named a second team All American.

Probably the best team in the country was Illinois. They were the undefeated champions of the Big 10 and lost only one non-conference game to Camp Grant. The Whiz Kids were a year older and absolutely superb. In their two games against their intrastate rivals of the Big 10 they whipped the University of Chicago 92-25 and Northwestern 86-44. In all, they outscored their opponents by nearly 2-1. But they declined an invitation to the NCAA tournament and the bid went instead to independent DePaul. It was the only time that a Big 10 team was not represented in the playoffs. The Whiz Kids missed their chance at a national title and were never to have another opportunity.

DePaul had a respectable 18-4 record. Their schedule was heavily loaded with games against army and navy bases around Chicago, which frequently had better teams than the colleges. Dartmouth, 19-2, again won the Ivy League and were invited for the third straight year. For the third year, too, they produced a different All American, Stan Skaug. They had routed Holy Cross 79-37 and several other games were not much closer.

New York University (17-4) was the first New York team to play in the tourney. There was some feeling they were not the best that the city had to offer, having lost to both St. Johns and Fordham. Even Manhattan had a better record, but these three schools went to the NIT. Another independent, Georgetown (19-4), was the choice to represent Region 3. Their claim to fame had been the 105 points scored against American University during the season, triple digit scores being extremely rare in those days. Southern and Southeast Conference schools were either bypassed or refused an invitation.

Texas (18-6) was the designated Region 6 school. Oklahoma (17-8), second to Kansas in the Big Six, was invited and accepted. Wyoming (27-2), the class of the Skyline, was also the class of the West. They had lost only to Duquesne and to non-college Denver Legion though admittedly some of the teams they played, like Poudre Valley Creamery whom they beat 64-27, were not that strong. Wyoming was one of the few teams to make a trip across the country to play outside their geographic region which was to prove a big factor in their favor. Washington (24-5), after disposing of Southern California in the PCC playoff, rounded out the field.

All in all this was a relatively inferior field. Certainly there were better teams in the country. Some had been snubbed for political or personal reasons while others had declined to participate. Examples in Regions 2, 3 and 4 have been mentioned. In Region 5 neither Creighton, which had won 19 straight games and was undefeated in the MVC, nor Kansas (22-6) was included. Oklahoma, with an inferior record, was the regional representative instead.

In Kansas City, Colorado had its problems with Kansas. After leading 27-20 at intermission the Buffalos allowed their opponents to go ahead twice before finally taking a close game 46-44. McCloud led the Colorado rally that dampened the enthusiasm of the hometown fans. Stanford suffered through a similar experience in the other first round action. Leading by 12 points at the half, they hit a cold spell in the second period and failed to score for seven minutes as Rice took a temporary lead. At this point Jim Pollard,

Stanford's best player since the legendary Hank Luisetti graduated in 1936, took matters into his own hands and put in eight quick points to spark his team to a 53-47 victory. In all he tallied 26 points, almost half of his team's total, and 12 of the 21 buckets made by Stanford.

The next night proved easier for Stanford as they disposed of Colorado 46-35. It was only the second loss of the season for the Buffalos. Pollard was high scorer again with 16 points. The deciding factor, though, was Stanford's defense which held Colorado's one-two scoring combination of McCloud and Doll to just 14 points.

Meanwhile in New Orleans, attendance had not picked up materially and those few who did show up saw a rather lackluster contest. Kentucky took an early lead which they maintained for seven minutes. Then Dartmouth, led by Munroe who eventually scored 20 points, moved into high gear and left the Wildcats panting in their wake. The final score, 47-28, told the story graphically.

In Kansas City Stanford waited a week for Dartmouth and the final showdown with misgiving. Pollard, their ace, had contracted the flu and would not be able to play. It was not unusual for a team to build around one outstanding player who did most of the scoring. But when that player became sick or injured, the team suffered the consequences. Most of the time the other members of the squad simply could not fill the gap. It was unfortunate for Stanford that at this crucial time their star player was in bed with a fever. (California athletes occasionally have a difficult time adjusting to severe climate changes and Kansas City in March is a much wetter and colder place than Palo Alto where Pollard was used to playing.)

These were undoubtedly the two most academically prestigious universities ever to meet in the tournament final. It was as close as the Ivy League ever got to a national basketball title and the only appearance for Stanford.* The two schools also had something else in common: they were both nicknamed the Indians.

Dartmouth led from tipoff until less than a minute remained to intermission. Then sophomore Howie Dallmar tied the score at 22-22 and Jack Dana's basket at the buzzer gave Stanford its first lead. The second half was all Stanford as Dallmar, Dana and Ed Voss picked up the slack left by Pollard's absence. The final score was 53-38.

In the first four years of the tournament, two schools from the Big 10 and two from the PCC had each won a national championship.

The NCAA moved its East playoffs to Madison Square Garden in New York, the fifth city in as many years to host them. After enduring small crowds in New Orleans and only slightly bigger ones in Madison, Indianapolis and Philadelphia, the program organizers decided that exposure in the big arena, not to mention the big bucks, would not hurt the tournament at all and might even take some wind out of the NIT's sails. Meanwhile the West

*Currently Stanford is the only school with a perfect record in NCAA tournament play.

regionals had found a home in Kansas City.

On March 24, 16,491 fans, several hundred less than had attended the NIT opening round the previous week, watched Dartmouth get off to a horrendous start against DePaul. It took them nearly eleven minutes to score their first field goal, in the meantime missing their first 34 shots (*New York Times*) from the field. George Mikan, 6' 9" center, scored 20 points for DePaul as they went on to win by a comfortable 46-35 margin.

There was more than one similarity between the opener and the nightcap, which pitted NYU against Georgetown. NYU, nearly as cold and disorganized as Dartmouth, also had to contend with a 6' 8" center, John Mahnken of the Hoyas. Mahnken also scored 20 points but 18 came in the first half, just one short of the NYU team total. The second half began disastrously for the Violets. Already ahead by 13, Georgetown swished in the first 12 points of the second period and later in the half added another ten straight for good measure. Their second half attack was more balanced and the result was a 55-36 victory. NYU, despite the home court advantage, just could not get untracked and their fans finally lapsed into silence.

George Mikan was not the only rookie in the DePaul contingent. It was also Ray Meyer's first year as a college coach. He had been a star player and two time captain at Notre Dame and was still in his twenties when he was offered the position at DePaul.* Meyer was aware of the potential game breaker he had acquired by grace and good fortune when Mikan enrolled at DePaul. He had devised an innovative training program for the gangly uncoordinated schoolboy who, according to Meyer, "would trip over the lines on the court." The regimen included exercises in dancing, boxing, jumping over chairs and rope skipping. Since DePaul did not have any dormitories Mikan had to commute from his home in Joliet, a daily three hour round trip. With the rigorous training practice and the long train ride, Mikan barely had time to study let alone have much time for fun. Maybe that was why, on his first trip to New York, Mikan spent the day of the East regional final walking all around the big city. The young sightseer, who suffered from fallen arches, finally returned on very tired feet just before game time. Meyer was livid, Mikan contrite and his teammates understandably shaken.

The East final between DePaul and Georgetown was a battle of centers with similar sounding names. Georgetown's Mahnken outscored DePaul's Mikan 17-11. Mahnken believed in scoring early and luckily for his team he did, because he had to sit out the last 10 minutes of the game with three fouls (only four were allowed up until 1944 when the present limit of five was

*Shortly thereafter the coach at Notre Dame suffered a fatal heart attack. Meyer was offered the post but declined, deciding to stay at DePaul instead.

introduced). In Mahnken's absence, Danny Kraus took over the floor leadership and with his playmaking and passing set up many of Georgetown's scores. Mikan's presence was felt more on defense than on offense. He stood in front of the basket (maybe to rest his sore feet), leaped and batted Georgetown's shots away as they headed toward the basket (goaltending was not outlawed for another year). After a while the Hoyas changed their approach and began banking their shots off the backboard. The tactic worked and they went on to win 53-49.

The first round in Kansas City matched Texas and Washington. Travel restrictions and lack of college opponents resulted in a strange situation. Texas was the first school the Huskies played outside their conference. Both teams used a racehorse style of play as they scooted from end to end, trying to put the ball in the basket before the defense could get set. Washington got off to a fast 16-4 start, led at the half 33-28, and was hanging on by a single point with six minutes left after John Hargis, Texas' All American, scored his thirtieth point on a one hander to make the score 53-52. A basket and a foul shot put the Huskies on top again. But the Longhorns got help from an unexpected source. Roy Cox, a 5′7″, seventeen year old freshman, destroyed Washington's hopes by popping in three straight baskets in the last two minutes as Texas won 59-55.

The presence of Gerald Tucker, Oklahoma's All American, was the only trump that kept the Sooners in the game against Wyoming. Without him, Wyoming's height proved too difficult to overcome. Unfortunately Tucker did not survive the first half. He fouled out after only 17 minutes trying to guard Milo Komenich and Jim Weir, Wyoming's big men, who scored 36 points between them. There was nobody on the Sooner bench who was up to the task, so the coach decided to leave him in. Oklahoma held onto a slim 25-22 lead at the intermission but lost ground in the second half, and Wyoming eventually won, 53-50.

The final was a real western shootout. Texas, looking as if they were going to run the Cowboys right off the court, if not the range, took a 21-9 lead in the first nine minutes. By half time Wyoming had cut the margin to six. They finally nosed ahead, 37-36, seven minutes into the second half. For a time, neither side was able to establish an advantage. The score was tied one last time at 41-41 after which Wyoming's Kenny Sailors scored a quick bucket and the Cowboys pulled away to lasso the Longhorns 58-54. John Hargis scored 29 points, giving him a total of 59 for two games, the best tourney average to date. It had been an exciting and closely contested regional as each winning team had had to come back from half time deficits.

For the first time in four years, the final was not held in Kansas City. It was staged instead in New York. The 13,206 fans who came to the Garden, though a respectable number, were considerably fewer than the capacity crowds during the NIT. After NYU's loss the local fans seemed to lose interest and the crowds declined to 14,000 for the semi-final and even fewer for the final. The game was decided not by the giants but by the playmakers.

Sailors, dribbling, penetrating, shooting or passing off, performed brilliantly. Kraus, his counterpart at Georgetown, had to sit out most of the second half with three personals. Without Kraus to feed him the ball, Mahnken was held to six points and Wyoming's height advantage allowed the Cowboys to control the boards. Nevertheless, with six minutes left in the game, Georgetown still held a tenuous 31-26 lead. At this point the Cowboys exploded with 20 points in two long thunderclaps of eleven and nine points sandwiched around a barely audible three point response by Georgetown. For the third time in as many games, Wyoming came from behind to win. The final score, Wyoming 46, Georgetown 34, did not indicate the closeness of the game which saw the teams separated by only three points, 37-34, with two minutes left to play. Sailors was voted the MVP of the tournament.

A few days later, before heading back to Wyoming, the Cowboys beat St. Johns, the NIT champion, 52-47 in a Red Cross benefit match.

1944

By 1944 the full effects of the war were being felt in intercollegiate sports as elsewhere. Schedules were altered frequently and schools played whichever quintet was available as lineups often changed from game to game. Under these conditions it was difficult to make comparisons between teams that played such disparate schedules. Compounding the confusion, much that occurred on the court that year went unreported or received only local coverage due to the shortage of newsprint. The best basketball teams in the country had "fort," "camp," "base," "field" and "station" appended to their names though none went to a postseason playoff. The U.S. Military Academy at West Point had a 15-0 record, but they did not enter a tourney either.

The schools that benefited most from the disruption caused by the war were those that had military training programs on campus and those that had outstanding freshmen, too young to be drafted. One such school was Dartmouth, which had incorporated several star basketball players onto its team as soon as they arrived at the Armed Forces training camp on campus. Dick McGuire had played most of the season for St. Johns where he had been voted the outstanding player in the New York area. Just before the end of the season he had been drafted and now exchanged his red shirt for Dartmouth's green. Besides McGuire, the Hanoverians had Bob Gale, who used to play for Cornell, and Harry Leggat, formerly of NYU. In addition, they came up with home grown Audley Brindley, the latest in a string of All Americans. Yale and Harvard did not compete in 1944 and Dartmouth had little trouble in taking the Ivy title for the seventh consecutive year and posting a

17-1 record. As a result, they accepted an invitation to participate in their fourth successive NCAA tournament. During the previous four years Dartmouth accumulated a 74-10 record, best in the country, but the 1944 squad was the finest they had ever put together; the feeling in Hanover, as well as elsewhere in the basketball world, was that this year they would go all the way. – and they did

Region 2 chose Temple, an independent with a so-so 13-8 record. The Big 10 was once again represented, by Ohio State (14-6) this time. The selection committee overlooked DePaul with a superior record (20-3) and their outstanding sophomore center, George Mikan. Ray Meyer had the feeling the only way he would coach in another NCAA tournament was to apply for admission to the Big 10. To make obvious what was apparent to all, DePaul beat Ohio State during the regular season. Feeling slighted, the Blue Demons went to the NIT where they lost in the final to St. Johns. Another surprise choice was Catholic University of Washington, D.C., the Region 3 representative. Though there were few games played in the Southern and Southeastern Conference, Kentucky compiled a 17-1 record and also went to the NIT. With the inclusion of Catholic and Ohio State, the NCAA tourney took on the look of an assemblage of bridesmaids.

The western teams were not much better. Washington (26-6) and California (7-3) won their respective divisions in the PCC, but the conference did not hold a playoff and neither school went to the tournament. Instead Pepperdine (21-11), which had played mostly military teams as well as such quintets as the San Pedro YMCA and 20th Century Fox, to whom they lost, was asked to participate and accepted.

The Big Six sent two schools to the playoffs, one-third of its entire conference. The reason was that Region 7, which normally sent the winner of the Skyline Conference, had no candidate since it had suspended competition for the duration. Oklahoma and Iowa State had tied for the title but it was Missouri and Iowa State which went to Kansas City. Missouri (9-8) had the worst record to date of any team to play in a postseason tournament. The best that could be said for the choice was they did not have far to travel to Kansas City and, therefore, would not have to use a lot of rationed fuel. Iowa State (13-3) was a low scoring team whose opponents averaged 30 points a game against them. This was attributable to a good defense or the substandard play of many wartime teams. Region 6 decided to invite either Rice or Arkansas, co-champions of the SWC, whichever would agree to go.

The East Regionals were again held in New York. Dartmouth, looking like champions already, routed Catholic 63-38. After leading 28-12 at intermission Dartmouth coasted the rest of the game, giving everyone on the squad some playing time. In the other first round game Temple stayed close to Ohio State for one half and trailed by only three points at intermission. But when the Buckeyes returned to the court they reeled off ten points in a row and won 57-47.

The next evening Dartmouth "outdrove, outshot, outplayed and outscored" Ohio State. Dartmouth started fast and simply ran the Buckeyes off the court in the first few minutes. They held a 28-14 lead before Ohio State pulled themselves together and closed the gap to 28-22 after 20 minutes. The Buckeyes caught up and vaulted into a 44-43 lead halfway through the second period. Leggat responded with two baskets and McGuire one. Ohio State made a last ditch effort and were threatening to take the lead again when Brindley poured in seven straight points to halt that rally. Despite Arnie Risen's 21 points, Ohio State fell short, and the Hanoverians reached the final on the strength of a 60-53 win. Brindley's play was decisive as he netted 28 points on 13 of 20 from the floor.

In Region 6, Arkansas had accepted an invitation to the tournament. Travelling to Kansas City by car, the Razorbacks were involved in a serious accident and had to drop out of the competition. The NCAA desperately needed an eighth team to complete the field. They looked around for a likely school and came up with Utah. The Utes had accepted an invitation to the NIT and had just lost to Kentucky in the first round. Utah was on its way home when it received a request from the NCAA: Would it please come to Kansas City to participate in the West regionals? Well, Kansas City is on the way to Ogden, Utah, and so they accepted. They were keenly disappointed at their early demise in New York and playing one or two more games before calling it a season would be fun.

Utah had one of the youngest teams in the country. They were a freshman dominated squad whose average age was only 18-½ years. Since there were so few schools playing basketball in their area, their record (18-4) had been achieved mostly against industrial amateur teams and service squads. Before participating in the New York tourney, they had played a total of three games against college opponents. Despite their fine record, featuring a good defense that had given up more than 50 points only twice all season, they were a big questionmark, especially in light of their inexperience.

In Municipal Auditorium, Kansas City, Utah disposed of Missouri rather easily, 45-35. The game was not as close as the score would indicate since at one stage the Utes had climbed to a 20 point lead. Their high scorer was Arnie Ferrin, an All American despite being just a freshman. In the other first round game, Iowa State upended Pepperdine 44-39. Then in the West regional final Utah rallied from a one point half time deficit to beat Iowa State 40-31.

For the second time in two weeks Utah packed its bags and headed for New York. Their return to Ogden would have to be postponed another week. Awaiting them was a powerful Dartmouth team that felt confident it would now achieve the national title that had eluded them two years earlier. Dartmouth was very strong offensively. They had scored 60 points against Catholic and Ohio State, a mark that had been reached only three times previously in the tournament.

The 14,990 fans in Madison Square Garden saw one of the closest, most exciting contests of that or any other year. In a low scoring game with Utah controlling the tempo, Dartmouth held an 18-17 lead at the end of the first half. The pressure seemed to affect Dartmouth more than it did their opponents. They made many mistakes and turned the ball over repeatedly. Their speed was counterbalanced by the quickness of Wat Misaka, Utah's 5' 7" guard. In the waning moments of the game Utah, nursing a slim lead, maintained possession of the ball. Four times they waived the opportunity of shooting a foul. (The rule at the time allowed the team that was fouled either to shoot from the free throw line or waive the shot and keep possession.) Dartmouth did get the ball back, though, and with three seconds left McGuire put in an angle set to tie the score 36-36.

The teams went into the first NCAA playoff overtime. Dartmouth drew first blood with a free throw. Each side then dueled from the foul line, Ferrin putting in four and Brindley one to make the score 40-38 in favor of Utah. With the seconds ticking away McGuire drove to the pivot and scored to tie the game for the last time. Utah held for the last shot. With only three seconds left Herb Wilkinson found the range and Utah claimed the championship 42-40. The team that was not even supposed to be in the tournament had won the top prize.

Utah stayed in New York for one more game—the Red Cross benefit match against the winner of the NIT, St. Johns. They won that game, too, 43-36. Ironically the Redmen had beaten Kentucky, the team that had ousted Utah in the semi-finals of the NIT. Had Utah not lost to Kentucky, they would not have had time to stop off in Kansas City for a try at the championship.

3

THE "TALLING" OF BASKETBALL 1945-1947

On the same day Utah won the national title, the Rules committee of the NCAA met in New York and made two far reaching changes—they banned goaltending and they increased the number of allowable personal fouls to five per player.

In the previous couple of years, basketball had witnessed the emergence of the first "giants" who began to dominate the game, especially on defense. (Anyone 6' 9" or over was considered a giant then.) They would park themselves in front of the defensive basket and slip the ball away just before it reached the hoop. Nat Holman, the coach of CCNY, once remarked of 6' 9" Mike Nowak of Loyola (Ill.) that once he was set it "was a physical impossibility" to score against him. There were, of course, ways of neutralizing a big man. LIU in its 1939 NIT win against Loyola placed one man in front and one behind Nowak. Another method used successfully by Georgetown against DePaul's George Mikan in the 1943 NCAA playoff was to bank their shots off the backboard, but this was an unnatural way of shooting and the adjustment difficult to make for a single game.

Over the years rules were changed in an attempt to minimize the effect of the big man. In 1937 the center jump after each basket was eliminated. In 1939 the three second rule, putting a limit on the time an offensive player could stay in the key area, was adopted. Various other suggestions were made and discussed. Phog Allen was in favor of raising the hoop to 12 feet. He maintained the only reason the basket had been established at ten feet was that Dr. James Naismith's YMCA in Springfield, Massachusetts, had a raised running track ten feet off the ground and the founder of basketball had to attach his peach baskets someplace. In a game between Columbia

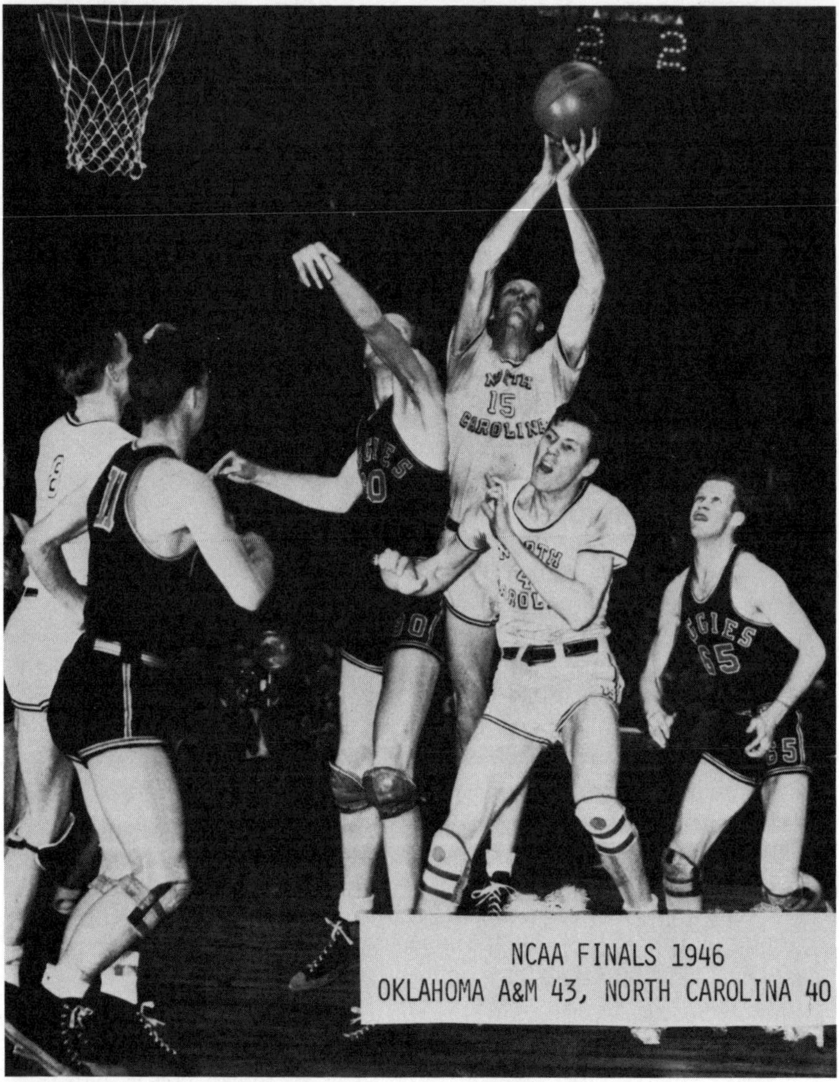

Bob Kurland (90), Oklahoma A&B's towering center, is out of position in the scramble for the ball early in the 1946 final game. Note the leather knee pads which were standard at the time.
(Oklahoma State University photo)

and Fordham, the schools experimented with a 12 foot key (double the current width) and a 21 foot circle beyond which a player could shoot and score a three point basket. The first change was adopted several years later for all basketball competition; the second by the professional American Basketball Association in 1969 and the National Basketball Association in 1979.

These measures were designed to reduce the effect of the taller players on offense. Corresponding changes were needed to reduce their devastating impact on defense. For instance, Oklahoma A and M, which had used a man-to-man defense for years, switched to a diamond-and-one zone with 7 foot Bob "Foothills" Kurland in the middle to bat basket-bound balls away. Thus the goaltending rule change which gave a basket to the offense if a defending player touched the ball on its downward flight to the hoop was long overdue. Then, in order to sweeten the impact of the change, the Rules Committee also increased the number of fouls which a player could be charged with before fouling out from four to five. This would have the effect of putting less pressure on the big man who, in his role of defender in the middle, picked up a high proportion of fouls (which frequently resulted in a star player getting into foul trouble and sitting on the bench for long periods of a game). Many, if not most, good teams of the period were built around one star who carried the brunt of the offense or defense or frequently both. Often such a star would score more than 50 percent of his team's points. For instance, Jim Pollard scored 26 of Stanford's 53 points in a semifinal game in 1942. John Hargis scored 30 of Texas' 59 points in a first round game in 1943, and Arnie Ferrin scored 22 of Utah's 40 points in the 1944 final, just to mention NCAA playoff games. The loss of such a player via fouls was often decisive in determining the outcome of a game. The effect of the rules' changes, it was hoped, would be higher scoring games and a less decisive role for the big man. The first did happen, the second did not.

1945

The giants of the game were 6' 9" George Mikan, 6' 11" Don Otten of Bowling Green and 7 foot Bob Kurland. Since they were too tall for the service, neither they nor other similar athletes had been drafted. The teams they played on were all finalists in postseason tournaments in 1945—DePaul and Bowling Green in the NIT and Oklahoma A and M in the NCAA.

The war, though it was nearly over, still had an effect on the basketball schedule and the year-end playoffs. Dartmouth, for the first time in eight years, did not win the Ivy League title and was replaced as the Region 1 representative by Tufts (10-5). NYU, which won 13 while losing 7, was the Region 2 choice. The Violets won most of their games by lop-sided scores, some by 20 points or more. Iowa won the Big 10 championship while losing only a single game all season, that to Illinois by one point. But they declined an invitation to the postseason tournament and it was Ohio State (14-4), the runner up, that went instead. DePaul, considered the number two team in the country behind Oklahoma A and M, was bypassed and instead went to the NIT. Kentucky (21-3), which had gone to the NIT the previous year, accepted a bid as the Region 3 choice. They finished second in the SEC but won the postseason conference playoff. Some nights the Wildcats were absolutely overwhelming, to which Arkansas State, whom they destroyed 75-6, could testify.

The Oklahoma A and M "Aggies," the representative from Region 5, could be overwhelming, too, but in a different way. Hank Iba, their coach, taught his players to play a tight defense and a ball control offense which would only take shots that had a high percentage chance of scoring. Their patience and self-control set the pace and pattern of the game which their opponents could rarely reverse. Iba was slowly becoming an anachronism as more teams went in for the fast breaking, quick shooting, racehorse type of offense. However, Iba's conservative approach never changed; he later suffered his biggest setback when the United States Olympic team, playing cautiously, lost to the USSR at the 1972 games for their only defeat in Olympic basketball competition. But as long as he had Kurland, Iba's tactics worked perfectly.

Though the Skyline had suspended operations, Utah (17-2) was selected from Region 7. Their only two losses had come at the hands of St. Johns and Ohio State. Arkansas, which finished second to Rice in the SWC, nonetheless became the Region 6 participant. The Razorbacks victimized Baylor and Texas A and M, their SWC opponents, four times during the season, winning three by 60 points or more. The PCC held no playoff and Oregon, the North Division winner, was extended an invitation which they accepted. Oregon had just completed a sneaker-shredding season during which they won 29 of 41 games. Aside from playing their North Division opponents almost addictively (they matched up with Washington State a total of seven time), Oregon was willing to play with just about anybody who could put five players with uniforms on the court. In their odyssey around the Northwest they lost to Fee's Musicers, the Seattle Coast Guard twice and the Vancouver J.C. Some of these losses may have been attributable to sheer exhaustion.

In the first round in New York, NYU trounced Tufts in a very sloppily played game, 59-44. The Violets were favored by 30 points which accounted for their lack of concentration. The other first round game, between Ohio State and Kentucky, was a replay of an earlier encounter in which the Wildcats eked out a win in double overtime. The extremely intense rematch was frequently interrupted by an official's whistle. A total of 39 infractions were called. Arnie Risen and Don Grate, Ohio State's All American duo, led the scoring although Risen collected four personals in the first half and had to sit down most of the second before eventually fouling out. Ohio State survived the hard fought contest, 45-37.

Two evening later Ohio State and NYU squared off before the first capacity crowd the NCAA had attracted in three years in New York. After a closely played first half, NYU found itself ten points down with two minutes to play. Six quick points cut Ohio State's lead to 62-58. With 1:14 to go one of the Buckeyes was fouled. Instead of waiving the free throw and keeping the ball, which was their right, they foolishly elected to shoot the foul. The shot was missed but luckily Ohio State got the rebound. Thirteen seconds later they were again at the line and again they missed. This time they were not so lucky as freshman Dolph Schayes of NYU took the ball downcourt and scored. Having discovered a tactic that worked, NYU fouled Ohio State almost as soon as they took possession. The Buckeyes swallowed the bait once more and for the third time in less than a minute went to the foul line. Apparently Coach Harold Olsen's stubbornness would not allow him to choose the more logical tactic of waiving the shot. By this time the noise in the arena had risen into the ultra-decibel range, and the pressure at the line was on the level of a bomb defusing operation. The attempt missed, the Violets grabbed the rebound and Don Forman hit a set shot with 26 seconds left to tie the game 62-62. There was no more scoring before the buzzer ended regulation time. In overtime, the teams traded buckets before the Buckeyes pulled ahead briefly 65-64. But not for long. In a final burst the Violets exploded for three baskets in 37 second to gain the final 70-65.

High scoring though it had been, that game had to take second place to the extravaganza Arkansas and Oregon put on in Kansas City. Breaking almost every scoring record for a NCAA playoff game, the Razorbacks edged the Ducks 79-76. The half time score, 47-34 in favor of Arkansas, could easily have been a final in any previous year; 6' 10" center George Kok led the scoring with 22 points but it remained for little Bill Flynt to tally the winning basket and free throw in the final seconds. In a down-to-the-wire finish the score was tied at 72, 74 and 76.

Oklahoma A and M had little trouble eliminating Utah 62-37 as Bob Kurland majestically put 28 points through the hoop. The Utes had suffered a crippling loss when their star player, Arnie Ferrin, was drafted into the service late in the season. Unimpressed by Arkansas' high scoring reputation, the Aggies threw up an almost impenetrable defense and easily won their semifinal game 68-41.

On Tuesday evening, March 24, another capacity crowd turned out for the seventh NCAA basketball final. The local fans had gorged themselves watching DePaul obliterate its three opponents by a total margin of 85 points on its way to the NIT crown. Now, their appetite aroused once more, they came to see if their hometown favorites could beat number one ranked Oklahoma A and M and the tallest of the tall, "Foothills" Kurland. This, too, was a rematch since the Aggies had won an earlier game against the Violets in the Garden, 44-41. This time the result was almost identical as the

Oklahomans led most of the way and won 49-45. Bob Kurland, who scored 22 points and was voted the MVP, and the Aggies' defense were too much for the local team.

The final curtain was about to descend on the 1945 season. However, one more game remained. A game that despite a steady diet of superb basketball over the past two weeks, no sports fan in New York wanted to miss—the now annual Red Cross Benefit game. A most fitting finale, it would pit NCAA champ Oklahoma A&M against NIT champ DePaul, the number one team against the number two team in the country, and the two towering superstars of the decade, Kurland against Mikan. The game, as is so often the case, was not half as exciting as the buildup. Mikan fouled out after just 14 minutes, one of the fastest exits on record, and the Aggies went on to win 52-44, the third win in as many games for the NCAA entry in the benefit series.

1946

The NYU quintet of 1946 was even stronger than the previous year's and they were again selected to represent Region 2. Led by Sid Tanenbaum, an All American, and coached by the canny Howard Cann, the Violets entered their last game of the season against traditional rival CCNY having lost but one game. They succumbed in this intra-city rumble but even so their 18-2 record was one of the best in the country. Ohio State (14-4) won the Big 10 and was also invited to its second successive tournament.

North Carolina beat Wake Forest twice during the season, then lost to them in the conference playoff. Nevertheless their 27-4 record was impressive enough so the selection committee decided on the Tarheels as the best in their region. However, many of their wins came at the expense of army and navy bases which were not as strong as they had been during the war. Kentucky with an equally respectable 17-2 record went to the NIT, and LSU and Duke, which won the SEC and Southern Conferences respectively, were uninvited by either tourney. Arbitrariness was a failing not unknown to selection committees.

At the end of the war many fine athletes returned to campuses around the country to resume their education and their playing careers. With their reappearance on the court, many schools had sudden reversals of fortune. Harvard, which had suffered through 2-12 and 2-13 campaigns the two previous years, suddenly blossomed to 19-1, losing only to Holy Cross. The Crimson was chosen as an independent since they did not play in the Ivy League that year.

Another school that pulled itself up by its sneaker strings was Baylor, winner in the SWC. Having endured a ghastly 0-14 season in 1945, the Bears made one of the most spectacular turnarounds in basketball history and finished the year with a 24-3 record due in large part to Jack Robinson. Colorado (11-5) in its last year in the Skyline (it was to join the Big Six the following year) was the Region 7 choice though Wyoming had a much better conference record. Idaho, long the doormat in the PCC, won the Northern Division and came within one game of playing in its first tournament. But California, winner in the Southern Division, beat them two of three and Idaho had to wait 36 years before making their tournament debut. The Golden Bears (29-4) were a ball control team on the order of Oklahoma A and M. In only two of their 33 games did they score as many as 60 points. Their inflated record was a result of the number of service teams they played.

Oklahoma A and M (28-2) was still the number one team in the country. Their two losses had come at the hands of DePaul and Bowling Green, each with a big center who could challenge Kurland. Fortunately for the Aggies, neither school had been invited to the tournament, primarily because the Region 4 selection committee felt that only a Big Ten school could represent that area of the Midwest. The only other team that might have stood a chance against the Oklahomans was Kansas, another Region 5 school. Kansas was the Big Six champ and had lost only one game, to Oklahoma A and M, until they met for the second time to determine the Region 5 representative.

Leaving little doubt who deserved the tournament bid, the Aggies defeated Kansas for a second time.

An indication of the type of player Kurland could have been under a different coach was provided in his last home game. Abandoning his slow down, deliberate offense for once, Iba instructed Kurland to go all out and make as many points as he could. He scored 58 as the Aggies beat St. Louis 86-33. They had previously beaten them 39-27. It is fair to say if Iba had been less conservative his team would have been even more successful.

Harvard prepared for its meeting with Ohio State by playing and defeating the Chelsea Naval Hospital three times. Even if they were playing the staff and not the patients, this was hardly an adequate warmup for the kind of competition the Ivy Leaguers would be facing in the tournament. It came as no surprise to the capacity crowd in Madison Square Garden, therefore, that Ohio State trimmed the Crimsons 46-38. After allowing Harvard an early 8-6 lead, the Buckeyes tied the score and never trailed again. The Bostonian's only NCAA appearance was short and unremarkable.

NYU's single loss, aside from its final game against CCNY, had been to North Carolina and now, by the luck of the draw, they had to face the Tarheels again in the first round. Nonetheless, NYU was favored by seven points on the basis of their three starters—Schayes, Tanenbaum and Don Forman. It soon became evident, however, that this was not their night. The Tarheels were not shooting much but they did not have to. They netted 12 of their first 20 shots from the floor, an incredible percentage for the time, when a 33 percent shooting average was considered creditable. John Dillon, North Carolina's All American forward, was performing admirably with his favored hook shot. Meanwhile NYU's trio of stars failed to respond, and the fans watched disconsolately as the Tarheels stomped NYU 57-49.

The semifinal match two nights later between North Carolina and Ohio State started with dulling ineptness and ended at a white hot pitch of excitement. For more than five minutes two big zeros faced each other on the scoreboard as neither team was able to score. Finally at the 5:20 mark Bones McKinney of North Carolina popped one home. Ohio State meanwhile did not score its first basket until nearly ten minutes had elapsed. Both teams were extremely tight and the score reflected this. Halfway through the first period, only twelve points had been chalked up, evenly divided between the sides. Then the Tarheels found the range and ran off 11 points in a row. The Buckeyes loosened up, too, and took the lead at the intermission 20-19. Things did not improve much for the Tarheels in the second half. McKinney fouled out with nine minutes to go. Dillon, who had been held scoreless in the first half, managed to make four of his unstoppable hook shots but was not as effective as he had been against NYU. The Tarheels had to play catch-up throughout the half. They stayed within overhaul range and with 20 seconds to go when North Carolina was only two points behind, 54-52, Bob Paxton sank a long set shot from 30 feet out to send the game into overtime. It was the third time in as many years New York fans witnessed an extra period tourney game. Hanging tough, the Tarheels scored 6 to Ohio State's 3 in the overtime and vaulted into the final 60-57.

In a first round game in Kansas City, Oklahoma A and M had little trouble hurdling Baylor. Kurland was almost single-handedly responsible for the 44-29 victory. Not only did his 20 points prove decisive, he also dominated the boards, threw outlet passes and fed off to teammates to collect several assists. In the other game California, led by southpaw Andy Wolfe who scored 17, clipped Colorado 50-44.

This set up a final between two strong defensive teams. Oklahoma A and M had given up an average of less than 32 points a game during the season and California was almost as stingy. The capacity audience of 9,000 fans saw Kurland dominate the game as he sank 12 of 23 shots while scoring 29 points. The Californians tried to change the pace by fast breaking, a tactic foreign to them. The Aggies refused to panic, though, and got back on defense quickly. They blunted California's momentum by slowing the tempo down again. By making the Bears play their game, they had little difficulty securing the victory, 52-35.

North Carolina and Oklahoma A and M were a contrast in styles as well as uniforms (the Tarheels wore T shirts with sleeves while the Aggies wore the more popular tank tops) as they squared off in New York three days later. It was too much Kurland again. McKinney at 6′ 6″ had his hands full. Gamely, he tried to hold Foothills from rampaging under the boards, but he was picking up costly fouls. After trailing by six points at the half, the Tarheels came within three after intermission. It was then that McKinney picked up his fifth personal and was gone. Kurland responded by scoring the next seven points for the Aggies. Still, North Carolina closed to within a point and might have taken the game but for the quick thinking and resourcefulness of A. L. Bennett. Seeking to inbound the ball with a few seconds left, Bennett found himself trapped by leaping, arm-waving Tarheels. He coolly rolled the ball along the floor to a teammate as if in a bowling alley. Seconds later the Oklahomans won 43-40 for their second consecutive national title. Bob Kurland, who made 72 points in three games for a low scoring team, was voted the MVP for the second year in a row. An innovation that year was a consolation between the semifinal losers. Ohio State beat California 63-45 for third place in the tourney.

After eight years of competition the national championship had been won twice by teams from each of four conferences—the Big 10, Pacific Coast Conference, Skyline Conference and the Missouri Valley Conference. So far not one independent had gone all the way but this was about to change.

1947

Many war-interrupted collegiate basketball careers were being completed in 1947. John Hargis was back with Texas and Gerald Tucker with Oklahoma. They were both All Americans again as they had been in 1943. Andy Phillip was back at Illinois, Danny Kraus at Georgetown, Arnie Ferrin at Utah, Kenny Sailors and Milo Komenich at Wyoming; familiar names and faces and all remembered appreciatively by playoff fans.

Holy Cross was a school without a gymnasium and consequently had to play all its games on the road. This did not faze the Crusaders in the least. Superbly coached by Doggie Julian, they won their first four games, suffered a slight lapse by losing their next three to North Carolina State, Wyoming and Duquesne (all three eventually landed in one of the two post-season tournaments), then won their last 20 of the season for a 24-3 record. The Crusaders were a logical choice to represent Region 1.

Another fine coach, Ben Carneval, brought his Navy squad into the tournament, the first time a service academy had accepted an invitation. Carneval had coached North Carolina to the tournament final against Oklahoma A and M the previous year and now he was back with a different school for another try at a national title. The only blemish on Navy's 16-1 record was inflicted by George Washington. The Midshipmen from Maryland were the choice of the Region 3 selection committee. Kentucky (32-2), winner of the SEC, and North Carolina State (24-4), winner of the Southern Conference, were both better regarded than Navy but ended up going to the NIT.

From Region 2 came CCNY (16-4) under Coach Nat Holman, as dedicated to fast breaking, wide open basketball as Iba was to disciplined ball control. CCNY was one of four New York schools (along with NYU, Long Island University and St. Johns) to play its home games in Madison Square Garden. Playing before as many as 18,000 hometown fans was certainly an advantage for the New York schools and they consistently produced winning teams. In the early years of the tournament, it was NYU and later CCNY that opted for the NCAA while St. Johns and LIU chose to play in the NIT. It was not until 1951 that St. Johns accepted their first NCAA playoff invitation and not until 1981 did LIU go.

CCNY, like Holy Cross, was a streaky team. All four losses had been in a short two week span during the middle of the season but they had rebounded well and won their last seven games. Wisconsin (15-5), the winner of the Big 10, completed the field in the East Regional. The Badgers had to return to Purdue after the regular season was finished to complete a game that was critical to the standings but had been suspended when a section of the bleachers collapsed. Wisconsin won and took the Big 10 championship by a game.

In the West the standout team was Texas which came within a single basket of a perfect season. Their only loss came against Oklahoma A and M and that by one point. Hargis was back from the service and this time he had help from teammate Slater Martin. An aggressive playmaker, the 5′ 10″ Martin would charge downcourt dribbling as if the ball was attached to his hand with a rubber band. Oklahoma (22-6), the Big Six champ, disposed of St. Louis, the Missouri Valley Conference titlist, to gain its playoff berth. The Sooners were led by Gerald Tucker, a lumbering, clumsy player while moving but solid, steady and immovable as a rock when planted under the basket. Given Tucker's limitations, the Sooners' strategy featured a strong defense and a set pattern on offense.

Wyoming won the Skyline and compiled a 22-4 record. Oregon State won its division in the PCC then went on to subdue UCLA for the right to play in the postseason tournament. As usual the PCC representative played the longest schedule of all the playoff entrants. The season spanned three stages. First came games against non-college teams before other schools started their schedule. The Beavers sharpened their claws on the likes of Preferred Stocks, Bruno Studio, Portland All Stars, and Fee's Rollerdrome, smashing them by 40 or 50 point margins, using them as sparring partners to limber up for more formidable opposition. The Beavers then headed for New York and played some East Coast schools. Finally, they returned home to finish their schedule against the other PCC North Division teams, each of whom they played four times. With such a long schedule, they developed stamina and were a good team in the clutch, winning three overtime games while losing none.

The opening round of the East regional in New York featured CCNY and Wisconsin. The Badgers got off to a fast start, sinking five of their first nine shots and leading 22-6 after seven and a half minutes. Midway through the first half they still held a 16 point margin when CCNY's speed began to assert itself. The Beavers cut the lead to ten before the players headed for the locker room. Shortly after intermission CCNY went on a scoring binge and tied the game at 39-39. The lead then changed hands several times before Phil Farbman's basket made the score 49-47 to put the Beavers ahead for good. Led by freshman Irwin Dambrot, CCNY raced to a 70-56 win that left the Badgers gasping in their wake.

In the other first round game the story was similar as Navy took an early 23-15 lead, only to see Holy Cross come back in the second half to win 55-47. The Crusaders were led by Joe Mullaney who scored 18 and George Kaftan who accounted for 15. A little-known freshman reserve named Bob Cousy had 3 points.

The following Saturday night Madison Square Garden was packed to the beams with fans plugging for an upset. But the favored Crusaders, looking for their twenty-second consecutive win, had played all season on foreign courts and were used to coping with hostile fans. The early going gave the Beavers' supporters some hope as Holy Cross took a long time to loosen up. The pressure may have been due more to the importance of the game than the fans' partisan reaction. Still it took them seven and a half minutes to connect for their first basket. With six minutes left in the first half they were trailing badly, 23-12. That jolted Holy Cross to life and they pumped in 13 points in a row to take the lead at intermission 27-25. Using the break to reorganize, CCNY stayed with the Crusaders until halfway through the second period. With the score tied 38-38 the Beavers fell apart even more dramatically than in the first half. They threw passes away, lost control of the backboards and shot erratically. With Kaftan dominating the boards and shouldering the brunt of the scoring (he eventually finished with 30 points, one off the tournament record), Holy Cross coasted to a 60-45 victory.

In Kansas City's Municipal Auditorium Oklahoma established a 14 point lead in the first twelve minutes, then nursed it carefully to edge Oregon State 56-54. The Beavers managed to tie the game at 46 with seven minutes left, but the Sooners were too strong defensively. With Tucker parked in the middle of the lane, the Oregonians had to shoot from outside but with little success. A contributing factor was the Sooners' success at the line. Oklahoma made their first 12 free throws and 16 of 23 overall while Oregon State could only respond with 10 of 19.

The other first round game was even closer. After Wyoming took a 27-24 lead at the half, Texas scored the first field goal of the second period; thereafter the teams were never separated by more than two points. Leading 40-39 with four minutes left the Wyoming Cowboys went into a stall. Three times they declined to shoot a free throw when fouled. Then Al Madsen of the Longhorns stole the ball from Floyd Volker and was fouled while driving to the hoop. He made one free throw to tie the game at 40. On the next play Jim Collins of the Cowboys was fouled but failed to convert and Texas retrieved the ball; 8,526 fans, screaming themselves hoarse, jumped to their feet as Slater Martin put in a one hander with 30 seconds remaining to win the game for Texas, 42-40.

An extra one thousand fans squeezed their way into the arena to watch Texas and Oklahoma, traditional rivals, battle for the right to go to New York and play for the championship. The contest they saw was, if anything, even closer and more exciting than the previous evening's games.

For Texas as well as for Oklahoma this was their third tournament appearance. Through some strange quadrennial clock these appearances occurred at regular intervals in 1939, 1943 and 1947. It seemed that every time one was invited so was the other, yet this was their first postseason meeting.

The game was a contrast in styles: the spirited downcourt gallop of the Texas mustangs led by Slater Martin against the defensive strategy of Oklahoma's circle of covered wagons anchored by Gerald Tucker. Running and shooting well, Texas plunged ahead at the intermission 29-22.

Back on the court the Sooners erupted for eight straight points to go ahead. They increased that margin to 41-34 with seven minutes to go. Then the pendulum swung back and the Longhorns rallied to tie the score at 53-53 on a bucket by Martin with 55 seconds showing on the clock. Moments later Madsen sank a free throw to put Texas ahead. It was showdown time for the Sooners. They worked the ball in to Tucker but he was too well guarded and elected to pass off to Ken Pryor. Finding more room outside, Pryor pumped in a long set shot—his only basket of the game—with 10 seconds to go to win 55-54. It was a bitter disappointment for Texas, only their second loss of the season and both by one point. The most disappointed Longhorn was Hargis who managed only nine points in each of the games while being completely upstaged by Martin.

In New York the fans jammed the Garden for the third time in a week. Though neither finalist was local, New York had a large Catholic population that rooted for the Crusaders, several of whom, including Kaftan, had gone to high school in the city. The game was brilliantly played and close most of the way with 11 ties and as many lead changes. Holy Cross started out with a deliberate, controlled offense in the first half, then switched to a running game in the second. With three minutes to go the Crusaders were ahead by only 48-45. Sprinting against the tiring Oklahomans they bagged 10 points to which the Sooners responded with a pair of meaningless free throws.

Thus Holy Cross became the first non-conference and first Region 1 school to win the NCAA title as well as the first East regional winner to do so in five years. George Kaftan was voted the MVP while future star Bob Cousy collected just 10 points in three games playing as a reserve guard. The Crusaders' ability to come from behind, which they did in each of their three victories, and a consistent defense—they allowed 47, 45 and 47 points—won them the championship.

In the consolation game for third place, Texas beat CCNY 54-50. As spectators' heads swivelled back and forth, two of the fastest breaking teams in the country fairly scorched the varnish off the Garden hardwood.

1948

But in 1948 most of that fine CCNY team was still in high school. Kentucky was rated the best team in the country and was naturally selected to play in the NCAA tournament, having just won their fifth consecutive SEC championship. Their two losses, against 31 wins, had been to Notre Dame and to Temple, each by one point. Their supercharged offense scored more than 75 points on nine occasions, recording blowouts against schools like Florida 87-31, Vanderbilt 79-43, Tulsa 72-18 and Creighton 65-23. If one was looking for a close, exciting contest, attending a Wildcat game was not the answer. In the Big 10, Michigan (15-5) won its first title since 1927. It had a stingy defense which in the four games prior to the tourney had given up an average of only 33 points. Columbia, though an Ivy League school, was selected as the Region 2 representative since it was geographically located in New York. The Lions had won 20 of 21 games, their only loss coming against Princeton.

The only school given a chance to beat Kentucky was Holy Cross (24-3). Just as in the previous year when they had won the title, the Crusaders entered the playoffs with a long string of victories—19 in all. As in the previous year they had been a streaky team, losing two of their games in back-to-back losses to St. Louis (the eventual winner of the NIT) and DePaul. They shared with Kentucky an emphasis on offense, twice going over the 100 mark, and the ability to overwhelm their opposition—as evidence a 90-35 destruction of Brown. Kaftan was back and so was Bob Cousy both with All American credentials.

In the West, Kansas State (21-4) the Big 7 (now that Colorado was included) champion, beat Oklahoma A and M, the MVC titlist 43-34 to become the Region 5 selectee. It was the Wildcats' second victory of the year against the Aggies who were thus shut out of the postseason play since St. Louis, the runner up in the conference, accepted an invitation to the NIT. The Baylor Bears (21-5) on the rebound again after an 11-11 season were the Region 6 choice. Baylor lost a regular season game to Oklahoma A and M, 22-21, that set a record of sorts for the glacial tempo of play. Wyoming (18-7) was the Skyline representative even though Brigham Young finished first in the conference. Washington (22-10), which ended the season in a tie with Oregon State, beat the Beavers in a one game playoff 59-42 and then knocked off California, which had won the South Division, two out of three.

In the opening round in New York, Kentucky had little trouble with Columbia. The Lions, led by Walt Budko, managed to stay even for only three and a half minutes. Thereafter Kentucky's speed, height, depth and experience were too much to overcome and they pulled away to a 76-53 victory. Holy Cross also encountered little difficulty in their game with Michigan. The Wolverines moved ahead in the first ten minutes 21-16 on red hot shooting. That prompted the Crusaders to kindle their own afterburners and they responded by streaking to a 34-27 half time advantage. Both sides were hitting the target consistently, sinking nearly 50 percent of their shots. In the second half the Wolverines cooled off considerably, but Holy Cross kept on scoring and walked away winners by 63-45. Cousy was high scorer with 23 points.

4

THE WILDCATS AND THE BEAVERS *1948-1950*

Once or twice in a decade a basketball team emerges that completely dominates the rest of the field. Writers record its feats in superlatives, young players pattern their styles after its stars, and coaches study its tactics. Its success is a blend of leadership by one or more players, superb coaching and team cohesion. To watch a team like this play is pure joy and though each opponent usually reserves its greatest effort to produce an upset, the fans invariably come to root for the favorite. Such teams become legends and they are usually identified by one or two stars who become legends in their own right. During the mid-1930's Stanford with Hank Luisetti was such a team. In the mid-1950's it was San Francisco with Bill Russell. Five years later it was Ohio State with Jerry Lucas and John Havlicek. In the later sixties it was UCLA with Lew Alcindor and most recently UCLA again with Bill Walton.

In the period 1947-1950 two such teams emerged, or rather one achieved greatness and the second showed potential for being every bit as great. However, tragedy, in the form of a bribery scandal, aborted its players' careers.

The first team was Kentucky which came close to winning the NIT in 1947 before bowing to Utah in the final. They then won the NCAA championship the next two years, compiling over a span of three years a record of 100 wins against 7 losses. Kentucky was blessed with no less than all three All Americans, Alex Groza, Ralph Beard and Wallace "Wah Wah" Jones, along with a supporting cast of players who would have been stars on any other team of the time—Cliff Barker, Dale Barnstable, Jim Line and Ken Rollins. Groza, Beard, Jones and Barker played as a unit for three years and when they

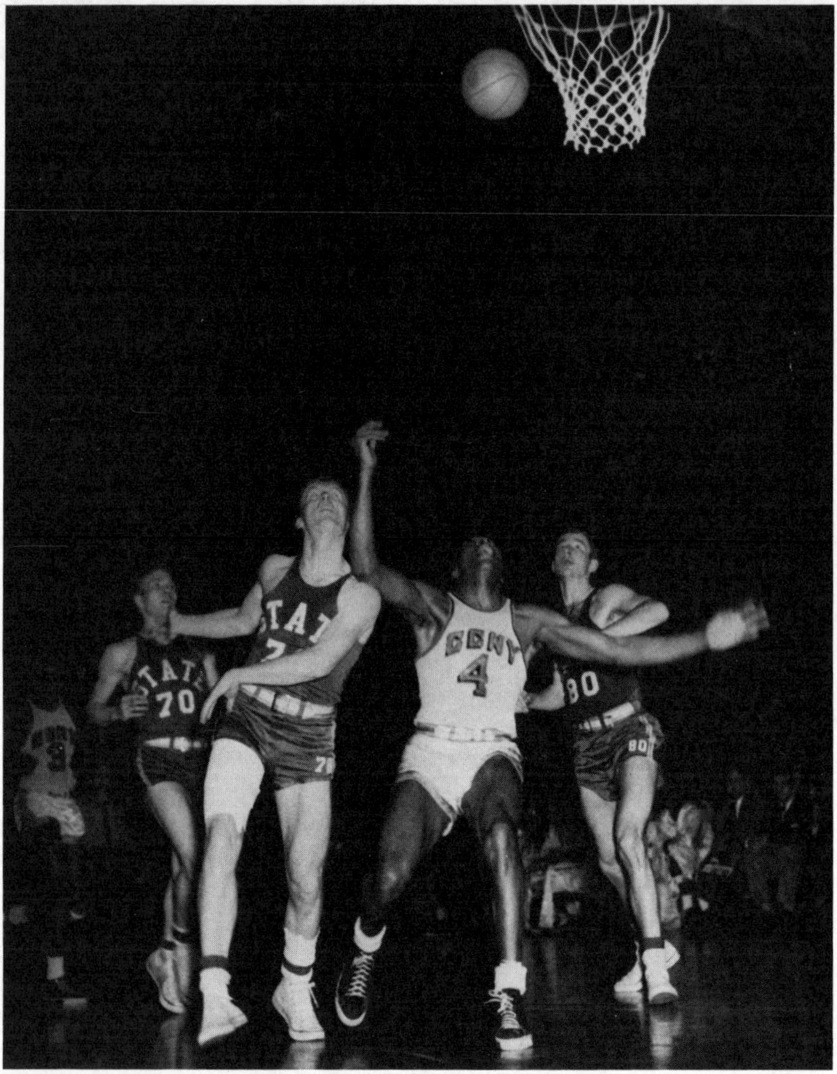

Ed Warner of CCNY spinning in an underhand shot while Dick Dickey (70), Vic Bubas (78), and Joe Harand (80) of North Carolina State wait for a possible rebound. CCNY won 78-73 in this 1950 semi-final contest. (Charles Vanon photo)

graduated, they formed their own professional team, the Indianapolis Olympians with Groza the president and on-court captain. The name they chose was a reminder that the Kentucky squad formed the nucleus of the United States Olympic team that won the gold medal in 1948.

No other college basketball team had until then (or has since) included three All Americans. Groza at 6′ 7″ was the center, high scorer, top rebounder and team leader. He was not only exceptionally tall but solidly built and difficult to move once he positioned himself. Ralph Beard, 5′ 10″, had speed to burn. An excellent shot from outside he was the team playmaker, passing off to Groza or whoever had the hot hand. Jones, a 6′ 4″ forward, complimented Groza and Beard and was solid in the clutch. The man who developed this remarkable squad was Adolph Rupp, the most successful coach in the history of basketball. By the beginning of the 1947-48 season Rupp's teams had already won 318 games while losing only 68.

The other team was CCNY; it reached its pinnacle of performance during the 1950 postseason tournaments. Ned Irish, the president of Madison Square Garden and the man who introduced college basketball to that arena, said of CCNY even before their double tournament victory in 1950: "Potentially they are one of the great college teams of all time" and "The best collection of players ever gathered at a New York school."

Another capacity crowd at the Garden gathered to watch what most anticipated would be the best match-up of the tourney. It was a confrontation between the two top teams in the tournament, with speed and height on one side (Kentucky) and superb ball control on the other (Holy Cross), and between two of the best tacticians in basketball, Adolph Rupp and Doggie Julian. Kentucky started the game by driving for the hoop and for 40 minutes never let up. They ran and ran and ran, blazing tracks to the basket. Kentucky went ahead to stay after only three and a half minutes and just before the half ended were ahead 36-23. Holy Cross closed that gap slightly just before the buzzer. Two quick Crusader buckets opened the second half and Rupp, taking no chances, called time out. The pause gave Kentucky a chance to regroup. Jones scored on a one hander and another from the top of the key, followed by a one hander by Groza and the Wildcats were gone. The final score was 60-52. Ken Rollins and Dale Barnstable covered Cousy like a tent and he managed only five points on frigid one-for-fourteen shooting from the floor.

In Kansas City, Wyoming turned up cold against Kansas State. The chill lasted for nearly ten minutes until the Cowboys made their first two pointer. Despite Mack Peyton's game-high 20 points, Wyoming found itself 19 behind at one point and Kansas State glided to a 58-48 decision.

The second game was played according to a completely different scenario. Washington, leading 34-17, went into a tailspin toward the end of the first half. They lost their shooting eye, stopped hustling and driving. As if caught in some internal blizzard their offense congealed and their defense froze. Trailing by eleven at the intermission, 37-26, Baylor scored ten to the

Huskies' two to open the second half cutting their deficit to three. Washington lost control of the backboards and committed one turnover after another. Coach Art McLarney called time out to settle his players. It worked, briefly, as the Huskies increased their lead to 42-38, but the Bears came back to tie the score at 44-44. The Pacific Coast champions pulled ahead again 50-46. Back came Baylor, led by Bill Johnson and Jack Robinson, to go in front 51-50. The score was tied four times at 53, 55, 58 and 60 before Johnson scored a basket to give Baylor a temporary 62-60 lead. Jim Nichols, who was high scorer for Washington, then tied it for the last time at 62. Nichols, who had collected four personals in the first half, had to play cautiously and this hampered Washington. Finally with 1:55 left Don Heathington put in the winning basket for Baylor. McLarney, deeply disappointed, no doubt remembered a similar game his players had blown in the second half against Texas in 1943. The next night Baylor came from behind again to eliminate Kansas State 60-52.

For the first time in years there were empty seats for a NCAA final—more than 2,000 of them. It was a dull game and neither team shot well, the Wildcats hitting only 30 percent and the Bears less than 25 percent. It was obvious Baylor was overmatched. Their strategy was to slow the pace down; but the only thing they succeeded in doing was to go scoreless for long stretches. Baylor took just one shot in the first four minutes. Meanwhile Kentucky had little trouble in putting the ball in the hoop. After 7:35 the Wildcats led 13-1. Five minutes later it was 24-7. For the rest of the game the Bears held their own but succumbed 58-42.

1949

Back from their triumph in the Olympics in London, Kentucky won its sixth successive SEC championship. They lost only one game while winning 29 and accepted invitations to both postseason tournaments. This was the first time since 1944 a team had been so honored. The NCAA East regionals were to be held in New York again and would not start until after the NIT was concluded so there would be no schedule conflict. As good as Kentucky had been in 1948 they were even better now. They averaged nearly 70 points a game and their average margin of victory was 25. They tore through their opponents like a tornado crossing the prairie leaving broken victims in their wake. They humiliated Mississippi 85-31, Georgia Tech 78-32, Georgia 95-40 and a strong St. Johns squad 57-30. The Wildcats were back with essentially the same team—only Ken Rollins had graduated.

Big 10 champion Illinois (19-3), paced by Dwight Eddleman, was almost as offensively prolific as Kentucky. Yale (20-8), the winner in the Ivy League, was the only new school in the tourney. They were led by Tony Lavelli who liked to play the accordion at least as much as he enjoyed playing basketball and sometimes entertained during half time. All American Lavelli had compiled 1921 points over a four year career and his 21.3 average was one of the highest in the country. He had an unstoppable hook shot which he launched—sometimes as far as 20 feet—while leaning away from the basket. However, Yale was too much of a one man team to be considered seriously and outside of two West Coast teams, to whom they lost, played exclusively against schools from the Northeast.

Villanova was the first Region 2 choice from outside New York City in five years. At times they could be very, very good—for instance in a 117-25 victory—and then at others they could be awful, as when they lost three times in a four-game stretch by a total of 71 points. After that debacle Villanova went on a strict military diet and bounced back with victories in their next four games against Navy, Naval Air Material Center, Fort Dix and Army. The star of the Wildcats was Paul Arizin who set a national record by scoring 82 points in one game.

The toughest conference that year was the MVC. Oklahoma A and M, St. Louis and Bradley were all rated in the top ten and any one of them would have made an excellent choice for the tournament. As it was, Oklahoma A and M (31-4) had to beat Nebraska to qualify as the Region 5 representative. In one span of 20 games the Aggies gave up fewer than 40 points in all but one. St. Louis and Bradley found some consolation by playing in the NIT.

Wyoming (25-8) won the Skyline race. Their schedule included only conference and other local schools. Oregon State (23-10), which beat UCLA in two of three games for the privilege of representing the PCC, also played exclusively against regional teams. Schools like Oregon State, Wyoming and Yale that did not play intersectionally were thus at a disadvantage during the postseason. Without experience against different styles played outside their regions, they found it difficult to adjust when confronted with them at tournament time.

The SWC choice was Arkansas (14-10) making its quadrennial appearance (they played previously in 1941 and 1945). Arkansas had some trouble getting out of the starting gate, losing five of their first six and eight of eleven. Luckily none of these was against a conference rival. They made the correct adjustments and ended by sharing the league title with Baylor and Rice, beating the latter in a one-game playoff, 50-34.

Madison Square Garden fans were looking forward to a basketball treat. Four of five first team All Americans—three from Kentucky and Lavelli of Yale—would be showcased by the NCAA playoff. (The fifth, Ed Macauley of St. Louis, in the NIT.)

Kentucky's dream of wearing both postseason tourney crowns evaporated in the quarterfinals of the NIT when they lost to Loyola (Ill.)—a game that was later found to have been fixed. They had to wait a week in New York, nursing what was left of their wounded pride, for the first round of the NCAA to begin.* Kentucky vented their frustration on Villanova in a tangle of Wildcats. Villanova took an early lead as they hit on six of their first seven shots. However, they were unable to maintain that kind of deadliness and Kentucky soon moved in front. It was a rough contest, frequently interrupted by the referee's whistle. Taking advantage of all opportunities, Kentucky bagged 23 from the line and beat Villanova by a record breaking score, 85-72. In a year when the average number of points scored by both teams was not quite one hundred, both teams acquitted themselves well offensively. Rupp, though pleased with the victory, remarked this was the most points ever given up by any of his teams. Scoring honors went to Groza and Arizin who each tallied 30. Jim Line contributed 21 points though neither Beard nor Jones could claim a basket.

With three minutes left in their game against Illinois, Yale found itself with a surprising five point lead. Ted Anderson and Walt Kersulis put in one handers for the Illini, but Yale answered with a free throw to make the score 67-65. Hoping to break Illinois momentum, the Bulldogs switched from man-to-man to a zone defense. It did not help. With less than two minutes remaining, first Anderson and then Kersulis struck again. The insurance was provided by Dick Foley who stole the ball and layed it in to give Illinois a 71-67 win. Lavelli scored 27, mostly on hook shots, but he had very little support.

In the regional final Kentucky wasted no time. They took an early lead and ran away from Illinois 76-47. Groza had another brilliant night and scored 27 while nobody on Illinois made it into double figures. Having been eliminated in the NIT by one team from Illinois, the Wildcats took their revenge on another.

In Kansas City before a capacity crowd of 10,200, Oregon State advanced at the expense of Arkansas 56-38. The game was much closer than the score indicated. With nine minutes left to play Arkansas enjoyed a slim lead, 30-29. Then the roof caved in. Oregon State went on a scoring binge that left the Razorbacks prostrate.

Oklahoma A and M playing their usual slowdown game found they needed some points in a hurry. They were trailing by five against Wyoming

---

*In 1949 the NIT decided to expand to 12 teams. Four were seeded and thereby drew a first round bye. Four New York schools competed—NYU, St. Johns, Manhattan and CCNY—but since none of them were seeded they all had to play in the first round. All four lost their games in what was called the "Manhattan Massacre." An even bigger and more incredible massacre awaited the seeded teams. Playing against the first round winners, nationally first ranked Kentucky, third ranked St. Louis, fifth ranked Western Kentucky and Utah, the top four seeded teams, all lost. Two nights' later seventh ranked Bradley and tenth ranked Bowling Green lost in the semifinals to upstart San Francisco, the eventual tournament winner, and Loyola (Ill.).

with 1:40 to play. Jack Shelton, a junior forward who had contributed ten points up till then, decided to take matters into his own hands. He scored two quick buckets. Then in the waning seconds a double foul resulted in a jump ball. Taking the tap Gale McArthur of the Aggies whipped the ball to the hot hand and Shelton put it through the hoop with four seconds remaining to give the Oklahomans a 40-39 win. Scanning the statistics after the game, Wyoming appreciated the hazards of playing against the Aggies. They made almost 50 percent of their shots but managed to get off only 31.

Wyoming's hot hand must have been contagious because the Aggies' accuracy from the field (17 of 38) and the foul line (16-19) went a long way towards eliminating Oregon State. Coach Amory Gill of the Beavers tried a variety of tactics including substituting a fresh quintet in place of his starters halfway through the first period, but nothing helped. Oregon State tallied only 11 points that half and the Aggies romped, 55-30.

For the first time since 1942 the final round was not played in Madison Square Garden. The regional winners flew to Seattle to play in the University of Washington's Edmundson Pavilion. It was a classic confrontation between the two winningest coaches in college basketball—one an advocate of ball control and strong defense, the other favoring a run-and-shoot style of play. It was also the only time Adolph Rupp and Hank Iba faced each other in an NCAA playoff.

If ever a player deserved the title Most Valuable it was Alex Groza in the final. He tallied 25 of Kentucky's 46 points—this in spite of the fact he sat out eight minutes of the second half with foul trouble. Reinserted in the lineup, he fouled out with five minutes to play. Thus he scored 25 points in only 27 minutes of action. He was so dominant while on the court that few of his teammates scored. Groza's total of 82 points in three games set a new NCAA playoff record. Oklahoma A and M played their usual ball control game, but Kentucky and Groza scored enough points to win, 46-36—their second consecutive championship, a feat previously accomplished only by A and M.

1950

One rule change had a profound effect on the 1950 season in general and the playoffs in particular. No longer could a team waive a foul in the latter part of a game in order to retain possession. Instead, the side fouled had to shoot the free throws, but they also kept the ball if the foul occurred in the last two minutes of the game. The rule was passed in order to reduce frequent interruptions in the closing minutes as the trailing team tried to gain possession of the ball. Its effect, however, was to reduce the game to 38 minutes since, with the advantage the rule change gave to the team ahead at that point, it was next to impossible to catch up.

The NIT was over for a week before the NCAA playoffs got underway. No Region 2 representation had been picked until CCNY surprised everyone except maybe its coach, Nat Holman, and his players by winning the NIT. CCNY (17-5) did not have the best record in the region nor in New York City—St. Johns was 22-4, LIU 20-4—but CCNY had beaten both of them as well as NYU, Fordham, Manhattan and St. Francis to become the unofficial city champion. An invitation to the NIT seemed logical, but a championship was definitely unlikely. In the first round the Beavers upset San Francisco, the defending NIT champions. In the quarter finals they were matched against third ranked Kentucky which was aiming to extend a 14 game win streak. The Wildcats had lost four of their starting five through graduation, but they still had Jim Line, and 7 foot sophomore center Bill Spivey was learning fast. You could have counted the number of teams better than the Wildcats in the time it takes the ball to drop through the hoop, but CCNY demolished them 89-50, the worst drubbing the Wildcats had ever suffered before or since. (After that game the Kentucky State Senate considered a resolution to drop the flag to half mast to mark the defeat.) Next came sixth ranked Duquesne which CCNY defeated to gain the final against the number one team in the country, Bradley. In an exciting finish CCNY polished off the Braves. The next day they accepted an invitation to play in the NCAA championships. Bradley, on the other hand, still had to qualify for its berth by defeating the Big 7 winner Kansas State.

The Beavers had not been particularly impressive at the start of the season. They won their first five against mediocre opponents, then lost to Oklahoma and UCLA, both better-than-average teams. A win over weak California did not enhance their prestige, but they gained momentum as the season progressed. The reason for the slow start was that CCNY had a starting five composed of four sophomores (freshmen were not eligible at the time) and one senior, Irv Dambrot, who had been a freshman on the 1947 tournament team. All were products of New York City high schools and each had to have the equivalent of a 3.0 scholastic average to be admitted to the college.

CCNY had no football team so that over the years most sports interest was focused on their basketball teams. They had an exceptional coach in Nat Holman, properly called Mr. Basketball, who had been a star with the Original Celtics. He had coached at CCNY, where he was paid $8,500 a year as an assistant professor, for 30 years and had either played with or observed every star of the game; but even he had to admit the hopefuls who greeted him on the opening day of practice were exceptional. Besides Dambrot there was Ed Warner, a 6′2″ forward, with the poise of a ballet dancer and the drive of a runaway bulldozer. There was 6′6″ Ed Roman who could stand in the corner and hit 18 foot one handers all night. And there was chunky Ed Roth and lithe Floyd Layne, a couple of solid guards. But it was not as individuals that they glittered. Rather it was the rhythm and fluidity they created as a team, like a machine whose power is measured only by its output and not the size nor the complexity of its parts. They blended and meshed and generated the kind of excitement still recalled fondly many years later. The 1950 Beavers peaked at exactly the right time. The unselfishness of their passing, the sharpness of their attack, the intensity of their drive for the basket was absolutely stunning. It was clinic basketball and pure joy to watch.

At least some of the players were products of the ghetto. Warner and Layne were black. Warner, and Sherman White, a contemporary at LIU, were among the first black stars in a sport that had, until then, been dominated almost exclusively by white athletes. It was not easy to attend school, play basketball and help support one's family. Warner, an orphan, provided for two brothers, a sister and did social work in Harlem.

CCNY, though impressive in the NIT, was not the favorite in the NCAA tournament. There were too many other good schools. Kentucky was not invited back to try for a third straight title. The Region 3 representative was North Carolina State (25-5). Though they had just won their fourth consecutive Southern Conference championship this was their first invitation to the tournament. They had defeated schools from all over the country, including an excellent LIU squad. The Wolfpack was fortunate in having two All Americans in Sam Ranzino and Dick Dickey, as well as the dependable Vic Bubas.

Ohio State, ranked number two behind Bradley, was the Big 10 winner. They had their own All American in Dick Schnittker. The Buckeyes had just completed their most successful season ever, losing only to DePaul, Bradley and Illinois while winning 21. The Region 1 choice was Holy Cross (27-2). The crusaders, aided by players from last year's freshman team that won 16 of 17, beat their first 26 components and then lost two in a row to Columbia and Yale. In the last game of the season they reversed that short losing streak, humiliating Fairfield by 48 points. Holy Cross, led by Bob Cousy (by now a senior), had an awesome offense and twice scored over 100 points. They were also very deep in talent and often played two platoon basketball, a tactic enjoying brief popularity that year. Some teams, including Holy Cross, would substitute five fresh players at periodic intervals. With well-rested players in the game they could, theoretically, maintain momentum and wear their opponents down. Fans and sports writers around the country were talking and writing about Cousy's phenomenal ball handling. He drove whoever was guarding him dizzy with his dazzling ability to dribble behind his back and change directions at eyeblinking speed. With his white T shirt under his uniform he was the focus of attention whenever he was on the court.

UCLA (25-5) became the PCC champion after beating Washington State two games to nil in the playoff. Baylor's 13-11 record was good enough to win the Southwest crown since only one other school in the conference was able to win more than 50 percent of its games. But even they were outclassed when they lost seven during one stretch of nine games. Brigham

Young's record was slightly better, 21-11, as they won in the Skyline but they, too, skidded temporarily when they lost seven of eight. However, they notched their last six, all against conference schools.

The MVC leader, Bradley (27-3), was voted the number one team in the country. Much of the credit belonged to Paul Unruh, an All American, and Gene "Squeaky" Melchiorre, a 5′8″ dynamo who often played forward because of his driving and jumping skills. Bradley was a small college with a student enrollment not much more than 3,000, most of them, including the players, from within 50 miles of the school in Peoria, Ill. They played in a tough league and had an even tougher schedule outside the conference, playing teams from all over the country including Hawaii.

The opening round games were played in New York and Kansas City as usual. By half time North Carolina State had opened a big gap over Holy Cross. The Crusaders came back and closed to within two before the Wolfpack restored matters to their satisfaction. New individual and team records were set as Ranzino tallied 32 to top fellow North Carolinian Glamack's nine year old mark, while Dickey contributed 25 to help the Wolfpack set a new team scoring record. The final 87-74 score might have been even higher, but North Carolina State lost Vic Bubas in the first half with a sprained ankle, and it seemed doubtful he would be able to play again in the tournament. Cousy led the Crusaders with 24 points though his shooting touch forsook him as he forced up 38 shots.

CCNY found itself in a close battle with second ranked Ohio State. The Beavers' strategy was to take center Ed Roman out of the post in order to open up a lane for Warner to drive for the basket. But the Buckeyes clogged the middle, forcing CCNY to shoot from outside. They adjusted well and, with Roman hitting from the corners and the others from medium and long range, gained a 40-all tie at the half.

After taking an early lead in the second half, with Ohio State stubbornly sticking with its zone defense, the Beavers simply held the ball for four and a half minutes, refusing to risk a shot from outside. Eventually the Buckeyes had to come out and go for the ball but it was too late. CCNY went into the last two minutes with a 56-54 lead and with the two minute foul rule in effect, they seemed safe. But then this superbly disciplined team suffered two lapses that almost cost them the game. The Beavers froze the ball effectively until Warner unexpectedly found himself completely free under the basket. Wanting to make absolutely sure of the easy layup, he took his time and, as if he was trapped in some slow motion charade, he leisurely sank the basket. The referee blew his whistle. No basket; three second violation. Ohio State could not score and CCNY got the ball back, but with 19 seconds left Ed Roman foolishly tried a layup and was called for an offensive foul. Ohio State made the free throw and put the ball in play. By this time their star Dick Schnittker, who had pumped in 26 points, fouled out and Bob Burkholder who took the final shot missed the mark. The 56-55 victory brought CCNY a step closer to a double tournament victory.

The semifinal game was equally close and just as exciting. CCNY held a slim 38-37 lead at the midway mark. Ranzino was as hot as a blowtorch in the second half. With his teammates repeatedly passing him the ball, he scored the first 16 points of the period for State. He might have done even more damage, but he fouled out at the peak of his eruption. CCNY still led 72-69 as the game entered the last two minutes. Ten seconds later Dickey scored on a layup to trim the margin to a single point. At 1:35 Warner was set up on a back door play and put in an easy layup. After State missed a shot, Layne was fouled by Dickey, his fifth, and made the penalty. With less than a minute showing on the clock, CCNY elected to freeze the ball, but a turnover gave the Wolfpack possession, an opportunity which they cashed immediately by depositing the ball in the net. Another bad pass gave North Carolina State (now down by only two points) the ball with 30 seconds left. Bubas, playing in spite of a painful ankle injury, missed and one of the Beavers grabbed the rebound. Three points by CCNY in the last 20 seconds made the final score 78-73. The Beavers were only one victory away from glory.

Meanwhile in Kansas City Bradley was having problems. After an evenly played first half which ended in a 33-33 tie, UCLA found itself leading by 57-50 with only seven minutes left to play. Bradley rose to the occasion and with a field goal and two free throws by Bill Mann and two jump shots by Unruh assumed a 58-57 lead with three minutes to go. This was just the opening salvo. Pushing the throttle to maximum, the Braves scored 15 points in the next three minutes to two for the Bruins. When the dust settled and time expired, Bradley was on top 73-59.

In still another close match Brigham Young took a sparse 26-25 lead over Baylor into the locker room and increased that slightly to 54-50 with one minute to go in the game. But Baylor had the ball and Don Heathington, shooting from long range, hit the cords to slice the lead in half. Again Baylor got the ball, and Gerald Cobb calmly sank a free throw to complete a 3 point play. BYU's Joe Nelson added a free throw to produce a string of fives on the scoreboard. The Cougars kept possession and played for the last shot. Then a turnover gave the Bears a last chance, and they worked the ball to Heatnington. Before he could get a shot off, he was fouled. Calmly stepping to the line with more than 10,000 fans creating a tunnel of hysteria, he sank the winning free throw with seven seconds to go for the 56-55 victory.

By the following evening both winning quintets were feeling the results of their semifinal exertions. Despite their 14 point underdog status, Baylor fought Bradley to a standstill in the first half, trailing only 35-32 at the break. There had been eight ties up till then, but now Bradley, living up to their number one ranking, began to pull away and only a late rush by the Bears made the final score close. Baylor held Unruh to seven points while their own star, Heathington, collected 26, but the Braves won the game 68-66.

Bradley returned to New York for their rematch with CCNY, to be played the following Tuesday. The Braves were exhausted. They had flown to New York to participate in the NIT. Then after their loss in the final, they flew back to Peoria, then on to Kansas City for a game against Kansas to determine the Region 5 representative. After their two wins in the NCAA western regional, it was back to Peoria and finally to New York. In the meantime CCNY did not have to stir from home, confining their travel to subways and buses between home, classroom and basketball court.

To conserve their energy the Braves opened the final with a zone defense. There was a second reason for this strategy. In nearly every game CCNY had won in both postseason tournaments, they managed to make the opposing team's top scorer foul out. Much of this was due to the Beavers' constant driving pressure. A zone defense seemed the most sensible answer to Bradley's problems. It did not work out that way, though. Taking a 39-32 lead into the locker room, the Beavers increased that to 58-47 halfway through the second half. They seemed in good shape although Roman had fouled out and Warner at 6′2″ had to take his place at center. At this point Bradley switched to a man-to-man defense and subjected CCNY to an all-court press. They paid the price. Before the game was over Unruh, Mann and Aaron Preece had fouled out and Melchiorre, Elmer Behnke and George Chianakas were on the brink with four each. However, the tactic had the effect of closing the gap, and the teams entered the last two minutes with CCNY enjoying only a five point lead. With the two minute rule in effect a margin of this magnitude was almost always sufficient to ensure victory. With 57 seconds to go the Beavers lead had climbed to 69-63 and the ecstatic fans were ready to storm onto the court. But the next 20 seconds froze everyone in their seats as the Braves scored five on two layins by Melchiorre and a free throw by Joe Stowell. Squeaky, the last of Bradley's stars on the court, was playing as if he had been tanked up with jet fuel. Streaking all over the court he took one pass and put it in, then stole the ball and scored again. Holman called time out to settle his team. Cheerleaders for the Lavender ran onto the court to orchestrate a rousing "Allagaroo!" But the Beaver players were definitely rattled now and within ten seconds a wild pass gave Bradley the ball again. Melchiorre drove the key and jumping to his utmost reach let fly for the basket. Dambrot, a full eight inches taller than Squeaky, timed his counter jump perfectly and deflected the ball to Norm Mager who, uncontested, drove the length of the court for the crusher. CCNY 71, Bradley 68.

It was all over. Hysterical fans and students swarmed onto the court. They had just witnessed something that had never happened before and never would again—a double tournament triumph, a grand slam of basketball. In order to achieve this, unranked CCNY had to defeat the 12th, 6th, 5th, 3rd, 2nd and finally the top ranked team in the country twice. No other school has ever come close to achieving that kind of dominance in tournament competition.

After the first 12 years of NCAA basketball tournaments Regions 1 and 2 had each produced a champion. The other Regions had two champions each, except for Region 6, which had yet to produce a winner.

5

SCANDAL AND EXPANSION 1951-1952

The 1950-51 season looked bright with prospect for CCNY and Bradley. Each had lost only one starter from the previous year—Dambrot of the Beavers and Unruh of the Braves. Many felt the former super-sophs of CCNY, now even more super as juniors, could become the number one quintet in the country. Of course they would have strong opposition from Kentucky with 7 foot Bill Spivey. Another school, LIU, with perhaps the best college basketball player in the country in Sherman White, won their first 16 games and was a definite contender for a tournament berth and a national championship. It all looked so promising—but that was before the black stain of scandal aborted hopes, careers and the ascendancy of New York college basketball. CCNY, Bradley, Kentucky, LIU and several other schools were all eventually implicated in the scandals.

Awareness that gambling had an effect on college basketball games did not begin with the revelations of 1951. In 1945 five Brooklyn College students admitted they had accepted money to lose purposely, or dump as it was called, a game to Akron. The scheme was discovered prior to the game, which was then cancelled, and the students expelled.* Four years later gamblers tried to bribe George Washington University's Dave Shapiro but he turned them in to the police. Rumors of other bribe attempts and fixed games surfaced from time to time, but it was not until 1951 that the lid blew

*The word student was used quite liberally in the case of one player who was not even enrolled in the college. Nobody, neither the coach nor his parents, knew of his special status. He left home every morning ostensibly to attend classes and spent the day hanging around the gym playing basketball.

Ronnie McGilvray (15) has a problem seeing the basket and looks as if he may pass off to Bob Zawoluk (30). Kansas routed St. Johns 80-63 in the 1952 final.
(Rich Clarkson photo)

right off the pot, revealing a mass of moral decay that besmirched players, coaches, recruiters and promoters. There were victims and villains enough to cast several horror stories but only a single hero. That honor went to Junius Kellogg, the star of Manhattan College in New York—an honest athlete who turned down a bribe. He was approached by former teammate Hank Poppe who offered him $1,000 to control the point spread of an upcoming game. Instead, he went to the police and the resulting investigation brought to light the scope of the game-fixing activity.

It is interesting to note that Kellogg, a black man, came from a school that took pride in maintaining a moral code. In the late 1940's several northern schools, notably Duquesne, had refused to play in tournaments that barred negros, but in all such cases the school included a black athlete on its squad. In 1948 Manhattan refused an invitation by the National Intercollegiate Association (which barred blacks) to participate in its basketball tourney even though it had no black players on its team at the time. That type of integrity must have transmitted itself to Kellogg.

A month after the original scandal was revealed, four players—Warner, Roman, Roth and Layne, the nucleus of the CCNY 1950 championship team—were arrested along with gambler Salvatore Sollazzo. The investigation spread and soon other New York players from NYU and LIU were implicated. The only major New York school untouched by the scandal was St. Johns. At the time CCNY was in the middle of a disappointing season, having already lost six games. It was soon discovered that four of those games had been deliberately dumped. LIU, which had won its first 16 games, lost its next four as the players who had not yet been arrested lost their concentration while waiting for a call from the DA's office. (The LIU players were cleverer than their CCNY counterparts because they were able to continue winning while shaving points to beat the spread, thus ensuring huge profits for the gamblers who were paying them.)

At first it looked as if the scandals were confined to New York schools and to games played in Madison Square Garden. Coaches around the country were quick to denounce the corrupting influence of the Garden and pointed an accusing finger at its president Ned Irish. Irish defended himself by denying he had promoted college basketball in that arena,claiming his sole function was that of landlord, a response that caused some hilarity in the basketball world. Phog Allen, the coach at Kansas, went so far as to accuse the NCAA of teaming up "with promoters to hold tournaments in an arena where everyone knows big time gamblers operate." This was an obviously hypocritical statement since Allen's teams had frequently played in the Garden. Nevertheless, the accusation stung the NCAA into announcing that after the 1951 tournament the playoffs would no longer be held in Madison Square Garden and recommended that its member schools not play there in the future.

The predominant feeling among coaches, especially outside New York and Philadelphia, was that they had lost control of the game as a result of its transfer to the big city arenas. This prompted a movement to bring the game back to the campus gymnasium. A planned postseason tournament to be held in Chicago in competition with the NIT was cancelled.

Bradley organized what it called its first annual National Campus postseason tournament. (It was also to be the **only** National Campus tournament.) In March, effervesced by a spirited "rah rah" atmosphere somewhat reminiscent of a revivalist convention, Bradley and seven other schools participated in the week-long campus event. A few months later Gene Melchiorre, Bill Mann and four other Bradley players were indicted for manipulating the outcome of a game played in the campus gymnasium. It became apparent that corruption could occur on campus as well as off.

Revelation of the scandals did not erupt in one big explosion but as a series of sizeable tremors which jarred the basketball community to its foundation over a period of almost two years. As the dimensions of the calamity became known, educators, coaches, writers, lawyers and judges unhesitatingly delivered their opinions, solicited or otherwise. At first most of the finger pointing focused on New York and the corruption created by the big city environment. (Senator Estes Kefauver of Tennessee was holding a series of hearings to determine the extent of organized crime in New York at the time.) Adolph Rupp smugly announced that gamblers could not touch his boys with a ten foot pole. He found out differently. Alex Groza, Ralph Beard and Dale Barnstable, now well paid professionals, confessed to having shaved points in the game they eventually lost to Loyola in the 1949 NIT and also in a game against Tennessee in Lexington.

After midwest and southern schools had been implicated, criticism focused on the commercialism that had crept into the sport. Here critics were on much firmer ground. For example, until 1938 LIU had played its home games in Brooklyn College of Pharmacy's 800 seat gymnasium. Then they switched to the Garden where the school netted more money in one game than they had over a full season in the old gymnasium. At Kentucky, gross income from basketball jumped from $42,000 in 1945 to $194,000 in 1951. Schools such as Bradley, St. Louis and Western Kentucky, to mention just three of many which could not afford a major college football team, found that with a relatively small investment they could develop a revenue producing first class basketball team. Arena owners were making huge profits from sellout crowds attracted by college basketball doubleheaders. Gamblers were wagering from $50 to $500 per contest and it was estimated that a total of $500,000 was bet on an average night in Madison Square Garden* while an additional ten million dollars changed hands around the country nightly during the season. It seemed everyone was making money except the players who were the reason for this bonanza. For the relatively slim pickings of a

*Ned Irish did try to curb gambling activity in the Garden by adding additional policemen and screening spectators for known gamblers. He also suggested that newspapers not print the point spread on local games.

$50 a week retainer and $1,000 for each game manipulated to the gambler's satisfaction, some athletes forfeited integrity and the chance at much bigger earnings in the future. Groza, Beard and Barnstable, who were already playing professionally, were barred from the NBA for life. Sherman White, who was looking forward to spending the winter of 1952 on a professional team, spent it instead in a jail cell—his potential for a $100,000 salary a shattered dream.

In April 1952, Judge Saul Streit handed down suspended sentences on the self-confessed Kentucky players. He took the occasion to deliver a scathing attack on Coach Rupp and the university's athletic program, calling its basketball team "the acme of commercialism," adding he had found "covert subsidization of players, ruthless exploitation of athletes, cribbing at examinations, illegal recruiting . . ." Not many college spokemen were in a stone-casting mood. They knew what was true at Kentucky was equally true at any number of other schools. Even at CCNY with its high academic standards investigation revealed the admission of Irv Dambrot and Al Roth had been based on grades that had been altered in their favor. There was sufficient blame to go around but few would accept it. The National Association of Basketball Coaches, for instance, trying to sound contrite, missed the mark by a wide margin when they passed a resolution in March, 1951 in which they stated: "In the desire to win games we have let players into the game who are not a credit to their school or to the sport."

There was no doubt college basketball was driving a large number of Americans bonkers during the winter months. But this was nothing compared to the atmosphere when March rolled around and playoff mania swept the country like an epidemic. Most of the excitement centered around high school state championships, but with CCNY's stirring double victory in 1950 and its resulting publicity, more colleges and their fans wanted the opportunity for a national championship. Many fine teams were not getting that opportunity due to the bias towards certain conference winners in most of the regions. In 1948, for instance, of the top ten teams in the county only top ranked Kentucky was invited to the NCAA playoffs. St. Louis (14-3), Bowling Green (27-6), Oklahoma A and M (27-4), Texas (20-5), North Carolina State (29-3), Western Kentucky (28-2), NYU (22-4), Illinois (15-5) and Notre Dame (17-7) were not invited; either they were not selected by the regional committee, or they played in the wrong conference, or they did not play in any conference in a region that selected only conference winners. In Region 4 the big 10 winner was assured of a bid. Other schools from the region like Bowling Green, Notre Dame, DePaul and Loyola, which annually produced excellent teams, remained uninvited. In Region 5, the Big Seven and Missouri Valley Conference champions fought it out annually for the privilege of playing in the tourney. In most years the MVC alone had enough good teams to fill half the spots in the playoffs. The same could be said of Region 3 where usually the winner of either the Southern or Southeastern Conference was selected by committee, never mind that **both** conference champions might be rated in the top ten. On the other hand, in 1947 Navy, with a 16-1 record, represented Region 3 while Kentucky (32-2) and North Carolina State (24-4) did not participate. It was high time to expand the tournament and bring in more schools that had in a de facto way been barred in the past.

In 1949 the NIT had expanded to 12 teams and before the 1951 season the NCAA decided to go it four better and doubled the size of its field. In effect two schools from each region would participate. However, conference affiliation rather than geographical area would determine eligibility for some schools, while non-conference schools would be picked as at-large entries based on location. In 1951, winners of the Yankee, Big 10, Southeast, Southern, Ivy, Big Seven, Missouri Valley, Southwest, Skyline, Border and Pacific Coast conferences were to receive automatic invitations and the selection committees would pick an additional five at-large schools—three from the east, two from the west. This still left several conferences unrepresented—the Ohio Valley and Mid American for instance—but their members could qualify as at-large selections. That year seven schools not previously in the tourney were extended invitations.

1951

East:

With expansion the directors of the tourney decided to hold first round games in Raleigh, N.C., New York and Kansas City. The first game at Raleigh was an interesting rematch between North Carolina State, winner of the Southern Conference for the fifth consecutive year, and Villanova, an at-large entry. State had lost only 4 games while winning 29, but two of those losses had come at the hands of Villanova and the Wolfpack was eager for revenge. It was not an easy task. North Carolina State had a strong offense that three times scored more than one hundred points in a game. Unfortunately, three of their starters—Paul Horvath, Vic Bubas and All American Sam Ranzino—were not going to be able to play since they had used up the three year eligibility allowed by the NCAA.

The second game was a confrontation between two Kentucky quintets—Louisville (19-7) and number one ranked Kentucky from nearby Lexington, with a 28-2 record (including a 21 game winning streak). Kentucky's opponents tried various tactics to spring an upset. Slowing the pace down, thereby producing a low scoring game, seemed the key to victory. For St. Louis it was; for others who tried a similar tactic it was not.

Kentucky had little trouble eliminating Louisville. From a 44-40 half time lead they slowly pulled away in the second half to win 79-68. In the first game Villanova's Wildcats continued their dominance over the Wolfpack until after the intermission Bill Kukoy of North Carolina State led his team to a 67-62 victory. Kukoy, getting a chance to start in place of one of the ineligible players, was credited with 27 points. North Carolina State had salvaged one game of three against Villanova, but it was the most important one.

Two more first round games were decided that evening in New York. St. Johns (22-3), the only major New York college untouched by scandal, was making its first tournament appearance. Coach Frank McGuire's boys had lost only to Kansas, Niagara and Dayton. Connecticut, with an identical 22-3 record, was the Yankee Conference winner. Their won-loss record looked impressive, but it had been achieved against relatively modest competition. All the Huskies' opponents came from the Northeast.

Columbia represented the Ivy League. They had won 22 games without a loss—the first undefeated team to play in the NCAA tourney. Their winning streak actually extended back 31 games to the end of the 1950 season. Columbia was playing under freshman coach Lou Rossini, only 29 years old, who had started the year as assistant to head coach Gordon Ridings. When Ridings suffered a heart attack the week before the season opener, Rossini was promoted to the top spot. The Lions had been established as co-favorites with Kentucky in the East regionals, not only on their record but also because of the way they overpowered their opponents. In only four contests was Columbia's winning margin less than ten points.

Their opponent in the first round was Illinois (19-4), loser of only one game in the Big 10. Due to their lack of height the Illini offense was built around their guards, Don Sunderlage and Rod Fletcher.

In the wake of the scandals, attendance at Madison Square Garden had plunged. The annual, traditional NYU-Notre Dame game had drawn only 9,000 spectators, about half that arena's capacity. So it was not surprising there were a few empty seats in the Garden, normally packed for a post-season tournament.

St. Johns had little trouble with Connecticut, extending a 34-19 half time lead to 54-27 before the Huskies made a run late in the game to make the final score a more respectable 63-52. Connecticut's high scorer with 22 was the colorfully named Yogi Yokabaskas.

Despite seven straight buckets by Illinois' Ted Beach, Columbia enjoyed a 45-38 period ending lead. It looked as if the Lions would sweep to their 32nd consecutive victory. But in the second half their fast break congealed while their turnovers zoomed. Illinois took control of the boards and with six minutes left had a fairly comfortable 70-61 lead. Baskets by Jack Molinas, Bob Reiss and John Azary cut that advantage in half. A foul shot by Beach and a layup by Sunderlage were offset by a pair of Columbia buckets and the margin was down to two. The two minute foul rule had been abandoned after only one year so that it was no longer a factor, but the side fouled could still elect to waive and retain possession. With time runing out, Fletcher drove to the hoop, scored, was fouled and elected to shoot to complete a three point play. That was the ball game as Illinois advanced to the next round 79-71. It was also the most points ever given up by Columbia.

North Carolina State and Kentucky travelled to New York to play Illinois and St. Johns in the East regional semifinals. Fletcher and Sunderlage, scoring 19 and 21 points respectively, were superb as they led Illinois to victory over North Carolina State. Each made 50 percent of his shots and Sunderlage contributed ten assists. The Wolfpack, behind by 11 at the half, came back to take the lead in the second period; but the Illini exploded for 11 straight points down the stretch and won 84-70.

In the other regional semifinal St. Johns emulated St. Louis' winning strategy by slowing the pace against Kentucky. It might have worked again except for the dreadful shooting of Jack McMahon (2 for 16) and All American "Zeke" Zawoluk (6 for 24). Bobby Watson, only 5′10″, shadowed McMahon all evening, completely destroying his usual poise. The Redmen started the second half leading by a point and things looked even brighter a few minutes later when Spivey picked up his fourth personal. But Adolph Rupp left him in the game. That move paid off as Spivey avoided any more fouls and the Wildcats soared to a 42-34 lead midway through the second half. The Redmen weren't through, though. They rallied to knot the score at 43-43. The Wildcats then took charge and scored the last 16 points, winning 59-43 as St. Johns' defense went completely to pieces.

Two evenings later Kentucky and Illinois squared off in the last NCAA tournament game to be played in New York for several years. Fletcher with 21 and Sunderlage with 20 led the Illini as usual. But the star of the game was Spivey, who scored 28 and picked off 16 rebounds, most of them in the second half. He fouled out with three minutes to play—the Wildcats leading 70-69 and the outcome still in doubt. Taking charge in Spivey's absence, Shelby Linville's jump shot gave Kentucky a little breathing room. Beach's free throw and a long set by Irv Bemoras tied the game for the tenth time with 50 seconds showing on the clock. Another jumper by Linville at :38 was matched nine seconds later by a Sunderlage layup. Kentucky maneuvered up court and Frank Ramsey, seeing Linville open, fed him a perfect pass which he converted with 17 seconds left for his third straight basket. Time out, Illinois. The last shot was set up for Sunderlage. He dribbled towards the basket and tried a hook shot that bounced off the rim as time ran out. Kentucky had barely survived 76-74.

West:

Eight teams gathered in Kansas City to participate in the West regional. Kansas State (22-3) was the favorite to win. A loss to LIU and a pummeling of Iowa State by 40 points marked the low and high points of the Wildcats' season. Their opening round opponent Arizona (24-4) was the first Border Conference school to play in the NCAA playoff. Arizona accepted invitations to both postseason tournaments (as did St. Johns, North Carolina State and Brigham Young) but they did not last long in either, having the misfortune of facing both eventual runners up in the early rounds.

Brigham Young (23-7) had the opportunity of duplicating CCNY's double triumph of a year earlier after taking the NIT the week before NCAA competition commenced. With Mel Hutchins at the top of his game, they had an outside chance of doing just that. San Jose State (18-11) was given even less chance. At one point during the season they slumped badly and lost five games in a row.

Oklahoma A and M (27-4), playing their usual ball control offense, won the MVC. Even the deliberate Aggies were beginning to score in the sixties and occasionally even the rarified seventies. Much of this prosperity was attributable to Gale McArthur, their first All American since Bob Kurland. But the whole team played tough and never quit. Twice they won double overtime games and once they went three overtimes to win. Their opening round opponent, Montana State, the first member of the Rocky Mountain Conference to receive a bid to the tourney, had played a blistering schedule, winning 24 of 35.

Texas A and M (17-11) won the SWC by the slimmest of margins in a special conference playoff. Not prolific, the Aggies offense managed to score more than 50 points on only eight occasions. Finally, there was Washington (22-5) which beat UCLA two straight to win the conference. The Huskies finished with a rush winning seven of their last eight to clinch their division in the PCC.

The opening game pitted Kansas State against Arizona in a fray of Wildcats. Arizona found Kansas State a little too much to handle and soon fell so far behind they were almost out of sight. Midway through the second half the Kansans had a 21 point lead. Coach Jack Gardner figured the game was won and substituted a completely new squad for his starters. This had an invigorating effect on Arizona. Going on a 12-5 binge Arizona began to close the huge gap. Kansas State was still ahead 59-45; but worse was to come as Arizona poured in eight more points while Kansas State was able to add only a single free throw. Now the lead had shrunk to seven and panic was oozing out of every Kansas State pore. Gardner called time and got his starters back in the game. It did not help. Arizona was rolling like some monstrous boulder down the side of a canyon, gathering momentum as it progressed. And there was plenty of time left. Jerry Dillon and Bill Schuff scored two more baskets for the underdogs. Kansas State just could not buy a field goal. Ice-cold in their shooting, they were losing cohesion and playing playground basketball. There were still 90 seconds left when Roger Johnson popped one to bring Arizona within one. They had made up 20 of the 21 point deficit. But that basket was the last hurrah. Kansas State, disdaining to shoot either from the floor or from the foul line, held on to the ball. In the final second they shot the first of a two shot foul to make the final score 61-59 but then waived the second. To Jack Gardner the final buzzer must have sounded sweeter than any angel's music. He knew he had been in a scrap and that his team was lucky to have got out alive.

The second game was less invigorating as BYU, with Mel Hutchins' 22 points leading the way, eliminated San Jose State 68-61.

The following evening Oklahoma A and M plodded over Montana State 50-46 and Washington wasted Texas A and M 62-40. The Texans were utterly futile in the first half sinking only 5 baskets in 31 tries. They overcame that trauma after intermission and trailed by only 48-40. The Huskies responded by filling the basket with 14 points while shutting off the Aggies for the rest of the game.

A confrontation between two excellent defensive teams resulted in Oklahoma A and M taking a 36-33 lead over Washington at the end of the half. The Huskies rallied after the intermission but a disputed referee's call became the turning point of the game. Trailing by one point, Washington's Jack Ward recovered a loose ball, drove to the basket and was intercepted by one of the Aggies. The Huskies claimed he had been fouled, but the referee called a jump ball. The Aggies controlled the tip, and Don Johnson scored the next two baskets to give them a 54-49 lead. Washington never came closer than four points again eventually losing 61-57.

Kansas State, finding cougars to be a lot tamer than wildcats, trimmed BYU 64-54. That set up the final between Oklahoma A and M and Kansas State—the second and third ranked teams in the country. The Aggies, playing their third game in as many nights, were obviously tired. Unprolific scorers at best, the Aggies were almost comatose and failed to score for the first seven minutes. The Wildcats, benefitting from an extra day's rest, simply ran them into the boards. Their 37-14 halftime lead was one of the most lopsided in tournament history. The Aggies managed to hold their own in the final 20 minutes but they were beat and beaten 68-44.

The scene now shifted to Minneapolis where another battle of Wildcats was about to decide the national championship. The 1951 tournament had been good to the favorites. Not a single upset had been recorded and the final was no exception.

Lew Hitch, Kansas State's 6′7″ center, kept Spivey in check for one half and the Big Seven champions left the court leading 29-27. Linville's free throw and Spivey's basket at the start of the second half gave Kentucky a lead they never relinquished. Hitch, exhausted by his efforts to guard Spivey, allowed the taller man to get free more frequently. In the first ten minutes of the second half Spivey, who had earlier been held in check, dropped in six buckets on his way to a 22 point evening. To make matters worse Kansas State hit a scoring drought and failed to connect for a full eight minutes. When it was over, Kentucky had the game 68-58 and their third national championship in four years.

1952

With Spivey back, 1952 looked as if it would be another good year for the Wildcats. Actually 1952 was an excellent year for Kentucky who were ranked number one again, but Spivey had little to do with that. The All American center left the team after he had been indicted for perjury in the basketball fixing scandals. He maintained he was innocent and his trial ended in a hung jury, but he never played for Kentucky again. The Wildcats did not miss him all that much. They had Cliff Hagan and Frank Ramsey, the latest in what seemed an inexhaustible line of All Americans. Losing only twice in 30 starts, the Wildcats obliterated most of their opponents. Mercilessly they ran up the score and humiliated their SEC rivals. They beat Mississippi 116-58, Mississippi State 110-66, Tulane 103-54, Florida 99-52, Georgia 99-55, Tennessee 95-40. They averaged more than 83 points a game and their average winning margin was 28 points. Three times they scored more than a hundred points and eleven times more than ninety. Only a one point loss to St. Louis and a four point loss to Minnesota kept them from an unbeaten season. Naturally, they were favored to win their regional and take the national title again.

The NCAA had decided to hold four regional playoffs: East, Mideast, Midwest and West, and then bring the four winners together—the Final Four they were called for the first time—a system that in a slightly modified way is still in effect today. Of the 16 schools in the 1952 tourney, ten were conference winners and six at-large picks.

East:

Beside Kentucky the East regional included Penn State (their first post season appearance), St. Johns and North Carolina State, for the sixth consecutive time the Southern Conference champion. Penn State (20-4) played most of the season as if the word lose was a four letter word. They won 17 of their first 18 but eventually tailed off. Even so their four defeats were by a total of only 11 points. They beat Pittsburgh early in the season 52-45. Their rematch turned into one of the lowest scoring games of modern times as Pittsburgh suspended almost all offensive effort. It did not help them as Penn State scored often enough to take a 24-9 decision.

St. Johns (22-4) had All American Bob Zawoluk back and beat all other New York teams, several of whom were still staggering from the previous year's scandals. North Carolina State (23-9) without Ranzino and Bubas was no longer the dominant squad it had been the previous two years and lost several games decisively, including one by 19 to Manhattan.

All four regionals commenced on March 21. The East regional was held in Raleigh, North Carolina's Reynolds Coliseum. Before 11,000 fans Kentucky trampled Penn State 82-54 with some spectacular shooting and play-making. The second game was closer. The Carolinians, playing before their local supporters, got off to a fast start, but St. Johns overhauled them and led by three at the intermission. In the second half the Redmen spurted to a 47-33 advantage and though the Wolfpack closed to within six they eventually wound up on the short end of a 60-49 score.

As Kentucky and St. Johns warmed up for the regional final they must have been thinking back to the last time they had met a couple of months earlier. On that occasion the Wildcats devastated the New Yorkers by the humiliating score of 81-40. There was little reason to suspect the outcome would be any different now. But that evening the capacity audience watched the Redmen execute the upset of the year as they stopped Kentucky's fast break along with their 23 game winning streak. Every time the Wildcats tried to break out St. Johns would be downcourt to meet and greet them. The Redmen attacked with a deliberate, controlled offense sparked by Zawoluk's 16 first half points (he added the same number in the second half, as many as the rest of his team combined). After 20 minutes the New Yorkers were leading 34-28, then added to their advantage to win 64-57. Along with Zawoluk's 32 points and Jack McMahon's 18, Ronnie MacGilvray's floor generalship was indispensable to St. John's success. Kentucky, playing somewhat overzealously on defense, saw four of their players foul out including center Cliff Hagan, their high scorer with 22 points. The Redmen survived a scare when Zawoluk was charged with his fourth personal with five minutes left in the game but he finished the contest.

Mideast:

In Chicago the Mideast regional included two of the top four teams in the country—second ranked Illinois (19-3) and fourth ranked Duquesne (21-1), as well as Princeton (16-9) and Dayton (24-3). The latter finished as the runner up to LaSalle in the recently concluded NIT. The Flyers had the distinction of being the first independent school selected from the Midwest. Led by second team All American "Monk" Meineke, Dayton had come within a whisker of completing a perfect season. They lost to St. Louis by two (they beat them in the NIT), lost to Miami (Ohio) by one and fell to Louisville in overtime.

Illinois hardly missed Don Sunderlage. His position was filled by Irv Bemoras and along with the returning Rod Fletcher the Illini continued to feature a strong guard oriented attack. Princeton, winner of the Ivy League, won their first three encounters and then went into a tailspin, losing their next six games, luckily none against league opponents. They finished strong, though, capturing 11 of 12.

Duquesne's only loss during the regular season came against Villanova in overtime. Later, after accepting an invitation to the NIT they bowed to LaSalle in the semifinals. The Dukes, though highly rated, played a relatively easy schedule, beating several weak teams by large margins. All in all, the Mideast regional looked like the toughest of the four, but surprisingly none of the teams made it to the final game.

In the first round in Chicago Duquesne was too strong for the Tigers. With Jim Tucker controlling the boards and firing quick outlet passes, the Dukes used the fast break to wear down Princeton. Ten points in a row broke the game open midway through the final half and decided matters for Duquesne, 60-49.

Illinois-Dayton was a repeat of the first game. With Dayton leading 49-47 Illinois scored ten unanswered points and soon put the game out of reach. Jim Bredar, a 5′10″ guard, led the winners with 19 points while Meineke connected for 18. The final score, 80-61, was an accurate reflection of the teams' relative abilities.

Illinois' strategy against Duquesne was to slow down their fast break and try to keep Tucker away from the backboard. That they succeeded on both counts was attributable to their strong defense. Six men played most of the game for Illinois, the scoring evenly distributed among them. Even though he didn't take as many rebounds Tucker still accounted for 29 points and with Dave Ricketts contributing 22 the two players made up almost the total Duquesne offense, such as it was. Illinois led most of the way and eliminated the Dukes 74-68.

Midwest:

Though Madison Square Garden was now officially off limits for the playoffs, the regional tournament was back at its familiar stand in Kansas City's Municipal Auditorium. The favorite of the Midwest regional was Phog Allen's Kansas Jayhawks. Crusty old Phog received his nickname while umpiring baseball games in the minor leagues. Whether the appellation was due to the feeling that his vision was impaired or the resemblance of his voice to a foghorn is not clear. Allen, dean of college basketball coaches, had participated in the game since its infancy, having graduated in 1905 from Kansas, where he played under Dr. Naismith, the founder of the sport. He was in his forty-second year of coaching, most of it at Kansas, and time was beginning to run out for him. He dearly wanted a national championship before retirement.

Allen had a way of exasperating people with his non-stop patter. He had opinions on everything relating to basketball and was never reluctant to express any of them, whether it was the height of the basket, the sinfulness of playing in Madison Square Garden or the amount of sideline coaching that ought to be allowed. Until the late forties coaches were not even allowed to talk to their players during time outs. How Allen survived this restriction is a mystery. During a game he would keep up a non-stop machine gun rattle of advice from the bench. His assistant would be likewise occupied so it was not unusual to hear one man scream, "Shoot," while the other cautioned, "Don't shoot." It was often confusing, but somehow the players managed to cope and more important, to win.

Phog Allen knew how to win. He also knew how to recruit. When he could not find the dominant player he was looking for in any local high school, he went to Terre Haute, Indiana, where he was able to persuade Clyde Lovellette to enroll at Kansas. Lovellette was not only tall, he was also beefy—a well-distributed 245 lbs. on a 6′9″ frame, and almost impossible to push around once planted under the basket. The press appropriately nicknamed him Man Mountain.

If one were charting Kansas' record in 1952 it would look like a straight line with a small cusp in the middle. They won their first 13 games, lost two in a row to Kansas State and Oklahoma A and M and then won the rest for a 22-2 record. Opposing them in the first round was Texas Christian (23-3) with the best record of any SWC school since Texas in 1947.

St. Louis (22-7) won the MVC. Their record was deceptive since four of these losses were by a single point and they had swamped Army and Marquette, two respectable teams, by 35 points each. Rounding out the Midwest quartet was New Mexico A and M (21-8), winner of the Border Conference, making their first tournament appearance. At Kansas City, St. Louis had little trouble disposing of New Mexico A and M, 62-53. Kansas had an even easier time of it against TCU—until the last few minutes, that is. Kansas led by ten at the midway mark and by 16 in the second half. TCU made it close at the end, but the Jayhawks were never in real danger as they took the game 68-64. Lovellette scored 31 points, but this was just an appetizer for the big man.

The next evening Lovellette moved into high gear and broke Ranzino's three-year-old individual scoring record by lofting 44 points through the cords, the first point-a-minute performance in the tourney. Though the rest of the Jayhawks found it difficult to locate the basket, Lovellette's shots seemed to be guided by radar. A good thing, because St. Louis held a 14-8 lead after 10 minutes. The first half ended with the teams even at 27 apiece. It was Lovellette who kept Kansas in the ball game as he scored 19 of their points or 70 percent of the total. The second half was all Kansas—or all Lovellette—as they pushed their final advantage to 74-55.

West:

If there was a favorite in the West regional, held at Corvallis, Oregon, it was Wyoming (27-6), champion of the Skyline Conference. The Cowboys were making their sixth NCAA tourney appearance, a record matched only by Kentucky. Wyoming liked to start their campaign against an opponent that would let them ease into the season without undue exertion. So for years they scheduled their first three games against Montana State and invariably swept them. They then challenged schools all around the western United States and even faced Canadian squads before finishing out the season against their Skyline opponents. This kind of exposure had much to do with their success over the years.

Santa Clara (15-10) and Oklahoma City (17-8) were a pair of at-large selections making their initial tournament appearance. In contrast to Wyoming, Santa Clara played mostly local schools and a few Skyline opponents. Their season did not exactly start with thundering success; it was not until their tenth game that they evened their record and began to win more often than they lost. Oklahoma City was a defense-minded team along the lines of their cross-state rivals Oklahoma A and M. They limited more than two-thirds of their opponents to fewer than 50 points.

UCLA (20-10) was the Pacific Coast Conference representative. Their record was actually worse than Washington (24-4), whom they had beaten in the traditional intra-conference playoff. It was sweet revenge for the Bruins who had been twice defeated by Washington during the season and eliminated by the Huskies in the previous year's playoff.

UCLA's fortune did not survive their clash with Santa Clara. After establishing a 35-31 advantage at the half, the Bruins allowed Santa Clara to surge ahead 50-49. A free throw and basket by Ron Livingston of UCLA put the Bruins on top again but Ken Sears, the Bronco's 6′7″ freshman*, knotted accounts at 52-52. UCLA forged ahead on a bucket by Ron Bane, but this was matched by Bob Peters who stole the ball and dribbled the length of the floor for a layup causing the last tie. UCLA, weakened by the loss via fouls of two fine rebounders, John Moore and Mike Hibler, lost control of the boards and collapsed. Santa Clara poured it on in the final minutes and won 68-59.

A low scoring game between two defensive teams saw Wyoming, in control all the way, eliminate Oklahoma City 54-48.

Santa Clara, using the same script in the regional final, overcame a three point half time deficit to go ahead by 12 against Wyoming. It looked like a safe lead until Wyoming, led by its hurtling guards, threw a scare into the Broncos. Little Leroy Esau pumped three long set shots through the hoop, slicing the lead in half, 51-45. Jim Young scored for the Broncos, but Esau retaliated with another bomb. Sears connected on a foul shot, but Esau responded again. Moe Radovich, playing the other guard position, then stole the ball twice and bang bang the Cowboys were within two with one minute left. Just as it looked as if Santa Clara's dream would turn into a nightmare, Dick Garibaldi swished one in for the Broncos sending them to the championship round in Seattle on the long end of a 56-53 score.

Final Four:

St. Johns, having eliminated number one Kentucky, now faced second ranked Illinois. The New Yorkers outrebounded their taller opponents and, propelled by a ten point spurt, established an early 28-18 advantage. Playing disciplined ball under the floor leadership of Ronnie MacGilvray, the Redmen took a 33-27 lead into the locker room. As soon as play resumed Illinois made their move, pulling even three times and finally leapfrogging

*Freshmen were again eligible due to the Korean War.

ahead 40-39. But St. Johns did not lose their concentration; after the lead tilted back and forth, they moved in front 48-45, nursing that slim margin for the next few minutes. With eight minutes still to go Zawoluk picked up his fourth personal but stayed in the game. The senior center played brilliantly, scoring ten of his 24 points in the final ten minutes. Holding a 58-55 advantage, the Redmen went into a semi-stall, interrupted by a layup off a rebound by Zawoluk and a foul by Solly Walker to give them a 61-55 edge. Then Herb Gerecke, a reserve guard (Illinois was deep in good guards) who had scored but two points until then, found the range on a set shot, stole the ball and was fouled while shooting. He missed the first free throw and Illinois decided to waive the second attempt. Again Gerecke scored, this time from the corner and now St. Johns led by only 61-59. Illinois hounded the Redmen relentlessly and with two seconds remaining stole the ball; Jim Bredar's desperate shot from midcourt at the buzzer missed and the slim margin held up.

The Kansas-Santa Clara contest was not nearly as close. The Broncos were unused to playing against such class competition. Two years earlier under the eight team setup they would not even have been invited to play in the tournament since prior to 1951 the Region 8 representative always came from the PCC. But here they were in the Final Four. Kansas quickly shattered any illusions Santa Clara may have had of going all the way. Lovellette cooled off slightly and scored only 33 points. But the Man Mountain who had led the nation in scoring with 795 points—averaging 28.4 a game—was the difference in the game. If there was any doubt of Lovellette's indispensability, it was dispelled in the second half when, with the Jayhawks ahead 65-41, Allen took his star out of the game. Santa Clara responded by scoring 13 of the next 14 points. The coach quickly reinserted Lovellette and Kansas won going away 74-55. Sears, the Bronco's star, was held to a single point before fouling out.

St. Johns, having eliminated the number one and two ranked teams in the country, had to get past the third ranked team to win the national crown. Theoretically, it should have been easier than their previous contests, but the game is played on the court and not in theory or in some newspaper poll. Kansas, showing more symmetry in the names of its lineup than in the balance of its attack, started Keller and Kenney at forward, Hoagland and Hoag at guard and, of course, Lovellette.

It was a hard-fought duel. Kansas was charged with 35 fouls and St. Johns with 25. But the outcome was never in doubt. Lovellette, hitting consistently on hooks and tip ins, scored 33 points. Thus in three of the four contests he had topped the previous individual scoring record. His total of 141 points for four games shattered the record set by Don Sunderlage by 58. At only one point in the game did it look as if St. Johns might have a chance—when Lovellette suffered his fourth personal early in the second half. He stayed in the game, however, without collecting another. The final score was Kansas 80, St. Johns 63—Phog Allen had the national championship he so coveted.

6

THE SCORING REVOLUTION 1953-1954

During the 1951-52 season fans watched impatiently as referees whistled an average 45 personal fouls per game, a record, and contests had more interruptions than action. On the day of the 1952 championship game the NCAA Rules Committee suggested some changes to the regulations governing fouls. These changes would have a significant effect on the game as it was played in 1953 and 1954. The committee made three recommendations which were adopted shortly thereafter. First, fouls could no longer be waived and free throws would have to be taken. Second, if a "one shot" defensive foul was called, and the free throw missed, the player who was fouled was allowed a second attempt. Third, all fouls in the last three minutes of a game would be two-shot fouls.

As a result, a lot more free throws were attempted and a lot more sunk than in any previous year. 1953 saw a 30 percent increase in free throw attempts over the previous year and an almost 10 percent increase in scoring—the biggest jump ever recorded. Bradley still holds the record for the most free throws made, and attempted, in one season—865 of 1263 in 1954. Frank Selvy's individual record of 355 free throw points that year has also survived. Accuracy from the line was an important factor in developing a winning team.

The intent of the changes was to reduce fouling. However, this was undermined, in many cases, by the statistical realities then prevailing. If a team with good free throw shooters could almost be guaranteed a point every time they were fouled, then the offensive strategy was to drive to the hoop and pick up as many fouls as possible. Even if one had to give the ball up after a successful foul shot, one was better off since field goal accuracy

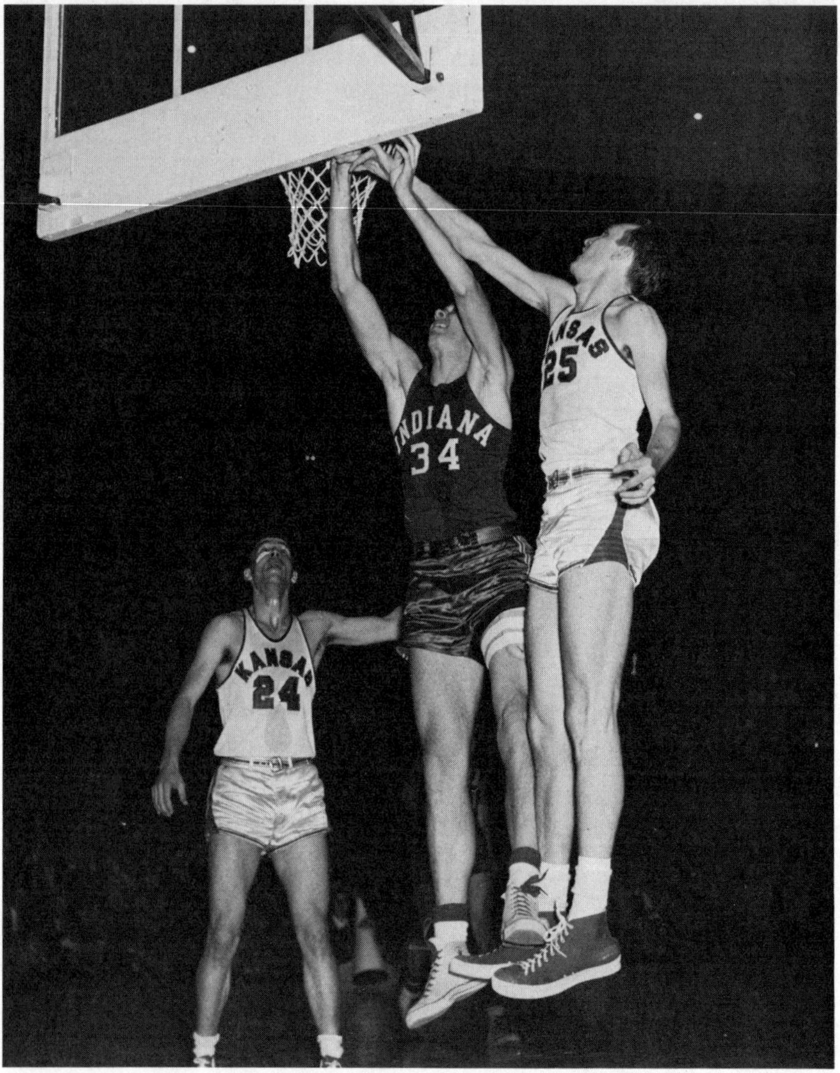

Don Schlundt of Indiana muscles his way between a pair of Kansas defenders in the 1953 final game. His team squeezed by the Jayhawks 69-68. (Indiana University photo)

was only about 35 percent at the time. Thus, by playing the percentages, a team had a better chance of scoring when an 80 percent free throw shooter was given two chances to make one point than a 35 percent shooter attempting to make two points from the floor.

Teams began concentrating on aggressive, fast breaking, explosive offenses as never before. Scores soared into the 80's and 90's and topping 100 points was no longer so extraordinary. There were a few exceptions such as Wyoming and Oklahoma A and M where Hank Iba preached the sanctity of defense and a deliberate, patterned offense. But by and large coaches were convinced higher scores meant more victories.

High scoring teams naturally meant high scoring players, and there were a bunch. Foremost among then was 6′3″ Frank Selvy of Furman. In 1953 he scored 63 points in one game. A year later he banged in 57, 58 and 100—the last being the all-time individual scoring record for a Division I player—on his way to a 41.2 point per game average. Then there was Bob Pettit, the 6′10″ LSU center, who scored 57 and 60 that same year and averaged 31.2 points per game. Not to be forgotten was Johnny O'Brien, at 5′9″ a swizzlestick among bean poles who nevertheless became the first player to score 1000 points in a season and later the first to top 3000 in a career. And in 1953 Bevo Francis from Rio Grande College (94 students) scored almost 2000 points and averaged 50 a game though the opposition was often junior college caliber.

In 1952 the teams participating in the NCAA tournament averaged 66.3 points per game. The next year teams appearing in the tourney had jammed an average of 72.4 points through the hoop.

1953

In 1953 the NCAA again decided to increase the size of the tournament field. A total of 22 schools competed, four more at-large teams and the winners of the Mid-American and Rocky Mountain conferences—both of which would in the future receive automatic invitations. In effect, every major basketball conference with the exception of the Yankee and Ohio Valley was now represented in the postseason competition, and even schools from those two conferences could be picked as one of the nine at-large selectees. Since the number of entrants dictated that some teams would have to play an extra game, a plan was devised whereby schools from some conferences would receive an opening round bye. The privileged conferences were those who had the better records in previous NCAA postseason competition.

It was a tournament of individual stars rather than great teams. Lovellette's scoring mark for a single game was broken after only one year and several other players came close to breaking it. Among the stars of the first magnitude were Bob Houbregs of Washington, Johnny O'Brien of Seattle, Bob Pettit of LSU, Don Schlundt of Indiana, Togo Pallazzi of Holy Cross and Bob Mattick of Oklahoma A and M. Almost as well regarded were B.H. Born of Kansas, Ernie Beck of Pennsylvania, Ron Feiereisel of DePaul and Bob Leonard of Indiana.

East:

In the East, Lebanon Valley, winner of 19 of 20 games, was an at-large selection. With an enrollment of 500, of which only half were men, it was the smallest school to compete in the NCAA playoffs. Their coach, the colorfully named George (Rinso) Marquette, was a proponent of the helter-skelter dribble toward the basket and shoot offense so popular at the time. This strategy was surprising in light of the Flying Dutchmen's lack of height. Only one starter, Leon Miller, topped six feet but true to their nickname, they all flew.

Fordham (18-7) started out the season on a high trajectory, winning their first 11 games and 15 of 17—losing only to St. Johns and Seton Hall, both ranked in the top ten. Then they suffered a power failure in the home stretch and crashed in their last three games. Holy Cross (18-5), the New England representative, was led by Togo Palazzi. The Crusaders, a high scoring team which averaged almost 80 points a game, got better as the season matured. After losing to Dartmouth early in the campaign, they socked them in a rematch 99-50. Navy (16-4), under Bern Carnevale, was another team that fitted the offensive mold.

Louisiana State University was the SEC champion, having bowed only once in 25 games. LSU's loss was against Tulsa, which had thumped them 84-58. They sneaked past Villanova on their next date. The temporary absence of Bob Pettit accounted for this brief lapse.

The unusual situation of a team other than Kentucky perched atop the Southeast Conference came about when the Wildcats were barred first by the SEC from conference competition and then suspended by the NCAA for a whole year. So Kentucky sat out the 1952-53 season and played a series of well-attended intrasquad games at its large new auditorium. Rupp fumed and bided his time planning for next season.

There was considerable satisfaction among rival coaches that Rupp and his Wildcats had received what they deserved. For years Kentucky had dominated their conference, often humiliating opponents by running up astronomical scores. The decision to ban Kentucky from conference competition for one year was as much motivated by a vindictive desire to cut Adolph Rupp down to size as it was by a feeling that disciplinary action was necessary. For the first time in ten years a Kentucky team was not playing in at least one postseason tournament.

Also among the missing was North Carolina State which, though they won the Southern Conference title for the eighth consecutive time, fell to Wake Forest (21-6) in that league's playoff. The Deacons, a charter participant in the NCAA tournament, had played in the inaugural game in 1939 and were making their first appearance in 15 years.

In the first round double header at the Philadelphia Palestra before a small crowd of 4,000, Lebanon Valley surprised everyone, though probably not themselves, by downing Fordham 80-67. The victory becomes even more remarkable when one considers the Rams not only had a substantial height advantage but also boasted the top rebounder in the country in Ed Conlin. But what the Flying Dutchmen lacked in size they made up for in quickness. They repeatedly stole the ball and raced in for easy layups. Tied at the half, Lebanon Valley simply wore Fordham down by running them into the hardwood. The Dutchmen were in remarkable condition since all five starters played the entire game while Fordham, using substitutes liberally, was unable to keep up.

The Pennsylvanians won the game at the free throw line, an indication of the Rams' inability to contain their opponents' repeated drives to the hoop. Outscored from the field, 31-26, Lebanon Valley sank 28 of 35 free throw attempts while the Rams made only five foul shots. The winner's Lou Sorrentino was high scorer with 30 including a perfect 12-for-12 from the line.

In the second game Holy Cross eliminated Navy 87-74 as Palazzi flipped in 30 points. Don Lange and Johnny Clune combined for 48 but they were the extent of the offense mustered by the Midshipmen.

The winners of the first round moved to Raleigh, North Carolina, three days later where they encountered the two Southern schools. For Lebanon Valley it was a tall order. Miller had to guard LSU's 6′10″center Bob Pettit and did a remarkably fine job, allowing his bigger counterpart 28 while scoring 26 points himself. At half time LSU held only a five point lead. The one thing keeping the Dutchmen in the game was free throws. Forty-three times they stood at the line, a result of the constant pressure they exerted on the Tigers. Before the end of the game five LSU players either fouled out or had four personals called against them. The Dutchmen started the same team that had gone all the way against Fordham. Not until the game was out of reach did Rinso Marquette make his first substitution. When it was over, LSU knew they had been in a ball game; their 89-76 victory was as hard won as any they had played that season.

Holy Cross had suffered its worst defeat ever at the hands of Wake Forest, 91-69, in that season's Dixie Classic, and they were hyped up for revenge. Palazzi, continuing his smouldering pace, scored 32 points, three more than the Deacon's Dickie Hemric, and also took control of the backboards. For the first time in eight games the Crusaders failed to score 80 points but they still won 79-71.

The next night LSU keyed their defense on Palazzi and held him to one bucket. The Tigers, ahead 41-33 at intermission, increased their advantage over Holy Cross to 18 points, only to see the Crusaders scramble back to within five. That was as close as they got as LSU led by Pettit's 29 points won 81-73.

Mideast:

Notre Dame (17-4), long a Midwest powerhouse, made its first postseason tournament appearance as one of three mideast at-large entries. Eastern Kentucky (16-8) by winning the Ohio Valley Conference was another as was DePaul (19-7). It was the first appearance for the Blue Demons since 1943 when George Mikan and Ray Meyer flashed briefly in the tournament spectacle. The Chicagoans were particularly tough on their own court. After romping over Notre Dame by 27 at home they were waxed on the Irish's court by 26, a swing of 53 points.

The Mid American Conference winner was Miami of Ohio (17-5). Of the five losses, four were by a total margin of only seven points. Their only substantial defeat was to Xavier, 110-91, a team they had beaten in their other meeting by 20—another illustration of the decisiveness of the home court. Pennsylvania (21-4), coached by Howie Dallmar, Stanford's hero in the 1943 championship game, won the Ivy League and Indiana, winners of 19 of 22, were tops in the Big 10. The Hoosiers stumbled early, losing two of their first three, but by just three points. Thereafter they were checked only by Minnesota by a field goal. The Hoosiers were paced by All American Don Schlundt, a 6′10″center nicknamed Mr. Inside, and guard Bob Leonard labeled Mr. Outside. This high scoring duo was backed by an excellent supporting cast.

The presence of Pennsylvania in the Mideast regional (while LSU played in the East) is another example of preferential treatment that was, and still is, given by the NCAA to schools from conferences with superior records in previous tournaments. Though they received a first round bye, the Quakers were shunted off to Chicago while LSU went to Raleigh.

In the first round at Fort Wayne, Notre Dame easily disposed of Eastern Kentucky 72-57. The second game, between DePaul and Miami, was much closer. The Blue Demons' supporters watched their team blow a 42-30 half time advantage as the Redskins tied the score at 53-53 midway through the second half. The last ten minutes was a see-saw struggle and it was not until three seconds before the buzzer, when Ronnie Feiereisel canned a jump shot assuring a 74-72 DePaul victory, that their rooters could relax.

The following Friday evening Pennsylvania held Notre Dame in check for the first half. Ernie Beck, the Quaker's All American center, put on a one man show for the fans in Chicago Stadium. In the second half, however, the Irish came back and with deadly foul shooting pulled away in the last five minutes to triumph 69-57. Beck's fine leadership and 25 points were wasted for the losers.

DePaul found itself in an almost impossible situation against Indiana—seven down with a minute to play—and then almost accomplished the impossible. It was 82-80 at the buzzer, giving the DePaul faithful another chance for cardiac collapse. Had DePaul managed to tie, it is doubtful they would have survived in overtime. By the end, four of their starters had fouled out and their star Feiereisel was burdened with four personals. The miracle was they got as close as they did against the number one team in the country. It was a total team effort inspired, no doubt, by the home crowd's support and was a tribute to Ray Meyer's coaching.

The following evening the two Hoosier schools squared off. It promised to be a bitter contest since the Irish had beaten their cross state rivals early in the season 71-70. The Indiana faithful saw the most spectacular one man show in a tournament dominated by star performances. Don Schlundt, who grew up in South Bend almost in Notre Dame's back yard, attacked the basket throughout the first half, sinking the last 11 points for Indiana as they took a 42-33 half time lead. In all he scored 30 points in the first 20 minutes, accounting for nearly three-fourths of his team's production. In the second half the Irish were able to adjust and check Schlundt more effectively but he still finished with 42. It was never close, the Bloomington Hoosiers outclassing the South Bend Hoosiers 79-66.

Midwest:

Only four schools were selected to play in the Midwest regional to be held in Kansas State's fieldhouse in Manhattan. Oklahoma A and M (22-6), showing a surprising offensive facet (they once scored 81 points against Colorado), won the MVC crown. They still led the country in defense, though, allowing no more than 60 points in 24 of their 28 games.

Besides the Aggies, Oklahoma City (18-4) and Texas Christian (14-7) also played a deliberate ball control game. The first half of TCU's season had been forgettable as the Horned Frogs compiled a 4-6 record. Thereafter they played mostly Southwest Conference opponents, a collectively weak lot, and won all but one of their remaining games. These three teams in the regional were among the top six defensive teams in the country.

Kansas State had been the favorite to snatch the Big Seven. However, defending champion Kansas (16-5) was an unexpected winner. They had lost their entire starting five, including Lovellette, to graduation. Only one man who had scored in the 1952 championship game was back. Looking over his squad prior to the season, Coach Allen had predicted gloomily, "I'll be surprised if they win five games."

In their opening round game against Oklahoma City, Kansas looked as good as last year's champions. The Jayhawks scored 48 in the first half against a team that had allowed an average of fewer than 55 points a game and was ranked number four in defense nationally; then they relaxed and coasted the rest of the way to win 73-65. The co-feature involved two very defense-oriented teams. With both squads playing cautiously, TCU clung to an old fashioned 29-28 advantage over Oklahoma A and M after 20 minutes. After the break the Aggies tuned up their offense and with Bob Mattick's 35 points leading the way, poured it on to win going away 71-54.

In the regional final Kansas, building on a 30-28 half time advantage, increased its lead near the end to 52-43. That should have been safe were it not for the absence of their two tallest players, B. H. Born and Harold Patterson, who had both fouled out. That left the Aggies' Mattick in control of the boards; his team came back to close to within two with only two minutes to go. But the Kelley brothers, Dean and Allen, scored four free throws between them to assure the Jayhawks another trip to the Final Four with a score of 61-55.

West:

The West regional resembled a Wild West shootout. The Chieftains of Seattle, the Cowboys of Hardin Simmons and the Broncos of Santa Clara, as well as Idaho State, were all whooping it up in the big first round showdown in Seattle while waiting in the corral were the Cowboys of Wyoming. The Miami Redskins and the Oklahoma City Chiefs had already bitten the dust in another regional, but confidence was high that Seattle University (27-2), making its tournament debut, would uphold Indian prestige. The Chieftains had lost only to Georgetown and to Gonzaga by two. They avenged that defeat by pasting their conquerors 109-68 in a rematch. Seattle was the second highest scoring team in the nation, averaging almost 89 points a game. Their 102-101 victory over NYU showed they often left their defense in the locker room. The only team to hold them to fewer than 70 points was Wyoming, but they had beaten the Cowboys anyway. Seattle was emerging as a basketball power. To help attain recognition they scheduled a game against the Harlem Globetrotters and actually beat them, the first defeat after 77 consecutive victories for the professionals.

Two players, the O'Brien twins, Johnny and Eddie from South Amboy, N.J., had put Seattle on the basketball map. No university would give them an athletic scholarship so they worked as bricklayers for a year, playing semi-pro baseball in their spare time. Al Brightman, the Seattle baseball coach, watched them on the diamond, liked what he saw and offered them a scholarship. It so happened Brightman was also the basketball coach at the university. There may have been some doubts in Brightman's mind. After all he had never seen the O'Briens play basketball and at 5′ 9″ the twins were not exactly the size to inspire awe on the court. Once the season began, though, all doubts evaporated. In 1952 Johnny O'Brien, the more prolific scorer of the two, became the first man to sink over a thousand points in a season. The following year he set a career high of more than 2500 points and was voted All American.

For Idaho State (18-6), the Rocky Mountain Conference winner, this was also their first tourney. The Bengals were flying high with a dozen victories in their last 13 outings.

Hardin Simmons were the Border Conference champs. Their 19-11 record was compiled almost exclusively against local teams, having played in Arizona, New Mexico, Oklahoma and Texas. Their only confrontation with a NCAA tournament school resulted in a loss to Oklahoma City. Santa Clara (18-6) repeated as the West Coast Athletic Conference titlist. Wyoming (20-8), despite winning the Skyline, was a team that had trouble scoring. In half their games they failed to crack the 60 point level. Besides they had lost twice to Seattle and, despite a first round bye, their prospects were not good. It was their seventh tourney appearance, more than any other team to date.

The team favored to take the regional, and picked by many to snatch it all, was Washington (27-2). Ranked second behind Indiana, this was the best Husky squad ever to step on a court. Strong defensively, they also had an All American Bob Houbregs, an awesome offensive threat. An early season loss to UCLA was followed by a string of 21 victories which ended when Idaho upset the Huskies. They had no difficulty in eliminating California in two games in the PCC playoff.

In the first round in Seattle, Santa Clara thrashed Hardin Simmons. It was no contest after the first three minutes as the Broncos dominated, building a 39-19 lead at half time, then going through the motions to post an 81-56 victory. The restless spectators would have left earlier, but most had come to see the second game. In that contest Seattle's O'Brien brothers came out steaming. The Chieftains led from start to finish, winning easily over Idaho State 88-77. Johnny "O" flipped 42 points through the cords and twin Eddie put in 21 more. It was strictly an O'Brien show as no other Seattle player hit double figures. The Bengals tried guarding Johnny from behind, but his teammates had no trouble getting the ball to him. The only consolation for Idaho State lay in 6′ 6″ super jumper Rick Bauer's 25 rebounds which broke Bill Spivey's tournament record. But then again, with two 5′ 9″ players playing against them, there was not much competition for rebounds.

Regional action moved to Corvallis, a big disappointment for the sports fans of Seattle. For the first time in tournament history two schools from the same city would be facing each other. Though located three miles apart, Seattle and Washington had never played each other. It was to be a battle between two teams with identical won-lost records, between a fine defensive and an excellent offensive team, between an established basketball power and a recently arrived Johnny (O'Brien) come lately. Both teams also had an All American.

It turned out not to be much of a contest. The Huskies clamped a lid on the O'Briens while Houbregs set a new tourney record of 45 points as Washington advanced 92-70. In the other game Santa Clara found the range in the second half to break up a close contest with Wyoming, winning 67-52.

Washington and Santa Clara were well matched in the regional final and the game was close, at least for the first three quarters*. Behind by eight near the end of the first half, the Huskies tallied six unanswered points to trail 30-28 at the intermission. Washington stayed close but did not take the lead until Houbregs put in seven points in a row for a 37-36 lead. Each quintet took turns moving in front; but when Houbregs sank a long set shot for a 51-50 lead, the Huskies were in front to stay. They eventually won 74-62. Houbregs was high for Washington with 34 while Sears had 23 for the Broncos.

Final Four:

The championship was to be decided in Kansas City. Indiana's one-two scoring combination, Schlundt and Leonard, played little more than half the game yet still managed to tally 29 and 22 points respectively as the Hoosiers eliminated LSU 80-67. Bob Pettit's 29 points paced the Tigers.

In the other semifinal Kansas had a super shooting night, hitting 50 percent of their attempts while Washington was glacier cold, making only 19 of 62 from the floor. The shorter but quicker Kansan's pressing defense so disconcerted Washington that in the first few minutes they committed seven turnovers—four steals and three violations. The only bright spot was Houbregs, who scored 18 points in the first 20 minutes and held B. H. Born, the Kansas center, in check. But Washington's star fouled out when the second half was barely underway and with him went the hopes of the Huskies. Free of his taller assignment, Born went on a scoring binge which eventually totalled 25 points. Without Houbregs, the Huskies suffered a total collapse (19 points in the final 20 minutes) and the Jayhawks had little difficulty stretching their margin. The scoreboard told the story—Kansas 79, Washington 53.

If there was a feeling of *deja-vu* during the championship game, it was understandable. The final matched the same two schools that had fought for the championship 13 years earlier on the same basketball court in Kansas City. It was a thrill-charged game from tipoff to buzzer. At no time were the teams separated by more than six points and by not more than three during the last quarter. At the end of the first ten minutes Indiana was ahead 21-19. At the half the score was tied and after three quarters it was Indiana on top 59-58.

Kansas played the same close checking, clinging, infuriating, hand-in-the-face defense so effective against Washington. Hoosier tempers flared as physical contact increased and Schlundt, Leonard and Charlie Kraak were given technicals, almost costing their team the game. Born was particularly aggressive for the Kansans on both offense and defense.

Dean Kelley drove in for a layup to tie the score at 68-68 while the capacity

---

*College games were played in four ten minute quarters from 1951 to 1954.

audience rocked the arena to its foundation. It looked as if the Jayhawks, the team that was going to be lucky if it won five games, was going to perform one last miracle. Indiana held the ball for the final shot but with 27 seconds left Kelley fouled Leonard, who had performed skillfully as the Hoosiers' floor leader. Leonard missed the first but under the rules was given a second attempt. He made that one. Kansas called time out, but Jerry Alberts' shot with six seconds left hit the rim and bounced away. Kansas had run out of miracles and Indiana, as in 1940, won the championship; this time it was 69-68.

In the consolation Washington beat LSU. It was their last significant victory for some time. After losing the entire starting quintet the Huskies, in an incredible turnaround, lost 14 of their first 15 games the following year.

1954

In 1954 scores went even higher than the previous year. Bevo Francis scored 113 points in his team's 134-91 victory over Hillsdale. Frank Selvy scored an even 100 in Furman's 149-95 rout of Newberry.

With the exception of Kansas' victory over Washington in the semifinals, the 1953 tournament games produced no upsets. The favorites won as predicted with Indiana, top ranked before the playoff, taking the top prize. By contrast, the 1954 tourney produced one upset after the other. Only four of the top ten schools were invited and none made it to the Final Four. Kentucky, undefeated in 25 games and probably the best team in the country, declined an invitation when their two All Americans Cliff Hagan and Frank Ramsey, along with Lou Tsiropoulos, were declared ineligible. All three were in their fifth year of college.

The 1954 Wildcats may well have been the best basketball team ever at Kentucky. After a year's suspension they came back with a vengeance, scoring more than 100 points six times and over 90 points on eleven occasions. Their average margin of victory was 27 points, the fourth time in the past six years the unmerciful Wildcats had led the country in that category. Though undefeated, they were ranked only second in the coaches' poll when three of the 35 voters, in a gesture of spite against Adolph Rupp, declined to even mention them on the ballot.

Other highly ranked teams like Western Kentucky, Duquesne and Holy Cross went to the NIT. So anxious were Madison Square Garden officials to deny the NCAA some quality teams, they extended invitations at the beginning of February, a full four weeks before the tournament was due to begin. Western Kentucky accepted, preferring a week in New York to an evening in Fort Wayne where the NCAA had scheduled its first round. Duquesne, determined to win the NIT, a goal that had eluded them many times, also went to New York. Yet the NIT was losing its appeal and would soon be relegated to scooping up the remains left them by the NCAA. Kansas was also shut out of the tournament when they lost a coin toss to Colorado whom they tied for the Big Seven title. The Jayhawks had a superior overall record, ranking seventh in the polls at season's end.

East:

In the East regional LaSalle (21-4) made their debut in the NCAA tournament. They had fallen to Niagara twice and lost another to Kentucky. Fordham (18-5) repeated, hoping they would not have to face another pesky opponent like Lebanon Valley.

North Carolina State (26-6) was the champion of the newly organized Atlantic Coast Conference, formed when seven schools split away from the Southern Conference and were joined by former independent Virginia. The Wolfpack played an eclectic schedule. Aside from their conference foes they played AAU teams such as the Peoria Caterpillars and the Phillips Oilers, as well as Rio Grande—the presence of Bevo Francis on the Rio Grande squad being the only excuse for that mismatch. With the stronger Southern Conference teams departing to form their own league, George Washington topped the shrunken standings. Their only two losses in 25 games came against ACC teams, North Carolina State and Maryland. Though impressive, their record was gained against local opponents only. The Colonials were led by Joe Holup, number one in field goal accuracy with a 57 percent mark.

Navy's 16-7 record was also deceptive. They looked fine when they won; but when they lost, they were thoroughly outclassed. In their seven losing outings they were capsized by an average of 12.5 points per game. Connecticut, with an impressive 23-2 record, was back as the New England representative. Their two losses were back-to-back defeats to Fordham and Colgate, neither of them basketball powers. However, the Uconns dished out some humiliating beatings to the less talented Yankee Conference members. They beat Maine twice 102-61 and 108-60 and New Hampshire 104-48. Their only win over a ranked team was a one point decision over Holy Cross.

Cornell (18-6) won the Ivy crown in the last second of the season when Henry Buncom scored his only basket of the night to eliminate Princeton 46-44. The teams had finished in a tie for first place at the end of the regular season. For Cornell it was their first Ivy League title in 30 years.

First round competition got off to a lively start in Buffalo's Memorial Auditorium. LaSalle, losing earlier to Niagara there, had their problems with Fordham, too. The game was tied on seven occasions, and the lead changed hands 14 times. The Rams, playing much better than the previous year, came back from a four point half time deficit to take the lead 66-65 on a

Bob Reese tap in with three minutes left. Tom Gola followed with a free throw to even the game once more. Fordham held the ball for a final shot and were successful when Dan Lyons tapped one in on a follow up shot with a few seconds showing on the clock. The Explorers called time immediately. Everyone expected Gola to attempt the last shot; but he took the inbounds pass instead and with most of the Rams collapsing on him, coolly passed the ball to Fran O'Malley standing alone under the basket. O'Malley flipped in a layup at the buzzer and the game went into overtime. With a second life LaSalle then put Fordham away 76-74 to advance to the next round; Gola sparked the Explorers with 28 points.

In the other game Navy came on strong in the second half, mostly on the shooting of John Clune, to defeat Connecticut 85-80. Clune's 42 points almost matched the rest of his team's total production.

In Durham, North Carolina, North Carolina State blew an 11 point lead but still outlasted George Washington 75-73. It was the Wolfpack's fifteenth consecutive win over the Colonials.

The Regional moved to Philadelphia where the next two games proved to be as exciting as the two in Buffalo. Trailing Navy 40-32 at the half, Cornell* rallied and tied the score at 57, with most of the damage inflicted by Lee Morton. Navy's Clune cooled off considerably but still tossed down 21 points. His teammate Don Lange contributed 29 more to take up some of the slack. But it was Ken McCally, scoreless till then, who was the hero for the Middies as he pumped a set shot through the cords with three seconds remaining to give his team a 69-67 triumph. Cornell's high man was Morton who accounted for 34 points despite playing all but two minutes of the second half with four personals.

After having survived Fordham and the Buffalo Auditorium, LaSalle stepped up their pace and knocked off North Carolina State 88-81 in the highest scoring NCAA tournament contest to date. Gola was Tom Terrific as he accumulated 26 points and 26 rebounds.

LaSalle was now moving into high gear, getting better from game to game. Playing at home before their voluble fans they sank Navy 64-48. The Explorers shuffled their way to a 21 all-half time tie. They heard some choice words from Coach Ken Loeffler and came out of the locker room with their motor humming. Eight straight points by Bob Maples broke the game open. Lange, after his fine game against Cornell, could account for only three points before fouling out. Gola with 22 also dominated the boards, gathering 24 rebounds.

---

*It is interesting to note the only school to receive a first round bye in the East Regional was Cornell. At the time the Ivy League had a better tournament record than the Southern Conference and the ACC was in its first year.

Mideast:

In the Mideast regional Penn State, playing an anemic schedule, won 14 of 19. Due to a quirk in the Mid American Conference schedule Toledo (13-9) won the league championship by half a game over Bowling Green. The latter had a much better record and beat Toledo twice during the season; but Toledo played one fewer game in the conference, accounting for the half game difference.

Notre Dame (20-2) lost only to Bradley and Indiana and were ranked fifth in the country. They made a shambles of their game against traditional rival NYU, winning 99-64. Loyola of New Orleans (15-8) was invited as an at-large entry, an invitation that would normally have gone to NIT-bound Western Kentucky. The level of their competition was decidedly inferior. Even so they found it difficult to cope with weak opponents. They were beaten by Spring Hill (twice) and Southern Mississippi. LSU (21-3), second to Kentucky in the SEC, went to the playoffs when the Wildcats declined an invitation. The Tigers played powerful offense and once scored 128 points. Still, LSU was unhappy about playing in the Mideast regional, the toughest of the four, rather than in the easier East where they had competed the previous year.

One reason the Mideast was so tough was the presence of Indiana, the defending champion and number one team in the nation again. Bob Leonard and Don Schlundt had become All Americans and Indiana had succumbed only to Northwestern in overtime, Iowa and Oregon State while chalking up 19 wins.

At Fort Wayne, Notre Dame had little trouble with Loyola and won 80-70 primarily because of better rebounding and aggressive play. The five Irish starters played the whole game and were led by Dick Rosenthal's 31 points while Loyola found Bob O'Donnel's 32 markers the only thing to cheer about.

Toledo also played without a single substitution—a big mistake. Leading Penn State through most of the game, the Rockets just ran out of fuel and flamed out at the end. With four minutes remaining Jesse Arnelle whipped in two baskets and Penn State was ahead to stay. The final score was 62-50.

The scene shifted to Iowa City where the first of the upsets occurred. It was jungle warfare as Penn State's Nittany Lions faced the LSU Tigers. The Southerners took an early 24-14 lead only to have Penn State rebound to establish a 34-32 half time advantage. Thereafter the lead seesawed back and forth until Ed Haag's jump shot gave the Lions their final lead. Despite All American Bob Pettit's 34 points, Penn State netted the Tigers 78-70.

The second game was a rematch between Indiana and Notre Dame. It was played at a level of ferocity that only traditional intrastate rivals can summon up. So intense was the action some players almost dropped from exhaustion. Rosenthal collapsed during a time out in the final minute of play but recovered to go back on the court, sinking the decisive free throw that proved to be the margin of victory for the Irish. Rosenthal played a superb defensive game, holding Schlundt to a single basket. Leonard scored a mere 11 points. In the latest installment of the Hoosier version of the running battle between the Hatfields and the McCoys, Notre Dame survived 65-64. It was sweet revenge for their regular season loss to the Hoosiers and even sweeter coming against the current national champion, number one in the country and the team that had knocked them out of the previous year's tourney.

Penn State and fans sensed another upset in the offing. The Irish peaked against Indiana and they seemed to lack motivation against the Nittany Lions. Arnelle stole the ball five times in the first half to set up his teammates for baskets. With the score 45-42 Haag made three consecutive set shots that looked to have been launched from the parking lot and Notre Dame was dead. Penn State poured it on, scoring 26 points in the final ten minutes to win 71-63.

Midwest:

The Midwest regional had one outstanding team, fourth ranked Oklahoma A and M. The Aggies who led the country in defense for the sixth time in seven years had limited their opponents to fewer than 50 points on ten occasions while completing a 23-4 season. Rice (22-4) was not in the same category as A and M despite a similar won-lost record. Oklahoma City (18-6) was again selected as an at-large school as was Bradley (15-12). The Braves, after playing in the MVC for three years, dropped out in 1951 to become independent. In 1954 they won barely half their games but this was deceptive since theirs was one of the toughest schedules in the country. Among their victims was Notre Dame. Still, they were the last school chosen by the selection committee. It was a decision forced on the committee when it was unable to find another at-large team with a better record than Bradley's. The Braves did not make that decision any easier by losing five of their last seven games.

Bradley's style was to race downcourt, head for the basket and penetrate whatever defense stood in their way. Abandoning the pass unless it moved them closer to the hoop, they put the ball on the floor, then drove, drove, drove all evening, challenging their opponents and picking up fouls by the bushel.

Colorado (11-9) was more lucky than good. After a disastrous start during which they dropped their first seven games, the Buffalos made the correct adjustments and began posting more Ws and fewer Ls. Luckily their early losses came mostly against non-conference foes. They finished in a tie with Kansas, which had a superior overall record, at the top of the Big Seven standings. That conference's rule for breaking ties was to flip a coin to decide which school would go to the NCAA tournament. Colorado made the right call and ended in the playoffs while Kansas remained home, contemplating the merits of being good versus being lucky.

Bradley was delighted to be in the tournament. They had been barred from postseason competition in 1953 as a result of violations uncovered during the bribery scandal investigation of 1951. Showing much poise they upended Oklahoma City in the first round 61-55.

The other three teams had drawn byes and they, along with Bradley, met in Stillwater, Oklahoma, the following Friday evening. In the first game it seemed as if the referee never stopped blowing his whistle. There was virtually no flow to the game as Colorado was stopped 34 times for infractions and Bradley 27 times—an average of one interruption every 40 seconds not including turnovers, time outs, end of quarters and substitutions. Not surprisingly, five players fouled out.

Leading by a point at the intermission, the Braves stretched that advantage over the course of the second half and went on to win 76-64. Since both teams made the same number of baskets the difference came at the foul line. Bob Carney of Bradley set a record of 23 free throws (in 26 attempts) that may never be broken. He finished the evening with 37 points. Altogether the Braves collected 38 points at the free throw line which, though high, was not unusual for them.

Oklahoma A and M, playing on their home court, and the only ranked team in the regional, was expected to have little difficulty in reaching the Final Four. Rice had other plans. Leading 22-18 at the end of a slow, deliberate first half they increased their margin to ten. The Aggies then pulled themselves together and slipped by the Owls 51-45. Scoring was evenly distributed; not a single player on either squad scored more than 12 points.

Everyone anticipated the Braves would be massacred by the home side in the regional final. But the teams deviated considerably from the script as the Braves were the ones who did the scalping.

No doubt the Aggies were complacent. Bob Mattick, their star, was getting married shortly and his mind was elsewhere. Then, too, Forddy Anderson—that great motivator—had told his men that the fans back in Peoria had taken up the basketball court, figuring the Braves would not survive the regional and that the season was over. The story was, of course, untrue but it fired up the players.

Up by 31-28 at the end of the half, Bradley took a 47-44 lead into the final quarter. They really turned it on in the last ten minutes, outscoring the Aggies 24-13 before their disbelieving fans, and advanced to the Final Four 71-57. It was the most points ever scored against an Aggie team in Stillwater.

Normally the Oklahomans rarely fouled, but the Braves attacked with such abandon they were forced to commit 30 fouls giving their opponents 29 points from the line. In the process four Aggies fouled out, to the considerable annoyance of Coach Iba and the local fans. Three Bradley players were also excused prematurely.

West:

In the West regional Idaho State (20-4) represented the Rocky Mountain Conference. Their season was highlighted by an 18 game winning streak bookended by losses in their first two games to Brigham Young and two more to Montana State to break their string. Seattle without the O'Briens had an even more impressive record. They blew their opening game to Wichita, then beat the same school the following night, inaugurating a string of 26 consecutive wins. Their 26-1 record was the best in the tournament, sufficient to have them ranked eleventh in the country.

Santa Clara (19-6) was an at-large selection while high scoring Texas Tech (20-4), playing mostly schools in the Southwest, was the Border Conference champion. Colorado A and M (22-5) were participating in their first tournament, having won in the Skyline. Among their losses were two to Seattle.

Southern California had a so-so 17-12 record. At one point in the season they lost four of five during a swing around the midwest. The scoring revolution was losing its momentum in the PCC and a 46-32 loss to California was an example of the lower scoring games that were to feature conference contests over the next few years. USC turned back Oregon State two games to one in the conference playoff to make the tournament.

For 28 minutes in Corvallis, Santa Clara and Texas Tech were locked in a tight duel. But with the score tied at 46 the Broncos broke the stalemate and led the rest of the way to win 73-64.

In the other game Seattle, comfortably ahead 41-32 at half time, suddenly found itself in a contest as Idaho State came back with a vengeance. Accurate shooting from the perimeter and a tough defense contributed to Idaho State's resurgence. They hit eight consecutive perimeter shots while holding Seattle scoreless to take a six point lead going into the last five minutes. But the Chieftains regrouped and knotted the score 66-66. Regaining possession, they held the ball for the final two minutes; but Joe Pehanick's last second attempt failed and the teams went into overtime.

State took an early lead and Seattle had to play catchup. Behind by four, the Chieftains tied the score on a pair of jump shots by Cal Bauer and evened it again when Stan Glowaski coolly dipped in two free throws with 18 seconds remaining. But Idaho State was not to be denied. Rick Bauer of the Bengals hooked for the basket, missed, but was fouled. With :04 remaining he calmly flipped two from the line to make it 77-75 as Seattle's winning streak became history. Still another upset in this upset dominated tournament.

Three nights later Colorado A and M and USC joined the first round winners in Corvallis. Neither of the regional semifinal contests was close. USC with a substantial height advantage eliminated Idaho State 75-59 and Santa Clara with a tough zone defense and a hustling fast break bombed the Aggies 73-50. The Broncos, making 50 percent of their shots, played excellent transition basketball and scored consistently on layups.

The regional final between the two California schools was a barn burner with the Trojans ahead most of the game but the Broncos within overhaul range. And overhaul they did as they moved ahead by three with seconds remaining. Things looked grim for USC until Roy Irvin muscled his way under the basket, tipped in the ball, was fouled in the process and completed the three point play. For the third time in the tournament an overtime was needed to decide the issue. Again Santa Clara had the lead, 65-64, with time running out. With 3 seconds left Tony Psaltis of the Trojans sank another free throw to send the game into another extra session—the first double overtime in NCAA tournament history.

A few seconds after action resumed USC capitalized on a converted foul to go on top 66-65. Bronco coach Bob Feerick then ordered his team to hold the ball for the final shot of the game. Frustrated by two successive last second comebacks by USC, Feerick was willing to take a chance in order not to give the Trojans a third opportunity. For four and a half minutes Santa Clara did nothing but stand with the ball just inside the center line. The Trojans similarly did nothing. They had the lead and were content to wait for the Broncos to make a move. The fans were the only ones in the arena showing any movement as they yelled and whistled for the action to resume. Finally, with 17 seconds left, Santa Clara stirred themselves; but their first pass was intercepted and USC held on to the ball for the remaining seconds.

Final Four:

The final rounds were held in Kansas City, the fifth time the city hosted the national championship. The two Pennsylvania teams opposed each other in one game. In a rather dull game LaSalle trounced Penn State 69-54. The Nittany Lions converted only 25 percent of their shots and were never in contention.

The other contest was a lot livelier as USC attempted to avenge a regular season loss to Bradley. The action was punctuated as were so many Bradley games by the frequent sound of the referee's whistle. Outscored from the floor, Bradley's frequent trips to the free throw line paid off handsomely. Still USC held a substantial 40-29 lead late in the first half before the Braves spurted to close the gap to six at the intermission. USC maintained their advantage through the third quarter. Then, just as they had done against Oklahoma A and M, Bradley spun into overdrive in the final ten minutes, outscoring the Trojans 23-14. Bob Carney hung a layup with 63 seconds left to put Bradley ahead 71-70 and they held on to win 74-72.

Thus it was that two schools, neither ranked in the top ten, one a desperation last minute choice, squared off in the championship game. In a tournament dominated by upsets Bradley was hoping for one more to make up for their defeat in the 1950 final to another underdog, CCNY. For a time it looked as if they might achieve their goal. Mining the mother load that had thus far brought them success, Bradley drove to the basket at every opportunity making LaSalle foul in the process. At the end of the half the Braves were ahead 43-42 and it looked as if the ultimate upset was in the making.

In the LaSalle dressing room Coach Ken Loeffler, as intelligent as he was feisty, decided on a new tactic. He switched from man-to-man to a zone defense. It stopped the Braves cold. Unable to penetrate the zone Bradley tried to hit from outside but their shooting was frigid. The Braves, who had shot 36 percent in the first half, could not even hit 20 percent in the second. Meanwhile, at the other end of the court LaSalle was ripping the cords for a total of 50 points. Led by sophomores Charles Singley and Frank Blatcher who each scored 23 and Gola, voted the MVP of the tournament, the Explorers ran away from Bradley. The final score, 92-76, was indicative of the superiority of the Philadelphia team. They made 37 baskets to 22 for Bradley. It was only the Braves' ability to pick up fouls that kept them in the game. Were it not for Loeffler's switch to a zone defense the game may easily have ended differently. The switch allowed Gola to remain under the basket where he appropriated almost every Bradley miss. Two of LaSalle's eight man squad, including Gola, fouled out and four others finished with four personals.

For Bradley their bubble had burst but there was some consolation for their Peoria supporters. That same evening the Peoria Caterpillars won the national AAU championship.

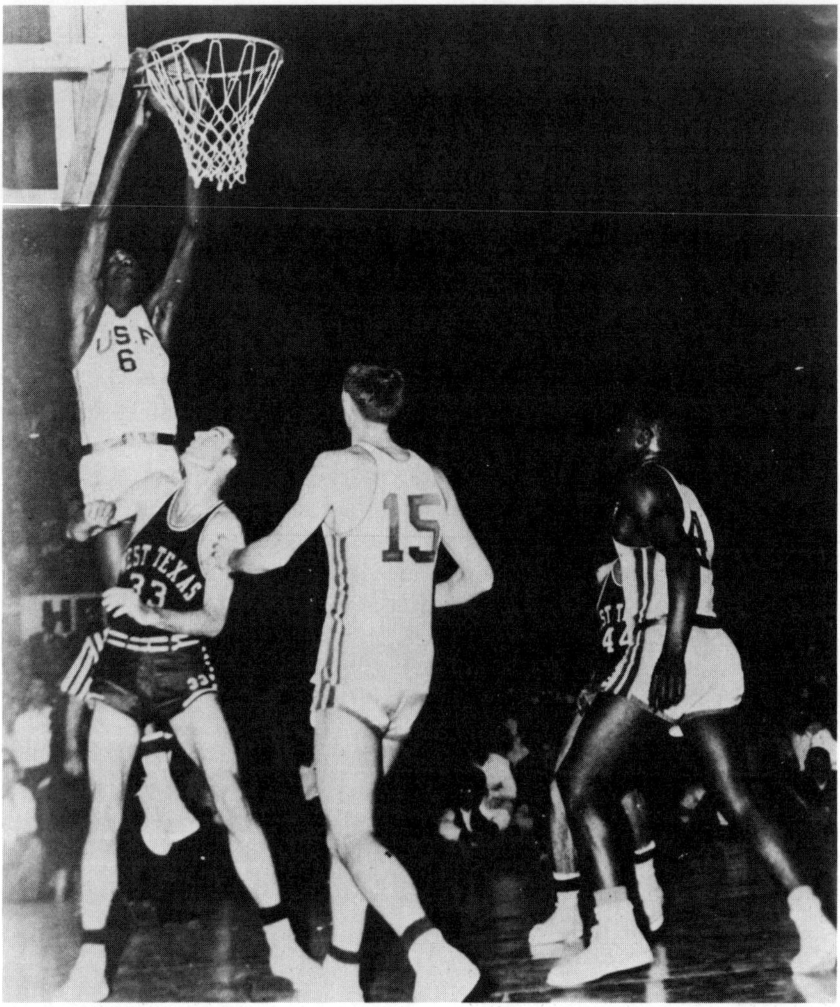

Bill Russell tips the ball through the hoop in San Francisco's first round action against West Texas State. The Dons went on to win the 1955 championship.
(University of San Francisco photo)

7

THE COUNTERREVOLUTION: DEFENSE IS ALIVE AND WELL IN SAN FRANCISCO

Despite the critics' complaints about the scores climbing to the century mark and beyond, run and shoot tactics, and defenses limited to snaring rebounds, the packed arenas echoed with the din of approval from delighted fans. Zone defenses were rarely used though they were often highly effective and the professional league barred them. Players were shooting more accurately, too, and 1955 saw the biggest jump in shooting percentage ever recorded—from 35% to almost 37%.

Some coaches, however, recognized there was a limit to the amount of firepower that could be used effectively. Furman, consistently among the leaders in point production in the early fifties, had not earned a tournament bid. Other schools which often scored over one hundred points found their opponents could also score as many and more. The trouble was few coaches knew very much about defensive tactics and how to apply them. Defense and especially the different types of zone are a little harder to teach than man-to-man and some coaches were just too lazy to be bothered. But when the pendulum swings far enough in one direction, as it obviously had by 1955, innovators are ready to try counter-measures which, if successful, are then copied by the less enterprising.

History was to show that a strong defense was a much better guarantee of success than a superior offense. In the decade 1951-1960, nine teams that led the nation in defense participated in the tournament and three won the national championship. By contrast, only four offense leaders were invited during this period and only one was a winner.

Prior to 1955, teams relying predominantly on a tough defense and a ball control offense were found almost exclusively in two small enclaves. One was Oklahoma where Hank Iba at Oklahoma A and M and Doyle Parrock at

Oklahoma City preached the benefits of controlling the opposition's output rather than filling the basket, hoping it would be enough to win. Some of this philosophy spilled over onto several teams in the SWC. The second enclave was the Pacific Coast where scores were invariably lower than in other areas.* And teams with good defenses won—not spectacularly, but they won. Still, it was not the kind of success to make coaches run to their gymnasia and change their tactics.

However, that was before Phil Woolpert and a 6′9″ jumping giraffe of a center named Bill Russell focused the media's attention on the success potential of a strong defense. Woolpert replaced Pete Newell as coach at San Francisco University, the latter having moved to Michigan State after putting the Dons on the basketball map with a NIT championship in 1949 and another tournament appearance in 1950.

It was no coincidence that Woolpert and Newell shared the same belief in defensive basketball tactics. They had been teammates at Loyola of California in the late thirties and learned the effectiveness of a strong defense from the same mentor, their coach Jim Needles.

Woolpert was hired from next door St. Ignatius High School were the Dons, lacking a gymnasium, played their home games. Success did not come immediately and he entered the 1955 season with a career losing record. Then Bill Russell put on a Don uniform and became the most potent defensive force in the history of college basketball.

Bill Russell was an ambidextrous shooter, the result of an uncle's attempt to convert young Bill from a natural righty into a southpaw. He was not much of a scorer from long or medium range but under the basket he sucked up every ball within reach and tipped, hooked or layed it in. Though Russell was only the second college player to average more than twenty points and twenty rebounds in a career (the first was Walter Dukes), his outstanding contribution came on the defensive end of the court. There he used his arms and hands to block opponent's shots, uncannily timing his liftoff with theirs. In every game fans would watch the same scene played over and over. A player would spring up for a seemingly open shot when, sailing through the air, would come Bill Russell, arm extended like a shiny black flail, and at the apogee of his leap, a hand would descend and hammer the ball back at the shooter's head or chest. Soon the mere idea of having one's shot smacked back in the face had an intimidating effect on a player so he began to hurry his shots or pass off rather than be humiliated. Bill Russell played the toughest defense in the country and it was not long before San Francisco was number one among college teams.

*During the fifteen years 1948-1962, with the single exception of 1951, the top defensive team in the country was either Oklahoma A and M or one of the Bay Area schools. In 1954, four of the top ten defensive teams came from the Pacific Coast and two from Oklahoma.

1955

In the 1955 basketball preseason balloting, not a single coach ranked San Francisco in the top ten. It was not until they had won the All College tournament in Oklahoma City during Christmas week that the Dons achieved that plateau. Then, as win followed win, they slowly rose until late in the season they were recognized by nearly everyone as the best team in the country. Their only loss was to UCLA in the campaign's third game, after which they reeled off twenty-one wins for a total of twenty-three for the year.

It was defense that did it. In half of their games they gave up 50 points or fewer. They subdued Oregon State 60-34 and San Jose State by 56-30. Only once did they allow more than 62 points—this in an atypical game in which they outscored Wichita State 94-75.

West:

In the West regional, San Francisco's opponents were definitely not in the same class as the Dons. Idaho State (18-7) had won the Rocky Mountain Conference for the third year in a row. West Texas State (15-6) was the Border Conference champion. Seattle (20-5), a high scoring quintet swimming against the current defensive strategy of other Pacific Coast schools, was the mirror image of San Francisco. Seattle's lowest production of the season was the 67 points they were held to by Oklahoma City. Otherwise, it was score as you please and the hell with defense.

Perhaps the only school given a chance to upset San Francisco was Oregon State (21-7). Anchored by 7′3″ Wade Halbrook, a rather temperamental player, introverted and self-conscious of his height, who once casually dropped out of school and off the team for a few days, the Beavers had a pretty potent defense of their own. They were excellently coached by "Slats" Gill, who had been with the Beavers since 1929. Besides, they had disposed of UCLA, the only conqueror of San Francisco, in the interdivision playoff two games to none. However, they had been beaten 60-34 by the Dons earlier in the season.

Utah, winner of the Skyline (23-3), was also highly regarded. Losses to Kentucky by five, to Brigham Young by two, and to USC by two, were the only setbacks in an otherwise extremely successful season. They beat LaSalle, the defending champion, and, as a tune-up for the tournament, whipped New Mexico 85-42 and Denver 99-70 in their last two games.

In the first round in San Francisco, Seattle was a little worried about playing Idaho State but not because they felt they did not have the better team. After all, they had beaten the Bengals three of four during the season. The contest was to be held on Tuesday evening. During the season the Chieftains had lost three of four on a Tuesday; they were a little worried the jinx would strike again.

This was the third consecutive year these schools faced each other in a first round match, each having won once. This year Seattle easily prevailed 80-63. Dick Stricklin of the winners scored only four in the first half but stuffed 16 in the second to lead his team. In the other game, San Francisco overwhelmed West Texas State 89-66 as Bill Russell scored 29 points in as many minutes.

Later in the week in Corvallis, the Dons again had little difficulty winning, this time against fourth ranked Utah. Russell, suffering from a cold, played only briefly but tallied thirteen points. In his absence, Jerry Mullen with 24 provided the needed offensive punch. Utah tried intimidating the Dons, who wound up taking 42 free throws, but that tactic did not work. Playing with great confidence even without Russell, San Francisco shot ahead 41-20 at intermission. In the second half, Utah got within eight but when Russell returned for a few minutes the advantage soared to 19 again. The Dons advanced 78-59.

In the other game, Oregon State, playing on its home court, Gill Coliseum (named for its longtime coach), converted hot shooting and the height advantage provided by Halbrook into a victory. Streaking ahead 18-8, the Beavers relaxed momentarily and allowed Seattle to get within four at 36-32. At half time the Beavers were in charge again. Two minutes into the second half, Gill removed Halbrook who had already scored twenty-one points. At the time his team was making sixty percent of its shots and was riddling Seattle's defense, such as it was. Towards the end, the Chieftains made the score respectable but Oregon State still won 83-71.

In the regional final, San Francisco found itself in the toughest game it had played since its loss to UCLA. Russell was still suffering from his cold but played anyway. To make matters worse for the Dons, Mullen, who was normally second to Russell in scoring, twisted his ankle in the first ten seconds, played with a limp and contributed only two free throws. On the brighter side Russell intimidated the taller Halbrook who could not outjump the Don's center. Halbrook found himself staring into Russell's palm most of the evening and became so disconcerted he attempted few of his deadly hook shots. Still, it was a struggle. San Francisco took the game by the narrowest of margins, 57-56.

Midwest:

The Midwest regional was a wasteland when it came to basketball talent and its two at-large teams were disasters. Nevertheless, one of them almost made it to the Final Four. Most basketball powers in the area belonged to a conference. The NCAA was committed to selecting two at-large teams so they had to pick the best of what was available. They chose Oklahoma City and Bradley, the latter from Illinois which logically would qualify it for the Mideast regional.

Oklahoma City (9-17) lost its first three games of the year and then struggled along the rest of the season winning one here and losing a couple there, even managing at one point to win three in a row. Bradley (7-19) was not quite so fortunate. They also lost their first three, but were never capable of putting a three game winning streak together. However, they did achieve a fourteen game **losing** streak which finally ended with a two point victory over Wichita. In fairness, the Braves played one of the most demanding schedules in the country and they won their last two games, thus entering the tournament on an up note.

Southern Methodist University (13-11) was another team that did not exactly scare any of its opponents. Its non-conference record was studded with defeats.

The class of the regional was Colorado. The Buffaloes also had a rocky start, losing four in a row in December, but then reeled off victories in thirteen of their next fourteen to extend their record to 16-5. Colorado had first hand experience of what it was like to play against a strong defense. They had been beaten twice by California, held to 44 and 46 points.

Tulsa (20-6) was making its first tourney appearance. They won the MVC mostly on the strength of their defense designed by Coach Clarence Iba. The Oklahoma connection was in evidence in two games played by the Hurricanes against intrastate rivals. Tulsa beat Oklahoma City 48-42 and Oklahoma State 47-44. The scores seemed to indicate that periods of the game were played with lids clamped over the baskets.

Maybe the NCAA was looking for a place for their two most embarrassing selections. They found a suitable site in El Reno, Oklahoma, population 10,000, where Bradley and Oklahoma City could play their first round game in relative obscurity. The Braves, having learned to win in Oklahoma the previous year, survived 69-65.

The regional continued in Manhattan, Kansas. Bradley, facing SMU for the second time, beat them again 81-79. The official scorer nearly caused a riot when he inadvertently pressed the buzzer with fifty-seven seconds left and Bradley ahead 79-78. SMU protested vigorously; when the error was discovered, the game resumed. Unfortunately for the Mustangs, though the final score was different, the outcome was the same. For Bradley it was their fourth straight win, their longest streak of the season. Colorado took Tulsa 69-59 after leading by only 34-33 at the half.

In a very rough final, Bradley came close to making the Final Four again, but foul trouble finally sank them. Bradley committed twice as many fouls as Colorado which connected on 33 of 47 attempts while four of the Braves fouled out. Bradley actually outscored the Buffaloes from the floor, but could not repair the damage Colorado was inflicting from the foul line. Bob Jeangerard scored 29 to pace Colorado to a 93-81 win.

Mideast:

In the Mideast, Kentucky, ranked number two in the country, was back in tournament competition after a two year absence. As usual the Wildcats (22-2) had had a very successful year. Both losses came against Georgia Tech which had an otherwise undistinguished season. The Georgians' first victory occurred in Lexington and was the Wildcats' first loss at home in 130 games. It was also Kentucky's first loss in the SEC since 1951. Prior to that they had not dropped a conference game since 1947. Their pride stung, they vented their anger and creamed a fine Tennessee team 104-61, in the season finale.

Another team with an identical 22-2 record but not as highly regarded was Marquette. It seemed as if the Warriors were pursuing some precise blueprint designed by a perverse computer. The Warriors lost their first game to Michigan State by 19 points. Then they busted 22 consecutive opponents but lost their last game to Notre Dame, again by 19 points. When they were good they were very, very good but when they were bad . . .

Iowa (17-5) won in the Big 10 when it split two very close games with runner-up Minnesota, one decided by one point and the other by two. Miami of Ohio (14-8) represented the Mid-American and Memphis State (17-4) was an at-large selection. The latter started 1-3 but won sixteen straight before dropping their last game. Penn State (17-8) rounded out the field. The Nittany Lions provided an example of the effect the home court had on most teams. They beat Colgate by nine at home but lost by 35 away. They beat Syracuse by 22 at home but lost at Syracuse by the same margin. Both series showed a swing of 44 points.

At Lexington, Kentucky, Penn State ousted Memphis State 59-55 despite playing very sloppy ball. Bad passes and poor shooting kept the score low. Penn State held Memphis State to just 19 first half points. The Tigers, who had amassed ninety points or more in fully half their games, had never scored fewer than 67 all season. In the other game, Marquette overcame Miami 90-79 after the teams had battled into overtime.

At Evanston in the second round, Iowa had few problems eliminating Penn State 82-53 in a game that was one sided from the opening tap. But the fans were amply compensated in the co-feature. Kentucky and Marquette, with identical pre-tourney records, stayed even through most of the game. The score was tied 16 times and the lead changed hands 25 times. Finally, ninth ranked Marquette went ahead by seven and stalled their way to a 79-71 victory in a mild upset. For Marquette, it was a team effort as five players hit double figures.

The next evening Iowa, ahead at half time 46-33, increased its lead to 19 points in the second period. Suddenly Marquette caught fire and closed the gap to a single point with less than two minutes remaining on the clock. The Warriors' supporters were in a frenzy—it looked as if their team's momentum would carry them to victory. Besides, Bill Logan, Iowa's 6′6″ center who had scored 31 points was out of the game on personal fouls. Desperately Iowa tried to freeze the ball and they succeeded. In the final seconds a couple of Hawkeye guards, Roy Johnson and Bill Seaberg, scored baskets to make the final score 86-81.

East:

In the East, defending champion LaSalle finished with the identical 21-4 record it had achieved the previous year. Tom Gola was voted to the All American team for the third time and repeated as the best rebounder in the country. LaSalle's four losses were all to schools in the top ten and their wins, like the one over Syracuse (103-54), were often by wide margins.

The third ranked Explorers were the East's hope for upsetting San Francisco. In Gola they felt they had the means to neutralize Bill Russell. In 1955, Gola had been voted the outstanding player to perform in San Francisco's Cow Place, Kansas City's Municipal Auditorium, Buffalo's Memorial Auditorium, Philadelphia's Convention Hall, University of Pennsylvania's Palestra, and New York's Madison Square Garden. His cuts and fakes kept the opponent's defense off balance and opened the middle for other players to score.

West Virginia (19-10) represented the Southern Conference. Fred Schaus, after graduating from West Virginia in 1949, went on to become a star in the NBA. After five years he decided to call it quits as a player and accept a coaching job at his alma mater. In 1955, as a very young rookie coach, he took his team to the NCAA tournament for the first time after defeating George Washington in overtime to take the conference playoff. West Virginia's weakness was primarily defense. They gave up over one hundred points on three occasions, never giving up fewer than 60. In one forgettable match they lost to Richmond by 40 points.

Yet if their game occasionally fell apart they were still one of the most entertaining teams to watch, due primarily to one Rod Hundley. "Hot Rod" was a one man show, a pale faced Harlem Globetrotter. He would twirl the ball on his fingertips, flip it over his back, pass it back and forth over his shoulders and, in general, act the clown before his appreciative audience. He was known to shoot fouls from behind his back and make an inbounds pass while facing away from the court. It was all a lot of fun, but it did not add up to good basketball.

Canisius (16-6) from Buffalo, NY, was also making its first appearance in the tourney as was Williams (17-1). Both were at-large selections. Villanova (16-9), the third Pennsylvania school in the tournament, had recorded victories over Canisius by 23 points and over North Carolina State twice, 107-96 and 91-78. This was quite an achievement considering the Wolfpack was sixth ranked and had a better record (28-4) than even LaSalle.

North Carolina State, which went over the century mark eight times and had an awesome offense, finished first in the ACC. Unfortunately, due to recruiting violations, they were banned from participating in the tournament and had to watch from the sidelines. Duke (20-7), second in the ACC, was selected instead.

Princeton (13-10) represented the Ivy League. The Tigers had finished in a three-way tie for the league lead and had a worse record than either tie-mate; but in a playoff Columbia beat Pennsylvania and Princeton beat Columbia, so they were in. For a while during the season it looked as if the Tigers were not going to be in anything except the cellar. They started the campaign losing seven of their first eight games. Once they started playing the weaker Ivy schools, things turned around. Princeton pulled themselves up by their sneaker strings and won twelve of fifteen to move into the tournament if not with a lot of talent, at least with some momentum.

After an absence of four years the NCAA tournament returned to Madison Square Garden. True, it was only first round competition but New York fans were treated to a triple header. There was a good crowd in spite of almost 4,000 empty seats. It was not quite like the old days.

In the first game, Canisius and Williams took turns scoring in spurts with the Buffalo team finally winning 73-60. Tony Moro of the losers was high man with 27 points. Then Villanova and Duke took the court. The Wildcats were leading by twelve with five minutes left in the game. Their starters were still in the game having played without a single substitution and they were beginning to wilt. The Blue Devils, seeing Villanova running out of gas, pressed harder and closed to within two at 71-69 with a minute to go. Fortunately for Villanova, one of their starters fouled out, and Jack Weissman came in fresh off the bench. He promptly scored a bucket and a free throw and the Wildcats shut off Duke's last gasp effort to win 74-73.

The final contest was not that close, but it did feature LaSalle's Tom Gola and West Virginia's Rod Hundley. It was Gola's twenty-third and last Garden appearance, the most ever by a visiting player. Sophomore Hundley brought a 23.9 scoring average into the game which included 38 points scored earlier against NYU in the Garden, a season high for the arena. The game was close in the first half until the Explorers netted 14 points in a row. Gola was having his problems scoring in the first twenty minutes, connecting on only one of eight. Yet he rebounded well and performed the playmaker's role excellently, feeding teammates so that the scoring was evenly distributed. In the second half LaSalle switched to a zone defense that had the Mountaineers baffled. On offense LaSalle ran off ten and twelve point spurts to win the game 95-61. LaSalle's total and the 34 point winning margin set new tournament records.

LaSalle and Princeton are less than fifty miles apart, and they both qualified as local schools when they met in Philadelphia's Palestra on March 11, 1955. Due to the Ivy playoff, Princeton was playing its fourth game in seven days. The strain was beginning to show. Gola, performing without strain and as graceful as ever, could not be contained. The obviously fatigued Tigers managed to hit only 21 percent of their throws as LaSalle romped to a 73-46 win.

The game between Canisius and Villanova was much closer. The Wildcats had lost to the Griffins during the season by 23. Now that they were playing closer to home, Villanova felt confident they could reverse that decision. The first half ended in a 39 all tie. Jack Devine of Villanova spent a good part of the period at the foul line, sinking 14 of 15 and with his four of seven from the floor had 22 points. The second half was just as close. With two minutes left the score was again knotted at 71 apiece. Canisius held for one last shot. John McCarthy dribbled the ball at center court as the clock ticked away. With fourteen seconds to go, McCarthy drove to the basket, was fouled and converted both tries to make the Griffins winners, 73-71. McCarthy's total of 28 was high for Canisius while teammate Hank Nowak made 27, matching Devine who led the Wildcats.

The Explorers, wearing their old style tee-shirts, took the court for the regional final and were greeted by a deafening roar. Thus encouraged they proceeded to make a shambles of the game. Gola was superb, scoring 30 and taking down 25 rebounds. When he fouled out with two minutes left in the game and the issue no longer in doubt, the spectators almost blew the roof off. It was Gola's last game in Philadelphia, and the fans rose to their feet and bellowed their appreciation. The only issue to be resolved was whether or not the Explorers would be the first team to score one hundred points in a NCAA tournament game. Canisius tried to freeze the ball which triggered a loud chorus of boos. LaSalle failed to hit triple digits but won the game 99-64, breaking their own tourney scoring and margin of victory records set against West Virginia earlier in the week.

Final Four:

The Final Four gathered in Kansas City the following weekend. LaSalle went ahead of Iowa early in the game and stayed there. The Jayhawks made a late run at the Explorers and drew within two with five minutes left, but that was as close as they got. With Gola contributing 23 points, LaSalle won their record ninth successive tourney game, 76-73.

In the other semi-final, San Francisco and Colorado played cautiously, and the game was a standoff until the Dons mounted a mini-surge in the final minutes before the intermission to take a 25-19 lead. In the second half the Dons played equally tough defense with Russell, who scored 24 points, dominating at both ends of the court. Unsurprisingly, San Francisco eliminated the Buffaloes 62-50 as they registered their twenty-fifth straight victory.

The final was everybody's dream game. The 1954 champion against the number one ranked team of 1955; the two best players in the country, Bill Russell and Tom Gola, facing each other; two outstanding coaches in Phil

Woolpert, the new prophet of defense, and the feisty, aggressive Ken Loeffler, an offense-oriented strategist. Loeffler had conceived the LaSalle weave. This was a device calling for the Explorers to pass the ball back and forth while players zigzagged across the court until one player got free for a high percentage shot. There was no doubt that LaSalle would score but could they score often enough against San Francisco's defense—a question that would shortly be answered.

The contest was anti-climatic. Bill Russell completely overshadowed Gola. Instead of using his star to guard Gola, Woolpert gave that defensive assignment to 6′1″ guard, K.C. Jones, the Don's playmaker on offense. Though six inches shorter than the Explorer's center, he was extremely quick and held Gola in check while scoring 24 points himself, one more than Russell. Loeffler devised a sliding zone, but its effect was minimal. In the final analysis, it was Bill Russell's first half contribution of 18 points and his dominance of the backboards that made the difference. He was voted the MVP as the Dons subdued LaSalle 77-63 to win their first national championship.

1956

The establishment of Bill Russell as a superstar coincided with, and some would say, contributed to the emergence of black basketball players on the national scene. Prior to the mid-fifties almost all players of star rank were white. The great Kentucky teams of the late forties and early fifties were all white as were such individual standouts as Lovellette, Gola, Cousy, Lavelli, Mikan and Kurland. Because of strict segregation in the southern schools their teams were all lily white. True, some eastern colleges, especially those which played in the large cities and some in the Big 10 and PCC included one or two black players on their squads. Among these were Duquesne with Dave Ricketts; CCNY with Ed Warner; Long Island University with Sherman White; and Seton Hall with Walt Dukes. Earlier Jackie Robinson had been a star player for UCLA. However, these were, by and large, exceptions.

By 1956, the pendulum had begun to swing in the opposite direction and such stars as Russell and K.C. Jones of San Francisco, Willie Naulls of UCLA and Si Green of Duquesne were recognized All Americans. By 1958 four of the five concensus All Americans were black.

In 1956, the Louisiana legislature passed a bill banning sporting events in which black and white athletes competed against each other. This was a reaction to the increasing militancy of the Black Freedom movement. The response from northern schools was quick. St. Louis, Notre Dame and Dayton which had been scheduled to play in the 1956 Sugar Bowl tournament declined invitations. Harvard, though it had no black players, cancelled a southern tour set for its basketball team; Cincinnati cancelled a game in Louisiana. But southern intransigence was flying in the face of basketball imperative.

The 1956 NCAA tournament was marked with a new awareness of the importance of containing the offense. Pete Newell's clinic for coaches with its emphasis on defense was drawing a lot more attention than it ever had before. San Francisco had just completed an undefeated season and looked unbeatable. Many coaches were looking for a means of slowing down the game, holding the ball for the high percentage shot and thus cutting down the amount of time their opponents held the ball. The most often used stratagem was to freeze if one's team had the ball and the lead late in the game. The stall became a feature of several crucial games in this tourney.

West:

San Francisco (25-0) was riding the crest of a fifty-one game winning streak, the longest by a major college. Besides Russell, they had a second All American in 6′1″ playmaker, K.C. Jones. Their success was based on a smothering defense that gave up an average of 49.5 points a game. Only three times did they allow as many as 60. They dominated teams so completely that their average winning margin of 21 points meant they scored 40 percent better than their opponents.

San Francisco's closest game was against crossbay rival California, coached by Newell,whom they outlasted 33-24. After taking a lead early in the game, California went into a stall. For eight minutes the Bears' Joe Hagler held the ball like an undelivered package without once passing or dribbling it. Gene Brown, waiting for the Dons to gain possession in order to get into the game, spent eight uncomfortable minutes crouched in front of the scorer's table. Woolpert, concentrating on the game, forgot all about him until a whispered voice asked, "Can I sit down now, Coach?" By this time, Woolpert, not to mention the fans, had had enough. Deciding to teach Newell a lesson in defensive tactics, he ordered the Dons into a full court press. In the next seven minutes the Dons outscored California 17-3 as they put inexorable pressure on the Bears' ball handlers. California persisted in not shooting and the contest ended with more than three times as many free throws as field goals.

Many felt UCLA (21-5) had the best chance of upsetting San Francisco in the tournament. For the first time since 1922, the PCC eliminated the two division setup and played as one undivided conference. UCLA was undefeated in their conference although they had their early season problems. They lost their first two to BYU, won the next two, lost two more, won two again, and then dropped one to San Francisco 70-53 in the finals of Madison Square Garden's Holiday Festival. The Bruins then got off the seesaw and, led by Willie Nauls, won their last 17.

Utah (21-5) were first in the Skyline. In one of the worst mismatches of the year, they clobbered Arizona 119-45. The return game was a little closer, the Utes winning by only 30 points. Idaho State (18-7), the perennial Rocky Mountain champion, lost twice to their perennial first round tournament foe, Seattle (17-9), in a preview of coming attractions.

Seattle nipped Idaho State again 68-66 in a first round game. Dick Stricklin, the Chieftains' high scorer, was injured prior to the game and was not at his best. Nevertheless, Seattle took a seven point lead into the locker room at intermission. Revived by the break, Idaho State came back strong. With the score knotted at 60 each, Seattle substitute Clair Markey, who scored all of his 13 points in the second half, made two free throws and connected on a jump shot. The Bengals responded with a pair of charity tosses, but Markey hit another jumper and Stricklin added two points to give Seattle an insurmountable 68-62 lead.

In Corvallis, Seattle faced a stronger opponent in Utah. This time the Chieftains were behind after the first twenty minutes but caught up. Gary Bergen, a key player in the Utes' running attack, returned to the bench with six minutes gone in the second half, charged with his fourth personal. Utah seemed to be in control with a 57-47 lead. But Seattle hustled back to even the score 66-66. Coach Jack Gardner reinserted Bergen who responded by sinking eight points in a row to break the game open for Utah. Bergen fouled out but by that time Utah had matters under control as they won 81-72.

San Francisco was under a severe handicap. Its All American playmaker, K.C. Jones, had been declared ineligible because he played one game in 1953 before undergoing an appendectomy and sitting out the rest of the season. The three year eligibility rule was in effect for postseason games and the Dons would have to get along without him. UCLA posed no problem for San Francisco. The Bruins were held to only four field goal attempts in the first ten minutes. Five minutes later they still had only two buckets. Meanwhile the Dons were scoring two points for every one the Bruins cashed. At the end UCLA made the score respectable but San Francisco advanced 72-61. Russell bagged 21 points but was outscored by Jones' replacement, sophomore Gene Brown, who tallied 21.

Utah tried running with San Francisco. Although they scored more points against the Dons than any other team that season, they still lost 92-77. San Francisco proved it had an offense, too, and that they could run as well if not better than most teams. Russell scored 27 and completed a productive weekend in which he accounted for 45 rebounds and about 20 blocked shots.

Midwest:

Surprising SMU (23-2), ranked sixth, was the favorite in the Midwest regional. Rarely had a Southwest Conference school posted such an impressive record. Starting with their first game, a 113-36 massacre of McMurray, they projected a champion's image. Their two losses had come against Kansas and Iowa, but these had been early in the year and they won their last 18.

The regional opposition was not all that imposing. Kansas State (16-7) was the Big Seven champ. Houston (19-5) had won the MVC with a good record but lost their last two games. Memphis State (20-6), an independent, was known for its high scoring games. They averaged 88 points, scored over one hundred on eight occasions and, in one blowout, recorded 138 points. For Memphis State, it was run and shoot all night.

Oklahoma City (18-6) was making its fifth consecutive tourney appearance, a new record. The Chiefs had played several interregional games against such schools as Seattle, Pennsylvania, Wyoming, and Western Kentucky and benefited from the experience. The team with the poorest record was Texas Tech (13-11), the Border Conference winner. They began the season as if the whole team were playing on one leg, losing eight of nine during one stretch. Subsequently, the Red Raiders began winning and found the hoop consistently, averaging 105 points in a four game outburst.

Because the teams representing the SWC had such a poor record in NCAA tournament play, SMU did not receive a first round bye. These went to schools representing conferences which had the best records in tournament competition over the previous five years. Since at-large schools had no conference record on which to base a decision to grant a bye, they always had to compete in first round games, a bias which the NCAA maintained until the field was expanded to 32 schools in 1974.

Texas Tech, spurning the underdog role, took a 35-33 half time lead and increased it after the break. SMU spent most of the second half trying to catch up. Finally, with six minutes to go, Joel Krog snaked in a layup to put the Mustangs ahead. For the next five minutes the Red Raiders refused to be shaken off. Then, with less than a minute left, 6′8″ center Jim Krebs gave the Mustangs a 68-65 edge. Nine seconds later Texas Tech's Gene Carpenter brought the Red Raiders back to within a point but SMU froze the ball the rest of the way to preserve its one point victory. Carpenter was high scorer with 22 in a losing cause but it was Krebs and Krog, who scored the last 15 points for SMU, who were the heroes.

In the other first round game Oklahoma City, after trailing by as many as twelve, exploded for 64 points in the second half to eliminate Memphis State 97-81.

The Oklahoma City chiefs, long known as a defense-oriented team, had become more offense-minded under their new coach Abe Lemons. They learned to adjust quickly. In Lawrence, Kansas, they faced Kansas State in the second round. This time they held an eighteen point lead and saw most of it melt away under a determined Wildcat counterattack. They held on, though, to win 97-93, their second 97 point performance in as many games. Oklahoma City and Kansas State played a team game which was reflected in the balanced scoring. Both teams had five men in double figures.

SMU, on the other hand, spent most of the evening trying to get the ball to Krebs, a fine scorer who once tallied 50 points against Texas, as Houston tried, often vainly, to screen him from his teammates. The Mustang center got his hands on the ball often enough to pop for 27 points, meanwhile holding the Cougar's 7 foot center Don Boldebuck to just 11. With a 16 point margin at the end of the half, SMU coasted to an 89-74 victory.

In the regional final, Oklahoma City had better luck defending Krebs but their scoring touch evaporated. After an early 8-8 tie, SMU went ahead to stay and eventually won 84-63. Although they were able to check Krebs, the Chiefs had less luck against Krog who pumped in 22 and Larry Showalter who chipped in 20.

Mideast:

Third ranked Dayton and seventh ranked Louisville accepted invitations to play in the NIT so the NCAA had to choose two lesser rated schools to complete the field in the Mideast regional. They picked Wayne State (17-1) and DePaul (16-7). The latter played a rather eclectic schedule with games against Milwaukee State, Illinois Normal, Manchester, Lewis as well as against San Francisco and Kentucky. They split their two games with the Wildcats.

Kentucky (19-5) finished second in the SEC to Alabama and were beaten decisively by trhe Crimson Tide 101-77. It was the most points ever given up by a Kentucky team. However, all five of Alabama's starters were seniors who had played four years and were consequently ineligible for postseason play. The Tide, therefore, declined a tournament invitation. Kentucky took revenge on Georgia Tech for the two losses they had pinned on the Wildcats the previous year by trouncing them 104-51. For good measure they also scrambled Georgia 143-66. These two scores did nothing to diminish Adolph Rupp's reputation for being merciless.

Iowa (17-5) was the preseason favorite to repeat as the Big 10 winner, and they did. But they had to overcome a horrendous start during which most of the experts counted them out of the race. In December they lost five of six including four in a row but after righting themselves, reeled off fourteen consecutive wins to end the season on the up slope.

Marshall (18-4) was the Mid American winner. Charlie Slack, relatively short at 6′5″, set a new individual NCAA rebounding record that still stands, 26 years later. One suspects he picked up so many rebounds because Marshall shot so often. The Big Green scored more than 100 points on six occasions but gave up 100 as often. Morehead State (17-9) was even more prolific. They registered three digit scores ten times and topped 90 a total of 19 times. These were wild bombing affairs in which anyone who had the ball felt it obligatory to heave it at the basket. Passing off was considered poor form. One memorable shootout was a 119-113 loss to Cincinnati.

The fans were expecting the same bombardment of the nets as Marshall and Morehead State took the court in a first round game in Fort Wayne. They were not disappointed. The Eagles had beaten the Big Green twice during the season, 102-89 and 108-103, and did so again, this time 107-92; Dan Swartz led the way with 39 points. It was the first time, other than in a consolation game, that a team had scored over 100 points in the tournament.

DePaul and Wayne battled on even terms and when the teams left the court after the first twenty minutes, Wayne was clinging to a narrow 37-36 lead. As soon as play resumed, DePaul reclaimed the lead but Bob Kendrick's jump shot gave Wayne the advantage again. With Kendrick and 5′11″ sophomore Clarence Straughn doing most of the scoring, Wayne built up a 53-43 lead only to see the Blue Demons flush eight points through the hoop, closing within two. Again Wayne pulled away with Straughn carrying most of the load. DePaul rallied once more and at 1:42 narrowed the margin to two again. One final effort by Kendrick and Straughn, who scored 27 points, gave Wayne the decision 72-63.

In the second round Wayne drew Kentucky, an awesome assignment for the small college. Unbelievably, they led the Wildcats at half time 34-32. The upset of the century was in the making, but Kentucky pulled themselves together in the second half and went on to an easy 84-64 win. Bob Burrow, the Wildcat center, tallied 33 points while a disappointed Straughn was limited to six.

The regional was held in Iowa City which meant the local Hawkeyes received substantial vocal support. They responded by overwhelming Morehead State 97-83 as Carl Cain sank 28 to lead his team. Four Eagles and two Hawkeyes were excused before the final buzzer as a total of 68 personals were assessed.

The following evening before a packed arena of frenzied, screaming hometown fans, Iowa took its fifteenth game in a row, upending Kentucky 89-77. Cain was again high man, this time with 34 points and Burrow, playing his last college game, checked in with 31.

East:

In the East, Connecticut (16-9) won the Yankee Conference as usual. Their success depended on a highpowered offense that never failed to score at least seventy points. Manhattan (16-7) under veteran coach Ken Norton matched Connecticut's offensive power. They had hung up at least seventy points per game, too. From Philadelphia came Temple (23-3), replacing LaSalle as that city's leading team. They had won their first thirteen games in a row, numbering among their victims highly ranked Kentucky. Their only losses came against Muhlenberg by one, Duquesne by two and St. Josephs.

Holy Cross (22-4), the top rebounding team in the country, represented New England. The Crusaders faced some tough opponents. Three of their four losses were to teams that were invited to the NCAA postseason tournament, including San Francisco. With All American Tom Heinsohn scoring a bunch, Holy Cross showed they were ready to take on anybody by topping one hundred in their last two games, including a 111-75 shellacking of Boston college.

Dartmouth (16-10) started well and then sailed into the doldrums in mid-season. The Indians had just about written off the season after losing nine of ten—seven in a row. Then, unexpectedly, they put together a ten game win streak to take the Ivy crown. West Virginia (21-8) with All American Rod Hundley averaging 26.6 points per game won the Southern Conference. Canisius (17-6) was an at-large entry.

North Carolina State (24-3) was the only ranked team in the regional. They were rated right behind undefeated San Francisco. All three losses had come in the ACC, probably the strongest basketball conference in the country. Three different ACC schools had been in the top ten at one time or another during the season including North Carolina, which had tied the Wolfpack for the conference championship. However, State copped the postseason tourney and the NCAA invitation.

Everett Case, a former high school coach in Indiana where he had won 726 games—almost 90 percent over 24 years—had come to Raleigh to take over the reins of the Wolfpack. Case was a real oddity. Despite his fantastic record he had never played organized basketball—not even in high-school! He also brought some of his Indiana stars with him and in his zeal to produce a champion, had been censured for recruiting violations. This resulted in the Wolfpack missing the 1955 tournament. Even with last year's suspension, North Carolina State was making its fifth tournament appearance in seven years. Case had a lot to do with the basketball madness that descended on Raleigh each winter. Several years earlier a game had to be cancelled when too many fans jammed into the gymnasium and refused to leave. Since then a new, much larger arena had been built and this one, too, was filled to capacity for each game. At the end of the season a total of 265,000 fans had watched State play at home, the highest attendance in the country.

The fans and Case were confident they could take the national championship this year. The prime reason for this optimism was 6′8″ All American Ron Shavlik. Case figured that given the level of the opposition, it should be simple to win their regional and then hold off San Francisco in the final. Unfortunately for the Wolfpack, they did not reckon on Shavlik's broken wrist or Canisius' determination.

On March 12, 1956, 14,522 New York fans saw two of the closest, most exciting games ever played in Madison Square Garden. In the first game a generally even first half ended with Temple, helped by a late scoring flurry, ahead of Holy Cross 40-37. With less than two minutes left in the game, the Owls were in front 72-67. Then a foul and a hook shot by Joe Hughes and a tip-in by Heinsohn evened the match. With six seconds left, Fred Cohen of Temple hit on a jumper to retake the lead. The Crusaders worked the ball quickly to Heinsohn who took a desperation shot that miraculously swished through the net. A great roar greeted the score to be followed a second later by an equally loud groan as the referee disallowed the goal claiming it came after the buzzer. One of the disappointed Crusader boosters attacked the referee before he had a chance to find safety in his locker room, but the score remained 74-72 in favor of Temple. Heinsohn was top scorer for Holy Cross with 26. Hal Lear and Guy Rodgers were high men for the Owls hitting for 26 and 18 respectively.

But the fans had seen nothing yet. They were about to witness the longest NCAA tournament game ever played as Canisius and North Carolina State took the court.

The freeze was a recognized weapon, used occasionally in the final minutes or seconds of a close game. However its use, or abuse, reached new dimensions in the East regional that year. Dave Markey's side jumper for Canisius at 2:40 left of the second half tied the game at 65-65. For the next two and one half minutes, the players acted as if shooting the ball at the hoop just was not in their game plan. A minor flurry ended regulation time with the score still knotted. Late in the first ovetime Canisius was leading 68-67 when Markey and Bob Kelly of the Griffins both failed to convert free throws, thereby missing an opportunity to put the game on ice. So when Phil Dinardo's jump shot with twenty seconds left put the Wolfpack ahead 69-68, it looked like the end of the season for Canisius. However, Hank Nowak was fouled with eight seconds left. With a chance to take the lead Nowak could do no better than make one of two tries.

The game went into a second overtime. Johnny Maglio of the Wolfpack grabbed the opening tipoff and sailed in unobstructed to put his team ahead 71-69 after only four seconds had elapsed. A little more than a minute later Nowak sank a rainbow hook to tie it again. The Griffins regained possession and froze the ball until with fifteen seconds left, they called a time out. The play they tried to set up did not work and the teams went into the third overtime.

If play had been deliberate until then, it became positively glacial now. Both teams having come this far were reluctant to make any offensive thrust, fearing that if it failed it would be their last. Canisius froze the ball for most of the third overtime; with twenty seconds left the Griffins called another time out. This set play was as unsuccessful as the one ending the second overtime so the teams, after a scoreless five minutes and still tied at 71-71, went into the fourth overtime.

By this time the fans were frustrated and becoming irate at the lack of action on the court. The coaches, sensing their players were approaching exhaustion from tension and court play, ordered them to resume action. The fourth overtime was quite lively but as the period waned, Canisius found itself a point short. But, with just four seconds left, Fran Corcoran snapped in a one handed jumper, his only basket of the marathon, to win it for Canisius 79-78. Corcoran was mobbed by a happy group of Griffins who finally got the last second shot they had been freezing the ball for all evening. North Carolina State, stunned by the upset, returned to Raleigh, wondering if they would have won if Ron Shavlik had not broken his wrist. Shavlik did play, though, and despite a brace led the Wolfpack with 25 points.

The following evening Connecticut won its first round game with Manhattan 84-75. It was a rematch of a regular season contest which saw the Jaspers beating Connecticut in overtime by three.

In the fourth first round match Dartmouth, behind by two at the half, watched a two point lead evaporate late in the game when West Virginia's Joedy Gardner sank a pair of free throws. There were still three minutes left in the game, but as far as Dartmouth was concerned, the action was over. Stealing a page from the Canisius playbook, the Indians froze the ball for the remainder of regulation time. Since they failed to score on a last-second shot, the teams went into overtime tied 59-59. An absolute chill descended on the court as Dartmouth spent most of the five minute session freezing the ball. The fans, a disappointingly small crowd filling only half the Garden, screamed for some offense but the Indians were content to wait. They almost waited too long. With four seconds left, Larry Blades tried a long desperation shot that was deflected by a Mountaineer player. But Blades retrieved the ball, shot again and connected with one second left to win the game for Dartmouth 61-59. Aside from not handling the ball very much in the last eight minutes, the Mountaineers could blame their loss on their poor performance at the free throw line where they made only 13 of 24 shots.

At the Philadelphia Palestra, the two prime practitioners of the deep freeze met in a second round contest. A war of nerves loomed. Some wondered whether Canisius or Dartmouth would make any offensive move toward the basket at all, whether the heat should be turned up in the Palestra or what it would take to defrost the teams if they went into another stall. There was no need for concern. Both teams played aggressively if not brilliantly and Canisius took the contest 66-58. Nowak's 29 points eased the way.

The second game went to Temple by an almost identical score, 65-59. Connecticut failed to tally 70 points for the first time that year. The story of the game was the brilliant shooting of 5′11″ guard Hal Lear. He made 18 of 27 shots, 4 of 5 fouls, two-thirds of his team's baskets, and 40 of his team's 65 points. His was a virtuoso one-man performance.

The final was held before 7,664 highly partisan and vocal fans urging Lear and the rest of the Owls on. But Canisius, having acquired the reputation of giant killer was thinking of Kansas City, not a return trip to Buffalo. The Griffins played the whole game without a single substitute. Strangely, neither Lear nor Nowak was able to make much impression on the scoreboard. The game turned on a single play as unusual as it was rare. With the score tied 58-58, the Griffins went into their Eskimo act and turned the temperature down on the court. What they did not expect was the aggressiveness with which Temple countered that tactic.

Bob Kelly found himself being forced into backcourt by a determined Jay Norman of Temple and the Griffins were thus relieved of the ball. Now it was

Temple's turn to freeze. With two seconds left, Guy Rodgers, who scored 22, passed to Lear who was immediately fouled by Joe Leone. Lear, who had been held to 12 thus far, converted both attempts as Temple advanced to the Final Four, 60-58.

Final Four:

The semifinals were scheduled for the Northwestern fieldhouse in Evanston, Illinois, for Thursday evening and the finals for Friday, a departure from the usual Friday-Saturday finale. San Francisco toyed with SMU through much of the first half, leading at one time 40-19. The Mustangs finished the period with a flurry and trailed by only 44-32. Back on the court SMU resumed where they left off and were closing fast. Ahead by only 46-40, the Dons pulled themselves together and won going away 86-68. Krebs outscored Russell 24 to 17 but the latter played a super game on defense. For the Dons, Mike Farmer was their high scorer with 26 points—18 in the first half.

In the other semifinal, it was Iowa's tall front court of Bill Schoof, Bill Logan and Carl Cain against Temple's sharpshooting backcourt of Lear and Rodgers. It was a game of brilliant individual efforts but in the end the Hawkeyes' height and strength was too much for the quicker Owls. Harry Litwack, in his fourth year as coach at Temple and already acquiring a reputation as a first class basketball strategist, tried various defenses against the Iowa trio but without success. The final score was Iowa 83-Temple 76 as Logan (36), Cain (20), and Schoof (18) provided almost the entire Iowa offense. Lear's 32 points and Rodger's 28 paced the Owls.

Iowa took an early lead over San Francisco in the final. Bill Russell, discussing the game later, said, "No, I wasn't nervous . . . I was just flat scared!" Playing scared must have done wonders for his game. The Dons overtook Iowa before intermission and later led by as many as 17. Iowa never got close again as the Dons won 83-71. It was their second consecutive NCAA Championship, their fifty-fifth win in a row and the first time any team had won the title while remaining undefeated. For Russell, it was an appropriate ending to a brilliant college career. He scored 26 points, grabbed 27 rebounds and blocked many shots. He went on to lead the U.S. Olympic basketball team to a gold medal before turning professional. Still, the MVP award went to Hal Lear who scored 48 against SMU in the third place consolation game, thus setting a new record of 160 points in the tournament. Lear's high scoring performance in a consolation game was to set a precedent for similar individual efforts in the future.

The Dons had put their winning streak on the line twice against teams having substantial streaks of their own. In the end it was SMU's 20 game and Iowa's 17 game streaks that ended while the Dons overcame the challenge to reign another year.

8

COACHING MADE THE DIFFERENCE 1957-1958

1957

East:

When St. Johns upset Kentucky in the 1952 East regional held in Raleigh, North Carolina, Frank McGuire, the Redmen's coach, must have made an excellent impression on the local fans. Soon after the season ended, McGuire accepted an offer to coach at North Carolina. Since then, his teams had improved to the point that by 1957, he was aiming for a national championship.

At the conclusion of the 1956 season, Phog Allen came to the end of his long and extremely successful career. In 46 years on the bench, the man who learned the game from the founder of the sport had won 771 games, more than any other coach. Now he had reached the mandatory retirement age of seventy and no amount of persuasion could change the minds of the University of Kansas regents to allow him to remain one more year. The reason Allen wanted to coach in 1957 was that he had landed the most sought after high school player in the country, seven foot tall Wilt Chamberlain. With Chamberlain eligible to play in 1957, the Jayhawks were almost guaranteed a national championship. Disappointed at the regent's decision, Allen turned the coaching over to his assistant, Dick Harp. It was Harp and McGuire who were destined to meet in what is generally accepted as the most dramatic tournament final ever played.

After McGuire left New York, he remained in contact with local high school basketball coaches and afficionados of the sport and these kept him well supplied with local players. It was McGuire's Mafia that sent a steady stream

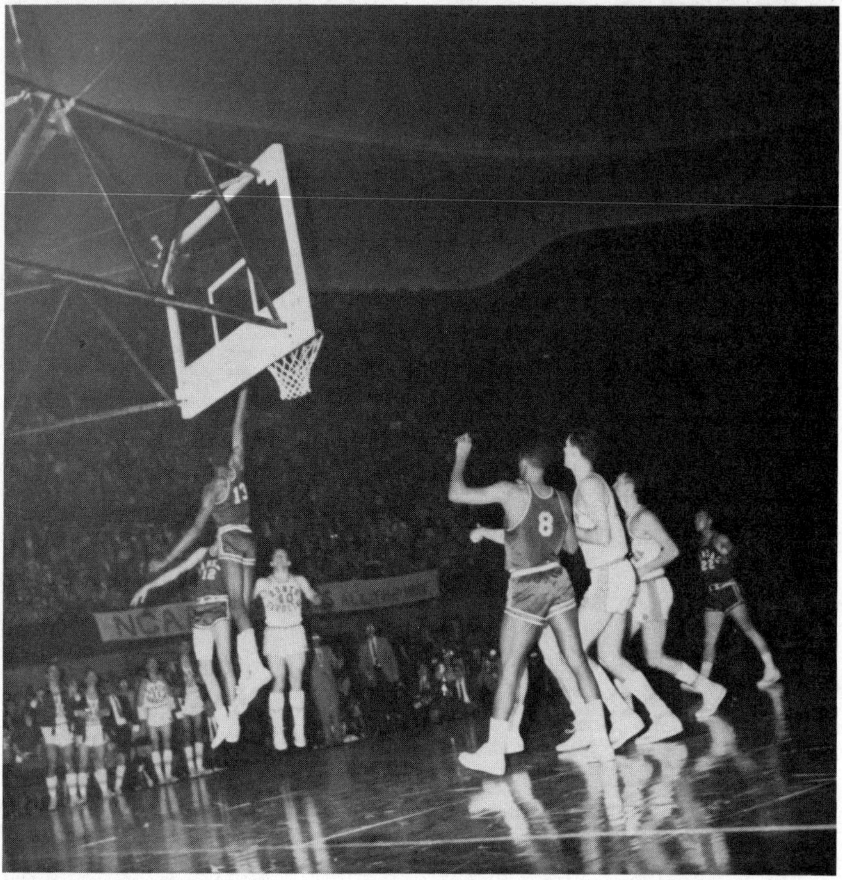

The final seconds of the third overtime in the 1957 final between North Carolina and Kansas. Wilt Chamberlain (13) has just blocked Tommy Kearns' (40) jumper. Kansas was ahead 53-52 but the Tarheels scored two more points to win the game.
(University of Kansas photo)

of New York's finest basketball talent south to Dixie. Roaming the gyms and playgrounds of New York, the unofficial scouts would buttonhole the best athletes and hold forth on the benefits of a basketball scholarship at North Carolina and the delights of campus life at Chapel Hill. Quite a few boys were impressed enough to make the trip south. Once a player arrived, McGuire, if he was impressed with the prospect, was usually able to get him to sign a letter of intent. There were also scouts in New York working for Case at North Carolina State but somehow McGuire managed to get the cream of the crop.

In 1957, the North Carolina starting quintet (one Jewish star and four Catholics) was the product of metropolitan New York schools. Probably the best of the lot was All American Lenny Rosenbluth of the Bronx. Almost as talented were Bob Cunningham of Manhattan; Joe Quigg and Pete Brennan of Brooklyn; and Tommy Kearns of New Jersey. The few local North Carolina boys on the squad spent most of the season on the bench occasionally seeing spot action to salve Tarheel pride. McGuire substituted sparingly (unlike his successor Dean Smith who brought the shuttle system to college basketball), but as long as he won games the local fans supported the carpetbaggers enthusiastically. It was a close knit squad having great confidence in itself. After surviving a four point deficit with 40 seconds to go against Maryland, a laughing Rosenbluth turned to his shaken coach and crowed, "Only 17 more to go!"

North Carolina, with a perfect 27-0 season, was the only undefeated school in the country in 1957 and was ranked number one. This was a remarkable accomplishment since the team played in what many considered the toughest conference of all.* This would change over the years until the ACC's record would be the third best behind the Big Ten and Pac Ten. It was a breakthrough for the Tarheels. For nine of the past ten years rival North Carolina State had won the conference championship, a situation that did not sit well in Chapel Hill.

The only team given a chance to defeat North Carolina in the East regional was seventh ranked West Virginia (25-4). Rod Hundley, now a senior, was playing in his last tournament. It would be the All American Mountaineer's third attempt to lead his team to a NCAA tournament win. Hundley had added to his repertoire of tricks and could now dribble with his knees and punch the ball into the basket with his fist. The rest of the regional opposition was not too formidable. THe highest scoring team in the country was Connecticut (17-7). As usual that record was achieved by victimizing weak conference opponents. The Huskies had bagged 118 and 124 points in their two games against Maine—the sixth time in four years they had scored over 100 points against this hapless team. Syracuse (16-6), was a fine squad with a problem—beating Buffalo area schools. They lost to Canisius twice

*The Atlantic Coast Conference schools had not been very successful in the NCAA Tournament. To date, they had won only nine while losing twelve and none of the four schools that had participated had a winning record.

and to Niagara once. Lafayette (22-3) was the Philadelphia area representative, winners of the Mid Atlantic non-conference.

Yale (18-7) was beaten five straight early in the season with three of the defeats coming at the hands of Big 10 schools. The Ivy Leaguers ensured their invitation to the tournament by squeezing past Dartmouth 57-56. The Eli's were led by guard Johnny Lee, a two-time High School All American at Erasmus Hall in Brooklyn.

Canisius (20-5) was an at-large selection. Its four overtime win over North Carolina the previous year gave the school a considerable amount of exposure. The Griffins, by playing a national rather than a regional schedule that included games against Seton Hall, Notre Dame, Marquette, Dayton, St. Bonaventure, Holy Cross and Villanova—all Catholic schools, as well as Alabama and Minnesota, were attempting to become a big time power.

Canisius took a step in the right direction by eliminating West Virginia in the first round in New York 64-56. The Griffin's two stars, Nowak and Leone, took turns dominating the action. Nowak scored 17 in the first half which ended with Canisius on top 34-18. Leone took up where Nowak left off and sank 16 in the second half. West Virginia climbed back within two points with six minutes to go, but Canisius put on a closing spurt that left their opponents floundering. For the unranked Griffins it was the second consecutive year they had ousted a top ten team in the first round. They were acquiring a reputation as a giant killer.

On the same program Connecticut, leading by two at the half, increased its advantage over Syracuse to 65-55 with slightly more than eight minutes left. At this point the Syracuse coach instructed his players to put on an all court press. Connecticut reacted by falling apart. They booted the ball away or had passes intercepted, committing one turnover after another. The Orangemen took advantage of nearly every opportunity. Within a span of six minutes they outscored the Huskies 22-3. Mercifully, the buzzer ended the carnage and Syracuse advanced, 82-76, to the next round.

Incredibly Yale and North Carolina left the court at half time tied 40-40 in the third game of the triple header. At 5:00 of the second half the Tarheels were grimly protecting a three point lead when the court finally stopped tilting against them. North Carolina went on an 8-0 spree and coasted the rest of the way as they dropped Yale 90-74. Giving away an average of three inches per man, a band of gutsy Elis had played the number one team in the country on even terms for 35 minutes. With Johnny Lee setting up plays and tallying 25 points himself, and the defense using a pressing zone that held the Tarheel's offense in check, Yale gave McGuire's boys an unexpected scare. In the end Yale paid the price for their aggressive defense. Four of their starters fouled out and their replacements were unable to hold North Carolina. For their part, the Tarheels used only six players and their starters carried the brunt of the load.

The regional moved to the Palestrain Philadelphia for second round competition. North Carolina had little trouble with Canisius and finished them off,

87-75, as Rosenbluth scored 39 points with some excellent shooting. Syracuse had a little more trouble with Lafayette. The Panthers hit for nine points in a row just before half time to close to within two. Syracuse prevailed, though, and took the game 75-71. The winner's Gary Clark was the leading scorer with 34 points.

In the regional final, Syracuse outscored North Carolina from the floor 24-17 but committed so many fouls trying to keep the Tarheels in check they lost the game at the free throw line. The Orangemen had a dreadful night, converting only 10 of 23 attempts. But it would have taken almost perfect shooting to overcome the Tarheels who made 33 of 45 foul shots to win 67-58.

Midwest:

The number two ranked team in the country was Kansas with a 21-2 record. They had been ranked first at the beginning of the season but after their first loss, North Carolina took over that spot. Both Jayhawk defeats were by two point margins—to Iowa State and to Oklahoma State. In a way, it was surprising that Kansas stumbled even twice. After all, they had Wilt "the Stilt" Chamberlain, who dominated every game in which he played. While a senior at Philadelphia's Overbrook High School, he averaged 45 points per game and was courted by 77 major colleges in the country as well as several smaller schools. He had selected Kansas as a result of a soft-sell campaign by Phog Allen (who made two trips to Philadelphia) and members of the local black community in Lawrence who suggested he would be of "great help to his race" if he enrolled at Kansas. Actually the whole town cooperated in trying to make Chamberlain feel comfortable and welcome. The color problem was important to Chamberlain. He turned down scholarship offers to break the color line at Missouri and North Carolina State because he did not want to be a token black in an all-white university.

In his first game as a sophomore, Chamberlain scored 52 points and hauled down 31 rebounds, both Kansas records, as he almost single-handledly beat Northwestern 87-69. Strangely, it was the most he would ever score in his college career. Eventually defenses would be designed to limit his point production by keeping him out from under the basket where he was deadly with tip-ins and stuffs. Still, he averaged close to 30 points per game during the season, usually with two or three men guarding him. As Frank McGuire said, "There might be somebody in the penitentiary who can handle him, but I guarantee you there is nobody in college."

One reason for Chamberlain's occasional poor performance was his personality. He was a shy, withdrawn young man, sensitive about his height. He suffered from the cultural shock of being transplanted from an urban ghetto to a small midwestern town and was unused to the ubiquitous attention his presence attracted. As a result he was not in the game emotionally.

He internalized many of his complaints, so it came as a big shock when he left school at the end of his junior year with a year's eligibility remaining.

The only team given chance to beat Kansas (and Chamberlain) in the Midwest regional was SMU (21-3). The Mustangs played just seven games outside their conference, and this lack of interregional competition hurt them. Krebs, the Mustangs' 6'8" all American center, was their high scorer and the keystone of the team. One admirer called him "the greatest Methodist since John Wesley and Doak Walker."

St. Louis (19-7) won the MVC crown. (Bradley, which had rejoined the conference, finished second and was invited to play in the NIT. Somehow they overcame their revulsion at playing in Madison Square Garden and eventually won the tournament.) The two at-large teams invited were Oklahoma City (17-8) and Loyola of Louisiana (14-11). Oklahoma City was making its sixth consecutive tourney appearance, playing under new coach Abe Lemons. Loyola, with the poorest record in the tourney, had dropped six of their last eight games.

Playing before their hometown fans, Oklahoma City blew Loyola off the court in the first half, taking a 38-16 lead into the locker room. The second half was a little closer but the Chiefs still advanced 76-55.

In the second round in Dallas the Chiefs upset St. Louis 75-66. The feature game had Kansas facing fourth ranked SMU. To get Chamberlain away from the basket and thus neutralize his rebounding advantage, Krebs came out of the low post and played in the corner. That tactic did not work too well since he missed consistently and Krebs finally resumed his place in the pivot from where he hooked the ball with slightly better results. Krebs' problem may have been a cold shooting night, but a more plausible reason was Chamberlain's intimidating presence, the kind of player that Krebs had not faced in the past. In any case, Chamberlain outscored Krebs 36-18 while taking fewer shots. On defense SMU used a 2-3 zone which collapsed on Chamberlain but often left other Jayhawks open. Kansas raced to a 15-4 lead and then let the Mustangs catch up. At half time the Kansans held a narrow 33-32 lead. The second half was just as close. With five minutes remaining and SMU ahead by three, Krebs fouled out, a common occurrence for anyone trying to guard Chamberlain. Kansas tied the score at the buzzer and the game went into overtime. Without their star center the Mustangs provided little resistance as Kansas overcame their toughest obstacle on their way to the final 73-65. In another second round contest Oklahoma City upset St. Louis 75-66.

The following evening Kansas took Oklahoma City 81-61 as Chamberlain tallied 30 and Hugh Reed made 26 for OCU. Lemons had noticed that Chamberlain raced straight down court to receive a lob pass for a stuff and directed a player to position himself at the top of the key to delay the Kansas center. The first half of the game was close but then Kansas moved ahead by 20 soon after the intermission, holding this advantage for the remainder of the game. At one point there was an angry outburst from the fans when

Chamberlain knocked over a Chief player but was not given a foul. Spectators threw coins and cushions (which were sold at the arena) on the court and the stands erupted in an explosion of boos and insults.

Mideast:

In the Mideast regional Pittsburgh (15-9) returned to tournament competition for the first time in sixteen years. Morehead State (19-7) represented the Ohio Valley Conference. They had finished in a tie with Western Kentucky but had a better overall season record. Notre Dame (18-7) had beaten Michigan State, and had also beaten Marquette twice, the second time by a lopsided 94-55 score.

Michigan State (14-8) had tied Indiana for the Big 10 title but were selected since they had beaten the Hoosiers in their only meeting. The Spartans had to overcome early season problems to enter their first tournament. After a 4-7 start (0-3 in the Big Ten), they won 10 of 11, losing only to traditional foe Michigan.

Miami of Ohio (17-7) topped the Mid American and third ranked Kentucky (22-4) won their conference as usual, losing two games by a single point. Also as usual, they found at least one team which they could pulverize; Loyola of Illinois was that year's unfortunate victim and the Wildcats ripped them 115-65.

In Columbus, Ohio, Notre Dame, leading all the way, eliminated Miami 89-77 as Tom Hawkins of the winners and Wayne Embry of the losers each scored 25 points.

The referee's whistle had as much to do with settling the outcome of the Pittsburgh-Morehead State game as the play of the respective teams. In a very rough contest, a total of 59 personals were assigned and seven starters from the two teams fouled out. Little Don Hennon (5′8″) of Pittsburgh was the star for the Panthers as he gunned 31 points through the cords. But it was Panther substitute John Laneve who was the ultimate hero. He scored on a jumper to win the game for Pittsburgh 86-85.

At Lexington the following weekend, Michigan State eliminated Notre Dame 85-83 in a very close game. The Spartans' scoring was evenly distributed as five men hit double figures. Kentucky, playing on its home court, had less trouble with Pittsburgh as they rolled to a 98-92 victory. Hennon fired in 24 points but teammate Bill Riser, deadly from the foul line, topped that with 30, including 16 of 17 free throws.

The following day Fordy Anderson, formerly at Bradley and now the Michigan State coach, took his boys fishing. His intention was to relax his players. After all Kentucky did not lose a game at home more than once every five years or so, especially not such an important one, and their last home court loss had come a mere two years ago. The benefit of the fishing trip was not apparent in the first half as the Wildcats swept to a 12 point lead. It looked like another Rupp runaway. But Anderson must have found the tonic in the locker room because the Spartans came back on the court a completely different team. By the midway mark of the second half, Michigan State had tied Kentucky 58-58. Charlie Bencie's layup put the Spartans in the lead to stay. In the last few minutes the Wildcats fell completely apart as Michigan State executed one of the most dramatic rallies in the tournament's history. The Spartans humiliated Kentucky in the second half, outscoring them 45-21 and recording the biggest upset of the tournament, 80-68.

West:

The team with the best record in the West regional was Idaho State (24-2). Despite a new coach the Bengals kept right on winning and dominating the Rocky Mountain Conference. Their only two defeats had come against Oklahoma City and Georgia Tech in back-to-back losses., The RMC schedule was structured so teams played each other in a series of two-game sets. Idaho State played eight consecutive such series and won them all. The Bengals did not have Seattle to contend with this year. The fifth ranked Chieftains, with an excellent 22-2 record and All American Elgin Baylor in the lineup, had accepted a trip to the NIT in New York.

Brigham Young (18-8), after losing three of their first four, rebounded to take the Skyline. Hardin Simmons (17-8) represented the Border Conference. San Francisco (18-6), after winning their first five of the season to extend their three year winning streak to sixty (a national record), were chilled by Illinois 62-33. One reason for the lopsided score was the frigid climate in the Illinois gym caused by the local management's practice of opening all the windows. The Dons, recently arrived from sunnier climes, literally froze. They were so cold they made only twelve baskets and hit a meager 22 percent of their shots from the floor. The traumatic effect of that defeat lasted for the next couple of weeks as San Francisco dropped three of their next four games but then recovered to win their conference. Still, that short slump cost them a place in the top ten at the end of the season.

California (20-4) was coached by Pete Newell who had left San Francisco for Michigan State in 1951. After four years in the Midwest he was back in the Bay Area. Newell, a leading proponent of defensive basketball, molded his California Bears into one of the stingiest teams in the country. Half their losses came against two teams who eventually made it to the Final Four—Kansas and San Francisco. California had an excellent team but their participation in the tournament was all but assured even before the season started as UCLA, Southern California and Washington were barred from postseason play for recruiting violations.

In a first round game in Pocatello, Idaho State beat Hardin-Simmons 68-57. The Bengals were led by Gail Siemen, who returned two weeks after

---

*Play-by-play announcers had a slight problem with a Jack Quiggle on one team and a Joe Quigg on the other. By the end of this drawn-out contest, at least one announcer had a slight quaver in his voice.

a leg operation to score 21 points and collect as many rebounds. Fans attending the second round games in Corvallis witnessed two dull, one-sided affairs. San Francisco, after moving into a 21 point half time lead, toyed with Idaho State, sinking them 66-51 to advance to the next round against California which had an even easier time prevailing over BYU 86-59.

California and San Francisco faced each other for the second time that year in the regional final. Newell and Woolpert, the top defensive strategists in the country (along with Hank Iba), sparred for forty minutes in a show-down of Bay Area schools. Defensive tactics kept the game tight and the score low. In the final seconds with the Dons ahead by two and time for only one more thrust, Newell inserted Joe Kapp, the school's gridiron quarter-back (and later quarterback with the Minnesota Vikings) to throw a long inbounds pass downcourt. Kapp threw a knuckler that spun downward short of the mark and was intercepted by Mike Farmer. Kapp forgot which sport he was playing and tackled Farmer who sank a pair of free throws, making the final score 50-46 in San Francisco's favor.

Final Four.

For the third time in the last four years, the Final Four gathered in Kansas City for the Championship Series. The first game was one of the closest ever contested anywhere. North Carolina and Michigan State were even at the end of the half, at the end of regulation time and at the end of the first and second overtime periods. The score was tied 18 times and only twice did either team have as much as a six point advantage. The Tarheels got off to a 6-0 lead, but Michigan State quickly closed the gap. After the first twenty minutes the score was knotted 29-29. Rosenbluth, the 6′5″ Tarheel center who averaged 28.2 points prior to the playoffs, was having trouble getting to the basket. Johnny Greene, the Spartan's sophomore sparkplug was playing him extremely tightly and he had to let fly from longer range than normal. Though he took almost half his team's shots he averaged only 26 percent. That hurt the Tarheels but he was their only player not in foul trouble. With two minutes remaining in the second half and the score tied 58-58, North Carolina held the ball for a final play. Only seconds remained as they moved to the basket. The shot missed, the ball bouncing off the rim to Jack Quiggle of the Spartans.* Quiggle turned and let fly from almost midcourt. Amazingly, the ball went through the hoop, but the referee ruled the buzzer had already sounded.

Michigan State went ahead in the first overtime only to see Pete Brennan collect a missed free throw and hit with a short side jumper, knotting the score at 64-64 just before the buzzer. In the second extra period, Rosenbluth got an early basket and Greene matched it with a tip in of a missed free throw. As the teams entered the third overtime session tied 66-66, the tension was high enough to power half the city. Again Rosenbluth got the Tarheels an early basket but again it was matched, this time by a side jumper from Quiggle. It was the eighteenth and last tie. Rosenbluth answered with a long jumper. Two free throws and another bucket gave the Tarheels their biggest lead since the opening minute and put the game on ice. The final score was 74-70 as North Carolina kept its spotless record intact.

The spectators were still limp as Kansas and San Francisco took the court. The Dons took an early 8-7 lead but thereafter it was all Kansas. Chamberlain, collecting 32 points on offense and playing almost flawless defense, completely intimidated the Dons. San Francisco shot a subpar 32% while the Jayhawks were converting an incredible 60% of their shots. Kansas outrebounded San Francisco almost two-to-one and the final score 80-56 reflected the dominance of the Midwesterners. It may have been Chamberlain's finest game against a major opponent. His scoring and rebounding showed confidence and alertness, and he played fine defense without picking up a single foul.

The next evening San Francisco beat Michigan State in the consolation game. After two years as champions, the Dons without Russell salvaged a third place finish, much higher than most expected and a tribute to Phil Woolpert's fine coaching.

Now the attention of the spectators, actually the whole country, focussed on the championship game. For the first time since 1949, the number one and number two teams in the country were playing each other for the title. Facing each other across the court were Frank McGuire, a veteran of years of the toughest basketball competition in the country, and rookie coach Dick Harp, a quiet, emotional man with a lot of tradition to live up to. He was Phog Allen's successor, possessed the best college basketball player in the country and was playing before a partisan crowd in an almost hometown atmosphere **and he was expected to win**. The teams were evenly matched and it was coaching that ultimately made the difference.

McGuire carefully studied the tactics used by the Jayhawks opponents during the season and probably learned most from a game that Iowa State won from Kansas 39-37 on a last second basket. Iowa State had played a very tight defense, assigning one man to guard Chamberlain from the front and the two forwards to collapse inward from the sides, thus pinching him off from the strong side of the court. In effect it was a 2-1-2 sliding zone. It left Kansas a lot of room to shoot from the corners, but it denied them the backboard which Chamberlain used so effectively to drain rebounds and sink tip ins. On offense, Iowa State had been extremely deliberate (as evidence the low score) and had taken only high percentage shots and when Chamberlain was not directly under the twine.

McGuire adopted this game plan almost without modification, adding his own wry twist as a psychological ploy to annoy Chamberlain. He had Tommy Kearns, his shortest starter at 5′11″, jump against Chamberlain at the opening tipoff. Another reason for this ploy may have been that McGuire knew that Wilt could outjump anybody on North Carolina, and he may as well have his tallest players try to intercept the tip before a Kansan could take off with it. The fans got a charge out of that ploy. One of the most vocal was Governor Luther Hodges who had seated himself on the North Carolina bench.

North Carolina played very deliberately, spreading out and firing from the corners, shooting only while facing the basket and when Chamberlain was out of position to block their attempts. They were leading 9-2 when Chamberlain scored his first bucket at 15:14. On defense, Kansas started the game playing a box and one (one man on Rosenbluth). But the Tarheels were so deadly from the perimeter, not missing a shot in the first 10 minutes, that the Jayhawks switched to a man-to-man. It gave the Tarheels less room to shoot, but it did not slow them down appreciably. At the end of the first half, North Carolina, firing 65 percent from the floor, was leading 29-22. Joe Quigg was playing Chamberlain as if they were laminated together. Consquently the Kansans could get nothing started offensively.

McGuire's defensive strategy was working. His collapsing zone was isolating Chamberlain from the ball. It left plenty of room for the other Jayhawks to shoot but they refused the opportunity. Harp could have moved Chamberlain out of the pivot but the big man was not particularly mobile and his scoring range was limited to about eight feet from the basket. If it had not been for their anemic 27 percent foul shooting, North Carolina might have broken the game open in the first twenty minutes.

It was a different Jayhawk squad that started the second half. Outscoring their opponents two to one, Kansas took a 40-37 lead with ten minutes to go. North Carolina tried to slow the pace, but still the Kansans came on. Then, inexplicably, with the Tarheels on the ropes and with a mere three point lead, the Jayhawks went into a freeze to protect their advantage. McGuire declared later this was the turning point of the game. After having played 55 minutes the previous evening, playing with almost no substitutions, with their starters in foul trouble (Quigg had four, Kearns and Rosenbluth, three each) and the momentum going against them, the Tarheels were exhausted, desperate and ready to be taken. They welcomed the respite and allowed Kansas to control the ball for five minutes. Then, having found their second wind and not having picked up any more fouls, they went about separating the Kansans from the ball. As the clock wound down to zero, the tension rose even higher than the night before, if that was possible. The atmosphere was incandescent. Pete Brennan and Chamberlain collided. Harp ran onto the court. McGuire bounded to the Kansas bench to protest Harp's action. A fight ensued with McGuire getting punched in the back of the head. The referees restored order on the court, but the stands were a bedlam.

Two minutes before the end of regulation time, Rosenbluth picked up his fifth foul and exited. Grimly, the Tarheels dug in and the clock ran out with the teams tied 46-46. Overtime again. The sides exchanged baskets, but there were long stretches of inactivity. Again the buzzer sounded. Second overtime. For five minutes the protagonists stalled, waiting for the one perfect opportunity to clinch the contest. The buzzer sounded again, the score still tied 48-48. Third overtime.

For the second time in slightly more than 24 hours, North Carolina was playing in a third overtime. The pressure was intense on both sides but probably more so on North Carolina. They had finished an undefeated season, survived the rugged ACC playoffs, beaten back Yale and then Michigan State in triple overtime; now with a perfect season within reach, a very tired quintet of Tarheels took the floor again. Four of them had played almost the entire game and last night's entire game, too—100 minutes of basketball. It was now or never, no more stalling.

Kearns got a basket and then two free throws to put North Carolina ahead 52-48. Earlier he had made only one charity toss out of five but in the clutch he found the range. Next Chamberlain scored, was fouled and completed a three point play. Then, with 31 seconds left, Gene Elston gave the Jayhawks the lead on a pair of free throws. Pandemonium in the stands. It was as if a twister had hit the arena. North Carolina calleo time out and set up a play. With six seconds left Quigg was fouled in the act of shooting and calmly sank both free throws. It was the Kansan's turn to call time out. Everyone was standing as the inbounds pass headed for Chamberlain, but Quigg stepped in front of the giant, wrestled the ball out of the air and held on. For North Carolina, a perfect ending—53-52.

1958

The years 1956-1962 saw some of the greatest basketball players in the history of the game compete on college courts throughout the land. Bill Russell, Wilt Chamberlain, Elgin Baylor, Oscar Robertson, Jerry West and Jerry Lucas thrilled the fans in the North, South, East, and West. Baylor, known as the Rabbit for his speed and jumping skills, started his college career at Idaho in 1955. He switched to Seattle, a perennial West Coast power, and sat out a year. In 1957, he led his team to the NIT and in 1958, the Chieftains were invited to the NCAA again. Baylor had been a high school All American in Washington, D.C., averaging 36 points per game. But his skill was not only as a scorer. He was also a brilliant rebounder and playmaker, an inspirational leader who ignited his teammates in a crucial game. Baylor was one of only seven players who averaged more than 20 points and 20 rebounds a game during his college career. In 1957 and 1958, he was the top rebounder in the country.

West:

Seattle (19-5) split their first eight games, losing to such powerhouses as San Francisco, Temple and Dayton (all in the top ten), but won 15 of their last 16. Their only loss during this stretch was to traditional rival Idaho State by three points. Idaho State (21-4) was making its sixth straight tournament appearance. Under their new coach, John Grayson, they emulated other west coast schools' emphasis on defense and held their opponents to an average of 54 points per game.

Arizona State (13-12) won the Border. As late as the halfway mark in the season, their record was an anemic 3 wins and 12 losses with victories over New Mexico Highland, Pacific and Loyola of Los Angeles—not exactly powerhouses on the court. Wyoming (13-13), another school with an inferior record, won the Skyline. The Cowboys had an abysmal 3-9 record outside their league while Utah, which finished second, had a much better overall mark but lost too many games in their conference. Wyoming was making its eighth tourney appearance, second only to Kentucky.

California (18-8) tied with Oregon State for the lead in the Pacific Coast Conference and then beat them in a playoff, 57-45. Third ranked San Francisco (24-1) was the top quintet in the Far West. It was just like the old Bill Russell days as the Dons recaptured the defensive title, limiting their opponents to only 50 points per game. And in Mike Farmer, they had another All American.

For the first time Idaho State, which beat Arizona State 72-68, and Seattle, which took Wyoming 88-51, both advanced to the second round. The schedule makers had switched the Border winner to the West regional, thus allowing Seattle and Idaho State to play separate opponents rather than each other. With a 51-25 half time lead Seattle rested most of their starters during the second half. Elgin Baylor played only slightly more than twenty minutes but scored 26 points and took down 18 rebounds.

The first round was completed in Berkeley and the winners now moved across the bay to the Cow Palace in San Francisco. A record crowd of more than 16,000 turned out for the next round. California, playing a superlative defensive game, halted Idaho State 54-43. The Bears committed only ten personal fouls and completely hamstrung the Bengals.

In the second contest Seattle avenged an earlier loss to the Dons by edging them 69-67. Baylor was superb. Phil Woolpert commented, "I don't know how anyone could see a better show than Baylor put on." Pete Newell, who had seen many great players, raved, "It was the greatest one man performance I have ever seen."

With Seattle trailing by four with seconds left before the end of the half, Baylor, surrounded by three Dons, grabbed a rebound and whipped the ball 90 feet down court to teammate Jerry Frizzell who made an easy layup. Though they were still ahead 33-31 that play had a stunning effect on the Dons. In the second half Farmer fouled out and then, with San Francisco ahead by only a point, Gene Brown picked up his fifth personal. Baylor's two foul shots put the Chieftains ahead. With their two best players on the bench, San Francisco held the ball until, with ten seconds left, Art Day put the ball up and was fouled. He converted his first attempt but missed his second, leaving the game tied.

Seattle called time. On the inbounds play Baylor got the ball and dribbled around for several seconds trying to get free or find an open man to pass to. With no alternative, Baylor fired from 40 feet and the ball dropped through the cords as the buzzer sounded. Baylor's statistics showed 35 points scored—half Seattle's output and more than any player had ever registered against a Woolpert team. He made 11 of 20 from the floor and 13 of 14 from the free throw line.

In the regional final Seattle again fell behind early, the Bears leading at the half 37-29. California's clinging defense prevented Seattle from launching their fast break and the Bears' Don McIntosh, firing from long range, connected five times in as many attempts to produce 14 first half points. The Bears could not find the range at the beginning of the second half, though, and it was not until the five minute mark that they made their first basket. Meanwhile Seattle was having greater success and a court length pass from Baylor to Charlie Brown who layed the ball in the hoop gave the Chieftains a 39-38 lead. California pulled ahead again by seven but then Seattle, playing pressure defense, caused several turnovers which they used to advantage. Two jumpers by Francis Saunders, who was playing despite a fractured cheek suffered in the Wyoming game, and a dunk by Baylor put Seattle back on top. Then Baylor was called for goaltending and a subsequent short flurry by California gave the Californians the lead once more, 57-56.

With the score 60-58 in favor of the Bears, Seattle came down court for a final play. Brown took a pass and hit on a 15 footer with 14 seconds remaining.

Regulation ended with the teams still deadlocked.

Brown was again the hero in overtime. In an almost identical situation, he arced a long jump shot into the basket with 15 seconds left to put Seattle ahead 64-62 and then iced the victory by making two free throws at the buzzer.

Midwest:

Kansas, with Chamberlain playing and a weak supporting cast, was beaten out of the Big Seven championship. The best of the Midwest was fourth ranked Kansas State (20-3). The Wildcats with their own All American, Bob Boozer, beat three other conference champions during the season—Arkansas, Indiana and California although they lost two of three to the Jayhawks of Kansas. For Oklahoma A and M (19-7) there were two significant switches. They were now called Oklahoma State and the school had dropped out of the Missouri Valley Conference. Due to begin playing in what would be called the Big Eight in 1959, they spent 1958 as an independent and were selected as an at-large entry.

Meanwhile the MVC had added Cincinnati, Houston and North Texas State, spreading that conference over a huge geographic area. The Cincinnati Bearcats (24-2) with All American Oscar Robertson, won the MVC crown their first year in the conference. The Big "O", the first sophomore to win the national scoring championship, impressed wherever he played. In Madison Square Garden, he scored 56 points, establishing a new record for that arena. In field houses and gymnasiums he performed before packed houses wherever he went. The Bearcats sparkled on offense but few realized they had a fine defense, too. Victories over Indiana State (105-49), Seton Hall (118-54), and North Texas State by a whopping seventy points (127-57), helped them establish the best average scoring margin in the country.

Arkansas (17-8), a low scoring quintet, tied with SMU for the SWC title, then beat them in a playoff. Loyola of New Orleans (16-8) was invited, more because there was an opening for an at-large team in the Midwest regional than on the basis of their record. This regional called for two at-large teams but the number of eligible non-conference schools could be counted on the fingers of one hand; and most of those played second class competition. As a result Oklahoma City, never an outstanding team, played in six consecutive tournaments in the 1950's. But in 1958 the Chiefs won barely half their games and Loyola went instead. The selection committee was lucky to have Oklahoma State compete as an at-large school for one season. The next year they would have to go clear out to the West Coast to find an at-large entry.

In the first round, Oklahoma State, playing on their home court in Stillwater, swept past Loyola 59-42. The Aggies were almost perfect from the line, sinking 23 of 24 foul shots, not surprising since they led the nation with a 79 percent free throw average.

In the second round Oklahoma State disposed of Arkansas even more easily, 65-40. No other team had been held to a lower score since the 1949 playoffs and though the level of competition was not that strong, limiting their opponents to 82 points in two games was a considerable defensive achievement. As in their first game, the Oklahomans' foul shooting was on target all evening. Arlen Clark, high scorer for the Aggies, made 12 of 13 free tosses.

It was a shame the number two and four teams in the country, Cincinnati and Kansas State, had to meet in such an early round, but the luck of the draw brought them together in the feature contest in Lawrence. After an exciting first period, Kansas State held a one point advantage and the two teams fought each other tooth and claw down the stretch. The Wildcats still clung to a one point edge as the clock approached zero. Then, with one second remaining, the Big "O" was fouled and went to the line with a chance to win the game. The partisan crowd set up an ear crackling din but it didn't seem to affect Robertson, who calmly lofted the tying point through the net. The Bearcat bench was all ready to rush on the court to mob Robertson but congratulations were premature. Oscar missed the second shot and the teams went into overtime, tied 74-74.* The Wildcats' height advantage had been a factor all evening and Kansas State eventually won the battle on the boards 52-37. When Connie Dierking, the Bearcats' center, and Barry Stevens fouled out late in the second half, this advantage became overwhelming; and when Robertson exited on five personals in the first minute of overtime, it spelled the end for Cincinnati. The trio of Dierking, Robertson and Stevens had scored 61 points among them and the Bearcat substitutes could not pick up the slack. With unheralded Roy De Witz's seven points doing most of the damage in overtime, Kansas State advanced 83-80.

Having disposed of the tough competition, the Wildcats had a relatively easy time in the regional final against Oklahoma State. Bob Boozer, hitting a remarkable 78% of his shots in the first half, led the Wildcats with 26 points. The huge forward wall of Boozer, Jack Parr and Wally Franks, all 6′8″ or over, took most of the rebounds, seldom allowing the Aggies more than one shot at the basket. Only 6′8″ Clark could match the tall Kansans, and his 24 points were insufficient for the task. The score was tied 23-23 in the first half, but Kansas State took off from there and stretched their lead to 61-41 before substitutes gave the Oklahomans the opportunity to make the final score more acceptable. In the end Kansas State prevailed 69-57. In the consolation Robertson scored 56 points for the second time that year as Cincinnati demolished Arkansas 97-62.

---

*Supposedly the referee had upset Robertson by counting off seconds. A strict interpretation of the rules called for the second of a two shot foul be completed within ten seconds of the first.

Mideast:

In the Mideast, Kentucky won the SEC championship as usual. However, their won-lost mark was only 19-6, their worst in 15 years. For the first time since the Associated Press and United Press began publishing team rankings, the Wildcats were not in the top ten at the end of the season. After a rocky early season when they won only four of their first seven, they improved but were hardly on a par with Adolph Rupp's previous teams. They lost to Auburn and barely beat Alabama in overtime. A loss there would have given Auburn the championship.

Indiana (13-10) was fortunate to be in the tournament. Only a win against St. Mary's interrupted a string of six losses at the start of the campaign. Two three-point victories over Michigan State, which had a much better overall record, and a 109-95 pounding of Purdue, their best game of the year. assured their Big ten championship. It was a struggle and the Hoosiers would not have gone as far as they did without their All American, Archie Dees.

The favorite in the regional was Notre Dame (22-4), ranked number seven, with high scoring Tom Hawkins in the pivot. Miami of Ohio (17-7) retained their Mid American title without a defeat. Their record outside that conference was an unimpressive 5-7 including three losses without a victory against Big ten teams. Tennessee Tech (19-6) won in the Ohio Valley Conference.

Rounding out the field was Pittsburgh (18-6) playing in the East regional. The only reason Pittsburgh had a winning record was 5′8″ All American Don Hennon whose 30 point average was one of the best in the country. Overshadowed in the land of the giants, he was not overlooked or underestimated. It was Don Hennon who single handedly brought Pittsburgh into the tournament. With an average supporting cast the Panthers might have gone as far as the championship round, but Hennon's teammates were hardly that.

In the first round, Miami of Ohio, after trailing by four, came back in the second half to beat Pittsburgh 82-77. It was the first tournament win for a Mid American conference school. For Pittsburgh, Hennon bagged 28 points but for once relinquished top scoring to Julius Pegues who looped 31 points into the basket. Meanwhile, the Irish swamped Tennessee Tech 94-61 as Hawkins contributed 30 points.

The next rounds were held in Lexington. This was a big advantage for Kentucky, which needed all the help it could get. The Wildcats, playing on their home court, toyed with Miami. Wayne Embry's 26 points and overall leadership was not enough to hold off Kentucky which advanced 94-70. In an Indiana shootout Notre Dame outlasted the Hoosiers 94-87. Dees' 28 points for Indiana was more than offset by Hawkins' 31 and John McCarthy's 29 for the Irish. Hawkins' driving layups gave Indiana fits and, unable to fend him off, they fouled repeatedly. Indiana actually outscored Notre Dame from the floor, but opportunities at the free throw line made the difference.

Kentucky, moving into ever higher gear, smothered Notre Dame in the regional final. Wildcat Ed Beck held Hawkins to just 15 points and Kentucky outrebounded the Irish 60-41. Mostly, it was the Kentucky defense that made the difference. After limiting Notre Dame to 31 points in the first half and establishing a twelve point lead, the Wildcats allowed their opponents a mere 25 in the second period. The final score was 89-56 and Kentucky advanced to their fifth Championship Series.

East:

The top team in the country, West Virginia (26-1), had a lot to look forward to. They had won four consecutive Southern conference crowns but had yet to win a postseason game. This was the year, felt the Mountaineers, that they would go all the way and there were many who agreed. Hot Rod Hundley had graduated but in Jerry West, a dynamic sophomore guard, and 6′10″ center Lloyd Sharrar, both All Americans, Coach Schaus found more than mere replacements. The Mountaineers had the second highest scoring average in the country, almost 87 points a game, and had gone over 100 points seven times. This was quite a feat in 1958 since the one and one free throw rule had been amended at the end of the previous season and, as a result, scoring had been reduced by five points a game.* West Virginia won the Kentucky Invitational Tournament by beating the host team and handing North Carolina its first loss in more than a year. The problem for the Mountaineers was they had not been tested. They played none of the other teams in the top ten. The only superior quintet they had faced aside from Kentucky had been Duke and the Blue Devils handed them their only loss. Victories over Virginia Military by 104-58 and 109-50 did not impress since they were not reinforced by wins over better teams. Thus, a big question mark was West Virginia.

Maryland (20-6) was sixth ranked and had the best season record in the ACC. Unfortunately, they lost five of their games to league opponents and finished fourth in the standings. Fortunately, the NCAA entry was determined by a postseason tourney. The Terrapins won that, upending North Carolina and first place Duke in the process.

Dartmouth (20-4) with Rudy LaRusso, the star they had plucked from the sidewalks of New York, won the Ivy League, and Connecticut (17-9) took the Yankee Conference for the fifth time in a row. Like Miami of Ohio, the Huskies beat all their league opponents. They scored over 100 points against Maine as if by habit, but they lost most of their non-conference games.

---

*The rule change had made the first six common fouls (those not committed in the act of shooting) in each half worth only one free throw. After six violations the rule reverted to the one and one situation.

Manhattan (15-8), an at-large selection from New York, lost to Navy by 30 points but beat Army by 20. Boston College (15-5), another at-large school, had a very fine record until they fumbled away their last three , two to cross-town Boston University. But these setbacks were but ripples compared to the wave of euphoria that spilled over the campus when the Eagles beat archrival Holy Cross. The Crusaders had beaten Boston College a total of 18 out of 19 times since World War II and had flayed the Eagles in their last six encounters by an **average** of more than 25 points.

Fifth ranked Temple (24-2) had a 23 game winning streak going into the playoffs. They had lost their second game of the season, an 85-83 triple overtime thriller, to Kentucky and, still groggy from that loss, had been set-back by Cincinnati in the next game. The Owls then started their string which included victories over Seattle and California and were hoping to stretch it to at least 27. Harry Litwak's squad was brilliantly coached. Hal Lear was gone but Guy Rodgers, his backcourt teammate, had become equally proficient and was picked to the All American team. The Owls also had speed and an excellent defense. The only thing they lacked was a big center.

The East regional got under way with another Madison Square Garden triple header. The first game saw Connecticut again unable to survive the first round. With LaRusso banging the boards and nestling the ball into the hoop for 24 points, Dartmouth had a relatively easy time disposing of the Huskies 75-64.

After watching one predictable outcome the fans, 5,000 less than a sellout, were anticipating another. So were the number one ranked Mountaineers who looked forward to moving on to Charlotte after an easy victory over underrated Manhattan. It would be their first NCAA victory after three disappointing outings in as many years.

Apparently nobody informed the Jaspers they were about to become West Virginia's first postseason victim. What Coach Ken Norton told his boys was to play the Mountaineers aggressively and they followed directions explicitly. It was a rough game. A total of 61 fouls were called—29 against Manhattan and 32 against West Virginia—as eight players, four from each team, fouled out. One player had barely worked up a sweat before he was whistled out of the game at 3:17 of the first half, the second followed him with less than a minute gone in the second half. Both West and Sharrar picked up their fifth personals late in the game and the Mountaineers were left without a leader.

Aggressiveness was working for the Jaspers in the first half as both teams played run-and-shoot, drive-and-penetrate basketball; defense appeared to be a foreign commodity not yet imported from California. After twenty minutes Manhattan led 56-49. Soon after the intermission Manhattan increased their lead to 15 points. Desperation leads to innovation so the Mountaineers switched to a zone and started pressing the New Yorkers all over the court.

It worked. With a little more than four minutes remaining, West Virginia tied the score 84-84. But West and Sharrar were gone by now and West Virginia could not maintain their momentum. Jack Powers put Manhattan on top again with a basket and the Jaspers scored three more times on free throws while holding the Mountaineers scoreless to register the biggest upset of the year, 89-84.

An 86-63 victory by Maryland over Boston College in the final game came as an anticlimax as many fans left early to celebrate.

The three winners and Temple gathered in Charlotte for the next round. Three days before St. Patrick's Day, the Jaspers and the green shirted Indians of Dartmouth took the court for a second round game. Dartmouth sprinted to an early 13-2 lead and retained command for the rest of the game. Manhattan showed none of the aggressiveness they displayed in New York. Increasing their advantage to 20 points in the second half, the Indians coasted to a 79-62 victory. LaRusso and Chuck Kaufman, another Brooklynite, did most of the damage for Dartmouth.

After taking a half time 39-32 lead over Maryland, Temple was cruising smoothly with a comfortable eleven point lead and only five minutes left to play. Four minutes later the Terrapins were within a point and taking charge. Temple hung on grimly but lost the ball on a turnover. Maryland was holding the ball for the last shot when, with 16 seconds remaining, Bill "Pickles" Kennedy stole the ball and fired a long lead pass to Rodgers. His attempt at the basket failed but he was fouled. Rodgers' first free throw was good; his second failed but Jay Norman maneuvered inside to tip the ball in for a three point play. A few seconds later it was over, and Temple reeled into the regional final 71-67.

The Owls had it easier against Dartmouth. The Indians, playing alert defense but inept offense, stole the ball three times in the first two and a half minutes but got nothing for it as they missed seven attempts from the floor. Their shooting did not improve much during the rest of the contest. Failing to penetrate Temple's sliding zone and unable to find the range from the perimeter, Dartmouth succumbed 69-50. However, the Indians out-rebounded their opponents by 19, underlining Temple's lack of height.

Final Four:

The last two rounds were played in Louisville's new Freedom Hall, an obvious advantage for Kentucky. The Wildcats had won the regional on their own home court, and now were due to play less than one hundred miles from their campus before some very partisan fans. It was the sort of advantage that had helped CCNY win the NIT and NCAA championships in 1950. Since the NCAA picked the site of the regionals and the finals before the season even started, it was impossible to be sure no college would have the home court edge. Still, the same sites were picked from year to year. From 1953 to 1957, the West regional was held in Corvallis, home of Oregon State. From 1954 to 1957, the East regional was held in Philadelphia and from

1958 to 1961, it was held in Charlotte, benefitting schools like Temple, LaSalle, North Carolina, North Carolina State and Duke. In nine of eleven years, from 1957 to 1967, either the Mideast regional or the final rounds or both were held either in Louisville or Lexington, Kentucky. In every year from 1953 to 1965, the Midwest regional or the final rounds or both were held in Kansas City or at the campuses of the University of Kansas or Kansas State. What this amounted to was a huge advantage for Kentucky and the two Kansas schools. This is not to say the NCAA deliberately picked gymnasia to give any college an edge but rather they chose arenas which could hold a sizable crowd and which were willing to stage the event. But the result was the aforementioned schools, especially Kentucky in 1958, were beneficiaries of the system.

Of the four teams in the Final Four, Temple played a zone defense almost exclusively. Kansas State used both a zone and man-to-man while Kentucky and Seattle defended man-to-man exclusively. This would later have a decisive effect on the outcome of the final game. In the first semifinal Kansas State, their towering front court averaging 6′9″, moved into an early 15-10 lead. Then Seattle started hitting from outside and overtook them 21-19. The Wildcats, trying to put more pressure on the Chieftains, switched from a zone to man-to-man but this did not help them much and Seattle ended the first half ahead 37-32. Baylor scored four successive baskets to start the second period. Meanwhile Kansas State hit a cold streak and went almost nine and a half minutes without scoring. Seattle pulled away and eventually won 73-51. Incredibly, Seattle outrebounded the taller Wildcats by a substantial 56-33 margin. Baylor, playing another of his superb games, accounted for 23 points as well as 22 rebounds—two thirds as many as Kansas State.

In the feature game, Kentucky, with four senior starters and junior Johnny Cox, battled Temple to a 33-33 half time standoff. Before a hysterically partisan crowd, the lead seesawed most of the game with neither side ahead by more than seven. With the clock winding down, it was Temple's turn to pull ahead. Rodgers' two free throws, capping a personal five minute, ten point burst, gave the Owls a 59-55 edge. When they regained the ball, Temple went into a freeze but with 1:19 to go, Kennedy drew a charging penalty and that was the break Kentucky was waiting for. Adrian Smith converted both throws in a one-and-one situation. A free throw by Temple and two more points from the line by Smith made the score 60-59 in favor of the Owls with just 43 seconds remaining.

Temple controlled the ball, and it looked as if they would run out the clock. In desperation, Cox fouled Rodgers. The All American stepped to the line with a chance to ice the game but missed his first throw. Ed Beck, who preempted the backboards all evening, grabbed the rebound and the Wildcats called time. The play Kentucky set up called for Cox to feed Vern Hatton who would take the shot. The play worked perfectly as Hatton scored on a layup with 14 seconds remaining to win the game for Kentucky 61-60 and end Temple's 25 game winning streak.

For Temple, it was a frustrating night. Rodgers' missed free throw was just the culmination of an evening's ineptitude at the foul line. In all, they converted just 10 of 20 opportunities (Kentucky made all but five of 28) considerably under their season's average, though they outscored Kentucky from the floor 25-19. For Hatton, it was the second time he had beaten Temple in three months. Previously he had arced a 47 foot set shot at the buzzer to defeat Temple in their triple overtime game.

A record 18,803 fans, the largest crowd to witness a NCAA tournament game, filed into Freedom Hall for the final game. It was the second pack of Wildcats Seattle would have to tame in a little more than 24 hours. The Chieftains were at the end of a very long road and they were tired. During the season they had travelled 19,000 miles, probaby the most by a college team to that date.

The courtside fans were overwhelmingly for Kentucky, but the Chieftains had their partisans too. John Lindtwed, Seattle *Times* reporter, wrote, "Seattle University's rookie coach in the NCAA basketball tournament will match wits with the meet's dean tonight and only the wildest-eyed Kentuckians think the University of Kentucky stands a chance against the Chiefs." Considering the source the author could be excused for his enthusiasm. However, he was 180 degrees off target. John Castellani was actually in his second year, having taken over from Al Brightman who had resigned to go back to college for a degree. Castellani was far from being in Rupp's league. He was a mediocre coach, a little too highly strung even for that profession, who happened to be blessed with an outstanding player in Elgin Baylor. Castellani was to resign a year later because of unsanctioned recruiting practices and join the Minneapolis Lakers where he lasted less than one season.

On the other hand, Adolph "The Baron" Rupp was the most successful active basketball coach in the country. He looked more like a butcher than a coach and had acquired a reputation for being brutal and overbearing. Rupp would have called it intensity. Fred Schaus reflected the majority opinion when he said, "He's not the most modest coach that ever came down the pike but he's the greatest." Tennessee coach Emmett Lowery commented, "Life doesn't hang on the result of a basketball game but it seems like it when you play Rupp." Graduated from Kansas where he had played for Phog Allen, Rupp came to Kentucky in 1930. Prior to his arrival, the Wildcats had employed 15 coaches in 26 years. In the next 27 years Rupp won 18 SEC championships, three national championships and one NIT crown. His worst record was in 1941 when he won 17 and lost 8. In other words, in more than a quarter century his teams had never lost more than a third of their games in any one year. In the championship game Rupp outcoached Castellani in the same way McGuire outcoached Harp the previous year.

In one respect the finalists were very different from the 1957 protagonists. Neither team had been ranked in the top ten. Seattle, a bit of an anomaly, was bidding to become the first at-large team to win the playoffs since CCNY won the title in 1950.

Rupp set his strategy—get Baylor out of the game and the Chieftains will collapse. He ordered his players to pass the ball to John Crigler whom Baylor was guarding. The tactic called for Crigler to dribble the baseline and go up for a shot as close to the hoop as he could penetrate. It worked. Baylor picked up three personals in the first ten minutes and Seattle had to revise their whole game plan. Crigler scored 11 of Kentucky's first 16 points. He was not a factor thereafter, but the damage had been done.

To their great credit, Seattle refused to fold and Baylor, hampered by personals and a painful rib injury incurred in the semifinal against Kansas State, did not foul out but he was not the threat he normally would have been.

At the half Seattle led 39-36, and there was still hope they could survive Baylor's handicap. Castellani decided to switch to a zone at the beginning of the second half to minimize the possibility of more fouls. Other players had been helping Baylor on defense and had run into foul trouble too. The move worked. Seattle actually widened their margin to six points; but when Baylor picked up his fourth personal after only three and a half minutes of the second period, gloom descended on the Seattle bench. Hatton and Cox began to hit the target regularly, Hatton from the inside after penetrating a zone which Seattle were unaccustomed to playing, and Cox from the outside, over the top of the zone. Gradually Kentucky caught up and passed the Chieftains to the delight and high-decibel approval of the fans. But Seattle was not through yet. Somehow Baylor, playing his last game and in jeopardy of fouling out any second, held the team together for a last effort. Seattle nosed in front 60-58, but almost immediately the Wildcats retrieved the advantage 61-60.

The end came with the suddenness of a long impending thunderstorm. Don Ogorek and Charlie Brown of the Chieftains fouled out. The Wildcats went on a tear during which Hatton and Cox accounted for 10 of 11 Kentucky points while Seattle scored but two. A few minutes later the game was over and Kentucky was champion again, 84-72. Baylor had 25 points, 19 rebounds and a fistfull of assists, setting up his teammates. He also received the MVP award. For the Wildcats, it was the 35-second half points by Cox and Hatton that spelled victory.

But in the final analysis coaching made the difference and for Rupp and the Kentucky team he had disparagingly nicknamed the Fiddlin' Five the reward was an unprecedented fourth national championship.

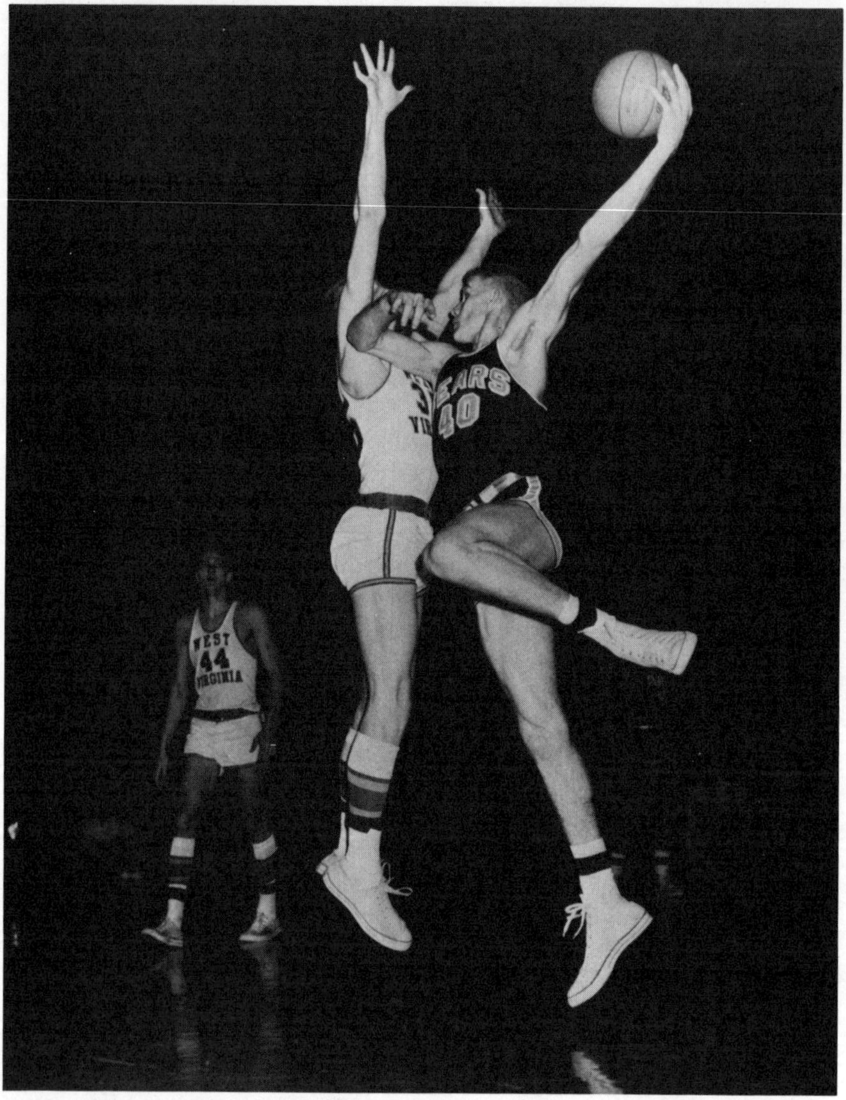

California's Darrall Imhoff is closely guarded but shows grace under pressure as he launches a shot in the 1959 final. His team nipped West Virginia 71-70. However, Jeery West (44) was voted the MVP.
(Ed Kirvan photo)

9

A TALE OF TWO JERRYS

1959-1960

1959

In 1959 the NCAA could look back on two decades of ever increasing success. Competition was keener, players were better and teams more diverse in playing styles. Attendance was up all over the country—approximately 15 million fans attended college basketball games in 1958—and tournament games, many played in larger arenas, were usually sold out.

One reason, and maybe the prime one, for the increased popularity of college basketball was the almost yearly emergence of some new superstar. In 1958 Jerry West and Oscar Robertson played their first varsity games. Although the Big "O" broke in more spectacularly, becoming the first sophomore to win the national scoring championship, their careers and personalities had much in common.

Robertson was a High School All American, three times All State at Crispus Attucks in Indianapolis, and led his team to a 45 game win streak and two state championships. He chose the University of Cincinnati because they played games against New York and Philadelphia schools in the large eastern arenas, thereby increasing their national exposure. But Robertson was not happy at Cincinnati. He was quiet and brooded a lot. "There's no real social life for me here," he once said, alluding to Cincinnati's proximity to the southern states. Segregation, officially or unofficially sanctioned, was still prevalent in many cities where Cincinnati played and it affected The Big "O". There were predictions he would leave school at the end of his junior year and play for the Harlem Globetrotters or another barnstorming team before playing for the National Basketball Association.*

*An NBA rule forbade drafting a college player before his class graduated.

Jerry West from Cabin Creek, West Virginia, was also a High School All American at East Bank; his team won the state championship in his senior year, too. In honor of their star player the school was renamed West Bank for a day. Jerry learned to play basketball from his older brother who coached him in the local playground and gymnasium before he was drafted and sent to Korea. He was killed in the war, giving Jerry added incentive to succeed as a player.

Fred Schaus visited Jerry's father in Cabin Creek, sat with him on his front porch a while and convinced him that his son would be well taken care of in Morgantown. Jerry needed a sympathetic ear. He was an introverted kid who grew increasingly upset by the publicity engendered by his skill.

West was best when challenged, when circumstances necessitated a super effort. Otherwise he had a tendency to loaf. This often resulted in early deficits, followed by spectacular comebacks and a rousing finish. In 14 of their 25 victories in 1959, West Virginia led by Jerry West, went on to victory after being behind at half time. With the proper incentive there was no telling how far West could and would go. By the tournament of 1959 West had acquired maturity and leadership qualities that almost singlehandedly propelled West Virginia into the finals.

There were other similarities between Robertson and West. In their sophomore years they each played on a team with a star center—Connie Dierking at Cincinnati and Lloyd Sharrar at West Virginia. Both centers graduated, leaving Robertson and West to carry a disproportionate burden in their junior and senior years. In 1959 and 1960 Cincinnati and West Virginia were essentially one man teams, and in showdown games neither could overcome disciplined team play. This was effectively demonstrated twice by Pete Newell's California Bears.

Over the years well-balanced teams have invariably defeated teams which relied on a single star player, regardless of his magnitude. A team with a strong defense and a single superstar may rise to the top of the heap, but this is not a contradiction. It takes five men to play good defense, helping each other out and switching assignments when necessary. Thus teams like Oklahoma A and M with Kurland and San Francisco with Russell can qualify as playing team basketball. Others such as Holy Cross and Kentucky in the late forties, CCNY in 1950, North Carolina in 1957 (which beat Kansas with Chamberlain) and Kentucky in 1958 (which beat Seattle with Baylor) were teams where talent blended to make the whole more successful than any outstanding individual. The exceptions are rare but should be mentioned. Only Kansas with Lovellette and LaSalle with Gola come to mind.

The burden on superstars like West and Robertson was enormous. Not only did they lead their team in scoring, they frequently headed the rebound and assist statistics, too. In 1959 Robertson was tops in all three categories for Cincinnati. The loss of such a player via the foul route has a devastating effect, and even early foul trouble effectively immobilizes him, which was the case with Baylor in the 1958 championship game.

East:

In 1959 West Virginia with a 25-4 record again won the Southern Conference crown. They had slipped out of the top ten but were still formidable. Two of their losses came in overtime, one in double overtime. Dartmouth (22-5) had better luck in extra period games, winning three of four. Tied with Princeton at the end of the Ivy schedule, they waited until the last second to gain a place in the tournament. Behind by one with three seconds to go, Dartmouth took the ball out of bounds and set up a play for LaRusso, who drove in for a layup at the buzzer, nipping Princeton 69-68. Connecticut (17-6) again outdistanced all other Yankee Conference foes.

Boston University (18-6) replaced Boston College as the year's at-large New England entry. The Terriers were anything if not consistent. They gave up exactly 55 points in seven different games against various offenses and playing styles. Navy, under veteran coach Ben Carnevale, won 16 and lost 5. St. Josephs with Jack Ramsey at the helm topped the newly organized Mid Atlantic Conference in its first official season. The Hawks won 22 of 25, losing to St. Johns twice and Kansas State once. In their final game they trounced Muhlenberg 103-66, but this was hardly the caliber of competition they would face in the tourney.

The class of the regional was sixth ranked North Carolina (20-4). The Tarheel squad still resembled a group of refugees from New York as eight of twelve members hailed from that metropolitan area. Doug Moe, a High School All American at Erasmus Hall in Brooklyn, York Larese and Louis Pucillo were the backbone of the team. North Carolina had been streaking for most of the season, winning 17 of their first 18, bouncing Cincinnati among others, but finally hit a slump and split their last six games. In the final of the ACC playoff, with a tournament berth assured, they were thrashed by North Carolina State 80-56. Earlier in the season they twice whipped the Wolfpack, but the latter were barred from postseason competition again because of recruiting violations. McGuire grumbled that his players had become complacent, had lost their will to win and needed to be shaken up.

The shaking occurred in Madison Square Garden in a first round match against Navy. When it was over, the season ended for the Tarheels as the Middies pulled a sizable upset 76-63. The lack of concentration which had afflicted North Carolina during the latter part of the season was evident in their poor defense and worse shooting. Navy completed nearly half their shots while North Carolina targeted only 33 percent. Besides, the Tarheels committed almost twice as many fouls as the Middies. In the scoring department, Larese, North Carolina's sophomore star, was shut out in the first half and tallied just eight points in total.

A hard fought first half between Connecticut and Boston University ended with the teams knotted at 35-35. Connecticut was hampered by the loss of Ed Martin, their leading rebounder, who had undergone an appendectomy the day before. Boston University began the second half as cold as a New England cod. They were shut out for the first five minutes and not until the twelve minute mark did they register their first basket. The Huskies opened an eight point gap but the Terriers, thawing rapidly, caught up and it was a dog fight the rest of the way. With 19 seconds left Ed Washington put Boston ahead 59-58 with two free throws. Regaining possession, Washington sank another foul shot with two seconds remaining assuring victory, 60-58. For Connecticut Jack Rose scored 28, 18 from the foul line, as they failed to advance for the sixth time in seven tournament appearances.

West Virginia, still looking for its first playoff victory, drew Dartmouth in the opening round. LaRusso committed four personals in the first half and was not a factor thereafter. In the meantime Jerry West was performing his magic, scoring 25, hauling down 15 rebounds and feeding teammates for more points. West Virginia easily earned their first tounament win, 82-68. It was also a first for a Southern Conference team.

With the secret of winning solved, the Mountaineers applied the formula again in Charlotte against St. Josephs. The Hawks proved to be a tougher foe than Dartmouth, though. St. Josephs, ahead 48-42 at the intermission, pulled away to a 67-49 advantage with thirteen minutes to go. At that point the Mountaineers hit the accelerator—**hard**—and took off. In a burst of incandescence seldom seen on a court, West Virginia flushed 46 points through the hoop in the last 13 minutes, each swish greeted by the swelling cheers of their fans. West, who had been having trouble converting from the foul line and was not finding many opportunities from the floor either, led the charge. He accounted for 21 points in just nine minutes, 14 of those coming in a four minute span of brilliant marksmanship. He totalled 36 points for the night on 12 for 22 field goal shooting. The Hawks fouled and fouled again trying to hold the Mountaineers. Altogether they were whistled 32 times and West Virginia converted 33 of 50 gift throws. One by one the desperate Hawks fouled out until four starters and one reserve were sitting on the bench. When the final buzzer sounded, the scoreboard showed West Virginia 95, St. Josephs 92.

The other second round game was a lot slower, and cleaner, too. Boston University led throughout the first half, which ended with the Terriers ahead of Navy 32-30. But they needed a free throw by Ed Washington with two and a half minutes left to lift them into a 52-52 regulation tie. In overtime, Jack Leaman's two charity tosses were the clincher for the Bean Towners, as they advanced 62-55. It was the eighth time that year the Terriers had given up exactly 55 points.

The regional final was a typical victory for West Virginia. Tied at the half, the Mountaineers fell behind after the intermission. Then for the fourteenth time in eighteen games West Virginia ignited a second half rally. Here was the kind of challenge Jerry West loved best. Rising to the occasion, West pumped ten straight points through the cords to give the Mountaineers a lead they never relinquished. They went on to win 86-82 to advance to Louisville.

Mideast:

Second ranked Kentucky (22-4) and third ranked Michigan State (19-3) were cofavored to take the Mideast regional. Neither one of them did. The Wildcats had finished second to Mississippi State (24-1) in the Southeast Conference but the latter was prevented from playing in the tournament by the Governor and the Regents lest they become contaminated while playing against black players. Mississippi's loss was Kentucky's gain. For the fifth year in a row the Wildcats posted an identical 12-2 record in their conference, losing only to Vanderbilt and Mississippi State. Of last year's starting team, Hatton, Smith, Crigler and Beck had graduated. Only Johnny Cox, now an All American, remained. But Rupp still had plenty of talent on his squad, and he was still stomping the doormats of the conference unmercifully as evidenced by blowouts over Georgia, 108-55, and Florida, 94-51.

High scoring Michigan State (19-3), with All American Johnny Green, had the best rebounding team in the country, the third highest ever recorded.

Two other Kentucky teams participated in the Mideast regional: Eastern Kentucky (16-5) and Louisville (16-10). Eastern Kentucky was the Ohio Valley representative. The highlight of their season was a victory over fifth ranked North Carolina State. Independent Louisville had completed an undemanding schedule. After losing their first game to Georgetown of Kentucky, hardly a basketball power, they won several games until they hit a midseason slump during which they lost five of six. A 32 point loss to Xavier (Ohio), a school with a losing record, did little to enhance their image.

Bowling Green (18-7) tied with Miami (Ohio) in the Mid American. After losing two close games to Miami during the regular season, the Falcons beat them when it mattered most in a 76-63 playoff showdown, thereby qualifying for the tourney. Marquette (22-4) won 17 of their first 18 but then stumbled. The Warriors were happiest when they could run and shoot; control tactics cramped their style. They split two games against Notre Dame, winning one by twenty as they scored 95 while losing the other by 16 when the Irish slowed the pace to a shuffle and held the Warriors to 36 points.

In Lexington in the first round Louisville eliminated Eastern Kentucky 77-63 as the winners' Don Goldstein tallied 25 points. In the non-Kentucky matchup, Marquette knocked out Bowling Green. Both coaches cleared their benches late in the game as the Warriors pulled away to an 89-71 win.

In the second round at the Northwestern University fieldhouse, Louisville and Kentucky opened the program in a Blue Grass special. It was only the second time these schools had ever met on the court.* It promised to be a walkover for the Wildcats. When they opened a 15 point gap in the first period, spectators began getting acquainted with their programs which were starting to look decidedly more interesting than the game. Louisville coach Peck Hickman, as good as any in a state blessed with fine coaches, called time

*The country is still waiting for number three.

out. He ordered his players to pressure the Wildcats at midcourt instead of waiting for them to get into their offensive patterns. It worked. By half time Louisville had cut the margin to eight and in the second half they overhauled Kentucky and then swept ahead by fifteen. The scoreboard told the whole shocking story: Louisville 76, Kentucky 61. It was a sweet victory for the Cardinals, who had lived a long time in the shadow of the Wildcats.

Michigan State conquered Maqrquette 74-69 in the nightcap, but it was the first game that had excited the fans and which they discussed on their way home.

Hickman had another trick up his ample sleeve and he sprang it on the Spartans in the regional finale. He had his three tallest men collapse on Johnny Green. And that tactic worked, too. After falling behind by three points at the intermission, Louisville sprayed twelve unanswered points through the iron to open the second half. The Cardinals were normally 36 percent shooters from the floor. In the final 20 minutes, just as the previous evening against Kentucky, they shot better than 50 percent. The result was a well-earned 88-81 Louisville victory. The "other" Kentucky team, which had shown so little during the regular season, rose to the occasion and eliminated the second and third ranked teams in the country. The Cardinals headed for home where the Final Four were to gather.

Midwest:

The Big Seven had become the Big Eight with the inclusion of Oklahoma State, formerly Oklahoma A and M. Chamberlain, with a year's elibility left, dropped out of school and without Wilt, Kansas was not a contender. The big man complained he was being roughed up too much under the boards, opposing players were picking on him, he could learn nothing new by playing another season of college ball. Besides, he wanted to earn some money to help support his parents. His father, a handyman, was barely able to support his family which included Wilt and eight siblings. Chamberlain joined the Harlem Globetrotters and barnstormed around the country and the world waiting for his class to graduate so he could enter the professional basketball ranks.

The number one team in the country was Big Eight champ Kansas State (24-1) which featured All American Bob Boozer and teammates Jack Parr and Wally Franks. All three players were over 6′8″ and the Wildcats sometimes played a triple post in which the tall men moved in and out of the pivot. It tended to get a little congested in the middle, though. State lost only to BYU but had to survive some nail biting finishes early in the season. In their first eleven games they won seven by three points or fewer. Later the victories became easier. Once they crushed a good Oklahoma squad 90-45.

Cincinnati (24-3), ranked fourth, beat out Bradley for the MVC title. The Braves were ranked eighth in one poll but another picked them above Cincinnati in fourth place. The Bearcats suffered a lapse a third of the way into the campaign when they lost both their games in the Dixie Classic, returning home to eke out an 85-84 double overtime victory over Bradley. It was their most crucial confrontation and turned out to be the turning point of the season. The Bearcats went on to win 16 in a row, a string broken only by a season finale flop against Bradley. The Braves were unfortunate to be playing in the same league with Cincinnati. Had they remained an independent or joined another conference they would undoubtedly have participated in the tournament. Five years earlier the Braves went all the way to the NCAA finals with a team that had a losing record and couldn't carry the current squad's ball bags. Bradley went to the NIT instead where they lost to St. Johns in the finals. Losing in the finals was becoming a bad habit for the Braves.

DePaul (12-9), Portland (19-7) and a very tall Texas Christian (19-5) team completed the regional field. DePaul toasted the new season by taking its first game from the Christian Brothers college while Portland twice doubled weak opponents—Nevada, 66-33, and Seattle Pacific, 86-43. Apparently the NCAA could find no other worthy at-large Midwestern team to compete in the regional and so had to reach out to the West Coast to find an opponent for DePaul.

In the first round played in Portland, DePaul eliminated the home team 57-56. Portland played the kind of ball control game indigenous to the Far West. The difference between the teams came down to their comparative success at the foul line. Each had 16 opportunities—the Blue Demons sinking 13 and the Pilots but 8.

In the second round at Lawrence, Kansas, Cincinnati led by Robertson's 34, nipped TCU 77-73. Kansas State had much less trouble with DePaul whom they defeated 102-70 for their twenty-first victory in a row.

The following evening before a packed house of 17,000 partisan rooters, Kansas State held a two point lead at the halfway mark. It looked as if the outcome would be a repeat of the previous year. The Wildcats posted a picket guard around the Big "O" so he was not free to go on his usual scoring rampage. In the second half the Bearcats switched tactics. Instead of trying to score, the many-talented Robertson became a playmaker, feeding open teammates for easy baskets. Consequently, Cincinnati overhauled the Wildcats and avenged their previous year's loss 85-75. Bob Boozer collected 32 points before fouling out.

West:

In the West ninth ranked California (21-4), the last PCC champion (the conference disbanded at the end of the year), was the choice to take the regional. Many felt they were underrated since three of their losses had been by no more than three points. The Golden Bears were also the best defensive team in the country, giving up more than 60 points only twice.

St. Marys (18-5) was making its tournament debut. Most of St. Mary's offense was generated by talented sophomore Tom Meschery. However, the Galloping Gaels relied as much on their defense as did most of the California schools. Idaho State (19-6) was invited as an at-large school since the Rocky Mountain Conference winner no longer rated an automatic invitation. They were not far behind California in fewest points allowed, having given up fewer than 50 points in almost half their games. The Bengals also led the country in average margin of victory, a result of several blowouts in no-contest contests, including four by more than 50 points.

Utah (21-5) won in the Skyline and New Mexico State (17-10) in the Border. The latter had a habit of leading off on the wrong foot. They usually started their season on the road where they had difficulty winning. In 1957 they had lost their first nine games of the season. In 1958 they improved and dropped only their first four; in 1959 they made a major breakthrough, winning their opening game in double overtime before crashing in their next five encounters.

In the opening round in Las Cruces, New Mexico, Idaho State squeaked past New Mexico State 62-61. By the end of the week the Bengals were themselves eliminated. In San Francisco's Cow Palace, St. Marys, led by Meschery and Leroy Doss, eliminated Idaho State 80-71. The losers wasted Jim Rodgers' 29 points.

In the other second round match California hounded Utah from tipoff to buzzer and forced them into 22 turnovers. Al Buch of California stole the ball from the befuddled Utes four times and the California defense blanketed their opponents so effectively not a single Utah player was able to reach double figures. The Bears' scoring was, as usual, evenly distributed. They held a 15 point lead at half time and had little trouble subduing the Utes 71-53.

The Bears found St. Marys even easier meat in the regional final. They had squeaked by the Gaels during the season by two points, but in the regional final they trounced them 66-46. It was a combination of California's impenetrable defense and ownership of the backboards that sealed the victory.

Final Four:

The final two rounds were again held in Louisville. The home team, the surprise of the tourney, gave their supporters some early hope. Trailing by eight in the first few minutes, Louisville rallied to overtake West Virginia 27-26. The Mountaineers then went on a 22-5 tear with West directing the assault, leaving the court at the intermission on the sweet side of a 48-32 score. West perpetrated most of the damage, claiming 27 points, passing, rebounding and defending outstandingly. The outcome in the second half was never in doubt as West Virginia attained the final, 94-79. Aside from West's virtuoso performance, the difference was West Virginia's speed, which Louisville could not match, and the Mountaineers' sharpshooting. They connected on 53 percent of their shots paced by West's 12 of 21 for a game high 38 points.

California knew that in order to win it would have to hold Robertson, the nation's leading scorer with a 33 point average, in check. They did so effectively by assigning Bob Dalton and Jack Grout the task of guarding the Big "O". Robertson was limited to 19 points and just one bucket in the second half.

Things began well for the Bears. They rambled to an eight point lead in the initial stages before hitting a cold spell. After twenty minutes the Bearcats enjoyed a 33-29 edge built on solid 50 percent accuracy from the floor. California, mired in a shooting slump, managed to connect only one-third of the time. There was a dramatic reversal after the intermission. California's iron curtain defense rang down and so did the Bearcats' scoring production. For the first nine minutes Cincinnati could not buy a basket. Every shot hit either rim, backboard, air or a California arm. The Bears took the lead and maintained it until the Bearcats were able to reorganize. With two minutes remaining the score was tied at 54 all. But Darrall Imhoff's hook shot gave the Bears their final lead and minutes later they were celebrating their 64-58 victory.

The championship game was a classic matchup of the number one defense in the country against the number two offense. So intense was the interest in the game it was used to resolve an incident in the Hamilton, Ohio, county jail. Inmates were warned that if a stolen club was not returned they would not be allowed to watch the game on television. Not only was the club returned promptly—but so were four others and three hacksaws besides.

It was the offense that was able to gear up first as the Mountaineers ran up a ten point surplus in the first nine minutes. Then California's dormant defense coalesced and forced West Virginia into costly turnovers. By half time the Bears were in control and halfway through the second period California extended their margin to twelve. The Bears' rooters could already taste the champagne. But the Mountaineers were not through. Borrowing a chapter from the California game book they threw a pressing defense at their opponents. The Bears lost their smoothness and threw the ball away repeatedly. The patented West Virginia comeback was in full swing. At 8:49 Jerry West's jumper made the score 59-53, slicing California's advantage in half. Four minutes later Jim Ritchie's set shot closed the gap to four. With less than a minute to go Imhoff was called for goaltending, the third of the game for the 6′10″ center, and California clung to a 69-68 lead. For forty seconds the PCC champions stalled until Imhoff popped from close range. The ball missed but bounced back to Imhoff, who tapped in his own rebound. West Virginia's final basket with five seconds left brought the Mountaineers back within a point, but the final buzzer sounded before they could get the ball again as California triumphed 71-70. In the final analysis it was the Bears' defense, despite giving up a season high of 70 points, that made the difference. They limited West Virginia to just 55 shots, not enough for even such sharpshooters as the Mountaineers. There was some consolation for them when West, who was credited with 28 points in the final and a record-tying 160 points for the tourney, was voted the MVP. But it was California's cohesive squad of five players, a team without a star, that overcame Cincinnati with Robertson and then West Virginia with West, two of the greatest individual performaers in the history of basketball.

1960

Mideast:

A new star appeared as the 1960 season unfolded. Jerry Lucas, a sophomore at Ohio State, was hailed as the best player in the Big Ten since Don Schlundt. Even that compliment was not doing him justice. Big Luke, as he was affectionately called, had been an All American at Middletown (Ohio) High School since his sophomore year, a three-time honor unequalled in prep school history. He also broke Chamberlain's record of most career points by a high school player. He had even been featured in an article in the *New York Times*. Lucas had sparked his team to 76 consecutive victories including two state championships in his sophomore and junior year. It was the 77th game that hurt. Middletown had reached the finals of the state championships for the third straight year, but was beaten by a single point in what was Luke's last high school game. He walked off the court like a champion, not looking back and with no regrets.

At 6′8″ Lucas could do everything—score, rebound, start and complete the fast break and defend superbly. At the end of his first varsity season at Ohio State he owned the best shooting percentage in the country, a scorching 63.7 percent. Though this slipped slightly in the following two years, when he graduated Luke owned the highest career field goal percentage ever recorded. His hook shots, layups and tip-ins were a perfectly timed composition of movement. Everything about his motion on the court was smooth and natural. He would scrape the ball off the defensive boards, peg it to a breaking forward or guard and arrive under the basket just in time for a tip-in if necessary.

But Jerry was more than a basketball player. He maintained a straight A average in high school and though 160 colleges offered him an athletic scholarship, he enrolled at Ohio State on an academic scholarship, no strings attached. Some personality characteristics are worth mentioning. He was very mature for his age, completely unflappable and extremely unselfish. All the publicity he received in high school left him without the feelings of self importance one would normally expect. His high school teammates, less admirable, resented all the attention Lucas received and often failed to pass him the ball when he had the best shot. His coach, trying to maintain solidarity on the team and understanding the jealousy Lucas' presence created, abstained from directing his players to pass the ball more often to their star center. In one game he benched Lucas after he had scored 38 points (the school record was 39), but when the other team caught up, he had to reinsert Big Luke who went on to score 44.

Ohio State was not a one man team though. Coach Fred Taylor was blessed with a talented supporting cast. Besides Lucas, the Buckeyes, whose 21-3 record ranked them third in the country, unveiled two other sophomores that year, John Havlicek and Mel Nowell. Along with junior Larry Siegfried and senior Joe Roberts they were the most potent scoring quintet in the country with an average of more than 91 points per game. One coach predicted that everyone on the starting five would play professional ball*. Substitute guard Bobby Knight, later to make his mark as a championship coach at Indiana, could have started for most other schools. If the team had one weakness it was on defense. They had given up 90 points in four games and had lost three of them: to Utah by five, to Kentucky by three, and to Indiana. Coach Taylor, knowing he had a problem and realizing it was probably the only thing standing between him and a NCAA championship, visited Pete Newell after the 1959 season and received some good advice. As the season progressed the Buckeyes' defense improved and in the playoffs they gave up an average of only 65 points per game.

After beating Wake Forest 77-69 in the curtain raiser, they banged in over 90 points in ten of their next eleven games. Some of the contests were hardly worthy of the name. They massacred Michigan 99-52, demolished Delaware 109-38, idled Iowa 75-47, powdered Pitt 94-49 and mauled Memphis State 94-55.

The Mideast regional also included Notre Dame (17-8) and Ohio University (16-6). The Bobcats after a mediocre year in 1959 had lost four starters and were picked for last in the Mid American. When they lost their first four of the season, they made the crystal ball gazers look like prophets. But they did an about flip, won 12 in a row and rose to the top of the standings.

Another high scoring quintet was independent Miami from Florida (23-3). The Hurricanes put considerable strain on the scoreboard, making it overflow to three digits on seven occasions. One memorable game saw them edging out South Carolina 107-106. In their last three outings before the tournament, they averaged 111 points. However, their schedule was studded with weak opponents and losses to Houston, Centenary and Stetson did nothing to enhance their reputation.

For the first time since 1954 Kentucky did not represent the SEC. Instead the nod went to Georgia Tech (21-5). The Yellowjackets beat the Wildcats twice, decisively, by 18 and 21 points. However, they dropped two to Auburn whose 12-2 record was the best in the conference. (Ineligibility kept Auburn out of the tourney.)

Since it would be unthinkable to have a NCAA tournament without a representative from the Blue Grass State, Western Kentucky (19-6) preserved the state's honor by winning the Ohio Valley. It was the first appearance for Coach Ed Diddle in the playoff in twenty years. High scoring or low scoring games, it made no difference to Diddle. His Hilltoppers showed their versatility by vanquishing Middle Tennessee 109-89 and 109-80 and Eastern Kentucky 38-20.

*They all did.

Diddle was approaching the end of a long coaching career dating back to 1923. He had won more than 700 games, second only to Phog Allen, and though he operated in the shadow of Adolph Rupp in Lexington, he outdistanced him by a wide margin in popularity. The likeable Diddle with his dead center hair part had played basketball and football with Bo McMillin at Centre College, the legendary Praying Colonels. Two years after graduation he accepted the coaching post at Western Kentucky and had been there ever since. An early advocate of the fast break Diddle taught his Hilltoppers to run their opponents into the boards. It was the kind of basketball that was popular in the big Eastern arenas, and Diddle had been invited to more NITs than any coach of a non-New York school. Now NCAA audiences would have a chance to see the fun loving Diddle go into his act, an animated performance which featured a big red bath towel which he waved, threw and chewed on throughout the game.

It resembled a track meet. Ten basketball players churning up and down the hardwood, shooting with abandon. It was the kind of game Diddle loved. Defense took a vacation, but he didn't mind as his Hilltoppers, led by Bobby Rascoe's 27 points, axed Miami 107-84 in a first round matchup in Lexington. Hilltopper fans sitting in place of the accustomed Wildcat rooters were ecstatic. In the other game Ohio University and Notre Dame played a close first half. The lead changed hands 11 times and when the buzzer sounded, the Irish were ahead for the moment by a point. Not for long, though. The Bobcats came out clawing in the second stanza and with some fine shooting by Howie Jolliff, who contributed 29 points, overcame Notre Dame 74-66.

The following Friday evening Diddle watched his team set a torrid pace as his thoroughbreds ran away from Ohio State in the first half 43-37. But in the second he spent a lot of time with his head buried in his red towel, unwilling to watch as the Buckeyes broke the game open. Within 90 seconds of the second tipoff Ohio State had the lead and proceeded to score 61 points in the final 20 minutes. Lucas' 36 points did most of the damage but the whole team contributed to the 98-79 pasting.

For Georgia Tech things were a little harder. Down by ten after 20 minutes they rallied to take a 49-48 lead on a pair of free throws by their All American Roger Kaiser. There were still five minutes left. Playing cautiously, Ohio University took the lead again on a pair of charity tosses. Dave Denton of the Rambling Wrecks then hit a jumper and added a free throw to put his team on top again. Georgia Tech held on in the final minutes and won 57-54. Kaiser had 25 points, including a perfect 11 for 11 from the line. The Bobcats' Jolliff banged 20 through the hoop but missed 5 of 7 foul shots that could have reversed the decision. The regional final went to Ohio State 86-69 in a lopsided contest.

Midwest:

Second ranked Cincinnati was favored in the Midwest regional. They had won all but one of their 26 games, losing only to Bradley by a point. The MVC was loaded that year including two of the top four teams in the country. Unfortunately for the fourth ranked Braves (23-2) they had to co-exist with the Bearcats in the same conference. Bradley with the best team in their history took the consolation prize and accepted a bid to the NIT where they made up a twelve point deficit in the final ten minutes to win the tournament by **eighteen** points over Providence.

Cincinnati was becoming accustomed to facing teams from Kansas in the regional. Still it took them almost three-quarters of the game to move ahead of the Jayhawks. Paul Hogue, their sophomore center, got into early foul trouble and played only six minutes of the first half and cautiously thereafter. Ahead 42-40 at the intermission Kansas added to their margin to lead 57-51 well into the second period. The Bearcats bore down and closed to within two at 63-61. Then Robertson flipped in 11 of the next 12 points and Kansas played catchup the rest of the way. With their starters playing almost the whole way the Jayhawks simply petered out. As usual Robertson was the deciding force. His 43 points amounted to more than half his team's total as Cincinnati advanced 82-71.

West:

California, like Cincinnati, lost only one game and narrowly beat out the Bearcats for top national ranking. They won 24 including two from USC the only team to beat them. California as usual was first class defensively, leading all others in that department. In 80 percent of their games they gave up fewer than 50 points. On offense they rarely taxed the official scorer either. But in one game against a fine Washington side they combined superlative offense and defense to crush the Huskies 79-39. They were still a team without an outstanding player though. Darrall Imhoff had been voted to the All American team as much for his leadership of a top ranked team as for any individual brilliance. His 13.7 scoring average was the lowest by an All American in eight years.

The old Pacific Coast Conference had broken up and five schools, those that considered themselves a kind of elite among equals, reformed to establish a new conference, rather pompously named the Western Universities Athletic Associations but more popularly if not very originally, the Big Five. The league consisted of California, Southern California, Stanford, UCLA and Washington and each played the other three times. Since they were formed too late to get official NCAA approval, two schools, California and USC, were invited to the tourney as at-large entries. USC (16-10) finished third but had a good enough record to merit an invitation.

New Mexico State (20-6), winners of the Border, had an excellent defense giving up more than 70 points only once. Idaho State (21-4) won its conference for the eighth straight time but was included as an at-large entry. They had won 17 in a row before succumbing to Seattle in the season finale by a surprising lopsided 89-53 score. Surprising, because they had earlier beaten the Chieftains by a similar margin, 94-58. The Bengals were undoubtedly looking ahead to the playoffs.

A third former PCC school, Oregon (16-9), was also selected for the West regional. Their record against the Big Five was a mediocre two wins, four losses. Santa Clara (18-7) tied with Loyola (Cal.) in their conference but took the postseason playoff 59-53.

Utah's starting five included a brilliant if inconsistent young sophomore Bill "The Hill" McGill. A two-time All American at Jefferson High School in Los Angeles, he had led the fifth ranked Redskins to a 24-2 season. Among their victims were Ohio State and several other good teams. Losses to tournament-bound Duke and Utah State stained an otherwise perfect record. However, they had nipped the latter in a rematch 77-75 to take the conference title by a game. (Utah State, ranked seventh, was almost as good as the Redskins, but suffered the same fate as another also ran, Bradley, spending an enjoyable week playing in the NIT and taking in the sights of N.Y.) One reason for Utah's success was they honed their skills against teams from every section of the country including Holy Cross, Duke, Ohio State and Washington State.

Cincinnati got off to a fast start led by Oscar Robertson. The Big "O" had decided to complete his eligibility and the three-time All American ended his career with his third scoring title, an unprecedented achievement. The Bearcats went over the century mark in three of their first four games. They murdered St. Bonaventure, one of the top ten, 96-56, in the Holiday Festival. During that tournament Robertson scorched Iowa with 50 points and pumped in a total of 122 in the three games at Madison Square Garden (New York always brought out the best in him). The Bearcats also exacted heavy punishment on less talented teams such as North Texas State 123-74, a game in which Robertson put on a superlative performance, scoring 62 points. Unsurprisingly, they topped everyone in average margin of victory.

Kansas and Kansas State could not have been more evenly matched. They split their two encounters and finished in a tie for the Big Eight crown. In a playoff Kansas (18-8) took the rubber match 84-82—in overtime, of course. Texas (18-6), playing only schools in the Southwest, won their conference. For the Longhorns it was their first tournament appearance in 13 years. Theirs had been a dramatic turnaround from an awful 4-20 record the previous year. The two at-large invitees were DePaul (15-6), which bowed twice to both Notre Dame and Western Kentucky, and Air Force (12-9). It was only the fourth year of competition for the newly created Academy, which lost their first five games and looked unprepared for major competition.

Unlike the previous year when they had to travel more than halfway across the country, DePaul took on Air Force in their back yard in Chicago. Despite phenomenal 70 percent shooting the Falcons were behind at the halfway mark. This because DePaul was also blistering the cords at almost the same rate, abetted by deadly foul shooting. This kind of marksmanship could not continue and the intermission cooled off the Falcons considerably. A switch to a shifting man-to-man defense by DePaul had a lot to do with Air Force missing their first seven tries and being blanked for three and a half minutes early in the second half. Meanwhile the Blue Demons showered the hoop and took a 60-45 lead. Air Force narrowed the margin but could not overtake, and DePaul advanced to the next round 69-63. Five-nine guard Howie Carl was the leading scorer for DePaul with 24. The 85 percent free throw shooter was the prime reason for DePaul's excellent 21 of 23 success from the line.

One swallow does not a spring make, nor one victory a champion. DePaul crashed in the second round when Cincinnati administered a 99-59 spanking, the worst in 23 years of tournament competition.* In the other regional semifinal Kansas pulled itself together in the second half after trailing Texas by four at the intermission. Wayne Hightower, who took the same trail from Overbrook High School to Kansas as Wilt Chamberlain, flipped eight straight points through the mesh to give Kansas a 68-63 lead they never relinquished. Hightower's 22 second half points gave him 34 for the night to share high scoring honors with Jay Arnette of Texas.

Given the geographical spread of the schools in the regional, it was felt advisable to hold the first round in three separate locations. In Provo, Utah, the Utes ousted USC 80-73. The local team, defending with much greater skill than the Trojans, had only 12 personals called against them while USC was whistled 26 times. Some blamed the disparity on local refereeing. John Rudometkin, the Trojan's star, scored 31 while McGill countered with 27.

The next evening California toyed with Idaho State in San Francisco. Leading 30-9, Coach Newell began to substitute reserves and the teams played on even terms for a few minutes. But until a minute before half time Idaho State was able to breach the Bears' defense for only three field goals. Back went the starters for the beginning of the second half, but they were soon out of the game again as California scored two points for each one the Bengals popped. The result was an inevitable rout, 71-44.

On the third evening Oregon spent most of its game with New Mexico State trying to catch up. Seven down at the half Oregon was still wallowing as the clock began ticking off the final ten minutes. However the Beavers broke out with 11 unanswered points to plow ahead 55-48 and went on to win 68-60.

Santa Clara, the only school to receive a bye, was chilled early by California. The Bears took a 9-1 lead and were never headed, extending their margin to as much as 23 points. It was a team oriented offense, typical of the Berkeley team, with well-distributed scoring. Santa Clara found the Bears' defense as impenetrable as had their predecessors. With subs playing much of the

*The Blue Demons almost did not make it to the tournament site. Their bus crashed on an icy highway in Kansas and they had to be rescued by a snowplow. The team spent most of the night in a rural police station huddled around a potbellied stove.

second half, California prevailed 69-49.

Utah had lost to the eventual national champion three times in the last five tournaments. This time they encountered equally formidable Oregon. The Utes, who had averaged 85 points a game during the season, were held to just five buckets and 19 points in the first half by one of the best executing defenses in the country. Chuck Rask sparked the Beavers' offense with his brilliant dribbling and playmaking. Billy McGill was limited to 6 points and fouled out with 12 minutes to go and his team far behind. By holding Utah 31 points below their average, Oregon posted an easy 65-54 victory.

In the regional final Oregon and California put on a display of hard checking, chest-to-chest, vicious basketball. With eight minutes remaining in the first half and California ahead 22-15, both defenses stiffened so effectively neither team scored a basket before the intermission. But California's smothering defense outlasted the Beavers and with Imhoff tallying 18 points, they forced their way into the Final Four again 70-49.

East:

In the East, Princeton (15-8) won the Ivy League. Things looked grim for the Tigers after they lost seven of their first ten. The last rites were about to be recited when the corpse revived and the men of Nassau streaked to a 12-1 finish.

St. Joseph (20-5) lost three close games, and a pair to Cincinnati that were not, one of them an incredible 123-79 pasting. Connecticut (17-8) won their seventh conference title in a row and their twelfth in the last thirteen. But after 28 wins in a row in one of the most one-sided rivalries in sports, Connecticut lost to Maine for the first time since 1945. Navy ended their season with the same record (16-5) as the previous year. West Virginia, winners of the Kentucky Invitational, was 24-4. Playing one of the longest schedules in college basketball, the Mountaineers were also prolific scorers. Six times they scored over 100 points and 15 times they hit in the nineties, including a 98-69 thrashing of an excellent NYU quintet. Only once were they held to fewer than 70 points and that against the country's best defense as California chilled them 65-45. Another setback that hurt was a loss to William and Mary, their first in 51 against Southern Conference teams.

NYU (19-3) had lost only to Iowa and to tournament participants St. Joseph and West Virginia. Howard Cann had resigned the previous year and was replaced by Lou Rossini who had moved over from Columbia. Another team with a new coach was Duke (15-10). In his first season Vic Bubas had finished no better than fourth in the ACC, losing twice to both North Carolina and Wake Forest who tied for first place. But in the postseason ACC tourney, the Blue Devils had squeezed by the Tarheels 71-69 when John Frye hit two clutch free tosses with nine seconds remaining, and then knocked off Wake Forest in the final 63-59 when the same super cool Mr. Frye looped four foul shots through the hoop in the final minute of the game.

As usual the East regional opened with a triple header in Madison Square Garden, this time attended by a respectable crowd of over 15,000 fans. Connecticut, using an offensive pattern unfamiliar to Rossini, moved to an early 19-9 lead. NYU looked sluggish, confused and unable to get the ball in to Tom Sanders, their center who was attracting the Huskies like red meat left in the woods. Finally the Violets' coach solved the puzzling pattern and the New Yorker's fast break took off, sparked by 5′8″ Russ Cunningham. NYU overhauled the Huskies long before the buzzer signalled the end of the half and they went on to win 78-59.

In another first round contest Duke proved too tall for Princeton. Duke's 6′8″ Doug Kistler scored 20 in the first half and effectively dominated the game so the Blue Devils had little trouble overpowering Princeton 84-60.

In the third matchup West Virginia, with All American senior Jerry West as usual spearheading the action, torpedoed Navy 94-86. He scored 34, retrieved 15 rebounds, was credited with six assists and played just as superbly on defense. Navy's high scorer Jay Metzler answered with 27 points, but his effort was not nearly enough.

Duke faced St. Josephs in one regional semifinal match. The North Carolinians led almost throughout, but St. Josephs had an opportunity to tie with :04 to play. Their final shot missed and the Blue Devils won 58-56. In the cofeature NYU had a chance to revenge an earlier drubbing in Morgantown. Al Barden of the Violets, who had been the high scorer against Connecticut, was assigned the task of containing Jerry West. He did so fairly effectively but committed enough fouls to force him to leave the game. Playing mostly a one-way game Barden was limited to three points.

NYU held a 27-18 lead halfway into the first period but the Mountaineers caught up and nudged ahead by a point at the break. The second half was a thriller. With Barden on the bench West took off, eventually garnering 34 points. But NYU stayed close and with just four seconds left little Russ Cunningham lofted a long shot, seemingly from the parking lot, which swished through the hoop to tie the score 77 all. The Violets controlled the overtime tipoff and, invoking a tried if not often true tactic, passed the ball back and forth for almost three minutes without taking a shot. The tactic backfired when Jim Warren stole the ball, passed to West who layed it in. NYU, forced to shoot, tied the score on a set by Ray Paprocky and then got possession again. Another 90 second delay ensued until Jim Reiss, a transfer student from West Virginia, untied it and nailed the coffin shut on his ex-teammates by sinking a field goal, his only one of the evening. A foul shot by Cunningham and a last second basket by the Mountaineers completed the scoring as NYU advanced 82-81. Sanders contributed 28 points to become high man for the Violets.

In the consolation game West Virginia bounced St. Josephs 106-100, the first time two teams had reached triple digit scoring in a NCAA playoff. It was West's last game as a collegian and as usual he was outstanding, looping 37 points through the hoop to give him a 36 point average for the regional.

The scoreboard showed NYU and Duke tied at 6-6 when Barden hit on a side jumper. NYU then went on a 12-2 tear and opened considerable daylight between themselves and the Blue Devils. Duke, which had started the game playing a zone, switched to man-to-man coverage when the Violets found no difficulty popping from long range. Neither defense was able to stop the New Yorkers, who controlled the action with their deliberate offense. Barden, freed from his strictly defensive assignment, ignited the attack; the rest of the team responded by completing 53 percent of their shots. Stretching their lead to 71-45, NYU coasted to win 74-59. It was their eleventh consecutive win and their 16th in the last 17.

Final Four:

The final two rounds were held in San Francisco's Cow Palace. Assembled were the number one, two and three teams in the country and NYU, the latter seemingly outclassed. It did not take long to confirm this assessment. Ohio State took an 8-0 lead and NYU never got closer than two. The Buckeyes' defense strangled their opponents while their slashing running attack piled up points on the scoreboard. Lucas, who scored 19 as did Siegfried, held Sanders to eight. NYU fell further and further behind land the Buckeyes won easily 76-54.

In a rematch of the previous year's semifinal Cincinnati and California, voted the two best teams in the country, gave the fans a much closer contest. Cincinnati took an early 20-11 lead but Robertson could not break free to score his usual basketful of points. Not until the 18 minute mark was he credited with his first bucket. Nine unanswered California points knotted the count at 20. Bill McClintock's two pointer then put the Bears ahead for good. Hogue, the Bearcat center, had been attracting foul calls all season and this game was no exception. He departed via five personals with a quarter of the game still to be played. With Robertson held to 18 points, the Bearcats' hopes died. For the second year in a row California's disciplined team play outmatched Cincinnati's one man show. The Bears were outstanding in all phases of the game, even sinking their first 21 foul attempts without a miss, as they moved to the final confrontation 77-69.

Robertson ended his career as had West on an up note scoring 32 in his team's victory over NYU in the consolation game. The three-time scoring champion, three-time player of the year finished the season with over 1,000 points, the second collegian in history to do so. He also shattered Frank Selvy's career scoring record by 400, falling just short of the 3,000 point plateau which was not pierced until ten years later.

The fans had come to see the best defensive team take on the best offensive team for the national championship. The Buckeyes, averaging 91 points a game, were the underdogs to the defending champion California Bears. One reason was that in a game of great defense versus great offense, it is the defense that normally dictates and prevails. Another reason was California's outstanding team play. Then again there was a "home" court advantage of sorts in San Francisco and experience in a game for the national championship. However, Ohio State under Taylor's excellent coaching was playing well defensively, too. Though blessed with great individual talent, the Buckeyes also played a strong team game. Lucas himself was one of the most unselfish players in the sport.

The final turned out to be not much of a contest. The boys from Columbus were incandescent as they completed 16 of 19 shots in the first half. On the other end California made only 29 percent of their attempts and as the teams exited after the first 20 minutes the scoreboard showed the Buckeyes ahead 37-19. The second half was almost a repeat of the first as Ohio State won their first national basketball championship 75-55. It was Ohio State's ability to control the game using California's tactics against them that decided the outcome. They shot only 41 times but made 31 of them for an outstanding 77 percent shooting average. Their defense was so tough they held California to 33 percent from the floor and Dick Doughty, the high scorer for the Bears, was limited to eleven points. Fred Taylor had learned his defense well from Newell and the student had beaten the teacher. Another important factor was the outstanding team play of the Buckeyes. All five starters hit double figures but none scored more than 16 points.

10

THE BOYS FROM THE BUCKEYE STATE

[1961-1963]

1961

Midwest:

At the end of the 1960 season Coach George Smith of Cincinnati was promoted to Athletic Director and his assistant Ed Jucker was given the coaching job. Smith, with the Big "O" shouldering most of the burden, had done a remarkable job directing the Bearcats to 73 regular season victories against only six defeats over the past three years and finishing third in the NCAA tournament the previous two years.

Jucker was faced with a dilemma: How to replace Robertson's and the other graduating players' scoring, representing an average of 60 points per game. Jucker decided he would convert Cincinnati from a run-and-shoot offensive squad to a team that could win with strong defense. He figured even if he lost more games, it would not look so bad if he could hold the score down, thereby losing by fewer points. It was a gamble he came close to losing and which the Cincinnati fans, accustomed to the scoring pyrotechnics of Robertson and company, would not have forgiven.

Jucker built his team around the rebounding of 220 lb. forward Bob Wiesenhahn and center Paul Hogue, whom one writer described as a tree trunk with glasses. A couple of speedy sophomores, Tony Yates and Tom Thacker, were added to the starting five, the first a short forward and the latter a guard who later developed into the best defensive backcourt man in the country. Senior guard Carl Bouldin completed the squad. They were not a good shooting team, but they made up for it game after game with a defense as inviting as a mine field, rebounding with hands that had a homing

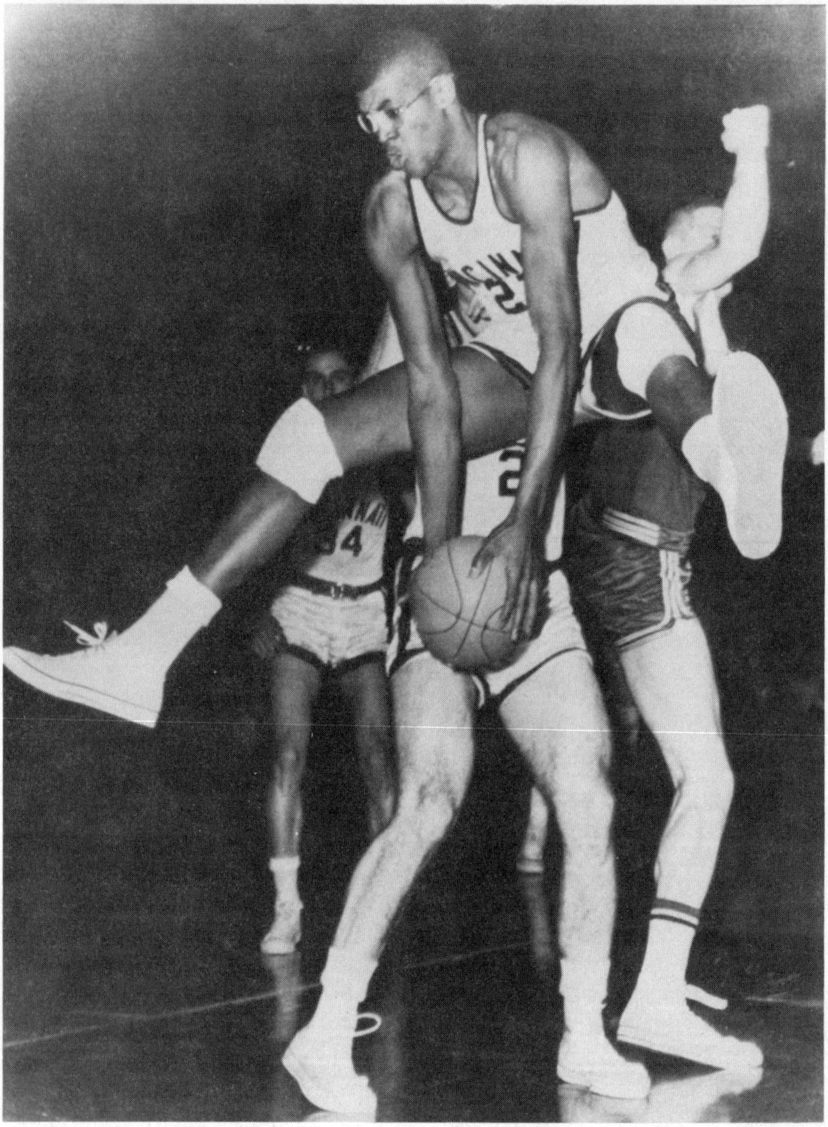

Paul Hogue of Cincinnati snares a rebound in the 1961 final against Ohio State. Effectively blocked out is John Havlicek (dark jersey). The Bearcats won 70-65 in overtime.
(World Wide Photo)

instinct for the ball and team play that was a marvel of discipline. The team was a reflection and product of Jucker's encompassing demand for exactness and precision of execution. There were no All Americans such as the Big "O" of past campaigns, nor a Jerry Lucas such as attended neighboring Ohio State nor a Chet Walker at conference rival Bradley, but as a team the Bearcats were outstanding and at the end of the year they were ranked second in the country.

They had had to struggle to reach that perch. Early losses to Seton Hall, to St. Louis by 17 and to Bradley by 19 made Jucker wonder whether his strategy would pay off. He decided to scrap his team's zone defense which was not containing anyone and switch to a pressing man-to-man. The Bearcats' defense jelled (in one game they flogged North Texas State 86-34), and they began winning consistently. By the end of the season they had won 23—18 in a row, including a one point decision over Bradley that assured them another conference crown—against three losses.

Houston (16-9) had left the MVC and was selected as an at-large team in the Midwest regional. With only one school in each conference invited to the NCAA tournament it was frustrating for the other excellent teams in the Missouri Valley to miss an opportunity at a national title. In their two games against Cincinnati, Houston had forced the Bearcats to play their best, but were still short ended in one by five points, the other in overtime. Marquette (16-10), another at-large selection, was a team with some ups and several yawning downs. Beating Kentucky in the final game did not make up for two disasters against Louisville and one against St. Bonaventure, all three losses by more than twenty points, and a 16 point beating at the hands of St. Johns. Fourth ranked Kansas State (21-4) and Texas Tech (14-9) completed the regional field.

With Houston playing at home and making 57 percent of their shots, they had little trouble with Marquette in the only first round contest. After building a huge half time lead on the scoring of Ted Luckenbill and Gary Phillips, Houston inserted their second stringers and held off Marquette to win 77-61.

In the second round Cincinnati eliminated Texas Tech 78-55 as Paul Hogue scored 24 and Kansas State dropped Houston 75-64. In the regional final Cincinnati, playing in the Sunflower State against one of the local teams for the third year in a row, faced Kansas State in a replay of the 1959 regional final. Tied 33-33 at the half, Cincinnati fell behind by seven with ten minutes to play. Tex Winter, the Wildcats' coach, had used Hogue as his point of attack. The junior, who was still foul prone, had to be removed with four personals early in the second half. Relentlessly the Bearcats slashed back and with five minutes to go Thacker's two pointer evened matters at 48. A flurry of baskets pumped up the score in the final minutes. Cincinnati had most of them as they reached the Final Four, 69-64, for the third time in as many years.

Mideast:

Ohio State, with four starters returning, continued where it had stopped the previous year. Voted the top team in the nation they won every game, most by considerable margins. They rolled over Army 103-54 and over Big 10 rivals Northwestern 79-45 and Indiana 100-65. In all, they beat their conference foes by an average of 22 points. Their closest and lowest scoring game was a 62-61 white knuckle victory over Iowa. Ray Cave of *Sports Illustrated* called the Buckeyes "the best basketball team of all time." Though the 1956 San Francisco team and the 1954 Kentucky team might have given him an argument, there was ample justification for that statement. Lucas was again a first team All American pick and Siegfried was a second team choice. Havlicek was one of the best defensive forwards the Big 10 had ever produced. And they were smart. The team maintained a B+ average scholastically. Their assistant coach claimed they were so quick to learn it was unnecessary to call a time out to tell them something new. He just yelled at them as they ran past the bench. Physically they were tall and husky with speed and stamina.

All of them were homegrown products of Ohio prep schools which may have accounted for how well they meshed as a unit. The Buckeyes were a coach's dream team.

There were two other teams from Ohio in the regional, making a total of four in the tourney. Ohio University (17-6) the Mid American winner, a money team when the chips were down, played and won three overtime games. Xavier (17-9), on the other hand, were erratic. They lost twice to Marquette but were one of only four teams to trip St. Josephs. A better at-large selection might have been Dayton, another Ohio team, but as usual they elected to go to the NIT.

Competing with the Ohio schools were three from Kentucky. Louisville (19-7) won their first 13, then hit considerable turbulence and went into a tailspin. In the second half of their season they lost more often than they won. Morehead State (18-8), on the other hand, saved their best for last. Tied with Eastern Kentucky and Western Kentucky for the Ohio Valley championship they disposed of the first by a point and the second in overtime in two classic Kentucky barn burners.

Kentucky, after being beaten seven times the previous year, slipped again dropping four of five in one short stretch to finish 18-8. Losing 15 games over two years was unprecedented for a team coached by the Baron, but still the Wildcats saved a slot for themselves in the tournament. They finished in a tie with Vanderbilt in the SEC, behind Mississippi State. But the Mississippi legislature would not let State compete against blacks and the Wildcats beat Vanderbilt in a rubber match playoff, so Rupp qualified for his twelfth NCAA tournament.

Two interstate contests marked the opening round in Louisville. When the shooting was over, the two schools south of the Ohio River had eliminated their northern opponents. Louisville and Ohio University took turns at holding slim leads. John Turner of the Cardinals was held to a single bucket in the first half, but found the range in the second and led his team to a 76-70 victory by notching 24, including a pair of clinching free throws. In the other match, another close one which also was tied at the half, Morehead overcame Xavier 71-66. Morehead committed only 11 fouls and Xavier missed most of the few opportunities they were given at the line. The Musketeers' abysmal 6-for-16 foul shooting cost them the game as they outscored Morehead from the floor by 5 baskets.

None of the combatants had far to travel for the next two rounds which took place in Louisville. The local team with the home court advantage threw an unholy scare into undefeated Ohio State. The Buckeyes, the only school from Ohio left against three teams from Kentucky, had to fight for their lives throughout the contest. The Cardinals assigned three defenders to guard Lucas, who scored only two baskets and nine points, the first time since elementary school he had not scored in double figures. But with Turner and 6′11″ Fred Sawyer guarding Lucas, other Buckeyes were left relatively free, including substitute Bobby Knight who scored eight points.

Ahead 26-25 at the break, Ohio State surrendered the lead in the second period and the Cardinals held a 54-49 advantage with 2:47 left to the delight of their voluble supporters. Then Havlicek arched a two pointer and Siegfried followed with a three point play to tie the score. Bedlam replaced uproar as Havlicek was called for travelling in the waning seconds. Louisville, setting up for a final play, threw a pass that went astray. It was recovered by Havlicek who floated the ball through the rim with six seconds to go to give the Buckeyes the edge 56-54. But it was not over yet. With only a second left Turner, high man with 25 points, went to the free throw line in a one-and-one situation with the opportunity to tie the game. He made the first and with more than 18,000 fans standing and holding their collective breath missed the second. Ohio State 56, Louisville 55.

The other affair was almost as close. Both Morehead State and Kentucky used only one substitute and their starters carried almost the entire burden. With the clock showing only two minutes to go, the Eagles had an opportunity for a stunning upset, trailing the Wildcats by a single point. But buckets by Bill Lickert, Carroll Burchett and Roger Newman saved the day for Kentucky who prevailed 71-64.

There were more than 1,000 empty seats the next night (due to Louisville's elimination) as the surviving Ohio and Kentucky team squared off. It seemed as if this was an entirely new squad of Buckeyes on the court, so different were they from their Louisville matchup. Kentucky tried desperately to contain Lucas but it was like trying to use a wooden shield to stop a buzzsaw. First 6′9″ Dave Jennings hounded Big Luke but the Wildcat picked up four fouls in nine minutes. Burchett was even less successful. He fouled out in only six minutes. Finally, Allen Feldhaus was brought in and he picked up only a couple of personals. In a tactical move, Coach Taylor had instructed Lucas to play closer to the hoop. He responded by scoring 33 points, missing only four of eighteen shots. He also brought down thirty rebounds!

The closest the Wildcats got was three points with 3:33 to play in the opening period. Ohio State increased the gap to eight at the half, then lost the Wildcats the rest of the way and won 87-74.

The only bright spot for Kentucky was Roger Newman's 31 points. Otherwise it was all Ohio State as they converted 60 percent of their floor attempts and outrebounded their opponents 51-29.

West:

Arizona State (21-5) earned the right to represent the Border Conference when they won a playoff with co-champion New Mexico State. The Sun Devils lost three games in a row early in the season but then righted themselves and won 18 of their last 20. Though a high scoring team, their defense had as many leaks as the Alamo after the shooting stopped. An example was the 119-103 shootout over Texas Western. USC (20-6) with All American John Rudometkin won the Big Five. USC was ranked fifth, surprising for a team which had absorbed six defeats. Seattle (18-7), making its first appearance since its loss to Kentucky in the 1958 final, once again earned an at-large berth. They played former PCC teams - Washington State, Idaho, Oregon and Oregon State—twice each in what amounted to an at-large conference.

Utah (21-6) was tops in the Skyline. After a surprising 21 point upset loss to Loyola of California in their opening tilt, they succumbed to Stanford but then reversed themselves by flogging Evansville 132-77. The schizophrenic Utes then headed East where they were staggered by St. Johns and St. Bonaventure. Home once more, they took off down victory lane and won every game until they were ambushed by Colorado State in their finale. This resulted in a conference tie between these two teams, but Utah qualified for the tournament by axing Colorado State 55-51 in a playoff. Loyola of California (19-6) completed the regional field.

A disappointingly small turnout in Portland saw two very exciting opening round matches. Rudometkin took a considerable amount of time finding the range, leaving the Trojans with a nine point deficit to make up starting the second half. The big Russian found the hole in the final 20 minutes to lead USC to an 81-79 win over Oregon.

Arizona State had to come from even further back. Behind by eleven at the break, the Sun Devils poured seven points through the hoop in the opening minutes of the second half before Seattle counter-attacked. The aroused Chieftains then returned the lead to nine but Arizona State tied matters at 60 apiece. With his team trailing by a point and 16 seconds to elimination, Seattle's Dave Mills went to the line for a pair. He made his first and then deliberately aimed for the rim, hoping a teammate would tip the ball in for a three point play. Unfortunately for Seattle an Arizona State player got to the ball first. The Sun Devils called time out to set up a play which worked when Gerry Hahn scored at the buzzer, giving Arizona State a 72-70 win. It was the first victory for a Border Conference team in ten tries. The difference was in the rebounding where the Sun Devils excelled 57 to 39.

Following the demise of both Pacific Northwest schools, an even slimmer crowd of 3,332 turned out for second round action. In both contests control of the boards was once again the key. Utah, paced by Billy McGill's 29 points and Jim Rhead's 23, hung on to almost twice as many rebounds as Loyola. With that kind of an edge Utah had little trouble advancing 91-75.

Arizona State won the battle of the boards 70-50 from USC and the game 86-71. They used two men to guard Rudometkin, one in relief of the other. The first fouled out after 25 minutes at which point his replacement came in to finish the job. Coach Ned Wulk's strategy worked as Rudometkin was limited to 21 not very damaging points. The biggest gun for the Sun Devils was 5′9″ whippet-quick Larry Armstrong, the shortest man on the court, who fired away from the perimeter and netted 27 points.

After gaining respectability for itself and the Border Conference, Arizona State bowed to Utah in the regional final. A string of 17 unanswered points by the Utes at the end of the first half helped scuttle the Sun Devils. Directly after their 88-80 triumph Utah booked a flight to Kansas City and the Final Four.

East:

The powerhouse of the East was St. Bonaventure (22-3), ranked third and making their initial tourney appearance. A loss to Ohio State by two, another to Duquesne in overtime and a third to Niagara were the only blots on a very successful season. The last loss hurt the most. Aiming for their one hundredth straight victory at home the Bonnies were upset by Niagara, another strong upstate New York team. Ninety-nine straight wins on their home court was not surprising, considering the pecularities, not to mention claustrophobia, of their 2,200 seat gymnasium, where the first row of fans had to tuck their feet under their seats to keep from tripping the players. A certain intimacy developed between the home team and the fans that had an intimidating effect on the visiting team.

Coach Eddie Donovan had built St. Bonaventure's offense around two men—forward Tom Stith, third highest scorer in the county, and guard Freddy Crawford. Stith had been an All American high school player at St. Francis in New York for two years and again the past two seasons in college. The Bonnies won 21 of their first 22, scoring over 100 points five times and clobbering their opponents by an average of 19.

St. Johns (20-4), playing in Madison Square Garden, hosted teams from around the country, thereby encountering a variety of styles of play. St. Josephs (22-4), winner in the Mid Atlantic, had played three other teams appearing in the regional during the regular season and recorded wins against St. Johns and Wake Forest while bowing to St. Bonaventure. The Hawks were streaking as the season wound down, taking their last 13 in a row.

Rhode Island (18-8) supplanted Connecticut as the Yankee Conference champion. Connecticut did not even finish second, that honor going to the perennial doormat, Maine, which under their new coach was gaining a measure of respect. Rhode Island was coached by Ernie Calverle who was remembered for having sunk the most spectacular basket in the history of the NIT—a tying 52 foot bomb at the buzzer for his team, Rhode Island. Princeton (17-6) won in the Ivy League.

That Duke, Wake Forest and North Carolina were all ranked in the top ten at season's end was an indication of ACC strength. Wake Forest (17-10) had finished second behind North Carolina in the standings, but took the postseason playoff by downing Duke in the final. Wake Forest had lost twice to the Tarheels but North Carolina had the misfortune of being eliminated in an earlier round of the playoff—and the playoff winner was always the conference's choice for the tournament. Bones McKinney, their coach, had experienced tournament pressure as a player when he starred for North Carolina in 1946.

The most surprising team in the regional was George Washington (9-16). They finished seventh in the Southern Conference (West Virginia had finished first as usual) and had only six victories at the end of the regular schedule. Then they won three playoff games in a row to earn the right to represent their conference in the tourney. Getting better and gaining confidence with each victory, the Colonials won their first by one point, their second by seven and the final by eleven. By this time they were about as high as their namesake monument.

Their euphoria evaporated in a first round bout with Princeton before a capacity crowd in Madison Square Garden. The Tigers outrebounded the taller Colonials by establishing better position under the boards. Al Kaemmerlen, Princeton's 6′4″ pivotman, fed teammates cutting in for easy inside shots. In the second half George Washington switched to a zone but Princeton, unfazed, started popping from outside, with Pete Campbell (27 points) and Art Hyland the principal sharpshooters. It was an easy 84-67 win for Princeton.

In the second game St. Johns, the favorite over Wake Forest, scampered to a 46-36 advantage at the half. All American Tony Jackson hitting from inside and Kevin Laughery from outside paced the Redmen's attack. Lumbering Wake Forest, always slow to start, began to pick up momentum in the second period. Len Chappell, a 6′8″, 240 lb. bull, preempted the middle as none of the Redmen could move him away from the basket. Repeatedly he muscled his way in to score on layups and dunk shots. Halfway through the period the Deacons pulled ahead 60-57 and set sail to a stunning 97-74 upset, having outscored St. Johns 61-28 in the second half. Chappell with 31 points was backed up by Alley Hart with 28 and Dave

Wiedman with 23. These three, scoring 61 of their combined 82 points in the second half, were the prime movers in the late developing romp. It was the only NCAA tournament game that Joe Lapchick ever coached. As a player on the Original Celtics and as a predecessor of Frank McGuire as coach of St. Johns, and later coach of the New York Knickerbockers, Lapchick was known as one of the finest minds in the sport. His return to St. Johns was unfortunately cut short.

The nightcap was the last NCAA tournament game to be played in Madison Square Garden. St. Bonaventure, basically a two man team, played true to form as Stith and Crawford split the Bonnies' first 19 points. But Rhode Island, with more evenly distributed scoring, were in control at the break. The shocked Bonnies began applying more pressure. Stith and Crawford, hitting with short jumpers and with needed help from Whitney Martin, erased the Rams' five point half time advantage. This trio eventually accounted for 35 of St. Bonaventure's 37 field goals. Crawford caged 34 points and Stith 29 as St. Bonaventure advanced 86-76.

In Charlotte St. Josephs and Princeton hooked up in a ragged second round matchup. Kaemmerlen again played a fine game at center and Campbell was once more the high scorer for the Tigers though half of his 24 points came on foul shots. But the Hawks were too strong. Princeton threatened in the waning moments when, behind by ten, they made eight free throws and a field goal to pull to within two. St. Josephs then cut off the rally to beat back the Tigers 72-67. In the second game St. Bonaventure faced the same dilemma as had St. Johns—how to move Chappell out of the slot. Short of renting a tow truck to haul him away there was little they could do. The big center clogged the middle and flushed 24 points through the hoop as the Deacons with a typical second half rally upset St. Bonaventure 78-73.

In the regional final the fans were treated to two colorful coaches putting on a show that for entertainment almost equalled the one on the court. On one side was Bones McKinney, his red socks winking along the sidelines, waving towels and a jacket. On the other Jack Ramsay of St. Josephs spent most of the game on one knee next to his seat in a prayerful, intense stance. Play was fast and furious in the opening minutes as both teams surged up and down court and the scoreboard blinked every few seconds to record the seesaw action. The score was knotted for the sixth time at 13-13 when St. Josephs went into overdrive and extended their advantage to 48-28 at the half. During their spree the Hawks neutralized Chappell by outhustling the slower Deacons and by pinpoint passing involving the whole team in the action. The Deacons awoke on schedule in the second period and narrowed the margin to five. But the revival had come too late this time and, though they more than doubled their first half production, the twenty point deficit was too much to make up. Chappell was again a pylon of muscle in the middle but his 32 points could not compensate for the six men who tallied in double figures for the Hawks, who advanced 96-86.

Final Four:

The final rounds were held in Kansas City for the eighth time. The favored Ohio teams had little difficulty winning. With Carl Bouldin and Paul Hogue leading the way Cincinnati eliminated Utah 82-67. McGill's individual standout performance was no match for the disciplined team play of the Bearcats.

Ohio State had an even easier time eliminating St. Josephs 95-69. The game started deceptively. Neither team was able to locate the net for the first three minutes. Then St. Josephs took a 5-0 lead and that spark ignited the Hawks' fans' hopes. But in the next 30 seconds Big Luke evened matters with two one handers and a foul. Suddenly the Buckeyes came to life and went on a scoring binge to take a 16-7 edge using their overall height superiority to good advantage. The rest of the game was boring except to diehard Buckeye fans. Lucas, who rarely shot more than 15 times, canned more than 90 percent of his shots—ten of eleven from the floor and nine of ten from the line for 29 points.

The consolation game for third place lasted almost three hours as St. Josephs and Utah required four overtimes to settle their dispute; the Philadelphians finally prevailed 127-120 in the highest scoring post-season game ever played. It was a meaningless contest but both sides played with nerve and abandon throughout.

An interesting incident occurred at the start of the first overtime. The Hawks' Bill Hay grabbed the tipoff, headed for the wrong basket and sank an unopposed layup much to the delight of Utah's players and fans. It all turned out right for St. Josephs as John Egan's 42 points paced the winners.

For the first time in the history of the tournament two teams from the same state were meeting in the final. Cincinnati and Ohio State are located within 100 miles of each other but in the sports world they are poles apart. The Big 10 considers itself the Ivy League of the Midwest. Long regarded the best football conference in the country, its schools were equally dominant in basketball. By the end of 1960 its members had won 41 playoff games and had taken the championship four times with three different schools achieving that honor. The Big 10 had been represented in 21 of 22 tournaments, a record unsurpassed by any other conference. By contrast the MVC was composed of an array of schools stretching from Ohio to Texas without any connection to the valley after which it was named. Its membership changed at frequent intervals as schools left and joined like some kind of floating dice game. Its academic standards were unremarkable and athletes who would never have been admitted by a Big 10 school were given scholarships in the MVC. Aside from Oklahoma State, which was now playing in the Big Eight, no member school had ever won a national basketball championship. Its record in the postseason tourney was only slightly better than average. Nevertheless it was one of the most competitive conferences in the country. Bradley, a perennial runner up, had been ranked high in the top ten for the past three years but had had to watch the playoffs from the sidelines. Thus, it was a classic confrontation in Kansas City between an establishment team "the best of all time," against the less endowed, poor neighbor, trying to carve a reputation for itself.

For the teams from the Buckeye State this was their first meeting since 1922. Both had long winning streaks entering the contest—Ohio State's stood at 32 games. Cincinnati's at 21.

The game was a barn burner from tipoff to final buzzer as each side played to its strength. The Bearcats with Hogue and Wiesenhahn retrieving most of the misses dominated the boards. Bulk and position proved more productive than height. And on defense the Bearcats slowed the Buckeyes fast break to a walk. Cincinnati also adjusted well. While Siegfried was helping guard Hogue, Bouldin (the man he normally defensed) made five long range baskets. During a time out Siegfried was instructed to go back to guarding his man. When he did Bouldin stopped shooting and passed off to Hogue.

At the half only a point separated the teams and neither side could shake free in the second period. With 56 seconds to go and Cincinnati clinging to a slim two point lead, Bobby Knight scored on a layup, his only bucket of the evening to tie the game 61-61. The Bearcats decided to stall and take the last shot. With :05 to go Tom Thacker got the ball inside and shot. It fell short and Lucas, grabbing it, called time out immediately. A court length pass and another time out positioned the inbounds play near the Buckeye basket with one second remaining but an alley oop pass from Havlicek to Lucas hovering over the rim did not click.

On the first play of the overtime Lucas fouled Hogue, a poor foul shooter who had missed three of four so far. This time Hogue was perfect, picking up both points. Havlicek's free throw was answered by Wiesenhahn's driving layup past Lucas, who was playing cautiously with four personals. Big Luke got those points back with a jump shot but Yates' free throw put Cincinnati ahead 66-64 entering the last minute. Siegfried cut the lead in half with one of two free throw attempts. The game was still up for grabs as the Bearcats went into a stall with 28 seconds to go. Never putting the ball on the floor Cincinnati passed it around until Yates was fouled and converted both shots. It was all over for Ohio State. A last desperation attempt by Lucas flew through the air and hit nothing. The Bearcats added two more points to win the title 70-65.

For the Buckeyes it was a shattering loss, a disappointing ending to what would otherwise have been a perfect season. For the Bearcats the victory was vindication for themselves and their conference. The fans from Ohio could be proud of both their teams and of Wittenberg College, too, the winner of the NCAA Division II Tournament.

1962

The 1962 season started under a cloud similar to one ten years before. The specter of player bribery surfaced again and schools not implicated in the earlier scandals discovered their student athletes had learned little from the past. Only ten years after prison terms, fines, suspended sentences and ruined professional careers had devastated college basketball, there were still a number of athletes willing to manipulate the scores for a payoff of a few hundred dollars. The players who were caught came primarily from the New York area (giving ammunition to that city's many critics) though several attended schools elsewhere. Implicated were students from NYU, St. Johns, Columbia, North Carolina, North Carolina State, Connecticut and St. Josephs. It was discovered that gamblers had even attempted to fix a NCAA playoff game. A NYU player tried to shave points in his team's first round contest with Connecticut in 1960 but the latter played so ineptly the Violets won by more than the point spread. As a result of the scandals, St. Josephs was deprived of its third place finish in 1961 because three of its players were found guilty of accepting bribes.

This time no players went to jail as they had in 1951 but there were severe repercussions nonetheless. The NCAA Basketball Committee recommended that postseason tourney games be played only in facilities owned and operated by educational institutions. It was the final blow for Madison Square Garden and no playoff games were scheduled in that arena again. North Carolina and North Carolina State cut their schedule to 16 games though this was increased again two years later as memory of the scandals dimmed. The Dixie Classic held in North Carolina was eliminated and the number of players these schools were allowed to recruit outside the conference area was reduced to two a year. This was a blow to Frank McGuire and his New York connections, and he resigned after the 1961 season to coach in the pros where recruiting regulations were less stringent. Everett Case remained at North Carolina State through the 1964 season.

The scandals almost ruined one budding professional career. Doug Moe of North Carolina, who accepted money to introduce teammates to gamblers though not to shave points, did not turn professional until years later when the ABA was formed. Most of the players implicated came from underpriviledged or emotionally deprived homes. They wanted something tangible, not just headlines, to relieve financial strain. The lure of easy money was something they found hard to resist. Some really desperately needed the very basics of life such as adequate clothing. Ray Paprocky of NYU was holding two jobs while studying because his wife was in the hospital. He gratefully accepted anything the gamblers offered him. Tim Cohane's revealing article in **Look** claimed that half the athletes involved were marginal students, lacking basic academic skills, who should not have been in college at all and would not have been had they not been excellent basketball players.

Many critics blamed the recruiting wars that all but shanghaied high school basketball stars onto major campuses around the country. Al McGuire, coaching at Belmont Abbey, claimed there were no secrets any more in basketball aside from recruiting.

Probably the roughest and most lucrative battles for talent were fought in the MVC. Academic standards were comparatively low and boys who would have had a hard time maintaining an acceptable scholastic average could almost be assured of four years of athletic eligibility and the possibility of a degree at the end of their senior year. Athletic directors and coaches could also promise national exposure in the major arenas around the country and the prospect of postseason play in both national tournaments, since the MVC allowed its schools to play in the NCAA and NIT tourneys.

Nearly every major college coach participated in the headhunting expeditions aimed at luring talented prospects to his campus. At the end of the season the coach and a few forceful and often well-heeled alumni would hit the road to call on a prospect, using their well-developed skills of persuasion on the coveted athletes or their parents. What they could offer was limited by the NCAA regulations and a violation of these restrictions, if discovered, resulted in, among other penalties, ineligibility for postseason play. Nevertheless coaches and alumni made wild promises to impressionable young men, most of whom they signed by bending if not breaking the rules. Recruiters did not feel bound by geographic limits and Rupp, Jucker, Jack Gardner of Utah, and George Ireland of Loyola to name but a few of many, criss-crossed the country in early spring, stocking up on talent for the future. The likes of Lucas, West, Robertson, McGill, Art Heyman and Barry Kramer, again to name but a few, were offered scholarships from 50, 75 and even more than 100 universities. Everyone it seemed was waiting to cash in on a young man's talents. Even the high school coach sometimes got in the act. It was alleged an occasional coach would charge recruiters a standard fee just for the privilege of talking to his basketball star, and a few were known to have demanded a coaching job (assistant or better) if they delivered the boy.

In such an atmosphere it is understandable that it was not hard to corrupt college players. In the wake of the scandals critics demanded that athletic staffs clean up their act. "Until then, young players, unable to resist the temptations offered by colleges, will be unable to resist the temptations of gamblers," editorialized one national magazine.*

But of course they did not clean up their act. More scandals followed a few years later and it was not until professional teams offered enormous salaries that gamblers discovered players were unwilling to take the risk of being caught and banned from professional basketball.

The high school graduating class of 1960 produced the most star-studded array of talent to hoist the round ball since peach baskets were used for other than collecting fruit. Jim Barnes, Ron Bonham, Joe Caldwell, Mel Counts, Connie Hawkins, Walt Hazzard, Barry Kramer, Jeff Mullins,

Cotton Nash, Paul Silas and Gary Bradds all started college varsity basketball in 1962. All but the last was an All American in high school. All but Hawkins played in the NCAA tournament. In 1962 coaches around the country welcomes these sophomores with open arms and fans slapped their palms red in appreciation.

Midwest:

At Cincinnati Ed Jucker had a lot less trouble replacing his departing seniors than he had the previous year. This time he had two sophomores, 6′5″ Ron Bonham and 6′8″ George Wilson, to man the **corners** and was able to move Tom Thacker to the backcourt where he joined Yates. Hogue remained at center. To emphasize the team play philosophy that he advocated he placed a sign "There is no I in TEAM" in the locker room. The Bearcats' strength lay in their defense. It put relentless pressure on their opponents, forcing them out of their accustomed patterns, thereby creating errors and turnovers. If they had any weakness it was their poor foul shooting and a habit of falling behind early and having to come from behind.

The Bearcats won 25 of 27 and 10 of their last 11, losing only to Wichita by a point and to Bradley by two in overtime. Crunching wins over Miami (Ohio) 63-30 and George Washington 83-43 showcased their stingy defense. They could spew points all night, too, as they did when they overpowered Wisconsin 107-71, the only team to upset Ohio State. Still they were the last school to earn a place in the tournament. At season's end they shared the conference lead with sixth ranked Bradley and had to beat them in a playoff to make the field. Bradley was consistently ranked in the top ten but just could not dislodge Cincinnati from the number one spot in the MVC. "After winning in the (Missouri) Valley," said Jucker, "the NCAA is a breeze." He had a point. The MVC schools lost most of their games within their conference while taking 75 percent of the games against outside opponents.

Other regional teams to qualify were Air Force (16-6), so disciplined they set a record of just eleven personal fouls per game, and Creighton (19-4), the best rebounding team in the country. The Blue Jays had been ambushed by two Big 10 schools and two from the New York area.

Texas Tech (18-6) tied with SMU in the Southwest Conference but beat them in a close playoff game 71-67. The Red Raiders opened their season with two cliffhangers—a double overtime win over Colorado, and a one point loss to Memphis State. Both schools turned up in the tournament, Memphis State with a mediocre 15-6 record and Colorado only slightly better at 18-6. Though Kansas State was ranked fifth nationally and had a much better overall record, they unfortunately lost two of their three games in the Big Eight. Colorado, a clutch outfit, won more than half their games by five points or fewer. While they did lose four in a row, all were outside the

**Newsweek,* June 5, 1961.

conference. By the end of the season the Buffalos had impressed the sports voters enough to be ranked eighth.

In the first round action, Texas Tech squeezed past Air Force 68-66. The young pilots kept themselves in the game by converting 88 percent of their free throws. On the other hand Creighton had to overcome poor foul shooting to get past Memphis State 87-83. It was an extremely rough game and all the Creighton starters except Paul Silas fouled out. Late in the game a fight broke out and two players were ejected. Silas, the best college rebounder since Charlie Slack almost a decade earlier, led all scorers with 27 points.

The two first round winners were quickly eliminated. Colorado took the measure of Texas Tech 67-60 and Cincinnati strangled Creighton with their doomsday defense 66-46 after holding the Blue Jays to 18 first half points. Creighton was so frustrated they sank only 8 of 41 first half shots then added just two more field goals in the first fourteen minutes of the second. It was not until Jucker benched his starters that Creighton was able to add some points to their anemic total. The final score was still 30 below their season average. Silas was the leading point man for Creighton with three buckets and 15 points. Nobody else had more than seven.

The defensive shield was up again in Cincinnati's win over Colorado. The Buffalo zone was tight but Bonham and Wilson found the target with medium range jumpers as they led the Bearcats with 14 and 12 points respectively in the first half. Ahead 28-26 with five and a half minutes to go in the period, the Bearcats accelerated to a 41-29 lead at intermission. The second half saw the Buffalos held to 17 points as Cincinnati frolicked to a 73-46 win. It was the third consecutive game, including the playoff victory over Bradley in which the Bearcats had held their opponents to 46 points.

Mideast:

Ohio State (23-1) was still the number one team in the country. Lucas, Havlicek and Nowell were now seniors. Gone was Larry Siegfried but in his place talented sophomore Garry Bradds had been added to the squad. Lucas had been voted to the All American team for a third time and Havlicek, a very underrated athlete playing in Lucas' shadow, had finally been given some recognition by being similarly honored. Lucas' scoring average had dropped three points primarily because he shot so infrequently, but his field goal percentage was the highest in the country for the third year in a row and his career percentage shattered the old record by a wide margin. He remained, as always, in complete control of himself, icy and calm, almost aloof under the most intense pressure, prompting one fan to inquire, "I wonder how old he was when he was born." The professional Cincinnati Royals could not wait for him to play his last college game. After all they had drafted him while he was still in high school.

Of all the games he played as a collegian, Big Luke was probably at his best in his team's 105-84 victory over UCLA in the semifinals of the Los Angeles Classic. In that game he scored 30 points finding the hoop 11 times in 13 attempts and 8 times in as many tries from the line besides retrieving 30 rebounds. John Wooden, the UCLA coach, was moved to congratulate Lucas after the game, calling him the most unselfish player he had ever seen. "It was a pleasure to lose to such a man. I have never said such a thing before. I never expect to again." Forrest Twogood, whose USC team Ohio State whipped in the final, was equally impressed. "It was the greatest performance I have ever seen," he said.

The Buckeyes sliced through their opponents like a shark cutting through a school of fish. Nobody got within ten points of Ohio State until March and then in one of the most surprising upsets of any season Wisconsin buried them by 19 points. The Buckeyes rebounded by beating Indiana 90-65 in their finale. This was more typical of the team whose margin of victory averaged 19 points.

One other quintet given a chance against Ohio State in the regional was Kentucky (22-2). They lost only to USC by two and to Mississippi State 49-44 in a game that had the pace of a minuet. Fourth ranked Mississippi State and third ranked Kentucky finished in a tie in the Southeast Conference, but it was the latter that went to the playoffs when the Bulldogs were refused permission once again by the Regents to play against blacks. Rupp was still running up scores against his unfortunate victims and during the season exploited Notre Dame 100-53. It was a much improved team over the previous year's squad, due primarily to the latest in Kentucky's long list of All Americans. This was sophomore Cotton Nash who, despite the name, came from Massachusetts.

There was also Bowling Green (21-3), which beat Michigan, Houston and Bradley among others, and Detroit (15-11), an at-large selection which had lost their last four decisions of the season. Detroit was led by Dave DeBusschere, the eighth highest scorer in the country. Two other eligible at-large teams, Loyola (Ill) and Dayton, with much better records than Detroit, elected to go to the NIT. Dayton, it seemed, was determined to win the NIT, a prize that had eluded them so often, before accepting an invitation to play in the NCAA.

Though they finished first in the Indiana Conference, Butler (20-5) was invited as an at-large team. Competition in that conference was not considered of high enough caliber to warrant an automatic inclusion in the tournament. Three losses to Big 10 schools cast doubt on their ability to handle major opponents. The Bulldogs were a well-drilled team under Paul Hinkle who since 1927 had won 456 games. Western Kentucky (16-8) rounded out the regional field. Ed Diddle's boys had a strange habit of losing games in pairs. Four times during the season they lost back-to-back games. It seemed as if they needed an extra game to regroup and get back on the winning track.

In the first round in Lexington, Western Kentucky eliminated Detroit 90-81 despite 38 points by DeBusschere. Dariel Carrier with 26 and Bobby Rascoe with 25 paced the winners. Butler sneaked by Bowling Greene 56-55 in a game decided at the foul line. Jerry Williams' two foul shots with 30 seconds to go won it for the Bulldogs.

Three of the four coaches assembled in Iowa City for the regional semi-finals had experience on their side while the fourth had the best talent available. Since it is talent that actually plays on the court while experience sits on the bench, it was the former that won out. Rupp, Diddle and Hinkle had 108 years of coaching experience among them plus almost 2,000 winning games to their credit. They all ranked among the top five winningest active coaches. Chuck Taylor had won only 89 games over four seasons but he had Lucas, Havlicek and company. No Mississippi gambler ever had a more powerful hand.

Kentucky, after a rocky start, subdued Butler 81-60, outscoring the Bulldogs by 20 points in the second half. Ohio State had an easier time against Western Kentucky and pranced to a 93-73 win. Five Buckeyes finished the game in double figures though Lucas, surprisingly, contributed only nine points.

The following evening Lucas was back to his old self, cashing 25 in the first half on the way to a 33 point performance. During one stretch Lucas banged in 23 of Ohio State's 25 points including three three-point plays in one sixty-second span of torrid action. Havlicek as usual was assigned to guard the other team's heaviest scoring forward, in this case Cotton Nash. He did such an effective job that Nash was finally benched by Rupp after his effectiveness was reduced to almost zero. The Buckeyes were rarely in trouble as they eliminated the Wildcats 74-64.

East:

There were no outstanding teams in the East regional. Wake Forest (18-8), which had finished with a rush after a so-so start (typical of the late blooming Deacons), captured 11 of their last 12, including six in a row against ACC schools, was the regional favorite. All American Len Chappell, fifth highest scorer in the country, and his teammates developed into a cohesive unit as the season progressed. A 49 point victory over Virginia showed them at their explosive best. Yale (17-6) won the Ivy crown and West Virginia (24-5) topped the Southern Conference. Fred Schaus had left to coach the Los Angeles Lakers, who had drafted Jerry West, his star pupil. He was replaced by George King who had inherited Rod Thorn, the latest in a line of All American Mountaineers. While Thorn was a high school student at Princeton, West Virginia, the state legislature passed a resolution declaring him a natural resource. It urged him to attend West Virginia University declaring that if he went elsewhere it would cause the state to suffer "irreparable harm."

Thorn, who sported West's number 44 and had the same first name as Hundley, was very different from his two predecessors. He was an excellent student—sixth in his class—intent on entering medical school, did not join a fraternity, did not date and in general was considered a loner. He was also an extremely intense person and frustration on or off court caused him to blow up. Fans took to booing his frequent tantrums which made him withdraw even further.

But on the court he was an excellent athlete who as a junior led his team in points, rebounds, and assists. There was much pressure on Thorn to perform well and the fans let him know it when he walked out on the court in the jersey with the now famous 44 on it.

Jack Kraft, Villanova's new mentor, entered the coaching ranks with elan as his Wildcats won their first 12 games. They skidded towards the end, losing four of five, but completed a respectable 19-6 season. St. Josephs (18-8) took first place in the Mid Atlantic with a mediocre team. They lost to St. Johns and Drake, both by 28 points, as well as to Albright and Pennsylvania among others. NYU (18-4) also lost to St. Johns—twice. The Redmen were the best team in New York but they elected to go to the NIT. However, there was another Indian tribe in the tournament—from the University of Massachusetts (15-8). These Redmen had taken the Yankee Conference though their record against non-league opponents was dismal. They were bulldogged by Rutgers (20), by Toledo (30), by Providence (34) and by Holy Cross (40)!

The first round, played for the last seven years in New York, was moved to Philadelphia's much smaller Palestra where only 9,200 fans showed up. With 6′7″ Charlie Fohlin controlling the backboard, Massachusetts moved ahead of NYU 21-20 in the early going. When his stars Happy Hairston and Barry Kramer were burdened with three personals each, Coach Rossini inserted three reserves, including captain Al Filardi. The change did not pay dividends immediately. The Redmen upped their advantage to 28-24 before Filardi sank four foul shots and stole the ball to feed a teammate for the go ahead basket. From then on NYU was in control and they salvaged the game 70-50.

West Virginia, which had handed Kraft his first coaching loss at midseason, seemed to have Villanova under control in the first period. After a locker room briefing, however, the Wildcats pounced on their opponents. With Hubie White, who scored 28 points, and Wally Jones, who added 27, firing from uptown and downtown, Villanova advanced to the next round 90-75.

Surprising Yale led Wake Forest by as many as seven though by midgame this had become a four point deficit. However, Wake Forest, apparently feeling the time was not ripe to make their usual late fire drill finish, gave the Eli another chance. At 2:42 Yale tied the count 76-76 and then almost pulled a stunning upset. But with two seconds remaining David Schumacher's free throw hit the rim and bounced free. Given a new lease the Deacons aroused themselves from their torpor during overtime. They finished in overdrive, clipping Yale 92-82.

In the first game of the second round, Wake Forest, playing as if they had come in out of the cold without warming up, shuffled through their usual frigid first half. They lacked cohesion, their patterns broke down and their defense sprang leaks, allowing St. Josephs easy baskets. Only Chappell's 34 points kept them in the game. St. Josephs led throughout except for two short intervals when the Deacons nudged in front by two points. With St. Josephs ahead 74-66 McKinney ordered his players into a full court press—an unusual and desperate move for such a slow, lumbering team. The Deacons nibbled at the lead but it was still 74-72 in favor of the Hawks as Bill Hoy stepped to the line for the clincher. He had sunk his four previous attempts but this time he missed. A Deacon clutched the rebound and fed Billy Packer who scored on a 15 foot jump shot to send the game into overtime. It was a repeat of the Yale game in the extra period. Wake Forest scored the first 12 points as they finally came to life. The Hawks were unable to connect until a little more than a minute remained. By then it was too late and Wake Forest advanced 96-85. In the two overtime sessions they had scored 38 points. To their exasperated fans forty minutes of regulation time seemed a long time for the Deacons to warm up.

The second game was almost as close. NYU needed no time at all to warm up in its contest with Villanova. They came out blazing in the first half, shot into a 12 point lead which shrank to two at the intermission. The Violets were apprehensive though. They had made 62 percent of their throws but still were unable to shake Villanova. With White arcing one ball after another through the cords, the Wildcats came back to take the lead. NYU surged ahead again briefly but White's three point play restored his team's advantage. The score was tied for the last time at 73 when Jones popped in two free throws to put the Cats on top for good. In the last 30 seconds NYU twice lost the ball on fumbles and succumbed 79-76. White had 31 points for the winners while Kramer and Hairston were high for the losers.

Following their script, Wake Forest fell behind Villanova at the end of the first half. Their fans were not worried. They had been there before. They reassured each other that overtime would bring out the best in their team. However, this time the Deacons did not wait as long to ignite. Early in the second half Chappel tied the score and Dave Wiedemann's set shot put Wake Forest ahead for keeps. The North Carolinian's were just too tall and powerful for the leaner Wildcats. They established position underneath the nets and would rarely allow Villanova more than one shot at the basket. During the last six minutes they swept the backboards so effectively the Wildcats had to settle for one field goal. Wake Forest won without an overtime 79-69.

West:

In the West regional Seattle (17-9) and Oregon State (22-4) were at-large entries. These two evenly matched teams had played each other twice, the Beavers winning the first in double overtime and the Chiefs copping the second by one point. The latter ended a 16 game winning string for Oregon State and precipitated a three game losing streak. Utah State (21-5) was making its first appearance since the year the tournament began. It was like a reunion of charter members of an exclusive club. Villanova, Wake Forest and Ohio State in addition to Utah State—one half of the original eight schools who played in 1939—participated in this tourney. But Utah State would not have appeared at all were it not for the probation slapped by the NCAA on Utah, which had finished ahead of State in the Skyline Conference. The Aggies credentials were further tarnished by losses in both regular season games against the Utes.

The first part of UCLA's (16-9) season resembled a seismograph track. They lost their first two to BYU, snapped back to win a pair, then dropped three in a row, including a 26 point shellacking to Houston. They then gained two decisions before absorbing an equal number of losses. The Bruins finally straightened out and won 12 of their last 14.

Pepperdine (19-6) won the West Coast Athletic Conference and made their first appearance since 1944. They were lightly regarded since they had played West coast Schools exclusively. Arizona State (23-3) was back with even more offensive punch then the previous year. They had been edged by Loyola (Ill.) by one basket for the team scoring title but their margin of victory was the highest in the country. The three losses had come in a row—to Indiana, Minnesota and the team that was sitting on the sidelines, Utah. On the other side of the ledger were overwhelming victories over Pasadena 130-65, Hardin-Simmons 110-65, Brigham Young 94-54, and Oregon 91-55.

In the first round Utah State led Arizona State 70-52 with five minutes to go but the Sun Devils were not ready to concede and hacked away at the Aggies' huge lead. Utah State hung on to win 78-73. In the second game Seattle tried ball control tactics to neutralize Oregon State's height advantage. Their defense was superb, (only three Beavers scored in the first half) and they were more consistent. But the taller Beavers, especially 7′0″ Mel Counts and 6′7″ Jay Carty, controlled the boards. Counts, a relatively inexperienced sophomore, picked up three fouls in the first half and added a fourth before the midpoint of the second. Carty, a forward, replaced him in the pivot and scored consistently from there, picking up 27 points. In order to contain Counts and Carty the Chieftains fouled frequently and the Beavers took full advantage by sinking 23 of 26 free throws. In the waning seconds Seattle's Tommy Shaules flipped in a two pointer to knot the score and the contest went into overtime. The Beavers, playing in their own arena, took a slim lead. Seattle battled back but two turnovers cost them the decision. First John Tresvant travelled a moment before caging a shot. Then with 33 seconds to go and two points down a forecourt-to-backcourt pass gave the ball to Oregon State which added two more to win 69-65.

Once more height and foul shooting helped Oregon State overcome their next opponent, Pepperdine. Counts was the dominant force off the boards again though he sat out part of the game after he picked up his fourth personal early in the second half. Trailing by 11, Pepperdine took advantage of Counts' absence. With the Waves threatening to catch up, Counts was quickly reinserted. Both teams had 24 opportunities from the line but the Beavers converted 19 times while the Waves made only 11. Just as in their game against Seattle Oregon State held a narrow lead as the last seconds faded away. With two seconds left and the Beavers ahead 69-66, Pepperdine's Lee Tinsley went to the line for two. He made the first and deliberately bounced the second off the backboard to try for a three point play. The referee blew his whistle and gave the ball to Oregon State since a rule states if the ball does not touch the rim on a missed foul it goes over the non-shooting team. The Beavers thus climbed to the next rung 69-67. Five Oregon State players scored in double figures, three sharing top honors with 15, though the bench made no scoring contribution.

UCLA had never won a postseason game except for a meaningless consolation contest in 1956. Every other team in the old PCC except Idaho had won at least one and three of them had won the national championship. It was not that UCLA did not have a good team most years, just that they always folded under tournament pressure. It seems strange now that UCLA has won 60 tournament games, more than twice as many as any other school except Kentucky and North Carolina, that it took them 25 years to post their first postseason victory.

Paced by the slick ball handling of Walt Hazzard, the Bruins experienced a moment of panic when their tallest starter, 6′5″ Fred Slaughter, fouled out. Utah State, trailing by 13 at the half, sensed the opportunity and led by Cornell Green pulled to within two at 63-61 before UCLA shut them down. When it was over UCLA had preailed 73-62, and was no longer a tournament virgin.

The second victory was only 24 hours away. Slaughter, who gave away seven inches to Counts, held the taller player in check. For once Counts stayed out of foul trouble but he and his teammates could not stop the much shorter but quicker and slicker Bruins from controlling the game. UCLA won going way 88-69. For the third time in as many games Oregon State scored exactly 69 points.

Final Four:

The first game in the penultimate round pitted Ohio State against Wake Forest. The most obvious difference between the teams was speed. It was like watching five thoroughbreds competing against five draught horses and the outcome was never in doubt. Lucas and Havlicek each sank half their shots though Havlicek outscored his more famous teammate. However it was Big Luke's rebounding and quick outlet passes that made the Buckeye fast break click. The pace set by Ohio State was so torrid it effectively killed off the Deacons and only once did they get closer than ten points in the second half. Chappell scored 27 in a losing cause as Ohio State advanced to the finals for the third straight year, 84-68. It would have been a happy group of Buckeyes heading for the locker room but for a chilling event that occurred eight minutes before the final buzzer. Lucas fell to the hardwood and had to be helped, limping, off the court.

In the nightcap the finely tuned Bearcats came out humming like a supercharged precision tooled engine. In the first five minutes they did not miss a shot and after scoring ten points in a row led UCLA 18-4. The Bruins switched to a 2-3 zone which immediately disengaged Cincinnati's drive. By the end of the first period UCLA had caught up and both sides settled down to a grim, closely contested battle. If not for Hogue the Bruins would have taken charge and won handily. The massive center accounted for 36 points, exactly half his team's total, on 12 of 18 from the floor and as many free throws. He also hauled down 19 rebounds. UCLA tried various combinations to contain him but none of the tactics worked, and two of the Bruins fouled out trying to guard him. In the second half neither side could gain more than a four point advantage. The lead changed hands seven times and the score was knotted ten times. Mostly UCLA was on top on the strength of Johnny Green's scintillating moves to the hoop. But just when it looked as if the Bruins might pull away, Hogue would tie the score or put the Bearcats ahead again. During one stretch he sank 14 points in a row.

At 3:20 Hogue produced the last tie. For more than two minutes neither side was able to take the lead. Cincinnati, in possession, decided to hold for a last shot. With ten seconds to go they called a time out to set up a play. It worked. The inbounds pass went to Tom Thacker who dribbled toward the basket and hooked in the winner. It was his only bucket in seven tries. Three seconds later the buzzer sounded, giving the Bearcats a 72-70 victory.

Lucas was in considerable pain the next day. His coach and teammates hovered around him but he assured them his knee was not too bad and that he could play. Still, as he walked onto the court to warm up, his strained knee heavily taped and braced, everyone could see he was limping. It was speculative just how effective he would be.

For the first time in tournament history the same two schools contended for the national championship for the second year in a row. The final was a real grudge match. Lucas had again been named Player of the Year and Fred Taylor was voted Coach of the Year. Once again Ohio State had topped Cincinnati in the polls as number one in the country. Two Buckeyes were on the All American team while none of the Bearcats had received that honor. To add insult to injured pride Governor Mike DiSalle of Ohio had honored Ohio State by pronouncing it an All American team and its players All Americans of the century without mentioning Cincinnati once. The Bearcats and their fans were enraged at the lack of recognition.*

*DiSalle did not win reelection in 1962 and his poor showing at the polls in Cincinnati had a lot to do with unseating him.

So the Bearcats were out to prove the so-called experts wrong, to prove they had been underrated and that they were indeed Number One. The Buckeyes, their great trio of Lucas, Havlicek and Nowell playing their final game, were just as determined to show that last year's loss was a fluke and to bring the national championship to Columbus once more. As the teams took the floor tension hung in the smoky air like the awareness of an alarm clock about to go off. Banners on one side of the arena urging GO GO OHIO and HATE STATE buttons on the other reflected the intensity of the feeling between the intrastate rivals.

For the first 12 minutes each team took turns holding narrow leads but with the score tied 21-21 the Bearcats forged ahead and for the rest of the period they responded with two for every point made by the Buckeyes. Ohio State tried containing the Bearcats by switching defenses. None of the various zones nor man-to-man worked. Desperately they moved to a half court and finally a full court press. The Bearcats maintained their poise and refused to fold. Executing their plays with finesse they picked their way through Ohio State's defense, patiently waiting for the good shots. Repeatedly the guards would break loose on change of direction plays set up by Wilson and Hogue and would either shoot from short range or pass off to an open man. Hogue alternated between high and low post confusing the Buckeyes on the switch so he was able to get free for several easy baskets. He and Thacker alternated in setting up plays and they both finished with more than 20 points. The disciplined offense was mirrored in a defense that smothered the Buckeyes while being assessed just ten personal fouls in the entire game. Though Lucas was obviously hampered by the brace on his knee, Hogue's tenacity was as much a factor in holding the big center to eleven points. Sophomore reserve Gary Bradds was inserted by Fred Taylor to take some of the pressure off Lucas and he responded well by scoring 15 points, more than any other Buckeye. But it was the rebounding of Hogue and Wilson that effectively stopped the Buckeyes' normally devastating fast break. They never got untracked as Cincinnati, showing great stamina despite only one substitution, controlled the pace of the game. The crack the Bearcats had opened late in the first half became a fissure and eventually developed into a crevasse. When the final buzzer sounded, Cincinnati had their second championship 71-59.

After the game Lucas disclaimed any excuses. "My knee didn't hurt but Hogue bothered me," he said, paying tribute to the man who outscored him 22-11 and won the tournament's MVP award. For Lucas it was only his ninth loss in a career going back to elementary school.

Meanwhile, only 50 miles away in Dayton, Ohio, the fans were celebrating just as boisterously. Their Dayton Flyers had won the NIT for the first time after finishing second 5 times in the previous 11 years. For the boys from the Buckeye State it was a night to remember.

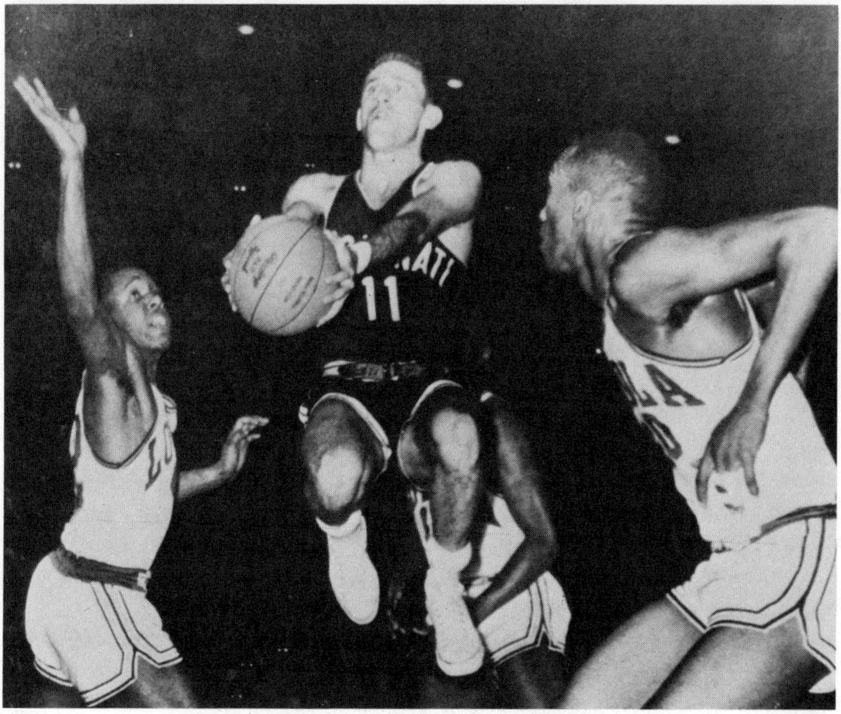

Cincinnati's Larry Shingleton finds some driving room for a layup attempt between Loyola defenders Ron Miller, Left, and Vic Rouse, right. This 1963 championship game went to Loyola 60-58 in overtime.
(AP Photo)

1963

Midwest:

As the 1963 tournament approached, the Cincinnati Bearcats had achieved several goals they felt they deserved the previous year—they were ranked number one, Ed Jucker was voted Coach of the Year and Ron Bonham and Tom Thacker had become All Americans. Even Governor Mike DiSalle had been defeated. The Bearcats (23-1) had completed a near perfect season, marred only by a 65-64 overtime loss to Wichita which broke a 37 game winning streak, the fifth longest in major college history and the longest since San Francisco's in 1957. They had not lost at home since 1957.

Prospects looked good for a third straight championship. Hogue was the only starter who had graduated and Jucker had shifted Wilson to center to replace him while Tom Thacker had moved to forward. Larry Shingleton took Thacker's place at guard. The Bearcats' long suit was their nationally top ranked defense. In their first three games they gave up an average of only 39 points. In seven of their first nine they gave up fewer than 50 points and the highest total they allowed was 65 in the overtime loss to Wichita. Given such a stingy defense it was remarkable that they also led the country in fewest personal fouls committed.

Even against the best teams the Bearcats were overwhelming. In one memorable double header in Chicago featuring the top three teams in the country at the time—Cincinnati, Loyola and Illinois—the Bearcats whipped Illinois by 20 points.

If they had one weakness it was their laxness in the initial stages of a game which frequently forced them to come from behind to win. It often provided the only excitement in an otherwise unstimulating exhibition of methodical execution.

Colorado (18-6) and Kansas State tied for the top spot in the Big Eight but the Buffalos were selected without having to compete in a playoff. Their superior overall record and the fact that they had beaten the Wildcats in both meetings during the season, including the last game, weighed in their favor.* Colorado was also a strong defensive team, limiting their opponents to fewer than 50 points on nine occasions.

Still another strong defense was exhibited by Texas Western (19-6), making their first tournament appearance. These tall Texans kept their opponent's score low by controlling the boards. They led the country in that department due mainly to Jim Barnes who latched on to more than a third of his team's rebounds. One school the Miners could not handle was Arizona State, who beat them twice by identical 63-60 scores.

Texas (18-6) represented the SWC. Texas was off to a rocky start winning only four of their first nine games. They dug in their spurs, though,

*For the first time since 1954 neither a Kansas nor a Kentucky school was selected.

and won the next 14 before losing to Baylor in the season finale. Oklahoma City (18-8) had an almost identical experience. After posting a 5-7 mark in the first half of the season they won 13 in a row before losing their last one to Houston. Colorado State (18-4), another independent, was proud of their All American, Bill Green, third leading scorer in the country, who had distinguished himself by sinking all 14 of his free throws in a NIT game two years before.

Texas gained revenge over Texas Western for an early season defeat by crushing the Miners 65-47 at Lubbock. In the other half of the double bill Oklahoma City guard Gay Hill took charge in the last minute of a closely contested game, firing six points through the hoop to give his side a 70-67 win over Colorado State.

In the next round Oklahoma City and Colorado displayed their talents in two sports—basketball and boxing. The game was interrupted when players began swinging at each other. Almost immediately both benches cleared and everyone was taking turns punching each other out. The scuffle threatened to degenerate into a riot and several fans were ready to throw more than just their fists. After everyone had their say and calm restored, the contest resumed; Colorado won the game 78-72. The winner of the fight was not announced!

Texas surprised Cincinnati by assuming an eight point lead in their second round game. The Bearcats switched to a full court press and caught up to the Longhorns at 26-26. By the end of the first half they had established a modest lead but they could not shake their stubborn opponents. Texas even outscored the Bearcats from the floor but gave Cincinnati too many tries at the foul line where Bonham, an 89 percent shooter, and his mates had few peers. It was Cincinnati's tough front court of Wilson, Bonham and Thacker who accounted for the 63 points that finally sank the Longhorns 73-68.

In an almost identical scenario the same trio determined the outcome of the regional final. Cincinnati trailed Colorado by nine before closing to within one at the intermission. Colorado was not ready to belly up, though. They spun two balls through the hoop at the start of the second half to lead 36-31. But the Bearcats did not lose their cool. Unemotionally and with precision they whittled away at Colorado's lead and then took charge.

In the next six minutes Bonham and Wilson bombed for 17 points between them to give Cincinnati a 48-42 edge. That advantage held up for the rest of the game as the Bearcats advanced to the Final Four for the fifth consecutive year, 67-60. This time the front court parked 55 points in the net.

Mideast:

Ohio State, ranked eighth in the country, was itching for another chance at a showdown with the Bearcats. Going into the last evening of the season, the Buckeyes were a game up in the Big 10 and failed to win it all by the narrowest of margins. They lost to Indiana 87-85 in overtime while Illinois, the runner up, held off Iowa 73-69. The resulting conference tie allowed Illinois (19-5) to go to the tourney since Big 10 rules did not permit a playoff but instead called for the school which had played there most recently to step aside in favor of the other. The fifth ranked Illini were well qualified to represent the Big 10. They did beat Ohio State during the season and had the fourth highest scoring offense in the country, though their defense had the consistency of wormwood. A split with Indiana in which they won the first 104-101 and lost the return match 103-100 is illustrative.

Tennessee Tech (16-7) took the Ohio Valley. They won the right to play in the tournament because of their ability to manhandle Morehead State, whom they whipped twice during the regular season. When the two finished in a tie for the league lead, the Eagles had even less trouble trouncing Morehead for a third time. But the Eagles were a mediocre team, as evidence a humiliating 107-83 defeat at the hands of Western Kentucky, which won only five games. Bowling Green (17-7) started their season with rubber burning acceleration. They won their first three by an average of 50 points but then hit the skids and lost five of seven. They then moved back into high gear, winning their last ten using the strength of All American Nate Thurmond at center and Howard Komives' howitzer shelling from the perimeter.

Notre Dame (17-8) and Loyola of Illinois (24-2) were at-large entries. Loyola was ranked fourth and had the top scoring squad in the country. They first came to national attention the previous year when they finished with a 23-4 record and placed third in the NIT. With four starters returning, they won their first 21 games and had little trouble gaining their initial NCAA tournament invitation. They were led by their outstanding All American Jerry Harkness, a 6′2″ guard from New York. Coach George Ireland had recruited the Ramblers' two tall men, 6′7″ Leslie Hunter and 6′6″ Vic Rouse, from the same high school in Nashville, Tennessee. After unsuccessfully trying to sign a local star, Ireland was consoled by the boys' coach, "Don't worry, I've got two boys graduating next year who are even better." He was right and better still he was able to deliver Rouse and Hunter as promised. These three along with Ron Miller gave Loyola four blacks on the starting squad, unusual even at a time when black players were becoming more common on the court. Though Harkness was their leader and driving force, the Ramblers' strategy was to involve the whole team in the game so that all five starters averaged double figures. The player with the hot hand was fed the ball. They reached triple digit scores in ten games, including their first six, a span during which they averaged 111 points a game. With all that offensive power few noted the Ramblers' underrated defense. Loyola was relaxed on defense but adequate when it had to be.

Loyola's success was attributable to George Ireland's excellent coaching and his rigorous training methods. These included running three to five miles a day, starting a month before actual basketball practice, jumping with weights attached to the feet and negotiating an obstacle course to improve agility. A Marine boot camp regimen might have been a welcome relief after some of the more exhausting practice sessions. Ireland's credo, "Discipline is 90 percent of winning," made him as popular as a drill sergeant. He forbade any talking during time out or practice and transgressors were banished to the bench. Still, he had the respect of his men with the result that a school without a previous tradition in any sport found itself close to the top of the basketball heap.

For the third time in five years Mississippi State (22-6) finished on top of the SEC but this time they decided to risk contamination and play in the tourney. The decision was reached by the coach and players and endorsed by the university's President and Board of Regents. Governor Ross Barnett, however, threatened to cut off funds to the school if they played a game against a team fielding a black player and sent a sheriff with a restraining order chasing after the Bulldogs. Team and coach sneaked across the state line to Tennessee barely ahead of the sheriff and lay low in an undisclosed motel until it was time to fly to the tournament site.

The conference was well represented. Mississippi State had six of their first seven lettermen returning and were well drilled in the give and go and drive to the baseline, the hallmark of Coach Babe McCarthy. One weakness was their lack of interregional competition since they were limited to playing against all white squads.

In the first round at Evanston, Illinois, Loyola obliterated Tennessee Tech 111-42 in the most one sided contest ever played in the NCAA tournament. The first half ended with the Ramblers on top 61-20, wondering whether the team they were playing were imposters. Ireland, who always found some reason for chewing his players out during the intermission, was for once speechless. The Ramblers' statistics gave clear evidence of their balanced offense. Their high scorer, Miller, made only 21 points while the other starters weighed in with 19, 18, 18 and 17 each. The winners also committed just seven fouls. In a more balanced contest Bowling Green upended Notre Dame 77-72 as Butch Komives lent the needed support with 34 points.

As the regional continued, Bowling Green barely succumbed to Illinois 70-67 despite Komives' 25 team-leading points. Loyola had cooled off considerably by the time they took the court against Mississippi State. The southerners scored the first seven points; it was not until nearly five minutes had elapsed that Loyola sank their first basket. By half time though, they had forged ahead 26-19. Despite the Bulldogs' effort to slow down the action the Ramblers took charge, mainly with the excellent board work of Harkness, Rouse and Hunter. It was ironic that Mississippi State, playing their first integrated game, should confront the team with more black players than any other in the tourney. All acted like gentlemen, very polite, as if afraid to give offense. The resulting action was timid if not boring. After the game, which the Ramblers won 61-51, McCarthy showed he was as good a diplomat as he was a coach when he stated, "I'm happy my boys could come just to see a team like Loyola play." In retrospect it was more a love-in than a basketball game.

In the regional final it was back to hardnosed power tactics. Loyola, which had given up fewer than a point a minute in the first half of their two previous games, allowed Illinois a generous 30 points in the initial period. In the second half the Ramblers, showing little strain, stretched their advantage over their better known intrastate rivals to 28 points. They pressured their opponents so relentlessly that Illinois turned the ball over 20 times. On offense Jerry Harkness slipped through for 33 points and though the Ramblers almost stopped scoring in the last few minutes, they still won convincingly 79-64.

East:

The East's best hope for a national champion was Duke (24-2) coached by Vic Bubas, no stranger to the playoff. He had been a star on the North Carolina State squad that almost upset CCNY in the 1950 tourney. Duke had lost back-to-back games to Davidson and Miami of Florida by almost identical scores—72-69 and 71-69—but otherwise they had been perfect. They won 19 straight before the tournament, beating powerhouses like West Virginia, 111-71, and ACC runner-up Wake Forest, 113-87. The Blue Devils were the country's deadliest team and four of the five starting sharp-shooters hit better than 50 percent of their shots. Deadliest among them were Jay Buckley and Jeff Mullins. The man who took most of the shots, though, was Art Heyman, Duke's All American senior, picked the Player of the Year by the coaches and media. Heyman, along with several other New York high school stars, had originally decided to go to North Carolina but changed his mind at the last minute. This had created some bad feelings between him and the Tarheels, and whenever Duke and North Carolina played the sparks flew. Heyman, an intense ball player, refused to let North Carolina intimidate him. In 1961, his rookie season, he completely out-played Doug Moe, the Tarheels' star. After Moe fouled out Heyman, now guarded by Larry Brown, had driven to the basket in the game's final seconds. There he collided with Brown's elbow which embedded itself in Heyman's mouth, causing considerable damage to his jaw and starting one of the biggest brawls in ACC history. Heyman and Brown were suspended for the remaining games of the schedule which guaranteed the feud would continue as long as Heyman played for the Blue Devils.

After Duke the talent in the regional dropped off drastically. NYU (17-3) had All American Barry Kramer. He had been heavily recruited by stronger powers but chose NYU because of its fine pre-medical program. Kramer was the second highest scorer in the country, averaging 29 points per game. West Virginia (21-7) had won the Southern Conference. St. Josephs (21-4) was undefeated in the Mid Atlantic. Connecticut (18-6) and Pittsburgh (19-5) were given almost no chance to advance.

Finally there was Princeton (19-5) under coach Butch van Breda Kolff and showcasing the finest sophomore in the country, Bill Bradley. Bradley was from Crystal City, Missouri, where he had twice made All American as a high school player and accumulated 3066 points in three years of varsity competition. He had also been a straight A student and a member of the National Honor Society. With those credentials he could have had an academic or an athletic scholarship to any university in the country. He first chose Duke but at the last minute he changed his mind and enrolled at Princeton. However, he refused to accept a scholarship, giving as his reason the fact that since his father was a bank president in Crystal City, his scholarship should go to a needier student.

Bradley was a coach's dream incarnate. He was an all-round player, talented in every phase of the sport, but his most developed skill was his ability to concentrate, especially when foul shooting. As a freshman he sank 57 free throws in a row. As a sophomore he hit the cords for an .893 free throw mark, second best in the country. "Dollar" Bill (the nickname came later after he signed a professional contract for a huge salary) was also the fifth highest scorer in the country in 1963.

Princeton lost four of five in a midseason slump but subdued its last nine opponents to tie Yale for the Ivy League lead and then beat the Eli in a playoff to earn the right to play in the tournament. Maybe their most significant win was a 15 point drubbing of Villanova on the latter's court, only the second loss at home for the Wildcats in ten years.

West Virginia needed some clutch free throw shooting from Ricki Ray before overcoming Connecticut in first round action at Philadelphia's Palestra. Rod Thorn was limping on a bad knee, but despite that handicap the Mountaineers pushed their advantage to ten points just before half time. After Gerry Manning put Connecticut ahead 52-50 on a corner jump, the teams shadowed each other and for most of the second period were never separated by more than two points. After Bill Maphis put West Virginia on top 68-67 the Mountaineers regained possession and went into a stall. Connecticut was unable to shake the ball loose and finally had to foul. Ricky Ray found himself camping out at the foul line and converted seven of eight attempts as West Virginia widened the gap to win 77-71.

St. Josephs had an even more difficult time subduing Princeton. The Hawks were playing in the first round thanks mostly to their failures in recent tourneys; the Mid Atlantic now had a worse record than the ACC schools in postseason play, thereby forcing the former conference's representative to forfeit its first round bye. (For years Mid Atlantic schools had received an opening round bye due to the excellent showing of LaSalle and Temple. But in three of the past four years St. Josephs had been eliminated in the first round.)

The Philadelphians took an early ten point lead but lost it when Princeton went on a 19-3 tear, to take a 29-23 lead. Bradley was the whole show as he accounted for 13 of the Tigers' first 15 points and assisted on the other bucket. St. Josephs regrouped towards the end of the half and cruised to a 33-31 half time advantage. Princeton emerged from the locker room in the second half and blew past the Hawks to recapture the lead. With five minutes to go they were ahead 73-62 and were still in front 77-72 when Bradley fouled out with 3:39 remaining. The Tigers failed to score another point and St. Josephs made the equalizer to knot the score before the buzzer. Without Bradley the Tigers could generate little in the way of an offense during the overtime and the Hawks advanced 82-81. Bradley scored 40 points (55 percent of his teams total at the time he fouled out) on 12 of 21 from the floor and an incredible 16 of 16 from the foul line.

NYU had an easier time against Pittsburgh which led only once in the contest. The Violets banged away with their heavy artillery, Kramer and Hairston, who unloaded for 37 and 29 points respectively as they hit on close to 60 percent of their shots.

One second round match pitted NYU against Duke. What had been a close game until slightly more than a minute to go in the first half turned into a rout as Duke converted a two point deficit into a nine point advantage. They swept past NYU with a seven point flurry before the buzzer then added three more to open the second half. With Heyman leading the fast break, Mullins popping for 25 points on offense and Herb Tison blocking shots on defense, Duke blew the Violets off the court. Heyman was the catalyst in the surge. Though his shooting was off he directed plays, assisted on baskets and was a potent rebounder. With eight minutes remaining in the game the Blue Devils were up by 18, then switched to their bench and coasted the rest of the way. The final score, 81-76, was not indicative of Duke's total mastery and, despite Kramer's 34 points, the Violets were never a factor after the intermission.

Another fine performance in a losing cause was Rod Thorn's 44 points. In a torrid shootout in the first half St. Josephs targeted 64 percent of their tosses while West Virginia, erratic by comparison, posted only a 50 percent mark. After taking a 21 point lead at the half the Hawks' advantage eroded under Thorn's blistering counterattack. With his knee repaired, Thorn was able to score consistently with his patented two handed jump shot. He hit three buckets within a 50 second span as the Mountaineers moved to within six. West Virginia tried to slow down the game but the Hawks, led by Jim Boyle's nine for eleven shooting, were too hot to be caught and advanced 97-88.

For the second successive game Heyman had a poor shooting night. Normally he took more than a third of his team's shots and when he was off the mark the Blue Devils had to scramble to win. Heyman, however, was still an important factor as he frequently looked one way and passed another to hit an open teammate for a high percentage shot. Mullins' 24 points helped as did Buckley's 18 rebounds but it was Duke's impenetrable zone that decided the contest. The Blue Devils' disciplined defense committed just six fouls.

It was St. Josephs' strategy to slow down the game and take the fast break, Duke's ultimate weapon, away from their opponents. St. Josephs moved to an early 10-1 lead but after a Duke time out Mullins hit three consecutive field goals. He repeated that feat in the last minute of the half, to give the Blue Devils a one point edge. As Duke's advantage increased in the final period the Hawks were forced to take risks.

As a result their slow down strategy collapsed and Duke's fast break was back in business. The Hawks, gambling on defense, fouled frequently so that Duke received 28 opportunities from the line, four times as many as St. Josephs. Only Tom Wynne's 29 points kept the Hawks in the game (Boyle was a frigid as he had been torrid against West Virginia), but Duke won their 20th consecutive game, 73-59.

West:

Stanford was favored to win their first conference championship since 1942. Entering the last weekend of the season, the tenth ranked Indians held a two game lead over UCLA, their closest competitor in the Big Five. The Indians had already beaten UCLA twice and only a complete collapse by Stanford and a sweep by UCLA could prevent them from going to the tourney. Unfortunately for Stanford their last two games were in Los Angeles. They lost to UCLA on Friday evening (their bad luck evening) which put the Bruins only one game back. On Saturday evening they tangled with USC. With the championship in the balance the teams went into overtime but Stanford was unable to meet the challenge. The same day UCLA trounced California, thus tying Stanford for the Big Five lead. Stanford, completely demoralized after blowing their lead, was no match for UCLA in the one game playoff in Los Angeles. For UCLA (20-7) it was a great comeback. In the tightest conference race ever contested on the Pacific Coast four of the five teams finished within a game of each other.

Arizona State (24-2) won the first Western Athletic Conference championship. The new league was composed of four former members of the Skyline Conference—Brigham Young, New Mexico, Utah and Wyoming—and two former Border Conference schools—Arizona and Arizona State. These two conferences disbanded and the remaining schools became independents. Third ranked Arizona State had lost only to Wichita* by two points and Wyoming by six. Utah State (20-6) lost four of their games to tournament teams, including two to Texas Western. San Francisco (18-7) dueled Santa Clara to the wire. Late in the season the Dons won a 62-61 thriller from their tough rival but Santa Clara held on to tie for the WCAC lead. San Francisco then duplicated their earlier win by taking a one game playoff from Santa Clara 66-65 on Dave Lee's free throw with two seconds remaining.

*Wichita, the runner up in the MVC was the number one giant killer that season. They had beaten tournament-bound Cincinnati, Loyola (Illinois), Texas Western and Arizona State as well as Big Ten co-champion Ohio State, among others.

Oregon State (19-7) lost three of its first five, including their opener against Seattle which they later avenged. The Beavers were a tough defensive team, giving up more than 70 points only once and that in an untypical 96-69 loss to Stanford. Mel Counts patrolled the middle but the man who made the offense work was playmaker Terry Baker, football All America, Heisman Trophy winner, Maxwell Trophy winner and *Sports Illustrated's* Sportsman of the Year.** He was an excellent student, too. Seattle (21-5) was another at-large selection. In contrast to Oregon State their strategy emphasized offense.

In the rubber match between Oregon State and Seattle, Ernie Dunston and John Tresvant tried in vain to contain Counts who tallied 30 points. Seattle's Eddie Miles, averaging almost 26 points, carried his team to a 44-43 lead soon after the intermission but the Chieftains could not maintain their advantage. Playing almost the entire game with the same five, Seattle faded in the closing minutes. They had one final opportunity when Miles, who had already scored 28, stepped to the line for a one and one with 15 seconds left and the Chieftains behind by two. He missed his first attempt and one of the Beavers gathered in the rebound. Oregon State held on to win 70-66. For the third straight year a frustrated Seattle quintet lost a first round game in the final seconds.

In the co-feature Arizona State won a come-from-behind victory from Utah State 79-75 in overtime. Not only were the teams well matched, they also produced well matched scorers. Wayne Estes of Utah State had 32 while his counterpart Joe Caldwell had 31.

Oregon State and San Francisco, another matched pair who played Big Defense very effectively and gave up baskets grudgingly, played a seesaw game in the second round in Provo. The game was not decided until Mel Counts put the Beavers ahead on a jump shot late in the second half and Oregon State held on to win 65-61. Counts and Baker accounted for 43 points between them for the winners.

UCLA's defense took a holiday when they faced Arizona State. The Sun Devils, pressing man-to-man, caused the Bruins to force their shots and miss consistently. Even UCLA shooting star Walt Hazzard was barely moving and accounted for just four points in the first half. Only one-quarter of UCLA's shots found their mark in the first period while Arizona State, their fast break unchecked, was hitting 59 percent of theirs. Sun Devils' coach Ned Wulk inserted his reserves in the second period but the result was still a humiliating 93-79 defeat for the Bruins.

The regional final was a dull affair. Oregon State's defense completely shackled Arizona State, especially in the second half when the high production Sun Devils scored only 27 points. The Beavers started fast and were in control throughout. With Mel Counts clogging the middle and redirecting

---

**The Heisman goes to college football's outstanding player; the Maxwell to the country's best amateur athlete.

Sun Devil shots and Steve Pauly blanketing Joe Caldwell, Oregon State had little trouble advancing to the Final Four in Louisville 83-65.

Final Four:

For Ed Jucker the setting was familiar. Exactly a year earlier he had stunned the Buckeyes and won a second consecutive national title. Now he was on the threshold of taking his third in a row, an unprecedented feat. The pressure was mounting. "It's like being the last egg in an incubator," he said. "Everybody's standing around waiting for you to crack."

The pressure did not seem to bother the Bearcats, particularly in their semifinal contest with Oregon State. The Beavers were unshakable in the first half and were only three points down at the midway mark. Counts was the hub of Oregon State's offense and Cincinnati had some trouble containing him but when he ran into foul trouble early in the second half, the Bearcats poured 16 unanswered points through the hoop and put the game on ice. The final 20 minutes became a nightmare for the Beavers; their opponents, working off a double screen at the foul line, tallied 50 points to their own anemic 19. It was not that Oregon State's shooting was so poor—just that they seldom got a shot off before the Bearcats' quick hands stole the ball or caused some other turnover. Counts, as usual, was his team's high scorer with 20 points but nobody else was able to contribute more than five; Terry Baker, normally the second highest scorer, was shut out completely. When the massacre was over, Cincinnati had won 80-46 and was one step away from another title. For Jucker it was his eighty-second career win against only six losses.

It was evident even in the early going that Duke's 20 game winning streak was about to hit a dead end. Loyola streaked to a 17 point lead and the Blue Devils spent the evening floundering in their wake trying to catch the rambling boys from Illinois. They managed to haul themselves into contention at 74-71 with three and a half minutes showing on the clock. Then the Ramblers kicked into overdrive and slammed home 20 points to Dukes' four and took the contest 94-75. The Ramblers' speed, deadly shooting and above all great balance (all the starters were in double figures) was too much for Duke, who relied too heavily on one man. Heyman, who scored 29 and had some help from Mullins, was simply outmanned.

It was the sharpshooters from Chicago, the nation's number one offensive team, against Cincinnati, the leading defensive team, in a final reminiscent of the 1960 showdown between Ohio State and California. Neither team substituted in the first half which saw the Bearcats control the pace throughout. Loyola, which had averaged 93 points a game during the season, was cold as its city's lakefront in January, missing 13 of its first 14 shots and converting fewer than 25 percent of their attempts from the floor in the first half.

When the Bearcats hit five of their first six shots, including three by

Bonham, at the beginning of the second half, Jucker might have been excused for starting to compose his victory statement. With less than 12 minutes left his team held a 45-30 lead and it looked doubtful that Loyola would reach the half century mark. Cincinnati was in total control, playing a deliberate, patterned, almost stylized game. The only problem was that they were picking up too many fouls. In the space of five minutes Yates and Wilson were charged with five infractions between them. When Wilson picked up his fourth, Jucker decided to go to his not particularly strong bench, and bring in Dale Heidotting in place of his center. It was the game's first substitution. At the same time he ordered the pace slowed even more, in effect a modest freeze. This effectively changed the tempo of the game and it made Cincinnati overly cautious. Slowly the Ramblers closed the gap—to twelve points, to nine, to five. After four minutes Jucker reinserted Wilson but the Bearcat's rhythm had been broken. They missed several crucial foul shots and committed mistakes creating turnovers—16 in the game to Loyola's 3.

Cincinnati's earlier momentum ground to a halt as Loyola accelerated. Their shooting did not improve particularly but they were throwing a lot of leather at the basket and eventually the ball began to drop in. On the other end of the court the Bearcats refused to shoot unless they had an almost sure two points. Suddenly the Ramblers were back in their groove. They began to fast break and all the hours of conditioning that Coach Ireland had inflicted on them began to pay off. Though Loyola's starters had played the whole game, they had more left than the exhausted Bearcats who were slow to get back on defense. At 4:29 Harkness sank his first field goal of the game. They were only his fourth and fifth points, but now, in the crunch, he began hitting consistently. With 45 seconds left Cincinnati was desperately hanging on to a lead that had shrunk to three. The arena was bedlam, approaching pandemonium. With twelve seconds remaining and the Bearcats ahead 53-52, Larry Shingleton was at the line for a one and one with a chance to frost the game. He made the first but missed the second. Harkness grabbed the rebound, flew downcourt and potted a ten footer. There were still five seconds showing on the clock but the dazed Bearcats failed to call time before the buzzer sounded. Overtime again—the second time in three years for Cincinnati.

The tipoff went to Harkness who layed it in to give the Ramblers a 56-54 lead after only five seconds. Everyone had to play cautiously. Half the players on the court had four fouls and the others were in nearly equal jeopardy. But this was no time for substitutes. Wilson tied it with a twisting layup; Ron Miller's 25 footer put Loyola ahead again. Thacker fired a court length pass over the heads of the pressing Ramblers which was hauled in by Shingleton, who scored his first and only field goal. Loyola held for the last shot but Shingleton tied up 5′10″ John Egan and forced a jump ball. Somehow the Ramblers controlled the tap and stalled for over a minute. Then, with eight seconds remaining, Harkness spotted Hunter alone at the free throw line. The feed was converted into a shot which hit the rim and bounced off to the right. Timing his jump perfectly Rouse grabbed the ball before it had travelled three feet and in one motion banked it into the basket as the last second ticked away. The Ramblers had a national championship on their first try.

The final score was 60-58 and it was Hunter and Rouse, the Tennessee connection, who drove the final nail, burying the Boys from the Buckeye State. A week earlier Wittenberg had lost the Division II championship to South Dakota State on a final second basket. It just was not Ohio's year.

11

THE WIZARD AND HIS PERFORMING BRUINS

1964-1965

1964

West:

UCLA coach John Wooden was not an easy man to know. Quiet and scholarly, he found enjoyment and relaxation in reading poetry, especially the nineteenth century English poets. John Keats was his favorite. On the court he was a strict disiplinarian, demanding much from his players and often getting more than they knew they possessed. He expected them to be able to play all-out for forty minutes at top speed.

As a youth he had led Martinsville (Indiana) High School to one state championship and had barely lost another in the final seconds. He had been an All American guard at Purdue in each of his three varsity years (1930 to 1932) and indeed he was once voted an **all-time** All American.

As a professional player he was considered the best dribbler in the game. Wooden had also been voted into the Basketball Hall of Fame, an honor shared by fewer than 20 players. He came to UCLA in 1949 after two years at Indiana State. His Bruin teams were eliminated in their opening games in NCAA tournament play in 1950, 1952 and 1956 and it was not until 1962 that they advanced to the next round. But during those years of frustration and failure Wooden was learning. He read books by theoreticians of the game, attended clinics, sought advice from coaches, and through trial and error applied those tactics that worked. When another team beat UCLA with a new offensive play or defensive alignment, he tried it himself. If it worked he incorporated it into the UCLA repertoire. Wooden, the teacher, was his own best student. By 1964 he was recognized as probably the most brilliant mentor in college basketball and was voted Coach of the Year.

Nobody ever heard John Wooden utter an expletive but he had a reputation of baiting referees without resorting to four letter words. He was not

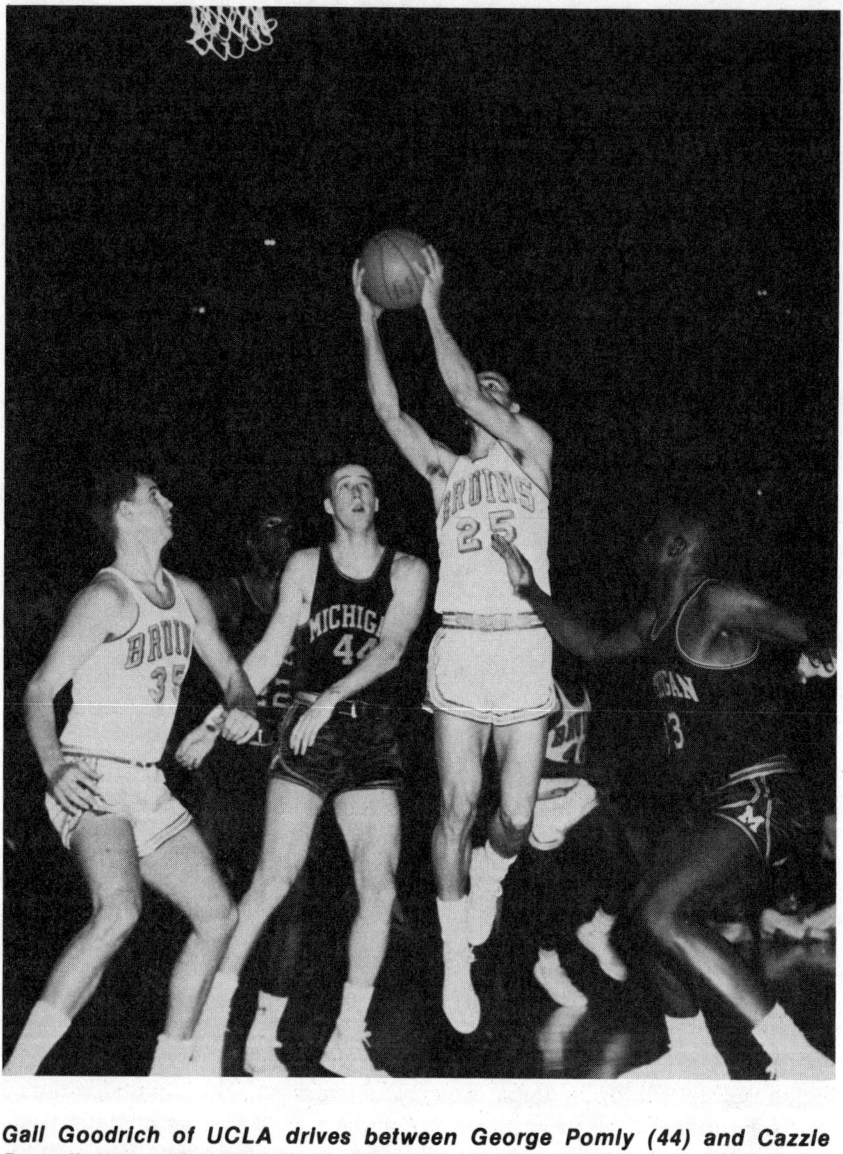

Gail Goodrich of UCLA drives between George Pomly (44) and Cazzie Russell (33) while Mike Lynn (35) gets ready to block out. UCLA beat Michigan 91-80 in the 1965 final to take their second consecutive title. (Norm Schindler photo)

above accusing an official of being a "homer," one who favors the home side, when playing on an opponent's court. The PCC was a referee's nightmare. They suffered abuse from coaches like Slats Gill of Oregon State, who held the record for fines assessed as a result of court altercations, and John Grayson of Washington, who once won a libel suit (later reversed) against John Lightner, a referee who had been attacked more than once by fans egged on by West Coast coaches. In this company of carpers, John Wooden was well able to hold his own.

By 1962, though, Wooden was definitely mellowing. Whereas he had formerly imposed silence on his players during team meals, he now relaxed his rules enough to allow the high spirited Bruins to express themselves verbally. The result was finer individual efforts without endangering team cohesiveness and a happier group of players.

The most happy-go-lucky member of the squad was Walt Hazzard, who had graduated from the same Philadelphia high school that had produced Wilt Chamberlain and Wayne Hightower. Walt was one of the most unselfish players in the game. He would come dribbling downcourt and, heading straight for the basket would, if his path was blocked, unleash a perfect pass to an open teammate. At first his passes, often emerging from between his legs or behind his back, would bounce off the unsuspecting receiver who expected Hazzard to shoot himself. Later when the players got used to him, Hazzard's passes found their targets and he piled up an impressive number of assists. With his fancy dribbling and passing, Hazzard was at first accused of showboating. He teamed with Gail Goodrich to complete one of the fastest backcourts in the country.

The 1964 Bruins were not heavily recruited. They just sort of gravitated to the UCLA campus, more it seemed for its ambience than its basketball tradition. They were a totally disparate group, yet together they performed magic. Coming from such different backgrounds it was remarkable how well they blended.

Hazzard was from an urban ghetto in Philadelphia. Kenny Washington, (who was invited to UCLA because Hazzard had told Wooden he was 6′5″ and weighed 230 lbs when in reality he was three inches shorter and sixty pounds lighter) came from rural South Carolina. A shy, slightly withdrawn young man, his cross country bus ride to Southern California left him overwhelmed and culture shocked. Jack Hirsch, a 6′3″ forward who could not shoot, had his Jewish roots in New York. Hirsch did not take the game very seriously, goofing off in practice and referring to Wooden by an overly familiar "J.W." Yet Hirsch could play defense. "He could take anything he wanted away from you," said Washington years later. "He played so you couldn't have your habits."

There was also Goodrich, the resident Californian and Fred Slaughter from Kansas City. Hazzard, Washington and Slaughter were black , Hirsch, Goodrich and Keith Erickson were white. Hazzard, Hirsch and Washington were Easterners, while most of the rest were from the West Coast with

Slaughter in between. Washington, Erickson and Doug McIntosh came from small towns, the others from metropolitan centers. There was a delicate balance on the team and with the Wizard of Westwood orchestrating this unzippered, footloose crew, the results were devastating.

Nobody picked the Bruins to finish in the top twenty in 1964 most probably because their tallest player was only 6′5″. But they made up for their lack of height with blazing speed, quickness and good team defense. Though they were the shortest team in the Big Six (Washington State was admitted as the sixth team), they led the conference in rebounding. On defense Wooden installed the zone press which pressured opponents in the backcourt before they had time to bring the ball over the center line and set up. This constant pressure on the ball handler was UCLA's most potent weapon and many teams fell apart in the face of the Bruins' relentless pursuit. In a game against Washington State, UCLA was ahead by only 15-14 when they switched to a zone press. By half time the Cougars had become completely unraveled and UCLA led 61-28. The team's height liability and the strategy employed by Wooden demanded unselfish teamwork and great stamina. The Bruins were not lacking in either.

UCLA surprised the experts by winning all their regular season games. They scored over 100 points five times. Their closest game was a 58-56 victory over California. They also beat tournament bound Creighton, Michigan and Kansas State and took the Los Angeles Classic during the Christmas recess.

The only school given a chance to beat them was Oregon State (25-3), winner of the Far West Classic. The secret in beating the Beavers was to clamp a lid on Mel Counts, a tall order at best. In their three losses Oregon State was held to 45, 53 and 55 points, their lowest point productions of the season. So if a team could hold the Beavers to fewer than 60 points it had an excellent chance of winning. Seattle (20-5), the most penalized team in the nation, was not able to do this and lost to the Beavers twice. Not surprisingly, given the war that raged between the referees and the coaches, five of the top six foul-smitten teams came from the West Coast.

Utah State (20-5), another at-large selection, had won 17 straight at mid-season. The Aggies' credentials were enhanced when they flew around the country to play intersectional rivals, thereby giving them national exposure. San Francisco (22-4) also took an extended trip, this one to the South, and came away with three early season losses. Thereafter the Dons won 18 in a row.

Normally a fine defensive team, the Dons dropped their guard twice, giving up 95 points to Miami and 97 to Oklahoma City. It was the most points ever allowed by a San Francisco team.

Arizona State (16-10) finished in a tie with New Mexico in the WAC. Though the latter had a better record, Arizona State was selected to go to the NCAA tourney while the Lobos went to the NIT where they were runners up. Arizona State won their first two but then lost four in a row. Their record continued to deteriorate until it reached 6-9 when the Sun Devils pulled themselves together and won 10 of their last 11.

In a replay of the previous year's first round overtime thriller, but with the outcome reversed, Utah State, powered by Wayne Estes' 38 points, nipped Arizona State 92-90. Caldwell and Art Becker paced the losers.

Another rematch, that between Seattle and Oregon State, was the evening's feature at Eugene, Oregon. The Beavers had replaced Idaho State as Seattle's perennial first round opponent. This was their third meeting in as many years and Seattle had yet to win a postseason game from the Beavers. Slats Gill badly wanted this game. He was due to retire at the end of the tournament after 36 years as coach at Oregon State. He had 599 victories to his credit and if he collected his 600th, it would mean going back to familiar Gill Auditorium in Corvallis to host the Far West regional semifinals and final.

As usual between such intense rivals it was an extremely physical game. The action seemed to be focused at the foul line which the players visited frequently. Five men fouled out of the game and as a result, they shot a near record 70 free throws. Seattle scored only 16 field goals while parking almost twice as many fouls.

The Chieftains' task was to contain Counts. Initially, too many Chiefs tried to guard the monumental center. Seattle changed tactics after Counts picked up his third foul in the first half and his fourth after only five minutes of the second. Still he managed to score 27 without fouling out; no other Beaver reached double figures.

Seattle was hitting less than 30 percent of their shots. They led briefly at 41-39 but then fell behind by ten and prospects looked grim when they still trailed 57-49 with only 3:25 left. But a sizzling rally in the next 69 seconds powered Seattle into the lead as they caromed nine points through the net.

On the next series Counts took a shot and missed. The Chieftains recovered and froze the ball for two minutes until Greg Vermillion sealed the victory with a pair of charity tosses, only twelve seconds remaining. The 61-57 verdict was sweet revenge for the victors. It was Gill's last game and he never did get victory number 600.

San Francisco won their 19th in a row by playing their usual outstanding defense against Utah State. They were sparked by Ollie Johnson's 26 points. Only three players were listed in the scoring column for the Aggies—Wayne Estes, Leroy Walker and Troy Collier. The rest were zipped.

UCLA seemed tired and disorganized. They committed 18 turnovers, 50 percent more than Seattle. Nevertheless they were leading 48-39 at the half and seemed to have the situation under control. Seattle whittled away at UCLA's lead and closed to within five only to see the Bruins flush eight points through the hoop in a minute and a half. The Chieftains surged again and took a 75-73 lead on a base line jumper by Rich Turney.

The teams played on even terms for several minutes until Hazzard and

Goodrich, the Bruin guards, shucked off their lethargy and became twin streaks blazing downcourt. A three point play by Kenny Washington, a bucket by Goodrich and a layup by Jack Hirsch settled the issue as UCLA advanced 95-90.

It was a brutally hard nosed affair. Six men fouled out and a total of 84 free throws were attempted. The game was significant for another reason, though nobody at the time could foresee that. It was the first win in what was to become a 38 game tournament win streak for the Bruins. Not until 1974 would they lose a postseason game.

The following night the odds that UCLA's streak would reach even two were not very high when they trailed San Francisco by 12 in the first half. In the first ten minutes their shooting was frigid as they sank just a pair of field goals. Towards the end of the half the Bruins thawed considerably, though they still lagged by eight at the buzzer. Following the intermission the combination of Goodrich and Hazzard again powered the Bruins into a 45-44 lead. UCLA dominated the rest of the game and won 76-72. A sparkling performance by Hazzard, who scored 14 points in as many minutes, sealed the victory.

East:

Fourth ranked Duke (23-4) was the class of the East. They beat Navy 121-63 and manhandled a good North Carolina squad, upending them by 35 points. They split a pair with the co-champions of the Big 10, sinking Ohio State but capsizing under a strong Michigan attack. By tourney time they had won 16 of their last 17 and were eager to improve on their previous year's third place finish. To help remind them of their goal the Blue Devils would play "Going to Kansas City," the site of the championship round, on their record player in the locker room before every game.

Princeton (19-7) was given an outside chance to make the Final Four if Bill Bradley, their All American, and fourth highest scorer in the country, could get some help from his mates. At times they contributed—during the Tigers 100-46 smashing of Dartmouth for instance—but mostly Princeton's was a one man show.

Bradley was such an attraction that his team spent the holidays visiting three different Christmas tournaments.

Villanova (21-3) and Temple (17-7) represented Philadelphia, which always seemed to have at least one team in the tournament. The city was known for its well-coached teams. There had been Ken Loeffler at LaSalle, Harry Litwak at Temple and Jack Ramsey at St. Josephs; now Villanova had young Jack Kraft, who had won his first 12 games as a varsity coach. By the end of 1964 his teams had compiled a 64-21 record.

Villanova was led by guard Bill Melchionni and Wally Jones, another graduate of Overbrook High School where he had teamed with Walt Hazzard. The Wildcats' victims included Temple and Princeton. They also walloped a pair of New Jersey teams—St. Peters by 83-42 and Seton Hall by 109-73.

St. Francis of New York and St. Francis of Pennsylvania both felt the Wildcats' claws—the first beaten 84-48 and the latter 113-59. This was ample reason for ranking Villanova number seven. In addition they had won the Holiday Festival.

Temple, probably the best coached team next to UCLA, was the least penalized squad in the country—and by a wide margin. Harry Litwak's boys were always well-disciplined.

Connecticut (14-10) was a strong defensive team. They had lost by a point to Rhode Island in the final game of the regular season, creating a tie between the teams for the Yankee Conference lead. In a playoff the Huskies had reversed that decision by making a microscopic improvement and edging Rhode Island 61-60. However, outside their conference Connecticut's record was a sorry 6 and 8. Providence (20-5) was making its first tournament appearance, though not the first for Joe Mullaney, its coach. He had played for Holy Cross when it won its championship in 1947.

The most surprising team was VMI (12-11), the first school from Virginia to participate in the tournament. It had finished fourth in the Southern Conference. Davidson (22-4) finished first but were eliminated by the Kaydets (82-81) in the semifinal of the playoff to determine the conference representative. During the regular season Davidson had clobbered VMI 129-91 and 70-58. However, the Southern Conference rule prevailed and a team whose victories exceeded its losses only on the last day of the season went to Philadelphia and tenth ranked Davidson went back to their classrooms.

It first looked as if the spell would last for at least another game but the ball turned into a virtual pumpkin for VMI in the second half of its opening round game with Princeton at the Palestra. The Tigers came up a point short at the half and were still trailing as the second period matured until Bob Haarlow's driving lay-in off a pass by Bill Bradley. Five more points gave the Tigers a 46-40 lead and a little later a 13 to 1 spurt assured them of the victory. Bradley's consistent play was reflected in the statistics as he accounted for 17 points in each half. He was also credited with eight assists and would have had many more if the other Tigers had been able to score off the many passes he fed them. Nonetheless Princeton broke out in the second half and outscored VMI by 27 points on 60 percent floor shooting, to win 86-60.

Connecticut and Temple played a slow, deliberate game, passing the ball around, waiting for the right opportunity. The problem was the Huskies often threw the ball away before the right opportunity presented itself. Connecticut had the taller team but the guards could not work the ball in close to them. Eventually they gave up and started shooting from long range. When they began hitting consistently, the Owls were forced to come out and try to block. This opened some lanes and the Huskies were able to get inside more often. Taking charge in the second half, the Huskies disappointed the Philadelphia fans by beating Temple 53-48.

There was some consolation for the local loyalists when Villanova upended Providence 77-66. Wally Jones wound his way through the Friars' defense to spark the Villanova offense.

The next stop for the winners was Raleigh where Duke awaited Villanova and Connecticut was to play Princeton. Connecticut again slowed the action down and a war of nerves ensued. Neither side could pull away as each took turns leading. No more than four points separated them throughout the contest. The taller Huskies, realizing Bradley was the Tigers' only threat, surrounded him with a wall of human redwoods so he seldom saw the ball. When he did, he was hounded and as a result drew a number of fouls. The extent to which Connecticut concentrated on Bradley and ignored his teammates was reflected in the free throw statistics. He was the only Princeton player to go to the foul line! With 73 seconds left in the game Bradley sank a 15 foot line-drive one-hander to tie the score for the last time at 50-50. Thirty seconds later Dom Perno gave Connecticut the lead again as he converted two free throws. Princeton worked the ball to Bradley but, with the clock showing only ten seconds, Perno came up behind the Tiger star and stole the ball to clinch the win 52-50. It was the furthest advance for a Yankee Conference team in the tournament and only their third postseason victory in the last 14 years.

Duke had a much easier time against Villanova. All American Mullins put on the one man show that Connecticut had denied Bradley as he accounted for half of Duke's scoring with 43 points. Two of those came from midcourt as the first half buzzer sounded, giving the Blue Devils a 49-33 lead. Mullins' quickness enabled him to maneuver free of the defense for an open shot. He also stole the ball six times from the nervous Wildcats. Shooting sensationally, Mullins was credited with 28 points during the first twenty minutes. By the end of the game he had hit his target 19 times in 28 tries. In the second half Villanova chipped away at Duke's lead and closed to within six. But with ten minutes to go Villanova's 6′7″ Jim Washington fouled out leaving two 6′10″ giants, Hack Tison and Jim Buckley of the Blue Devils, in control of the boards. Duke pulled away again and won 87-73.

In the regional final Connecticut tried unsuccessfully to slow the pace. Husky coach Fred Shabel, who had been an assistant at Duke the previous year, watched as the players he had recruited ran his team into the boards. Their height advantage against earlier opponents was cancelled out by Tison and Buckley. After seven minutes the Blue Devils had sprung into a 20-6 lead with Mullins accounting for half his team's points. Duke showed no respect for the Husky zone as they accelerated around and through it like a pack of cheetahs. Mullins shot from every point of the compass in the first period, contributing 23 points to Dukes' 62-27 advantage. The second half was not much pleasanter for Connecticut. Unstoppable, the blue Devils won 101-54 and made reservations for Kansas City.

Mideast:

In 1963 there was a slight drop in scoring over the previous year due to tighter defenses. In 1964, however, scoring was up again by almost ten points as field goal accuracy increased and coaches learned methods of overcoming zone presses. Seventeen teams averaged over 85 points per game; only two had reached that mark in 1963. Seven players averaged over 30 points per game, a level not achieved the previous year.

Thus it was that Loyola (Ill) which led the country in scoring in 1963 was only fifth a year later with an almost identical average of 91.3 points. The Ramblers (20-5) had to find a replacement for Jerry Harkness, who had graduated, but the rest of the team remained intact. To compensate for the loss of his star, feisty Coach Ireland modified his defense by substituting a half court press for his usual full zone. Nine times Loyola hit triple digits and fifteen times they recorded 90 points or more. They started the season under a full head of steam, averaging 104 points over the first five games. Later they swept past Morehead State 127-85 and Marshall 117-63.

Third ranked Kentucky (21-4) was back in the tournament after a one year lapse. The Wildcats featured versatile Cotton Nash, an All American who played guard, forward and center, switching positions depending on the need. The Wildcats won two Christmas tournaments—their own Kentucky Invitational and the Sugar Bowl. They also beat Duke, as well as 20 of their first 22 opponents. They ranked high offensively, posting scores of 100, 101, 102, 103, 104, 105, 107 and 108 points. Wide open basketball was their style but they could also handle a control type offense, beating Tennessee 42-38. Adolph Rupp was mellowing. He was nowhere near as rigid as he used to be. He was even willing at times to experiment from the tried and true he had been teaching for thirty years. On some occasions he even tried that heresy—the zone defense.

For the second year in a row Ohio State tied for the Big 10 championship, this time with Michigan. The Buckeyes missed the opportunity to take the crown outright by losing to the Wolverines 81-80 in their last game, a situation reminiscent of their final game the previous year against Indiana. Big 10 rules sent the Wolverines (20-4), who were in any case considered the second best team in the nation, to the tournament. Michigan had started strongly, winning 15 of their first 16 before hitting a few snags. The prime reason for the Wolverine's success was rookie guard Cazzie Russell, an All American selection at year end. Russell had graduated from Chicago's Carver High School where he led his school to the City Championship during his senior year. Russell's hero was Oscar Robertson, whom he patterned himself after. He almost enrolled at the University of Cincinnati before deciding to come to Ann Arbor.

Murray State (16-8), after losing five of six and splitting their first 14, reversed their fortunes and won nine of their last ten to take the Ohio Valley. Louisville (15-10), playing their last season as an independent before joining the MVC, was selected as an at-large entry. Ohio University (19-5) won the Mid American and split two with Louisville, taking the finale from the Cardinals.

The two teams met again, for the third time, in an opening round match at Evanston. The Cardinals, who led by five at the intermission, continued their dominance in the second half. It was uphill all the way for the Bobcats and the only thing that kept them in the game was their frequent trips to the foul line. However, it was a free throw by Louisville's Judd Rothman that tied the game 65-65 and sent it into overtime. Ohio wasted little time and sped to a 69-65 advantage in the opening minute of the second session though Louisville tied it once more. As the final seconds ticked away Jerry Jackson and Paul Storey dumped the final free throws through the mesh to give the Bobcats a 71-69 victory.

For the second year in a row Loyola scored over a hundred points against an Ohio Valley team in the first round though this time the game was much closer. The Thoroughbreds of Murray State stampeded to a 21-8 lead. But in the next two minutes the Ramblers caught fire and scored 15 rapid-fire points. They kept pouring it on and spun off to a 101-91 victory. All five Rambler starters scored in double figures.

The Mideast regional continued in Minneapolis where less than 10,000 fans showed up for the semifinals, considerably fewer than had attended the high school state championship. Ohio streaked to a 40-24 advantage over Kentucky at half time and maintained that lead to score the upset of the tourney, 85-69. The Bobcats' clinging defense held Kentucky in check from start to finish. Nash, who had earlier broken Alex Groza's record to become the school career scoring leader, was held to one basket in the first half. He finished with just ten points, considerably below his average.

Michigan, making its first tournament appearance in 13 years, was as tight as a new shoe as they tipped off against the defending champions. Loyola broke away to an early lead but was soon overhauled. Hunter of the Ramblers and Bill Buntin of the Wolverines provided the offensive charge as the sides remained closely linked until the end. Michigan, leading 82-80 with twelve seconds remaining, was trying to wait out the clock when Loyola's Jim Coleman stole the ball and headed downcourt. A slight hesitation resulted in a travelling violation and Michigan, aided by a pair of free throws by Bob Cantrell, won 84-80.

Attempting to accomplish what their fellow Buckeyes had failed to do—beat Michigan—the Bobcats engaged the Wolverines in a bruising, defensive struggle. The game was so physical that Coach Dave Strack of Michigan shuffled his players in and out of the game to keep them fresh. The outcome was decided under the boards where 225 lb., 6′4″ Don Hilt of Ohio and 250 lb. Buntin used their bulk to try to establish position. Muscle overcame finesse and the bigger Wolverines prevailed 69-57.

Midwest:

In the Midwest, Cincinnati's six year reign over the MVC came to an end. Wichita (21-5) tied Drake for the conference championship, then beat them in a playoff. It was Wichita's first NCAA tournament, an honor that should have come sooner and would have had they been playing in a less competitive conference. (Not a single school, not even last place North Texas State with a 7-17 mark, had a losing record against non-conference foes.) The Shockers' moment of truth came late in February. After losing to Bradley by two and Drake by one, they faced Cincinnati and reversed the tide by gaining a one point decision.

On the other hand, Texas A and M (18-6) came from a weak conference. Though 13-1 in conference standings, they split their ten games with non-conference opponents. Oklahoma City (15-10) and Texas Western (23-2) were at-large selections. The latter was ranked ninth but played a relatively easy schedule. They lost to Washington in the second game of the season and later succumbed to Arizona State by two points. The Miners were coached by Don Haskins, who had played at Oklahoma A and M under Hank Iba. This accounted for their grudging defense, second tightest in the country. Another blessing was Jim Barnes, a 29 point scorer and one of the top rebounders of the year.

Even better than Barnes, though, was Paul Silas of Creighton (21-5), another at-large entry. Silas had compiled the second best career rebounding mark ever recorded. He was only the fourth man to average more than 20 points and 20 rebounds over a varsity career, joining Walter Dukes, Bill Russell and Elgin Baylor in that select circle. Silas snatched more balls from the boards in each of his three seasons than anybody else. Kansas State (20-5) rounded out the field.

The first round of the regional was played in Dallas, where two Texas and two non-Texas teams were paired. Texas Western, down by three at the half, rallied behind Barnes' 24 second period points to defeat Texas A and M 68-62. Barnes collected 42 in all but the difference, as in so many tourney games that year, came at the foul line where the Miners had more than twice as many opportunities as the Aggies.

Creighton and Oklahoma City had split a pair of regular season games, neither of which were very close. The rubber match fit that pattern, too. Creighton tripped the Chiefs 89-78 as Silas set an arena record with 27 rebounds and Elton McGriff, normally a seven point scorer, fired 25 for the Bluejays.

Wichita, hosting the regional and playing in their first tournament game, appeared nervous at first, but encouraged by their fans, they swooped to a 15 point lead. Creighton refused to quit and came back in the second half to trail by just three. Wichita Coach Ralph Miller looked over his bench and sent Larry Nosich, a reserve forward who had scored just 18 points all year, into the game. It was an inspired choice because Nosich immediately responded by scoring six points in a row. The momentum created by that splurge lifted Wichita to an 84-68 win.

A torpidly paced first half in which the teams combined to score an anemic 44 points opened the co-feature. Both sides thawed somewhat in the second half. Kansas State's 1-3-1 zone limited Jim Barnes to just four points, 25 below his norm, and nine rebounds as the Wildcats disposed of Texas Western 64-60. Again free throws made the difference; Kansas State made twice as many trips to the free throw line as the Miners.

The Wildcats used the same zone against the Shockers in the regional final. Wichita, at the short end of a 46-33 first half score, blitzed for 20 points in the first five minutes of the second period with Dave Stallworth, Wichita's All American, sparking the comeback. The Shockers were set to take the lead when the Wildcats regrouped and pulled away again. Wichita's famous pressing defense could not contain Kansas State's fast break. The speedy Wildcats simply moved the ball downcourt and set up quickly, depriving the press of its effectiveness. With Willie Murrell pointing the way with 28 the Wildcats celebrated a 94-86 victory and made reservations in Kansas City. worth's 37 points highlighted a brilliant performance in a losing cause.

Final Four:

Just as nobody picked the Bruins to be Number One before the season, hardly any of the experts picked them to emerge champions at Kansas City. Most tagged either Michigan or Duke in the favorite's role. The Wolverines were not only tall, but meaty too. With guard Cazzie Russell contributing to the already muscular front court of Larry Tregoning, Oliver Darden and Bill Buntin, they could overpower any opponent. Russell would often drive for the baseline, giving Michigan in effect a third forward. No doubt the strongest team in the Final Four, Michigan lacked only speed and ball handling agility. Duke was determined to exploit this vulnerability.

The Blue Devils had been stung by an earlier 16 point loss to Michigan. In that game Buntin had outrebounded Buckley 18-2. The Blue Devils, who had played a somewhat ineffective zone during their first encounter, opened with a man-to-man and the switch paid off. After spotting Michigan an early lead, Duke cranked up their fast break which they seemed able to spring loose a lot faster off their new defense. By the end of the half they were comfortably in front. Though not as strong as the Wolverines, the Blue Devils matched up well in height and grabbed most of the rebounds, especially off the offensive boards where Buckley outhustled Buntin. Buckley had 25 points to go with his 14 rebounds, thereby atoning for his ineffectiveness in the previous loss to Michigan. Despite playing on a gimpy ankle which required a pain killing shot before the tipoff, Russell's shooting eye was as good as ever and he bombed for 31 points. But Duke's ability to set the tempo with an effective fast break was the deciding factor in their 91-80 victory.

UCLA and Kansas State traded baskets during much of the first period which ended with the Bruins ahead 43-41. Aside from Hazzard, who seemed capable of dribbling through a brick wall, the Bruins had a hard time penetrating their opponents' pressing 1-3-1 zone. Poor foul shooting by the Wildcats, who canned fewer than half their shots, kept them from taking command. Even so they were ahead 75-70 late in the game. A mini-surge by the Bruins tied the count. Kansas State called what in hindsight was an injudicious time out. Suddenly, to the accompaniment of a rafter rattling welcome,the UCLA cheerleaders, who had been delayed in flight by bad weather, rushed onto the court, stripping their street clothes off as they came. It was one of the most dramatic entrances ever witnessed in the tournament and the turning point of the game. The effect on the Bruins was immediate. Six unanswered points followed and UCLA, which had been down by five just three minutes earlier, took a six point lead. The cheerleaders leaped and tumbled, the fans screamed and the players, their adrenalin pumping, held on to win 90-84. Erickson paced the Bruins with 28 while Murrell was one point better for the losers.

The final featured the two fastest quintets in the tournament if not the country. The Blue Devils had a distinct edge in height with Tison and Buckley able to see right over the top of the tallest Bruin. For the first twelve minutes the advantage seesawed from one side to the other. The score was tied for the eighth time at 27-27 when Buckley put Duke ahead with a free throw. Two more by the tall forward established the high water mark for the Blue Devils.

Suddenly UCLA exploded for 16 points in a row in just two and a half minutes of brilliant basketball, to led 43-30. The sizzling Bruins just blew the Demons away. With their cheerleaders now established at courtside and their fans in full cry, they went into hyperdrive. Hazzard, spearheading the awesome zone press which pinned their opponents in the backcourt, was the catalyst who launched the Bruins into orbit. He stole the ball several times, dribbled around his guard, set up plays, fed his teammates and in general so shocked the normally steady Devils that they committed 29 turnovers. Hazzard only collected 11 points himself but he was responsible for many of Goodrich's 27 and the 26 points scored by supersub Kenny Washington, who came in for Erickson.

Center Jack Hirsch played the high post thus keeping Buckley away from the basket. All the Bruins helped out by playing outstanding team defense. They collapsed around the basket, blocked out, established position and hauled down eight more rebounds than Duke. Washington alone grabbed 12 boards which was two more than both of Duke's giants retrieved between them. UCLA's 98-83 triumph was their first national championship. It was also their thirtieth win in an undefeated season. The 98 points scored by UCLA still stands as the most in a final round. It was a happy moment for Coach of the Year Wooden but the happiest Bruin of all was Walt Hazzard who, in his final game as a collegian, was recognized as the MVP of the tournament.

1965

Mideast:

In 1965 despite a better record than Michigan, the Bruins were relegated to number two by both wire services in the final polls. The number one Wolverines (21-3) had lost two one point decisions—to Nebraska which ended the season with just ten wins, and to St. Johns in the final of the Holiday Festival in New York. They also bowed to Ohio State in the final game of the year though they had earlier trounced the Buckeyes 100-61. Cazzie Russell, now a junior, was an All American again and led the high scoring Wolverines with a 25 point per game average. Most of the starters, who averaged 6′5″ and 200 lbs., were hefty enough to have made the football team. Michigan, long a gridiron power, was experiencing basketball euphoria for the first time. In 1963 they had sold eleven season tickets for the roundball game; by 1965, 600 were snapped up.

Michigan was a scoring machine. They had been held to less than 80 only in the losses to St. Johns and Nebraska. Normally Russell and Buntin led the point parade (accounting for 21 of the final 29 points in a narrow victory over Wichita, number one at the time) while the rest of the team outmuscled the opposition for the ball. But the Wolverines lacked a quarterback, a man who could impose some discipline on their helter-skelter offense. The team also lacked a killer instinct. They often lost leads and had to hustle to recover. This overconfidence was especially true against weaker opponents. They had to hustle late in the game to overcome deficits and allowed huge leads to melt away as in the loss to St. Johns.

Fifth ranked Vanderbilt (23-3) beat Kentucky twice and ended the season by trouncing LSU 106-69. They also claimed the Sugar Bowl trophy, dismantling Louisville in the final 80-47. The SEC was no longer Adolph Rupp's fief. His Wildcats finished fifth with a 15-10 record, adequate by most standards but their worst in 38 years. Eastern Kentucky (19-5) was the state's only representative. Ohio University won the Mid-American again with a 19-6 record after subduing co-champion Miami in a playoff.

DePaul (16-8) and Dayton (21-5) were the at-large selections. DePaul had an excellent record until they lost five of their last seven, including two to a mediocre Notre Dame team. Dayton, having finally won the NIT and anxious to try the NCAA tournament, was forced to sit on the sidelines in 1963 and 1964 when the NCAA placed them on probation for the usual recruiting violations. Now the Flyers, who had often passed up the NCAA tournament for a trip to New York, were anxious to add a national championship to their trophy case. Dayton's schedule was not difficult but they did sweep three Loyolas, beating the schools located in Illinois, Louisiana and California. The Flyers were playing their first season under Don Donoher, who had replaced the late Tom Blackburn for whom he starred in the early Fifties.

It was a close first half between Dayton and Ohio, in one Mideast regional opening round match. With five minutes remaining, the Bobcats, ahead 57-52, went into a stall to protect their lead. The strategy misfired as the Flyers, sparked by 6′11″ Henry Finkel, caught their opponents as time expired. It was Bob Sullivan's field goal and Bill Cassidy's two free throws in the last 34 seconds that ultimately gave Dayton a 66-65 victory, but it was Finkel's 27 points that earlier kept the Flyers in the game.

The DePaul - Eastern Kentucky contest (if it could be called such) was a yawner by comparison. Though Eastern Kentucky managed to stay within hailing distance of the Blue Demons in the initial period, they lost sight of them in the final 20 minutes. The game ended with DePaul on top 99-52, outscoring the Maroons 56-19 in the final 20 minutes. For the third successive year the Ohio Valley representative had been humiliated in the first round.

Dayton found itself outclassed against Michigan when the Wolverines' strength nullified the taller but leaner Dayton center. Finkel, the second best shooter in the country with a 65 percent average, was manhandled by the beefier Wolverines. They muscled him away from the basket and harried him throughout. With their best scorer neutralized the Flyers were unable to generate much offense. After taking a 17 point lead into the locker room, Michigan played their reserves most of the second half and still won handily 98-71. For once the Wolverines were concentrating.

The co-feature at Lexington was a lot closer. DePaul, waging an uphill battle, came back to tie their game with Vanderbilt on a ten foot jump shot by Jim Murphy with 12 seconds remaining. However, the Commodores rallied in overtime to win 83-78.

The regional final was just as close. Michigan lost their concentration and as a consequence found themselves in a fight for survival. The Wolverines were outrebounded by Vanderbilt and when faced with opportunities at the line could cash in on only half of them. Behind by a point at the mid-mark, Michigan let the game slip further away in the second half. Although he had to play the entire second half with four fouls, Clyde Lee's 28 points and 20 rebounds provided most of the impetus for the Commodores. It was concentration time for the Wolverines and they responded. With seven minutes remaining Cazzie Russell, who had not been a factor until now, fired five baskets in as many minutes, including a jumper that put Michigan in front 81-80. Ninety seconds later the game was over and Michigan had advanced to the Final Four, 87-85. Russell and Buntin paced the winners with 26 points a piece.

East:

Never had the East regional seen such fine teams. The Northeast and the Mid Atlantic states were loaded with talent. Not all the best schools made it to the regional. Two that did not were seventh ranked Davidson and ninth ranked Duke, thanks to the fact that both schools played in the only two conferences which held postseason tournaments. For the second year in a row Davidson, which had lost only one game during the regular season, finished first in the Southern Conference but lost in the league playoff. West Virginia finished fourth. Their 14-14 record included two lopsided losses to Davidson but in the conference semifinals they snapped Davidson's 23 game win streak 74-72. West Virginia then beat William and Mary in double overtime in the finals to qualify for a trip to a NCAA regional. Anyone who would have predicted at midseason that the Mountaineers would play in the tournament risked ridicule. West Virginia staggered to four victories in their final 15 games and suffered through six losses in a row before exploding in their finale against Virginia Tech, 127-73. This massacre, which avenged an earlier embarassment, gave them a shot in the arm and the confidence to charge through the conference playoffs undefeated.

An almost identical situation developed in the ACC. Runner-up North Carolina State (20-4) under Coach Press Maravich defeated first place Duke in the playoff final although the Blue Devils had twice beaten the Wolfpack earlier in the schedule. So overpowering was the ACC, the only teams the Wolfpack lost to were conference rivals from the state of North Carolina.

Connecticut (23-2) took the Yankee Conference, as usual, and led the country in margin of victory. As usual, too, the Huskies victimized other New England teams in their conference. They smashed Vermont by 45 and 47 points, Maine by 36 and New Hampshire by 48. Worst of all was a drubbing of American University by 55 points. Connecticut's dominance was attributable to their superior rebounding, led by Toby Kimball, who owned the boards and shot 57 percent besides. The Huskies lost only to Virginia and Holy Cross.

Penn State (20-3) was one of three at-large schools in the regional. An opening game loss to Maryland by a point was taken in stride, but a 121-88 humiliation at the hands of Duke stung. The Nittany Lions lashed back in their next outing, squashing Carnegie Tech 69-36. They sailed through the remainder of their schedule in a breeze.

St. Josephs (25-1) and Providence (22-1) were ranked third and fourth. Providence was the only team to beat the Hawks while another Philadelphia school, Villanova, spoiled Providence's chance for an undefeated season. Friar coach Mullaney had averaged 20 wins per year over the last 11 seasons and his teams had triumphed on almost three out of every four court appearances. Providence lost four starters from 1964 and most analysts expected this to be a rebuilding year. For Mullaney there was no such thing. Structuring his team around 6′3″ sophomore Jim Walker, he proceeded to win his first 19 games with a squad of apprentices. Jim Walker was used to winning, though. He had sparked his high school team in Boston to 49 wins against only one loss in his final two years on the varsity.

St. Josephs featured a 6′4″ center, Cliff Anderson, and 6′5″ guard, Matt Guokas. Resourcefulness was obligatory in that shark tank, the Palestra. Visiting teams were dispatched as a matter of course, but when it came to intracity competition among Pennsylvania, Temple, LaSalle, Villanova and St. Josephs, the fans witnessed the equivalent of a World War I air aces dogfight. Such rivalries did not make it easy to achieve spotless records. Still, the Hawks beat all their Philadelphia opponents as well as handing Davidson their only loss prior to their upset in the Southern Conference playoff. They also conquered MVC champion Wichita.

A few miles from Philadelphia, Princeton (19-5) was making headlines too, primarily because of repeat All American, Bill Bradley, now a senior. Bradley was tops in free throw percentage and failed to lead the country in free throws scored for the third year in a row only because Rick Barry of Miami camped at the foul line an average of 23 times a game. Still, Bradley drew a disproportionate number of fouls on his team. If one could stop Bradley one would almost certainly beat Princeton, was a reasonable assumption. Even drawing that much defensive attention he still ranked third in scoring.

The Tigers, though not in the top ten, were by the end of the season a much improved team and highly underrated. They had lost four of their five games by two points or fewer and were on a ten game roll at season's end. What Princeton lacked was support for Bradley. They had the habit of looking to him to get them out of trouble, thereby putting an inordinate amount of the burden on his shoulders. Then one day Bradley got hurt. Although he did not miss a game he was excused from practice. His teammates learned to play without him and gained enough confidence in themselves to assume more responsibility during a real game. It showed at the tail end of the schedule as Princeton won their last seven by an average of 23 points.

Earlier in the season though, Princeton without Bradley was the equivalent of a car without an ignition key. Seldom had a quintet relied so completely on one man. What Bradley meant to Princeton became vividly evident in a semifinal game during the Holiday Festival against top ranked Michigan. Princeton was given almost no chance of upsetting the Wolverines. Yet with 4:37 to play they were ahead 75-63. Then Bradley fouled out. Scoring 41 points, taking down nine rebounds and contributing four assists, he held his man to one point and was credited with several steals. Furthermore, when one of the Tiger guards was benched Bradley, normally a forward, switched to guard and brought the ball upcourt. With Bradley out of the game the Tigers collapsed like a tent in a monsoon. Michigan went on a 17-3 rip and won the game 80-78. Later, Michigan coach Dave Strack admitted to the disconsolate Bradley, "We didn't deserve that."

Six teams, all playing at the top of their game, met in the Palestra for a first round triple header. For 32 minutes Penn State's excellent zone kept Bradley in check. He had scored just twelve points, well below his norm. With the score 45-42 in favor of the Nittany Lions, Bradley found a seam in the zone and drove through for a three point play that tied matters. Another layup by Bradley created another tie at 49. A minute later Bradley knotted the count again 52-52 on a pair of free throws. When Penn State moved in front by a pair Bradley missed a shot but put in his own rebound to even the score at 54. Finally, an almost automatic pair of Bradley foul shots put Princeton ahead 58-56 with 51 seconds to go. The Tigers went on to win 60-58.

A pair of 15 game winning streaks were on the line as Connecticut and St. Josephs squared away in another first round match. The Huskies streaked from the opening tip to take a 17-6 lead. The Hawks spent five minutes trying to locate the hoop with little success but by half time they were down by only seven. It was unheard of for St. Josephs to lose at the Palestra. They tightened their defense causing Connecticut to hit a cold streak similar to the one that had numbed the Hawks. St. Josephs struggled but won 67-61 despite an excellent performance by Kimball who hauled down 29 rebounds.

Providence had little trouble with overmatched West Virginia. Using a twenty point half time lead as a springboard they vaulted over the Mountaineers 91-67.

The second round began. Princeton limited North Carolina State to 16 points in the first period and had little trouble solving the Wolfpack zone to score an easy 66-48 victory. Larry Worsley was the only State player in double figures while Bradley naturally took scoring honors with 27 points. Providence and St. Josephs had only two losses between them when they took the court in the second game. The teams were locked in an epic struggle for the second time that year when time ran out with the sides even at 61 apiece. But Providence stuffed twenty points through the cords in the overtime session and won 81-73, verifying the result of their first encounter earlier in the year.

Princeton had improved its showing every year since Bradley put on a Tiger uniform. In 1963 they lost in the opening round. The previous year they lost in the second round and now they were playing for the right to go to Portland for the championship series. Both finalists had a young starting quintet. Providence had only one experienced starter while Princeton started two sophomores, two juniors and Bradley.

Joe Mullaney assigned Jim Walker to guard Bill Bradley. Walker was not very successful and fouled out with five minutes remaining in the game. The rest of the Friars fared no better because for once Bradley played with a supporting cast that deserved star billing. Ed Hummer did not miss a shot all night, making a perfect four for four from the field as well as all five free throws while taking charge of the backboards, too. Bob Haarlow and Robinson Brown each had an outstanding night. Princeton played excellently in the first half to take a commanding 47-34 lead but the 12,653 fans in Cole Fieldhouse had seen nothing yet. In the second period Princeton unlimbered their guns and let fly with a barrage rarely seen on any basketball court. During one twelve minute stretch the Tigers did not miss a shot from floor or line. When the dust cleared Princeton had made 62 points in the half (73 percent shooting from the floor and 88 percent from the line) on the way to a 109-69 blowout victory—and this against the fourth ranked team in the country. Bradley's statistics showed he had hit 70 percent of his shots, a perfect 13 for 13 from the foul line, for a total of 41 points to go with nine assists and ten rebounds.

Midwest:

None of the schools participating in the Midwest regional were solid enough to be included in the top ten. Oklahoma State (19-6) had topped the Big Eight. They had been beaten by Southern Illinois in their opener 78-55. Such penetration of Henry Iba's forces called for a stiffening of the Aggies' defense and they held the rest of their opponents to fewer than 70 points over the next 24 games to finish second in the country defensively. Wichita's All American Dave Stallworth had graduated at midseason and Dave Bowman had failed to retain his eligibility after running into academic difficulties. The Shockers (19-7) were trying to adapt to the loss of these two outstanding tall men but few expected them to survive the opening round. Earlier in the year they overwhelmed Pittsburgh 109-58 but lately the scores had been much closer.

SMU (16-7) had tied Texas for second place in the SWC behind Texas Tech. But the Red Raiders were barred from postseason competition because they inadvertently used an ineligible player and so SMU went to the tournament.

A couple of high scoring independents rounded out the field—Notre Dame (15-11), which went over 100 points seven times, and Houston (18-8), which did it six times. The Fighting Irish hit a slump in the middle of the season when they twice lost three in a row but did respectably well at both ends of the season. In their first four games they averaged 104 points and subsequently bombed Kentucky 111-97 and Houston 110-80. No one had ever scored that many points on a Rupp team.

Houston lost four of their first half dozen but improved dramatically as the season matured. This was particularly true of their scoring output. Seldom had a team played such contrasting styles within a single season. At mid-season their scoring went from thrifty to profligate in one quick step. Early in the year they beat Auburn 50-48 and Texas A and M 59-48 while falling before North Texas State 60-48. Later they found their collective shooting eye and shattered North Texas State 117-83 (a swing of 46 points) and Trinity 139-87.

The NCAA had decided to hold the Midwest and West regional first round games in the same location. So a double header was held in Lubbock, Texas, before a mini-audience of only 4,500. Host Texas Tech had to watch from the sidelines though they might well have been able to beat all four teams. Houston, which had been victimized by Notre Dame by 30 points early in the schedule, refused to die so easily this time especially since the whole team now qualified for sharpshooters' badges. The Cougars clawed their way back from a nine point half time deficit to tie matters 88-88 in regulation. Both sides had six men in double figures. The Irish's individual totals were 18, 17, 17, 17, 16 and 13 (in a display of balanced scoring). But it was Ed Winch, shut out until then, who hoisted a pair of free throws for Houston six seconds before the end of overtime to clinch the 99-98 victory.

Neither Texas school survived the second round. Oklahoma State jammed all those fine shooters from Houston, allowing them only 22 points in the first half. At game's end only one Cougar had more than three field goals as Oklahoma State advanced 75-60. In the co-featured matchup, Wichita nipped SMU 86-81 in a rough game in which three Mustang players fouled out. Kelly Pete of the Shockers stepped into the breach left by Stallworth and plunged 31 points through the hoop.

The following evening it was Oklahoma State's turn to turn dry. Not one Aggie reached dougle figures. The Shockers started the contest with their usual bustling, fast break offense but when their advantage reached 17-7 they put on the brakes. Holding the ball for long stretches and waiting for the high percentage shot, Wichita did an excellent imitation of their opponent's normal offense. The Aggies found it difficult to disrupt the tactic they usually employed themselves. Occasionally Wichita would catch the Oklahoman's off balance and start a fast break for a quick two points. In all the Shockers took just 29 shots as they eliminated the Aggies 54-46. The slow tempo allowed Wichita, a team with a weak bench, to play without a substitute. Pete had 19 to lead Wichita again.

West:

UCLA (24-2) had no difficulty winning their conference, which had bulged to eight schools with the admission of Oregon and Oregon State. The Pac Eight was almost identical with the old PCC except for the absence of Idaho. Hazzard had graduated but Gail Goodrich filled his All American slot. UCLA had also added a brilliant sophomore, Edgar Lacey. The Bruins lost their first game to Illinois 110-83 and later fell to Iowa by five, inducing a sense of superiority in the Big Ten. However, they won the rest of their games, including the Milwaukee Invitational and Los Angeles Classic tourneys, and were undefeated in their conference.

The 1964 BYU freshman team, which had averaged 109 points per game, was incorporated into the varsity as a unit. Their output was a decisive factor in bringing home 21 victories against five losses. In one-third of their appearances, BYU passed 100 points to give them the second highest point production in the country. They beat Ohio State 112-71, Arizona State 111-102, Air Force 110-77, Creighton 109-74, Santa Clara 109-80 and Oregon 109-80. Nothing second rate about those opponents. The Cougars loved to bomb the hoop, winning 10 games by 20 points or more. One would almost have had to nail a lid on the basket to stop them. Only once were they held to fewer than 70 points. That was against Wichita and the Shockers later beat them again for good measure.

Tenth ranked San Francisco (22-4) lost only once in the WCAC. The Dons, the William Tells of the tournament, were led by Ollie Johnson who succeeded on 60 percent of his shots. Colorado State (16-7) and Oklahoma City (19-9) were the two independents in the West regional. Oklahoma City would normally have participated in the Midwest but good independents were scarce on the coast. Abe Lemons, the Chiefs' coach, was in his tenth year and still devoted to run-and-shoot basketball. A charming and witty man, Lemons was considered the Will Rogers of basketball, always good for a chuckle and an insight into the vagaries of the game. Lemons had never been given a first name, just the initials A.E. When he entered the service he was required to state his first name. So he inserted a B between his initials and became Abe. Later he was sorry he had not inserted the letter C.

As mentioned earlier the Chiefs and Colorado State completed a first round twin bill in Lubbock, Texas, which also saw Houston beating Notre Dame. Colorado State, ahead by a basket at intermission, allowed the Chiefs to run up a nine point second half lead before storming back in the flickering minutes to tie at 68-68. The Chiefs, who played the entire game without a substitution, were running out of gas. Gambling on one shot, Oklahoma City held the ball and were rewarded when high scorer Charlie Hunter hit a last second jumper from the corner to win it, 70-68. Sonny Bustion paced the Rams with 30.

Oklahoma City was not as fortunate against San Francisco. The second round game went to the Dons 91-67 as Ollie Johnson took charge and scored 35.

Surprising Brigham Young threw a scare into UCLA when they led the Bruins 30-27 in the first half. But a pair of three bucket bursts by Erickson—the first salvo coming in one 45 second span—bracketed a solo field goal by Edgar Lacey and the Bruins catapulted into a commanding lead. It was typical of them to amass points in huge gulps, blazing streaks that would cause their opponents to come apart at the joints. After the Erickson attack the Bruins had little trouble tranquillizing the dazed Cougars 100-76. Despite Erickson's brief flurry it was Goodrich's 40 points that led all scorers.

In contrast to the two laughers in the semis, the regional final was a very exciting contest with the winner in doubt until almost the end. San Francisco versus UCLA was becoming a staple in the West regional. The two California powerhouses were meeting for the fourth time. With five and a half minutes remaining, Charlie James put San Francisco ahead 83-82. Then the Bruins went to their patented zone press which shook the Dons so badly they coughed the ball up three times in less than two minutes. First Mike Lynn evened matters with a free throw; a steal by Kenny Washington and a pass to Goodrich for a layup put the Bruins ahead for good. A three point play and the Dons were licked. All this in 90 seconds. Goodrich's eight points in the last five minutes helped seal the 101-93 victory. His 30 and Erickson's 29 shared scoring honors for the Bruins while Johnson's 37 was tops for San Francisco.

Final Four:

Portland, Oregon, was the site of the Final Four. The field consisted of the two top ranked teams in the country and two decided underdogs. In contrast to the previous year few believed UCLA could be beaten. Coach Jack Gardner conceded that UCLA had its weaknesses: "Goodrich can't dribble too well with his left foot," was his sarcastic comment.

UCLA shocked Wichita 108-89, thus winning their third 100 point playoff game in a row. It was not even as close as the score. The Bruins had a 65-38 half time lead and threatened to break every offensive tournament record until Wooden mercifully substituted for his starters. Goodrich streaked for 28 points in 27 minutes while Jaime Thompson tallied 36 for the Shockers. It is doubtful even Stallworth and Bowman at their best could have made a difference.

When Princeton lost in the Holiday Festival to Michigan, their only opportunity for revenge would be in Portland. The chances were slim. No Ivy League school had gone this far since Dartmouth in 1944, but incredibly three months later here were the Tigers two wins away from the national title, with Michigan the next obstacle. In many ways the game was a replay of their first encounter. Bradley scored 13 of Princeton's first 15 points to give his team a slim lead. Princeton was still ahead 34-29 when Bradley was charged with his third personal with almost four minutes still remaining in the first half. The Tigers game began to disintegrate. By half time Michigan had drawn ahead 40-36. After the break Princeton switched from a pressing man-to-man to a zone. However, it was impossible to keep the quicker Wolverines and especially Russell and Buntin from infiltrating the zone and penetrating to the basket. On offense Princeton seldom got off more than one shot as Michigan took down almost twice the number of rebounds as the Tigers. Bradley picked up his fourth personal after only a minute of the second half and fouled out 14 minutes later with Michigan ahead by eight. It was, for Princeton rooters, a matter of dèja vu. The Tigers went into their folding act and Michigan surged to a 93-76 victory. Bradley was superb again with 29 points while Russell contributed 28 to the Michigan cause.

In the consolation match for third place Princeton dumped Wichita 118-86. It was Bradley's last game for Princeton and his mates consistently fed him the ball. The Princeton star never shone brighter as he pocketed 22 of 29 shots from the floor, hit 14 of 15 from the foul line and retrieved 17 rebounds. He could easily have scored 70 points had he not passed off often. As it was he set a new record of 58 points in one game and 177 points for the tournament. The latter record still stands. When Bill Bradley left the game, the appreciative fans gave him one of the longest and most enthusiastic standing ovations ever given a player.

The final was anticlimatic (as many UCLA finals were to be over the next ten years). Strangely, considering UCLA had one player who scored almost half its points, the Bruins played a brilliant team game. This was especially true on defense where their full court zone press hounded Michigan mercilessly. They also outrebounded the taller, huskier Wolverines and outhustled them for every loose ball.

Michigan led 20-13 when UCLA detonated another of their explosive bursts to draw even at 24. Seconds later the Bruins charged into the lead and left the Wolverines sputtering behind. It was not much of a contest as UCLA rambled 91-80, but the spectators stayed to see if any Michigan player could hold Goodrich. The answer was no. Though Darden, Buntin and Tregoning, all three at least four inches taller than he, tried guarding him they all fouled out in the attempt. There was no holding Goodrich that night. The small guard loved to dribble and he loved even more to shoot. He penetrated every defense contrived by Strack and either got free for easy close-in baskets or was fouled in the act of shooting. In all he took 20 shots from the line and successfully converted 18. Altogether Goodrich had 42 points to his credit, giving him 140 for the tournament.

The game could have gotten away from the Bruins early in the first half when Erickson injured his leg and had to sit down. But Kenny Washington replaced him and for the second time in as many title games shrugged off the pressure, and earned the title of supersub. He finished second to Goodrich with 17 points. Russell had 28 in a losing cause.

It had been a tourney of monumental scoring. Bradley deservedly won the MVP prize with a 35.4 average, though Goodrich's 35 was almost as high, the third best ever achieved in the tournament. UCLA's average of 100 points per game shattered the previous mark. The Bruins went home confident a third straight championship awaited them in twelve months. And, maybe even four or five or six as Lew Alcindor*, the most sought after high school player in the country, was about to announce his intention to enroll at UCLA.

*Now known as Kareem Abdul Jabbar.

Coach Adolph Rupp (fifth from left) of Kentucky and some of his "runts" looking dejected as the 1966 championship slips away. Texas Western scored a stunning upset 72-65.
(Lexington Herald-Leader photo)

12

MINING THE MOTHER LODE 1966

1966

Midwest:

1966 was the year UCLA did **not** win the national championship, the year Kentucky rocketed back to the top of the rankings and the year a relatively unknown school from El Paso spoiled Adolph Rupp's bid for a fifth title and put Texas on the basketball map. It was also the year urban ghettos in America exploded in a violent confrontation between blacks and whites, a confrontation that found its counterpart on a basketball court in Maryland on the night of the championship game.

Coach Don Haskins had assembled a group of brilliant young ballplayers at Texas Western*. The five starters were all black and they came from the metropolitan ghettos of America. At center was 6′8″, 240 pound Dave Lattin, a mean looking Sonny Liston type. The playmaker was 5′10″ Bobby Joe Hill, from the slums of Gary, Indiana. He was a brilliant dribbler, quick as a water beetle and unrelenting on defense, often stripping an opponent of the ball and driving in for easy layups. A pair of Willies, Cager and Worsley, were recruited from ghetto schools of New York. Worsley was only 5′6″ but made up for his lack of height by an incandescent intensity that would lift his team out of a temporary slump. Nevil Shed, Orsten Artis and Harry Fluornoy, all blacks, made up the rest of the regulars who played the greater part of every game.

---

*Now called University of Texas at El Paso (UTEP)

Haskins was a defense-minded coach. He played under Henry Iba at Oklahoma A and M, and adopted the clinging defensive tactics of his mentor. He was also an excellent recruiter, convincing some of the best high school players to commit themselves to a college without a basketball tradition in a remote corner of the country. It helped that the school's academic requirements were not very strict.

Texas Western (23-1) did not play a single school ranked in the top ten during the regular season. Scanning their schedule, one would find Eastern New Mexico, East Texas State, Pan American, Weber State and others with equally forgettable names. But after the Christmas holiday tournaments they and Kentucky remained the only major undefeated teams in the country. The Wildcats and the Miners matched victories until the final weekend of the season when each had a 23 game win streak snapped—the Wildcats by Tennessee and the Miners by Seattle, 74-72, in a West Coast game marked by notorious hometown officiating. By this time Texas Western was ranked third but was given only an outside chance of winning the national title. They had achieved their success primarily on their fine defense, fifth best in the country, and their NCAA leading rebounding.

Oklahoma City (24-4) was as point prolific as always. Twelve times they pushed into triple digits, topped by a 138-114 triumph over TCU. They climaxed their season by averaging 113 points in their final four games.

SMU (16-8) copped the Southwest Conference title but had to win their last ten to do it after a disappointing 6-8 start. Kansas (22-3) was another team that played excellently down the stretch. After Jo Jo White became eligible early in February the Jayhawks won nine games by an average of 24 points and climbed to fourth place in the polls. They had lost previously to UCLA, USC and Nebraska but avenged the last by burying the Cornhuskers 110-73. Rounding out the regional field was Cincinnati (21-5).

In a classic confrontation between defense and offense, Texas Western outscored Oklahoma City 89-74 in a first round match in Wichita. Hill had been benched because of poor playing and did not start. However, with the Chiefs ahead 21-13 Haskins inserted his playmaker and Hill responded by tallying 13 points in six minutes as the Miners went on a 20-6 tear to take a 33-27 lead. Despite the presence of Jim Ware, the country's leading rebounder, the Miners dominated the boards 55-31.

The second round was played in Lubbock, Texas, where the Miners again came from behind. This time they were down by six to Cincinnati at intermission but rebounded to tie the score after forty minutes 69-69. It was a wild game in which Shed lost his composure, threw a punch at an opponent, and was ejected. With eleven seconds remaining Cager missed a free throw that would have won the game in regulation time. But he made up for it in overtime as he accounted for six of his team's nine points. Lattin's contribution was a game high of 29 points as the Miners slipped past Cincinnati 78-76 and advanced to the regional final. In the co-feature SMU and Kansas played to a 46-46 half time standoff. The surprising Mustangs then galloped ahead and held a 58-57 lead before the Jayhawks rallied to win 76-70.

Third ranked Texas Western and fourth ranked Kansas confirmed the rankings, staging one of the closest, most exciting games ever seen in the tournament. The Miners held a narrow lead after 20 minutes and still maintained a three point edge with seconds to play. Al Lopes' three point play nullified that advantage and, for the second night in a row, Texas Western found itself in overtime. Walt Wesley, Kansas' All American, and Lattin traded buckets but much of the time was spent setting up for the perfect shot. With the score tied once more and the clock showing just seven seconds, Jo Jo White arced a 32 foot jumper through the hoop and the Jayhawk supporters erupted. Not for long. The referee disallowed the basket, pointing to the baseline where White's foot had rested for a split second before the shot. The last seconds expired without additional incident.

In the second overtime the Miners moved quickly ahead on Cager's hoop and free throws by Hill, Shed and Artis. Kansas rallied as Lopes expoded for three field goals and a foul, but Cager, who thrived in pressure situations, once again produced the winning basket as Texas Western nipped Kansas 81-80 for their second extra-period victory in as many nights. Despite their first two wins over two top ten teams the Miners were not given much chance in the championship round, experts citing their ragged play and lack of finesse as the reason.

Mideast:

To everyone's surprise, including Adolph Rupp's, Kentucky (24-1) had an outstanding season. The previous year had been Rupp's worst in 35 years of coaching. The Wildcats had finished fifth in their conference. Now, with almost the same members returning, they were acclaimed the team of the year. The talent was there: Larry Conley from Ashland, Kentucky, Pat Riley from Schenectady, N.Y., and Louis Dampier, an All American from Indianapolis. What the Wildcats lacked was height. They were aptly but affectionately called Rupp's Runts since their tallest starter, center Thad Jaracz, was only 6′5″.

The team's strength was its cohesiveness. The players really liked each other, a fact reflected in their unselfish play on the court. They were looser and under less discipline than any of Rupp's previous teams. The Baron had mellowed and the affection for each other that enveloped the players included their coach, too. He had always commanded respect but rarely affection and he responded by joking with his players, occasionally asking one of them for advice. Rupp disliked and distrusted the zone. But with so many teams using it and with his squad's lack of height, he reluctantly began experimenting with a 1-3-1, though he never admitted that it was in fact a zone.

Despite their success, the Wildcat's road to the Final Four was a minefield of potential disaster. There were no patsies in the Mideast regional. Western Kentucky (23-2) had lost only to Dayton and Vanderbilt. They were led by Clem Haskins, who had scored 55 in a game the previous year. Dayton (22-4) had beaten Western Kentucky by twenty points and had upset St. Josephs in Philadelphia, a rare feat.

Michigan (17-7) still had Oliver Darden and All American Cazzie Russell. Cazzie finished his college career by scoring better than 30 points a game that season. The Wolverine defense was suspect, though, and they had to score bushels in order to assure victory. Only three times did they allow fewer than 70 points. In their final seven games they notched over 100 points five times—and lost the other two. Fifth ranked Loyola of Illinois (22-2), a typical, high scoring George Ireland team, had lost only to Oklahoma City and Wichita. Miami of Ohio (18-6), after losing three of their first five, righted themselves and took the Mid American.

Dayton eliminated Miami in a first round match 58-51. The Flyers, using a deliberate attack, were paced by sharpshooter Henry Finkel with 25 points. Western Kentucky sparred with Loyola on even terms in the first half; but they broke the game open when they sank nine of their first ten shots to start the second period. The game turned into a rout with the Hilltoppers emerging with a 105-86 victory. The Ohio Valley conference representative had been badly mauled the previous three tourneys and since it was Loyola which had done the mauling on two of these occasions, the victory was doubly sweet.

Neither winner survived the next round. Dayton led Kentucky into the second half and would not relinquish the lead until seven straight points by Dampier erased a five point Flyer lead. Dayton refused to be shaken off, however, and surged once more to move ahead 76-75. But despite control of the boards and Finkel's 36 points, the Flyers eventually fell to the Wildcats 86-79. Dampier with 34 points and Riley with 29 were the twin prongs of Kentucky's attack.

Michigan trailed Western Kentucky well into the second period but when the Hilltoppers, who had only substituted once, ran themselves to exhaustion, the Wolverines methodically closed the gap, and finally took a one point lead. In the waning seconds Steve Cunningham grabbed a loose ball, faked Cazzie Russell out of his sneakers, and twirled in a layup to move the Hilltoppers on top again 79-78. After a jump ball at center court Russell was fouled by Greg Smith and, at the 0:11 mark, found the net on both free throws to win it for Michigan 80-79.

Cazzie Russell's 19 second half points sparked a Michigan rally against Kentucky in the regional final. It was not enough, however, to overcome a substantial lead the Wildcats had built when the Wolverines could not find the hole early in the game. It was Cazzie's last college game. He played brilliantly but without support. Kentucky's 84-77 win put them into the national semifinals for the sixth time.

East:

Davidson (20-5) finally broke the jinx and won the Southern Conference postseason tourney. Fred Hetzel, their star the previous two years, had graduated but All American Dick Snyder remained to lead the Wildcats. Snyder was an all round athlete—a star quarterback at his North Canton, Ohio, high school, and a fine outfielder and pitcher on the baseball diamond. He had chosen basketball and Davidson over 75 other colleges that had recruited him. Another school that had bootstrapped itself into the tournament was Syracuse (21-5). Just three years earlier Syracuse had lost 27 games in a row. But that was before Dave Bing, their All American guard, and Coach Fred Lewis arrived. Bing was the fifth highest scorer in the country and the Orangemen averaged one hundred points per game, the first time this had ever been accomplished.* Both Davidson and Syracuse made half of their attempts from the field.

Providence (22-4) was another at large-team which featured an All American, Jim Walker, and the best free throw shooter in the country, Bill Blair. They had won the Holiday Festival final as Walker filled the nets with 50 points. The country's smallest state was also represented by Rhode Island (20-7) which had lost to Connecticut in the season finale, thus tying the schools for the Yankee Conference title. The Rams survived the tie breaker, 67-62.

The two schools given the best chance of copping the regional were Duke (23-3) and St. Josephs (22-4). Duke had taken two from UCLA on consecutive evenings and bounced Michigan in their only confrontation. Bob Verga and Jack Marin were both second team All Americans and Mike Lewis from Missoula, Montana, was as good. Despite the individual talent the Blue Devils played an unselfish, team-oriented basketball. Besides they were intelligent and flexible enough to adjust to different tactics. When South Carolina slowed things down, Duke beat them anyway, 41-38. When North Carolina State loitered with the ball for long stretches during their conference playoff semifinal, Duke patiently waited them out and prevailed 21-20 in one of the lowest scoring games of the past twenty years. Understandably, the Blue Devils were ranked second at the close of the season. season.

Sixth ranked St. Josephs was making its seventh appearance in the last eight years, though to date they had had little success in postseason competition. But the Hawks began gathering momentum in the closing stages of the campaign. During the season they had taken the Quaker City Tournament, beating the other Philadelphia schools, smashed Seton Hall 110-64, Bowling Green 98-55 and Temple twice—97-65 and 105-74. St. Josephs

*Houston also averaged one hundred points per game. In general schools were shooting and scoring at a faster clip than ever. Since 1963 field goal attempts per game had increased by ten and combined scores—by both teams—were up 16 points.

was as formidable as any team in the tournament but at home they were almost invincible. At the Palestra the St. Josephs' rooters, encouraged by a student in a hawk uniform and egged on by bawdy, sophomoric signs penned by imaginative fans and by drums and general hoopla, achieved a level of mania unequalled in college basketball circles. One observer called St. Josephs "the most selfconsciously vibrant college." The Hawks' opponents not only had to deal with the quintet on the court but also with the abuse—especially to the eardrums—of the most rabid, partisan fans in the country and the combination was invariably too much to overcome. When on the rare occasion St. Josephs did lose in the Palestra, it was usually to another Philadelphia school.

Pennsylvania won the Ivy crown but declined to participate after a prolonged controversy over the 1.6 ruling. This was a requirement that all students maintain at least a C- average in order to be eligible for NCAA-sponsored tournaments. Pennsylvania claimed the NCAA had no jurisdiction over academic standards, and in any case Ivy standards required students to maintain a higher than 1.6 average. The Quakers refused to recognize the NCAA standard and at the last moment they took a walk. That gave Syracuse, their first round opponent, a bye. It was the first time an at-large entry had been given a free trip to the next round.

St. Josephs, who had defeated Providence by 19 in their last game of the season, restaged that rout in the first round. It was also a measure of revenge for the previous year's overtime loss. The Friars held the early lead but the taller Hawks broke down their opponent's steady, deliberate maneuvers. The Hawks also collapsed around Jim Walker, with two or three defenders seemingly grafted to his body most of the time. As the game progressed Providence became less and less effective. They managed only 19 points in the second half and only two field goals in the last nine minutes as St. Josephs ousted them 65-48.

Davidson had even less trouble subduing Rhode Island. The Wildcats were just too tall for their foes. Rod Knowles, 6′8″, pumped in 39 points though Dick Snyder, who got into early foul trouble and was not needed much, had only eleven, which was five lower than his previous worst showing. Davidson toyed with the Rams before crushing them 95-65.

The All American matchup between Bing and Snyder was the highlight of the second round game between Syracuse and Davidson. The teams battled on even terms for most of the initial period but after a 24-24 tie a hook by Jim Boeheim (future coach at his alma mater) sounded the opening chord in a well-orchestrated 19-3 flourish by Syracuse. The Orangemen's pressing defense and their quickness overcame Davidson's height advantage. Bing and Snyder neutralized each other but the other Syracuse players out-hustled and out-jumped their matchups. It was their tough defense more than their free wheeling scoring that won the game for Syracuse 94-78.

It was too bad two of the top six teams had to play each other so early in the tournament. Duke was returning to the court on which they had captured the ACC playoff and so had a slight psychological advantage. Their strength lay in controlling the boards, primarily by Marin and Lewis, the leading leapers on the second best rebounding team in the country. St. Josephs relied on the fast break, triggered by Guokas and the zone press which Coach Jack Ramsay copied from UCLA.

With seven minutes left in the game Duke enjoyed a comfortable ten point edge. The Hawks reached for the throttle and blasted to within two at 0:48. With the ball in a deep freeze St. Josephs had to foul. They concentrated on Marin but he calmly flushed four points through the hoop in two trips to the line to preserve the 76-74 victory.

Syracuse tried a full court press almost from the start of their regional title match with Duke. The Blue Devils shrugged off the pressure and shot into a 16 point lead after only 11 minutes. Two ten-point bursts punctuated by Verga's pops from the corner accounted for the early Duke edge. But Syracuse retaliated and an 11-2 flurry sparked by Bing brought them within three. The Duke zone and a substantial height advantage prevented Syracuse from penetrating inside and the Blue Devils stretched their advantage once more.

The Orangemen were not yet through, though. Every time Duke looked as if it had put the game away Syracuse came charging back. In the second half their speed twice helped them build temporary leads, the last time a 74-72 edge at 5:43. In the end Duke's height advantage proved decisive. Syracuse could not contain the Devil's swarming attach and were forced to foul. In the second half Bing was fettered and scored only one point. As a result Duke was able to post a 91-81 victory and go to the Final Four for the third time in four years.

West:

UCLA had been favored to take the Pac Eight and maybe even win an unprecedented third straight national title. Keith Erickson and Gail Goodrich had graduated but Wooden still had exceptional talent returning, players like Mike Lynn, Edgar Lacey, Kenny Washington and Fred Goss. Unfortunately, Goss was lost for the season and the others never jelled. After losing two in a row to Duke early in the season, the team never recovered and finished behind Oregon State (20-6) despite crushing the Beavers 79-35 in their best game of the season. It was the first time since 1958 that a national champion did not return to defend its title.

The Beavers were the best defensive team in the country, holding their opponents to fewer than 50 points on ten occasions. After winning their opener the Beavers lost three in a row but righted themselves in time.

Houston (21-5) and Utah (21-6) were scoring machines by contrast. Houston barely edged Syracuse to lead the country's colleges in scoring. In half their games they eclipsed one hundred points, including a 152-108 whipping of Texas Wesleyan. That game set a record for the most points by two teams and nine Cougars scored in double figures. In a 140-87 devastation of Southwestern, sophomore Elvin Hayes rocketed to national attention by tallying 55 points. The Cougars lost their first three but then settled down and succumbed only twice more—to Maryland by a point and to Dayton by two.

Utah carved an equally impressive swath. Five times they soared over 120 points. Like Houston, they looked to a leader to provide the impetus during these scoring blizzards. Jerry Chambers provided that spark with a 28 point per game average.

However, the team was handicapped when it lost its captain, George Fisher, who broke his leg in the final game of the season. It was all too familiar to Coach Gardner who had lost a key player when he barely missed national titles in 1951 and 1961.

Colorado State, playing a short 21 game schedule, were 14 and 7 and Pacific (22-4), making their first NCAA tournament appearance after winning the WCAC, completed the West regional.

Wichita hosted both the Midwest and West regional opening round contests. Texas Western, winner of the first, were joined by their fellow Texans from Houston who upended Colorado State 82-76. The losers played a spirited man-to-man defense and held Houston to 18 points below their average, but to no avail. A strong team effort was reflected in double digit scoring by all five Ram starters. Sophomore Elvin Hayes, far below form, accounted for only 18 points but 5′11″ Joe Hamood peppered the basket for 23 and was the point man in the Cougars' full court zone press that harried Colorado State throughout.

Four nights later the top offensive team met the top defensive team in Los Angeles' Pauley Pavilion. It was UCLA's new home court but the Bruins were merely spectators. Oregon State played their usual deliberate, grinding style which effectively put the brakes on the Cougar scoring machine. The Beavers took just 42 shots but made 26 of them. So economical were they in their movements, their starters played the entire game without showing much strain. Meanwhile Houston was heaving the ball at the basket with less success, missing more shots than the Beavers even attempted. This barrage gave them a two point lead at the half. But in the second period Oregon State, led by Rick Whelan's torrid eleven for fourteen from the floor, rallied to win 63-60. Hayes was held to just 14 points.

Equally hot was Jerry Chambers of Utah who hit on eight of his first nine attempts on the way to a 40 point performance. Pacific whittled a 16 point Utah lead to four at 6:45 but the Redskins went into a stall and hung on to win 83-74.

The following evening Oregon State tried the same tactics on another scoring powerhouse with considerably less success. Utah, ahead 30-23 in the waning minutes of the first half, shrugged off the plodding Beavers and their suffocating defense and plugged nine unanswered points through the hoop to take a commanding lead. The Beavers played catchup the rest of the game but could never get their offense unlimbered. Besides, Utah owned the backboards and went to the free throw line three times as often as the Beavers. Chambers as usual led his team with 33 points in the 70-64 victory.

Final Four:

The final rounds were played in Maryland's Cole Fieldhouse. For three of the Final Four the road to Cole had been rocky. Kentucky and Duke had to wage comebacks in the second halves of their regional final and Texas Western had to survive an overtime and a double overtime to gain their berth. Only Utah had had it easy. But there was a total turnabout in the first semifinal game as the Miners, who led most of the game, had little difficulty subduing Utah 85-78 despite a virtuoso performance by Chambers accounting for 38 points.*

The featured game was Kentucky versus Duke, the number one and two ranked teams in the country. Many were disappointed that these two were in the same half of the draw and felt this was going to be the climactic game of the tourney. The survivor was almost sure to take the title.

The Kentucky runts were at a considerable disadvantage. Not only were they matched against the second best rebounding team in the country, but forward Larry Conley was sick with what was diagnosed as either a stomach virus or food poisoning. Conley spent the day in his motel room bed but dragged himself to the fieldhouse and dressed for the game. Duke's initial defensive move was a zone but when the Wildcats had little trouble penetrating it and shooting over the top, they switched to a man-to-man. Kentucky also began with their 1-3-1 zone but turned to their tried and true man-to-man when Duke showed a similar lack of respect. Surprisingly, the quicker but far shorter Wildcats were holding their own off the boards, primarily because Jaracz was having an outstanding night. However, when he collected his third foul in the first half Rupp had to sit him down. Duke responded by sweeping the backboards and mounting an attack that brought them from eight points down to five up. Kentucky managed to close the gap to a single point as the buzzer sounded the end of the first half.

Jaracz was reinserted in the second period and this evened the battle of the boards. With Dampier directing the offense the Wildcats swept into the lead. Thereafter the teams traded baskets for a spell and the score was knotted six times before a pair of free throws by Conley gave Kentucky a 73-71 advantage. With a minute remaining Conley grabbed an errant Blue Devil shot, drove the length of the court and laid the ball through the hoop to score what turned out to be the deciding bucket. It gave Kentucky a 79-72

---

*The result may have been influenced by an incident which occurred prior to the start of the season. Haskins, who was an excellent defensive tactician. had asked Jack Gardner if he could attend some Utah practices in preseason because he wanted to observe the superb fast break employed by the Utes. Gardner invited him to spend a week in Salt Lake City watching the drills, little realizing he would have to face Texas Western in the Final Four four months later.

lead and they fought off a last second Duke flurry to win 83-79. Jack Marin headed the Blue Devil scoring with 29 points while Dampier paced the Wildcats with 23. Verga, who was also under the weather, had just four.

The tourney had been dubbed the Last Chance Tournament. The expectation was that UCLA would win the next three titles when Lew Alcindor and the other Bruin super-freshmen became eligible in 1967. Little did anybody suspect that it would be eight years before a school other than UCLA would win a championship.

Rupp, whose coaching career was drawing to a close, may have felt this was his last chance to win his record breaking fifth national championship. The Baron donned his lucky brown suit (he actually had several brown suits but from more than three feet away they all looked alike) and hoped Conley would hold up for one more night and that Pat Riley's sore foot would not hamper him excessively. Haskins, who had done a superb job getting his collection of brilliant, unpredictable, independent, exhibitionist ghetto kids to play together as a team, was preparing for the most important game of his life and trying to keep his team's cockiness from becoming overconfidence. Kentucky's five white starters contrasted sharply with Texas Western's five black starters. Never had there been such a clear confrontation in a national final between the haves and the have nots, the establishment and the emerging newcomers, the kids who had grown up among green lawns and picket fences and those who had dodged rats and picked their way down garbage-strewn streets.

Though heavily favored, the Wildcats were once more facing an excellent rebounding team—better even than Duke—and would therefore have to be on target all night. The Miners' devastating, pressing, man-to-man defense was a factor from the start. Two pivotal plays came early in the game. After ten minutes, the Miners had a scant one point lead. Then Bobby Joe Hill twice stole the ball in a span of ten seconds, drove downcourt and laid the ball in to give Texas Western a 14-9 lead. They were never headed again. Several times Kentucky threatened to overhaul their opponents but each time they were thwarted and the Miners pulled away again. One play exemplified the intensity with which Texas Western played all night. Lattin, the Miners' massive 240 lb. center, received the ball and slam-dunked it home, almost ripping the hoop off its moorings. He landed squarely on Riley's sore foot which had been fitted with a sneaker cut out especially to relieve the pressure!

During the intermission Rupp tried to rally his players. He reminded them they would never be able to raise their heads in Lexington if they let these black boys beat them. Desire was there and Kentucky even had the fans with them but it was evident it was not to be the Wildcats' night. Haskins used a three guard lineup in the second half—Artis, Hill and Worlsey—with Cager and Lattin up front. They put merciless pressure on the Wildcats and drove for the basket repeatedly. Kentucky, unable to keep their opponents away from the hoop, fouled often and the Miners took advantage of almost every opportunity. They cashed 26 of 27 free throw attempts in a span that covered almost the entire game. Jaracz fouled out, leaving Lattin to patrol the backboards almost without opposition. At the final buzzer it was Texas Western 72, Kentucky 65.

Duke won the consolation game but Chambers score 32 points for Utah. This gave him a total of 143 points for the tourney, thereby breaking Lovellette's 14 year old record for four games. He was voted the tournament's MVP.

Texas Western was the first school from its state to win the national title. It was also the fourth independent to do so, the first since another quintet of blacks had won that honor for Loyola. It was not an easy road to the championship. On the way to the summit Texas Western had to beat four former national champions—Cincinnati, Kansas, Utah and Kentucky.

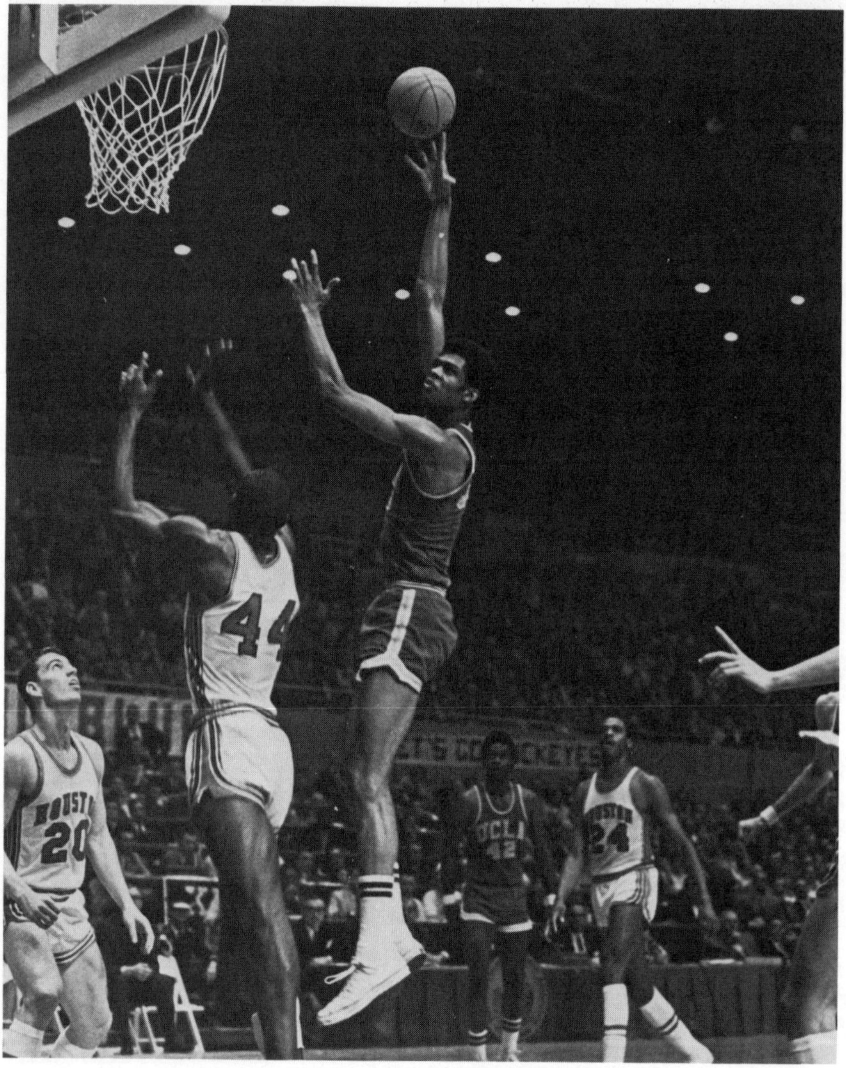

Lew Alcindor's sky hook leaves Elvin Hayes (44) flat footed. The Bruins' 101-69 semi-final victory in 1968 avenged their one point loss in the Houston Astrodome earlier in the season.
(Norm Schindler photo)

13

THE BIG A AND THE BIG E

1967-1968

Just before opening their 1965-66 schedule the UCLA varsity played a game against the Brubabes, the Bruin freshmen, and lost 75-60. UCLA was ranked number one in preseason polls but after that game there was good reason to believe the Brubabes were the best quintet in the land. Towering over his teammates, 7′1½″ from his size 16 D sneakers to his short curly hair, Lew Alcindor was the centerpiece of that freshman team. He had been the most sought after prep basketball player in the country; when he decided to enroll at UCLA, most experts were willing to concede them a national title in each year of Alcindor's eligibility.

The Big "A" had already reached his full height as a sophomore at Power Memorial Academy in New York City. Under Coach Jack Donohue he had come to the attention of every coach in the country when he was included on the high school All American team. Considering that high school games are only 32 minutes long, his point output could be extrapolated to over 30 and his rebounds to more than 20 in a college situation. And he was still only a junior. In his senior year he was acclaimed as a three-time All American and was the object of desire of more than 100 coaches and recruiters from all over the country. His statistics were phenomenal and besides he was a bright and intelligent boy in the top ten percent of his class. Several national

---

*There is some disagreement on the height Alcindor finally reached. Estimates ran as high as 7′5″.

magazines wrote articles about him. Southern schools were willing to integrate just to have him put on their uniform, alumni made job offers to Lew's father, a transit policeman with a modest income, and athletic departments hinted that a coaching job would be waiting for Donohue if he could induce his pupil to enroll at their school. Unfortunately for them, none of the recruiters were allowed to talk to Alcindor. Donohue permitted them to enter his gym to watch Lew practice but he refused to let them speak to him. Once a recruiter said "Hello, Lew" to the seven foot giant and was promptly shown the door. If a scout or coach approached Lew he was told to "see my coach." And Donohue protected the privacy of his star player.

Aside from handling the press and the visiting recruiters, Donohue was trying to steer Power Memorial to a third successive undefeated season but after 52 victories in a row the team lost its only game in the three Alcindor years by a point to De Matha on the winner's court. By this time Alcindor had narrowed his choice to UCLA or St. Johns. He had been approached by Ralph Bunche, the Nobel Prize winning United Nations mediator, and Willie Naulls, a former professional basketball player. Both were black and both were UCLA alumni. They convinced him to fly to Los Angeles and visit the Bruins' campus. When he returned, he was ready to announce his intention to enroll at UCLA*, which caused a lot of disappointed coaches to pack their bags and look elsewhere for a dominating center.

In the fall of 1966 Lew Alcindor registered at UCLA as a journalism major. So good were the undefeated freshman quintet that they drew as many spectators as the varsity when they played. In the preseason game in which the Brubabes beat the varsity, Alcindor scored 31 points. In his first regular freshman game he tallied 43, equalling the other team's total in a 119-43 blowout.

Still, Wooden was not satisfied with Alcindor's skills. He prevailed on Jay Carty, a former Oregon State star forward and doctoral candidate at UCLA, to give Big Lew some private instruction. Every day Carty and Alcindor would play one-on-one in the gym until the young center learned not to fade away from the basket, to time his jumps perfectly and to move laterally as well as he did forward and backward. With his private coach and John Wooden both concentrating their considerable teaching ability on him, Alcindor quickly developed his raw potential into the skills of a star basketball pivotman.

But UCLA was far from a one star attraction. Three other sophomores, two of them All Americans in high school, joined Alcindor on the varsity. Lynn Shackelford, a 6′5″ forward from Burbank, California, who shot 62 percent from the floor during his freshman year, and Lucius Allen, a 6′2″ guard

---

*Joe Lapchick's retirement from St. Johns was also a contributing factor in Alcindor's decision.

from Kansas City, Kansas, were the two All Americans. Allen had also helped his school to a state title. Kenny Heitz, a 6′3″ swing man who could play forward or guard, had also been mentioned for national honors. These four joined junior Mike Warren, a 5′11″ playmaker, to complete one of the most devastating college quintets ever assembled on a basketball floor. There were two seniors scheduled to open the season but Edgar Lacey, another high school All American (John Wooden seemed to have cornered the market in that rare commodity) had injured a leg and was lost for the season and Mike Lynn had been suspended when caught with a forged credit card. Lynn was later reinstated.

There was rhythm and poetry not only in their play but also in their names which fit together as smoothly as their styles to create this superb team. There was Lew Alcindor and Lucius Allen (L.A. and L.A.), Mike Warren and Mike Lynn, Mike Lynn and Lynn Shakelford. Sometimes reporters would become lyrical and call Lew and Lucius the Luclans or Lewclans depending on who was more outstanding that night.

Wooden developed his strategy to play to the strength of his Bruins. He placed Alcindor in the low post which opened the area around the key when opponents collapsed around the big center, thereby allowing his hot shooting forwards to pop from medium range. He also retained the fast break which was invariably triggered by Alcindor's outlet passes. The zone press was used less often than before, mostly because it was unnecessary when the Bruins sailed out of sight on the wings of a huge lead. When UCLA did press, Alcindor's enormous reach made the inbounds play as difficult as throwing a rock past a windmill going full tilt. Pressure, if not always on the full court, was the way to play the game according to Wooden.

Though blessed with this cornucopia of talent, John Wooden had his work cut out. Could he succeed in molding these egos, these examples of individual brilliance into a team, to blend their skills into a unit without destroying each man's unique talent? Wooden, the teacher and inspirational coach, did succeed. As one former player put it: "He makes you believe you can do anything." Wooden also lived up to his credo that he would rather command respect than demand it. But he did demand unselfishness from his players. They were not to seek headlines nor to accumulate fancy statistics. They were to submerge their own ambitions for the good of the team, not an easy lesson to learn when one had been the focus of attention back home on the local high school team. The Bruins' coach taught his players to pass off to an open man rather than take a contested shot. He also asked the player who caught the pass and scored to acknowledge the play by some signal such as a wink or a wave. But shooting was not the most important aspect of the game for Wooden. "By taking the emphasis off shooting," he said, "I think you strengthen the idea of team play and make boys not only willing but eager to sacrifice themselves for the group." He liked to use Bill Russell as an example of a man with the temperament to sacrifice his scoring ability in return for team success. Over the years it was as much his dedication to team play as his star ball players that made UCLA the most successful team in the history of college sports.

1967

West:

In 1967 UCLA did not lose a game while winning 26. They opened the season against Southern California, whipping them 105-90. The Trojans used a man-to-man defense to contain Alcindor, who responded by twirling 56 points through the hoop (later he scored 61 against Washington State). Not even Chamberlain or Robertson had had such an unveiling. That was also the last time anyone tried defending Alcindor one-to-one. From then on it was different variations of zone defenses thrown up at the Bruins. The second time the teams met, the Bruins won 107-83 in the final of the Los Angeles Classic. By the third encounter the Trojans were wiser and stalled through most of the game. Alcindor was held to 12 points, the lowest production of his career. When the Bruins got the lead, Wooden retaliated and for the first time in his life ordered a stall, too. UCLA held the ball for nine minutes without shooting. The game went into overtime before the Bruins pulled it out 40-35. Oregon tried the same maneuver after suffering a 100-66 thrashing and wound up on the short end of a 34-25 count. For the rest of the season UCLA's opponents used more conventional tactics with the same lack of success.

Alcindor finished the season second in scoring, seventh in rebounding and tops in field goal percentage, sinking two of every three shots taken. It was the best shooting percentage ever achieved. Alcindor often resorted to the dunk but this shot was doomed when, at the end of the season, the NCAA rules committee voted to outlaw it.

UCLA as a team was third in scoring despite the two stall ball games, and first in shooting percentage. They were also among the top 20 in defense and subsequently led the country in margin of victory—a whopping 26 points, second only to the mark achieved by Kentucky in 1954.

Matched against the Bruins in the West regional was Pacific (23-3), repeating as WCAC champion. They had digested their first three opponents before being dumped three in a row themselves. The Waves then soaked the rest of their opponents without a setback. During one home stretch they gamboled to four successive victories by a cumulative 129 point margin. Pacific's main strength lay in the rebounding and scoring of Keith Swagerty. The 6′7″ center was fourth in the country in rebounds and broke Bill Russell's career conference scoring record.

Wyoming (15-12) tied BYU for the lead in the WAC but outpointed them in a playoff. The Cowboys' undistinguished record included losses to UC Santa Barbara, Nevada Southern and BYU. By season's end they had scored just nine points more than they had allowed.

Seattle (17-8), led by ponderous Tom Workman, and Texas Western (20-5) were included in the West regional, though the Texans played more than a thousand miles from the Pacific. The Miners were just a shadow of the team that won the title 12 months earlier. Gone were Flournoy and Artis via graduation, Shed via ineligibility (he had played for another school as a freshman) and Bobby Joe Hill who had dropped out of school. That left only the two Willies—Cager and Worsley—and Dave Lattin. Texas Western had more trouble against teams from New Mexico than any other. They lost all three bouts with New Mexico and New Mexico State. Against Seattle they split a pair but recorded wins against tourney-bound Kansas and SMU.

The rubber match between Seattle and Texas Western occurred in the first round on a neutral court in Fort Collins, Colorado. Only slightly more than 4,000 spectators showed up to witness a ragged, penalty-infested game. Seattle, always an aggressive team, collected 28 personals which the Miners converted into 32 points off free throws, more than they scored from the field. It looked for a time as if the only points in the game would come from the line; Seattle went ten minutes without a basket while Texas Western suffered an even longer dry spell. Then Malkin Strong broke the drought to put the Chieftains ahead 19-16. In the second half Workman, the Chieftain's 6′7″, 230 lb. center, sprained an ankle when he went down in a heap under the basket. That loss and Wee Willie Worsley's second half performance doomed Seattle. The little fireplug guard's 19 second half points, his playmaking, his quickness and drive proved to be the sparks igniting the Miners to a 62-54 victory. It was a poor shooting night for both teams and the Texans made just 15 field goals.

Round two began with Pacific eliminating Texas Western 72-63. Worlsey again directed the Miners but this time scored only 13 as his teammates' frigid shooting paved the way to defeat. After falling behind early, the Miners rallied in the second half to come within four, only two minutes remaining. The Waves froze the ball and a succession of fouls by Texas Western cost them the services of Lattin.

UCLA was already ahead 12-6 when an 18 point Bruin avalanche totally buried Wyoming. By half time UCLA was leading 55-18 and the massacre was well on its way. Wooden mercifully cleared his bench even before the intermission. For some reason the Cowboys' coach stuck with his starters throughout the game. Whether Wyoming substitutions would have resulted in a wider or narrower margin of victory is impossible to say but at least five Cowboys would have been less exhausted. A full court zone press forced 19 turnovers and Alcindor dropped 29 points into the bucket in 29 minutes. The 109-60 result was hardly surprising.

What was surprising was Pacific's 50 rebounds to just 35 for UCLA the following evening and an early 21-21 tie. At that point a minor sonic boom of ten unanswered points propelled the Bruins into a comfortable if not convincing 37-27 half time lead. When they scored the first five points of the second session it looked like another runaway until the Waves rolled back on the good outside shooting of Dave Fox, Bob Krulish and Pat Foley and the outstanding rebounding of Swagerty. With seven and a half minutes to go, the Bruins were only seven points up which aroused the fans to a fine level of hysteria. But UCLA exploded once more and won 80-64 to take their usual place in the Final Four. Alcindor, with 38 points, was the deciding factor, while the rest of the Bruins were held pretty much in check.

Midwest:

Houston coach Guy Lewis had assembled some enormous firepower on the Cougar hardwood. It was generated by some massive young men, the most noticable being the talented Big E—Elvin Hayes. Aside from their substantial skills as the two premier basketball players of their time, Hayes had little in common with Alcindor. The Big E came from the small town of Rayville, Louisiana. Though an excellent player in high school he had not made the varsity until his junior year and had not been selected as an All American prep school player. Five inches shorter than the willowy Alcindor, he was considerably brawnier but possessed remarkable agility, coordination and finesse for a 6′8″, 235 lb. man. Many compared him to Bill Russell because of his ability to find the optimum spot on the court and to insinuate himself between the man taking a shot and the basket. Hayes was noted for his shotblocking, both legal and otherwise—during the 1967 season he averaged four goaltending calls per game. The in-your-face volleyball type spike seemed to give him great pleasure.

However, the Big E was not the team player Russell had been, nor was he as unselfish. Hayes was always calling for the ball and shooting at the hoop even when another man was more open. Passing off just was not his style. He was an excellent marksman, though, his favorite shots a ten to fifteen foot jumper and the dunk before it was outlawed. Hayes was also critical of others while enamored with his own skills. After he outscored and outrebounded Alcindor in their first encounter he remarked to the media after the game that the Bruin center was overrated and not as good as the press had reported. The quieter, less flamboyant Alcindor approached him later and accepted some "advice" from the Big E.

The Cougar supporting cast was almost as spectacular as that of the Bruins. They averaged almost 6′8″ and 235 lbs., the smallest one being 6′5″ Don Chaney. Melvin Bell at 240 lbs. and Don Kruse and Ken Spain, both 235 lbs., completed this hulking quintet. They intimidated their opponents with their bulk no less than with their height, and they cut through their overmatched opponents like a pack of over-enthusiastic barracudas. Guy Lewis liked to have them dress alike in Cougar red-and-white blazers. Decked out in their flashy attire they made almost as big an impression in a hotel lobby as they did on the court.

Houston (23-3) was ranked sixth. They lost only to Michigan, Washington and Notre Dame though their schedule was soft and sprinkled with schools such as Hawaii, Nevada Southern, Lamar Tech., Albuquerque, Arkansas State and St. Mary's of Texas, most of which they beat by lopsided scores (the last by 64 points). And the Cougars so loved to bomb the basket, their opponents considered themselves fortunate if they could hold them to 90 points.

SMU's (19-5) record was not as good as it looked. The Mustangs, the weakest of the three Texas teams in the tournament, lost three of their first four and then stabilized, but eight of their victories were achieved by three points or fewer. Fourth ranked Kansas (22-3) relied on a stout defense to pull them through. Sometimes this was not enough as, for example, a 68-44 debacle at the hands of St. Johns.

Peck Hickman had retired from Louisville after 23 years and 444 victories. He would undoubtedly have loved to have coached the Cardinals at least until All American Westley Unseld graduated. The 1967 tournament featured many fine rebounders but the 6′7″, 250 lb. monolithic Unseld was the best—better than Hayes or Alcindor. He finished third in the country in that department, disappointing for him since he had been number two the previous year.

Unseld had been an All American at Seneca High School in Louisville where he led his team to the state championship, beating Breckenridge in the final. Breckenridge, in turn, won the state title the following year. The sparkplug on that team was a young man by the name of Butch Beard, also an All American. By some high stepping, fast talking recruiting Hickman had snared both Beard and Unseld for Louisville, quite an accomplishment considering Rupp normally had first crack at Kentucky's star products. Rupp wanted Unseld badly and he was prepared to open Kentucky's doors to its first black basketball player; but Wes wanted to stay in Louisville where his parents could watch him play. Unseld was the complete team player. Unselfish, modest and self-effacing, he never made demands on his coach or fellow players. When he was issued his uniform, he found his shorts were too tight and rather than ask for a bigger size took them home so his mother could let them out.*

Louisville (23-3) won their first MVC crown, losing only to Southern Illinois (which went on to win the NIT), Cincinnati and Wichita. They rang up 13 straight wins at the beginning of the season including two successive decision by more than 50 points each, granted against weak opponents. The

*Unseld was drafted by the Baltimore Bullets after the 1968 season. The Bullets jumped from last place to first in one year with basically the same team plus Unseld. He was voted the league's most valuable player in his rookie season.

competition got tougher in the Quaker City Tournament but they won that, too, beating an excellent Princeton squad, undefeated at the time.

New Mexico State (15-10) completed the regional field. They had lost four of their first six and did not go over .500 until their eleventh game. The Aggies played almost exclusively against local teams in an area of the country not known for its basketball tradition.

In the first round the Aggies gave Houston a tussle they had not anticipated. They shut everyone of the Cougars down with the exception of Hayes and headed into the locker room with a two point half time lead. Hayes was the outstanding Cougar as he tallied 19 of his teams 23 points. Seldom had a player taken over so completely (which may have been part of the problem). The Aggies' cloying defense hardly let up in the second half. Each man shadowed his counterpart and the Cougars, who had averaged 93 points per game, just could not settle into their free wheeling offense. Only once was either team able to go ahead by as many as four points. Though State was able to dictate the tempo throughout, Houston survived 59-58 with Hayes' 30 points pointing the way.

Hayes cooled off somewhat in the next round against Kansas and scored only 19 points but Don Chaney picked up the slack with 20. Houston was held considerably below their average but still beat Kansas 66-53, though the losers were playing on their home court. Louisville, which had not played competitively for three weeks, came up short against SMU, the upset of the tourney. The long layoff affected Louisville's foul shooting a lot worse than their floor markmanship. They shot 56 percent from the field but sank just 5 of 14 free throws. Beard, in particular, was wild as he made two of seven. The Mustangs held Beard to 14 and Unseld to 18 but it took a layup by Denny Holman in the last three seconds to nail down the 83-81 SMU victory.

The next evening the Texas showdown between Houston and SMU gave 17,000 fans a lot to rave about. The score was tied seven times before Houston opened a little daylight. The Cougars, building on a six point halftime edge, extended their advantage to 14 points only to have the Mustangs pull even at 71-71 on Chuck Beasley's 20 foot jumper. Melvin Bell reestablished Houston's lead 50 seconds later and they went on to win 83-75. Hayes pumped in 31 points for the Cougars.

Mideast:

The favorites in the Mideast regional were seventh ranked Western Kentucky (23-2) and ninth ranked Tennessee (21-5). The Hilltoppers with their first All American, Clem Haskins, lost their opener to Vanderbilt but then ripped off 21 victories before being subdued by Murray State. They feasted on second rate quintets like Tampa, which they flogged 123-57.

Tennessee was making its tournament debut. Kentucky, the perennial SEC champion, had stumbled to a 13-13 season, their worst under Coach Rupp who barely avoided his first losing season in 37 years. Tennessee was coached by Ray Mears, even more of a fanatic about defense than Henry Iba. He had coached Wittenberg to a national small college title in 1961. In his last three years there, his teams had the best Division II defense in the country and Mears retained this miserly strategy when he switched to Tennessee. The Volunteers were sixth defensively in 1964 and number one the following year. Scoring points against Mears was like squeezing air out of a basketball. They were also a very disciplined team and averaged fewer than 15 fouls per game. Aside from Rupp and Doggie Julian (now at Dartmouth), no active coach had won a greater percentage of his games than Mears.

Toledo (23-1) lost only to Marshall but were unranked, due primarily to a soft schedule. Indiana (17-7) was one of the weakest teams ever to represent the Big 10. They had won five games by a field goal or less and had barely tied Michigan State for first place. The Hoosiers went to the tournament because the Spartans had been there more recently. Still, it was an improvement over their previous year's last place finish. Dayton (21-5) and Virginia Tech (18-6) were at-large entries. The underrated Flyers had won almost half their games by more than 20 points.

Virginia Tech was making its first tourney appearance, too, and they were not expected to last long. They had lost to their first round opponent Toledo, 90-71, in the final game of the season. But in a dramatic turnaround the Gobblers reversed that decision by eliminating Toledo 82-76.

In the nightcap at Lexington, Western Kentucky rolled to a 35-25 first half lead over Dayton. The Flyers then unleashed Don May, a 6′4″ jumping jack who ended the year with 31 more rebounds than the Big "E". His game-high 26 points triggered the surge. Pulling even briefly at 50-50, Dayton leaped ahead by five with nine minutes remaining. The Hilltoppers were far from through, though. Dwight Smith's layup at the buzzer to tie the score at 62 saved Western Kentucky, if only temporarily. Flyer's Rudy Waterman scored three quick points to open the extra session, then fouled out. The Hilltoppers surged back once more but Dayton was not to be denied. Bob Hooper fired their last four points—the deciding bucket, a 20 foot jump shot, coming with three seconds remaining to seal the 69-67 victory.

Conference teams continued to take a beating at the hands of the independents as the regional resumed in Evanston. Virginia Tech aided by Glen Combs' 29 points eliminated Indiana 79-70.

Dayton had considerably more trouble subduing Tennessee but eventually pulled out a one point victory against a miserly defense. The Tennessee offense was predictable. Their strategy was to get the ball to Ron Widby, who normally scored a third of the Volunteers' points. Dayton switched to a 1-2-2 zone from their more familiar man-to-man and had little difficulty in solving Tennessee's offensive pattern. At the end it was Hooper who came through in the clutch once more. With the score tied 50-50, he sank the go-ahead point with :24 remaining. Another pair of free throws for Dayton provided insurance as Tennessee's final second bucket made the score 53-52. Dayton missed only one free throw in 14 attempts, another factor in their victory.

The regional final was an unusual confrontation of independents. Once again the Flyers' sharpshooting from the line gave them an edge. They hit on 17 of 20 shots and May, who was high man with 28 points, converted 10 of 11 himself. The first half was extremely close and after 20 minutes the Flyers were barely ahead, 28-27. The Gobblers overtook Dayton and slowly pulled away to a 62-52 edge at 8:15. With the Final Four in sight, Tech suddenly could not buy a basket. Five free throws by May and goals by Hooper and Waterman launched a rally culminating in a 64-64 deadlock at 1:48. The Gobblers held the ball for a final shot. That attempt was aborted as they booted the ball away in the final seconds.

For the second time in the tourney Dayton found itself in overtime. For more than three minutes the score rermained unchanged until Waterman netted a charity toss. May added a layup and four more points followed from Dayton's favorite spot, the free throw line, as Tech tried unsuccessfully to steal the ball. The game ended with Dayton on top 71-66.

East:

Twenty years after playing on a national champion, Bob Cousy was once more part of the tournament scene, this time as a coach. After retiring from the Boston Celtics the ex-Crusader had accepted a post at Boston College—Holy Cross' bitter rival. Boston College (19-2) had qualified for an at-large berth in the East regional. Their only losses were to Utah and Fordham. As a result they had broken into the top ten on a plateau never previously reach by B.C. The Eagles played a 2-3 zone defense, enabling their tall front line to hit the boards hard. On offense Steve Adelman did most of the scoring while 5′11″ Mike Evans, who was credited with 16 assists in a match with Providence, quarterbacked the team.

Not to take anything away from Cousy, probably the best coached team in the regional was Temple (20-7) under Harry Litwak. The Owls were disciplined—they were the second least penalized team in the country—and they were consistent—in two thirds of their games they limited their opponents to between 58 and 70 points. Connecticut (17-6) regained its Yankee Conference dominance and, as usual, tore into Maine 109-65 and 114-88. The Huskies had problems with Boston schools though, losing twice to Holy Cross and once to Boston College. West Virginia (19-8) had made a remarkable recovery after having been 7-8 at midseason. Their early problems were due to a porous defense which once gave up 118 points to Syracuse.

St. Johns (22-3) lost to Marquette and was edged by Northwestern and Canisius each by a single basket. They beat fourth ranked Kansas decisively but mysteriously failed to make the top ten. Back after an eight year absence was third ranked North Carolina (24-4), now under Coach Dean Smith. Smith was every bit as good a recruiter as his predecessor

Frank McGuire. Three prep All Americans had been enticed to enroll at Chapel Hill, including Bob Lewis and Larry Miller. Playing in the heart of the tobacco country it was perhaps natural they would be labeled the L and M boys. Both were 6′3″ though Miller, an outstanding shooter, played forward while Lewis, recruited as a prolific scorer, had become a playmaking guard to give his team better balance. Backing them up were 6′4″ Dick Grubar, 6′8″ Bill Bunting and 6′10″ center Rusty Clarke. The tall redhead had led Fayetteville to the North Carolina High School championship in 1965 and Dean Smith was able to save on his travel budget recruiting him.

Princeton (23-2), after spending a year recovering from the loss of Bradley, was once more atop the Ivy League. They had lost only to Louisville in the final of the Quaker City Tournament, and to Cornell. They had beaten North Carolina in Chapel Hill 91-81 at a time when the Tarheels were ranked second behind UCLA. No longer ignored by the national press, nor referred to condescendingly as "just an Ivy team," the Tigers were ranked fifth. Princeton's attack was generated by a trio of tall forwards—6′9″ Chris Thomforde, 6′6″ John Haarlow and 6′6″ Ed Hummer. They were fed by a couple of short but scooter-fast guards, Gary Walters and Joe Heiser. Hummer, who played with Bradley as a sophomore, had been a prep star on a state champion in Virginia. Thomforde, a slim timber-tall towhead, resembled a Viking warrior, though his aim was to go into the Lutheran ministry.

As with UCLA, so, too, did Princeton's league opponents try to overcome superior talent by "stallball" tactics, a move which had fans screaming for a shot clock. After losing to the Tigers by 74 points, Dartmouth tried to hold down the score in their rematch by holding onto the ball. They took the opening tap and refused to shoot for the first ten minutes. Only 30 attempts at the hoop were made in the game, Princeton flinging up 11. They won 30-16 though their margin of victory was 60 fewer than in their first encounter. Pennsylvania tried the same tactic. Neither side worked up much of a sweat standing around and waiting. A pressing man-to-man finally shook the ball loose from the Quakers. In the final minutes the ball began swishing through the net the way it was intended to and Princeton won going away 25-16.

Another example of stallball occurred in the first round game between Connecticut and Boston College. Coach Shabel of the Huskies called it a "tempo situation" but by any name it was freezing the ball. Boston College fans shouted expletives at the Huskies, who mostly dribbled around aimlessly. The first half ended with Connecticut ahead 14-13. Adelman took charge after the intermission and plopped seven straight points through the hoop. This forced Connecticut to open up. Midway through the second half the Eagles had a 13 point lead and coasted to a 48-42 victory.

Elsewhere Temple spent most of the evening trying to catch St. Johns with little success. The Owls resorted to a tight zone but the Redmen, using a very deliberate attack, penetrated often enough to win 57-53.

Princeton had to rely heavily on their guards as their front line was plagued by early fouls against West Virginia. Thomforde was assessed four in the first half and had to be benched. Robbie Brown, his replacement, fouled out and Ed Hummer played the last part of the game with four infractions against him. Given all those trips to the line, West Virginia made little use of their opportunities, chalking up just eleven points in 25 tries. But West Virginia's leaky defense had apparently been well caulked in preparation for the tournament. The Mountaineer zone resisted the Tigers' penetration attempts so guard Joe Heiser began firing from outside. His 12 field goals delivered from long range proved decisive. He also held Dave Reaser 17 points below his average. Princeton struggled to an unconvincing 68-57 victory.

Free throw shooting played the decisive role in both second round games. Princeton and North Carolina bumbled through a close but ragged engagement. The L and M boys both played below par and their teammates were not much better. Princeton, led by Heiser's scoring again, was shooting well but allowing North Carolina to stay close by giving them too many opportunities from the stripe. For a time it looked as if neither team wanted the game very much. Even the Princeton coach tried his hand. Late in the game he became so incensed at the referees, he was slapped with a technical. Bobby Lewis stepped to the line and sank the free throw. The Tigers would have loved to have that point back since it almost certainly cost them the game. With 16 seconds on the clock Heiser scored on a short jump shot to tie matters at 63 and the teams went into overtime.

North Carolina held the ball until two minutes had run off waiting for a good shot. Tension was sliding the fans to the edge of their seats when Lewis drove in, scored on a layup, was fouled and completed the three point play. Then the floodgates opened and the Tarheels stampeded to a 78-70 victory to avenge their earlier loss to Princeton. Lewis scored seven points in the extra session, matching his total for the first 40 minutes. North Carolina made only two buckets during overtime but was a perfect eleven-for-eleven from the line. Princeton scored seven more baskets than the Tarheels but had 22 fewer chances from the line and blew half of those.

In the co-attraction, the referee's whistle tooted counterpoint to the alternate cheering and groaning of the fans. Most of the time the infractions were against St. Johns, and Boston College took advantage of almost every opportunity. Despite the whistle accompaniment, the Redmen steamed to a two point lead at the break which they proceeded to expand in the second period. Then in a stretch of less than four and a half minutes the Eagles turned a nine point deficit into a slim lead. In this brief span they hit on two field goals and 14 straight free throws. Sonny Dove, St. Johns' All American, spent a good part of the game on the bench with four personals. When he returned, he fouled out almost immediately. Another drought lasting six minutes saw the Eagles shut out from the floor but again beating a path to the free throw line. In all, Boston College made 25 of 27 free throws in the second half, including their final 21 in a row.

Despite all the interruptionns the game was still excitingly close. With

Boston College ahead 61-60 the Redmen held the ball for a final thrust, but with 14 seconds remaining Bill Evans stole Carmine Calzonetti's pass and was immediately fouled. Naturally he made both ends of a one and one opportunity. St. Johns' final bucket only made the score close again but did not change the outcome as Boston College advanced 63-62.

The Eagles tore out of the blocks in the regional final and were leading 12-3 before the Tarheels counterattacked. They tied the score 21-21 and when Larry Miller tallied on a pair of free throws, North Carolina was in the lead for keeps. The Eagles hung close for a time and were only trailing by two at the intermission. But their opponents switched to a zone in the second half and shut down Adelman, Eagle high scorer, holding him to nine points. On the opposite end of the floor Lewis reverted to a scorer, a role he had not played in some time, and clicked off 31 points. Rusty Clark, with 18 points and an equal number of rebounds, helped the Tarheels control the game. It was the fast break, constantly revitalized by fresh troops sent in by Smith, that eventually ground Boston College into submission. They just could not match the Tarheels' bench strength. For the fifth time in six years the ACC representative won the regional final, this time by a 96-80 score.

Final Four:

The national championship was to be decided in Louisville again. For Coach Dean Smith, participation in the final two rounds must have brought back memories of his playing days. Fifteen years earlier his Kansas team had won the championship under Phog Allen. It was Smith's first Final Four, but far from his last. In 1967, his North Carolina squad took an early 9-2 lead against Dayton but then the Cinderella team of the tourney staged a comeback and went on to win 76-62. Don May, who had a string of 13 baskets without a miss, was outstanding with 34 points. The Flyers also shut down the L and M boys, limiting them to a combined total of 24 points.

The second contest was even more one-sided. Many had expected Houston would give UCLA a tussle but none materialized. The Cougars used a collapsing zone to hobble Alcindor with Hayes, Bell and Don Kruse forming a picket line around the young center. But this left the rest of the Bruins relatively open and they scored consistently, Warren from outside and Schackelford and Allen from short range. Houston nosed in front 19-18 but the patented UCLA deluge, an 11 point whirlwind rally, settled matters early. UCLA had the situation well in hand and won 72-58. Hayes outscored Alcindor 25 to 19 and outrebounded him 24-20 but it was only a skirmish. The battle had been won by UCLA. Later the Big E told reporters he was not that impressed by Alcindor. He pointed out his shortcomings and implied that he had a lot to learn before he would become as good as Elvin.

The final was anticlimatic. Dayton never had a chance. From 1960 to 1966 both finalists had been ranked among the top three at the end of the season. No Cinderella team had reached the final since West Virginia and

California met in 1959. For ten years final games (with the exception of 1960 and UCLA's two championships in 1964 and 1965) had been relatively close affairs. This year a new trend began. UCLA consistently emerged as the Western champion but over the next seven years their opponent in the final would be a team either unranked or short of being the cream at the top. And the finals were mostly one-sided affairs.

In short, UCLA was just too tall and too talented for Dayton. Alcindor, Allen, Shackelford and Warren all scored in double digits. The Flyers started with a man-to-man defense then switched to a zone. Neither was effective. The defense to stop the Bruins had not yet been invented. Dayton tried to run with the Bruins, then tried to slow the game down. They tried just about every tactic ever attempted and then discarded by every frustrated team that had fallen to UCLA. It was back to the drawing board but unfortunately there was no tomorrow. With five minutes remaining and the Bruins ahead 76-47, Wooden removed his starters. The relieved Flyers responded with a flurry but the final score was still lopsided 79-64. For UCLA it was their twelfth straight postseason victory, a new record. It was also their third title in four years and their star Alcindor was voted the MVP, an honor he would earn twice more.

1968

Why did 52,693 basketball fans fill the Houston Astrodome to capacity for a midseason non-conference game? Why attend a game where the vast majority of the audience could just about make out the numbers of the players and the closest spectator was seated a hundred feet from courtside? The reason was simply that this had been billed the "Game of the Decade," if not the game of the century, as some overenthusiastic promoters claimed. For once the game lived up to its billing.

On January 20, 1968 number one ranked UCLA travelled to Houston to play the number two ranked Cougars and the normally football crazy state of Texas went loony over the contest. Promoters claimed they could have sold 75,000 tickets had seats been available. As it was, the crowd was more than twice the size of the previous record witnessing a college basketball game and almost three times the size of the previous year's national championship attendance. The national press was there in force and the game was televised coast-to-coast. Since the Astrodome did not have a basketball court, the Los Angeles Sports Arena hardwood was shipped to Houston at a cost of $10,000!

Houston had won 17 in a row since its defeat in the 1967 semifinals while UCLA had a 47 game streak cooking. The teams seemed evenly matched. However, Alcindor was not in top shape. He had suffered an eye injury several days before and had missed the previous two games. The showdown was close and exciting throughout. At intermission Houston held a three point lead and Hayes, who was playing probably the best game of his career, had scored 29 points. He penetrated the Bruin defense with twisting, driving layups and when he could not get close he bombed from medium range with his deadly accurate jump shots. But UCLA would not be shaken off. They came back to tie the game at 54, 65 and finally 69. But now their string had run out and Hayes at the foul line popped in his 38th and 39th points to win it for Houston 71-69. The Big E had clearly outplayed Big Lew who had been held to just 15 points, though early in the contest the Bruin center managed to block several of Hayes' shots. Hayes had also won the battle of the boards. Though not decisive, the victory elevated the Cougars to the number one position in the polls. UCLA, their 47 game win streak, the second longest on record, at an end limped back to Los Angeles, taking the basketball court with them. The Bruins observed that the national championship was to be held in Los Angeles in March and they vowed revenge when they and the Cougars would meet, as everyone expected, in the semifinals. "I hope they come to L.A. undefeated," said Lucius Allen.

Five weeks later Houston set a new national scoring record when they savaged Valparaiso 158-81. Hayes connected on 77 percent of his shots and steered 62 points through the hoop. In the contest prior to the Valparaiso win, they defeated Texas at Arlington 130-75 so that in two consecutive games they outscored their opponents 288-156. Admittedly Houston's schedule was soft and they played only seven games on the road, yet they beat three Big 10 schools by substantial margins and were rarely pressed. Their closest game, aside from the one against UCLA, was a 45-43 win over North Texas State in the final of the Rainbow Classic. The Cougars' opponents discovered the only chance they had of winning was to slow the game down. It was only stallball tactics in several games that prevented Houston from averaging more than 100 points per game. As it was they topped that mark 17 times, including their last 11 decisions. They led the country in scoring, rebound average and margin of victory. The Big E had over 1000 points to his credit, a feat accomplished only twice before in the regular season and he finished third in scoring and rebounding. He averaged better than 37 points a game and would have been the top scorer in nearly any other year, except that 1968 produced a couple of rapid fire sophomores, Pistol Pete Maravich and Calvin Murphy.

Midwest:

The Midwest regional included four other schools but they may as well have stayed home for all the opposition they could provide Houston. Best of the rest was eighth ranked Louisville (20-6). Led by their All American Wes Unseld, who finished fourth nationally in rebounding and shooting, right behind Hayes and Alcindor respectively, the Cardinals overcame early season problems to capture their last 12 games. After Louisville, the competition dropped off sharply. Loyola of Illinois (15-8) lost twice to a sub par Wichita team. Their major achievement was a win over well-regarded Kansas. Kansas State (19-7) copped the Big Eight crown, barely. One-third of their conference victories were by two points or fewer. It was the last campaign for their long time coach, Tex Winter, who moved on to Washington at the end of the season. Finally there was TCU (14-10), which lost five of their first seven.

Houston, in its quest for a perfect season, had little trouble eliminating Loyola 94-76. The Cougars opened a 19 point lead after the first 20 minutes and glided home easily. The Big E was responsible for better than half of Houston's production with 49 points as well as preempting the rebounding with some help from Ken Spain.

Almost as easy was the Cougars' second round victory over Louisville. It was a classic battle of rebounders, a confrontation of board sweepers, a joust between the 260 lb. pylon playing center for Louisville and the 235 lb. bull at forward for Houston. It was a *mano-a-mano* duel before an appreciative audience, and once again it was Hayes who was superior. He outrebounded Unseld 24-22 and outscored him 35-23. But while the action in the middle was torrid, more significant developments were occurring on the periphery. Chaney repeatedly stole the ball from the slower Cardinals and the Louisville coach later admitted, "He tore us apart." Most of the steals came during the middle of the first half when, following a 12-8 Louisville advantage, the Cougars streaked to a 33-15 lead. With control of the offensive board, Houston was able to maintain that margin by scoring often on follow up efforts. At the buzzer it was Houston 91-75.

Kansas State was ahead through most of its game with TCU, once by as many as 13. But the Frogs eventually solved Kansas State's zone and pulled in front on Mickey McCarty's layup with 90 seconds remaining, then added to their lead to win 77-72.

The result of the regional final between the two Texas schools was a foregone conclusion—only the margin of Houston's victory was in doubt. At half time Houston was ahead 59-26 and in the second half both benches enjoyed the opportunity of participating. A dozen TCU players, starters and substitutes, played and all of them scored though only one, Tommy Gowan, was in double figures. Hayes had 39 points for Houston giving him 123 for the regional in three games. He also grabbed 25 rebounds.

West:

At the end of the season UCLA (25-1) was ranked second behind Houston but the Bruins posted a wider scoring margin while completing a much tougher schedule. Aside from the two point loss to Houston the Bruins were in only two close games all season—an opening game 73-71 victory at Purdue, a sort of homecoming for Wooden who was a three-time All American there, and a 55-52 slow motion affair against Oregon State. Starting with the second game of the season they trampled over their opponents like a herd of stampeding buffalo. No team, no defense, nothing could hold them. During one ten game stretch they averaged 105 points and won by an **average** of 36.2 points.* And this against major powers such as Wichita, Notre Dame and Bradley. Never before had there been such a streak, never had one team outclassed its opponents so thoroughly over such a long stretch. Coaches tried every zone ever devised to stop the Bruins. They attempted to run with them, to stall, to double and triple team Alcindor, to roughhouse the big center so he might retaliate and be ejected from the game. Nothing succeeded. The Bruins juggernaut just kept rolling on, as unstoppable as a tidal wave.

UCLA was among the leaders in scoring and rebounding but their strongest suit was not one that could be measured statistically. They were a team in the purest sense and in every game they were maturing, gaining experience in playing as a unit and though most of the starters were juniors, this was their second year together with almost no changes. Lucius Allen had joined Alcindor as an All American. Mike Lynn had been reinstated as a starter. Shackelford, Warren and Heitz were veterans now. Returning from their smarting defeat in Houston, they regrouped and pointed to the day in March when Houston would come riding onto their turf.

There were some good teams in the West regional but none in the same class as UCLA. New Mexico (23-3), making its first appearance in the tour-

*The margins of victory were 34, 41, 36, 51, 40, 41, 33, 28, 28 and 30.

nament, won their first 18 and were ranked seventh. Their arch rival, New Mexico State (21-5), was also selected, as an at-large entry, despite two losses to the Lobos. Santa Clara (21-3) won the first Cable Car Classic, then travelled to BYU where they beat the Cougars by five. The following night, in one of the most surprising reversals, they were blown out of the arena by the same team 91-46. Still reeling, the Broncos were ambushed by NYU 93-88 in the next game. They pulled themselves together, stiffened their defense, and except for a narrow defeat by San Francisco, took the remainder of their games.

A new conference, the Big Sky, was represented in the regional for the first time. It had been organized four years earlier from the fallout of three other mountain state conferences and a couple of independents. One of the latter, Weber State (21-5) under Coach Dick Motta, captured the conference championship and made their first NCAA postseason appearance.

Weber State did not survive the first round, losing to New Mexico State 68-57. It was the first win for the Aggies in five playoff appearances and their reward was a second round date with that basketball meatgrinder, UCLA.

It took place before more than 15,000 partisan fans in Albuquerque, New Mexico. Lobo supporters were looking forward to a double treat. First, they expected their home town team would easily eliminate Santa Clara, and then they anticipated a slaughter by the Bruins of their detested arch rivals from Las Cruces. Somehow that script was misplaced. Santa Clara had little trouble sinking New Mexico 86-73, scorching the cords with 72 percent efficiency in the first half.

On the other hand UCLA had their hands full with the Aggies. Tenacious defense and a control offense that took only high percentage shots was State's strategy and it kept UCLA from running away with the game. After 20 minutes the score was tied 28-28. UCLA had played some masterful games but rarely had they been exciting. This was one of the rare ones. Even the Lobo fans joined the small group of Aggie supporters and somewhat reluctantly cheered the hustling underdogs. State dictated the tempo, denying the Bruins their normal free wheeling, fast paced game and forcing them to play in an unaccustomed deliberate style. Several times in the second half New Mexico State forged ahead and it looked for a time as if the upset of the year was in the making. But the tide turned against the Aggies when, with 6:25 to go in the game, Sam Lacey—their 6′9″ center—fouled out, followed a minute later by power forward 6′6″ Richard Collins. Without the driving force behind the hustling, tenacious defense, the Aggies' bubble burst. Unchallenged, Alcindor dominated the final minutes and UCLA won going away 58-49. Alcindor finished with 28 points and 23 rebounds, remarkable in a low scoring, low shooting game. But the Aggies might still have won had they shown greater accuracy from the foul line where they sank just 11 of 25 attempts.

The regional final was anticlimatic. UCLA trounced Santa Clara 87-66 with Alcindor shooting rarely but effectively. He took only eight shots but found the target on six of them. New Mexico State settled some old scores in the consolation by defeating the Lobos 62-58 in a game that was much more enthusiastically received than the finale.

Mideast:

Kentucky (21-4), making its sixteenth NCAA postseason appearance, was favored to take the Mideast regional. The fifth ranked Wildcats had barely nosed out Tennessee and Vanderbilt for the SEC title. They were travelling less outside the South and had played only five intersectional contests during the season. Another close race occurred in the Big Ten where Ohio State and Iowa tied for the lead. The conference had finally decided to hold a one game playoff in case of a tie and the Buckeyes stopped the Hawkeyes, reversing the result of a regular season meeting. (Under the old rule Iowa would have gone to the tournament since Ohio State had gone more recently.) East Tennessee State (18-6) also survived a playoff in the Ohio Valley after they had finished in a tie with Murray State.

Bowling Green (18-6) represented the Mid American while Marquette (21-5) and Florida State (19-7) were at-large selections. Al McGuire, the colorful, pepper-tongued scrapper from New York City, was making his initial appearance in the NCAA tournament as coach of Marquette. His Warriors were extremely tough on their home court where they had won 12 games without a loss by an average of 22 points. Strangely, they had given up exactly 57 points on five occasions, including four games in a row, which led to speculation that the scoreboard did not function above that mark. But the score also indicated McGuire had left his stamp on this team, namely a defense that regularly imposed a curfew on their opponents attack.

Florida State (19-8) had a colorful pilot too—Hugh Durham, who had just completed his second year at the helm of the Seminoles. His first had produced a lackluster 11-16 record. Now Florida State was in the process of climbing out of college basketball's minor league and beginning to run with the major college pack. Their schedule still included matches with Florida Presbyterian, Samford and Valdosta State but they also faced Ohio State, North Carolina and Georgia Tech. Their offense was the fifth best in the country due to some heavy hitting against schools that believed defense was best left to the federal government. A sampling of scores showed them beating Louisiana State 130-100, Miami 122-93, Jacksonville 106-65 and Citadel 93-50.

East Tennessee State and Florida State were both making their tournament debuts when they clashed in a first round tilt. The Buccaneers skewered the Seminoles 79-69, holding them to 22 points below their season scoring average.

George Thompson was the most productive Warrior with 33 points but it took a pair of long bombs from Jim Burke to nip Bowling Green 72-71 and send Marquette into the next round in Lexington.

Their reception was hardly friendly. Kentucky, playing in familiar surroundings blasted Marquette 107-89 as Dan Issel found the mark with 36 points. Kentucky's 6′8″ center accounted for 26 in the first period and was on target all evening, directing 14 of 18 shots through the ring. In the second game Ohio State beat East Tennessee State 79-72 after almost dissipating an eighteen point second half lead.

The unpredictable Buckeyes surprised many when they sailed to a 44-40 advantage over Kentucky in the regional final. But the Wildcats rewarded their supporters by climaxing a spirited rally at the 5:00 minute mark with the tying point. Thereafter, each lead change produced a rise in the pandemonium level. With 26 seconds left, Issel brought Kentucky rooters to their feet when he scored to give the Wildcats an 81-80 lead. But three seconds before the buzzer Dave Sorenson put in a mini-jumper from five feet to fix them in their seats and shortly after send them gloomily home. The 82-81 decision was Kentucky's first loss at home that year.

East:

Houston was not the only undefeated school in the tourney. St. Bonaventure, a small Catholic school from Olean, in upstate New York, had won all 22 games on their schedule. However the Bonnies had not been tested by any in the top ten nor had they faced a tournament-bound team. Given their easy schedule and close calls against Toledo and Fairfield, it was surprising they were ranked as high as third at season's end. Most impressive of the Bonnies was 6′11″, 265 lb. Bob Lanier who had made the All American team in this his sophomore year.

Boston College (17-7) lost to UCLA by only seven points, a considerable achievement, and to St. Johns twice by narrow margins. St. Johns (19-7) was the third* at-large school selected. The Redmen were involved in ten games in which the margin of victory was two points or less, almost causing Lou Carneseca, their explosive coach, cardiac arrest. But St. Johns, a cool squad in the final seconds, won a majority of the white knucklers.

Ivy League champ Columbia (21-4) also qualified. Bookend losses to Cornell in the league opener and to Princeton in the finale, bracketed 12 consecutive Ivy wins. The loss to Princeton caused a tie at the top of the standings but the Lions crushed the Tigers in a playoff by 18 points.

After absorbing three straight defeats early in the season Columbia reversed their fortunes, beat St. Johns in the final of the Holiday Festival and proceeded to rattle off 16 wins. The string was interrupted only when Princeton caught the Lions without their seven foot center, who was nursing an injured ankle. An earlier 17 point loss to Cornell was avenged by a 93-51

*The reason for three Northeast independents was the NCAA had decided that in light of their sorry 3-15 record in the post season playoff, the Yankee Conference winner would no longer get an automatic invitation.

drubbing of the same team (a 59 point swing). Because it was such a young team, it was slow in jelling but once maturity and momentum had been achieved, the national pollsters ranked them sixth.

Coach Jack Rohan had played on the last Columbia quintet to participate in the NCAA playoffs back in 1951. The success of his team rested on three brilliant hometown athletes. Dave Newmark, a 7 foot center, Jim McMillian, a 6′5″ forward, both from Brooklyn, and Heyward Dotson, a 6′4″ guard from Staten Island, were the trio who made the Lions roar. Dotson later became a Rhodes Scholar emulating Bill Bradley, another Ivy League basketball star. McMillian and Dotson, especially, were the heavy artillery that the Lions relied upon to put numbers on the scoreboard. In the final of the Holiday Festival they accounted for 29 of Columbia's 33 second half points. McMillian also scored 37 in the playoff against Princeton.

LaSalle (20-7), back for the first time since their loss to San Francisco in the NCAA final 13 years ago, was far from being a tournament threat. They had lost three of their first eight games—by 17, 21 and 23 points—and had improved only marginally since. Davidson (22-4) had again weathered the Southern Conference playoff. The highlights of their season had been a first place finish in the Charlotte Invitational, a 16 point defeat of St. Johns in New York, and a 21 point thrashing of Michigan.

The favorite in the regional, despite the Bonnies' perfect record, was fourth ranked North Carolina (25-3). Like Davidson they also lost to Vanderbilt and won a Christmas tourney—the Far West Classic, normally an Oregon State prerogative. Both southern schools had also broken the color barrier for the first time. Black stars Charlie Scott of North Carolina and Mike Maloy of Davidson had been heavily recruited while playing high school ball in New York City. Both had decided to pioneer in the new racially altered environment of the South.

Led by All America Larry Miller, the remaining half of the L and M pair, the Tarheels had won 20 in a row before losing their final pair of regular season games by identical 87-86 scores. Second place Duke was lured into a couple of stallball games in the ACC playoff, the second a 12-10 record-setting (for least points scored and probably also for inertia) study in frustration which ended with the Blue Devils' elimination. As a result North Carolina had a relatively easy road to the ACC championship.

Regional competition got underway in College Park, Maryland, and Kingston, Rhode Island. LaSalle made two decisions before the game, both of which backfired. In order to cage the Lions they chose to open with a man-to-man defense and to overplay McMillian. After Columbia scored the first five points, the Explorers switched to their more familiar zone without noticeable effect on their opponents, who never trailed and won 83-69. With LaSalle concentrating their defense on McMillian, Dotson found himself free frequently enough to lead his team with 32 points.

There were almost as many New Yorkers on the Davidson squad as on St. Johns' when the teams took the court. Though only a sophomore, Maloy had assumed leadership of the Wildcats. His supporting cast was tall—taller than St. Johns—and the Redmen had to struggle to overcome a 6 point half-time deficit. They pulled ahead briefly by a point several times in the second half, but the loss of Rudy Bogad, their most effective big man who fouled out with five minutes remaining, was the turning point. Davidson's height advantage was the deciding factor the rest of the way and they won 79-70.

St. Bonaventure had achieved the third best field goal average in the country and proceeded to shoot the lights out against Boston College. Coach Larry Weise of the Bonnies used his starters for most of the game. His dependence on his starters and reluctance to go to his bench would turn out to be critical for the Bonnies. On the other side of the court Cousy substituted more frequently, perhaps looking for the right combination and nine of his Eagles shared the scoring load. But the broad-based offense was not enough. With Bill Butler's 34 points and Bob Lanier's 32 pacing their attack, St. Bonaventure prevailed 102-93.

The number three, four, six and nine ranked teams assembled in Raleigh the following weekend to decide the regional represntative to the Final Four. It was one of the choicest fields ever assembled and, at least from the ratings, one of the most competitive. The two North Carolina schools had an advantage playing in their home state. The two New York schools were relying on their big centers and their hot shooting.

St. Bonaventure, facing their first high ranked team, were simply outclassed and outraced by North Carolina. Rusty Clark beat Lanier off the boards and the rest of the team showed their heels to the Bonnies. Jet propelled Tarheels flashed up and down court without letup. Dean Smith, substituting frequently as was his style, did not give St. Bonaventure time to catch their breath. The Bonnies kept their starters in the game most of the time and before the end they were clearly close to exhaustion. When it was over, North Carolina had won 91-72 and St. Bonaventure's 25 game win streak was over.

The second game was closer. Columbia, playing sloppily, turned the ball over frequently allowing Davidson to go ahead by as many as ten points in the first period. The Wildcats' pressure defense, which frequently employed a full court press, unnerved the Lions. Dotson and McMillian, both still sophomores, were unsteady and got into foul trouble while Newmark, still bothered by an injured ankle, was less effective than usual. In the second half, though, the Lions overcame their jitters and rallied to tie at 55-55. With two seconds remaining and the teams still even, Bruce Metz of Columbia stood at the line in a one and one situation. Just before he was to take the deciding shot, Davidson coach Lefty Driesell called time out. A minute later Metz approached the free throw line once more and again Driesell called time. Finally Metz approached the line for the third time; but now the pressure had the better of him and he missed the shot sending the teams into overtime. Rod Knowles put Davidson ahead with a bucket but Newmark matched that. However, four straight free throws by the Wildcats insured them a place in the regional final with a 61-59 victory.

Davidson was handicapped in the regional final when 6′6″ Doug Cook was unable to suit up because of an injury received in the game against Columbia. Still the Wildcats held a 34-28 lead at the intermission. It was a very physical game and after a while, with Dean Smith shuffling fresh troops into his lineup, the pace began to affect Davidson which did not have the Tarheels' bench strength. It was still either team's game with six minutes to go and North Carolina on top 54-52. Then the Tarheels spurted 8-2 and, though the Wildcats' pressure tactics resulted in some steals in the final minutes, they were never able to recapture the lead. A lay-in by Larry Miller in the final minute capped the hard fought 70-66 victory.

Final Four:

For the second year in a row North Carolina faced a team from Ohio in a semifinal. In one of the most forgettable contests played at a championship site the Tarheels whipped Ohio State 80-66. One reason it was forgettable was that Houston and UCLA were playing the "rematch of the century" on the same program. "Remember the Astrodome" UCLA rooters implored and the Bruin players never forgot that humiliation.

Houston was still undefeated. Guy Lewis had been voted Coach of the Year. Elvin Hayes was the Player of the Year. Defeating UCLA again would be the final jewel in the crown the Cougars felt was theirs ever since that evening in January. Hayes comment on Alcindor, "I don't think he's what they say he is," stung not only that fine center but his Bruin teammates, too. Wooden's opinion on the protagonists showed more balance and was considerably more diplomatic. "Elvin is more physical but Lew is more maneuverable," he said. "Elvin is a better outside player. But Lew is definitely more of a team player." There did seem one cause for Houston concern, though. Cougars' starting guard George Reynold was declared ineligible and he was replaced by Vern Lewis, the coach's son.

To the millions who had watched UCLA and Houston via television in the Astrodome there was something familiar on their screens aside from the players and the coaches. The teams were playing on the same court again, reassembled in Los Angeles after its short sojourn in Houston. This time all the players were healthy, though Edgar Lacey had quit the team after a dispute with Wooden—an outcome of the game in the Astrodome. Wooden claimed Lacey had refused to reenter the game after he had been told to go in. Lacey denied the accusation and there were conflicting versions from the Bruin players of what had occurred on the bench. Lacey, a highly emotional player, also accused his coach of ruining his natural shot by changing his shooting style. Wooden had picked Mike Lynn to take Lacey's place and he had fit in well.

The great rematch turned out to be no match at all. With the skill of masters, the Bruins proceeded to give the Cougars a demonstration in the finest points of team basketball. Not one starter scored more than 19, nor did one score fewer than 14. Each craftsman was a specialist yet all blended their skills like the ingredients in some classic recipe to produce a superb result. Alcindor, with skyhooks and tap ins, Lynn who scored eight times on just ten shots with sets and jumpers, and Allen, with driving layups after his mates cleared a lane to the bucket, were the leading scorers. Shackelford shadowed Hayes and held him to ten points, the ebb mark of his career. Warren was the floor captain who directed the slashing attack. On defense the men from Westwood played their usual zone press, which so flustered Houston they lost the ball several times before they could even bring it over the center line. One reason was that Hayes, who seemed too loose and overconfident, did not come back to help out. Once over the line the Bruins reformed into a diamond-and-one defense devised by assistant coach Jerry Norman. It worked effectively in containing the high scoring Cougars who shot only 28 percent from the floor. UCLA gained a 53-31 half time lead and after rocketing to a 44 point advantage coasted to a 101-69 triumph. Wooden mercifully sent in his substitutes to mop up after gaining sufficient satisfaction from this reversal of the Astrodome defeat. Even Guy Lewis was moved to comment, "That was the greatest exhibition of basketball I've ever seen in my life." It was also, incidentally, the end of Houston's 32 game win streak.

The finale was once again anticlimatic. North Carolina outshone the Bruins in only one department—their uniforms. The Tarheels were able to wear their traditional blue (with an added touch of class provided by the players' numbers stitched to their socks) while UCLA had to settle for white. In every other respect, though, the Californians prevailed. The Tarheels started the game by going into their four corners stall and the fans hooted their disapproval at such deep freeze tactics during a national final. But in short order, Warren, and then Allen, stole the ball, which enabled UCLA to establish a lead and forced North Carolina out of its shell. It was not much of a contest. Compelled by the score to mount an attack, the Tarheels had to back off and shoot from outside when Alcindor batted the ball back in their faces several times. The players in white had less trouble scoring from close range as they worked the ball inside to Alcindor who accounted for 15 baskets. The second half was punctuated by short Bruin spurts of seven, eight and nine points. When the final buzzer sounded UCLA had the game and the championship 78-55, the widest margin of victory in a NCAA final.

14

ALL THE WAY WITH UCLA *1969-1971*

1969

When UCLA lost to USC in their final game 46-44 on a last second field goal (their first defeat ever in Pauley Pavillion after 52 wins), it released mixed emotions among the Bruins and their opponents—exhilaration in the enemy camp because for the second time in 24 hours a team had stayed with the Bruins for 40 minutes—and more. (UCLA had barely sneaked by USC the night before in double overtime.) So it was possible to beat the unbeatables. True, it was their only defeat of the season after 25 victories, their first loss in the Pac Eight in three years and only their second overall in this span. True, for Alcindor it was only his fourth taste of defeat in **seven** years. But USC showed great tenacity when they came back after what must have been a bitterly disappointing two overtime setback, the kind of tenacity that would be required to upset the number one Bruins in the tournament.

The Bruins were disappointed they had once more failed to finish with an undefeated season. On the other hand, there was relief that the pressure of a win streak reaching 41 games had been lifted. But the emotion that was uppermost, not only in Los Angeles but all over the country, was anticipation. Could UCLA take three national titles in a row, something never before accomplished? Very few doubted they would.

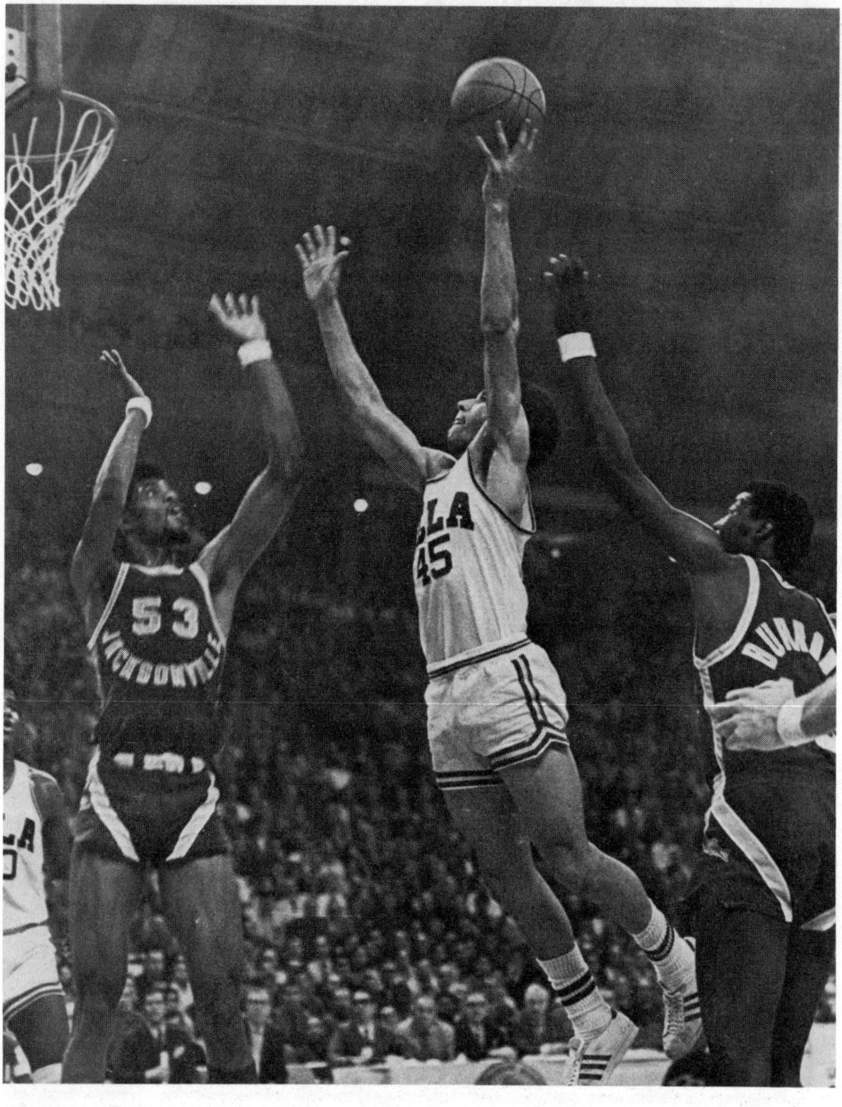

Henry Bibby (45) of UCLA is a foot shorter than Artis Gilmore (53) but he is at least two feet off the ground as he lays the ball in over the Jacksonville center. UCLA won their sixth championship by beating Jacksonville 80-69 in the 1970 final.
(Norm Schindler photo)

West:

Alcindor, All American once again, was still the central pillar around which John Wooden spun his offense and defense. For a change the defense, one of the best in the country, was superior. Maybe that was because UCLA was operating with a new backcourt. Lucius Allen had been suspended during the off season for possession of marijuana and John Warren had graduated. In their places were sophomore John Vallely and journeyman Kenny Heitz, who hard started at forward as a sophomore, been relegated to the bench when Mike Lynn reclaimed his starting position, and now in his senior year was reincarnated as a guard. To replace Lynn, who had also graduated, Wooden turned to 6′6″ Curtis Rowe who had averaged 32 points on the undefeated freshman squad the year before.

Aside from a superior defense, UCLA could put the ball in the hole and they were consistent. During one six game stretch they allowed exactly 64 points in five contests while the sixth opponent was permitted 67 points. A 100-64 rout of Houston at Pauley completed the revenge against the now Hayesless Cougars. Alcindor returned to the city from which he had been lured to UCLA, when the Bruins participated in, and naturally won, the New York Holiday Festival.

The only other school on the West Coast given even a remote chance to unseat UCLA was Santa Clara (27-1). The Broncos were ranked third, having lost only to San Jose State by four points. They had gone to two Christmas tournaments, the Cable Car Classic and the Rainbow Classic, and had won them both. The Broncos were coached by Dick Garibaldi, who as a player at Santa Clara clinched the regional title game against Wyoming in 1952.

The Bronco's strength rested on their uncharitable defense, which held the opposition to 60 points or fewer in half their games, and in their front line of Dennis Awtrey at center and twins Bud and Ralph Ogden at forward. All three were San Jose products. On the other hand, the team had little finesse, was slow, and its passing game was barely mediocre. Yet the players, especially the front court, were extremely physical, punishing anyone attempting to invade the middle.

Two other fine teams, but not as well tested because of easier schedules, were New Mexico State (23-3) and Weber State (25-2). New Mexico State, off and running from the opening tipoff in December, reeled in 16 victories before stumbling with back-to-back losses against arch rival, New Mexico. They lost only to West Texas State (by a bucket) the rest of the way. Weber State had a less auspicious start. They also lost to West Texas State but in their opening game. The rest of the season consisted of a procession of victories, most by substantial margins, interrupted only once by a 100-62 trouncing at Seattle.

Seattle (19-7) was making its eleventh tournament appearance. Coach Bucky Buckwalter had reached across the country to recruit Tom Little, a prep All American at Mackin High School in Washington, D.C.*

The Western Athletic Conference teams were bunched as tight as a school of fish. After the final whistle, only two games separated the top and bottom teams. Wyoming beat BYU in the last game, causing a tie for first place between the two. A playoff was won by Brigham Young (16-11). The Cougars struggled most of the season, and were no better than 9-9 at one point.

For the first time, the NCAA scheduled all opening round games for Saturday. Regional and National semifinals were played on Thursday night while the finals were again held on Saturday night.

The regional opened at the new Pan American Center in Las Cruces, New Mexico, home of the Aggies. The home side had little trouble with BYU whom they had defeated earlier in the year. With 6′10″ center Sam Lacey doing heavy boardwork, New Mexico State out-rebounded the Cougars 62-35. Ahead by four at the intermission, the Aggies established dominance early in the second half, and after stretching their advantage to 17 points, won 74-62.

Weber State, seeking revenge for its humiliating beating, was ahead by nine with less than seven minutes to go, when Seattle began chipping away at the lead. Seven unanswered points were followed by Lou West's goaltending, giving Weber a little breathing room. A basket by the Chieftains made the score 69-67. But with 1:53 remaining, Tom Little missed two free throws that would have tied matters and Weber State held on to win 75-73.

In the second round in Los Angeles, Santa Clara blew an 18 point lead and were fortunate to salvage a 63-59 overtime decision against Weber State. With six seconds on the clock and the score tied, the Wildcats' Dave Sackolwitz succumbed to the pressure and missed a pair of free throws that probably would have won the game.

Foul shooting was not a showcase event in the second game either. UCLA converted only three of ten attempts and Alcindor missed all five of his efforts. The Bruins, nevertheless, had little trouble eliminating New Mexico State 53-38. The Aggies' total was the lowest in NCAA postseason competition since the 1949 final when Kentucky allowed Oklahoma A and M just 36 points. The Aggies brought that statistic on themselves by their deliberate slug-paced attack. On defense they threw up a Siegfried Line zone and collapsed as many as four men on Alcindor. But when UCLA struck for seven consecutive points at the start of the second period, the Aggies were forced to open up and this speeded their demise.

*Mackin was an incubator of basketball stars. In the Fifties it had developed Elgin Baylor who had almost brought Seattle a national title. Little's teammate at Mackin was Austin Carr who went to Notre Dame and was about to rewrite several NCAA tournament records.

The teams with the two best records in the tournament faced each other in the regional final. The Broncos were confident their guards could get the ball to the high scoring forwards, so they rejected stall tactics and decided to attack with confidence. It was a serious miscalculation. The Bruins went into their full court press from the beginning, and Santa Clara had trouble getting the ball across midcourt, let alone feeding their tall men. It took them three and a half minutes to get off their first shot. By that time, UCLA had an 11-0 lead which soon became 18-2. The Bruins were harassing the Broncos so severely they caused eleven turnovers in the first 14 minutes. By half time, UCLA was 21 points ahead and the game was no longer in doubt, if it ever had been. Wooden replaced his starters after the first five minutes of the second half, and twelve Bruins contributed to the final score.

Santa Clara had only Awtrey in double figures. They shot an anemic 35 percent while UCLA was gunning at a 57 percent rate. The degree by which the Bruins outplayed the losers was reflected in the 90-52 final score.

East:

On the other side of the continent, the best team in the East was not even eligible to play. LaSalle (23-1), returning to the glory days when Tom Gola had led them to a national championship, was ranked second under their new coach—Tom Gola. But the Explorers had been slapped by the NCAA for recruiting violations and were banned from the tournament. During the season they had beaten Villanova, St. Josephs and Duquesne, three teams that were to play in the East regional. St. Josephs (17-10) represented the Mid Atlantic conference instead. The Hawks had squeezed past Temple by one point in the postseason playoff after having lost to them earlier by 20. Disappointed, Temple consoled themselves by accepting an invitation to play in the NIT which they won without much effort.

Two other Pennsylvania schools were represented in the regional, ninth ranked Duquesne (19-4) making its first tourney appearance in 17 years, and tenth ranked Villanova (21-4). Three of Villanova's losses were to teams ranked in the top ten. They whacked St. Josephs though, by 25 points. That game in the Palestra was highlighted by a fight between the teams' mascots. When it was over, the Wildcat was snarling triumphantly and the Hawk was forced to retire to the dressing room suffering from more than just ruffled feathers.

Columbia had a better overall record than Princeton (19-6) but dropped three in the Ivy League, while all Princeton's losses were outside the conference. Columbia was also hurt when Dave Newmark left school and signed a professional contract. Under their new coach, Pete Carril, Princeton became increasingly a defense-oriented team.* They won their final eleven games, and in eight of their last nine they allowed fewer than 60 points. Princeton had a tough schedule, half their losses coming at the hands of three of the top five teams in the country. The Tigers featured Chris Thomforde, Jeff Petrie and John Hummer (who had led Washington and Lee High

School to the state championship just like his brother three years before).

St. Johns (22-4) was ranked eighth. They had lost decisively to UCLA in the final of the Holiday Festival but had trounced Niagara (97-60) with Calvin Murphy, flattened North Carolina, and were one of only two teams to defeat fifth ranked Davidson.

Fourth ranked North Carolina (25-3) had hoped for a rematch against UCLA in the Holiday Festival, but St. Johns derailed them in the semifinals, thereby postponing any confrontation possibilities until the national championship. All told, six of the top ten came from the East and five of them, all but LaSalle, were in the same regional. It was not an uncommon imbalance and one that favored UCLA. The best teams in the East invariably knocked each other off while UCLA sailed serenely into the finals.

A sparse crowd of only 7,600 fans, most of them Davidson rooters, greeted the teams in first round action in Raleigh. In a melee of Wildcats, Villanova, due mainly to Howard Porter's deadly 10 to 15 foot jumpers, held a slight 37-35 advantage over Davidson at the end of the first half. Porter had 15 points by then, but he had also gathered three personals. When the Villanova star picked up his third foul with two minutes remaining until intermission, he left the game, precipitating a Davidson surge which brought them from nine points to within two.

The second period saw Villanova maintain their lead until Porter was charged with his fourth foul. Maloy, who was being guarded by Porter, stepped to the line and swish, the score was tied. Exit Porter again. Davidson responded by clicking off ten straight points. By the time the Villanova star was hastily recalled, it was too late. Davidson went into their four corner delay and strung out the game 75-61.

The second contest was a confrontation between two very deliberate teams. No helter-skelter, pell-mell, race-track, board-scorching encounter here. St. Johns took an early 11-2 lead over Princeton. Not until five minutes had passed did the Tigers notch their first bucket. Then Hummer and Petrie combined to score the next 19 points for Princeton. Joe DePre and Carmine Calzonetti were assigned to guard Petrie, the leading scorer in the Ivy League, but neither had much success. Finally, John Warren got the assignment and achieved the desired effect. Petrie was held scoreless in the final eight minutes of the half.

Hummer and Thomforde sparked a second half rally that gave Princeton their first lead at 49-48. St. Johns called time out to make a tactical switch to a 1-3-1 zone. Bill Paultz of the Redmen forced a shot which missed, grabbed his own rebound, and passed to Calzonetti who drove in to start a three point play. It was the turning point. In an almost exact replay of the first game, St. Johns added eight unanswered points to take a 59-49 lead, then slowed the pace and won 72-63.

---

*Offensive teams were still dominant. None of the top six defensive units made it to the tournament.

In Kingston, Rhode Island, before a miniscule gathering of 1,400 (one of the smallest ever to witness a NCAA playoff), Duquesne whipped St. Josephs convincingly, 74-52.

Both second round games were decided at the foul line and the one-sided way in which the referees called infractions in favor of the two North Carolina schools drew substantial criticism from St. Johns, Duquesne and even non-partisan fans. Though both Davidson and North Carolina were playing on a neutral court, College Park was an ACC town with Southern sympathies, and most of the fans were supporters of the Tarheels and Wildcats. In both games the winners were outscored by a substantial margin from the field.

St. Johns was charged with 27 fouls to eleven called against Davidson. This translated into 9 points for St. Johns and 31 for Davidson. The difference was just too much to overcome. Mike Maloy, who had gone to high school within dribbling distance of the St. Johns' campus, scored 35 points, including a perfect 13 for 13 from the line. Warren was sizzling in the opening period, shooting eight for thirteen from the floor, but could not buy a bucket in the final frame. A slim one point lead was pumped into an eleven point bulge by an early second half Davidson surge. Then the Wildcats ran into a cold snap, but frequent excursions to the foul line maintained their advantage. The whistle blew and blew and blew and always it seemed to be blowing for Davidson. The Wildcats eventually went into their four corner stall, and for the second year in a row Davidson eliminated the Redmen, this time 79-69.

In the co-feature, North Carolina trekked to the foul line 33 times to Duquesne's 17. Again the referees seemed to be favoring the Southerners. The Tarheels built a 14 point lead which looked safe with twelve minutes left. The Dukes, however, came storming back, and it took the extraordinary leadership of Charlie Scott to nail down the victory. His 22 points paced the Tarheels, but even more important he twice fed center Lee Dedmon under the hoop for easy baskets in the final minute. Using all the help they could get from Scott and the referees, the Tarheels spiked Duquesne 79-78.

Saturday night's contest was a rerun of the previous year's regional final. The Tarheels' Dick Grubar was hurt, so the versatile Scott had to switch from his normal forward position to plug the gap at guard. Scott responded by pulling the trigger consistently with 15 to 25 feet one-handed jump shots just as he had in leading the Tarheels with 40 points in the ACC final. But his biggest contribution came on defense when he was switched back to forward. Bill Bunting, Lee Dedmon and Rusty Clark, unable to cope with Maloy, were picking up fouls like mosquito bites on a picnic. So Scott was assigned to guard Maloy, and he did an effective job of shutting the taller man down. It seemed natural that the two All Americans, the only two black players on the floor, should end up guarding each other.

The atmosphere in the fieldhouse was electric from the start. Both sides were pistol hot, and the fans responded by an almost continuous outburst of emotion. Nine times the score was tied in the first twenty minutes; 23 times the lead changed hands. As time expired, North Carolina was temporarily ahead, 47-46.

The second half was almost as tight. Davidson regained the lead and held it for most of the session, but the Tarheels never allowed them to pull away. Finally, with four and a half minutes left, Clark gave his team a temporary lead, 80-79. The seconds fled into history as each side scrambled to protect one point advantages. Sixty seconds from the end, with the score tied, the Wildcats controlled the ball, holding it for the final shot. Forty seconds later that hope evaporated when Jerry Kroll was called for charging.

North Carolina called time to set up the final play. Everyone knew who would take the last shot. Scott was the hottest man on the floor. He had scored 30 points, ten of North Carolina's last fifteen and was shooting 75 percent in the second half. Though they were all aware that the ball was going to Scott, nobody was able to stop him from firing it home with two seconds to go to tame the Wildcats 87-85. For the third year in a row, the Tarheels had advanced to the Final Four and for the seventh time in the last eight years, the ACC representative had won the East regional. None had gone all the way, however.

Mideast:

The Mideast regional featured the two highest scoring teams in the tourney as well as the two highest scoring players. Sixth ranked Purdue (20-4) featured All American Rick Mount, averaging 33 points per game, the second best scorer (behind Pete Maravich), in the country.* Mount, a 6′4″ junior guard, was called Rick the Rocket and the Great Gunner for his ball launching skills. He was a pure shooter who ignored virtually every other aspect of the game to concentrate on putting the ball in the hole. A local boy from Lebanon, Indiana, Rick had twice been selected to the prep school All American team. Hoosiers around the state breathed a sigh of relief when this blond kid, looking like a Mark Twain character with his hair combed strangely inward toward the middle of his head, decided to enroll at one of the local universities.

For Purdue it was their first tournament appearance but not their first invitation. In 1940 they had spurned a bid and neighboring Indiana had gone instead, winning their first national championship. The Boilermakers were not about to make the same mistake twice. Purdue had lost their opener to visiting UCLA and three others by three, four and five points. In their final two games, they trounced Michigan, 116-87, and Indiana, 120-76, which boosted them to the national scoring title.

The third highest scoring quintet was Kentucky (22-4) which also had an All American high scorer in 6′9″ center Dan Issel. A pair of Mikes—Pratt and Casey—completed the high scoring front line. The Wildcats had reached

*Mount was one of the 3Ms, which also included Maravich of LSU, Calvin Murphy of Niagara, point production kept scorekeepers hopping throughout the season.

triple digit scores ten times, but their defense was as consistent as spring weather.

Notre Dame coach John Dee spent as much time recruiting players in the District of Columbia as Frank McGuire did in New York. His catch was equally bountiful. Notre Dame (20-6) had three starters from the Washington area—Austin Carr, whose coach at Mackin had been a teammate of Dee, and Sid Catlett and Bob Whitmore, both from DeMatha, the school that had beaten Power Memorial in Alcindor's final year. Big Lew got some measure of satisfaction when UCLA romped over the Irish early in the season. Marquette (22-4) featured 6′1″ Dean Meminger from New York City. His coach, Al McGuire (no relation to Frank), had good connections in the city, too, and harvested an abundant crop. Dean the Dream was an average shot from outside but was able to squirm his way to the basket consistently for layups.

The long shots were Miami of Ohio (14-10), whose non-conference record was a sorry 4-8, and Murray State (22-5) which tied Morehead State for first place in the Ohio Valley Conference. Considering Morehead State had trounced them earlier by 33 points, and they had won six conference games by no more than a goal or two, the 94-76 playoff result was quite an eye opener.

Marquette had little trouble eliminating Murray State 82-62 in the opening round. Notre Dame was hampered considerably when Austin Carr injured his ankle and played only a spectator's role in the second half of their game against Miami. The star for the Redskins was 5′9″ Mike Wren, who scooted around the court with the ball like a jet-propelled water bug. He only scored two field goals, but Irish bodies intruded so frequently into his darting path he was awarded thirteen free throws, twelve of which he made. A pressing defense also caused the unsteady Irish to commit many turnovers, allowing Miami to advance 63-60.

The following Thursday Purdue disposed of Miami 91-71 as Mount framed 32 points in the hoop. In the other contest Marquette effectively tied up Issel, limiting him to just two shots in the final 20 minutes. The game was very rough, not only on the court where six players fouled out, but also on the sidelines where Rupp and McGuire got into a yapping match that was to have repercussions a year later. Who won the battle of the mouth is open for debate, but Marquette won the game 81-74.

Injuries continued to be a factor in the regional. Herm Gilliam, Purdue's leading rebounder, was hampered by a sore ankle and saw limited duty. Chuck Bavis, the Boilermaker's seven foot center, did not play at all. That balanced the odds, which may even have been in Marquette's favor since the game was played in Madison, Wisconsin before a partisan crowd. Victory seemed within the Warriors' grasp when Ric Cobb stepped to the line for a pair of free throws, down by a point and with two seconds remaining. A deafening roar greeted Cobb's first shot which evened the score. A groan almost as loud announced the missed second shot.

The game went into overtime. Gilliam opened the scoring in the extra session with a pair of charity tosses. Marquette tied it at 69. Purdue moved ahead by two again. Meminger's short jump tied it once more. Mount promptly untied it with a one hander from the corner. George Thompson knotted matters for the third time when he drove in for a layup to make the score 73-73. The Boilermakers maneuvered the ball to Mount for the last shot, and the sharpshooting guard hit the bullseye with two seconds remaining, giving Purdue the game 75-73. Thompson had 28 in a losing cause and Mount 26 to lead Purdue.

Midwest:

The Midwest regional was not the place to look for a championship team. The Big Eight and the MVC, which normally produced at least one contender, had fallen on lean days. Representatives of the two conferences had won just one postseason game between them in the last three years. The MVC especially had been weakened by the 1.6 rule which required that college athletes must have at least a C- average to be eligible for an athletic scholarship. Previously, the conference members had been quite generous in the scholarships they handed out to marginal students.

Drake (23-4) tied with Louisville at the top of the MVC but beat them in a playoff on a neutral court 77-73. This was necessary since Drake had won their previous encounter at home, 101-67, and lost at Louisville by 14—a swing of 48 points.

Trinity of Texas (19-4), the winner of the Southland Conference but selected as an at-large team, was making its first appearance. Trinity's record was better than it looked. They had lost three by a single point.

On the other hand Texas A and M's 17-7 record looked a lot better than it actually was. The Aggies had won a half dozen games by one point, two others by a pair, and lost three contests by 19, 22 and 23. By season's end they had scored just 20 total points more than the opposition.

After three years of being shut out of the playoffs, the State of Colorado sent two teams to the tournament. Colorado (20-6) won the Big Eight and Colorado State (15-6) was invited as an at-large team. The latter had recently joined the WAC but was as yet ineligible for a title. The Rams had completed an abbreviated schedule by losing their final three. Matching players in the backcourt proved easy for State which had recruited twins Lloyd and Floyd Kerr.

The NCAA had decided to add two at-large teams to the Midwest regional (they also added one to the West regional to bring the tournament to 25 teams), but since there were insufficient quality teams in the area, they had to import one from elsewhere. The honor went to Dayton (20-6) which played in the Eastern time zone. Notre Dame and Marquette may have been more appropriate, but Notre Dame had become a fixture in the Mideast regional and Marquette refused to move. The Flyers began the season explosively, winning nine of their first ten and ripping their opponents by an average of 22 points a game. The remainder of the schedule was not as satisfying and reached a low point when Cincinnati shot down the Flyers 96-60. Houston, which had graduated the Big E, failed to make the playoffs for the first time in five years.

Dayton, trailing by as many as ten in the first half of their opening round contest against Colorado State, came back to take a 49-45 lead with three minutes remaining. Then Cliff Shegogg of the Rams sank a pair of free throws and followed up with a lay-in to even the score. With the final seconds blinking away, Lloyd Kerr stole the ball and was fouled. His free throw proved to be the winning margin as the Rams took a close one 52-50. Texas A and M had less trouble disposing of Trinity 81-66.

Drake, in turn, found little resistance in eliminating Texas A and M 81-63 as the regional continued in Manhattan, Kansas. In a more spirited contest Colorado State upset Colorado 64-56 despite an outstanding performance by Cliff Meely who strung the nets for 32 points for the losers, representing almost 60 percent of his team's total.

The regional final was one of the most exciting ever seen in the tournament. It was a game of fleeting leads and transient deadlocks. Twenty times the score was tied, and seventeen times the advantage changed hands. Drake nosed in front 38-37 at intermission. With 2:48 remaining, the Bulldogs were still ahead by a point. Lloyd and Floyd were performing well for the Rams, but at this point the Bulldogs unleashed their own matched pair—a pair of Garys—who came off the bench to ice the game. First Gary Odom tipped in a rebound, was fouled and completed the three point play to give Drake a 77-73 lead. Then when the Bulldogs got the ball back, Gary Zeller's short jumper put the game out of reach. Drake in its first NCAA tourney advanced to the Final Four, 84-77, where it joined Purdue, another first time participant, UCLA and North Carolina in Louisville.

Final Four:

Purdue's starting backcourt of Rick Mount and Bill Keller accounted for 56 points and between them destroyed North Carolina 92-65. The Boilermakers ran the Tarheels silly and put so much pressure on their ball handlers they caused 29 turnovers, almost three times the number Purdue committed. The Tarheels' front court averaged 6′9″ but Purdue's speed overcame that height advantage and the quicker Boilermakers grabbed 14 more rebounds. Charley Scott was held to 16 points, and for the second time that year North Carolina missed its opportunity for a rematch against UCLA by losing a tournament semifinal. It was also North Carolina's third demise in as many years after reaching the Final Four.

The Bulldogs were definitely the underdogs in their match against UCLA. But they refused to roll over and came snarling back every time the Bruins looked ready to pull away. Drake used unorthodox tactics that the Bruins had rarely seen in the last three years. First they ran with the Bruins and actually outraced them. They also played them man-to-man and got away with it. Wooden experimented towards the end of the first half by putting four forwards and a guard into the game, trying to overwhelm the Bulldogs with size and height. Drake retaliated by harassing the Bruins so energetically they jarred the ball loose from the usually unflappable Uclans.

With the help of turnovers, they scored seven straight and wiped out a Bruin lead. Every time the game tilted in UCLA's direction, the Bulldogs would bounce back. They simply refused to quit. Unaccustomed to being guarded man-to-man, the Bruins had trouble getting the ball in to Alcindor. His teammates danced and weaved around him like youngsters around a maypole and often had to shoot themselves when trying to connect with Big Lew appeared too risky.

The problem for Drake was they were fouling too much. UCLA was awarded 44 free throws and rang up 29 points from the line—20 by Alcindor and Vallely alone.

The second half had passed its midmark when UCLA made one of its patented rushes, clicking off nine unanswered points, seven by Vallely, while Drake misfired seven times without a hit. Drake was in a hole, 14 points down and only a few minutes left. But tenacity, the mark of the Bulldogs, enabled them to mount one last charge led by Willie McCarter. With less than half a minute remaining, the Bruins looked safe with an 83-78 edge. Yet McCarter's jump shot at :20, repossession, and a tip in by Dolph Pulliam off a missed McCarter jump shot brought Drake within a point with nine seconds still on the clock. Absolute frenzy greeted Pulliam's field goal. UCLA could not believe what was happening. But the possibility of defeat had an energizing effect on the Bruins and they controlled the ball the rest of the way. Shackelford's two free throws at the buzzer were superfluous. UCLA had finally collared the Bulldogs 85-82. Alcindor was credited with 25 points and 21 rebounds while Vallely picked up 29 points mostly from outside.

The final was a rematch between Wooden's alma mater and the team he had coached for 20 years. UCLA and Purdue had opened the season against each other and now, through a strange coincidence, they were about to be on stage for the last act before the final curtain descended. Mount, who had missed a crucial foul shot in the final seconds with the score tied in the opener, was anxious to redeem himself.

As usual when the Bruins were contending for the championship, the final scene was anti-climactic. For all practical purposes the game was over midway through the first period. With the score knotted 6-6, UCLA hummed eight consecutive points into the net, collected its breath briefly, then went on a 12-4 spree. By this time the score was 26-10, and the voters were already writing Alcindor's name on their ballot for MVP—an honor he earned for the third year in a row. Big Lew scored 24 points in the first half on his way to a 37-point night. Meanwhile, Mount found the hoop only three times in eighteen tries. He did better in the second half and triggered 28 points for the Boilermakers, but it was not enough and too late. UCLA took their third straight championship even more easily than the 89-76 score indicated. It was also UCLA and Wooden's fifth title in six years. Both accomplishments were firsts in the tournament.

Once more, all was right in Westwood. Wooden was once again Coach of the Year and Alcindor, Player of the Year. UCLA during the reign of Alcindor and his supporting cast had won 88 and lost 2—one by a point, the other by two—in three years of competition in one of the strongest conferences in the country and against some of the most talented teams, all of them prepared for and aching to beat the Bruins. Besides, they had now won twenty consecutive games in the postseason tournament, where no other team had won more than ten in a row before.

The Bruins should have been sky high after the final win, but the victory party in a Louisville restaurant was distinctly downbeat. Most of the players were just grateful it was over—that the pressure had lifted. The seniors, especially, were relieved. After all, they had won two national titles before, and they had been expected to win again. The juniors and sophomores were relieved, too. If there was any friction on the team, it was over the question of playing time. The reserves resented the amount of time the starters spent on the court and the amount of attention they received from the mass media. Considering their success, the Bruins were not a happy group.

They sat in the restaurant, letting the emotion of the evening drain away, not boisterous or clubby but each in his own way savoring the victory and the championship it brought. Some had expected Lucius Allen to put in an appearance, but he did not show up. Talking about Allen, the players remembered the others who had quit or been forced to leave the team—Edgar Lacey over a disagreement with Wooden and Mike Lynn after a brush with the law. The last three years had seen the Bruins reach the summit three times; it had also seen some of their teammates buckle under the pressure.

1970

West:

The 1970 Bruins were a much happier group, and Wooden was delighted to go back to tactics which he had shelved during Big Lew's tenure. For three years he had felt somewhat useless—just let the boys go out and play. Now he dusted off and revitalized the full court press, the fast break, the deft passing, and all the tricks that Wooden had innovated in the early and mid Sixties. They even used a zone occasionally, but it was not as effective as their man-to-man (Oregon was able to penetrate it without too much trouble and gave UCLA their worst beating in four years). The Bruins enjoyed themselves more and surprisingly, though they were not expected to, they won almost as often as the previous year. Their 24-2 record was good enough to rank them second in the country at the end of the season behind Kentucky. Alcindor, Shackelford and Heitz had graduated, but their place had been filled quite adequately by subs Steve Patterson, Sidney Wicks and sophomore Henry Bibby. In no way could Patterson at center be compared to Alcindor, but the Bruins played a more cohesive team game and helped each other in their varying assignments. Wicks, in particular, as the power forward on the team was helpful to Patterson, shouldering some of the center's burden, especially on defense and in rebouding.

If UCLA played unselfishly, displaying the finest exhibition of team basketball, it was due more to their coach than to the collection of raw talent assembled on the court at Pauley Pavillion. Wooden was concerned about his boys to the point where they resented his intrusions into their daily lives outside the basketball arena. And he had trouble relating to his black stars. Brought up in rural Indiana, Wooden found it difficult to understand the urban and ghetto-educated blacks and their need to express themselves. This led to some friction but it rarely spread outside the confines of the gym.

On the court Wooden was an absolute dictator. He determined where each player could shoot from, allowing some to post from longer range than others. He forbade any hot dogging, bragging, loafing, selfishness or criticism of teammates. He drilled into them repeatedly the need to keep their hands up on defense, to assume every shot will miss and thus collapse on the basket, to stay in condition, to acknowledge a pass that leads to a basket. In a word, Wooden's inspiration was based on discipline.

Though he never stated it, Wooden had a tremendous urge to win. This outwardly mild-mannered church deacon took second place to no man when it came to referee baiting. With a rolled up program he would devastate the men in the striped shirts; it took a great deal of fortitude for an official not to be intimidated. Wooden was not above raising the thermostat in the old B.O. Barn (where UCLA had once played their home games) so visiting teams wilted from the heat, thus giving the Bruins one of the best home court records in the country. The temperature in Pauley Pavillion was more stable, but UCLA continued almost unbeatable at home as Wooden and the UCLA aura worked their special magic. And the post-Alcindor Bruins were not without credentials. Forward Curtis Rowe and guard Henry Bibby had both been prep All Americans.

It was not until 22 games into the season that UCLA tasted defeat, losing at Oregon by 13 points. Three games later USC nipped the Bruins 87-86 and that was it. Only two losses, but still the worst record by a UCLA team in four years!

Until they had a few games under their belts, the national champions had several rocky moments. A couple of one-point-victories over Princeton and Minnesota caused some concern among their supporters who wondered whether the new kids could carry on the winning tradition. Such uncertainty did not last long. Aside from the two narrow victories, they clobbered six other teams, all major colleges, in their first eight games by an average margin of 41 points. Victories over Texas 99-54, LSU 133-84, Georgia Tech 121-90, Notre Dame 108-77, Miami 127-69 and Stanford 120-90 dispelled the doubts of their followers.

None of the other schools in the West regional were ranked in the top ten. Santa Clara (22-5) won the revised WCAC which had replaced San Jose State and University of California, Santa Barbara with University of Nevada, Las Vegas and University of Nevada, Reno. The Broncos won the Cable Car Classic for the third year in a row and added the Las Vegas Classic for good measure. That amounted to a total of five classics in three years—a distinctly classy if not classic performance.

Weber State (20-6) suffered half their losses on their own court which was unusual for them. However, they humbled Gonzaga by 48 points before losing to them in Spokane. Texas, El Paso (17-7) (formerly Texas Western and popularly known as UTEP) won the WAC their first year in the league. High scoring Utah State (20-6) scored in triple digits eight times. Their most prolific outburst was a 125-108 extravaganza over St. Peters. New Mexico State, which victimized UTEP and Utah State twice each, was selected to play in another regional.

Then there was Long Beach State (23-3), which won the Pacific Coast Athletic Association but was invited as an at-large entry. The 49ers were making their first apperarance in the tournament. A short trip to the Southwest cost them their three losses in a span of four games, but they completed the season with a string of 18 consecutive victories.

Long Beach State beat Weber State 92-73 in a first round match. The 49ers utilized a dense zone, causing the Wildcats to shoot an anemic 36 percent and limiting their star, Willie Sojourner, to 13 points. The winners also controlled the boards and shot well, extending their winning streak to 19.

There was some torrid shooting in the co-feature as a couple of hot-shot Nates—Williams of Utah State and Archibald of UTEP—singed the cords in the duel of the Wasatch. Coach Ladell Anderson, knowing it would be suicidal to try to contain Archibald with his normal man to man, deployed his men in a zone. Archibald missed his first shot, then connected on his next ten attempts. Williams made eight in a row in the first half and ten of twelve in the game. Archibald finished with 36 points, Williams with 31 and teammate Marv Roberts contributed 30.

The Aggies were ahead by twelve at intermission but the Miners rallied to close to within four. Unfortunately for Haskins, he protested a referee's call too vigorously and was slapped with two technicals. Utah State accepted the gifts and effectively killed the rally by claiming the next ten points on the way to a 91-81 win.

In the second round UCLA had little trouble ending Long Beach State's string. The starters played most of the game and unselfishly distributed the scoring so that all were in double figures, but none had more than 20 points in the 88-65 victory.

The co-attraction between Santa Clara and Utah State turned into a real scrap in the final 20 minutes. After allowing the Broncos to build a four point halftime lead, Utah State counterattacked, sparked by Nate Williams' point-a-minute scoring. Williams, a spring action sophomore forward, four times stole the ball and streaked downcourt to register. The Aggies opened up some daylight with a 65-58 lead but Santa Clara strung ten straight points together, the last two on a layup by Awtrey with 2:13 to go. Twenty seconds later Marv Roberts' layup brought Utah State within one again. The Broncos froze the ball until the Aggies fouled Bruce Bochte, who missed both his attempts from the line. The second miss was grabbed by Ed Epps, the best one-on-one player on Utah State, who ended the suspense by floating a side jumper through the net with 13 seconds left to put the Aggies ahead 69-68. Then Williams committed his fifth larceny of the half to end the Broncos' hopes.

In the regional final Epps broke a 42-42 tie, shocking UCLA into counteraction. It was the last advantage for the Aggies as the Bruins poured nine straight points in the net, six by Curtis Rowe. The rest of the game resembled a mopping up operation as UCLA won their twenty second consecutive NCAA tournament game, 101-79. Roberts led Utah State with 33 points while Rowe and Wicks each collected 26.

Midwest:

The only team (other than UCLA) west of the Mississippi ranked in the top ten was New Mexico State (23-2), number five. The Aggies lost only to Creighton and Baylor in rematches after having whipped them both initially. The meat of the Aggie team were New York imports including 5′9″ Charlie Criss and the man they called the Roadrunner, Milton Horne, though any roadrunning he did before coming West must have been in heavy traffic. In all, State had attracted six player from New York and one from New Jersey.

Kansas State (19-7) won in the Big Eight, and Drake (21-6), after surviving three losses in a row in December, topped the MVC once again. Rice

(14-10) was a disaster even for the football oriented SWC. Even their record was deceiving. The Owls gave up more points than they scored, lost six of their first nine, were humbled by Georgia Tech by 30 points and by North Carolina twice by an average of 19, and succumbed to lightly regarded Sam Houston. Besides, they won three SWC games by a single point. The next four schools in the conference all scored more points than they gave up, and the league could undoubtedly have been better represented.

Houston (24-3) was held to 66 points in an upset loss to St. Mary's of Texas but reversed the outcome in a stunning turnabout, 118-77. Dayton (19-7) was a substitute choice after eighth ranked Marquette (22-3) refused an invitation and headed for New York where they won the NIT. The reason for Marquette's withdrawal was the NCAA's decision to move the Warriors to the Midwest regional instead of letting them compete in the Mideast, their normal spot. Al McGuire was incensed on discovering the change of venue and accused Adolph Rupp, with whom he had clashed verbally in a previous tourney, of exerting influence with the NCAA tournament committee. Dayton, which was even further east than Marquette, gratefully accepted the invitation.

The Flyers travelled all the way to Fort Worth for their first round game against Houston, then travelled right back after losing to them 71-64. The game was close until the Cougars' Tom Gribben tied the count at 57-57 and Tim Welch twice stole the ball, scoring each time, to give Houston a lead they never relinquished. New Mexico State meanwhile devoured Rice 101-77.

New Mexico State almost blew a 17 point lead before eliminating Kansas State 70-66 the following weekend at Lawrence. The Wildcats triggered their rally by outsnatching the taller Aggies by 14 rebounds. Meanwhile New Mexico State's strategy called for them to clear a driving lane to the hoop for Jim Collins. The maneuver succeeded, and Collins set a new Aggie career scoring mark during the game. In the other match Drake also lost a huge lead but recovered in time to hand Houston their fourth loss of the season, 92-87.

Two days later New Mexico State's trio of guards, Collins, Criss and Horne, combined to score 53 points. Every time the Roadrunner entered the game the fans would greet him with shouts of "beep-beep" and he responded with an exhibition of fancy dribbling and jet-propelled drives to the basket. Collins and Criss scored from the periphery and Sam Lacey claimed 24 balls off the boards. That combination was just too much for the Bulldogs who lost four starters via fouls during the course of the game. After leading 19-18 Drake turned helpless as the Aggies outscored them 27-11 to take a commanding lead at the half. This time New Mexico State did not blow and triumphed 87-78 to qualify for their first Final Four.

Mideast:

The strength of the tournament was concentrated in the Mideast regional. Kentucky, Jacksonville, Iowa, Notre Dame and Western Kentucky had suffered just 14 losses among them. None of them was shy of firing the ball, and the regional resembled an all night shooting gallery, not surprising with four of the top five offensive teams participating. Every game except one saw the combined score total over 200 points as defense took a vacation. The fans loved it.

Number one Kentucky (25-1) was led by their All American center, gap-toothed Dan Issel who had averaged 33 points a game. The Wildcats had lost only to Vanderbilt after winning their first 15 games, including a 102-100 thriller over Notre Dame. Kentucky had achieved triple-digit scoring 15 times during the season, and it looked as if the Wildcats would give Rupp one more national championship before his imminent retirement. Only two other schools had scored better than the Wildcats.

Ninth ranked Notre Dame (20-6) had reveled in some memorable bombing binges such as a 135-88 pasting of St. Peters (a team whose schedule showed more guts than sense) and a 121-114 flak duel with Butler. They had also been on the receiving end while being staggered by UCLA by 30 points. The Irish were paced by All American Austin Carr, the highest scorer in Notre Dame history. Carr had averaged 38 points per game, second only to Pete Maravich, and was considered the best pure shooter in college. A special stacked offense had been devised by Coach Johnny Dee in which Carr, normally a guard, was used as a third forward and given additional scoring opportunities by setting him up with picks set by the other forwards.

Jacksonville (25-1) was making its initial tournament appearance after climbing to fourth place in the polls. The Dolphins played in aptly named Swisher Gym where they wore the nets off the baskets. Their prodigious scoring came mostly at the expense of second and third rate opponents. Fodder for their offensive barrages was provided by Biscayne 130-65, Virgin Islands 114-66, Mercer 102-62 and Richmond twice 113-77 and 88-49, which created the feeling the Dolphins were overrated or at least had not been properly tested yet.

There was nothing overrated about Artis Gilmore, their 7′2″ center (not counting a fierce Afro hairdo that added at least three inches to his height). Gilmore later became only the fifth man to average more than 20 points and 20 rebounds per game during his college career. In 1970 he led the country in rebounding and scored 26 points per game besides. But there was another dimension to Gilmore as well. In a regional dominated by shooters, he stood out as a superb defensive player. In a game against Harvard, he blocked 16 shots, and in every other contest he had an intimidating effect on the opposing gunners.

Gilmore, one of ten children, had grown up in Chipley, Florida and then moved to Dotham, Alabama, where he had been an All American in high school. After graduation he had gone to Gardner-Webb, a junior college, for two years where he became a JC All American. He was joined on the Dolphins by another seven foot junior college transfer with the classy name of Pembrook Burrows III. Rounding out the monumental forward wall was 6′10″ Rod McIntyre, making the Dolphins taller than most professional teams. Quarterbacking the attack was 5′10″ Vaughn Wedeking, who had been a star prep player in Evansville. Wedeking had influenced Greg Nelson and Rex Morgan, two of his buddies attending the University of Evansville, to transfer to Jacksonville. Nelson and Morgan had been important cogs in Evansville's undefeated freshman squad. With an Artis, a Pembrook, a Vaughn and a Rex, the Dolphins, if nothing else, had to be leading the country in the fancy name department.

Coach Joe Williams, who in his white double breasted suit and red shirt looked even nattier than Guy Lewis, was delighted with his team, whatever their names. All but ignored in the preseason polls, the Dolphins had lost only to Florida State, a team they later defeated. They first came to national attention when they won the Evansville Invitational, beating the host team 100-70. It was a homecoming of sorts for Wedeking, Nelson and Morgan, who impressed the hometown folks and their former teammates with the new company they were keeping.

Iowa (19-4) lost four of their first seven but then ran off 16 straight wins and were undefeated in their conference. They opened the Big Ten campaign on a positive note by tripping defending champion Purdue 94-88 despite Mount's 53 points. It was also Purdue's first home-court setback in 31 games. Having struck that major chord, the Hawkeye bandwagon was off and rolling.

Coach Ralph Miller had achieved a minor miracle. His team finished with a 12-12 record in 1969 and lost four of its first six players. But he also acquired Fred Brown, a junior college transfer, who could score from just about anywhere including the last row of seats. Now in his last year at Iowa before moving on to Oregon State, Miller had assembled a team that could flood the basket with leather. In their last four games, all against Big Ten teams, they averaged 114 points and finished the year as the second most prolific team in the country. They were as deadly from the floor as from the free throw line and were among the top three in shooting accuracy in both departments. Defense was an entirely different matter. It seemed at times that the Hawkeyes were willing to give up an open shoot just so that they could get their hands on the ball again.

Seventh ranked Iowa was sparked by John Johnson and the team came to be called J.J. and the Dealers. The Hawkeyes dealt themselves their best hand in a 108-107 title clinching victory over Purdue, in which Mount again went on a binge, this time tallying 61 points in another losing cause.

Western Kentucky (22-2) won their last 16 in a row after losing in the final of the Jayhawk Classic to Kansas by 23 points. Ohio University (20-4) seemed out of place in such talented company but they, too, made their mark, notably four victories against Big Ten schools in their first four games. They were a hard nosed team that averaged more than 23 personal fouls a game.

Austin Carr set a new NCAA tournament record with 61 points as Notre Dame extinguished Ohio 112-82 in the regional curtain raiser. His 35 points in the first half and statistics which included 25 of 44 field goals and 11 of 14 free throws, set the tone for the remainder of the regional.

The heavy artillery continued in the second game as Jacksonville eliminated Western Kentucky 109-96. It was a classic battle of seven foot centers and Gilmore bested the Hilltoppers' 7′1″ McDaniels 30-29. McDaniels might have scored more, but he fouled out with eight and a half minutes remaining trying to contain Gilmore. The big difference between the two giants was in the rebounding department where Gilmore had a 19 to 8 edge. On defense the big Dolphin center blocked nine shots.

The survivors moved on to Columbus, Ohio. By half time the Irish had built a 53-48 lead over favored Kentucky, but the number one ranked Wildcats rallied, scoring 61 points in the second half to salvage the contest 109-99. Once again Carr accounted for more than half his team's output, this time strumming the cords for 52 points. Issel's 44 points would have been the high scoring mark in most tournaments. Luckily for Kentucky, he received considerably more support from his teammates than did Carr.

The contest between Jacksonville and Iowa was marked by another scoring deluge. It was a thriller all the way. The Dolphins held a narrow 50-49 advantage after the first 20 minutes. Iowa spent most of the second half trying to catch up. They finally pulled even at 100-100 with one minute remaining, nudging in front 103-102—only to have Burrows tip in a rebound at the buzzer to give Jacksonville a 104-103 win. Gilmore matched his opening round production of 30 points, and Fred Brown popped 27 for the Hawkeyes.

The first shot Issel took in the regional final was slammed back in his face by the ham-handed Gilmore. Duly impressed, Issel was far from the awesome presence he had been throughout the season. True, he eventually scored 28 points, but he fouled out with ten minutes remaining while trying unsuccessfully to contain Gilmore. Mike Pratt and two Wildcat substitutes were also waved out of the game before the final buzzer, while the Dolphins suffered no personnel losses. Gilmore was less a scoring threat in this game than an intimidator and ball hawk off the boards where he collected 20 rebounds. Rex Morgan took scoring honors for Jacksonville with 28 points, but the Dolphin's most potent weapon was their playmaker Chip Dublin. The little guy in the land of the giants set up Gilmore, Morgan and the rest of the Dolphins. In addition, Dublin hung eleven points on the scoreboard in the last twelve minutes of the first half to pace a Jacksonville surge that resulted in a 52-45 lead at the intermission.

The Dolphins increased that advantage to 13 and still led by ten at 5:54. Kentucky rallied to cut the margin to a basket late in the game but with the clock showing 27 seconds Morgan iced the upset with a pair of charity tosses. The Dolphins had made believers out of those who had scoffed at this upstart team with the soft schedule and the crazy names, by stunning the number one team in the country 106-100 and moving on to the Final Four in their first NCAA tournament.

In keeping with the pattern set throughout the regional, Iowa poured it on to beat Notre Dame 121-106 in the consolation. A total of 195 shots were fired at the hoops in a cannonade seldom witnessed in peacetime. Run, shoot—run, shoot—run, shoot. It was like watching ten men imitating a popcorn popper. When it was all over and the nets finally hung limp, several records had been shattered. The Hawkeyes registered 75 points in the first half. Carr with 45 points (his worst showing in three games) accumulated 158 points in the tourney, the second best in 32 years and 15 points more than Jerry Chambers achieved in **four** games. Only Bill Bradley's 177 points, scored in five games, topped Carr's feat. The Hawkeyes and the Irish had a combined score of 227 points, a fitting finale to a regional that was a scorekeeper's nightmare. In addition, Iowa's 121 points was the most scored in a regulation game and Notre Dame's 105.7 points per game average was another new record, though they managed to lose two of three.

East:

The tall and the short of it in the East regional were a pair of All Americans: 6′11″ center Bob Lanier of St. Bonaventure and 5′9″ guard Calvin Murphy of Niagara. Both attended small Catholic colleges in upstate N.Y., both had averaged 29 points per game and were among the top ten scorers in the country.

The third ranked Bonnies (25-1) were one of four teams in the tournament which had lost only once—Jacksonville, Kentucky and Pennsylvania were the others. They bowed to Villanova by two points but so overwhelmed their other opponents they led the nation in margin of victory. They captured the Holiday Festival tournament, trouncing Purdue by 16 in the final. In that game Lanier upstaged Mount by scoring 50 points on phenomenal 18 for 22 field goal shooting. Affectionately known as Buffalo Bob, Lanier was a genial giant who wore size 19 sneakers and tipped the scales at 270 lbs. Despite his bulk, he was one of the most graceful and light footed centers ever to play the game. He also had a soft touch from outside as well as close range. His supporting cast included 6′5″ Matt Gantt and 5′11″ playmaker Billy Kalbaugh. Lanier, Gantt and Greg Garry, all black, were nicknamed the Soul Patrol.

Niagara (21-5) featured Calvin Murphy, not only one of the finest scorers in the country but a state baton twirling champion as well. Murphy averaged a sparkling 49 points per game on the freshman team. Despite his size he could jump high enough to dunk the ball and was called for goaltending more than once. Murphy was one of the 3M super sophs of 1968 (Mount, Maravich and Murphy). In that year he was national scoring runner up and in

1969 he was third. But in 1970 he carried less of the scoring burden, thus bringing his teammates more into the flow of the game. As a result Niagara's record improved and they received their first invitation to the tournament. The Purple Eagles won their first eleven but fell to Villanova and were twice crushed by St. Bonaventure, once by 36 points.

Pennsylvania (25-1) was one of three Philadelphia schools to compete in the tournament. After losing to Purdue by three in the Holiday Festival, the Quakers reeled off 18 straight and finished the season by polishing off Cornell 97-63. Even with such an outstanding record, Penn was not ranked in the top ten due no doubt to the pollsters' prejudice against Ivy League teams whom many thought played a soft schedule. The Quakers were led by star sophomores, Corky Calhoun and Bob Morse. Villanova (20-6) lost to three different Ivy League schools but had regrouped at the tail end of the season and averaged 112 points in their final three games.

The Mid Atlantic had experienced better years. By 1970 its stock had plummetted so far that Temple (15-12) emerged as the conference representative. Only one of its twelve teams lost fewer than ten games. The Owls were molting fast, barely winning their first three by a total of six points, then dropping six of their next eight. The rest of the conference teams were equally weak which kept their playoff chances alive. In confrontations with the Big Five in Philadelphia they were able to subdue only LaSalle while being raked by such lightweights as West Chester and Hofstra.

The two southern schools were Davidson (22-4) and North Carolina State (22-6). Both coaches were making their tournament debut after replacing experienced mentors who had seen considerable postseason action. At Davidson Terry Holland had taken over from Lefty Driesell when he moved on to Maryland, promising to make the Terrapins "the UCLA of the East." At North Carolina State Norm Sloan stepped into the vacancy created when Ev Case resigned. Case had since died and when his will was opened, it was discovered he had left most of his $200,000 estate to 57 Wolfpack players whom he had coached, among them Sloan.

The winner of the ACC during the regular season was sixth ranked South Carolina. They were undefeated in league competition, a considerable accomplishment in the cutthroat atmosphere of that conference. Five games behind in second place came the Wolfpack, beaten twice by South Carolina, the second time by 16 points just a week before the playoffs.

For several years almost every ACC playoff had been marked by at least one game played in a deep freeze. The ultimate in this exercise of tundra tactics was a 12-10 standathon win by North Carolina State over Duke in 1968. This year was no different. Clemson tried the same tactics against South Carolina in the first round of the ACC playoffs, but the Gamecocks survived 34-33. They also knocked over Wake Forest in the next round but lost the services of their star John Roche, the only man to have been named ACC Player of the Year in his first two seasons. Late in the game, with the issue no longer in doubt, Roche fell and tore ligaments in his ankle. He participated in the playoff final against North Carolina State but was almost ineffective, wobbling on an ankle that could barely support him. The Wolfpack reached back two years to recreate their successful game plan against Duke and applied it to South Carolina. The result was a 42-39 double overtime upset in a game where the action was at best intermittent. Tied 35-35 after forty minutes and 37-37 after the first overtime, the contest was finally decided when the Wolfpacks' Ed Leftwich stole the ball from Roche and curled in a layup with 22 seconds to go. The unfortunate Gamecocks could not even accept an invitation to play in the NIT because NCAA rules forbade a host school from playing in another tournament. The East regional was scheduled for Columbia, South Carolina.

The three first round matches were held in three separate locations. At Princeton, Penn suffered from a bad case of tournament jitters as they blew one opportunity after another against Niagara. They had little trouble penetrating but just could not stuff the ball into the hole from close up, not even on second and third attempts. Still, they were on the heavy end of a 33-24 score with intermission relief to regroup in sight. Then a purple streak by the Eagles closed the gap to a single point.

In the second half Niagara further tightened their zone so that Pennsylvania found it increasingly difficult to find their way to the basket. The Quakers' aim from long range was no better than from underneath. Meanwhile Murphy, mercury swift and equally elusive, was all over the court, leading the fast break and charging toward the hoop. The Eagles worked the ball well, and more often than not it was Murphy who took the shot. He scored 23 second half points for a game high of 35 and led Niagara to a 79-69 victory. Pennsylvania's frigid 32.5 percent shooting, more than anything else, was responsible for the rupture in their 18 game win streak. The cold Quakers would become an almost annual tournament sight.

St. Bonaventure and Davidson played a close if not particularly exciting first half which ended with the Wildcats ahead 36-34. They expanded their lead to 47-40 after six and a half minutes of the second half. At that point the Bonnies switched to a pressing man-to-man defense and turned the game around. They had waited for the right moment to crowd Davidson, certain they could not keep it up throughout a game or it would exhaust them. A Lanier jumper tied the count at 54-54. After that St. Bonaventure pulled away, surviving a slight scare when Lanier was hit with his fourth personal. Kalbaugh took charge of St. Bonaventure's offense, directing the flow with nine assists. His total of 17 points all came in the final 20 minutes. But it was Lanier's delicate bulk on both ends of the court that ensured St. Bonaventure's 85-72 declawing of the Wildcats. He amassed 28 points which was matched by Davidson's Brian Adrian. Mike Maloy was limited to 13.

Both teams were playing at home as Villanova and Temple squared off at the Palestra. Temple made a fight of it until Tom Wieczerak fouled out with the score tied and more than six minutes left to play. The loss of their leader and a harrassing second half zone press were too much for the Owls to overcome. Villanova had hurt themselves earlier by missing too many shots from the foul line, but seven consecutive free throws in the last three minutes sealed the verdict and the Wildcats, the only surviving Philadelphia team, advanced 77-69.

In Columbia, North Carolina State waited for Villanova and the two other Catholic schools. As Fred Handler, St. Bonaventure's assistant coach, put it: "At a tournament like this you find out who's closer to God." The local Gamecock fans vented their frustration by adopting the Bonnies and vehemently booing the Wolfpack. St. Bonaventure hardly needed the encouragement. Despite Vann Williford's 35 points the Wolfpack were unable to mount much of an offense. Lanier sucked up 19 rebounds to control the boards and his agile moves allowed him to gain position both inside and outside to pop for 24 points. It turned out to be an easy 80-68 win for the Bonnies.

Villanova had beaten Niagara four times in as many meetings over the previous three years and had devised a defense to defuse Murphy. Their system was to put pressure on the ball handlers feeding the star guard. Whenever the Eagles launched their offense, the man with the ball attracted traffic like a circus performer giving away free balloons. Niagara was denied room to maneuver, and passing inside became almost impossible. So effective was Villanova's pressing zone that Murphy attempted his first field goal only after more than four minutes elapsed, and did not sink his first bucket until midway through the first period. He finished with 18 points, considerably below his average. The Wildcats' front court of Clarence Smith, Sammy Sims and Howard Porter collected 44 rebounds, more than the entire Niagara squad. Porter also tallied 29 points in Villanova's easy 98-73 win.

Both Coach Larry Weise of St. Bonaventure and Jack Kraft of Villanova did not like pulling their starters out of the game regardless of the score. Often stars like Lanier and Porter would play a full forty minutes, even when the outcome was no longer in doubt. This practice was to cost the Bonnies dearly.

The contest was never close. St. Bonaventure's advantage was 16 points at the intermission, ballooning to 26 six minutes into the second session. Lanier, playing flawlessly, had already been credited with 26 points and there were still nine minutes remaining. He was often double and triple teamed, but would pass of to Gantt or another teammate or pull out of the traffic to launch his soft shots. It was sheer hubris to leave Lanier in at that stage of the game. There was no need to roll up the score. He should have been on the bench, watching his teammates mop up, but instead he was in the center of a mass of swirling bodies when he went up for a rebound and crashed heavily on the hardwood like a Douglas fir hitting the forest floor. As Lanier sprawled awkwardly trying to protect the ball, Villanova's Chris Ford fell across him, ripping ligaments in Lanier's knee. Even then Weise did not remove him. Lanier limped around for a few seconds, then called time out.

He hobbled to the bench, his collegiate career over. It was to all intents and purposes the end for St Bonaventure's tournament chances, too. The Bonnies won the battle 97-74 and avenged their only defeat of the year. However, they lost the war when Lanier entered a hospital the next day to undergo knee surgery. Without him, St. Bonaventure's flight to College Park was just a round trip in futility.

Final Four:

Three independents and UCLA arrived in College Park, Maryland, for the ultimate confrontation. Jacksonville, the dark horse, bedded down in the same hotel occupied by the UTEP Miners during their run for the championship in 1966. St. Bonaventure practiced the adjustments it was forced to make now that Lanier was hors de combat. A confrontation between Artis Gilmore and Bob Lanier would have been the classic matchup basketball fans yearned for. There were many who felt the Bonnies would have taken the less experienced Dolphins and then rolled over UCLA to become the first independent northeast team to capture the national championship in twenty years. But it was not to be. St. Bonaventure's demise did not come without a struggle. Gantt moved to center but at 6′5″, the tallest Bonnie outside a hospital gave away nine inches to Gilmore who tallied 29 and claimed 21 rebounds. The game started deceptively. After six minutes the scrappy quintet from Olean, N.Y., owned a 13-3 lead and Jacksonville had potted only one basket. St. Bonaventure's answer to the taller Dolphins was to run them into the boards and this worked at first. But Jacksonville hoisted the ball to Gilmore over Gantt's outstretched fingers; the big center had little trouble flicking it in from close range. Morgan was having almost equal success from outside. The Bonnies refused to fold and were down by only four points with a couple of minutes to go, but the effort of containing the Dolphins' offense had a decisive effect on the outcome. Four St. Bonaventure players, including three starters, fouled out, and though the Bonnies bagged seven more field goals than Jacksonville, they were outscored at the foul line by a massive 37-15 margin. The scrappy Bonnies made it close all the way, but the Dolphins finally put them away 91-83.

UCLA had a much easier time of it against New Mexico State in the other semifinal. In an effort reminiscent of the 1964 and 1965 Bruin teams, UCLA simply wiped out the Aggies with their high speed attack. Flashing downcourt like so many winged Mercurys, the well-conditioned Bruin starters played 38 minutes before being pulled by Wooden. New Mexico State flopped trying to keep up with the torrid pace and their composure disintegrated in the face of UCLA's zone press—another reminder of the days of Hazzard and Goodrich. The Aggies were hampered by the loss of their center, who twisted an ankle, and scored only eight points before retiring. The acrobatic Collins picked up some of the slack by tallying 28 points, mostly on jump shots. It was not enough as UCLA advanced to the final—again. The score was 93-77.

As in the previous year, UCLA was not facing the best the East had to offer. Kentucky and St. Bonaventure were more highly regarded than Jacksonville, but the Dolphins had beaten both so it was proper they should have their chance.

The Dolphins were bidding to become the first team since Loyola to win the title in their first tourney appearance. This time they were not caught napping at the start of the game. They took an early 12-4 lead and within ten minutes were ahead by nine. UCLA was not helping themselves by committing ten turnovers in as many minutes. In the critical battle in the middle Gilmore was outpositioning Wicks. Center Steven Patterson would normally have been guarding the Dolphin pivot man, but Wooden had given the assignment to Wicks. When Sidney heard of his task, he thought he would be more effective fronting the center, but Wooden refused to listen. Wicks was playing behind Gilmore when he picked up his second personal in the first four minutes. Wooden saw the problem and during a time out agreed with Wicks; he made the adjustment by moving Wicks in front of Gilmore. The move worked and Wicks picked up only one more foul the rest of the game. Gilmore, however, was unable to adjust. Wicks, seven inches shorter, outrebounded Gilmore and even blocked four of his shots.

With Wicks properly positioned, the tide turned. With 1:20 to go in the first half, a fast break capped by Bibby's field goal resulted in a 37-36 UCLA lead. The Bruins added four more unanswered points before the buzzer.

"The most intimidating man in basketball" is what Wicks had been called. He certainly lived up to his reputation in the second half. The extent to which Gilmore felt intimidated cannot be measured statistically. However, he missed his first five shots of the second period, going 16 minutes without recording a point. He fouled out with two minutes left in the game followed shortly thereafter by Rex Morgan. Meanwhile Wicks was hitting from under the basket, Rowe popping from the corner, Patterson lobbing from the vicinity of the foul line, and Vallely was finding the range from all over the court. UCLA stepped up the pace and beat the tired Dolphins, the second best rebounders in the country, off the boards 50-38. On defense UCLA used an imaginative and highly effective man-to-man on the guards while protecting the middle with a three man zone. It worked so well that Jacksonville's rare opportunities from the foul line amounted to only seven points. It was a complete reversal from the Dolphins' semifinal game and a tribute to the Bruins defense.

The final score favored UCLA 80-69, but the game was not as close as the score indicated. Later in the locker room Curtis Rowe crowed: "Every time somebody mentions the three in a row, they say Lew did it. Now we just proved four other men from that team could play basketball."

1971

The 1970-1971 season was marked by long win streaks spun by Marquette, Long Beach State, Kansas and Pennsylvania. Marquette and Pennsylvania both had perfect records, yet it was UCLA that was ranked first at the end of the season. There was even doubt for a time which Los Angeles school, UCLA or USC, would represent the Pac Eight in the tournament. Both entered the final game, a head-to-head confrontation, with identical 24-1 records. A win for the Trojans would have tied them with the Bruins at the top of the conference standings, but UCLA prevailed, retaining their number one ranking while USC was ranked fifth. By eliminating the Trojans, UCLA practially ensured themselves another trip to the Final Four since there was no other team in their regional that could stay on the same court with them.

East:

The East regional was the one many felt would ultimately produce the team to give UCLA its toughest competition in years. Candidates for the role of giant killer were Pennsylvania (26-0), ranked third—the highest ever by an Ivy League school—South Carolina (23-4), ranked sixth, and a surprising Fordham quintet (24-2), ranked ninth. The rest of the teams in the regional were not given much chance to survive even the first round.

Penn was now 51-1 over two seasons, their only loss by a slender three points. The Quakers had all the ingredients of a championship team—a strong front line of Calhoun and Morse at the forwards flanking Phil Hankinson at center, and a pair of greyhouds, Steve Bilsky and Dave Wohl, in the backcourt. A fancy dribbler, Bilsky was also a skilled free throw shooter while Wohl quarterbacked the offense. Penn's closest game was a 62-58 victory over St. Josephs in an intracity brouhaha. They also vanquished tourney-bound Villanova and Ohio State.

South Carolina (23-4), with their usual complement of New York athletes, finished second behind North Carolina in the ACC (all losses coming in intraconference games). The Gamecocks had been given a vicious kick in the shorts by Lady Luck the previous year when Roche's injury contributed to a hairline loss in the ACC playoff final. But the lady is fickle; a year later she was beaming at the Gamecocks. This time they were matched against North Carolina in the final. The Tarheels held a 51-50 lead with seconds left in the game when the referee called a jump ball following a scramble on the floor. Jumping for the Tarheels was 6′10″ Lee Dedmon, for the Gamecocks 6′3″ Kevin Joyce. North Carolina needed only to control the tap to win the game. It looked as if for the second year in a row South Carolina would be denied their first NCAA tournament invitation by a last second defeat. But the luck of the Irish prevailed. Timing his jump perfectly, Joyce soared as if jet assisted and tapped the ball to Tom Owens under the hoop. His layup just beat the final buzzer.

Coach Frank McGuire, the Irish pied piper, lured another bunch of high school stars from up north. After stowing their carpetbags, this ensemble of tough, streetwise kids from the sidewalks and parochial schools of New York had their fans from Dixie stamping, whistling and hollering throughout the season. At one corner was All American John Roche who did most of the ball handling and controlled the Gamecock offense; at the other, Kevin Joyce. In his senior year Roche had guided LaSalle Academy to the Catholic high school championship in New York over Rice Academy and had held Dean Meminger, to one field goal. McGuire was sometimes criticized for letting Roche handle the ball so much since he had two 6′10″ redwoods on the team. But Roche had a natural feel for the game enabling him to see patterns developing and thus direct the action to take advantage of them.

At center was 6′10″ Tom Owens, Roche's teammate at LaSalle. At one forward, 6′10″ Tom Riker, at the other a savage 6′8″, 240 lb. thunderball John Ribock, the only starter not from New York.

McGuire was not particularly loved around the conference. Maybe it was his tendency to recruit boys from New York or maybe it was his sense of style—he was undoubtedly the best dressed basketball coach in the country—but there was no doubt resentment had a lot to do with it. After all, McGuire was taking this third school to the NCAA (previously he had gone with St. Johns and North Carolina) and nobody had ever done that before.

For the first time in 17 years Fordham (24-2) was in the tournament, their fortunes buoyed by their freshman coach Richard "Digger" Phelps. Not much was expected from the Rams. Their record a year ago had been 10-15 and the team was too short, said the experts, to compete against major opponents. True, the Ram starters averaged just 6′2″ and their tallest player was a comparative shrimp at 6′5″, but they responded to Phelps' inspired coaching to complete Fordham's best season ever. Led by 6′2″ Charlie Yelverton, the team's leading scorer and rebounder, the Rams lost only to Temple by a point and scared undefeated Marquette before bowing to them in overtime. One highlight of a very successful season was a 56 point victory over host Rochester in the final of the Kodak Classic. Rarely had a team suffered such a shellacking on their own court.

One team that was fortunate to be in the regional was Furman (15-11), making its first tourney appearance. The Southern Conference along with the ACC were the only leagues which sent the winner of a postseason playoff to the tournament.* As happened so often in the past, conference champion Davidson went into its playoff swoon and was eliminated. Things could have been worse. The team Furman beat in the playoff final was Richmond (7-21) which had been Virginia Military's only victim during their 1-25 season!

Until the start of the playoff, Furman had barely kept their heads above .500, padding their record with conquests of Wofford, Presbyterian and

*Yet the ACC playoff rarely went to an underdog whereas this happened frequently in the SC.

Newberry, while taking it on the chin from Jacksonville, 94-60, and South Carolina, 118-83. But the Paladins had the distinction of being the only team to sock Davidson during the regular season and they knocked them out of the playoffs, too.

Four schools from Pennsylvania participated in the regional—three of them from Philadelphia. St. Josephs (19-8) had uncharacteristically lost four times at home and had fallen twice to Villanova and Pennsylvania. Duquesne (21-3) lost only to Boston College, Pittsburgh and Western Kentucky. Among their victims was Villanova.

For ten years Jack Kraft had been at the helm of Villanova (23-6) and ten times he led his team into a postseason tournament; five had been NIT bids and this was his fifth NCAA. Only once, however, had Kraft come close to a championship, a narrow defeat by St. Johns in the final of the 1965 NIT. This year did not look too promising either, though there were signs the Wildcats might have been underrated. Four of their six losses were to teams that had been invited to the tournament. They had an All American in 6′8″ forward Howard Porter. He was supported by some talented ball handlers and scorers including Tom Inglesby, Hank Siemiontkowski and Chris Ford.

The Wildcats had travelled more than 18,000 miles during the season. They paused at times off the beaten basketball track to display their skills in places such as Fargo and Grand Forks, where they bested North Dakota State 94-61 and North Dakota 103-63. A more traditional rival was DePaul whom Villanova sacked 99-59.

In the first round in New York, Fordham had little trouble subduing Furman 105-74. Phelps ordered his men to harrass the Paladins with a pressing man-to-man three-quarter court defense. The maneuver worked. The Rams hounded Furman so effectively they coughed up the ball repeatedly. Yelverton was high scorer for Fordham with 30 points and pulled down 19 rebounds besides.

That left the four Pennsylvania schools to battle for the remaining second round berths. Villanova and St. Josephs fought it out in the familiar surroundings of the Palestra. The Hawks moved in front 19-12 in the first half as Mike Bantom contributed eight of those points for St. Josephs. Villanova then took off and scored 13 of the next 14 points. Their speed and rebounding superiority (an overwhelming 56-34 off the boards) asserted itself and they were never headed. The Wildcats built a big lead mainly on a devastating fast break triggered by Chris Ford. It proved substantial enough to withstand a late rally and Villanova registered a decisive 93-75 victory.

With Garry and Barry Nelson, a pair of 6′10″ twins, and 6′7″ Mickey Davis, Duquesne enjoyed a height advantage over Penn they wished to exploit. Their tactic was to drive inside and try to make the Quakers foul. To promote confusion, they switched frequently between a zone and man-to-man. But Quaker discipline prevailed. They set picks for Morse, who had a hot hand in the opening half, and their overall quickness allowed them to overcome the Dukes' height advantage. Morse tallied 16 of Pennsylvania's first 22 points and had twenty of his team's 32 at the midway mark. He cooled down in the second half but Wohl, Penn's floor leader, picked up the slack and was credited with eleven points in the last nine minutes.

Toward the end, as it became apparent that the Quakers would remain undefeated, the partisan Duquesne fans who had travelled to nearby Morgantown, W.Va. for the game, became increasingly unruly. Bottles and cans skittered across the court and a bag of chicken feed exploded on the hardwood, stopping the game. Raucus Duquesne fans vented their frustrations in increasingly menacing ways but the result was unalterable: Pennsylvania 70, Duquesne 65.

South Carolina suspected Pennsylvania might try to stall since that tactic had been used so successfully against them in the past (at midseason the Gamecocks lost back-to-back contests at Maryland 31-30 and Virginia 50-49). Coaches are quick at copying success. But the Quakers played their standard game in this second round matchup and won going away 79-64. It was close in the first period and the Gamecocks barely led at intermission, 37-36. Calhoun checked Roche successfully while Morse and Wohl added points to the Quaker side of the ledger. Penn was especially brilliant from the line where they sank 19 consecutive shots in the second half.

It was a one man show for Fordham against a team effort by Villanova. Yelverton accounted for 16 of the Rams' first 24 points, but picked up his third personal with eight and a half minutes to go in the first half and Villanova ahead by two. With Yelverton on the bench, the Rams sagged. They tried to contain Villanova's explosive fast break by pressuring them in their backcourt. Villanova's response was a long outlet pass off a defensive rebound or, if no one was free downcourt, a criss-crossing pass pattern to beat the press.

Yelverton returned in the second half and finished with 32 points; but his individual effort was not nearly enough as Villanova stopped the Rams 85-75.

In the regional final Pennsylvania, undefeated, victors in 28 contests including one over their opponent, were expected to have little difficulty penning the Wildcats and becoming the first Ivy team to advance to the Final Four since Bill Bradley led the Tigers of Princeton in 1965. The result was one of the most stunning upsets ever witnessed not only in the playoff but on any court anywhere. It was not just that Villanova won, but how they achieved their victory. The Wildcats played a near perfect game, classic basketball the way it is taught in a clinic but almost never occurs under real playing condition, especially under tournament pressure. "I don't think we made a mistake in the first half," said an incredulous Jack Kraft after the game. After the initial twenty minutes Villanova led 43-22. If the Quakers thought this huge lead would make the Wildcats complacent, they were in for an even greater shock in the second half. If anything, Villanova was more intense than before and rattled off 16 points the first five minutes after the intermission. The Wildcats owned the backboards, shot 62 percent from the field, and their defense was as solid as Hoover Dam. Best of all was their transition game which whipsawed the ball back to the Pennsylvania end of the court for easy buckets. Porter with 35 points and Siemiontkowski with 20 led the attack. Not a single Quaker scored in double figures. Remarkably, Villanova collected just eight personal fouls while holding the Quakers in check.

As usual Kraft left his starters in for almost the entire game, yanking them only in the last couple of minutes. By that time it was just a question of numbers—Villanova 90 Pennsylvania 47. Fordham sank South Carolina for third place, helped by 22 free throw attempts without a miss.

Mideast:

The only other undefeated team in the country at the end of the regular season was second ranked Marquette (26-0). They were marked by a fine defense, third best in the country, and featured Dean Meminger, an All American guard who could penetrate.

A remarkable thing about Marquette, considering the free spirits on the team, was the disciplined way in which they played, especially on defense. It was a tribute to McGuire's recruiting and coaching skills. Opposite Meminger, at the other guard position, was Allie McGuire, the coach's son (no recruiting problem there). Jim Chones plugged the middle. The local boy from nearby Racine was the tallest sample of raw talent to enroll at Marquette. Rounding out the starting quintet was Bob Lackey—a mean, sinister-looking enforcer—at one forward, and Gary Brell at the other. Brell, a self-proclaimed hippy, had a reputation for being a bit of a flake. He wore his blond hair long, à la General Custer, and averted his head from the American flag during the singing of the national anthem as a sign of protect against the war in Vietnam.

They all played with zest and flair, each displaying his own particular charisma on the court. McGuire encouraged this élan by dressing his team in the most dazzling uniforms. One year it was horizontal hoop stripes; another it was a large cannonball, front and back, on which the numbers were stitched; still another time the school's name appeared below the numbers. And there was the season that arrowheads appeared on the side of the jersey, later replaced by tiger stripes. But the ultimate was the year the Warriors appeared in electric blue and gold uniforms which looked as if they were designed to glow in the dark in case of a power shortage. Though Dean Smith and North Carolina might not have concurred, Marquette was the team that set the style in basketball apparel.

Jacksonville (22-3) looked ready to advance to the finals once again. They had a new coach, Tom Wasdin, but the team was essentially the same except for Rex Morgan who had graduated. Gilmore signed off his memorable career by scoring 25 points, retrieving 28 rebounds and blocking 13 shots in his last regular season game. Once again he led the nation in rebounding, setting a new all-time record for career rebounds per game. Naturally, he was selected to the All American team. Despite suffering only two one point losses to Houston and Wake Forest and a defeat at Western Kentucky, the Dolphins were not rated in the top ten, due to a patty cake schedule that still included contests against Valdosta State, Southern Alabama and Mercer. Even leading the country in field goal accuracy and scoring did little to change Jacksonville's image as an average team among pygmies. Still the Dolphins' firepower was awesome. They averaged 127 points in their first four games, a string that included deluging Biscayne 132-88 and St. Peters 152-106. Later they trounced Miami 124-82 and at the end of the season they had averaged over one hundred points a game for the second straight year.

Kentucky (22-4) was right behind the Doilphins in the scoring race, though their defense was the third worst in their conference. The polls ranked the Wildcats eighth, but it was at the pole ends of the season that they performed best, averaging 106 points over the first and last five games. Issel had graduated but in his place was a 7′2″ sophomore, Tom Payne, the first black player to make Rupp's team.

Western Kentucky's fortunes pivoted around Jim McDaniels, their seven foot All American center and the fifth best scorer in the country. The Hilltoppers (20-5) had lost to South Carolina by two points in the final of the Holiday Festival. Tenth ranked Ohio State (19-5) also had a soaring center in Luke Witte. With 6′11″ Chones, 7′2″ Gilmore, 7′2″ Payne, 7′0″ McDaniels and 7′0″ Witte, the regional resembled a convention of lodgepole pines.

The only school without a dominating pivotman was Miami of Ohio (20-4). The Redskins split their first six games, then posted wins in 17 of their next 18.

Miami's streak ended abruptly when a close game turned into a route as Marquette, usually a low scoring team, stitched 19 points through the nets in the first ten minutes of the final period. However, that was the only offensive burst in an otherwise uninspired game. Meminger and Chones provided almost the only offensive punch generated by the Warriers as each notched 21 points. They were also the only ones to score from the line as Marquette's free throw shooting failed repeatedly. But the very deliberate Warriors still gained their thirty-ninth victory in a row, 62-47.

In the co-feature Jacksonville streaked to lead Western Kentucky by 18 points and looked capable of passing the hundred mark easily. At the half they had the better of a 44-30 score. After the intermission, though, the Dolphins' offense decelerated like a mechanical toy winding down as they turned the ball over repeatedly. Exhorted by their fans waving red towels and Big Mac signs, the Hilltoppers counterattacked and with 8:45 to go overtook Jacksonville. The final turnover proved fatal to the Dolphins. After McDaniels twice reached into the lane in the final 90 seconds to tip in missed free throws for tying buckets, the Dolphins maneuvered for a final winning shot. With five seconds left, Ernie Fleming was called for a double dribble. On the inbounds play, Gary Sundmacker found Clarence Glover, who had lost his defender, to score an easy layup with just two seconds remaining. The 74-72 decision reversed the previous year's first round outcome. It was only the second time that season Jacksonville had been held to fewer than 75 points. McDaniels outscored Gilmore 23 to 12 in the battle of the All American centers.

For the first time the Mideast regional was held in the deep South. Athens, Georgia, hosted a classic Bluegrass matchup between Kentucky and Western Kentucky that supporters of both universities had been looking forward to for a long time. For more than fifty years these two basketball powers had been playing in the same state but had never faced each other on a court. The confrontation was a disappointment. McDaniels completely dominated Tom Payne, outscoring him 35-15 and the Wildcats were never in the game. The Hilltopper center also gathered eleven rebounds, stepped to the line eleven times and sank eleven free throws. But this was not a one man performance. Western Kentucky's racehorse offense and pressing defense were as much responsible for the outcome as Big Mac's outstanding play. When it was over, Western Kentucky had upset Kentucky 107-83, the worst defeat ever for the Wildcats in the tournament.

Marquette put its long win streak on the line against Ohio State and for a time the Warriors looked as if they would notch their fortieth straight without strain. Using a pressing man-to-man, Marquette boomed to a 13 point lead in the first half. One of the maxims guiding Al McGuire's coaching was you stopped pressing when your team got a double digit lead. So McGuire switched to a zone defense which effectively broke Marquette's momentum. Poor foul shooting and the loss of Meminger via penalties in the final critical minutes compounded the Warriors problems. Still it was not until 69 seconds remained, when Witte curled in a layup, that Ohio State finally took the lead 58-57 after having played catchup since the opening minute. Decidedly flustered by now, Marquette squandered three opportunities to retake the lead. Their last chance melted away when Allie McGuire stepped on the line during an inbound pass with seven seconds left. A pair of Buckeye free throws and a meaningless Marquette basket made the final score 60-59.

If anything characterized the Mideast regional it was come from behind victories. Once again, the Hilltoppers suffered an early defensive lapse. The score was knotted 19-19 when Ohio State sprayed 14 points through the cords in four and a half minutes to just two for their opponents.

Big Mac then led a comeback, swishing five of his team's next six field goals. But it was not until more than eleven minutes into the second half that Glover's free throw pulled Western Kentucky even again at 53-53. Once more they fell behind but were saved from elimination when a short jumper by Rex Bailey with :11 to go found its mark. It created a 69-69 tie which remained unchanged until the horn.

Glover and Jim Cleamons of the Buckeyes, who had both been held below their average, now spearheaded their team's attack. Cleamons, who had spent most of the second half on the bench with four personals, came in and scored three of his four field goals in the five minute session. It was not enough. Glover scored on a tip in after a missed shot by McDaniels, then added another bucket and a pair of free throws. Glover scored only eleven points but all came at critical moments and his 22 rebounds was tops for both sides. Once again Big Mac bested another seven foot center, this time outscoring Witte 31 to 23, though he received ample support from the other starters, all of whom were in double digits. Allan Hornyak paced the losers with 26. It all added up to an 81-78 overtime win for Western Kentucky.

Midwest:

The only ranked team in the Midwest regional was number four, Kansas, (25-1) whose record had been smeared only by Louisville. At tournament time the Jayhawks were on a 19 game win streak though the last four, which included two overtime affairs, were close. They played pressure defense, zone or man-to-man, depending on their opponents' weakness. Cementing the middle was 6′10″ Dave Robisch, a bulky 240 pounder who was difficult to move once he planted himself.

The previous year the NCAA selection committee tried to move Marquette from its usual Mideast regional berth into the Midwest regional. Marquette balked and went to the NIT. In 1971 the committee did the same thing to Notre Dame (19-7). The Irish were more accommodating and accepted the invitation, even though the Mideast regional was scheduled for their campus.

Notre Dame played a nightmare schedule. Five of their losses were to schools good enough to be invited to the tournament. Their only other defeats had come against Indiana (three points) and Illinois (two). But Notre Dame was also the only team to beat UCLA and ambush Kentucky and Louisville, too. The Irish had an explosive offense led by Austin Carr, their All American guard. Carr almost single handedly beat UCLA, lofting 46 into the hole, including 15 of the last 17 Irish points. He had also driven Sidney Wicks, the man who shackled Artis Gilmore, to distraction and out of the game on fouls. During the season Carr had averaged 38 points per game, second best in the country, on 55 percent shooting.

The hot Irish recorded their most lopsided win against NYU 106-68. It was the last in a long and memorable series that had inaugurated college basketball in Madison Square Garden and which ultimately led to the great popularity of the sport. It was also NYU's last season as the school dropped the sport at the end of the year.

Two other at-large selections were Houston (21-6) and New Mexico State (19-7). The latter was due to join the MVC the following year expanding that conference's boundary even further west.

The MVC race went down to the wire and resulted in a three-way first place tie among St. Louis, Louisville and Drake. Louisville eliminated St. Louis in a playoff and then Drake (19-7), which had suffered a total collapse against Louisville 94-52 just two weeks before, caged the Cardinals 86-71. The unpredictable Bulldogs had blown hot and cold all year. They alternated between winning streaks and slumps, losing three of four at one time, four of five at another. Typical were two confrontations with Bradley. They lost to the Braves by three and then levelled them 113-78.

TCU (15-11) won the Southwest Conference but little else. They posted just four non-league victories in their first twelve games before facing easier conference opponents.

The opening round of the regional was held at Hofheinz Pavillion in Houston. (The national championship was also scheduled for Houston but in the Astrodome.) The Cougars had travelled almost 20,000 miles during the season, second only to Hawaii, and a home-sweet-home court advantage was greatly appreciated.

The partisan fans sat on their hands for most of the first half as New Mexico State sailed to a 32-13 advantage after twelve and a half minutes before Houston rallied to close the gap to eight points at intermission. The Cougars were shooting as if suffering from frostbite, making only two buckets in the first eight minutes and hitting 27 percent for the entire half. But they thawed considerably in the second half to rally behind Dwight Davis who rattled the rims for 30 points. After a long uphill slog, Davis' two free throws gave Houston its first lead 67-66 with 1:59 to go. Eleven seconds later Poo Welch nailed down the game with a three point play. Final score: Houston 72, New Mexico State 69.

It was fun rooting for Poo Welch but TCU fans also had their favorite—Goo Kennedy (not to mention Coco Villareal). Neither Good nor Coco was a match for Austin Carr who scored his one thousandth point of the season during the game—the only man aside from Maravich to do so in consecutive seasons.

TCU stayed even with the Irish for ten minutes but then Carr went on a rampage and tallied 18 points as his team outscored the Horned Frogs 27-14 before the buzzer. Early in the second half TCU closed the gap. But just as the pursuers were about to overhaul, James Williams (who had finally managed to bring Carr under control) fouled out and the Irish soared again. The Washington, D.C., connection of Carr and Collis Jones netted 52 and 26 points respectively. The 102-94 decision boosted Notre Dame into the second round against Drake.

For the first time in two years of postseason competition, a team managed to hold Carr reasonably in check—if 26 points is reasonable. Ahead 39-32 at intermission, the Bulldogs slowed the pace to a shuffle and led by eight with five minutes to go. Carr, who had been shackled by Bobby Jones throughout, finally slipped free and flashed five points on the scoreboard in 16 seconds and gave the Irish a 62-60 advantage. Desperately Drake bombarded the basket and four times the ball bounced around the rim before Al Sakys holed the tying field goal five seconds before the buzzer. Though they had scored only 23 points in the previous twenty minutes, the Bulldogs now abandoned their deliberate tactics and tossed in 17 in overtime to triumph 79-72.

The second game matched Kansas and Houston. Though the Jayhawks had prevailed in the regular season contest between them, it was the Cougars this time who set the pace for most of the game. Trailing by three, Kansas streaked with eleven consecutive points to take a 49-41 lead. Bud Stallworth, who contributed 20 second half points, accounted for seven during that barrage. Houston regrouped and made a run at the Jayhawks but Robisch converted seven straight free throw opportunities in the last two minutes to pull the game out 78-77. Robisch with 29 and Stallworth with 25 were high scorers for Kansas while Welch led Houston with 28.

In the regional final, Kansas once again practiced brinksmanship until the final buzzer. Again they played catchup for a major part of the game. Down by as many as ten to Drake in the second half, Kansas watched the clock wind down before coming to life. Another chapter in "The Perils of Kansas" unfolded as Robisch snaked in for a three point play to tie the score 55-55. Action boiled at both ends of the court. Three Bulldogs and two Jayhawks fouled out. In the final few minutes Kansas took command, then held on to win 73-71. It was the Jayhawks' twenty-first win in a row and their sixth in as many games by five points or fewer.

In the contest for third place Houston whipped Notre Dame 119-106 in a game reminiscent of the previous year's consolation which Iowa had won by an almost identical score. During the previous two years the Irish had scored over a hundred points four times and just missed once with 99, yet they won only two in that time. Carr, playing his final college game, was credited with 47 points, which equalled his average over the past two tournaments and by far the best ever achieved.

West:

The West regional included three schools from Utah and three from California. Long Beach State (22-4) was undefeated in the PCAA but were again an at-large selection. The Forty Niners were coached by the controversial and colorful Jerry Tarkanian who had the Long Beach machine finely tuned by season's end with 15 victories in a row. Pacific (21-5) were led by 6′10″ John Gianelli, one of the top rebounders in the country. The Big Sky Conference was becoming known as Weber State and the seven dwarfs. Weber State's (21-5) title was almost as predictable as the blizzards that howled across the conference campuses and occasionally disrupted schedules. This year was no different as they finished four games ahead of second place Idaho.

Utah State (20-6) had started the season by beating Ohio State, but then stumbled badly against BYU, absorbing a 111-83 pasting. They recovered to sweep the All-College Tournament.

BYU (17-9), the third school from Utah, also started strong, winning their first three games. The Cougars then flew to the West Coast where they were jolted by a total of 74 points in their next three appearances. In all, they won only four games on the road, not very impressive for a team with national championship aspirations. The most prominent and visible member of BYU's weird and wonderful cast was Kesimir Cosic, the 6′11″ center from Yugoslavia who could barely make himself understood in English. One thing he learned quickly, though, was the American way of showboating. Nightly this misplaced character would put on a show—clapping his hands, dancing, laughing, jabbering in a mixture of his nature tongue and what passed for English. Probably the most unorthodox center in college basketball history, Cosic loved to bring the ball upcourt, lead the fast break, shoot from as far as thirty feet and from any crazy angle that struck his fancy and make fancy passes to startled teammates. In a word, the Hot Rod Hundley of the Balkans! Generally, though, Cosic preferred shooting to passing off. The rest of the Cougars resented this and his publicity-seeking capers. Nevertheless, he was still the main attraction and that helped fill the almost completed 22,000 seat Marriott Activities Center in Provo, Utah.

Number one UCLA (25-1) had two close calls, both during a single weekend in Oregon. They barely escaped with their conference record untarnished after they outlasted Oregon 69-68 and Oregon State 67-65. The Bruins were not as fortunate when they travelled to South Bend to play Notre Dame. Austin Carr saved one of his super spectacular performances for the visitors; not even the leechlike defense of Sidney Wicks could hold him to fewer than 46 points. The Irish won more easily than the 89-82 score indicated.

In the first round of the regional, BYU tripped Utah State 91-82 on the loser's home court. Only Nate Williams' 29 points for State kept the score respectable. Cosic as usual was the top performer for BYU—in more ways than one—and tallied 30. It was an extremely physical game during which three Utah State starters fouled out and BYU made 33 of 44 charity throws.

Long Beach State displayed a tight zone which Weber State found difficult to penetrate. Well-handcuffed was Willie Sojourner, Weber State's leading scorer, who did not even reach double figures. Still, his presence gave his teammates a psychological lift and, when he fouled out with seven minutes to go with Weber State down by only five, the heart went out of the Wildcats. George Trapp and Ed Ratleff, who contributed a game high 31 points, scored the next seven points between them and the Forty Niners prevailed, 77-66.

The winners moved down the road a piece to Salt Lake City where they were joined by the remaining California teams. Pacific was slow, but Long Beach State did not take advantage until the second half, by which time they were 13 points down. Then, almost as an afterthought, the Forty Niners took their fast break out of storage. Moving into high gear they blazed tracks in the hardwood, making up the 13 point deficit not once but twice, eliminating Pacific 78-65.

Facing UCLA was enough to daunt any coach, but Stan Watts was grateful just to be there. He had undergone cancer surgery a year earlier and felt lucky to be alive. For a time his BYU Cougars challenged the Bruins and matched them point for point. The score was tied 25 each when UCLA moved into high gear. An hour later the last Utah team was out of the tournament 91-73. Cosic had a poor scoring night for him but he latched onto 23 rebounds, half the Cougar total. So evenly was the Bruin scoring distributed that four men bagged six field goals while two others chalked up five. Nine different players scored at least one basket; six hit double figures. Henry Bibby, with 15 points, was high scorer for the Bruins.

This was the come-from-behind tournament. Kansas had twice trailed in their regional, Western Kentucky had overcome 18 and 14 point deficits, Houston persevered after falling 19 behind, and Ohio State was down by 13 to Marquette before eliminating the Warriors, the same deficit that Long Beach State had overcome. UCLA with its top ranking was not expected to play the role of the late challenger but they had to in order to survive against Long Beach State.

Down by four at the intermission the Bruins slipped further behind as the second period matured. By almost midway through the session, the Forty Niners had secured a 44-33 advantage. To make matters worse for the flagging Bruins, Wicks was on the bench with four personals. The fans in Salt Lake City, deprived of their last local team, adopted the Forty Niners and roared for an upset.

However, last rites for the Bruins were definitely premature. Wooden made a couple of adjustments, reinserted Wicks, and substituted 6′6″ John Ecker for guard Terry Schofield. That left just Bibby as the lone guard. With the taller lineup the patient made a swift recovery. Bibby's jumper from the outer reaches tied the score 50-50 at 6:06. It was State that began to wilt, and when Ratleff, their 6′6″ guard and leading scorer, fouled out less than a minute later, it was almost time to blow taps over the Forty Niners. Still, they went down fighting. Suddenly points became scarcer than fish in the Salt Lake. Five minutes produced just three for each side. But Wicks, who until then had made only four of eight free throws, stepped to the line with 25 seconds left and hit a pair to give UCLA a 55-53 lead. Thirteen seconds after that, boom-boom, he sank another pair and UCLA had their thirtieth consecutive tournament win. The final score was 57-55 and the Bruins, shooting a forgettable 29 percent, were lucky to have won. "We did everything we had to do . . . We did everything we wanted to do to win," said Tarkanian philosophically.

Final Four:

The surviving foursome flew to Houston. The final two doubleheaders were to be played in the Astrodome. The second biggest crowd ever to watch a college basketball game streamed through the turnstiles the following Thursday evening. The court was raised four feet off the stadium floor in order to improve visibility for the fans; however, the players were in constant danger of hurtling over the brink and courtside spectators were eyeball to sneaker with the action. Most of the 31,428 fans, though, were still no closer than 150 feet from courtside. But for the four finalists who were to receive $60,000 each, the attendance was what made the size of the check possible. The International Cheerleading Foundation had voted the Kansas and UCLA cheerleaders the best in the country, and the two squads were wildly demonstrative as their teams took the court in one semi-final game. UCLA seemed in control until the Jayhawks rallied at the start of the second half and threatened to vault into the lead. The Bruins were ahead, 39-37, when Dave Robisch made an apparent tie-breaking jump shot—but was detected travelling before the throw. That reversal was the turning point, and UCLA took off again to win 68-60. Wicks, who always got the most difficult defensive assignment, held Robisch to 17 points.

Villanova's clogging zone defense denied Western Kentucky bombers their short range shots. Undeterred, they took three heaves for each of Villanova's two, maintaining a large lead in shots taken if not in baskets scored. Before he retired, center Hank Siemiontkowski notched 31 points, mostly from the top of the key when McDaniel did not follow him outside. McDaniel rarely saw the ball on offense as Villanova's zone kept passes from reaching their target underneath.

Villanova was true to form with five men playing the entire first forty minutes until Siemiontkowski fouled out with just four seconds left and the score tied 74-74. Jerry Dunn's adrenaline was pumping madly as he stepped to the line the center of a churning chorus of more than 30,000 voices. He missed the first of a one-and-one opportunity and the teams went into overtime.

Joe McDowell took Siemiontkowski's place as the teams headed into overtime. With twelve seconds showing on the clock, Howard Porter flipped a baseline jumper hoopward. Swish, the game was knotted again 85-85. For the first time since 1957, a Final Four game went into double overtime. Four of the Wildcats were approaching their fiftieth minute on the court and could be expected to be weary. Yet it was Western Kentucky that began to sag. They controlled the ball for a minute and a half, but showed nothing for their effort as they missed three shots and had two blocked by the unflagging Porter. His fade-away jumper from the left corner gave Villanova the lead for good following the Hilltoppers' last miss. A few seconds later McDaniel fouled out and the Wildcat defense range down the curtain. Exhausted but jubilant, the winners bounded off the court, 92-89 winners. They were the first Northeast college to get to the final since their fellow Philadelphians from LaSalle did it in 1955.

The Hilltoppers outrebounded Villanova and outscored them from the floor (by taking 32 more shots). However, their ineptitude from the line, their third sub par performance in four games, cost them the decision.

For the first time in twenty years a final failed to attract a sellout crowd. Still, more than 31,000 fans is a sizable turnout. To John Wooden and Bruin fans it must have brought back painful memories of the classic struggle between Houston and UCLA under the Dome in 1968. To add to its other credits UCLA could claim to have been the attraction at the three best attended college basketball programs.

Jack Kraft's approach to the sport had always been based on two principles—a lightning fast break and an impenetrable 2-3 zone defense. In order to win, Wooden would have to neutralize one or both of these. First, he dusted off his old zone press, forcing Villanova out of their running game into a set pattern offense. Then he told Bibby and Schofield to shoot over the zone in the first half and the guards' long range accuracy and some buckets from Patterson from the top of the key helped build a first half lead that reached eleven points. At that point Wooden called for a stall. This was totally against his principles and he later claimed he dictated the maneuver to draw the Rules Committee's attention—with a national championship at stake—to the need for some relief from such tactics. His more immediate goal was to make the Wildcats abandon their zone. This they refused to do but managed to close the gap to eight before the half time buzzer.

In the second half the Bruins continued their stall, dribbling the ball idly or holding it just inside the center line. Exasperatedly, Clarence Smith yelled at Bibby, "Don't be pussy cats!" Finally, after five minutes Kraft called time out and instructed his players to switch to a man-to-man. Patterson responded by shaking free from Siemiontkowski underneath and UCLA's advantage ballooned to twelve. Then surprisingly, the Wildcats began to achieve better results with their new defense. A couple of steals whittled the margin to eight, then six, then four. The Bruins were becoming more and more deliberate. They only attempted twelve shots in the entire half. Besides, Villanova made the startling discovery that they could play man-to-man as effectively as a zone. Porter completely shackled Wicks, holding him to seven points while he paced the Wildcats with 25 of his own. Only Patterson could not be contained. He plied the basket for a career high of 29 points in this his final college game, exiting a hero. With 2:28 to go Villanova crept to within three points, but that was as close as they got. The crusher was a goaltending call against Porter as he batted away a Patterson layup. When the scoreboard clock showed a row of zeros, UCLA had their fifth consecutive title, their closest to date but a 68-62 victory to be savored nonetheless.

With only a few seconds left and the outcome no longer in doubt, Wooden was presented with a token of affection he will always remember. A time out had been called and as Sidney Wicks, who had been something of a problem to his coach, got up to take the court again he turned back to Wooden and with a rare smile said: "Coach, you're really something!"

15

THE WALTON GANG 1972-1973

1972

When Alcindor graduated in 1969, an understandable wave of relief flooded university campuses around the country. The feeling was widespread that UCLA was now vulnerable and that mortal athletes from other institutions could now inflict retribution on them. That this was only a dream was quickly established by a team that included Sidney Wicks, Curtis Rowe and Steve Patterson and carried on the winning habit, hardly missing a victory on the way to two more championships. But after the 1971 final the Bruins were faced with the loss of four starters, a turnover even more drastic than the one in 1969. Only Henry Bibby returned to begin practice in the fall of 1972.

Once more hope sprang unquenched among the also rans that the Bruins would now really be reduced to more human proportions. But once more John Wooden, the Wizard of Westwood, had shown great foresight; relief was waiting in the wings in the person of a loquacious, intense, and-above all talented redhead, Bill Walton.

Just like Alcindor, Walton arrived with a supporting cast of talented sophomores. There was 6′6″ forward Keith Wilkes, and 6′4″ guard Greg Lee. Wooden promoted substitute 6′5″ forward Larry Farmer* to starter and with Bibby . . . *voila,* another juggernaut. The bench was skilled enough to have been starters at almost any other school. Sven Nater was perhaps the second best college center in the country behind Walton and, during 1972 at

*Farmer became coach at UCLA following the 1981 season.

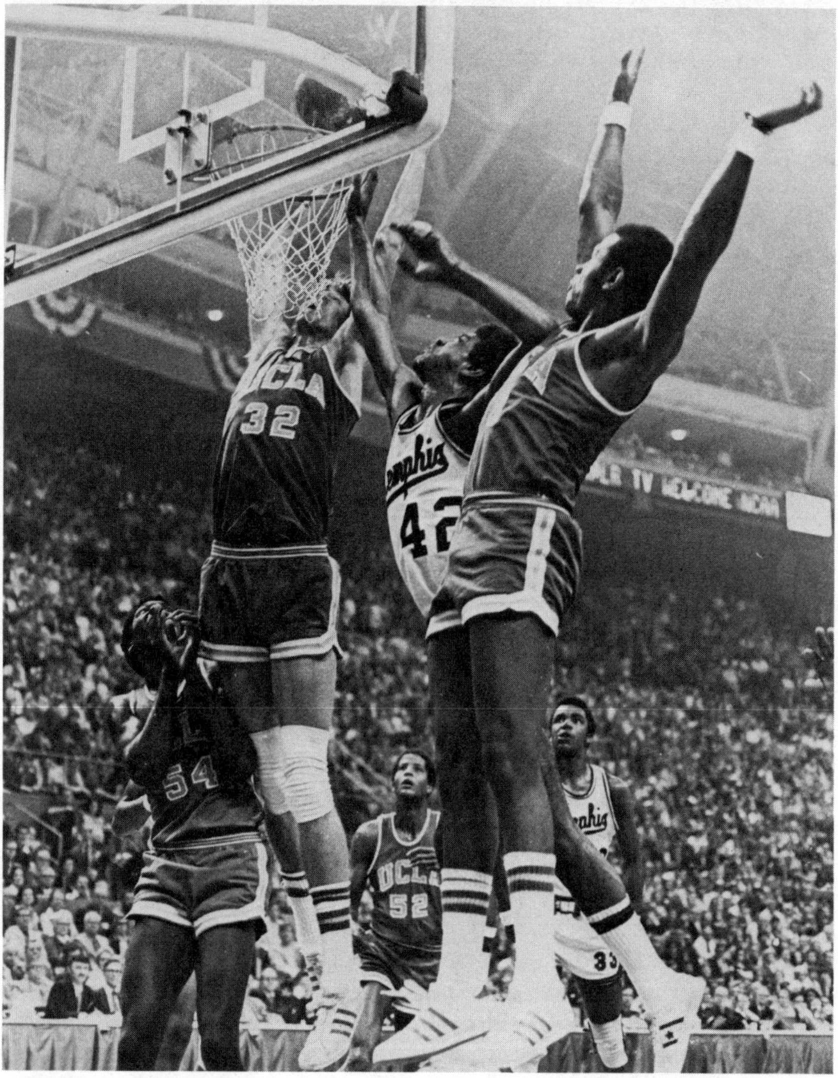

Two more points for UCLA as Bill Walton stuffs for the Bruins during their 87-66 win over Memphis State in the 1973 final. Walton missed only once in 22 goal attempts and was voted the MVP.
(Norm Schindler photo)

least, probably the best on defense. "It really helps me to play against him every day in practice," claimed the big redhead. Tommy Curtis, another sophomore, and Larry Hollyfield backed up the guards.

But it was Walton who gave the UCLA Bruins distinction and their tag—the Walton Gang. Bill had guided Helix High School of LaMesa, California, to a 29-2 record as a junior and a 33-0 season in his senior year. That was the year Walton had averaged 29 points per game on seventy percent shooting from the floor. A well-proportioned 6′11″, the redhead would clog the middle, forcing opponents to take more perimeter shots than they wanted. If the ball was not holed Walton was inevitably there to gather it in, uncoil the outlet pass, and trigger another fast break so dear to Wooden's heart. Wooden loved to see the Bruins run, and this team erupted downcourt more often than any other since the days of Gail Goodrich.

There were those who tried to compare Walton with Alcindor—a foolish exercise. The two men were entirely different, not only in the way they played but off the court, too. Alcindor was an only child who grew up in the big city. In some ways a loner, Alcindor rarely spoke in public. Walton, on the other hand, was an extrovert who argued with referees whenever he felt mistreated.

Walton had three brothers, all tall, all athletes. His formative years were spent in a suburb of San Diego where his father worked for the Welfare Department. Walton was a very intense person both on and off the court. He had assimiliated some rather definite ideas on racial and class injustice, probably from his parents, and was never afraid to voice an opinion. Concerned with the underpriviledged, he spent a good deal of time giving his support to causes. Though he had his share of ego, Bill was a team player who would always give his teammates a large share of the credit. He applied his high standards as much to his own game as anyone else's, and his self-criticism after a resounding Bruin victory sounded out of place among less driven athletes. Wooden felt Walton was too emotional for his own good.

Individually each Bruin was a star. All the starters except Farmer had been All American in high school. Even without Walton, Lee and Bibby might have led UCLA to another championship. After all, Lee had twice been voted Los Angeles High School Player of the Year. Yet they blended their individual talents to produce what may be the best college basketball team ever assembled. On defense Wooden used the zone press frequently. A 1-2-2 offense seemed to produce the most satisfactory results with Lee at the point and Walton and Wilkes deep. Wilkes would occasionally rotate to the high post. "The idea is to put each player where he can work to maximum efficiency," was Wooden's explanation for his tactics.

By season's end UCLA was undefeated in 26 games. For the first time since such statistics were compiled, a team finished in the top ten in both offense and defense. Their margin of victory was greater than 32 points per game, shattering the previous mark by five. The Bruins were in the top ten in every major statistic with the exception of free throw shooting. They were fourth in scoring offense, eighth in average points allowed, fourth in field goal accuracy and eighth in rebounds. Individually, Walton had the fourth best shooting percentage in the country.

UCLA opened the season with a 105-49 massacre of Citadel. This was followed by six consecutive victories in which the Bruins scored over a hundred points. They stripped Iowa 106-72, Iowa State 110-81, Texas A and M 116-53, Notre Dame 114-56, TCU 119-81 and Texas 115-65. No team had ever inaugurated a season so explosively against major college competition—and that included UCLA in the Alcindor era. Later they smashed Pac Eight members as convincingly as they dispatched non-conference foes. They defeated California 82-43, USC 81-56, Washington 109-70 and Washington State 85-55. Twelve times they scored in triple digits. Their lowest production was a 57-32 victory over Notre Dame. The Irish, after having absorbed a loss by almost sixty points, slowed down the game in their rematch, losing by only 25 points—a moral victory of sorts. The closest any team came to upsetting the Bruins was a 78-72 UCLA win over Oregon State.

Naturally the Bruins were ranked number one. Just as naturally, other colleges that had welcomed the 1971-72 campaign with great expectations reluctantly gave up any hope of a national championship for another three years when who knows whom Wooden would unveil as Walton's successor.

In one way UCLA used their top ranking to obtain a scheduling advantage over their rivals. Since so many schools wanted to play the Bruins and thus draw national attention if they could upset the Californians, Wooden was able to demand and get more home games than most other schools. Aside from conference clashes, UCLA seldom played away from cozy Pauley Pavillion, Notre Dame being a perennial exception. It was as if UCLA was ready to take on all challengers as long as they were willing to play in Pauley Pavillion. Their first eight contests (in the broadest sense of the word) were played at home and included the Bruin Classic which was a euphemism for an invitation to a massacre.

West:

Confronting UCLA in the West regional were a couple of fair teams, though not in the Bruins' class. Long Beach State (23-3), under Tarkanian, finished the season ranked fifth. Until the dynamic Armenian-American energized the Forty Niners, they had completed only six winning seasons. Many basketball coaches and administrators were suspicious of the charismatic Tarkanian, pointing to the rag-tag group of dropouts, misfits and problem kids who had gravitated to Long Beach State, several after failing elsewhere. Yet he had molded them into a premium basketball team. There was, for instance, 6′11″ Nate Stephens, the Marco Polo of college basketball, attending his sixth college. Stephens devoted long periods of the day to sleeping and had to be roused to go to daily practice. Lamont King was a dropout from the University of Michigan and belligerent Leonard Gray, the enforcer on the team, had come from the University of Kansas. Leading this band of refugees was Ed Ratleff, a junior, who had already become an All American. Lazy though they were, some with a history of being discipline problems, the Forty Niners seemed to respond positively to this tough season. Whatever his secret, Tarkanian had few problems making his players produce.

For the first time in three years the Forty Niners were in the tournament, not as an at-large selection but as the representative of the PCAA, whose winner was now accorded an automatic invitation by the NCAA.

Another strong quintet was Brigham Young (21-4). Coach Stan Watt's players, including a melange of Finns, a somewhat dippy Yugoslav, plus a better-than-average content of home grown talent, achieved a solidly successful season—good enough to make the top ten.

Weber State (17-9) won their fifth consecutive Big Sky Conference but because of a marshmallow schedule were not well tested.

Hawaii (24-2) was making its first tournament appearance. The Rainbows were probably the most colorfully uniformed team in the country with their flower print shorts. They were coached by gabby Red Rocha who had the reputation of holding the all-time record for lobby sitting as a professional player. Hawaii played most of their games at home where visiting teams, enjoying a brief respite from the chill back home, would be enticed with parties on balmy beaches. The visitors' loss of concentration would inevitably give the Hawaiians an advantage which they were not reluctant to exploit. Hawaii won all 19 games at home. While making two brief forays to the mainland, they lost twice in California where there were distractions of a different sort.

Rounding out the regional was San Francisco (19-7). They had limped to a 4-5 record before making adjustments and taking off during the last two-thirds of the season. The Idaho State fieldhouse was filled with 14,000 spectators who had wandered in from the cold. It was a remarkably big crowd considering no Idaho school was represented, but then, most of the cars in the parking lot had Utah plates.

Hawaii had acclimation difficulties and fell to Weber State 91-64. The contest was reasonably close for 20 minutes but in the latter stages the Rainbows got into foul trouble and fell further behind. With eleven minutes left, four Hawaii starters had collected four personals each and one by one they retired after committing their fifth. Weber State stepped to the line 52 times—their starters alone took 40 shots—and sank 33 attempts. Even their rebounding, fourth best in the country, failed the Rainbows.

BYU set the pace from the opening minute until the final 60 seconds of their game with Long Beach State. They were ahead by as many as ten as Cosic went wild, netting 21 points in the first half. But the taller Forty Niners, averaging 6′7″, wore down the Cougars and finally drew even on Glenn McDonald's 15 foot jump shot at :39. Cosic had cooled off considerably and contributed just six points after the intermission. In the overtime, fellow Cougar Doug Richards sprayed seven points through the ring to keep BYU in the game. An exchange of buckets kept the outcome in doubt until the final seconds. A layup by Lamont King gave Long Beach State its first lead, 89-88, since the opening minute. King and Chuck Terry then assured the outcome by hitting four consecutive foul shots in the final 17 seconds as the Forty Niners picked their way to a 95-90 triumph. It was one of the few close games in a tournament that was marked by lopsided scores.

The winners advanced to Provo where UCLA hardly worked up a sweat eliminating Weber State, 90-58, though Wooden was displeased with his team's lackadaisical effort. Eleven Bruins appeared on the scoresheet, five posting double figures. Long Beach State's victory over San Francisco was almost as easy. The Dons became unraveled early, never able to put together any sort of cohesive effort. Their offense was marred by 20 turnovers. They shot erratically, as if the whole team was afflicted with palsy. The Forty Niners coasted to a 75-55 decision.

Two days later UCLA eliminated Long Beach State in another laugher 73-57. Greg Lee held Ratleff to just two points in the first period. The Bruins devastated their opponents with their smothering full court press while Walton waited downcourt to swat basketballs back at the Forty Niners, should they thread their way through the traps. A long-range mortar barrage by Bibby led the Bruins who advanced to the Final Four for the sixth consecutive year.

East:

North Carolina (23-4) was second ranked but to compare them to UCLA was like saying Gaul was the second most powerful country next to the Roman Empire. The Tarheels had scattered Rice 127-69 in their opener, but two games later had been ambushed at Princeton by 16 points. Three more losses to other ACC teams, none by more than two points, followed at decent intervals. This did not tarnish the Tarheels standing because the ACC was considered the toughest conference in the country.* Five of seven teams had winning records and most of their losses came outside the conference. North Carolia and Maryland dropped seven games between them but only one each outside the conference. Dean Smith convinced Bob McAdoo, the most promising junior college player the previous year, to enroll at Chapel Hill and the 6′9″ center had taken charge and been accorded All American honors. (The following season he was gone; declaring he was a hardship case, he allowed himself to be drafted by the pros.) Dean Smith's aggressive, full tilt, attacking offense had given the Tarheels the best shooting percentage in the country and by a margin so wide the same difference bracketed the next 20 teams.

*Maryland (23-5) won the NIT final by 31 points.

South Carolina (22-4) had left the ACC at the end of the previous year and was an at-large entry. McGuire was unhappy about this independent status forced upon him, he claimed, by the football coaches who felt it would help their recruiting if they could switch to a more independent schedule. Another reason given was the more restrictive academic requirements of the ACC compared to the 1.6 standard set by the NCAA.

Because the Gamecocks had to replace the 14-game ACC schedule, McGuire had a considerable problem. His former pupil at St. Johns, Al McGuire, came to the rescue and booked a series of games between his Marquette team and South Carolina. After all, it was Frank who had been instrumental in getting him his first college head coaching job at Belmont Abbey. The sixth ranked Gamecocks looked to their All American center Tom Riker for leadership. A sharpshooting bunch, they had the third best field goal percentage in the country. Early in the season they won the Cable Car Classic. Later they lost to three tournament-bound teams—Villanova, Marquette and Houston.

The third point of the Carolina compass was represented by East Carolina (14-14). Prior to the Southern Conference postseason playoff, East Carolina lost three more games than it won and allowed three points more per game than it scored. They recorded losses in five of their first six games, and a four-game winning streak was the high point of the Pirates' regular season. Four losses in a row climaxed by a 35 point mugging in their season finale left the Pirates with a sense of having hit the canvas. As usual, Davidson was perched at the top of the conference standings and just as predicatably they were ousted in the playoffs—by East Carolina in the semi-finals. The Prirates completed their improbable sweep to the NCAA by sneaking past conference runner-up Furman in the final, a 77-75 overtime win.

There were also three teams from Pennsylvania—Temple (21-7), with Harry Litwak in his twentieth year at the helm, Villanova (19-6) and Pennsylvania (24-2). The Quakers were ranked third behind UCLA and North Carolina, duplicating their high finish in the polls in 1971. They had lost just three games in the regular season in as many years, equalling UCLA's glittering record. Only Princeton and Temple had tarnished Pennyslvania's slate. A new coach, Chuck Daly, instilled some aggressiveness into the once stodgy Quakers. He also moved 6′7″ Calhoun to guard and along with veterans Hankinson and Morse in the front court Penn had a formidable rebounding trio. The forwards could also shoot well from the perimeter.

Providence (21-5) were led by two local boys from Rhode Island—Ernie DiGregorio and Marvin Barnes. The latter had guided his high school to two state championships.

In the first round Villanova pricked East Carolina's bubble. For 21 minutes the game was a barnburner with the score knotted 13 times. Ford kept his team in the ballgame with ten of Villanova's first twelve points. Thirty seconds after the second half tip off, Jim Fairly brought East Carolina even on a pair of charity throws. That was it for the Pirates, though. An 18-6 spurt boosted Villanova into a commanding lead; excellent long distance shooting kept them there. Kraft, a cautious man, kept his starters in the game until the last minute, long after the issue was settled. The final score was 85-70.

Pennsylvania had some trouble solving Providence's 2-3, 1-3-1 and 3-2 zone press. The Friars frequently switched from one to the other, causing some confusion in Quaker ranks. Only Morse, who somehow got open during switches, scored consistently. It was Pennsylvania's defense that swung the game their way. Hankinson shadowed Barnes, who had averaged 22 points during the season, not giving him room under the basket and holding him to seven; Calhoun was simply too tall for 6 foot DiGregorio.

The Quakers lead mushroomed to 21 points, dropped slightly, and settled finally at 76-60.

A pressure zone also caused South Carolina headaches in their match with Temple. Ahead by four at intermission, the upstart Owls increased their advantage to 36-26 a few minutes into the second half. The Gamecocks tried to feed Riker inside, but the Owl zone pinched off that strategy. A Kevin Joyce jumper tied the score, 47-47, with 4:44 to go. Field goals by Riker and Danny Traylor gave South Carolina some breathing room, but a pair of buckets by Temple tied the score again with less than a minute remaining. The Gamecocks held the ball for a final shot, taken rather dramatically by Joyce. With the last tick of the clock fading into history he arced a 24-foot fallaway jumper through the hoop and never taking his eyes off the ball, sprawled awkwardly on the hardwood. The basket gave South Carolina its first tournament victory 53-51.

North Carolina joined the three first round winners as regional action continued. Scoring in persistent rallies, the Tarheels were almost out of sight of South Carolina by the end of the first half. By then they were ahead 51-32 on their way to a 92-69 blowout. Riker, the pillar of the Gamecocks, did not score his first basket until 6:40 remained.

A grim rematch between two Philadelphia schools, Pennsylvania and Villanova, provided the co-attraction. The Quakers were determined to revenge their humiliating defeat in the previous year's regional final. Many of the players involved in that debacle were still with the senior-dominated team. Pennsylvania had defeated Villanova during the season but the Quakers lusted for more during the playoffs.

Penn started with a controlled offense. Slowly, steadily they pulled ahead until they were in front by 16 midway through the second half. The Wildcats stormed back and got within three but the Quakers repulsed the charge and won going away 78-67. The veteran trio of Hankinson, Morse and Calhoun pooled 63 points, while Siemiontkowski and Tom Inglesby led the Wildcats with 43 points between them.

Pennsylvania was in the regional final once more, with an opportunity to atone for last year's collapse. However, they were facing an entirely different strategist in Coach Dean Smith. Whereas Jack Kraft refused to substitute unless a player was injured, or fouled out, or the game was no longer in doubt (and sometimes not even then), Smith used the revolving door approach in an effort to wear his opponent down. Sometimes he would even insert five fresh bodies into the game at one time. By the end of the first seven minutes, he had already involved 11 players. Using aggressive tactics and accurate shooting, they bulled their way to a two point advantage at the intermission. Four minutes later the second and third ranked teams in the country were tied 40-40. But Dennis Wuycik, a native Pennsylvanian, put the Tarheels in front permanently when he streaked in for a layup to start a three point play. The Quakers hit only two field goals in the next ten minutes, making only a quarter of their shots in the last half. Scoring droughts were becoming a perennial tournament problem for Pennsylvania and they finished the game almost as disorganized as they had the previous year. Excellent defense, especially by Bill Chamberlain on Calhoun who was limited to seven points, helped the Tarheels advance to the Final Four, 73-59, for the fourth time in six years.

Midwest:

After serving as Wooden's assistant for three years, Denny Crum left UCLA to take over the head coaching job at Louisville. In January 1971 Cardinal coach John Dromo had suffered a heart attack and had to retire. Crum's career in Westwood was marked by success—he had recruited Walton—but had also been punctuated by frequent flareups with Wooden. The most publicized of these occurred during the final in the Astrodome against Villanova. Wooden and Crum began jawing at each other over a substitution change and had to be restrained by Henry Bibby. It was the last of several confrontations between the two. Wooden would not tolerate any subordinate who questioned his authority, and Crum's future at UCLA dimmed almost to extinction.

Crum quickly whipped his first Louisville team into shape. Dropping their opener and the finale, the Cardinals won all but one in between. Unfortunately for Louisville (24-3), their last two defeats were inflicted by Memphis State which tied the schools for the lead in the MVC. A tiebreaking victory assured Crum of his first NCAA tournament as head coach.

The SWC also ended in a tie. Five days before the end of the season, five teams shared first place. In the final standings four schools finished within a game of each other with Texas and SMU locked at the top. Texas (18-7) beat SMU in a playoff 91-89. The Longhorns were going no place until their coach inserted Harry Larrabee into the starting lineup midway through the season. They responded by winning nine of their last ten.

Kansas State (18-8) won the Big Eight. But it was the three at-large schools in the Midwest regional that generated the most interest. All three were among the top ten offensive quintets in the country. Houston (20-6) had tallied over 100 points ten times. Like UCLA and Hawaii, Houston preferred the comforts—and the inevitable triumphs—of home. They played only nine on foreign courts and slunk home in defeat five times.

Marshall (23-3) made it into triple digits nine times. They had been expelled from the Mid American Conference three years earlier for recruiting violations. As an at-large team they could be assigned to any regional the tournament committee picked, which is why the Thundering Herd from West Virginia found itself playing in the Midwest regional. Despite their impressive won-lost record, their schedule was well-laced with cream puffs. Not once did they defeat a member of the top twenty.

But it was Southwest Louisiana in its very first year of Division I competition, that drew banner headlines wherever they played. The eighth ranked Ragin' Cajuns of the bayou featured the highest scorer in the country, guard Dwight Lamar, who averaged 36 points a game. The year before he had led Division II in scoring. He was supported by a strong front line of 6′9″ Roy Ebron, 6′8″ Wilbert Loftin and 6′7″ Fred Saunders. But Lamar was the drive shaft who made the Southwest Louisiana engine turn. His whirling, darting, change-of-direction swoops at the basket faked the defense out of their shorts. And the man nicknamed "Bo Pete" could also pop from outside. There were few places on the court from which he did not score.

The spacious Pan American Center in Las Cruces was three-quarters empty when Texas upset Houston 85-74 in a first round match. The Cougar attack was limited almost exclusively to Dwight Davis and Steve Newsome and that was insufficient. The sparse crowd also witnessed a wild clash between the Ragin' Cajuns and the Thundering Herd in the co-feature. It was as explosive as any shootout on a dusty main street in the Old Southwest. When the dust had settled and the court stopped shaking, Southwest Louisiana with the help of 35 hits by Lamar and 33 by Ebron had lassoed Marshall 112-101. Five players scored more than 20 points and 195 shots were launched. The combined total of 71 attempts from the line is telling evidence of the ferocity of the action.

For 15 years at least one Midwest regional round had been played at either Kansas, Kansas State or Wichita. Now the regional bypassed the Sunflower State and moved to Ames, Iowa.

Roy Ebron, weak due to a cold, was able to contribute only one point in the first half against Louisville. Lamar picked up the slack and scored 18 as SWL romped to a 14-point lead in the first half. This melted to five though at the intermission. Louisville's All American Jim Price shadowed Lamar in the second half. As a result Lamar became erratic, though this did not discourage him from shooting just as often. In the first ten minutes of the second period Price held Lamar to zero baskets while contributing to a Cardinal wave that swept them into a 68-58 lead. AT 2:26 Louisville was up 86-74 when the Cajuns went on the warpath with eight straight points in little more than a minute. But Price's bucket with 25 seconds to go put the game out of reach. Lamar, despite his drought, chalked up 29 points while Price led his mates with 25. Lamar's almost obsessive cannonade added up to 42 shots taken—almost half his team's total—with only 14 buckets to show for it. The result was an 88-84 Louisville victory.

In the second game Kansas State took a commanding lead only to see Texas leapfrog the Wildcats and head into the final 4:41 with a 48-47 lead. But David Hall tipped in a rebound, adding seven more points in a 13-2 Kansas State spree to drive the Longhorns out of the tournament 66-55.

On the following Saturday Louisville raced to a 40-20 lead before Kansas State staged a comeback which eventually brought them within three of the seemingly stalled Cardinals. Lon Kruger, who had been shut out in the first half, fueled the rally with 14 points. The Cardinals put the game away finally, when they converted a pair of late free throws and Jim Price stole the ball to preserve the win, 72-65. Price's 25 points and six steals were deciding factors.

Mideast:

In the 33 years of its existence the NCAA tournament included nearly every major university in the country, nearly all the teams in the major conferences, and representatives from almost every state. Eight of the Big Ten teams, for instance, had participated. Thus it was surprising that no school from Minnesota had ever played in the NCAA tourney. The University of Minnesota decided to do something about that. The athletic department set out to recruit a top coach. They came up with Bill Musselman, head coach at Ashland, a small college in Ohio. Musselman had established his reputation there as a strict disciplinairan and defensive strategist par excellence. His teams at Ashland were so tight they led the NCAA Division II in fewest average points allowed in each of Musselman's last five years. In 1969 Ashland allowed only 33.9 points per game, the lowest in twenty years.

Musselman installed his straightjacket defense at Minnesota; not surprisingly, the Gophers (17-6) led the country in that department. Only twice did they allow more than 70 points. However, Minnesota did not produce many points either, several times failing to score 50 points. Two victories over Purdue, 49-48 and 48-43, were typical examples of the tight checking contests they played. The deliberate style on offense and sticky defense which often anesthetized spectators elsewhere seemed to attract even bigger crowds to Minnesota home games, especially when the Gophers began to win regularly. Whereas Minnesota had previously played to a half empty arena, it was now almost impossible to get tickets.

There was another feature of the program drawing fans to Minnesota home games and that was the pregame warmup show. The Gophers would put on a spectacle unduplicated in college ranks, patterned on the one performed by the Harlem Globetrotters but without the dimension of innocent fun. Accompanied by throbbing music and dancing spotlights, the Gophers performed their intricate passing drills and fancy dribbling rhythms, whipping their fans into emotional bursts of frenzy. Musselman insisted it was intended to motivate the players, but with its overtones of *sturm und drang* it compared favorably to a Nazi party rally. The exercise seemed to psych the

Minnesotans, fans as well as players, but not necessarily to desirable actions. A riot always seemed an elbow-jab away.

Musselman wanted an instant winner. Impatient to prove himself, he tried to instill a win-at-any-price spirit. His slogan "Defeat is worse than death because you have to live with defeat," left no doubt about his feelings.

Since Musselman was unwilling to wait and recruit through the normal high school channels he harvested the junior colleges and the core of the Gopher squad was composed of transfer students. Almost all came from the black ghettos where they had played the game on concrete courts since they were old enough to handle a basketball. The fancy passing and dribbling was a normal development of their desire to imitate the great black stars of the Globetrotters and in the professional ranks. Unfortunately many of them did not possess the scholastic qualifications to enter college directly from high school.

The nucleus of the Minnesota team was composed of solid 6′8″ Jim Brewer, 6′9″ Corky Taylor and the MVP in the Big Ten, 6′7″ Clyde Turner. Ron Behagen, the number two scorer, and Dave Winfield rounded out the starting five.

On January 25 Ohio State travelled to Minneapolis. The pivotal game to decide first place in the Big Ten attracted a full house. The Gophers performed their usual pre-game warmup ritual. Hyped by the Gopher drill, the crowd mood resembled that of a frenzied mob. As Minnesota fell behind late in the game and defeat seemed inevitable, spectators began throwing debris on the court. With 36 seconds left and the Buckeyes ahead 50-44, Ohio State's Witte drove in for a layup. As his feet left the court a Gopher stepped in front of him and sent him sprawling. Taylor, with what looked like a sportsmanlike gesture, reached down to help Witte to his feet. No sooner was he up than Taylor kneed him in the groin., The giant center collapsed in agony. As if on cue Minnesota fans rushed onto the court and began attacking the Ohio State players. Behagen ran over to Witte and began stamping what looked like a Mexican hat dance on Witte's face and neck. By the time Behagen was pulled away, Witte's head was a bloody mess. He was rushed to the hospital along with two teammates, where it was discovered he had suffered a concussion.

Brewer and Winfield also participated in the assault. There was undoubtedly some racial overtones to the riot. One black Buckeye player later recalled the Minnesota athletes left him alone and singled out the white players for punishment.

The result of the fracas was that Behagen and Taylor were suspended for the rest of the season, including the playoffs. Fred Taylor, coach of the Buckeyes, accused Musselman of "brutalizing and animalizing his players." Unrepentant Musselman, still trying to get his team up for each game, dedicated the season to Behagen and Taylor and called the Gophers "a team with a mission." The newspapers, emphasizing the racial implications of the riot, blared: "The law of the jungle should not be tolerated."

Late in the season Bobby Knight, who had assumed the coaching reins at Indiana, knocked his former team out of the running for the Big Ten title by beating Ohio State 65-57. A Buckeye win would have created a tie between them and Minnesota and have necessitated a playoff. Luckily the basketball world was spared a renewal of hostilities and the Gophers won their first conference title since 1937.

The team given the best chance to cop the regional was Marquette (24-2). They, too, were crippled by the loss of a key player. Jim Chones, their star player, had been unhappy for some time. A chronic complainer, he felt that his considerable skills were being wasted in college, that his contribution went unappreciated, and that the referees were targetting him for punishment. At the end of his sophomore year Chones was offered $625,000 to turn professional but decided to stay at Marquette. Undoubtedly he had second thoughts afterwards. After all he had a widowed mother who worked in a restaurant in order to support Jim and five other children. It was unclear whether the New York Nets of the ABA approached Chones or whether he indicated to them that he was available. In any event, he was offered a take-it-or-leave-it 1.5 million dollar contract by the Nets three weeks before the end of the regular season. The offer was too generous to turn down. With his coach's blessing, Chones packed his sneakers and departed. Al McGuire, brutally honest as always, claimed he would have accepted the offer. "How can I tell **him** to turn it down?"

Still, it was a bitter disappointment to lose his junior star who was eligible to participate in two more postseason tournaments. The difference made by Chones was evident from the records Marquette posted before and after he left. With Chones, the Warriors were 21-0 and ranked second just below UCLA. Without him they won three and lost two, falling to seventh.

Still on the team was Allie McGuire, the coach's son. Three times his scoring in the dying seconds decided a ball game for the Warriors. Even more important, his playmaking skills cemented the offense. Allie was a dedicated team player. Without him it is doubtful the team would have meshed as smoothly. The other players occasionally lost their concentration and lapsed into one-on-one confrontations. Then the younger McGuire would rally the Warriors with his crisp passing and superior court presence. He displayed leadership on the other end of the court, too, by running the press so effectively that Marquette finished with the fourth best defense in the country. Unfortunately, McGuire was anemic and had to be rested from time to time.

The Warriors won their own tournament, the Milwaukee Classic, humbling Georgetown in the final, 88-44, after surviving a squeeker against Frank McGuire's Gamecocks. Marquette also sacked Minnesota 55-40 in a confrontation of tenacious defenses. But Marquette was badly beaten by Detroit, 70-49, the week following Chones' departure and also lost their finale to New Mexico State.

Kentucky (20-6) tied with Tennessee at the top of the Southeast Conference, but was awarded the tournament slot on the basis of two regular season wins over the Volunteers, a pair of close shaves decided by one and two points. Tom Payne had gone the way of Jim Chones and others who had aborted their college careers to become pros. The Wildcats, although an excellent team, had the misfortune of suffering from lost weekends. Three times they lost back-to-back games, though in between they rattled off substantial winning streaks.

Another close race developed in the Mid American. Ohio (15-10) tied with Toledo which had a better overall record. However, the Bobcats, who had twice sunk Toledo during the season, turned the trick for the third time, 69-67, in a playoff. At one point the Bobcats were 3-6, a streak which included a five-game losing skein. Paradoxically they managed to beat Ohio State and Indiana, runners up to Minnesota in the Big Ten, during this period.

An even closer race marked the Ohio Valley. Six of the eight teams finished the season with a total of eleven losses each, four with identical 15-11 records. Eastern Kentucky, Morehead State and Western Kentucky completed their season in a dead heat with Eastern Kentucky (15-10) eventually emerging as the conference representative.

Florida State (23-5) completed the Mideast regional field. Emerging from three years probation for recruiting violations, one of the stiffest penalties ever handed out by the NCAA, the Seminoles still included some of the players who had caused their suspension. After returning from a disastrous trip to Hawaii where they lost twice to the host team, they won back-to-back Christmas tournaments in the Far West Classic and the Senior Bowl. (The first encounter in Hawaii was stopped with the score 30-10 in favor of Hawaii when Coach Hugh Durham pulled his Seminoles off the court after a heated dispute.) An easy schedule which included Oglethorpe, Stetson, Valdosta State and Mercer lubricated Florida State's way to tenth place in the year end basketball poll.

In the first round Marquette had little difficulty subduing Ohio. Unable to cope with a full court press the Bobcats were blanked for five and a half minutes during which Marquette built a 23-10 lead which they increased to 38-20 at the intermission on torrid 68 percent shooting. The Bobcats found the hole only one third of the time over the course of the game. Marquette hardly worked up a sweat in winning 73-49.

The fans found themselves more involved in the second game. Eastern Kentucky led by as many as 13 points in the initial half only to watch Florida State come blitzing back to take an eight-point advantage at the intermission. The Colonels rallied again and, as the clock wound down, the scores converged at 79. With 1:37 remaining, Florida State's Ronnie King completed a three-point play followed twelve seconds later by an Eastern Kentucky layup to cut the gap to one. With 20 seconds left Daryl Dunagan of the Colonels stepped to the line for a pair. He had previously made eight of eight free throws but in the clutch, with a chance to win the game, he blew both attempts. Faced with the same opportunity twelve seconds later, King converted his attempt, leaving the Colonels insufficient time to set up for a tying bucket. Six Seminoles scored in double figures, led by the shortest man on the court—5′7″ Otto Petty. The narrow 83-81 win over a relatively weak opponent gave no indication how far the Seminoles would go in the playoffs.

Two days after the first round, the NCAA suspended Marquette and threatened to send Ohio University to the next round in their place. The dispute arose when Bob Lackey refused to sign an affidavit that he had not signed a professional contract. McGuire counselled Lackey not to sign without consulting a lawyer. After thinking it over for several hours, and with the knowledge that the NCAA could make their suspension stick, Lackey signed and Marquette was reinstated. As Minnesota dribbled onto the court to start their warmup for their second round game in Dayton, they were greeted by an unnerving storm of boos and jeers cascading down from the rows and tiers holding more than 13,000 Ohio fans. The early going favored the Gophers, though, and they led 22-18 before Florida State put together a 17-7 surge that gave them the lead for good. Without the suspended Behagen and Taylor, the Gophers were easily scalped by the Seminoles 70-56. The result gave the fans a great deal of satisfaction.

At the break Marquette held a sliver thin, one-point lead over Kentucky. So far the second round game's tempo had been dictated by McGuire. But in the locker room Rupp made two decisive adjustments. He directed his players to switch to a zone, a defense that Kentucky rarely used, and waved the Wildcats into a fast break offense that effectively broke the back of the Warriors' full court press. As a result of this change of pace, Marquette's normally tight defense leaked 52 second half points. Confused by the board-burning Wildcats directed by Ron Lyons, their 5′10″ sparkplug, Marquette fouled repeatedly. By tote-up time, three Warriors had fouled out. The opportunistic Wildcats swished 29 of 34 free throw attempts, 14 of 15 in the second half. Without Chones, Marquette also lost the battle of the boards and a season that had promised so much came to an abrupt end; Kentucky prevailed 85-69.

In the regional final, Florida State took Kentucky apart 73-54 after leading all the way. For more than eight minutes during the second half Kentucky could not buy a field goal. Fast as the Wildcats had been against Marquette, they could not keep up with the Seminoles. They careened down the court like a pack of jaguars and their quickness on defense caused the well-coached Wildcats to commit 24 turnovers. Reggie Royals, the Seminole's 6′11″ center, swept the boards while King paced the winners with 22 points. But the most infuriating player on the court—to Kentucky—was the mercurial Petty who scooted between, around and even sometimes it seemed under his taller opponents to register 13 points (including a perfect nine for nine from the line), eight assists and, incredibly, six rebounds. It was a measure of Florida State's team oriented style that a different player had been high scorer in each of the Seminole's three victories.

For Rupp it was a bitter defeat and may have evoked comparison to a similar loss to Texas Western in 1966. The Kentucky Board of Regents indicated they expected him to resign since he had reached the mandatory retirement age. Rupp, like Phog Allen before him, asked for one more year so he could try once again for his fifth national championship. His request was rejected and Kentucky's loss to Florida State was his last game. From his very first game in 1930—a 67-19 squashing of Georgetown of Kentucky—the Baron of the Bluegrass had set his stamp of excellence on the Wildcats. To be ousted by an upstart like Florida State playing in only its second tournament seemed unfair.

Final Four:

When Denny Crum brought his Louisville Cardinals into the Final Four, he was in familiar territory. The championship was to be decided in Los Angeles where Crum, brilliant and ambitious to run the whole show, had spent years sitting on the bench next to Wooden. Now he had his opportunity and his opponent in the semifinal would be the team he had helped to recruit. It was Crum who had discovered Walton as a high school junior in San Diego. He rushed back to Westwood to report his discovery to Wooden who was on the court conducting practice. "The greatest prospect I have ever seen," raved Crum. Wooden could not believe that Crum included Alcindor in that appraisal. When Crum insisted that Walton was indeed a better prospect than Alcindor, Wooden invited his assistant into his office, "And close the door after you."

Crum could have used Walton in Louisville. The Cardinals, with fine talent at every other position, lacked a good center. The need was glaringly apparent when UCLA sprang to an early lead; Walton rammed home 16 of UCLA's first 20 points on the way to a 33 point performance. The big redhead also clogged the middle on defense, halting traffic in the lane as effectively as a landslide blocking an interstate highway. After UCLA finished toying with the Cardinals, they put in their reserves who mopped up in the 96-77 laugher. It would have been understandable had Crum looked wistfully at the UCLA bench once or twice.

North Carolina was a strong favorite to burst Florida State's bubble. Ordinarily the Tarheels would have worn their opponents down by liberally substituting fresh players from a well-stocked bench. Their pressing man-to-man-defense had utterly frustrated Pennsylvania as well as many lesser teams. This time the mercury swift Seminoles simply ran North Carolina into exhaustion. Florida State players, directed by the elusive Petty, breezed by the Tarheels so frequently the latter were reduced to fouling just to keep their opponents from getting uncontested baskets. Though they outrebounded and outscored the Seminoles from the floor, they lost the game when they permitted Florida State to go to the free throw line at the rate of almost one a minute. Hugh Durham's men led by as many as 23 points, but then relaxed and frittered away most of the huge lead allowing North Carolina to close to within five points with five minutes remaining. Timely scoring by Wuycik and a swarming, harassing man-to-man defense lifted the Tarheels to within a hair of resurrection. But the Seminoles stiffened their defense, regrouped in a zone and won 79-75. McAdoo, who had been quiet in the Tarheels' previous two games, was the high scorer with 24 points, though he fouled out with almost ten minutes remaining. Thus, he was not around when the Tarheels made their belated run at the Seminoles.

The championship game was the tightest in nine years and the closest that any team had come to UCLA in a title match. Paced by King's 27 points, most of them on deadly corner jumpers, the stubborn Seminoles succumbed, but not before extending the Bruins to a maximum effort. Good outside shooting gave Florida State a 21-14 lead after six and a half minutes. This was the biggest deficit that UCLA faced all year. Quickly they pulled even as Walton scored his first basket midway through the first half to tie at 21. After the initial dry spell the Bruins were able to get the ball in to Walton over Royals and Larry McCray, a pair of 6′11″ defenders. The redhead began hitting from close range and UCLA waved goodby to the outclassed Seminoles. Florida State's speed, which had provided them with one victory after another, was neutralized when UCLA, the steadiest and coolest team in the country, refused to panic.

When Walton picked up his fourth personal at the midmark of the second half and had to sit down, apprehension on the bench was brief. Nater filled in adequately; when Walton returned six minutes later, Florida State had only improved their position by two points and were still down nine. Even so, the Bruins were forced into a late stall as Florida State mounted a game counterattack. They crept back to within five but time ran out on the gutty Seminoles when the score reached 81-76. Walton was credited with 20 rebounds and 24 points despite his interlude on the bench and was voted the MVP of the tournament. In the consolation North Carolina swept Louisville 105-91 in a game that saw both teams parade to the foul line to take 81 shots.

1973

The times, they were changing. Basketball interest was soaring. There were close to 200 major or Division I universities competing, plus many more in Division II and III and a host of Junior Colleges. Professional basketball was also expanding as two leagues competed in an undeclared war to lure, outbid, pirate or attract by any means, fair, foul, legal or illegal, the best talent available. The object was to get a college player's signature on a pro contract before anyone else. This kind of cutthroat competition led two professional teams to sign Howard Porter and Jim McDaniels before their schools had finished their season schedules. Since both Villanova and

Western Kentucky went all the way to the Final Four in 1971, both colleges were forced by the NCAA to forfeit all tournament victories and to return $60,000 each had earned by getting there. McDaniels promised to reimburse Western Kentucky for the money they lost because of his indiscretion, but he never did. The school claimed it would not have accepted even if the money had been returned.

The older National Basketball Association had imposed on itself regulations forbidding any team to draft a college player before his class graduated. For that reason Wilt Chamberlain who left school at the end of his junior year had to barnstorm for a year before being allowed to play in the NBA. The newer American Basketball Association, attempting to survive with limited resources, overcame its scruples early and began raiding colleges for outstanding underclassmen. The NBA retaliated by creating a "hardship case" category. This allowed—nay encouraged—any college player if he was a big enough star regardless of his class, to declare himself too poor to remain in school and make himself eligible for the draft.

Jim Chones was not in this category since he was plucked from Marquette before the draft though other ABA teams had given the New York Nets permission to go after Chones.

However, Bob McAdoo of North Carolina, Tom Payne of Kentucky, George McGinnis of Indiana and Julius Erving of Massachusetts, to name only a few, were drafted while they still had at least a year of eligibility left. Later they were joined by Michigan's Campy Russell, Marquette's Maurice Lucas and Notre Dame's Gary Brokaw. Other college players such as Bill Walton and later David Thompson of North Carolina State were tempted with multi-million dollar pacts but turned them down to continue their amateur careers. "You can only wear one suit at a time, drive one car and eat three meals a day," philosophized Thompson. The battle for undergraduate talent continued fiercely over several years in the early Seventies. It reached its ultimate limit when Moses Malone, a high school graduate who had signed a letter of intent to enroll at Maryland, was induced to sign a pro contract with the Utah Stars a few weeks before he was due to register for his first college class.

Maryland coach Lefty Driesell was incensed at the loss of a boy who had averaged 38 points and 23 rebounds as a senior and was the most sought after high school player in the country. It was a hypocritical reaction. Malone had promised several other coaches he would accept their offers for an athletic scholarship, but changed his mind every time he was shown around another campus. Driesell had snatched Malone from the clutches of another coach and he happened to be the last in a line of recruiters ready to promise the potential superstar whatever he could get away with.

Basketball players were a highly valued commodity. Each spring the scramble was on to sign the tallest, quickest, brawniest, deadliest, highest-jumping high school player. Coaches and assistants would hire recruiters to jet around the country and enlist alumni to contact the best prospect. In the maneuvering and jockeying for advantage, recruiters would promise almost anything that was legal and, in some cases, quite a bit that was against NCAA regulations. In some cases money, a car, sexual favors and free trips home for the holidays were used as inducements. Regardless of the subject a prospective undergraduate was interested in, the school wanting him had "one of the outstanding departments in the country." A senior who was Jewish and considering Marquette was told that Al McGuire's best friend was Jewish.

Often there was collaboration to make an academically weak student eligible for a scholarship. There were also instances of deliberately falsified grades on high school transcripts, often without the knowledge of the student. This happened in the case of Bernard King who graduated from a Brooklyn, New York, high school and accepted a scholarship at Tennessee. When news that the NCAA was investigating leaked out, the University felt the matter was of such importance (for the school as much as for King), they sent the Vice Chancellor, the Athletic Director and the Assistant to the President to New York to investigate. The three arrived back in Tennessee after having ascertained that some of King's grades had been lowered while others had been raised by the culprit who had falsified them. The university breathed a sigh of relief and King, temporarily suspended, was reinstated after only one game.

Many graduates who were unable to gain admission to a four year university went to a junior college, sometimes with the collusion of a college interested in signing that athlete. After competing in junior college for a year, and being carefully tutored, the player would transfer to the university that originally wanted him. Wichita sponsored at least one senior in this way and was put on probation for it. Other high school seniors with substandard grades enrolled in a junior college, played there for a year or two gaining, if not better grades, at least experience in playing against college level competition. If they had enough court talent, they would be offered scholarships to a four year institution after a year or two and become the well known "juco transfer."

Artis Gilmore, Bob McAdoo, Fred Brown and Larry Kenon were just some of the collegiate stars of the early seventies who transferred from junior college. Some coaches, like Wooden, avoided "juco" transfers, preferring to mold and develop an athlete over his four year undergraduate career. Others experimented. One ingredient in Al McGuire's winning player mix always included a junior college transfer. Dean Smith, who landed McAdoo and watched him develop into an All American, became soured on transfer students when his big center packed up after only one year with the Tarheels and turned professional. There were those who harvested juco players like a cash crop. Among these was Bill Musselman, who combed the junior colleges seeking to bring Minnesota a championship immediately and at any price. The Western Athletic and the Missouri Valley were two conferences which spread the welcome mat for juco transfers. This was particularly true at Wyoming and Wichita and later at New Mexico. But a coach who depended on instant help from the ranks of junior colleges was taking a risk, as Hugh Durham discovered to his regret. Florida State was favored to make it back to the Final Four in 1973, but it took six years for the Seminoles to qualify for the tournament again. Durham's team was destroyed by juco transfer Benny Clyde, a brilliant player, whose attitude fragmented all cohesion on the squad. As a youngster growing up in poverty, Clyde had been in trouble with the law and developed into a bitter, suspicious, moody youth with asocial habits. Still, Durham took a chance with him despite warnings from Clyde's hometown adviser. The coach tried a relaxed, easy-going approach on his problem player when he might have been better advised to be stricter. Discipline was not in Clyde's vocabulary. Durham hoped his teammates would help straighten out the rebellious potential star. Quite the reverse happened. The rest of the Seminoles became infected by Clyde's showboating and general egocentric attitude toward the game. "He really brought them down this year," said Ron Harris, a graduate student at the time. "A lot of dudes look up to Clyde and follow him. If he wanted to do it fancy, everybody wanted to do it fancy. If Clyde wanted to spin and take the ball through his legs, then Petty wanted to and Johnson wanted to. Everybody wanted the spotlight." The result was a fractured team.

Whichever means the coaches used, recruiting was the indispensable overture without which a major college team could not perform. Most coaches hated it. Some turned it over to assistants who spent more time recruiting than attending court practices and games. George Raveling, first at Villanova, then at Maryland, was one of the best and snared Howard Porter for Jack Kraft and Len Elmore, John Lucas and Tom McMillen for Lefty Driesell.

Wooden disliked recruiting, but then he did not have to do it. Given his reputation and that of UCLA, the best players in the country came to him. In general he preferred to encourage only California students to enroll at UCLA. He rarely courted those from the East, with the possible exception of Alcindor. Once in a Bruin uniform, the player was encouraged to make that extra effort, thus perpetuating the winning tradition. Said Wooden, "Subconsciously they are almost afraid to fail."

For others, the need to recruit aggressively overcame their desire to coach. Bob Cousy resigned from his post, bitterly denouncing the humiliating practices of his former profession. "You get a kid to come to your school nowadays by licking his boots . . . Once you have actually committed yourself to actually beg him to come, there can never be a player-coach relationship. The kid is the boss."

As if there was not enough turmoil on and off the court the NCAA decided to inject a new element into the potent brew. Starting with the 1972-73 season freshmen were declared eligible to participate in varsity games. This was strictly voluntary and though there was some dissent and considerable apprehension, most independents and conferences (with the exception of the Ivy League) allowed freshmen to play. (The change was made for economic reasons, permitting schools to save money by combining their freshman, junior varsity and varsity programs.) Competition for places on the varsity was particularly stiff since freshmen and sophomores both became eligible in 1973. This caused considerable unhappiness among veterans and freshmen alike—the veterans because some of them were replaced in the lineup by first year players, and the freshmen because many had been promised by recruitors that they would start and found themselves avoiding splinters on the bench instead. By the end of the year no freshman with the exception of James "Fly" Williams had made a significant impact on the fortunes of his school.

Another major change was a new foul rule. It made the first six common fouls (those not called in the act of shooting or in the backcourt) non-shooting violations. Starting with the seventh, the player fouled was presented with a one-and-one opportunity from the line—that is he was given a bonus shot if he made his first attempt. The result was lower scores with less interruption of the game flow. In 1972 there were 12 teams averaging more than 90 points, led by Oral Roberts with 105. A year later there were just six with Oral Roberts again leading, this time with just 97 points.

Midwest:

The MVC was on the rebound. This was due mainly to two new coaches, Denny Crum at Louisville and Gene Bartow at Memphis State. Crum had taken the Cardinals to the Final Four in 1972 but then lost his entire starting quintet. Undeterred, Crum rebuilt the team and finished just one game behind MVC champion Memphis State (21-5).

The Tigers lost three of their first five when forward Ronnie Robinson was injured but rebounded well once he returned to the lineup, and Larry Kenon began to fit into Bartow's offense with his domination of the boards. Kenon had five fewer rebounds than Bill Walton over the course of the season. Memphis State had one strange weakness—licking the Louis. They lost to St. Louis, Louisville and Louisiana State. Still, their publicity director plugged an old song for which he had written new lyrics. Called "Meet Me in St. Louis, Wooden," it was an invitation to UCLA to play in the championship game to be held in St. Louis in March.

Texas Tech (19-7) won the SWC after practicing brinksmanship the envy of diplomats and high wire performers everywhere. They won four of six overtime games and three contests that were decided by a point. Thus, more than one-third of their victories had the sides within a point of each other at the end of the regulation 40 minutes. Kansas State (22-4) took the Big Eight in a more pedestrian manner.

Southwest Louisiana (23-3) won in the Southland Conference but was once again selected as an at-large team. Dwight Lamar repeated as an All

American but dropped to sixth in the scoring race with a 29 point average. His team meanwhile finished with the second best offense while 12 times soaring over 100 points. Every game was a scoring orgy, a running and shooting circus. Defense was as unknown as meditation at Mardi Gras.

The Ragin' Cajuns rampaged frequently but aside from Houston, to whom they lost, their schedule was undemanding. A 120-78 battering by Jacksonville was a shocker but not nearly as shocking as the revelations (announced by the NCAA just before the game) that Southwest Louisiana had been found guilty of more than 100 violations. These included payments to players and giving fraudulent tests to keep them eligible. The Ragin' Cajuns were subdued for once as they took the floor against Jacksonville and played their worst game of the year. They were still traumatized in their next contest, trailing Cincinnati by 19 at the half, Coach Beryl Shipley must have fired some jolting words at his players in the locker room because they returned to the court vastly energized and outscored the Bearcats by 25 points to win.

The rest of the season was played in the law courts as much as on the basketball courts. The NCAA wanted to ban Southwest Louisiana from its postseason tournament, but the school successfully thwarted that by taking legal action. After the season, however, the Cajuns were finished as a team. The NCAA banned them from any college competition for two years, the players scattered to enroll in other colleges around the country and Coach Shipley, in a final blast, denounced everyone including the Southland Conference which he called a Mickey Mouse league.

South Carolina (20-6) found itself in the unfamiliar Midwest regional. There were at-large teams such as Marquette that were closer than South Carolina. However, the selection committee, mindful of the temperamental McGuire, moved the Gamecocks instead. The number of independent teams was shrinking, especially in the West. Such perennial tournament participants as New Mexico State and Seattle were now conference members and Houston was scheduled to rejoin the SWC.

South Carolina, in the space of two years, had completely revamped its schedule. Not one ACC team remained; instead the Gamecocks played a national sampling that showed either a brilliant imagination or a desperate attempt to fill out their slate. Games were played against Nevada-Las Vegas, Fairfield, Dubuque, Stetson, Georgia Southern, Lafayette, Toledo, Michigan State, Notre Dame and ten Catholic schools to which Frank McGuire had close ties. The Gamecocks were also invited to the Holiday Festival where McGuire's men lost to his old school, St. Johns, in the final, accompanied by the familiar hullabaloo of Madison Square Garden. Though the Gamecocks lost but six times, they were well beaten on each occasion, losing by an average of 11 points.

As usual McGuire had raided the New York parochial schools to build the nucleus for his team. Brian Winters and Kevin Joyce, a pair of All American teammates at Arcbishop Molloy High School were joined by Mike Dunleavy from Brooklyn. They made up a triumvirate of scrappy Irish Mafia players, the essence of the McGuire style.

The favorite to take the regional was seventh ranked Houston (23-3), making their eighth appearance in nine years. If they got past their first opponent, which was a fair assumption, they would be playing the next two rounds in Hofheinz Paviliion, their home court where they had lost just once in four years. The Cougars reflected the reputation of their home state. They were a big team and they did things in a big way. Dwight Jones, their 6′10″ center, had led his high school to the Texas State championship in 1970. He was supported by 6′10″ forward Maurice Presley and 6′8″ forward Steve Newsome. There was no fall off at guard where 6′9″ Louis Dunbar overshadowed his more normal-sized opponents. Wherever the Cougars played, the court seemed more congested than usual with those sturdy bodies and flaring Afros bouncing from baseline to baseline. Dunbar, an unselfish player, helped settle the team that had been fragmented by a feud between Jones and the departed Dwight Davis the previous season.

The Cougars were also noted for their spectacular performances though not all were boastworthy. In one game they retrieved 88 rebounds, in another they committed 38 turnovers and once they scored 74 points in a half. They liked to stay close to home and played only eight of 26 games away, only five outside of the state, a drastic change from previous years. Losses to Creighton by one point, to Indiana by three, and Seattle by four, stood between Houston and a perfect season. With their height and offensive punch the Cougars finished in the top five in both team rebounding and scoring.

Through some misguided scheduling the NCAA had matched the two best teams in the regional in the first round. Held in Wichita, the contest was a rematch between Southwest Louisiana and Houston. The teams had identical records and the first half reflected the evenness of the sides. But Roy Ebron came out smoking to start the second half and the Cajuns were ahead by 13 points before the Cougars could apply the brakes. Guy Lewis ordered a full court press and Houston hauled to within a point at 62-61. Eight unanswered points put SWL in command again and Houston was unable to produce another threat. The Ragin' Cajuns swept to a 102-89 triumph, avenging their earlier loss in Houston. Lamar's 35 points and Ebron's 23 were more than enough to overcome a balanced Cougar attack.

In the co-feature Texas Tech and South Carolina fought to a 30-30 first half stalemate. Neither team could get ahead by more than five points in the final period until the Gamecocks put on a minisurge in the last five minutes. Kevin Joyce's basket and four free throws iced the contest as South Carolina advanced 78-70.

Hofheinz Pavilion was filled to capacity the following Thursday evening but the fans were not as raucus as when Houston played host. Kansas State geared down the action to neutralize the Cajuns' power shooting. They spurted into a 22-8 lead and held on to win 66-63, despite a determined effort by their opponents who closed to within a point with 4:19 left. The tough Wildcat defense held Lamar to 18 points and the Cajuns as a team to their lowest output of the season.

Memphis State, led by Larry Kenon's 34 points, had little difficulty subduing South Carolina 90-76. Gene Bartow's patented zone trap defense and well coordinated team offense kept the Tigers in control throughout. It was Memphis State's first victory in four tournament appearances.

Two days later the Tigers had their offense purring again. Kansas State used a man-to-man and several variation of a zone but none of the defenses seemd to bother the Tigers. They continued to bomb the basket even after their two tall men, Kenon and Wes Westfall, got into foul trouble, hitting 60 percent of their field goals and 90 percent of their foul shots. Larry Finch, nicknamed Tubby, a mere 6′2″ sapling among the redwoods, scored 32 points including a perfect twelve-for-twelve from the line. Surprising Memphis State won easily 92-72 and advanced to the Final Four, the second MVC team to do so in as many years.

Mideast:

Probably the best team in the Mideast was third ranked Minnesota (20-4). Entering the final weekend of the season Minnesota had a 20-2 record and had to win just one of their last two games for at least a share of the Big Ten title. The opposition was not formidable—Iowa (a second division team) at home and last place Northwestern, which had won just four games all season, away. The Gophers lost to Iowa for the second time that year by two points and then were stunned in the biggest Big Ten upset of the year by Northwestern 90-74. As a result Indiana (19-5) won the championship, and Minnesota, which had dropped all their games in conference play, headed for the NIT. For Bobby Knight (who had played for Ohio State's national champions in 1960) this was his first NCAA tournament as a coach. Beating out Minnesota came as a double pleasure for Knight—first because Musselman was the defending Big Ten champion and the favorite to repeat, the second because Knight had never forgiven Musselman for what the Gophers had done to Ohio State in the bloody attack of the previous season.

Kentucky (19-7) won the SEC in their first year under Rupp's successor Joe Hall. Rupp had lost his fight to remain as coach of the Wildcats even though his friends and thousands of Kentucky fans had waged an enthusiastic campaign to waive the mandatory retirement age of 70. "They can leave me with my team or they may as well take me out to the Lexington cemetery" had been Rupp's assessment of what the Wildcats meant to him. They struggled to win their conference, finishing a game ahead of three other schools.

They lost twice to Vanderbilt and even bowed to a weak Mississippi side. At midseason their record in the SEC was 5-4 and Rupp adherents were screaming for the return of the Baron. But the Wildcats swept their last nine conference games, bombarding the basket with more than 90 points in six of their last seven games.

Miami of Ohio (18-8) took the Mid American. A 102-92 ambush of North Carolina at Chapel Hill was one of the surprises of the year. The Tarheels, in the final stages of their conference race, were presumably not concentrating. Jacksonville (21-5) was back after a year's absence. Three of their losses had come against tournament entries—Houston, Providence and Long Beach State. Marquette (23-3) fell only to Notre Dame, Minnesota and Long Beach State. The harshest blow had been the loss to Notre Dame when a last second toss by Dwight Clay found the mark. It snapped Marquette's 81 game win streak at home. A very quick quintet, they moved the ball well, dominated the boards and played their usual grudging defense.

The surprise team in the regional was Austin Peay (21-5) making their first postseason appearance anywhere. They lost three games by two points each and the other two by one. In other words, a total of eight points separated them from a perfect season. The man most responsible for Austin Peay's meteoric rise from last to first in the Ohio Valley Conference was a 6′5″ freshman forward from Brooklyn with a nickname that only partially described his many talents: James "Fly" Williams. Williams barely negotiated his way through high school. A product of Brownsville, one of New York's worst slums, he learned the game by tossing balls into a garbage can. He was spotted by Rodney Parker who played fairy godfather to the Fly by arranging for him to attend a private prep school on Long Island in his senior year. Parker then brought Williams to the attention of officials at Austin Peay.

The Fly was a one-man offense. Fed consistently by fellow Brooklynite Danny Odums, he finished fifth in the country in scoring with a 30 point average and twice tallied 51 points in a game. He propelled the Governors into third place in total offense, a display of whirlwind scoring which included 17 games over 90 points. Wherever Austin Peay played they filled the arena with fans waving flyswatters. At home it was standing room only as the Governors soared from obscurity to prominence on the wings of the Fly.

But Williams was a difficult man to incorporate into the team. Temperamental and cocky, he would direct his teammates, screaming criticisms when they did not meet his expectations. Worse, Williams attempted to subvert Coach Lake Kelly by second-guessing him and sometimes ignoring him when he did not wish to submit to his discipline. A moody player, he was alternately extroverted and withdrawn, much of it due to the difficulty of adjusting to life at a small college in Tennessee.

The Mideast regional got underway in Dayton. Miami skipped to a modest 12-6 lead over Marquette but when the Warriors retaliated by netting 16 of the next 18 points, the Ohioans were done. When Larry McNeill, Marquette's center, fouled out with ten minutes left, Maurice Lucas took over and scored 24 points to pace the Warriors to an easy 77-62 victory.

In another first round match Austin Peay headed for the locker room ten points to the good over Jacksonville. The Dolphins lashed back, though, and tied the contest 75-75 on Jimmy Clark's field goal with 27 seconds showing on the clock. Four seconds before the end Williams retired all the waving flyswatters by canning a short jumper to give the Governors a 77-75 win.

Austin Peay, distinctive in their pin stripe shorts, were the sentimental if not the betting favorites in their second round match against Kentucky. The Governors were ahead by four at the break and had their fans in an uproar throughout the second half which ended in a 92-92 deadlock. "Fly" Williams' emotionally immature outbursts against his fellow players did not help the Governors' cause, but when they moved ahead 96-92 to start the overtime period it looked as if they might actually pull a colossal upset. However, the Wildcats responded with eight points in a row and the Fly's basket with 1:39 remaining only cut the gap to two. Kentucky took the ball out-of-bounds and proceeded to put the game out-of-reach. Three straight buckets by Larry Stamper, who until then had contributed just four points, iced the contest for the Wildcats 106-100. Jim Andrews' deadeye shooting (77 percent from the floor) led Kentucky with 30 points. Ed Childress, Howard Jackson and "Fly" Williams each scored over 20 points to ignite the Governors.

Marquette had never beaten a Big Ten team in the playoffs but when they returned to the court after the intermission sporting a three point lead over Indiana and increased that to ten, it looked as if they were going to score a breakthrough. With less than 15 minutes remaining Marquette was in command 53-43 when the Hoosiers flared ahead after a 16-4 splurge. Both sides were shooting with radar-like precision from the field. The Warriors knotted the count but Indiana forged into the lead again on a pair of free throws by Steve Downing. Sparked by Downing (who netted 29 points) and John Ritter, the Hoosiers broke down the Warriors' pressure defense and cruised to a 75-69 decision.

The first five Kentucky balls swished through the net in the regional final against Indiana. But the Hoosiers, with Andrews again spearheading the attack, caught and passed them soon after. Starting the second half Joe Hall, who did not share Rupp's aversion to a zone, moved the Wildcats into a 1-3-1 pressing defense. The flustered Hoosiers watched their substantial lead shrink until a tip in by Andrews at 11:22 tied matters at 59. A basket by Jimmy Dan Conner for the lead was greeted by a joyful blast from the Wildcat cheering section.

It was now Knight's turn to select the right page from his tactic book. He repositioned Quinn Buckner in the high post where he could either pop with either medium jumpers or pass off to Steve Downing under the basket. It did not take long for Buckner and Downing to put Indiana in the saddle once more but Bob Guyette brought the Wildcat fans to their feet again when he squared accounts at 63-63. Indiana refused to quit. Downing's layup with four minutes to go spelled the beginning of the end. It was Indiana the rest of the way as they hustled into the Final Four for the first time in twenty years 72-65.

East:

Aside from UCLA, basketball power flourished most vigorously in the East and specifically the ACC. At one time during the season three ACC teams were ranked two, three and four. By the end of the campaign North Carolina State was undefeated and ranked second, North Carolina was ranked eighth and Maryland, the ACC tournament runner-up, was number nine. Since State was on a year's probation, Maryland (22-6) was invited to the postseason entertainment. Had the Terrapins not belonged to the ACC, they might well have been undefeated since all six losses came in league competition. (They were 13-0 against non-conference opponents.) The conference was so competitive that even when tail-end Wake Forest bumped second place North Carolina out of the ACC playoffs, few basketball experts in the tobacco state were shocked. The trio of North Carolina State, Maryland and North Carolina also finished with the top three marks in field goal accuracy **in the country.**

North Carolina State, the only undefeated team aside from UCLA, sat out the tournament in frustration because the NCAA had placed them on probation, along with Duke, for illegally recruiting David Thompson. The 6′4″ All American guard was so outstanding that the machinations to secure his enrollment leading to the suspension of two universities in pursuit of his talent was almost understandable.

Maryland had come closer to defeating the Wolfpack than any other school, losing to them twice by two points, the last time in the ACC playoff final. Bursting out of the starting gate like a nuclear submarine crew on shore leave, they devastated Brown in their opener, 127-82, showing their offensive punch. In their second game they demonstrated their fine defense by polishing off Richmond 82-50. The Terrapins ticked off nine more wins before hosting North Carolina State.

Maryland featured an outstanding player at each position. At center, Len Elmore from Power Memorial, Alcindor's old alma mater, was a superb ing rebounder and shot blocker; at forward, Tom McMillen, had been the most sought after high school player of 1969; and at guard, John Lucas was a steady team leader. McMillen, aside from being an All American, was also the brainiest power forward in the college ranks. A pre-med student with a 3.8 average, he was about to receive a Rhodes scholarship, an honor which he later turned down to enter professional basketball. The one element Maryland missed was speed, especially by the guards who at times were accused of lacking hustle.

The director of this talent bank was the colorful ex-Davidson reinsman Lefty Driesell. When he moved to Maryland, Driesell had vowed grandiosely to make the Terrapins "the UCLA of the East." So far, after four years, he was considerably short of his objective and the media, always looking to tweak the brash Driesell, never let him forget that remark.

Rarely had college basketball produced a showman who delighted in performing for his audience as Lefty. Unlike the *sturm and drang* of a Musselman or the hometown cornball folksiness of an Abe Lemons, Lefty drew his inspiration from Hollywood—which may have been one way of bringing the Los Angeles influence to Maryland. Driesell's command post was a director's chair with the word Lefty printed on the canvas back. When he entered Cole Pavilion he would stab the air with two fingers spread in a V sign and the band would respond with a chorus of "Hail to the Chief" while the fans bellowed their approval.

Normally a pleasant man, Driesell raged whenever someone tried to take away what he considered rightfully his, whether a player whom he thought he had recruited or a referee's decision that he felt he deserved. When his temper flared he was liable to do anything including removing his jacket and using it for a doormat.

The only southern school in the regional was Furman (20-8). The Palladins had finished second behind Davidson but had ousted them in the postseason playoff.* Joe Williams, who had coached Jacksonville to the NCAA final three years before, was now directing Furman. His former team did not treat their old mentor kindly, though. Furman met Jacksonville twice during the season and dropped both games. Williams had brought his power offense tactics, so successful at Jacksonville, with him. Eight times the Palladins broke through to post triple digit scores. But the value of their defense was only slightly greater than Confederate banknotes. A 118-115 loss to Mercer was just one example.

Fifth ranked Providence (24-2) had lost only to Santa Clara and UCLA on unfriendly territory far from home. Sparked by All American guard Ernie DiGregorio and Marvin Barnes, a brilliant pair who complemented each other's talents perfectly, the Friars won their last 14. Ernie D., as he was called much to the relief of the typesetters' union, quarterbacked the team, fed Barnes and the other men in the forecourt and still averaged 24 points a game. Barnes outrebounded everyone in the country except Kermit Washington of American University, which played a much easier schedule than Providence. Both DiGregorio and Barnes were hometown boys. The Friars also had Kevin Stacom, an import from Queens, N.Y., who took his training so seriously he spent his summer dribbling a basketball for miles along the sidewalks of New York.

Pennsylvania (20-5) completed another successful campaign though they lost two more than they had over their previous three regular seasons.

---

*Poor Davidson. Players arrived and graduated. Coaches screamed themselves hoarse and quit. Still, the Wildcats seemed to be afflicted with an inability to win their conference playoff and the berth in the NCAA tourney that went with it. NIne times in the last ten years Davidson had won the Southern Conference crown and five times, including the three previous years, they had been knocked out in the playoffs.

A niggardly defense made the Quakers the runners up in scoring defense. Another Big Five school from Philadelphia, St. Josephs (22-5), dropped three in a row as the season blossomed but then scooted to a ten game win streak.

St. Johns (19-6) reversed that scenario. They surged to a 17-2 record, then dropped four of their last six. This was cause for concern since three of these defeats were to teams who were also in the East regional—Syracuse, St. Josephs and Providence. Decisive 40 point victories over Georgetown and Dartmouth and the first loss pinned on Villanova at their gym in six years had made St. Johns the class of the East until their late season swoon. In December, Coach Frank Mulzoff had guided the Redmen to the Holiday Festival final where they trimmed South Carolina. Mulzoff, who had played for Frank McGuire in 1952, got considerable satisfaction in beating his old coach while directing his old team. Since both South Carolina and St. Johns featured local city players almost exclusively, the final became a showcase of the city game whose participants, on both sides, had known each other since high school and before.

The Redmen would undoubtedly have been even stronger if Mel Davis, the fourth best rebounder in the country in 1972, had been available. The St. Johns star was sidelined the entire season after undergoing knee surgery. Billy Schaeffer assumed the leadership role in his absence, and made up with his sharpshooting what the team had lost in rebounding strength.

Since the NCAA attempted to schedule opening round games so schools did not play in their home arenas, attendance was poor at each of the three first round sites. Only 3,000 showed up in Philadelphia as Syracuse (22-4) confronted Furman. The Orangemen had matters under control most of the way until Furman closed the gap to three points with 56 seconds left. The Palladins were forced to foul but picked the wrong man. Jim Lee with a 89 percent success average from the line confidently dropped in a pair. A brief Furman flurry made no difference in the outcome as Syracuse eked out an 83-82 decision.

Meanwhile in Virginia, before a house that was two-thirds empty, a Philadelphia and a New York team that would have filled arenas in their hometowns, played an absorbing, closely contested game. It was charged with tactical moves, short, intense burts of scoring, but was ultimately won by the individual efforts of a trio of Quaker sophomores.

St. Johns moved ahead 21-16 as Schaeffer found the range early, flushing a dozen points through the cords in as many minutes. Penn rallied to put 12 of the next 14 points on the scoreboard and led at half time 38-32. They pulled away to a 56-47 advantage before the Redmen talled 11 unanswered points. The charge was led by center Ed Searcy. Meanwhile Schaeffer, who had ignited the team earlier, was smothered by sophomore Bob Bigelow who shadowed him all over the court.

With a two point lead and possession, the Redmen scattered into a spread offense, a New York version of North Carolina's four corners. The

Quakers were patient and eventually forced a turnover. A pair of free throws tied the score 58-58. Mel Utley's foul shot put St. Johns on top again at 2:29. But Pennsylvania had the ball and in less than a minute sophomore John Jablonski's two pointer vaulted them into the lead again. In the final 30 seconds a third sophomore, John Beecroft, iced the game with a pair from the line to give Pennsylvania a 62-61 decision. Jablonski's and Beecroft's points were important but by holding Schaeffer to just four points in the last 28 minutes, Bigelow's contribution was decisive.

Back at the St. Johns' gym another sparse turnout watched Providence and St. Josephs lay it to each other in the latest installment of that historic rivalry. The game lacked tension and some of the local St. Johns' fans probably had an ear cocked to the progress of their team in Virginia. The Hawks used a zone in the first half but switched to a man-to-man when they fell behind after the first 20 minutes. Plagued by early foul trouble, the Hawks' 6′9″ Mike Bantom sat down for six minutes while Barnes, able to penetrate inside, now went on a rampage. Back in the lineup Bantom had to play cautiously but was still St. Josephs' leading scorer with 23. The game passed out of the Hawks' reach in the first five minutes of the second session. Ernie D., who had been sluggish up till then, caught fire and netted nine of the Friars' next 13 points to break the game open. He finished with 31 in an 89-76 winning effort.

For only the second time in 15 years the state of North Carolina was not represented in the East regional. Nevertheless, an enthusiastic sellout crowd welcomed the survivors to Charlotte. After all, the ACC was still represented.

Syracuse hoped to avenge their defeat by Maryland in the previous year's NIT. For 25 minutes they kept pace, but with the scoreboard favoring the Terrapins 43-41, Driesell's men sustained a three minute, 12 point burst. Syracuse was never able to come close again. They tried to neutralize their opponents' height and speed by deploying a zone, but the latter's pressure offense and physical superiority eventually wore the Orangemen down. Maryland's bulk asserted itself most strongly under the boards where they outrebounded Syracuse almost two-to-one. A well-balanced attack distributed the scoring evenly among their starters, all of whom wound up in double figures. Maryland was barely extended in an easy 91-75 victory. In the co-feature Marvin Barnes was literally unstoppable as he made all ten of his field goal attempts. Ernie D. complimented that performance by claiming ten assists. Stacom's seven of nine from the field, Nehru King's seven of eleven and Charles Crawford's perfect six for six gave the Friars a dazzling 65 percent shooting performance from the floor. Besides, they missed only one foul shot.

Energized by DiGregorio's fancy dribbling (between the legs) and passing (behind the back), Providence was downcourt and had scored before Penn had a chance to set up. The slower Quakers were helpless against that type of onslaught. They were also suffering from their annual postseason chills (or maybe the draft created by the swift Friars affected them) and were unable to plant the ball in the hoop. Providence started with a man-to-man defense but switched to a zone when Barnes picked up his third personal in the first period. Neither defense made much difference as the ice cold Quakers shot only 27 percent in the first half and 35 percent for the game. Providence breezed to an 87-65 victory.

It was quickness and aggressiveness (Providence) versus height (Maryland) in the regional final. Ernie D. was so pumped up he committed five offensive fouls and was whistled for a technical to boot, all in the space of 28 minutes. His intensity also accounted for 24 first half points.

The first period was played at a pace that almost wore grooves in the Charlotte court. Back and forth the teams hurtled like shuttles gone berserk. Eleven times the lead changed as neither side could shake free of the other. The fans loved it. They screamed and applauded both teams but especially Earnie D's aggressiveness.

Maryland held a slim 51-50 lead at the half. After a brief exchange of points Providence went on a tear, scoring ten straight as they slashed through Maryland's 1-3-1 zone with ease. They were still ten ahead with almost 12 minutes left to play when DiGregorio streaked in for a layup, scattering the taller Elmore across the baseline. Credited with the basket, his twenty-ninth and thirtieth points of the evening, he was also handed his fifth personal. Shocked, Providence retreated into a zone and held the slower Terrapins at bay for the remainder of the game to gain their first berth in the Final Four. DiGregorio's star performance and Kevin Stacom's 24 points in a supporting role made the difference in the 103-89 showdown.

West:

In the West, the Wizard of Westwood had directed UCLA (30-0) to a second successive undefeated year. The high point of the season occurred on a trip to the Midwest where they were scheduled to play their only two non-conference games away from home. In Chicago Stadium they whipped Loyola of Illinois for their sixtieth consecutive victory, tying with San Francisco for the longest winning streak in college basketball history. Ironically, Loyola was also San Francisco's sixtieth victim. Coincidental was the presence of Illinois and Notre Dame on the same doubleheader program. Illinois was the team that had broken San Francisco's streak and the Irish were the last team to beat the Bruins in 1971.

Two days later UCLA travelled to South Bend. If there was any apprehension that Notre Dame might break the streak it was not apparent on the UCLA bench. They coolly and mechanically whipped the Irish to set a new consecutive win record of 61 which they extended every time they played for the rest of the season. The string of victories rolled on, each one seemingly easier than the previous one. Their closest encounter came at Oregon State where the Bruins always had trouble winning and where they registered a hard fought 73-67 decision. The Bruins were unbeatable.

Whereas the emphasis in 1972 was on an explosive offense, Wooden now drilled his team to excel as a defensive unit. UCLA scored over 100 points only once, against Providence, but had the fifth best defense in the country. The switch from offense to defense was most apparent in the play of Walton. He patrolled the lane like a predator guarding his lair and rarely did anyone get by him. If an opponent managed to get a shot off before Walton slammed the ball away, or missed the attempt, that was the only shot he got—Walton or Keith Wilkes would gobble the rebound. Walton's effectiveness on both ends of the court were reflected in the year-end statistics which showed him in the top five in shooting percentage and rebounding. Walton was a total ball player and natural leader. "The best player ever to put on a pair of basketball shorts" was what Wooden's assistant Frank Arnold once called him. He was naturally picked for the All American team which included teammate Wilkes.

However, Walton and Wilkes were not the entire team. Sven Nater, 6′11″, 250 lbs, born in Amsterdam, Holland, was the best backup center in college basketball and conceivably the second best center outside the pros. A good shooter—the leading scorer in the Olympic tryouts—his only weakness was defense. Nater was the team jokester, hamming it up on the bench. In a broader sense he typified the team which loved to have a good time, to frolic, horse around, drink a few beers. They enjoyed themselves between games. "We have this great UCLA Image," confided one of the Bruins, bragging a little, "and nobody suspects we're a bunch of law-breaking degenerates."

Larry Farmer, who played in the corner opposite Wilkes, had been the vice-president of his honor society in high school. A cool dresser sporting the most current "rags," he boasted he had taught Sidney Wicks and Curtis Rowe all they knew about clothes.

Long Beach State (24-2) was the only school given even the slimmest chance to beat UCLA in the regional. The Forty Niners resembled a finely tuned machine designed explicitly for throwing a ball through a hoop. This was not unusual considering their coach, Jerry Tarkanian, was the grand guru of the run-and-gun faith. They totalled at least 90 points in their first eight games. In one memorable three-game set they swept their opponents by an average of 40 points. The Forty Niners participated in three Christmas holiday tournaments and won them all, including the All College Tournament in Oklahoma City.

San Francisco (22-4) had bowed to UCLA by 28 points. Oklahoma City (21-5) in its last year under Abe Lemons suffered from a leaky defense and twice allowed 106 points. Weber State (20-6) won the Big Sky for the umpteenth time though they had to make a midseason correction after losing five of seven. After that the Wildcats rolled to victory in their last 12 games and ran away from the rest of the conference.

Arizona State (18-7) finished a game ahead of three other WAC schools in an extremely tight finish. Though they were knocked over twice by BYU, they were at least safe from the Cougars. The NCAA had threatened the

WAC with the loss of their automatic tournament berth if it allowed BYU to become conference champion. The reason for the NCAA's ire was the presence of Cosic who had passed the age of eligibility (24 years) set for a foreign player. Arizona State got the WAC off the hook.

In the first round, Oklahoma City suffered a defensive lapse or relapse against Arizona State and was never a factor after the intermission. They looked almost exclusively to their 6′11″, 260 lb. hulk, Ozie Edwards, who turned in a 31 point performance. ASU spread the scoring among nine of the ten men who suited up. These were not token appearances, either, as each scored at least five points. The Sun Devils' team effort was rewarded with a 103-78 win.

Long Beach State and Weber State squared off for the third time in four years and as in the two previous games, the Forty Niners prevailed. The Californians were cruising along with a ten point lead late in the first period when the aptly named Brady Small, a bullet-quick, 5′11″ guard, ignited a Weber State rally. Small popped from all over the court in leading Weber State to a narrow half time lead. But the disciplined Forty Niners applied increased pressure on their opponents in the second half and Weber began to fall apart like a rose in a steam bath. The entire starting team with the exception of Small almost fouled out as disorganization increased with the size of the deficit. At the end it was Long Beach State's game 88-75. Ratleff and Leonard Gray divided 50 points evenly to take scoring honors.

As if UCLA did not have enough of an advantage, the West regional had been scheduled for Pauley Pavilion. The Bruins disposed of Arizona State with ease. Larry Hollyfield led the first half charge with 18 points but Walton was the eventual point leader with 28. With a huge lead the Wizard pulled his starters with six minutes to go, leaned back and watched the substitutes coast to a 98-81 win.

San Francisco's upset of Long Beach State was not so remarkable considering the injuries to Ratleff, who had jammed two fingers in practice earlier in the week. Favoring the injured members he tore a tendon in another finger, leaving him precious little to shoot with. As a result the crippled Ratleff made only four of 18 shots. The Forty Niners were behind but not out of it when guard Mike Quick flushed eight straight points through the hoop to give the Dons a substantial lead they never lost. Quick's 25 were a major factor in San Francisco's 77-67 advance.

Two days later UCLA fans sat stunned as San Francisco moved to a 16-9 advantage. It was the first time all season the Bruins had been so far behind. Wooden called time and inserted Tommy Curtis who responded with three long rainbows, to recharge the Bruin attack. The Dons very effectively slowed down the pace and also collapsed on Walton, sealing him off from his teammates. At the midmark UCLA had nosed ahead 23-22 but it was still anyone's game. With Walton contained, Wooden directed his men to attack from outside. Wilkes and Curtis both unlimbered, sending long-range payloads arcing through the net. With Curtis directing the offense, Walton preempting the boards, and San Francisco's shots bouncing off target, UCLA surged to a 41-28 lead on the way to a 54-39 victory.

Final Four:

St. Louis was the setting for the final two rounds. The NCAA tournament committee had made two changes since 1972. First, the semifinal round was to be played on Saturday afternoon and the national championship on the following Monday evening. Second, there would no longer be an automatic East versus West confrontation in the final. For the last few years the strongest basketball teams, with the exception of UCLA, of course, had competed in the East and Mideast regionals. The overall power of the ACC and the Big Ten, along with perennial SEC champion Kentucky and strong independents in the East and Midwest, tended to put the tournament out of balance. In effect the talented teams in the eastern part of the country knocked each other cut while UCLA landed in the final after barely working up a sweat. The committee, therefore, decided to match up the winners of the West and the Mideast regionals and those of the East and Midwest in the semifinals. In the future, regional champions were to rotate, and this led to the fateful confrontation between the West and East regional representatives the following year.

UCLA had indeed been fortunate. Over the years, one team or another that seemed to have the manpower to deflect the Bruins from the championship were derailed before the final round or did not compete at all. In 1969 second ranked LaSalle was on probation and did not play. In 1970 Bob Lanier, who might have been able to neutralize Sidney Wicks, was injured in a semifinal game against Jacksonville. In 1971 undefeated (at the time) and second ranked Marquette lost their star Jim Chones three weeks before the end of the season. In 1972 second ranked North Carolina was tripped by the upstarts from Florida State.

In 1973 fortune smiled even more brightly on a team already blessed with an abundance of talent. Undefeated and second ranked North Carolina State was barred from the tourney due to recruiting violations. Third ranked Minnesota incredibly had blown the Big Ten title on the last weekend of the season. Fourth ranked Long Beach State had been disposed of by San Francisco. The only school in the top five that remained was Providence and tragedy was about to strike the Friars, all but assuring the Bruins another national title.

As the first semifinal approached the seven and a half minute mark, Providence enjoyed a comfortable 24-16 lead over Memphis State. DiGregorio had eleven points already and had taken charge of the slashing Friar attack. It looked as if they would at least have a chance at avenging their early season loss to UCLA. It was then that Marvin Barnes crashed to the hardwood and limped to the bench. Providence's bench was thin. They were basically a six man unit and without Barnes, who had averaged 19 rebounds a game, they were in deep trouble. The muscular center was the only Friar able to contain 6′9″ Larry Kenon. Providence regrouped and even stretched their advantage. By intermission they still held a sizable nine point lead. Ernie D. was playing as if not only the reputation of the team but the school and the whole state of Rhode Island rested on him. Like a bumper car at an amusement park he scooted everywhere, shot from every point of the compass. In the first half he either scored or assisted on all but four of Providence's 22 baskets.

Gene Bartow apparently made the correct adjustments in the locker room because when they took the floor for the second half, they switched to a more patterned offense which immediately paid off. The Tigers set up Kenon repeatedly with pin point passes under the basket. Larry not only filled the hoop, scoring a total of 28 points, but without interference from Barnes was able to harvest 22 rebounds. Barnes returned to action in the second period but hobbled as he was, was no factor at all. Unable to jump, he finished with just three boards.

The Tigers caught Providence after five minutes of the second half. For a while neither side could establish dominance but Ron Robinson's field goal, giving the Tigers a 76-75 edge, proved to be the turning point. The Friar's dreams began to fade at about the same time as their energy. Stacom and Charles Crawford fouled out, attempting too strenuously perhaps to compensate for Barnes. Ernie D., also trying to shoulder too much of the burden, simply ran out of gas. Memphis State vacuumed the boards, outrebounding Providence 54-39. They also outpointed them, 98-85.

For two-thirds of the game it was a familiar scenario to the more than 19,000 fans in the St. Louis Checkerdome. It could have been a rerun of any one of UCLA's runaway wins. Ahead of Indiana at intermission, 40-22, mostly on the strength of an unanswered 18 point boom—the kind familiar to all UCLA fans—the Bruins were 20 points ahead after 27 minutes. They were only a couple of minutes away from inserting the reserves to mop up when either Indiana found the right combination or the Bruins got careless or both. But the next seven minutes saw the Hoosiers crash like a huge Pacific comber, engulfing more and more of UCLA's dwindling lead until only a field goal separated the teams. First the Bruins stopped pressing, then they lost their momentum and began to commit turnovers. A three second violation, a throw-in infraction, missed shots, and the Bruins began to crumble. Walton picked up his third and fourth personals during a 17 point Indiana rally which saw UCLA blanked on the scoreboard in a span of 3:43. Later Wooden admitted that for the first time that year his team lost their poise.

Almost ten minutes were left with UCLA clinging to a narrow 54-51 lead. On the next play Walton crashed into his counterpart, Steve Downing. Bruin fans groaned but the referee called the foul on the Hoosier center. The comber had reached the high water mark.

Wooden inserted Curtis and Dave Meyers into the lineup. Curtis seemed to have a stabilizing effect on the Bruins as he had in the San Francisco game. Suddenly the scoring blizzard died down. In the next four minutes Indiana crept another point closer but Downing, their big man, fouled out after gathering 26 points and slowly the Hoosier wave began to recede. The Bruins settled down and ran off the next ten points as Indiana failed to cash in on five straight sorties downcourt. Curtis, who finished with 22, sparked the comeback while Walton's 17 rebounds were also a critical factor in the 70-59 victory. Once again the Bruins triumphed but this time they had known fear, even if only for a few minutes.

Like jazz, Memphis State had come up the Mississippi River, except now they were bringing with them a different sound. The fifteenth ranked Tigers had a loyal following that included soul singer Issac Hayes who brought his music and his friends to St. Louis with the team. And then there was that popular favorite which the team's publicity director had been singing all season—an invitation that was about to be accepted—"Meet Me in St. Louis, Wooden."

Gene Bartow knew his team absolutely had to stop Walton. He assigned his frontcourt, Ron Robinson, Wes Westfall and Larry Kenon, to sag on the tall redhead. Kenon and Walton apparently played each other too tight to suit the referees. Whistles blew, arms pointed at the two centers and before long they were both in foul trouble. Kenon exited first, drawing his third personal after only 6:23. While he was gone the Bruins opened a nine point gap. He returned after a brief rest and a few minutes later it was Walton's turn to pick up his third. At that point UCLA enjoyed a six point edge. With Walton on the bench the UCLA attack foundered. They added just two more points to their total and allowed the Tigers to knot the score just before the half.

Memphis State went ahead briefly early in the second period on a pair of free throws by Larry Finch. When the Bruins regained the lead on three baskets by Walton, Kenon evened matters 45-45 with a pair of his own. With his great reach and mobility, the big redhead now took charge. Picking lob passes out of the air in the vicinity of the rim, he simply tipped the ball through the hoop. Greg Lee was the main feeder on the alley-oop play and finished with 14 assists. Walton continued his one man blitz, scoring 14 of his team's first 20 points of the second half as UCLA pulled away to a ten point lead. However, Memphis State sliced that to six and with more than half the period remaining Walton collected his fourth foul. Wooden left him in the game, a decision that was later vindicated.

The Tigers tried driving on Walton but failed to disqualify him. The one to foul out was Memphis State's Westfall while Robinson collected his fourth. Playing with superb control, Walton continued his assault as the UCLA advantage mounted. At the final buzzer it was UCLA 87 Memphis State 66. Walton had scored 21 baskets on 22 shots, accumulating 44 points, the finest performance ever in a championship game. He was voted the MVP for the second year in a row. The Memphis State front court trio, who tried to hold Walton, scored just 26 points among them.

It was UCLA's and Wooden's seventh consecutive championship. By now the postgame ceremony was becoming familiar to the Wizard of Westwood. Maybe he even had the time to reflect that if freshmen had been eligible in 1966, this would probably have been his tenth straight championship.

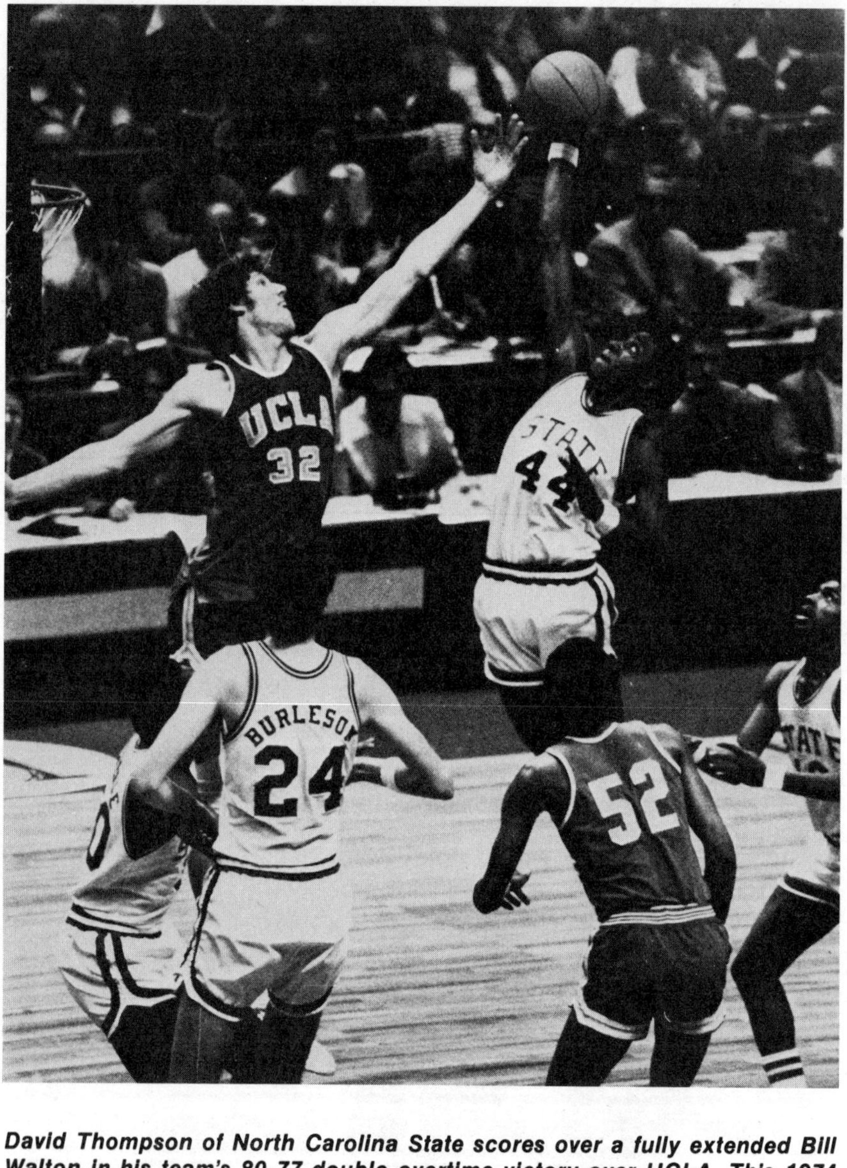

David Thompson of North Carolina State scores over a fully extended Bill Walton in his team's 80-77 double overtime victory over UCLA. This 1974 semi-final contest broke UCLA's 38 game tournament winning streak. (Hugh Morton Photo)

16

A LAST HURRAH 1974-1975

1974

East:

North Carolina State knew they could not compete in the 1973 postseason tournament. Rather than sulk or take a "what does it matter" attitude, the Wolfpack extended itself in every game, showing a considerable amount of class and determination. They played in the toughest conference in the land, won the conference title, the postseason playoff and beat teams in the top ten six times to boot. They were rewarded with a perfect season. Had they gone to the last round and confronted UCLA, it is doubtful they would have defeated them. A team of sophomores and juniors, North Carolina State needed another year of playing together before taking on the Bruins.

The Pack ranged from pocket size, through medium, to monumental. Monty Towe, at 5′6″, was one of the shortest starters on a major college basketball team. When someone suggested to Coach Norm Sloan that he recruit Towe, he shot back, not too kindly, "You got the wrong team. It's Florida State that runs a circus." The fireplug guard, four letter man in high school (basketball, football, baseball and golf) did enroll at North Carolina State and it did not take long for Sloan to change his mind about him. Towe showed that not only could he play the tall man's game, he would be the Wolfpack's floor leader. He was a superb dribbler, as small men usually are, moving the ball slickly behind his back and between his legs to keep the defense off-balance. He was not afraid to confront much taller men, letting them bang into him to collect offensive fouls. He was a casualty of so many collisions one wondered whether those giants were able to see him. He would also hustle after every loose ball, diving headlong on the hardwood if that was necessary. The big difference between Towe and most other players was his attitude. He was determined to play—and to win. He played healthy and he played hurt, once with a cast to protect a broken wrist, another time in a mask guarding a broken nose. "It's something inside," said Sloan, shaking his head in admiration.

The man giving a fair imitation of the Eiffel Towar was 7′4″ Tommy Burleson, the tallest center in college basketball. Burleson was still working on his confidence; centers who were considerably shorter were able to intimidate him. However, he was learning quickly. Not quite the defensive equal of Walton, his wingspread alone would daunt those who encroached on his territory. At times Burleson played with great intensity, but it usually required somebody or something to arouse the moody giant.

The medium-sized player, at least in basketball terms, was 6′4″ David Thompson. This remarkable athlete was coveted by so many colleges while a senior in high school, the resulting recruiting war caused two schools to be put on probation. North Carolina State at least landed Thompson; the other suffered the penalty without any compensating reward.

Thompson came from Shelby, North Carolina, where his father, a janitor, raised David and ten other Thompson children. He was different from other black basketball players. Most of those came from urban ghettoes, whereas Thompson grew up in a shack at the end of a dirt road. But he shared the ghetto youths' love for the game, their fluid motions, their unwasted efforts. An intelligent, popular player, he was content to finish college rather than rush off to the professional leagues at the first lucrative offer. Probably his greatest talent, aside from his court sense and his scoring, was his ability to outleap defenders several inches taller. Thompson could jump 42 inches off the floor and he and Towe perfected a play which started with the pocket guard lofting a high lob toward the net and ended with Thompson tipping it in while hovering just above the rim. The alley-oop play required near perfect timing and coordination. Some observers swore that if Thompson mistimed his leap, he could hover just below the rafters until such time as the ball was delivered.

In 1974, North Carolina State's record was 26-1, their only loss an 81-66 whipping by UCLA in their third game. They won the ACC regular season title. Then in the final of the playoff, they struggled with Maryland in an overtime tilt before qualifying for the national championship playoff 103-100. The game in Greensboro, North Carolina, was one of the most exciting ever played in the ACC tournament, quite an accomplishment considering the competition. Both teams shot better than 55 per cent. Burleson played an inspired game, scoring 38 points, and Towe flipped in a pair of free throws with six seconds remaining in overtime to win it for the Wolfpack. Actually, three ACC teams could have performed creditably in the NCAA tournament. North Carolina State, North Carolina and Maryland were all ranked among the top five teams in the country. Aside from a pair of losses to

UCLA, none of the three had been beaten by other than conference foes. The conference as a whole won 80 per cent of its games against outside teams.

The Wolfpack opened their season with a pair of laughers, chewing up East Carolina 79-47 and Vermont 97-42. But then UCLA wiped the smile away when they temporarily derailed the Wolfpack juggernaut. North Carolina State got back on the track with a 94-60 thrashing of Georgia. They followed this up with Sugar Bowl and Big Four tournament victories. By the end of the season, North Carolina State had won 53 of their last 54 over a two year span. The team was ranked number one, Sloan was voted Coach of the Year and Thompson was honored with the Player of the Year award.

Statistically, the Wolfpack was near the top, too. They had the fourth best offense in the country with All American Thompson's 26 points per game showing the way.

Providence (26-3) was just a hair weaker than in 1973. The eighth ranked Friars had graduated DiGregorio but still featured Barnes, the nation's leading rebounder. The temperamental center had been arrested earlier for slugging a teammate with a tire iron. His lack of discipline may have hurt him in court but on the court he was outstanding, earning for himself an All American berth. Providence lost only to Western Kentucky, Purdue and Duquesne but ambushed Jacksonville in their own gym by sixteen points.

Pennsylvania (21-5) won the Ivy title for the fifth straight time. An excellent defensive squad, they beat Cornell 87-36 and Columbia 73-36 in back-to-back contests. Furman (21-7) fell four times to ACC teams but did a lot better in their own conference. South Carolina (22-4) was invited as an independent.

It was Coach Jack McKinney's last year at the helm at St. Josephs (19-10). The Hawks' harrying defense kept them in contention in games throughout their long season. Whenever the defense broke down, which occured during a couple of slides that lingered like an epidemic, the Hawks lost. But they won in batches, too, taking their first five, losing six of nine, rebounding with six in a row, then succumbing four times. They recovered in time and triumphed in their last five outings including a victory over LaSalle in the Mid Atlantic playoff.

Pittsburgh (22-3) had the second longest winning streak in the country. After losing their opener to West Virginia, they counted 21 straight victims. The Panthers fell to Penn State and South Carolina before inflicting a revenge victory over West Virginia in their season finale.

Nine of twelve members of the Panther team, including all five starters, were from the Pittsburgh area. (The best high school player in the area, and one that Pittsburgh coach Charles Ridl had tried very hard to recruit, had escaped to Marquette. With Maurice Lucas, Pittsburgh might well have finished undefeated.) Despite the presence of a star of All American Billy Knight's magnitude, the Panthers were an unselfish, team-oriented group. Substituting lavishly from a well-stocked bench, Ridl was able to wear down opponents with wave after wave of court length sprinters.

Pittsburgh's switching defenses held St. Josephs to 16 field goals in an opening round encounter. Scoring was sparse. At the break the Hawks had just 16 points. Twenty playing minutes later they were ousted 54-42. Equal point distribution among the Panthers resulted in Mickey Martin taking high scoring honors with 12 points.

Furman scored an upset over South Carolina, 75-67, in a game played in the hollow privacy of the Palestra—a bare 1,042 spectators on hand. This was probably the smallest crowd to attend a NCAA playoff since before World War II. The Gamecocks, with such fine players as Mike Dunleavy, Brian Winters and Alex English, all of whom became professional stars, were unceremoniously whisked from the scene by an inferior Furman team.

Penn and Providence had split their encounters in the previous two East regionals. Now in a rubber match in the St. John's gym, the Quakers went into their annual swoon. Marvin Barnes was closely guarded and it took 15 minutes before he was able to score his first bucket. By the end of the half he had eight points and was just getting into his rhythm. Barnes pumped in ten of Providence's first 16 points of the second period as the Friars opened up a 12 point bulge. The muscular center erased the boards to trigger the Providence fast break, which was leaving scorched tracks in the Redmen's floor. Aside from sophomore John Engles' 27 points and Ron Haigler's 19, none of the Quakers seemed involved in the contest. For Providence, Barnes with 26 points, 17 rebounds and four blocked shots, was simply uncontainable; they swept to an 84-69 win.

In Raleigh a capacity crowd watched Knight catapult 34 points through the net, leading Pittsburgh to an 81-78 win over stubborn Furman. In the nightcap, North Carolina State shot a cool 39 per cent but still finished off Providence without much difficulty, scorching the Friars 92-78. The difference was Thompson, who hit for 40 points—24 in the first half—and Burleson, who plucked 24 balls off the backboard and the rim. Each team had an equal number of baskets but North Carolina State had double the opportunities from the free throw line and capitalized on them.

The regional final was supposed to be a predictable affair. The Wolfpack, playing on its home court, was heavily favored to beat a clearly outmanned Pittsburgh crew. The outcome was as predicted, but what developed before another capacity house fairly tingled with drama. Midway through the first half with the Wolfpack ahead 24-19, Thompson launched himself into the air on one of his coiled spring leaps, failed to complete his attempted tip in, bounced off teammate Phil Spence and crashed headlong to the court. Play stopped. Coach, trainer, doctor and players assembled around the prostrate body. It took four minutes for Thompson to regain consciousness and several more to lift him onto a stretcher and wheel him off the court. Meanwhile 12,400 partisan fans hushed, wondering whether this was going to be the end of North Carolina State's hopes as it had been for St. Bonaventure in 1970 (when they lost Lanier) and Providence the previous year (when Barnes was injured). It looked as if UCLA would once again miss facing their toughest potential opponent at full strength.

The game continued. A grim, determined Burleson took up the scoring slack left by Thompson's absence as he fired 26 points into the hoop. He got valuable assistance from Towe at the other end of the height spectrum. Their concentration was evident as neither missed any of his 15 free throw attempts. The Wolfpack had a total of 37 opportunities from the line as the Panthers fouled repeatedly, trying to check their determined opponents. The Wolfpack also governed the backboards by an almost two-to-one edge. The final score, 100 to 72, was fairly representative of the difference between the teams.

But the news off the court provided the real drama of the day. The announcement at the start of the second half that x-rays showed Thompson had not suffered a fracture or any other serious damage was greeted with the biggest cheer of the evening. Shortly after that Thompson reappeared in Reynold's Auditorium with a huge white bandage covering 15 stitches lacing the top of his head and sat down on the North Carolina State bench. Upon seeing the white-domed star, the fans jumped to their feet and erupted in an explosion of relief and welcome.

West:

All was not right in Westwood. On the court UCLA was devastating, at least for the first half of the season, but in their leisure time several of the Bruins were experimenting with alternate life styles and John Wooden found that increasingly difficult to accept. An edginess developed between the veteran coach, whose roots and values were drawn from his small town Indiana origins, and his players, who favored the California counter culture. They experimented with meditation and vegetarianism. Often it seemed as if they were bored with practise, with dedication to basketball, with winning. What else did they have to prove? Every game they won broke yet again the record they had set in the previous one. They did not even feel pressure any more, just the burden of a winning streak which they had by the tail and which they did not want to let go, but whose presence threatened to overwhelm them. Every team they faced was up for the Bruins. Every team pulled out all the stops in hopes of upsetting the Bruins. Playing basketball was not fun any more.

Three times number one UCLA faced a second ranked challenger, all pretenders to the throne. Their first was against Maryland—who still featured McMillen, Elmore and Lucas—at Pauley Pavilion. It was the Bruins' second game, the opener for the visitors. The media billed it as the first meeting between the UCLA of the East and the UCLA of the West. Driesell still was not laughing. He had prepared all summer for this game and his boys almost pulled off an upset. The Bruins were leading 65-57 when the Terrapins rallied in the dying minutes and pulled to 65-64. As the final seconds ticked off, Maryland's John Lucas shot for the winning field goal but Dave Meyers managed to block it to preserve the one point victory.

The second confrontation between the number one and two teams in the country came in St. Louis. North Carolina State believed they could have beaten UCLA in the 1973 national championships had they not been placed on probation by the NCAA. To prove that, was of course impossible. But the Wolfpack's athletic department tried for the next best thing—a challenge to UCLA to meet on a neutral court early in the 1973-74 season. The game was proposed to the television networks and one of them was able to arrange for the match to take place in mid-December in St. Louis, site of the previous year's final.

North Carolina State had won 29 straight and UCLA had won 79 in a row when they met in a contest that had all the buildup of a national championship. Walton picked up four quick fouls in the first half and spent 21 minutes sitting restlessly on the bench, watching his team hang on desperately. The Wolfpack could take little advantage of Walton's absence primarily because Keith Wilkes, UCLA's other All American, had attached himself to Thompson like a second shadow. Still, it was anyone's game when Walton returned with the score tied 54-54 and nine and a half minutes left to play. It was as if a faulty connection had been fixed. The Bruins immediately went into overdrive, accelerating past the rapidly unraveling Wolfpack. Burleson became the most flustered of the Pack as Walton stuffed him into his pocket and lost him. When the patented Bruin boom was spent, they had added 19 points to their score while allowing North Carolina State just two. At the end of the game with UCLA on top 84-66, there was no doubt which team deserved to be Number One.

The Bruins won their next two games against Ohio University and St. Bonaventure by 47 and 52 points. When they opened their Pac Eight schedule with a humiliating 100-48 defeat of Washington at the loser's gym, all seemed right with the Bruins again. A 92-56 laugher over California preceded a trip to the Midwest where they beat Iowa for their eighty-eighth consecutive win.

Their next game was against undefeated Notre Dame at South Bend. With the eclipse of North Carolina State, the Irish had become the number two team in the country. There was something fateful about this confrontation with Notre Dame, apart from the fact that this would be the third time UCLA was to play a number two ranked challenger. The last loss suffered by the Bruins had been in South Bend. Notre Dame had also been the Bruin's sixty-first victim, breaking the old record set by San Francisco. Having lived in South Bend and coached at the local high school, Wooden felt mixed emotions about playing there.

Except for a back injury to Walton, who had not played in 12 days and was wearing a corset under his jersey, UCLA seemed to have little to worry about. To date they had won games by an average of 26 points. None of the players had lost a game during their college careers. Besides, the Irish center, John Shumate, was a mere 6′9″.

After taking a 17 point lead in the first half, UCLA was still ahead 70-59 with the final buzzer just three and a half minutes away. Consecutive victory number eighty-nine seemed assured. But for UCLA time literally ran out. They committed one turnover after another as hysteria lashed the Irish fans into a roaring mob. Notre Dame scored the last 12 points, capped by a bucket from Dwight Clay, the same man who had scored the deciding points when the Irish snapped Marquette's 81-game home-victory streak. The final score was 71-70. It was the only time Notre Dame held the lead.

Disappointed? Yes, after all this was the first loss for any of the Bruins in more than a thousand days. For Walton, who had not been on the losing side since his junior year in high school, this was his first defeat in 154 games. In some ways the debacle in South Bend resembled the loss in the Astrodome in 1968. As before, it involved the number one and two teams. UCLA fell by one point on their opponent's boards and their star center (Alcindor then, Walton now) was not completely healed after an injury. The similarity became even stronger when UCLA hosted Notre Dame a week later and trounced them 94-75. After the game, Phelps told his team, "Get me to Greensboro (site of the NCAA playoffs) and I'll find a way to beat UCLA."

The pressure was now off the Bruins but their performance became, at best, uneven. One game they were brilliant, blasting Santa Clara 96-54; two weeks later they dropped a pair in Oregon on what became known as "the lost weekend." It was the first time in eight years that UCLA had been defeated two games in a row. Both Oregon and Oregon State used pressing man-to-man defenses, often double-teaming Walton to force an atypical number of turnovers by the normally poised Bruins. By the time they staggered home, they found themselves tied with USC for the lead in the Pac Eight.

The Bruins barely brushed by Stanford 62-60 and visited USC for their final game still tied, the conference title and a tourney bid at stake. For two hours the Bruins forgot their beads, their protest marches, their new cults and concentrated on basketball. Summoning an all-out effort from their hoard of talent, the Bruins dazzled USC into submission. The Trojans, a powerhouse with a 22-3 record and ranked seventh, were crushed in the first 20 minutes which ended with UCLA ahead 47-13. The second half saw USC make the score a more respectable 82-52. Still UCLA was in the tournament in quest of its eighth straight championship.

Both San Francisco (18-8) and New Mexico (20-6) streaked to their conference titles. The Dons won their opener, then dropped six of their next seven (including five in a row). They then recovered to cop 16 of their last 18.

New Mexico won their first dozen, scoring more than 100 points in half of them, then skidded to six losses in their next nine games. Another turnabout brought them victories in their last five. The Lobos seemed to take particular pleasure in thumping weaker teams. They ran up the score against North Dakota 105-61, Texas Tech 102-65, Columbia 109-56 and Minnesota 102-

68. At home the Lobos were undefeated in 15 games yet this was offset by a losing record on the road.

If UTEP had beaten New Mexico on the final day of the season, the WAC would have ended in a five way tie and the league might still have been qualifying a champion by the time the NCAA was winding up. As it was, three schools finished in a tie for second just behind the Lobos. This was not unusual in the conference. Only four times in the previous eight years had the title been decided before the last day of the season. The conference was situated in a part of the country that had recently contacted a particularly virulent strain of basketball fever. Schools in the conference responded by building bigger and more modern arenas. The one at Brigham Young seated in excess of 22,000. Not surprisingly, WAC teams played before almost a million fans in 1974.

Norm Ellenberger, the Lobo coach, was known as "the Hippie" for his very current ensembles. These consisted of a variety of gaucho shirts, plunging deeply at the neck, and an assortment of local Indian turquoise jewelry. Despite appearances, Ellenberger could be tough. Distrubed by the team's recent problems and the questionable values of some of his players, two of whom were arrested for theft, he warned, "We are going upstream and everyone better have a paddle."

For the first time in six years Weber State did not win in the Big Sky. That honor went to Idaho State which nipped Montana 60-57 in a playoff after the schools had tied for first place. Though Weber State had dominated their conference for almost a decade, they had only won two opening round games in postseason play and had never advanced beyond the second round in six tries.

Long Beach State (24-2) had their best team ever. They lost a pair by two points each and were undefeated in their conference. Unfortunately for them they were accused of paying their athletes, a practice frowned upon by the NCAA. Not only did that body bar the Forty Niners from the tournament but they also voided their participation in 1971, 1972 and 1973.

In their place the PCAA sent Los Angeles State (17-9), a much inferior team. They had been whipped twice by Long Beach State by a total of 44 points.

The final team in the West regional hailed from the Eastern time zone. Dayton (19-7) coach Don Donoher was not complaining. His Flyer's fortunes had dipped at midseason when they dropped four of five. However, they recovered to snag their last seven including a victory over second ranked Notre Dame, 97-82, in the season finale. Though the Irish were probably looking past Dayton to their first round opponent, the outcome was still completely unexpected, especially the margin of victory.

It was Los Angeles State's first tournament and the small group of Diablo fans were feeling exhuberant as their team led Dayton 65-62 in the opening match. But at that point the Flyers took off and soared to a nine point lead with five minutes remaining. They maintained their advantage to survive 88-80. The trio of Don Smith, Mike Sylvester and freshman sensation Johnny Davis contributed 74 points. All made better than 50 percent of their shots and none missed a free throw.

In the nightcap at Pocatello, the home town Idaho State Bengals, making their first tourney appearance in 14 years, were eliminated 73-65 by New Mexico.

As the teams headed for the locker room at half time UCLA seemed to have matters under control in their second round match with Dayton. Behind by 17 at one point, the Flyers closed the gap but the Bruins, who looked to be back in early season form, were still ahead 48-36 at the buzzer. Donoher's strategy to deny Walton the ball by collapsing on the big redhead did not seem to be working since it often left Wilkes and Dave Meyers free.

The second half saw a reversal of fortunes. Slowly the Flyers climbed back into contention. With Don Smith and Mike Sylvester showing the way, Dayton found itself with the score tied 80-80 late in the game and in possession of the ball. Some teams go for years before scoring a major upset. It looked as if the Flyers were about to pull their second one in as many weeks. With four seconds on the clock, Smith's jumper bounced away and the Bruins received a reprieve to extend their playoff string.

In the first overtime both Wilkes and Meyers, who was leading the Bruins with 28 points, fouled out. Since Mike Curtis had the flu and played only briefly, the Bruins were forced to go to their bench to find the resources to keep their hopes alive. Tension built like the funnel of a life threatening tornado. UCLA fought to survive to defend its national title. Donoher, one of the game's most underrated and overlooked coaches, tried one tactic after another to fell UCLA and avenge their defeat in the 1967 final when the Bruins had won the first of their seven consecutive titles. The efforts cancelled out. The buzzer sounded with the teams still even at 88-88.

The arena was a raging amphitheatre of raw emotion as 13,314 fans howled themselves into a frenzy. Up and down court raced the Bruins and Flyers, exhausted yet hardly slowing the pace. This was unlike other crucial overtime contests in which one team will hold the ball for minutes for the last winning shot. Not here. Neither team was holding anything back. They were both taking their chances, putting the ball in the air, letting their skills, not the clock, decide. Thus, each side scored ten points in the second overtime.

An explosion of cheers greeted the teams as they took the court for the third extra session. Walton, the country's second best percentage shooter, had been playing as if in a cage. Showing greater mobility than before, the Bruin center started the period by hooking a field goal through the hoop. This was followed shortly by Gary Franklin's steal and layup to give the Bruins a 102-98 advantage. Suddenly, the Flyers seemed to falter like a kite running out of wind. Walton's five points in the overtime and the depth of the UCLA bench were too much for the plucky Flyers and they fell short 111-100.

Dayton had played on the thin edge of elimination for more than fifty minutes. Smith's 26 points and Sylvesters' 36 were the major factors keeping them in the game. But they had been outrebounded by a substantial margin, outscored by eleven field goals and all their starters except Smith had four fouls. Nonetheless, they hung in and came closer to eliminating the Bruins than any team since 1963.

San Francisco's 64-61 victory over New Mexico came as an anticlimax. So did UCLA's win over San Francisco two days later. Meyers and Walton had led the Bruins in their marathon against Dayton. This time it was Wilkes' 27 points that fired the Bruins.

San Francisco, using a deliberate attack, slowed the pace to a shuffle. This resulted in a searing drought in the first five minutes. Patiently UCLA waited for their opportunities and by half time they had a twelve point lead matching the one against Dayton. But this time UCLA was more alert. They were guilty of just seven turnovers and were charged with only ten fouls. With 4:15 remaining, the Bruins were ahead 77-50 when Wooden began removing his starters. A few minutes later UCLA had chalked up their 38th consecutive playoff victory by an 83-60 score.

Mideast:

The Mideast regional featured two outstanding independents and four schools which had just survived extremely tight conference races, three of them deadlocks.

Ever since he had left Fordham to coach at Notre Dame, Digger Phelps had been waiting for a year like this. With All American John Shumate and Gary Brokaw, a pair of talents from New Jersey, pointing the Irish toward the tournament, Notre Dame won 24 while losing two—the rematch at UCLA and the finale at Dayton. Phelps also got help from Adrian Dantley, a freshman guard from the Washington, D.C. area, breeding ground of several former Notre Dame stars. Dantley had attended basketball-famous DeMatha. His presence helped bolster an Irish team that was already talent laden. The previous year they had failed by a point to win the NIT though Shumate, their 6′9″ center, had been voted the tournament's MVP. Among other feats he had, at one point, sunk 20 field goals in a row. In 1974 he was the country's fourth best shooter and was the prime reason why Notre Dame was first as a team in that department.

The Irish looked unstoppable in their first nine games which included three victories over Big Ten teams on the loser's court, a 15 point roasting of Kentucky in Lexington and one-sided decisions over a handfull of lesser teams. St. Louis, Denver and Valparaiso were thrashed by 30, 40 and 50 points respectively. Ranked second, then first, the Irish eventually settled back in the runner-up slot behind North Carolina State.

Marquette (22-4), the other at-large team in the regional, was the second choice to advance to the Final Four. A young team, they had nevertheless won their first ten games. Losses to South Carolina, Creighton and Notre Dame, all tourney-bound, had tarnished their standing only slightly. The Warriors, as usual, were an excellent defensive group—fourth best in points allowed.

Austin Peay (17-9) finished in a tie with Morehead State on top of the Ohio Valley standings. They were selected on the basis of two regular season wins over Morehead. Flashy "Fly" Williams was the third best scorer in the country with a 27 point average. However, his self control had not kept pace with his ability.

Ohio University (16-10) struggled during the early going, losing four of their first six including a 110-63 blowout at UCLA. But a 71-70 heartstop win over Bowling Green in their final game gave them the conference title, which helped to wipe out some of the earlier unpleasant memories.

The SEC provided some surprises. Kentucky, an almost perennial champion, came close to achieving its first losing season since before Rupp became coach in Lexington more than forty years earlier. The Wildcats were 13-13 and alumni were screaming for Joe Hall's dismissal. Rupp's presence around the campus and his advice freely given (though not necessarily solicited) did not make Hall's job any easier.

Tied at the top of the SEC were Alabama and Vanderbilt (23-3). However, since the latter had beaten the Crimson Tide twice and had a slightly better overall record, a playoff was considered unnecessary and the Commodores were picked for the tournament. Alabama came close though. Their two losses to Vanderbilt were by one and two point margins.

Sixth ranked Vanderbilt was distinguished by its free throw shooters, collectively the best in the country by a wide margin. Terry Compton from Horse Cave, Kentucky, was the most deadly of the Commodores.

The most surprising team in the regional was Michigan (21-4). They had been picked to finish near the bottom of the Big Ten but with hustle, determination and more than an average dose of luck, the Wolverines tied favored Indiana for the conference title. They then disposed of the Hoosiers in a playoff, 75-67.

The last Michigan team to go to the playoffs featured Cazzie Russell. Now the Wolverines had another All American Russell—Campanella "Campy" Russell. Coach Johnny Orr's bubbling, enthusiastic personality was reflected in the team's attitude towards the game. Orr wanted to make sure his players forgot a loss and concentrated on the next game. His positive outlook helped prevent losing streaks and minimized the depressing aftermath of defeat. After losing by 20 to UCLA in the final of the Bruin Classic, the Wolverines returned home and checked favored Indiana in their Big Ten opener. Similarly, after a disappointing one point loss to Purdue, they travelled to Iowa where they won by two. They later smashed Purdue 111-84 in a return engagement. Altogether, they sneaked by five Big Ten teams by two points or less.

Notre Dame swamped Austin Peay in a Mideast regional first round contest in Terre Haute, Indiana. The Irish Big Three—Shumate, Dantley and Brokaw—all scored at least 20 points while the Fly sparked a fizzling Governor attack with 26. The Irish prevailed 108-66 using a fifty bucket bombardment while Austin Peay was able to respond with only half that total. Some time after the game, officials at Austin Peay suspended Williams indefinitely. They also admitted to the NCAA that they had been misinterpreting entrance requirements for the last five years. The admission came a little late. The university was put on probation and its appearances in the 1973 and 1974 tournaments were voided. Fly Williams could hardly have cared. By the time his school was baring all, he had already signed a contract to play professional basketball.

In the co-feature, Marquette downed Ohio 85-59. Ten straight points at the start of the second half allowed the Warriors to pull away to their seventh playoff win in a row over the Mid-American representative. The only jarring note was a technical foul against Al McGuire, an ominous sign of things to come.

Marquette discovered a propitious omen when they checked into their motel in Tuscaloosa, Alabama, site of the final two rounds of the regional. Running through town was the Black Warrior River. A more concrete indication of Marquette's changing fortune occurred just before their clash with Vanderbilt. As McGuire's black warriors dressed, someone came rushing into the locker room, shouting in disbelief, "Michigan beat Notre Dame!!"

It was true. The Irish, conquerors of UCLA, the number two team in the country, had fallen to a team that three months earlier had been picked to be the doormat of their league.

There was little doubt where the sentiments of the Alabama fans lay. Poor Digger Phelps was the innocent victim of a backlash caused by Notre Dame's football victory over Alabama in the Sugar Bowl on New Year's Day. The loss had cost Alabama the mythical national championship. Unnerved, maybe, by the hostile reception, the Irish missed 11 of their first 12 shots. After 14 minutes Michigan was steaming ahead 28-8 leaving their opponent waterlogged. But the Irish were far from sunk. A furious counterattack in the waning minutes of the period closed the gap to five. Riding the crest of their momentum, Notre Dame continued their assault after intermission and crept ahead 54-52 much to the disgust of the Alabama fans.

But that was the high water mark for the Irish. Russell rallied the Wolverines as he had often done before to retrieve seemingly lost causes. With the local fans bellowing their approval, Michigan in the final minutes took charge and blitzed their way to a 77-68 victory. Russell had 36 points and incredibly held Adrian Dantley to just two. Shumate carried the brunt of the Irish attack with 34.

Elated Marquette made short work of Vanderbilt. Not surprisingly, the foul shooting was deadly. Best in the country, Vanderbilt made 21 of 22 and the disciplined Warriors connected 13 times in 14 tries.

With its most formidable threat eliminated, Marquette was the favorite to go to the Final Four. Nevertheless, they would first have to oust the Big Ten champion, something they had been unable to do in five tries over the last 20 years. Marquette had also never made it past the regional in eight tournaments. But then there had never been a Black Warrior river running through town, either.

McGuire assigned freshman Bo Ellis the man-sized task of guarding Russell. The strategy of trying to slow the Wolverine fast breaking attack was nothing new to the Warriors who had been a ball control team for years. Whether it was regional final jitters, Marquette's defense, or the more evenly divided partisanship of the crowd, Michigan had a hard time getting out of the blocks. Trailing 15-5 after committing ten early turnovers, the Wolverines uncorked their fast break—but briefly. Still it was enough to get their stalled offense moving again. With 1:18 to go in the first half, McGuire blew his top when Wolverine C.J. Kupec was awarded a pair of free throws. The referee added a technical and Kupec made all three to give Michigan a 39-31 lead. Fourteen seconds later the referee pointed his finger at McGuire again. It looked as if the Warrior skipper was about to dig his team a hole they would not be able to climb out of. However, McGuire was lucky this time. Russell missed the free throw and a six point Marquette flurry brought the Warriors within two at the buzzer.

Michigan maintained its lead through most of the second period though Marquette never allowed its opponent to get too far ahead. Finally a three point play by bench warmer Rick Campbell gave Marquette its first lead of the half 63-62. The sides battled evenly for several tense minutes. Ellis' bank shot put his team up 70-68 with two and a half minutes to go. The lead was bolstered when Dave Delsman hit both ends of a crucial one-and-one opportunity. Russell, who had been limited to 19 points by super-shadow Ellis, tried to take charge and single handedly save his team once again. He had his opportunities. His hook shot at 19:22 brought the Wolverines within two. Thirteen seconds later Lloyd Walton of Marquette was fouled, missed and Michigan had the ball again. A feed to Russell in the left corner resulted in an air ball. After a lively scramble, the referee's whistle signalled a jump ball. Gaining possession once more, Michigan realized this was their last opportunity and fed Russell again. He fired from his favorite spot in the corner but the ball bounced off the side of the backboard as the buzzer heralded Marquette's and McGuire's first regional championship. As his players swarmed around congratulating their coach, tenseness turned to relief and then to elation. Ever brash, McGuire announced, "I personally think we're going to be dynamite down in Greensboro!"

Notre Dame returned to form in the consolation and beat Vanderbilt 118-88. It was the sixth time in their last nine tournament outings the Irish had scored over a hundred points.

Midwest:

The teams in the Midwest regional had little to recommend them. None was good enough to be ranked in the top ten. One did not even have a winning record. Texas (12-14) finished first in the SWC, a notoriously weak league. Not since George Washington's participation in 1961, the result of an upset in a conference playoff, had a side with a losing record qualified. It was also the first time a regular season major conference champion had lost more games than it won.

The Longhorns were still at the starting gate midway through the season. They dropped their first nine, smacked Army, then fell twice more. No team had ever made the tournament after posting a 1-11 mark at midseason. It is doubtful whether a single Texas fan thought they could recover to finish at the top of their conference. But the SWC season had not even begun. The league opener provided a hint of things to come. The Longhorns obliterated TCU 104-53. It was completely unexpected, as if someone had lit a prairie fire and turned a group of docile cows into a thundering, stampeding herd of range cattle. The Longhorns went on to win 11 league games while dropping three by one, two and four points respectively. Texas Tech, the runner-up, had a much better total record—17 wins and 9 defeats—but dropped four conference games including heartbreaking one, two and three point losses. The crusher was a 75-74 setback to Texas on its own court.

Another race undecided until the final minute occurred in the MVC. In the deciding match Louisville (21-5) beat Bradley 87-84 as Junior Bridgeman completed a three point play with the clock at seven seconds. A Bradley win would have created a conference tie. Kansas with the same 21-5 record claimed the Big Eight title. Their's was an unspectacular team. Not until a season-ending 112-76 shellacking of Missouri did they display much power.

Three independents completed the field in the regional. Oral Roberts was the third team in the regional with a 21-5 mark. They had rehearsed for this, their first NCAA tournament, by appearing in the NIT the previous two years, Averaging 95 points per game, the Titans were the second highest scoring team in the country (the highest in the tourney) and had netted over 100 points ten times during the campaign.

Creighton (21-6) was returning for the first time since graduating Paul Silas. Its schedule was undemanding but the team took no school for granted. The Bluejays riddled Regis 93-38 in its opener, then hurdled such patsies as South Dakota State, Augustana, University of California at Irvine, and the holy trio of St. Thomas, St. Cloud and St. Johns of Minnesota. Creighton played only one ranked school, Marquette, and to their credit, beat them on the Warriors' home court, probably the second most difficult feat in college basketball, next to winning in Pauley Pavilion.

The Bluejays almost rivalled Henry Kissinger in the number of miles they covered during the three year period, 1972-74. The travelingest school in the country, they visited 20 states and logged 65,000 miles, not counting their trips up and down the court.

The 1974 Creighton squad was unusual in another respect. In an era when the majority of basketball players were black, the Bluejays fielded a starting five that was entirely white. The game had changed so much in the last ten years, this was considered noteworthy.

Syracuse (19-6) was imported into the regional because there were so few qualified midwestern non-conference schools. Dayton and Marquette were the closest geographically but the former had been shipped to the West and the NCAA selection committee knew better than to tangle with Al McGuire. So they tapped Syracuse, whose claim to distinction consisted of a 110-53 assault on Bucknell and little else.

Aside from a lackluster field, the regional suffered from the uncertainty of a playing site. Originally scheduled for Las Cruces, New Mexico, it was shifted to Wichita State. But when that school was put on probation the regional site was moved again to Manhattan, Kansas. Finally, after a third switch, the floating tournament came to rest in Tulsa, on the campus of Oral Roberts.

The first round was scheduled for Denton, Texas, and surprisingly that is where it was played. After a dead even first half, Creighton turned on the juice and won handily over Texas 77-61. The Bluejays hooped 15 points in a row during one second period stretch to leave the Longhorns tied, branded and hors de combat.

Oral Roberts, with the incentive of a home court advantage awaiting them in the next two rounds, brushed past Syracuse 86-82. The Titans held a one point lead at half time but were tied after 40 minutes. Greg McDougald and Sam McCants combined for six free throws in the overtime to give Oral Roberts the edge.

The second round in Tulsa featured two games which exhibited radically contrasting styles of play. In the curtain raiser Kansas rallied from a first half deficit to eliminate Creighton, a game in which the action was sparse and the pace glacial. With 45 seconds flashing on the scoreboard, freshman Roger Morningstar's basket sent Kansas into a 55-54 lead. Ten seconds later the Jayhawks regained possession and were able to freeze the ball the rest of the way.

Skating on the thin edge of elimination once again, Oral Roberts fought Louisville to a 51-51 standoff in the first period of the nightcap. The contest was played at a furious pace before 10,575 wildly partisan fans. Nearly everyone, except for the Cardinal cheerleaders, their mascot and a pocketful of supporters, was pulling for Oral Roberts. The Titans were again led by their Gaelic connection of McDougald and McCants. The latter accounted for 30 points while McDougald made the only significant defensive play of the second half in a game totally dominated by offensive tactics.

With Oral Roberts barely ahead, McDougald blocked a Cardinal shot in the last minute of play to preserve the Titan's edge. Shortly thereafter, the buzzer sounded with the home side ahead 96-93. The fans were ecstatic.

Apparently so was Ken Trickey, Oral Roberts' coach, who went off to do some liquid celebrating. Later that night Trickey was arrested for drunken driving. When Oral Roberts, President of the university bearing his name, heard of the incident, he immediately suspended his coach. Cooler heads must have convinced Mr. Roberts of the risk he was taking. The Titan fans were capable of rioting and the alumni could be expected to take fiscal revenge if their school lost because their coach was suspended. The Titans were within a game of the Final Four. President Roberts reconsidered. This intensely religious man summoned Trickey and after praying with him, reinstated the coach. He gave as his reason that God wanted Trickey to coach against Kansas.

If that was the case, it is probable the Heavenly Father is a Jayhawk fan. Kansas sprinted to an early 15 point lead, but the Titans rebounded to trail by only a point at the intermission. In the second half they took charge, running offensive patterns that Kansas was unable to stop. With 2:50 remaining, Oral Roberts was in command 81-74. The Titans should have abandoned their run-and-gun tactics in favor of a stall, but they were either incapable of holding the ball or were convinced they had the game wrapped up. Regardless, the Jayhawks tied the score on Tom Smith's foul shot, a pair of long range bombs by Morningstar and Dale Greenlee, and a layup by Rick Suttle. Kansas had a chance to win it when they took possession in the last minute with the score 81-81. But a fluke infraction (when Tom Kivisto stepped on the midcourt stripe) gave the Titans the ball at 19:25. President Roberts might have seen the intervention of God on that call, but his team was unable to take advantage and the contest went into overtime, the second of the playoffs for the Titans and their third cliffhanger.

Kansas got out in front in the extra period. They were still leading by the slimmest margin when Smith gave them breathing room with a basket at 1:06 of the overtime, to make the score 91-88. Just 38 seconds later, McCants' tipin brought the Titans within one again. Smith, who had just five points total but four in the overtime when it mattered, then scored the clincher with five seconds remaining. Kansas won 93-90.

Final Four:

The Final Four assembled in Greensboro, North Carolina, the following weekend. Just like CCNY in 1950 and Kentucky in 1958, North Carolina State had the home court advantage throughout the tournament. With the East regional in Raleigh and the championship rounds down the road from the Wolfpack campus, the top ranked team in the country was the natural favorite. But first it would have to get past UCLA, since the draw matched the East against the West regional winners this time. Despite its loss to Notre Dame, its lost weekend in Oregon, its cliffhanging triple-over-time, heart-stopping win over Dayton, UCLA was—after all—UCLA. Beside

Walton, Wilkes and company (not to mention the Wizard of Westwood), the 38 consecutive postseason wins was a psychological barrier that would have to be breached. Some felt that since the Bruins had handled the Wolfpack so easily in their game in St. Louis, they would be able to repeat the performance. But that had been on a neutral court. Now UCLA would have to contend with State on its home turf. Besides, Burleson had matured considerably, demonstrated by his leadership in the regional final.

Norm Sloan prepared well for UCLA. On defense he wanted to neutralize Walton with Burleson. He also wanted to deny Wilkes the back door play so he had the very quick Thompson, fully recovered from his head injury, playing the All American. Both moves worked well. On offense he had to break UCLA's press. To accomplish that he unleashed Towe and the little waterbug scooted around and through the unnerved Bruins to loosen up the suffocating press.

Thompson was playing as well as ever. Taking off from the foul circle, he rose in a graceful arc to lay the ball into the hoop, his leap covering what looked like an impossible distance. Or he would rendezvous at the top of his leap with the ball served up by the helpful Towe.

After 20 minutes of excitement the teams retired to their locker rooms tied, 35-35. After the intermission the Bruins swept ahead 49-38 and threatened to break the game open. It was then that Burleson asserted himself. He snatched the rebound of a missed shot out of Walton's hands and layed it in to the seat-rattling cheers of more than 15,000 fans. Still, with eleven minutes remaining, the Bruins were eleven points up. The Wolfpack cause looked bleak as UCLA fought off every challenge. It was 61-53 for the Bruins and precious seconds were ticking away when the giant-to-midget triumvirate of Burleson, Thompson and Towe took command. They were to score the last 24 Wolfpack points among them. Firing off ten straight points, NC State took the lead 63-61. During their outburst, they managed to isolate Walton from his mates and the other Bruins began to take forced, erratic shots. Sloan's strategy of moving his opponents a little further away from the basket was succeeding.

However, UCLA was not about to expire quietly. They tied the game and Walton's bucket at 2:22 gave the Bruins the upper hand again. A few seconds later Tim Stoddard assisted on a Thompson basket from underneath. Regaining possession, the Wolfpack held the ball for most of the final two minutes but a go-ahead shot by Stoddard with nine seconds left missed.

Greg Lee and Burleson traded field goals, the only scoring in the first overtime. Once more State held the ball for the last shot. With ten seconds left in the extra session, Thompson drove for the basket. As the Bruins converged on leaping David, he passed to Burleson who fired—but hit only the rim.

As the teams lined up for the start of the second overtime, veteran observers were probably thinking of the 1957 semifinal between North Carolina and Michigan State, a triple overtime affair. UCLA, however, was not willing to extend this game any further. They swished seven unanswered points, four by Walton, three by Wilkes, in just over a minute and a half to establish a commanding 74-67 advantage.

North Carolina State was finished. The Walton Gang would go out in glory. Everyone but the Wolfpack knew it (or maybe also Notre Dame who had been in a similar situation in South Bend). Their scoring trio cranked up again and with a furious assault, aided by two missed UCLA shots and a State interception, closed to within a point. With 1:16 left, Meyers missed the first of a one-and-one. At the other end of the court Thompson banked one in over Wilkes to give North Carolina State the lead 76-75. The suddenly ineffective Bruins brought the ball down court but Lee's one hander was off the mark. Two foul shots by Thompson, a steal by Burleson off a pass intended for Walton and a clinching pair of free throws by Towe with just 12 seconds on the scoreboard sealed the verdict. North Carolina State 80, UCLA 77 in double overtime. Walton's 29 points were more than offset by Thompson's 28 and Burleson's 20.

The Bruin streak was snapped. The Walton Gang had been hunted down by the Pack in supremely dramatic fashion. The fans were euphoric. The rest of the tournament would be anticlimactic.

UCLA had nothing to be ashamed of. It took a supreme effort on their opponent's home territory to oust the Bruins from competition for the first time in ten years. Even with victory in their grasp, a seven point lead with three and a half minutes left, UCLA did not deign to go into a freeze. Like champions, they put their streak on the line, and it took an explosive 13-3 Wolfpack spree to eliminate the Bruins. The chance that another team will surpass UCLA's record is next to nil.

The tournament to date had had two overtime contests, a double overtime and a triple overtime game. What to do for an encore? It seemed that Kansas, with a one point victory and an overtime decision to its credit, was the most likely candidate to provide more fireworks.

In the other semifinal, Marquette watched their seven point lead dissipate in a sluggish first half which ended with the Jayhawks on top 24-23. As usual, Kansas was giving their fans sweaty palms but what McGuire was giving his players was a lot better than that. In the locker room between periods, he gave them such a severe tongue-lashing that Lloyd Walton announced he would not play the second half and promptly undressed and got into the shower. His teammates pleaded with him to reconsider and finally Walton towelled off and put on his uniform again. He was a little late getting back on the court because the trainer had to tape him up again.

It was a different, and cleaner, Warrior team that took the court in the second half. They assumed the lead for good shortly after the tipoff and qualified for their first national final 64-51.

After UCLA had beaten Kansas for third place, the Warriors and the Wolfpack, neither of whom had ever won a national championship, were greeted by a deafening soundwave as they entered the arena. "We might have had more tough games to get here than any other team in NCAA history," said Norm Sloan. Frank McGuire of the 1957 North Carolina Tarheels might have disputed him.

This time it was Marquette who trailed, by eight. But they bounced back to grab a 28-27 edge. On the next possession, Marcus Washington ran into David Thompson and was called for charging. Instantly, McGuire was off the bench waving his arms and shouting at the referee. New York Al's juices were flowing in the best tradition of a street fighter. He had picked up one technical foul against Ohio, two against Michigan, had bawled his team out so severely that at least one of them was ready to quit and now he was ready to take on the referees—the world no doubt, if need be. He was hit with a technical. Seconds later, Bo Ellis blocked a shot by Phil Spence and one official called goaltending. McGuire shot up again and was immediately slapped with another tecnical—his fifth of the playoffs. It was strange how a man who could extract such disciplined play from his players could lose control over his own emotions so often.

That was the turning point of the game. From being down a point, the Wolfpack took a 37-28 lead just before intermission. The two technicals had been costly—ten points to be precise (two Thompson free throws, two technicals, two field goals after keeping the ball and the goaltending bucket). Besides, Marquette's momentum had been stalled. They had managed to slow down NC State and make them play Marquette's brand of deliberate ball. Ellis, Marquette's talented freshman and standout defensive star, gave away seven inches to Burleson but still held the giant to 14 points. Now as the shocked Warriors tried to regroup, State picked up the pace, sprang their fast break loose and took control. The contest became a runaway as a subdued McGuire hugged the bench. Once enjoying a 19 point spread, the Wolfpack relaxed but still won 76-64. Thompson led his team with 21 points and was given the MVP award.

McGuire gave his opponent due credit. "North Carolina State is a better ball club than Marquette. Officials never win or lose a game." Irascible as ever he added, "I would rather not discuss the calls because I'm absolutely correct." Still McGuire blamed himself in the privacy of his team's locker room. Maurice Lucas, who had accounted for 21 points, responded philosophically, "We go uptown together and we go downtown together."

1975

The NCAA expanded its tournament to 32 teams for the 1974-75 season. There were several reasons for this but the primary one was the opportunity for collecting more revenue from additional attendance and expanded television coverage. The postseason classic had become ever more popular, measured by the size of the television audience and the number of reporters covering the event.

Another reason for expansion was that excellent teams were excluded because they finished behind the conference champion or lost in the postseason playoff that determined the tourney selectee. This was especially true in the strongest conferences such as the Pac Eight—dominated by UCLA—the Big Ten and the ACC. In 1974, for instance, three schools in the top ten, North Carolina, Maryland and USC, were left out of the tournament because they finished behind North Carolina State and UCLA. The sudden-death jeopardy of the ACC and the Southern Conference deprived several deserving teams of a shot at a national championship. Davidson and Maryland (coincidentally, both coached by Lefty Driesell) had been prime victims of this setup.

The NCAA decided to invite seven additional conference teams, runners-up in most cases but not necessarily so. They would be distributed among the four regionals in such a way that they would always be in a separate draw from their conference's champion. In this way, two schools from the same conference could never meet, except, of course, in the final. The NCAA did not designate the conferences from which they would pick two schools. This would vary, depending on the merit of the teams. In 1975, the conferences sending a pair of schools to the tourney were the ACC, the Big Ten, the SEC, the Big Eight, the MVC, the Pac Eight and the WAC. All but the last had been given automatic first round byes over the years because their teams posted better records in the tournament than other league representatives.

At-large entries were unaffected. There was to be one additional eastern school but it would replace an at-large western selection. There were many more independent schools in the East. The four eastern teams selected would be the winners of division playoffs within a loosely organized body of 39 universities calling themselves the Eastern College Athletic Conference. The designated divisions were geographic in scope and represented New England, Upstate New York, Metropolitan New York and New Jersey and Southern Tier (Pennsylvania to Maryland and West Virginia). A selection committee would pick four schools from each division and the result of the elimination playoff would determine each devision's representative.

Another reason given for the expansion was that the new setup would eliminate first round byes, thus making a fairer and more balanced tournament. There were also some who said the NCAA wanted to kill off the NIT, which in any case was tottering and looked as if it was about to go under. But the NIT posed no threat to the NCAA and was not funneling any substantial money or interest away from the younger tournament.

Given all these reasons, seven schools that had never played in the tournament were given an opportunity to participate under the new expanded format. They were Alabama, Central Michigan, Middle Tennessee, Montana, Nevada-Las Vegas, Rutgers and San Diego State.

A trend was developing in college basketball. No longer was it sufficient for a player to be tall, he had to be broad, too. This was especially true of the forwards and centers, though hefty 6′6″ guards were not uncommon. The beanpole player was less evident and the huskier athletes were in greater demand. In the past coaches had been wary of the heavier player, preferring a more mobile man, but the new breed being fed into the ranks by the country's high schools was also fast and quick to react.

In an era of specialization, a new position was being created—the power forward. He was merely fast compared to the small forward (6′4″ to 6′7″) who could fly. Team strategy now called for overwhelming your opponent not only with speed, accuracy and ball handling, but with raw muscle, too. With a strong bench, a team could literally grind other teams into exhaustion.

The primary exponents of the new strategy were Joe Hall at Kentucky, Bobby Knight at Indiana, and Denny Crum at Louisville. These three schools were located in the fundamentalist basketball belt of America where games were played in a hothouse atmosphere, resembling more closely a holy war than an athletic contest. In Lexington, Bloomington and Louisville, coaches were expected to be front runners in the state-of-the-art of the sport, the point men, so to say, in the combat zone.

Mideast:

For Joe Hall, the 1974 season had been traumatic. After a 13-13 season, Wildcat fans were ready to turn the coach out to pasture in the bluegrass with other thoroughbreds who could no longer handle the pace. But in 1975, Hall scrapped the old Rupp system of speed and finesse and developed a new system based on height and brawn. When the Wildcats stepped on the hardwood, the basketball floor seemed smaller or more crowded. Hall, recruiting well, stocked the Wildcats with young John Bunyans. A freshman quartet consisting of a matched pair of centers, Rick Robey and Mike Phillips, both 6′10″ and massive, 6′7″, 245 lb. James Lee and 6′5″ Jack Givens, the smallest of the newcomers, joined an established squad of more moderately sized players. Kevin Grevey, 6′5″, an All American, was at one forward, Bob Guyette, a Rhodes scholar candidate at the other and Jimmy Dan Conner and Mike Flynn were the guards. With a lineup like that and the strength of its bench, Kentucky played at full bore throughout the game. Its shock tactics drew many fouls but Hall had the substitutes to bring in when necessary. The sixth ranked Wildcats were 22-4 during the regular season and were the highest scoring team in the tournament, fourth best in the country. They were tied by Alabama for the SEC title but since they had whipped the Crimson Tide in both their encounters, wearing down their opponents until they wilted, Kentucky was declared the conference champion. A stinging defeat at Indiana (24 points) wounded Wildcat pride, but they posted significant victories over Notre Dame, North Carolina and Kansas, whom they humiliated 100-63. Hall was not above being brutal, the way Rupp had been, by allowing his boys to run up the score against outclassed teams. The Wildcats humbled Mississippi State 118-80 and 112-79, LSU 115-80 and Auburn 119-76, after that team had the nerve to upset Kentucky in their first encounter of the season. Florida held the Wildcats to 58 points, their lowest score of the year.

Indiana (29-0) is a natural rival to Kentucky. The two schools compete for some of the best young talent in the country and play before the most demanding fans. Indiana, too, had been successful in recruiting a tall, strong team. At center was 6′11″ Kent Benson, tipping the scales at a solid 245 lbs., while All American Scott May and Steve Green played in the corners. But it was Quinn Buckner and Bobby Wilkerson, a pair of cat-quick guards, who were the energizing force that drove the team. They set up the offense and applied decisive pressure when the Hoosiers were on defense. Buckner was a complete athlete, a one-of-a-kind. He had been an All American football and basketball player in high school and won letters in both sports at Indiana, though he dropped football after the 1975 season. Wilkerson and May had been ineligible to play as freshmen since their high school grades were not good enough to earn them scholarships. But they were patient, sticking around to receive their scholarships as sophomores. Indiana's bench was not as strong as Kentucky's. But they had one of the best sixth men in the game, John Laskowski, who was inserted at critical moments and was a dependable scorer.

Knight had a way of inspiring confidence in his men. Despite being a martinet, he brought out the best in them. Some may have disliked him but they could not help but admire his coaching talent. There were those who said he had mellowed. He screamed at referees less frequently and kicked fewer chairs; but he was still a driven man who had his sights firmly set on a national championship.

The undefeated Hoosiers were ranked number one. From their opening game, a 113-60 massacre of Tennessee Tech, Indiana was ticketed for the top. Given the opposition, the game was hardly a measure of Indiana's strength. But their third match, a 98-74 romp over Kentucky, left few disbelievers. In that contest, Knight fetched Hall a rap on the back of the head during a mild dispute. Knight called it a "friendly tap" but it stung, and not just physically. In the next 14 games, Indiana scored over 90 points eleven times. They thrashed Texas A and M, the eventual winner of the SWC, 90-55 on the losers' court, then polished off Nebraska 97-60 in the final of the Hoosier Classic. They went to Hawaii where they ran away with the Rainbow Classic and returned to start their Big Ten conference schedule.

Indiana stormed past Ohio State 102-71, Michigan State 107-52 (the Spartans had just suspended ten black players in a racial dispute), Iowa 102-49, Purdue 104-71, Michigan 74-48 and Wisconsin 93-58. They beat every conference team by 20 points or more at least once. No team had ever devastated the Big Ten so completely. Their average margin of victory was 22 points against superior opposition. The Hoosiers' closest call was an 83-82 squeaker over Purdue.

The Indiana express was hurtling down the track toward a national championship with seemingly nothing along the way to stop them—when someone threw a switch which slowed, though it did not stop, the Hoosiers. Four games before the season closed, May fractured his non-shooting arm. The difference the All American made was quickly apparent. The Hoosiers almost lost their next game to Purdue. With May playing, Indiana's defense had given up an average of 63 points per game; without him they allowed an average of 82 points.

Marquette (23-3) was ranked fifth and as usual had one of the best defenses in the country. They lost only to Louisville, Cincinnati and Pittsburgh. In two untypically high scoring efforts, they erased Georgia 100-70 and Fordham 101-64. It was rare for the Warriors to go over the century mark.

Central Michigan (20-5), in its second year of Division I competition, triumphed in the Mid-American in a typical conference finish. Seven times in the last ten years the conference crown had been claimed on the final day of the season. It was no different in 1975. A last second field goal by Denny Parks beat Western Michigan, tying the Chippewas with Bowling Green and Toledo entering the final contest. They then squeezed by Bowling Green 82-80 in overtime while Toledo was losing. Jim McElroy accounted for all of Central Michigan's points in the extra session. But despite the last second heroics of McElroy and Parks, it was Dan Roundfield who led the Chippewas. His 61 percent shooting average was fourth best in the country.

Georgetown (15-9) was making its first NCAA appearance since the war year of 1943 when only eight teams had competed. The Hoyas suffered through a six game losing slump at midseason when Coach John Thompson benched a starter for cutting classes. Losing to Randolph Macon, Fairfield, Seton Hall, American and St. Peters did little to enhance their prestige. They rallied somewhat in the closing stages and were invited to the ECAC playoff for the Southern Tier. Surprisingly, the Hoyas conquered George Washington, a team that had tripped them earlier, and West Virginia to earn their place in the tournament.

The best defensive team in the country was UTEP (20-5). Rarely will a team score twice as many points as their adversary but UTEP did it twice. They obliterated Sul Ross 84-32 and Wayland Baptist 68-29. Given a weak enough apponent, it seemed the Miners were capable of recording a shutout. Only once did UTEP give up as many as 70 points and that against Arizona State, the only team to finish ahead of them in the WAC.

Oregon State (18-10) featured another young bull, ham-shouldered Lonnie Shelton who carried a well-distributed 240 lbs. on a 6′8″ frame. The Oregonians were the first Pac Eight team aside from UCLA to make the tourney in nine years. Though their record was not especially distinctive, the Beavers had finished second in a tough conference. They had won eight of their first nine, then lost momentum, dropping four in a row, and struggled through the rest of the season. For Ralph Miller this was the third school he had coached to the tournament (after Wichita and Iowa) tying him in that department with Frank McGuire.

Middle Tennessee (23-4) finished first in the Ohio Valley. But the reason they were in the tourney was because the conference had inaugurated a postseason playoff (only the schools finishing in the first four positions were eligible to participate) and the Blue Raiders had won. Until 1975, only the ACC, the Southern Conference and the Mid Atlantic had postseason playoffs. But the tournament eligibility of more than one school from the same conference started a new trend. It may be that the Ohio Valley was the first to realize that if a conference was to hold a playoff and the league winner was beaten, then the NCAA would be more likely to pick both the playoff champion and the regular season leader. Though the NCAA was obligated to take only the playoff champion, that is the way it often worked out.

Oregon State and Middle Tennessee, unused to tournament pressure, displayed a lot of nervousness in the initial stages of their match. The Beavers turned the ball over 14 times and the Blue Raiders 17 times in the first half which ended with the west coast team leading 30-19. Both sides settled down in the second period and the scoring picked up. In the end, Oregon State's power fueled them to a 78-67 decision. Shelton led all scorers with 23 points.

Two of the best defenses in the country were on display as Indiana and UTEP probed for openings in the nightcap. Indiana had a difficult time locating the hoop, hitting only 36 percent of their shots in the first half and only slightly better in the second. It was the Hoosier defense that pulled them through. They dominated the boards, boxed out well and clogged the middle. Their height and strength were also a big advantage. Eight times jump balls were contested and Indiana took possession after each one. Midway through the second half, Knight's men were ahead 62-36, then coasted to win 78-53. Offensively, the Hoosiers were not very productive. Laskowski, May's replacement, was high man with 15. May himself played only the last 51 seconds with a soft cast on his arm.

At Tuscaloosa, Central Michigan and Georgetown battled through a tight game that was decided only after the final buzzer on a referee's decision that was as controversial as any in the tournament. With two and a half minutes remaining, the Chippewas were ahead 75-71. In the next 60 seconds, Derrick Jackson swished one from downtown and Larry Long drove in for a layup for Georgetown to tie the score. The Hoyas regained the ball and held for the last shot. They may have waited too long. Seeing the clock was about to register double zero, Jonathan Smith lunged for the hoop, missed, and was whistled for charging. Leonard Drake, the only Chippewa starter who had not been to the line yet, calmly sank a pair to scuttle the Hoyas 77-75. Georgetown was understandably angry at the officiating. They had only seven free throw tries to 28 for Central Michigan, while outscoring their foes 35 to 28 from the floor.

The co-feature matched Marquette and Kentucky, the fifth and sixth best teams in the country. The Wildcats sped to a 13-4 advantage and then were overhauled by Marquette, who put together a 21-4 surge over a ten minute span. Conner was on the bench in foul trouble during a good portion of that streak. Six quick points by Phillips closed the gap late in the period but the Warriors had the lead 28-25 at the intermission. Conner's presence sparked Kentucky to a 49-36 edge after ten minutes. Thereafter, Marquette's defense crumbled completely as Kentucky pulled away to win 76-54 on a 51 point second-half scoring binge.

The next two rounds in Dayton attracted a much larger turnout. Kentucky with Phillips, Robey, Guyette and Dan Hall, all 6′9″ and 230 lbs. or more, wore down Central Michigan until the Chippewa resistance faded. The Wildcats scored on their last 14 shots as they took a rather easy 90-73 decision. Indiana posted an equally easy win over Oregon State, easy despite the misleading 81-71 score. The Hoosiers were up by 21 points at the break. At 7:21 of the first half, Shelton, who often ran into foul trouble, picked up his fourth personal and watched most of the game from the perspective of the bench. He played only eleven minutes. In his absence, Benson had a field day, dominating the rebounding and bagging 23 points. Green was even more productive with 34, 17 in each half. May, still hampered with a cast, played only three minutes.

The fans streamed into Dayton, a city almost equidistant from Bloomington and Lexington, to witness an emotional rematch between two bitter rivals deployed almost as much muscle on the run as a cattle stampede. Coach Hall had nursed his resentment at the humiliating defeat in Bloomington and at Knight's "light tap" for more than three months. Besides, the Wildcats had another old score to settle—their loss to the Hoosiers in the 1973 regional final. Hall decided to use a little psychology to fire up the Wildcats, if indeed they needed it at all. Before the game, he chalked four words on the blackboard in the locker room. Nets. Bus. Police. Celebration. He explained each carefully. First, after the game, the Wildcats were to use scissors to cut the nets down. A knife might cause an accident. Then they would enter the bus but would not be allowed to take any girl friends with them. A police escort would be waiting for them to escort the bus to Lexington. And finally, there would be a victory celebration in Lexington.

Hall had prepared his team well. They came to Dayton early to practice. Hall planned a 50 minute session but the Wildcats were so sharp, he called off practice after a quarter of an hour. The mix of veterans and freshmen created the right blend of enthusiasm and competition on the squad. The Wildcats were sky high when they exited the locker room.

Knight decided to use some psychology of his own. He started May, who was guarded by Grevey, but the ailing forward was largely ineffective. There was some question whether Kentucky was quick enough to stay with Indiana, but they showed much agility and that, combined with their coolness under pressure, and determination, made up for any deficiency. The Wildcats' pressing zone forced Indiana into 20 turnovers. The one Hoosier they could not stop was Benson, who popped 33 points through the hoop and gathered 23 rebounds. Robey and Phillips fouled out trying to contain him and Guyette, who finished with four personals, had to be shifted to center for eight minutes. Hall did not mind giving up fouls because his bench depth allowed him to maintain pressure throughout the contest. Indiana's disciplined troops tried to control the game by slowing down the action, but Kentucky kept shooting, shooting, shooting. For 32 minutes, the game was a standoff. Tied 44-44 at the half, the teams were still locked in an 81-81 struggle. The court resembled a battlefield. Bodies collided and went sprawling. The rough, bruising contest began to take its toll on the Hoosiers. Kentucky, having softened them up, went in for the kill. Robey and Grevey scored eight unanswered points in three minutes to give their team an 89-81 lead. Indiana struggled back but it was too late. The final buzzer went off with the Wildcats on top 92-90. The Hoosiers were no longer undefeated.

The chain of events that followed occurred just the way Hall outlined them on his blackboard. The jubilant Wildcats cut down the nets, ran out to the bus which swept them away to Cincinnati where they crossed the Ohio River into Kentucky. Awaiting them was a state police escort. When they got to Fayette county, the escort was joined by motorcycles from the sheriff's office and finally by the Lexington police as they crossed the city line. A wild victory celebration was waiting for them on the university campus.

Midwest:

The class of the Midwest regional were third ranked Louisville (24-2) and fourth ranked Maryland (22-4). Louisville, bowing only to Bradley and Tulsa, reaped victories in their first 13 outings, including a 112-67 pasting of North Texas State. The Cardinals, a moody bunch, were led by Wes Cox, namesake of an earlier Louisville star, and Junior Bridgeman. Coach Crum's strategy paralled that of Joe Hall—substitute frequently and freely and wear down your opponents with shock tactics. After each mass substitution, Cardinal opponents would have to brace themselves for a fresh red and black wave. The outspoken Crum, who was once described as having "the charm and persistance of a storm window salesman," had his hands full with a squad of brilliant individualists trying to play a team game. Then, too, the sometimes up—too often down—Cardinals seemed to lack motivation against weaker opponents and had to be prodded constantly to keep from loafing.

And when it came to outspoken, nobody could top Lefty Driesell. But the Maryland coach was still speechless (for a while at least) after Moses Malone decided to give up his basketball scholarship at Maryland and join the professional ranks. Driesell came close to an undefeated regular season in 1975, even without Malone, losing only to UCLA, Clemson and North Carolina—all strong teams. Then in the ACC playoffs, Maryland bowed to NC State 87-85 after having waylaid them twice during the season. So what was Maryland doing in the Midwest regional? Since the school finished with the best record in the conference, they received an invitation under the expanded format but were banished to another regional. Still, it was another example of Driesell's futile effort to win a postseason playoff after his team had taken the conference title. He must have wondered why he had not applied for a coaching job in the Big Ten, where there was no conference postseason playoff, and made some team the UCLA of the Midwest.

Statistically, the Terrapins were ranked high in four departments. They had the highest field goal accuracy in the country, the fourth best free throw percentage, the third best rebounding and their margin of victory was topped only by Indiana and the University of North Carolina, Charlotte. Their most amazing statistical superiority, however, was in the rebounding department. Playing most of their games in the toughest conference in the land (three ACC schools again made the top ten at season's end), using a three-guard lineup, the Terrapins number three ranking looked even more impressive. The reason for the three guards was that neither John Lucas nor Mo Howard nor Brad Davis could be allowed to sit on the bench; they were all that good. Besides, Driesell had to plug a hole in the front court left by the defection of Malone.

Lucas was the best of the three. Some said he was every bit the equal of David Thompson, though his jumping ability was as weak as Thompson's was extraordinary. No matter. Lucas was so quick, he was around his man and up for a shot while the faked-out defender was still heading in the wrong direction. On defense, he was undetachable. Lucas was a natural athlete who excelled in any sport he picked up. He shone on another court too, the one laid out for tennis. In high school, he won 92 matches in a row and was the state champion for three years. As a college sophomore, Lucas was the ACC singles champion. No doubt he could have become a successful tennis pro.

Another school that might have been ranked number one except for defections to the pros was Notre Dame (17-7). The war between the two professional leagues was approaching resolution. Either the ABA would disband or be incorporated into the older NBA. Whatever the future, college stars wanted to cash in on lucrative contracts before the bidding wars ended. Brokaw and Shumate decamped with another year of eligibility remaining, leaving Digger Phelps with only Adrian Dantley to build around. At 6′5″, 210 lbs, Dantley was another example of the slab-of-beef build that characterized the trend in basketball. The sophomore, the second best scorer in the country, was picked as an All American, leading to speculation of what might have been if Shumate and Brokaw had remained. At the end of the season, the Irish were starting an all freshman and sophomore quintet.

The Irish won their first four, lapsed to drop four of their next five, then pulled out of their spin to record that rarest of feats—a triumph over UCLA at Pauley Pavilion. In retrospect, the mini-slump did not look so damaging. The Irish succumbed to some powerful foes—Indiana, Maryland, UCLA and Kentucky, all ranked in the top six at the end of the year. Later, the Irish dropped one to fifth ranked Marquette, confirming the contention that they played the toughest schedule outside of the ACC. As the season ended Notre Dame, having gained experience and maturity, pulled out the stops and creamed Fordham 98-61 and got a measure of revenge by dismembering Dayton 102-69.

The rest of the field in the regional was forgettable. Kansas (19-7) had crumbled before Kentucky 100-63. Texas A and M (20-6) had collapsed before Indiana 90-55 and despite playing in three holiday tourneys captured only one. Rutgers (22-6) had beaten St. Peters and St. Johns in the ECAC playoff to reach the tournament.

Creighton (20-6) owned a center who was atypical, an exceptional free throw shooter. Besides leading his team in scoring he was also the third best in the country from the charity stripe, missing only 13 times all season. Another player of note was Rick Apke, the coach's younger brother. The Bluejays played cardiac ball nearly every time they took the floor either because they played well-matched opponents or because they could not stand prosperity long enough to nail down a win.

Cincinnati (21-5) was sputtering for most of the first month of the season. They split their first ten, dropping back-to-back-games to Navy and Harvard in the Volunteer Classic, not anything to write home about. The Bearcats then pulled out the throttle and went the rest of the season, 16 games, undefeated.

In one opening round game Kansas was unable to find a legal means of stopping the Irish. The referees called every infraction in sight so that six Jayhawks fouled out. Notre Dame went to the line 27 times in the first period on their way to a 12 point lead. Their total of 35 free throws, in 50 tries, was the most scored from the line in the last ten years of tournament play, Dantley alone taking 21 foul shots. If not for the current foul rule, they would have registered a new record. But Kansas' foul per minute performance *was* a tourney record. They made a run at the Irish early in the second half and cut their lead to two. Dantley led a counterattack as his team moved ahead by 18 and eventually salvaged a 77-71 victory. Dantley's 19 points in the last 11 minutes, to make a game high 33, was decisive. Despite being outscored 31-21 from the field, Notre Dame was able to win comfortably, thanks to Kansas infractions.

Junior Bidgeman did for Louisville what Dantley performed for Notre Dame! He kept the Cardinals in the game in the first half dominated by Rutgers. Phil Sellers gave the Knights a slight lead just before the midgame buzzer but after the intermission Allen Murphy's three consecutive buckets put Louisville ahead to stay. Rutgers kept within overhaul distance until the 13:00 mark when Bridgeman's three point play and another basket by the senior forward broke the game open. By this time, too, Louisville's superior defenses, stronger rebounding and deeper bench had begun to take their toll on a tiring Rutgers squad. Louisville raced off with a 91-78 victory. Bridgeman with 36 points on 15 for 18 shooting and Sellers with 29 points paced their respective teams.

After a slow first half, which saw Cincinnati ahead of Texas A and M 37-27, the teams went on a scoring binge, showering the nets with 102 points. When the blizzard was over, the Bearcats, with the assistance of freshman Steve Collier's 20 points, had disposed of the Texans 87-79. Maryland had to work a little harder to shake off Creighton who made a comeback early in the second half but fell short. Brookins had 25 points for the Bluejays and missed only one of eight from the line.

In second round action, Notre Dame was behind even before the opening tip. Phelps had failed to give the officials his starting lineup and Maryland was awarded a technical foul shot. Nontheless, the Irish shrugged it off and boomed to a 15-5 lead. The Terrapins, a very patient team, retained their poise and slowly narrowed the gap. They overtook Notre Dame before the intermission and began pulling away in the second half before Notre Dame scurried to within two with 9:25 to go. With Lucas directing an effective press, the Terrapins pulled away once more and won 83-71. Lucas was able to hold Dantley to 25 points while scoring 24 himself. The rest of the Irish were not a factor.

The co-feature was marked by a pair of Louisville scoring bursts that decided Cincinnati's fate and broke their 17 game win streak. With the Bearcats on top 11-10, Louisville, an on-again, off-again team all year, ripped off 15 consecutive points, launched by a pair of Bridgeman buckets. Unable to concentrate for very long, the Cardinals allowed Cincinnati back into the game. With the score tied at 29, Crum sent substitute Ike Whitfield into the game to stir the now torpid Cardinals. He responded by hitting four straight field goals in a 10-0 Louisville burst. They were his only points of the game but helped Louisville post its twenty-sixth victory 78-63.

The Terrapins were supposed to be the deadeyes of the tournament but it was Louisville that performed like William Tell in the regional final. A small turnout, (5,700), filling only a portion of the vast Pan American Center, watched Louisville scorch Maryland as it connected on two-thirds of its shots in the first five minutes. Maryland, which had trouble finding the hole, never caught up after the Cardinals' initial explosion. Louisville won despite sub performances from their usual saviors. Bridgeman had only a single point in the first half, picked up his fourth personal after five minutes of the second and had to play cautiously for the rest of the game. Wesley Cox was hurt but he played, doped up with pain-killing injections that cut down his effectiveness. Substitute Phil Bond took up the slack and played a superlative game, scoring 23 points and limiting Brad Davis to just eight. Though Lucas paced Maryland with 27 points, his guardmates, Davis and Howard, were able to contribute only ten points before both fouled out.

East:

Like a pride of lions pursuing and then fighting over a prize, the members of the ACC tore into each other all season long. Only one, Virginia (12-13), had a losing record and that was because it played so many games against conference foes. Wake Forest, with the worst record in the ACC, lost only twice (by a total of seven points) outside the conference. North Carolina's only non-conference defeat came at Kentucky.

Next to the NCAA tournament, the ACC postseason playoff is the most closely watched tourney in the country. The winner was invariably one of the North Carolina schools and in seven of the previous eight years it was either the Tarheels or the Wolfpack that survived. Winning the ACC and the playoffs was tantamount to receiving a ticket to the Final Four. Since 1962, nine teams had won that double prize and all had gone on to take their regional.

Tickets to the ACC playoff were normally available only as a reward for a substantial scholarship donation. The fans got their money's worth because the games were invariably the closest and most exciting of the season. The NCAA tournament was almost an anticlimax for the winner. 1975 was no exception. All games were in the gut-rotating, palm-tingling class. None of them ended with the teams more than six points apart at the final buzzer. North Carolina (21-7) finished second in the ACC and were immediately assaulted in the first round of the playoff by last place Wake Forest who treated them like a Division II upstart. With 50 seconds to go, Wake Forest was leading by eight points. Instead of slowing down and using caution, the Deacons, caught up in the euphoria of the moment, continued to play with abandon. They whipped a long pass downcourt that nicked the overhead scoreboard. This rattled the Deacons considerably. The Tarheels forced three more turnovers and when Wake Forest missed two critical free throws, North Carolina was able to tie and advance 101-100 in overtime.

In one semifinal, the Tarheels had to survive another overtime before sliding by Clemson. Meanwhile in the other semifinal, North Carolina State edged Maryland. Down 15 points with four minutes to go, the Terrapins were about to have last rites pronounced when they performed one of the all-time revival acts. With an explosive charge, Maryland proved that the anticipation of their demise was entirely premature. To the accompaniment of the screams of their frenzied fans, Maryland bounced back to lead 85-84 with nine seconds to buzzer time. But Kenny Carr's three point play was the silver bullet that did the Terrapins in. Despite the victory, the Wolfpack were concerned when David Thompson developed leg cramps during the contest. With Burleson graduated, Thompson was State's only offensive threat.

In the ACC final, North Carolina State, who had to win in order to get a tournament invitation, fought their cross-state rivals until the last second before sprawling 70-66. It was the first time since 1966 that the national champion was unable to defend his crown and came as a great disappointment to State. With some of the most talented players in the country and with a three year record of 79-7, the Wolfpack was able to qualify for only one NCAA tournament. They even declined an invitation to the NIT, deeming it a tournament of losers.

With the imminent departure of David Thompson, a new star was rising in the ACC to take his place. Phil Ford, a freshman guard at North Carolina was voted the most valuable player in the playoff, partly on the basis of his 26 point average but mostly on his team leadership qualities. Besides Ford, Coach Dean Smith had the services of Mitch Kupchak at center, 6′11″ Tom LaGarde at strong forward and whippet-quick Walt Davis at the other forward. Their supporting cast could have made the starting lineup on any other college team. Actually, Dean Smith's liberal substitution policy gave the whole bench substantial playing time, narrowing the gap that existed on other teams between the starters and the mop up crew. With a surplus of fine starters, the Tarheels finished second in field goal accuracy right behind Maryland, reinforcing the ACC's reputation as the deadliest conference in the country.

Syracuse (20-7) was a better team than their record indicated. They dropped five games by four points or less and trampled Army 95-59. Boston College, the other ECAC team, had an identical 20-7 record. They qualified by hurdling Connecticut and Holy Cross in the ECAC New England division playoff. Furman (22-6) was undefeated in the Southern Conference. A pivotal player in their lineup was Clyde Mayes, the nation's fourth best rebounder. Pennsylvania (23-4) won their sixth straight Ivy crown. They fell to LaSalle by a pair and to Princeton, their closest challenger, by a point. Beating Columbia by 44 points was noteworthy but not remarkable, since the Lions had been almost everyone's doormat for years. LaSalle (22-6) won the Dayton Invitational and the Sugar Bowl as well as going undefeated against all five Philadelphia intracity rivals. A three-game losing streak just before the Mid-Atlantic playoffs tarnished their reputation.

Two midwestern conference runners up competed in the East Regional. Kansas State (18-8) finished behind Kansas in the Big Eight. The Wildcats had been embarrassed by the conference champs 91-53 in one of the most lopsided contests of this long arch-rivalry. New Mexico State (20-6) was the runner up in the MVC and second to UTEP in scoring defense. Matched up in thrift shooting contests, UTEP and New Mexico State split the pair, the Texans winning 48-41 and the Aggies 61-39.

The Aggies of New Mexico were easy to spot. They were the last major college to play in the old fashioned, short sleeved T-shirts. Maybe North Carolina used that visibility to avoid the Aggies' annoying defense in their opening round game. The Tarheels controlled the pace and, once ahead, nudged the Aggies out of their deliberate set patterns. Using a fast break primed by fresh bodies inserted by Smith, the Tarheels mowed down New Mexico State 17-2 over a five and a half minute span early in the second period. That made the score 66-47 for North Carolina and the rest was more of the same. Smith used 14 players to wear the losers down. As a result, half a dozen Tarheels were in double digits. The final score was 93-69. The shocked Aggies had given up 33 points more than their average and the 54 points they allowed in the second half was more than they had given up in ten complete games during the season. It was also the most points scored on them in more than eight years.

Boston College was more frugal than North Carolina. They used just six men against Furman to achieve the same purpose. The score was knotted eight times in the second half until, with seven minutes to go, BC (led by Will Morrison), moved ahead to stay and won 82-76. An oddity of the contest was Furman's shutout from the freethrow line. They got just two chances (both by Mayes) and missed them both. Meanwhile, the Eagles accepted 26 opportunities and converted 20 of them. Most of the calls against Furman were of the two-shot variety. The game was not untypical in this respect. In each of the four first round games, one team was favored with at least twice as many foul shots as the other. Uneven refereeing? Or defenses that could not cope? Probably just a little of each.

In Philadelphia, Syracuse and LaSalle played a close second half, too. The score was tied nine times, the last coming at the end of regulation time. With 35 overtime seconds showing on the clock, the teams were still knotted 81-81 when Rudy Hackett, a 30 point scorer for Syracuse, threaded a pretty pass to Kevin King who layed it up and in. Four more markers, all on free throws, insured the victory 87-83. Once again, free throws made a big contribution to the Orangemen's victory as they sank 19 to 7 for LaSalle. Losing Joe Bryant, their high scorer, on five personals also hurt the Explorers.

At least once in every recent regional, it seemed Penn's shooting became touched with permafrost. Since Kansas State's defense could hardly induce such cold shooting and since the Quakers were playing at home, the 40-28 half time Wildcat lead could only be explained by Penn's annual postseason swoon. They started closing in the final minutes of the first period (trailing by 17 at the time) but fell behind by 17 again as Chuck Williams' first three shots of the second half found their mark. Kansas State had effectively barred the middle and the Quakers' long range bombs were off target most of the game. A better than two-to-one advantge at the line for Kansas State did not help any either. The Quakers rallied towards the end but Kansas

State, with Williams and Carl Gerlach sharing scoring honors, held on to win 69-62. A sad day for Philadelphia as both home teams lost.

Kansas State, barely ahead at intermission, broke open their second round game against Boston College in the first ten minutes of the second half. Scoring two points to every one for BC during this stretch, the Wildcats built up a 15 point lead on their way to a 74-65 victory. Williams blazed his way to 24 points in the second period and 32 for the game. He was abetted by Gerlach with 20 points.

Despite phenomenal shooting by North Carolina, they were unable to open much of a gap between themselves and Syracuse. Ahead 30-21 and threatening to break the game open, the Tarheels allowed Syracuse six points in a row to cut the deficit. Still, it took almost thirty minutes for Syracuse to move ahead. Jim Williams' breakaway basket gave them a temporary 51-50 lead. That launched an electrifying duel decided dramatically at the final buzzer. Eleven times the lead seesawed between the protagonists. True to form, Smith shuttled fresh players in and out of the lineup but Syracuse refused to fold. In the backcourt, Smith stuck with Ford and Brad Hoffman. Both were sizzling and they accounted for 26 of North Carolina's 34 second half points.

With 27 seconds left, North Carolina was protecting a one point lead by running their four corners delay. The tactic called for the point guard to direct the attack and, therefore, he handled the ball most of the time while the other players spread to the periphery. Suddenly, Ford found himself double-teamed by a pair of aggressive Orangemen. Trapped, the freshman looked for a teammate to pass to but under intense pressure threw the ball out of bounds instead. Syracuse took over and worked the ball to Jim Lee, who hit a twenty footer with only three seconds on the clock. Smith called time and diagrammed a play Wake Forest had used successfully on the Tarheels in the recent ACC playoff. It called for Kupchak to throw the ball to reserve guard John Kuester, who was to move parallel to the baseline and then pass the ball back to Kupchak or whoever was open. But Williams stepped in front of Kuester, intercepted the ball, and was immediately fouled. His free throw cinched the victory for Syracuse 78-76. North Carolina had hit 65 percent of their floor shots while Syracuse was just a touch less torrid with 59 percent. That meant rebounds were rather scarce. Actually, there were only 51 in the whole game. It was the first time a Smith-coached team had lost in a regional, this after ten straight victories resulting in four appearances in the Final Four.

Syracuse, after one overtime victory and a last-second win, was developing a reputation as a team with an ice water circulation system and an overheated fan section. But Coach Roy Danforth and the Syracuse loyalists had to withstand another assault on their nerves when Syracuse, trailing Kansas State by a bucket at half time, caught up at 46-46 four minutes after intermission and fought it out, swish by swish, the rest of the way. With the clock running down, the Wildcats took a 66-62 lead. Just when it looked as if

Syracuse had run out of miracles, they flipped eight straight points through the net to go ahead 70-66. Chuckie Williams bagged six of the next eight points to put Kansas State ahead again 74-72 at 1:31. A pair of free throws by Lee 26 seconds later tied the count. The Wildcats held for the last shot. Everyone in the arena knew who would take it but Williams still managed to get free in the corner and arched one in with five seconds left for what appeared to be the game winner.

It was just too soon. Against Syracuse, five seconds was a lifetime. After a time out, the Orangemen declined to take the air route. Instead, Jim Williams dribbled the length of the court and delivered the ball to Hackett, who spun like a dervish while propelling the ball into the basket as the buzzer sounded and several thousand Syracuse fans went berserk. Hackett tallied the first field goal of the overtime which was matched by red hot Chuckie Williams. But the Orangemen exploded, scoring a total of 19 points in the extra period—11 by Williams and Lee—to swamp Kansas State 95-87 and advance to San Diego and the Final Four.

Chuckie Williams was spectacular with 35 points but he could not do it all himself. He received some help from guardmate Mike Evans, looking somewhat grotesque playing with a plastic mask to protect an injury. He got none from center Gerlach who was shut out and fouled out.

West:

UCLA (23-3) had lost four starters including two All Americans. Only forward Dave Meyers was left. Known as the Spider Man, Meyers was such a fierce competitor and played with such intensity that he received more than his share of injuries. He played nonetheless, gritting his teeth and giving his all. He was well-supported by some experienced lettermen. Marques Johnson played the opposite corner while gregarious Richard Washington was Walton's replacement at center. The guards, Pete Trgovich and Andre McCarter, were not up to the standard of previous UCLA backcourts but were adequate to the task. Though not as awesome as the Walton Gang, the 1975 Bruins were a more cohesive unit than they had been with the controversial center.

This version of the Bruins was not as deep as in the past. Johnson had to be relieved earlier than normal because he was recovering slowly from an attack of hepatitis. The bench had little experience. Thus, it was surprising that the team lost only to Notre Dame, Stanford and Washington (the first time the Huskies had beaten UCLA in 13 years). The last was a 103-81 drubbing in Seattle, the worst defeat suffered by a UCLA squad in ten years and the third worst by a Wooden team. The Bruins had a considerable schedule advantage. They played only eight games on the road: seven conference opponents and Notre Dame. At home, they were invincible, beating, among others, Oklahoma 111-66, California 107-72 and Stanford—in a vengeful rematch—93-59.

Success enveloped UCLA like a royal mantle. The second ranked Bruins seemed able to rise to each occasion that demanded an added burst of effort, an extra measure of dedication. And it was all due to the Wizard, John Wooden. His success was based on drilling his teams in the basics so they would perform better than any other quintet. Certainly UCLA presented no surprises. Their opponents knew what to expect but were helpless to do anything about it. Stress the fundamentals, drill by rote, repetitive conditioning. It made the Bruins awesome, developing their stamina and allowing them to apply relentless pressure for forty minutes. (As a psychological ploy, Wooden refused to call the first time out.) Familiarity and repetition also governed the pregame program. Meals were served exactly four hours before the tipoffs and were followed by naps.

The team could be compared to a well-greased, finely-tuned, broken-in machine in which each player had a defined task. Brilliant as his players were individually, Wooden demanded that they submerge their egos and their talents to the needs of the team. Many UCLA graduates went on to become stars in professional basketball, but under Wooden they were expected to play within the limits he imposed. This could mean anything from sitting for long periods on the bench to shooting only from designated areas. Besides the loss of individuality, the athletes were expected to keep their emotions under control, a demand Wooden found harder to impose over the years and which led to increasing confrontations.

Though he refused to change his training practices, Wooden did adjust his tight discipline in other areas. He relaxed his dress code. He learned to adapt to the changing value patterns of Californians in the seventies, though his own values never changed; he learned even to accept the eccentricities and new counterculture lifestyles of his players. To Wooden, the development and the well-being of his men was even more important than winning. "You are here for an education. That comes first. Basketball comes second," he told them.

Still, Wooden was not as rigid as he seemed. He was aware that no rules, policies, ideas, tactics, or programs were unchanging or unchangeable. Why else would he have a sign prominently displayed in his office which read "It's what you learn after you know it all that counts"?

There were several unfamiliar uniforms on display in the West regional. For four teams this was their first tourney. A fifth had not participated in that regional before. None of them were given much of a chance against UCLA but rated just below the Bruins were two excellent squads—eighth ranked Arizona State (23-3) and tenth ranked Alabama (22-4). Arizona State had taken the WAC while Alabama tied Kentucky in the SEC. However, the Crimson Tide fumbled both their games against the Wildcats, on each occasion by five points, and thus were declared the runner up and banished to the West regional. Alabama had a chance to cop the conference crown outright by beating Auburn in their regular season finale but were ambushed by their arch rivals and had to settle for second place. The Tide were anchored by 6′10″ pivotman Leon Douglas, the first All American produced by the university. With the admission of blacks, Alabama's basketball fortunes flourished. Coach C. M. Newton looked around and found he was homesteading a gold mine. He did not have far to prospect, either, to hit the mother lode which seemed to run in a thick seam through the state's Black Belt. All five Tide starters were black and all were locally grown.

Michigan (19-7), second in their conference, was another carpetbagger in the regional. Russell, their star in 1974, had decamped for the pros. Still, they had lost only one game—to Southern Illinois—outside the powerful Big Ten.

Two of the six PCAC teams were on probation and not eligible for postseason competition. San Diego State with a mediocre record (14-12) finished second to Long Beach State, one of the ineligible schools. The Aztecs had dropped five of their first seven and were unimpressive against any tough opponent. University of Nevada-Las Vegas (22-4), where Jerry Tarkanian had found refuge after being driven from Long Beach State following that school's suspension, was first in the WCAC.

The controversial coach had installed his run-and-gun tactics and the Rebels had been renamed the Running Rebels to mark the transition. UNLV bombed San Francisco 113-103 in one memorable cannonade, just one of seven times they exceeded the century mark.

Montana (20-6), from the Big Sky, had a way of rebounding that showed they were learning quickly under Coach Jud Heathcote. They lost to Hawaii 83-69, then belted them 93-62 the next day, a swing of 45 points. They fell to Idaho State 49-47, but slaughtered them the following week 67-36. They also trumped Idaho 81-49. Consistently keeping their opponents off balance, the Grizzlies exhibited the finest defense in the northwest quadrant of the country. Utah State (21-5) lost twice to Utah but strung out 15 victories in their last 16 games.

By playing on its home court in Tempe, where they had never lost, Arizona State got a break in its opening round game against Alabama. The Sun Devils swamped the Tide in the first half, building a 22 point lead at one point. A clinging man-to-man full court press harassed Alabama into committing 14 turnovers, a statistic that included seven successful steals. The most larcenous of the Sun Devils was Lionel Hollins, an extremely quick guard. Alabama, led by Leon Douglas' 29 points and 21 rebounds, closed the gap in the second half and might even have taken the lead if their foul shooting had not been quite so atrocious. The chief culprit was Douglas who missed 9 of 14 shots. At one point, Douglas missed five in a row. Had they fallen in, they would have proved useful; Arizona State held on to win by only three points, 97-94.

San Diego State might also have pulled their game out against UNLV if they had been able to hit more than the rim from the foul line. (Three of the four teams at Tempe had problems finding the hole from the charity stripe.) Forty percent from the line just was not good enough as the Running Rebels galloped over the Aztecs 90-80. For the first 20 minutes, San Diego made it close; the lead seesawed back and forth ten times in the last five minutes of the period. After the break, UNLV streaked ahead, bumping the margin to as many as 20 points. The losers were breathless, unable to catch up. Ricky Sobers and Eddie Owens, with 21 points each, split the scoring laurels for the winners.

The other two first round contests were held in Pullman, Washington. Paced by the 25 points of Eric Hays, Montana came from behind in the second half to oust Utah State 69-63. The Grizzlies' pressure defense caused Utah State to force their shots, resulting in more ricochet than "bombs away." Blair Reed of the Aggies was the worst culprit, missing all ten of his shots. It was a particularly satisfying win for Coach Heathecote who had been an assistant at Washington State in Pullman.

Michigan almost pulled the upset of the year in the co-feature. Leading UCLA 50-46 at the intermission, mostly as a result of some fine shooting by C. J. Kupec and John Robinson, the Wolverines fell behind in the second half as the dormant Bruin defense revived and Johnson, Washington and Meyers took control of the boards. With 1:23 to go and UCLA up 87-85, Wayman Britt coolly converted a pair of free throws to equalize for Michigan. As the seconds flashed off the clock, neither team was able to break the deadlock. In the overtime, UCLA controlled the tip and Johnson was fouled after just three seconds. A pair of conversions from the line, a layup by Washington and another turnaround bucket by the Bruin center, all in less than a minute, were enough to finish off the Wolverines. At the buzzer, UCLA was pulling away 103-91. Just as in 1974, UCLA had survived an opening tourney game against an unlikely challenger.

The following week it was Montana's turn to scare the Bruins witless. Although they were in front most of the way, UCLA could not pull away from the pursuing Grizzlies. Hays picked up where he had left off against Utah State and flushed nine balls through the cords in as many trys. Dave Meyers, four inches taller but not as quick, was faked out several times while guarding the Montana star. Meyers' problem was compounded by sore legs that had been getting progresively worse during the season as he launched himself after loose balls, absorbed the shock of rebounding and spared himself not at all in careening after faster men. Hays had considerably more trouble with the referee. He was standing behind the man with the whistle when the latter called a foul and signalled so wildly he smacked Hays in the face with enough force to send him to his knees as if poleaxed. Hays got up groggily, shaking the bells out of his head, and resumed playing.

With a little over a minute to play, UCLA was ahead by only a field goal but a point from the line by Johnson and two more by Trgovich finished off the Grizzlies. The final score was 67-64. For Montana, all but one basket had come off the hands of their scoring trio of Hays, Larry Smedley and Ken McKenzie, but it was Hays' 32 points, half the Grizzlies' total, that carried the team.

Arizona State, down by eight points late in their contest with UNLV, recovered to win 84-81 in the other regional semifinal.

If Meyers had a difficult time guarding Hays, it was nothing compared to what Arizona State's 6′2″ Rudy White encountered trying to contain 6′6″ Marques Johnson in the regional final. Johnson, whose previous best was 22 points, chalked up 13 in the first ten minutes and finished with 35. The Bruin forward rebounded well, stole the ball, took advantage of every opportunity and became a one-man destruction unit. White chased him all game with about as much success as a Keystone Kop. Johnson's performance was atypical for a team coached by Wooden which usually spread the scoring load more evenly. But Meyers was suffering from several leg injuries and was performing below par so Johnson was forced to compensate. A 29-15 rebounding edge in the first half insured a substantial Bruin lead at intermission. The 89-75 win came as no surprise to the 8,834 fans. It was, however, to be the only game of the five they played in the tournament that the Bruins did not have to struggle to win.

Final Four:

San Diego is just a short hop south of Los Angeles so UCLA could almost be considered the home team of the Final Four. Off their performance in the regional, they would need all the help they could get. Meyers' legs were giving him constant pain and Johnson was weak from his recent bout with hepatitis. The Bruins were not in good shape. It was the first appearance in the Final Four since 1966 for Kentucky and the first time ever for Syracuse.

Louisville and UCLA were scheduled for a repeat performance of their semifinal confrontation of three years ago. And it was quite a match. What the sixth game of the 1976 World Series between Boston and Cincinnati was to baseball, what the overtime championship game between New York and Baltimore in 1959 was to football, the Louisville-UCLA clash was to college basketball. Many called it the greatest game they had ever witnessed. Certainly it had drama for a whole tournament and its aftermath was a terse announcement that shocked the basketball world.

It was a game of confrontations. Wooden against Crum, the old master versus his former upstart assistant, Trgovich against Bridgeman—the two had been teammates on an East Chicago high school team that took the Indiana state championship. Now they were guarding each other. Louisville breezed to a nine point lead which UCLA reduced to four by intermission. The Cardinals continued to dominate in the second half. Though Trgovich had effectively shut off Bridgeman's scoring—the Louisville forward failed to make a basket in the last 37 minutes of the game—he and Wesley Cox were unbeatable off the boards. The pair hauled down 31 rebounds, almost as many as the entire Bruin team.

The game entered its final minute with Louisville in front 65-61. Meyers, a clutch player, took a shot which was blocked by Bill Bunton. He recovered, shot again and Bunton batted the ball away cleanly once more. Meyers chased after the ball but it was Washington who came up with it. The Bruin center shot over Bunton a third time but this time Bunton got a piece of Washington. A pair of free throws, each followed by a mini explosion from the Bruin fans, narrowed the gap to two. On the ensuing in-bounds play, UCLA put so much pressure on the passer that Johnson was able to intercept the ball. A wave of hysteria greeted the move, and when Johnson swished the tying points into the basket with 35 seconds left it was as if a tsunami had shaken the walls and roof of the arena.

No more scoring occurred before the buzzer and so UCLA found itself in a semifinal overtime contest just as it had 12 months previously against North Carolina State. It was also the seventh time UCLA was entering an overtime period in two tourneys, a record of sorts.

The Cardinals' Allen Murphy went to work immediately. He scored seven of Louisville's nine points in the extra session to give him 33 in the game. His team was still leading 74-71 when, with 1:18 left, Meyers sank a pair from the line. The Cardinals got the ball back and with 50 seconds on the clock, called time out. One could almost hear the wheels spinning in Crum's head as he strategized on the bench. It was obvious Louisville would try to freeze the ball to protect their miniscule lead. What was questionable was Crum's decision to replace his high scorer, Murphy, with Terry Howard, his designated dribbler. It was true nobody on the Cardinals could handle the ball as well as Howard but this was a pressure situation and, as a substitute, he had had comparatively little game experience.

UCLA took risks trying to separate Howard from the ball but it seemed to be glued to the little dribbler's fingers. Finally, with just 15 seconds staring down at them from the scoreboard, Wooden took a calculated risk. He directed one of his Bruins to foul Howard. On the surface it looked like a bad gamble. Howard had been to the line 28 times during the season and he had not missed once. But he had also never been under such intense pressure and the Bruin fans did not make it any easier when they raised the decibel level several more notches, if that was possible. If Howard could sink both ends of the one-and-one opportunity, it was all over for UCLA. But he missed.

UCLA got the rebound and immediately called time. They set up a play that worked to perfection—a feed from Jim Spillane to Washington at the baseline. He turned, jumped and spilled a sweet little seven footer through the net. There were three seconds left but it was all over. UCLA had won 75-74. The Bruins clustered around Wooden congratulating each other while pandemonium rocked the stadium.

The players were physically and emotionally exhausted when Wooden dropped his bombshell in the locker room. The final on Monday evening would be the last college game he would ever coach. "I'm bowing out," he said. "I don't want to. I have to." Wooden had not been sleeping well lately. He was 64 and had suffered a mild heart attack in 1972. Schedules were longer, recruiting more competitive, athletes more difficult to control. It was time to quit. The shocked Bruins listened to their coach and vowed they would send him into retirement a winner.

Meanwhile, in the other semifinal, Kentucky and Syracuse had turned the court into a combat zone. Never before had tournament fans seen such a physical, brutally tough game. The body contact was more like that found at a football game or a roller derby while the contest was played to the accompaniment of an almost continuous obligato of the referee's whistle. A total of 61 fouls were called and if not for the new foul rule, the free throw stripe might have been worn away from all the traffic. As it was, 70 free throws were attempted, four players fouled out and six others were on the brink with four personals. The players might have derived greater benefit from orderlies and nurses than referees, so punishing was the action.

It was Syracuse that took most of the punishment. The taller and bigger Wildcats pounded the Orangemen into submission, winning the battle off the boards 57-40. Badly outplayed in the first half, Syracuse lost any chance of recovering when they went scoreless for the first four minutes after the break. Kentucky continued pounding until, mercifully, the buzzer sounded with the Wildcats ahead 95-79. When it was over, Joe Hall said with a straight face, "I think the officials did a good job controlling the game."

On Monday night, Louisville beat Syracuse in overtime for third place in the tourney. It was the third overtime game for Syracuse since the playoffs started and their fourth in six games over the last two years. With their sense for dramatic finishes, especially their last second win over North Carolina, the Orangemen had fulfilled any fan's dream of gangbuster endings.

But the fans had come to see the national championship decided between the two most successful teams in the history of the NCAA tournament; two teams that astonishingly had never met in post-season competition. Kentucky versus UCLA. The ultimate showdown. And it was Johnny Wooden's farewell party, too. How much more drama could one college basketball game support?

Once again, it was speed and finesse against height and strength. But the Bruins overcame their opponent's advantage. They out-rebounded their bigger foes because Washington and Ralph Drollinger boxed out well. Besides, the Bruin centers held their counterparts to just eight points while scoring 38. They and the rest of their teammates simply executed better. Andre McCarter ran the offense, fed the forecourt and was credited with 14 assists. Trgovich, with both thighs heavily taped, performed another defensive assignment superlatively, this time on Jimmy Dan Conner, and provided the impetus when neither side could establish any kind of lead. Meyers was outstanding in every phase of the game. Five times the teams were tied in the first half and 15 times the lead changed hands; but when Trgovich tallied ten of UCLA's last twelve points of the period, the Bruins opened a small lead that was to grow substantially. With eight minutes gone in the second half, the Bruins enjoyed a 66-56 edge.

Then the Wildcats counterattacked. Led by Kevin Grevey who, in the absence of any scoring contribution from Phillips and Robey—the latter fouled out after netting just two points—tallied a season high of 34 points, the SEC champions flung themselves on the exhausted Bruins using fresh troops every few minutes. They came in waves, stunning their groggy opponents with their shock tactics. They accepted penalties, replacing players in foul trouble with new ones from a seemingly inexhaustible bench. Meanwhile, UCLA was hanging in with just one substitution. Meyers, Washington, Trgovich and McCarter played the entire game but Johnson just did not have the stamina to stay in a fully forty minutes. Wooden replaced him with Drollinger, who played center, and moved Washington into Johnson's forward position. Drollinger did a remarkable job getting 13 rebounds and ten points while holding the fort until Marques could recover.

As Kentucky closed the gap, it was questionable whether Wooden's ironmen would last, let alone beat the Wildcats. Having played a draining overtime game just two days earlier, the Bruins were running on weak batteries. Lines of exhaustion traced their faces. Meyers, running on sore legs, was playing on raw guts and little else. With 6:49 to go, UCLA was nursing the last point of their lead, a 76-75 advantage, when the turning point occurred. Meyers went up for a jumper and came down on top of Grevey. The referee pointed a finger at Meyers and called a charging foul. Frustrated because his shot had not gone in and seeing the Bruin lead about to disappear, the intense forward began screaming at the official. He was given a technical for his outburst.

As if shot from a cannon, John Wooden catapulted onto the court. His face purple with rage, he charged the referees like a wild rhino. "You crook," he spat at one official. To the thousands at San Diego and millions more watching on television, this was a side of the mild, gentlemanly coach they had never seen before. But it was just as much a part of the persona of this fiercely competitive man as the more publicized side. In the fading minutes of his career, with the championship seemingly slipping away, Wooden reverted to the style that had given him the reputation as the most merciless referee baiter in his conference long before he won his first national title. He advanced to the free throw line and jawed at the referee, holding up the game while Grevey stood uncomfortably by waiting to shoot his free throws.

Joe Hall started onto the court, demanding that the game continue. The referee pointed his finger at Hall, warning him that if he took one more step he would be given a technical. Why didn't the referee give Wooden a technical, Hall wanted to know. To have done that under the circumstances would have required a referee with more courage than probably existed. Wooden was not McGuire. He was, after all, Wooden. It was like citing, if not God, then certainly one of the major archangels. To have given him a technical now would have been unthinkable. He got away with it and it changed the momentum of the game. With a chance for a five point play, the Wildcats came up empty. Grevey was so shaken by the incident and the delay that he missed the technical, missed the first of a one-and-one and when Kentucky took possession, they were called for an illegal pick (which might never have been called had Wooden not intimidated the referees) and gave up the ball.

Even more important, Wooden's outburst gave the Bruins a chance to catch their breath. With renewed strength they pulled away again and won their tenth championship in twelve years by a 92-85 final score. It was a fitting farewell present for the Wizard of Westwood.

17

OF KNIGHTS AND STREET FIGHTERS *1976-1977*

1976

In contrast to Kentucky's wild celebration and police-escorted triumphal return to Lexington following their win in the regional at Dayton, the retreat to Bloomington by the Indiana Hoosiers resembled a funeral procession. Bobby Knight and his players were more than disappointed. But for most of them there would be another chance the following year. Of the starters, only Steve Green was a senior and he was ably replaced by Tom Abernethy. The rest of the squad was back, more experienced, more determined, and if possible, stronger. Once more they sailed through an undefeated season and were ranked number one. This time they were led by two All Americans—Benson for the first time and May who repeated.

Mostly, though, winning was a result of team effort. None of the Hoosier's dominated any statistical department, nor did the team appear in the top five in any measurable aspect of the sport though they mustered one of the strongest defenses in the country. This was quite a turnabout for Bloomington. Defense was an aspect of the sport almost unknown at Indiana before Knight's arrival. However, through his association with his former coach Fred Taylor, Knight had become friendly with Pete Newell and was now one of the most enthusiastic disciples of the guru of defensive basketball.

Indiana fans were certain they could have beaten UCLA if only they had survived the regional. A match was arranged in St. Louis, a neutral site, similar to the UCLA-North Carolina State confrontation there two years ago. It was presented on national television and was the season opener for both

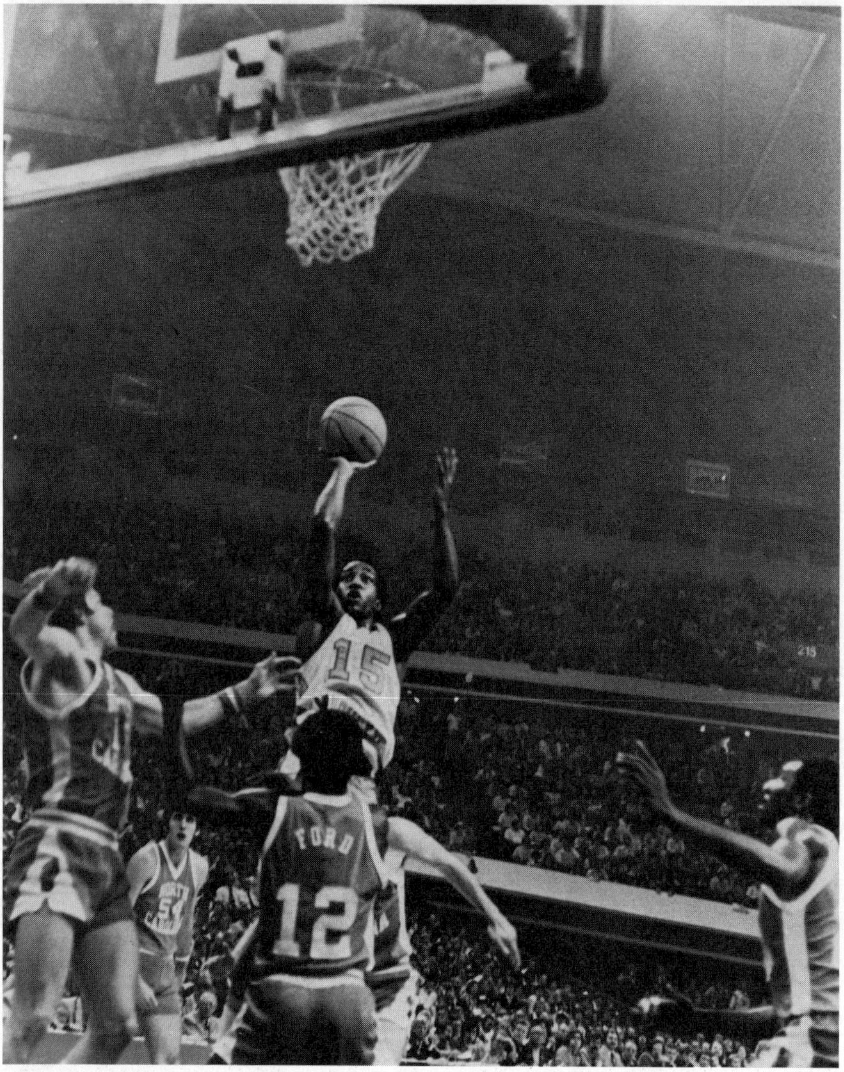

Butch Lee of Marquette is surrounded by Tarheels as he drives for another bucket in his team's 67-59 victory in the 1977 final. (Marquette University photo)

teams. With so much attention focused on the game it was an opportunity for each to establish itself as the favorite for the national title. Everyone expected a close contest.

It was nothing of the sort. After leading by 26 points, Indiana let down towards the end and won 84-64. May burned the Bruins with 33 points. For the first time since 1961 UCLA had lost a season opener. Three outings later Indiana avenged the regional final loss to Kentucky, then captured the Indiana Classic and the Holiday Festival in New York. They were outstanding in these two tourneys, trampling Georgia 93-56, Virginia Tech 101-74 and a trio of New York schools—Columbia, Manhattan and an excellent St. Johns squad—by an average margin of 30 points.

The Hoosiers suffered a mild slump at midseason, meaning they won by slighter margins. It was the result of effective zones deployed by opponents, but Knight countered by deviating from his normal disciplined attack and allowed his players to freelance once in a while, even springing a fast break on his opponents from time to time. Narrow victories over Ohio State and Purdue were followed by more laughers.

Though May, the Player of the Year, and Benson got most of the headlines, Indiana's bruising guards established the pattern for the team's success. On defense they intimidated. On offense they moved the ball around and set picks that enabled the open player to get off an uncontested shot.

The one outstanding characteristic of the team was its discipline, a reflection of Knight's strict coaching methods. Like Wooden, he never got fancy. Instead he stressed the fundamentals—pressing man-to-man defense, sealing off the passing lanes, setting screens and taking only high percentage shots on offense. He believed basketball was a game of mistakes and the team that made fewer would win. As a result of hard practice his men were always in top condition. That and the fact that he started four players 6'7" or over had a very intimidating effect on Indiana's opponents. By the end of the 1976 season they had won 59 straight regular season games.

Knight's strictness encompassed all aspects of the team's activity. His dress regulations made the Hoosiers the neatest basketball players in the country. During practice he imposed silence and booted all uninvited spectators out of the gym. Knight had been exposed to the strict regimentation at West Point where he was appointed head basketball coach at the tender age of 24. His personal idol was General Patton and he also had high regard for Vince Lombardi, Earl Blaik and Woody Hayes, a trio of coaches from a rival sport. This martinet shared with his heros, Patton and Hayes, the disturbing habit of smacking people in public. Aside from the "light tap" to Joe Hall's head during a game in 1974, he also conked Benson and yanked Jim Wisman off the court by his jersey during a televised game against Michigan. His relatively short career was marked by screaming showdowns with referees, enough kicked chairs and scorers' tables to stock several garage sales, and so many technicals that it earned him the nickname Bobby T. "Everyone is entitled to overreact once in a while," he claimed. To Knight the "once in a while" came more frequently than to most.

Despite his volcanic temper and insulting behavior, he gained the respect of most of his players. On those occasions that he humiliated a player publicly, the victim would come to Knight's defense and admit he had it coming. Over the years praise flowed from players and ex-players alike. And there was no doubt Knight was a very fine coach. His intensity was contagious. This quality was especially evident in the game against UCLA and contrasted with the more relaxed play of the Bruins under Gene Bartow, their benign new coach.

In six years as Army coach Knight took his team to the NIT three times. Because of restrictions at the Academy which limited the height of cadets to no more than 6′6″ , Knight was never able to field a tall lineup. So he stressed defense and Army led the country in that department three times, was second once and third another time. His teams beat archrival Navy in each of his six seasons at the Point.

Mideast:

Indiana would have been the overwhelming choice to advance to the Final Four were it not for second ranked Marquette (25-1), sixth ranked North Carolina (25-3) and seventh ranked Alabama (22-4) also participating in the Mideast regional. Marquette lost only to Minnesota 77-73 on the winner's court. It was the most points given up by the Warriors all season as their normally parsimonious defense broke down temporarily. After that slip they tore off 21 wins in a row. Included in that streak were a pair of blowouts, 82-48 and 74-49 over Xavier of Ohio, a school with a winning record.

For the first time in years McGuire retained his team intact. In recent memory he had lost stars such as Maurice Lucas and Jim Chones to one or the other of the professional leagues before their college eligibility expired. With the war between the professional teams about over, all the eligible Warriors returned to play. Foremost among them was All American Earl Tatum with one of the deadliest shots in the game and the very intense Lloyd Walton who was the team's quarterback.

North Carolina was in the Mideast regional because they lost to Virginia in the final of the ACC playoff. The latter went to the East regional. Aside from that defeat they had been bested only by NC State and Wake Forest. Mitch Kupchak at center and Phil Ford at guard were a tandem of All Americans (making a total of five in this, the toughest of the four regionals).

For the fourth time in as many years Alabama posted 22 wins. A well-coached squad under C. M. Newton, who had played at Kentucky under Rupp, the Crimson Tide developed a talent for pulling games out in the final minutes. Four times in their last five confrontations they came from behind in the second half to win.

The rest of the teams in the regional were not shabby either. Western Michigan (24-2) lost only to Toledo and Notre Dame. Western Kentucky (20-8) finished on top of the Ohio Valley and also won its postseason playoff. They suffered through two brief slumps, losing four of five each time. Their major problem was a defense which resembled a wool dress after the moths had finished dinner. Six times they allowed 90 points and the net result was four defeats.

Virginia Tech (21-6) was one of three teams from its state in the tourney. Basketball fans looking for close, exciting games would have been well advised to steer clear of the Gobblers. They feasted on weaker teams and were themselves devoured by the class schools on their schedule. Only once in their first 14 games was the point difference fewer than ten. The Gobblers won eight of the first ten, seven by 27 points or more. But they bowed to Indiana 101-74 and lost five of six *vis a vis* tournament teams.

St. Johns (23-4) was selected despite losing to Rutgers in the ECAC playoff. The New Yorkers had copped the BYU Classic and advanced to the Holiday Festival final before being blown away by Indiana. Unfortunately for the Redmen they had to face the Hoosiers again in a first round regional encounter. This time it was to take place in the more hostile environs of South Bend, just a short ride from the Indiana campus. It was the second straight encounter with an undefeated team for St. Johns—they had fallen to Rutgers in the final game of the season—and an honor they would as soon have foregone.

The Redmen opened with a man-to-man, then switched, but May hit consistently with medium range jumpers to nullify the zone. Despite the spectacular playmaking of Frank Alagia, St. Johns fell behind by seven at the half. They got within a point in the second period but then Indiana surged with a 19-4 burst in less than seven minutes. St. Johns was unable to contain their opponent's fast break nor counter with one of their own. Directing operations, Buckner fed May and Benson who contributed 33 and 20 points respectively. Knight was not taking any chances. He played his starters for most of the game which Indiana won 90-70, the starters sharing 81 points among them. For Indiana, the second conquest of St. Johns was easier than the first. It was a good omen since three of the five teams that Indiana would have to face in the tournament had been their victims earlier in the season.

Neither Western Michigan nor Virginia Tech seemed able to locate the basket in the other attraction. Since the Michigan team was making its first tournament appearance and the Virginians only their second, the pressure may have affected their shooting. Still it was a livelier contest than the Indiana-St. Johns debacle. The Broncos, trailing by 13 points in the second half, came storming back late in the game. Jeff Tyson, their high scorer, missed a 25 foot jumper with 77 seconds left. Given a second chance, he connected from the same spot 35 seconds later tying the count at 65. Neither side could score again before the buzzer. By now momentum had moved to Western Michigan and they sprinted away in the overtime to survive 77-67.

Meanwhile in Dayton Marquette clobbered Western Kentucky (79-60) for their twenty-second consecutive victory.

Inevitably two teams in the top ten had to face each other in the first round of this power packed regional and just as inevitably one had to lose. Unfortunately for them North Carolina drew Alabama as their opponent. It cost Dean Smith his first opening round defeat. Leon Douglas swished 35 points through the nets and gathered 17 rebounds to lead Alabama to an easy 79-64 victory. The value of Phil Ford to the Tarheels was underlined when their point guard, bothered by a sore ankle, sank just one bucket in five attempts. But with probably the best starting lineup ever to take the court for the Tarheels, and an adequate bench, they should have been capable of overcoming Alabama.* The prime culprit was Kupchak who was unable to stop Douglas and scored just eight points on weak shooting.

The following Thursday in Baton Rouge it was Benson who was having early problems with Douglas. He was in foul trouble and forced to sit down for six crucial minutes in the second half during which Alabama revived from a 12 point deficit to take a 69-68 lead with less than four minutes remaining. The scoreboard remained unchanged for the next two minutes until May dented the cords. Free throws by Abernethy and Wilkerson iced the decision for the Hoosier, 74-69. It was a close call for the Hoosiers who were well-matched in size and speed. What stopped Alabama was Indiana's ability to clog the middle, thus keeping Douglas from one of his explosive performances, and the Tide's failure from the sin stripe. Douglas scored only 12 points on 30 percent shooting and his success from the line was only slightly better. In all, Alabama made just half their fouls.

Marquette had a surprisingly difficult time with Western Michigan. The clock had eaten up most of the second half and the Warriors were still down by one. Unbelievably, they were also being outrebounded by a wide margin as the Broncos' Tom Cutter snatched almost half his teams' total. The turning point came when Butch Lee stole the ball from Marty Murray and layed the ball in to give his team the lead. With guards Lee and Walton penetrating for layups, the Warriors turned it on to notch another victory 62-57.

What should have been the national title game was played two days later between the two top ranked teams in the country—one with a 29 game winning streak, the other a slightly more modest 23. It was also a confrontation between the sport's two most volatile coaches.

May, Indiana's leading scorer, was charged with three personals in the first seven minutes and retreated to the bench for the rest of the half. At first it did not seem to affect the Hoosiers. They were ahead by three when he left and their lead blossomed to eleven. The Warriors subsequently rallied to trail by only a point at the intermission.

May was present at the second half tipoff. His defensive assignment was Tatum, normally an outside shooter. Instead of abandoning his modus operandus and driving on May to try to get him to foul out, Tatum continued bombing from the outside. This proved to be highly successful and Tatum

*North Carolina's five starters and one reserve all became starters in the NBA.

finished as the only Warrior in double figures. It also allowed May to continue in the game without collecting any more personals, a great comfort to Indiana.

The teams shadowed each other throughout the second period. Walton was playing despite an injury received against Western Michigan. He made only one-for-nine from the floor but the game was still up for grabs when at :25 Wilkerson approached the line in a one-and-one situation. McGuire flew off his chair to spew some choice words in the direction of the referees. They unhesitatingly slapped him with his second technical of the game. The 14,150 fans were stunned. The roar of the crowd trailed away as if someone had pulled the plug. When the fans recovered, shock was replaced with bitterness and some pity for the Warrior coach. Not even Indiana fans could find comfort from the call. Wilkerson bagged his two foul shots, the two technicals were sunk and Indiana kept the ball. They scored eight points in the final 25 seconds to qualify for the Final Four by a 65-56 score.

After the buzzer McGuire went over to Walton and put his arm around the player's shoulder. That intense, temperamental young man shrugged him off and walked away. Commenting later on his long history of getting hit with technicals in crucial situations a subdued McGuire said: "Personally I think I affect my teams in tournaments. If Marquette gets into another tournament when I'm still around I think I'll let my assistants handle it. I won't come to another tournament." But he did.

East:

There also was another school with a perfect record in the tournament. Despite a not very taxing schedule, Rutgers (28-0) achieved considerable recognition by scoring at least 90 points in 15 of their first 16 games. They even managed to score 75 points against Princeton, the best defensive team in the country, nine more than any other team accomplished.

The Scarlet Knights were paced by All American Phil Sellers, an intense individual who collected technicals as if they were currency. Temperamental and unpredictable, Sellers would criticize a teammate as easily as an opponent. As self-centered as he was brilliant, Sellers seemed to feel the team would fall apart without him. Actually six or seven players contributed to the team's success, including rookie James Bailey who would come into his own the following year as one of the country's fiercest dunkers. Even if most of the team was flat, as least one member could always be counted on to spark the Knights to victory. Though short—Bailey was the only one over 6′5″—they intimidated opponents almost as much by their menacing stares as by their hard-nosed tactics. Three had beards, creating an even meaner impression.

Coach Tom Young was quite lenient with his boys, leading to a chronic lack of discipline. Given the easy schedule, this did not prove an insurmountable handicap during the season. It did contribute to a helter-skelter offense which featured a blistering fast break attack.

The ACC representative was, surprisingly, Virginia (18-11), making their initial tourney appearance. After intense pressure from Lefty Driesell, the ACC agreed to hold its annual Armageddon in the Capital Center in Landover, Maryland, the first time it had been held outside the state of North Carolina. Driesell figured this was the year he would win a postseason tourney. He figured incorrectly and to add insult to painful experience, it was Terry Holland's Virginia Cavaliers who ousted Maryland in the second round. Holland had been a player under Driesell at Davidson and then had coached at the school when the latter moved to Maryland. Holland himself had departed for the ACC in 1975.

The third team from Virginia (joining VPI and UVA) was Virginia Military Institute (20-9) the Southern Conference titlist. Hardly in the same class as the ACC, the Southern Conference had only two schools, VMI and William and Mary, with more victories than defeats. This was the Keydet's first winning season since 1941—an incredible stretch of 25 years of waiting until next year.

Tennessee's (21-5) pride was All American Bernard King. It was he whose high school grades had caused the panic flight of Tennessee administrators to Brooklyn to check the records for themselves. King was half of the Bernie and Ernie Show. The other half was Ernie Grunfeld, also from New York but from a different neighborhood. It would have been difficult to find two players with more dissimilar background, style and appearance.

King was black and had lived in a rapidly disintegrating slum area. Grunfeld was white and Jewish and, though born in Rumania, had grown up in the relatively affluent suburb of Forest Hills. King was thin, 6′7″ and lightning quick. Grunfeld was a stocky 6′6″ and never made anyone check his stopwatch. They complemented one another and together they caused their coach to change his style of play from his favored defensive posture to run-and-gun tactics which took advantage of King's quick release and superior rebounding. With Bernie and Ernie and Mike Jackson (also from New York) Coach Ray Mears adopted the star system. The three New Yorkers accounted for 75 percent of the Volunteer scoring, King and Grunfeld each averaging 25 points. Mears encouraged this individualism by placing cardboard cutouts of his players in the lobby of the gymnasium and painting their names in orange, the team color, over their cubicles.

The best defense in the country by far was deployed by Princeton (22-4). Only four times did they give up as many as 60 points and only once more than 66, that against Rutgers. They throttled Penn 63-39 and in their next game suffocated William and Mary 64-43. The Tigers were not exactly prolific, breaching the 70 point mark only three times. Their disciplined, deliberate offensive patterns were designed for springing a man loose for high percentage opportunities. The offense was so controlled it bordered on boring.

Princeton's Pete Carril was the latest in a line of coaches who stressed tight defense. Iba, Newell, Haskins, Mears, Musselman, Knight and now Carril. At 5′7″, haphazardly dressed in a rumpled suit and shedding cigar ashes as he walked, Pete Carril with his sad basset eyes could easily be mistaken for Peter Falk's television detective, Columbo. During a game he would patrol the sideline with an agitated expression, baiting the referees and playing the persecuted martyr role to the hilt. A demanding type, who often resorted to screaming at his players, Carril dedicated himself to teaching the fundamentals of the sport and stressed the team concept.

DePaul (19-8), back in the tournament after eleven years of frustration and failure, had an undistinguished season aside from a 118-62 pasting of Marshall. Two fine rebounding teams completed the East regional field. Hofstra (18-11), making its maiden appearance, had John Irving, the country's number three rebounder while Connecticut (18-9) countered with John Thomas just a fingertip behind in fourth place. The Huskies were the ECAC New England representative. A consistent team early in the season, they scored exactly 83 points in half of their first dozen games. Later they became more erratic. In back-to-back games against New Hampshire they lost the first by three points and rebounded to take the rematch 99-54.

At Providence in the first round, Hofstra's Flying Dutchmen soared to a 43-30 lead over Connecticut at the break. Midway through the second half, they were still 15 points ahead when they hit a brick wall. The collapse was triggered by the benching of four Dutchmen, including Irving who ran into foul trouble. The Huskies shrank the gap and then went ahead to take the game 80-78.

The second contest was a rematch between two New Jersey schools located 20 miles from each other but whose playing styles were poles apart. Princeton forced Rutgers, the fourth highest scoring team in the country, to play at its tempo which was considerably below the speed limit. The Knights, suffering from a scoring famine, nevertheless held a 48-41 lead with 8:22 to play. Five minutes later Princeton trailed by only three. Showing astonishing self control and admirable patience as the pitiless clock spun the numbers down to zero, Princeton passed the ball around until Barnes Hauptfuhrer found an opening and brought the Tigers to within a point. With Rutgers trying to freeze the ball, their opponents were forced to foul. Mike Dabney stepped to the line but missed the front end of a one-and-one situation. Princeton got the ball back and the Knights were in danger of being toppled for the first time. Again the Tigers moved the ball around until with four seconds left it rested in the hands of substitute Pete Molloy. Ed Jordan fouled him immediately. It was a smart move. Molloy had not scored a point. Furthermore, he was a poor foul shooter, standing at nine for sixteen for the season. He had not scored from the line since December. The Rutgers' coach called time out and then called time again "just to make him (Molloy) think about it some more." Still, as Molloy finally stepped to the line, many Rutgers fans were thinking like Phil Sellers: "There goes the season." However, Young's psychological ploy worked and Molloy's shot hit the back of the rim and bounced away. Despite being held scoreless in the final four and a half minutes, the high scoring Scarlet Knights eked out a 54-53 heartstopper.

The same day at another site Ron Norwood poured 21 points through the mesh in the last 14 minutes to pace DePaul to a 69-60 victory over Virginia. In the co-feature VMI scored a ringing upset over Tennessee 81-75. King, who had suffered a dislocated finger, did not play and Grunfeld, despite 36 points, was unable to carry the Volunteers by himself.

Al Weston and Joe Welton, a pair of 5′10″ Connecticut guards, had scored 41 points between them in the Huskies' first round win. Now against Rutgers in Greensboro they again provided most of the offense in the first half. They cooled off during the intermission, however, and sputtered the rest of the way. Rutgers, led by guard Ed Jordan, put intense pressure on the Husky pair. Connecticut's moves became tentative and Rutgers was able to peel away eight steals. Thomas succeeded in his specialty and picked off 19 rebounds but it was not enough as Rutgers prevailed 93-79 to remain alive and still unbeaten.

VMI eliminated DePaul in a tight checking contest in which 57 fouls were whistled and five Blue Demons were sent to the bench with five personals. VMI might have prevailed in regulation had they been able to sink more than half their 42 opportunities from the line. As it was they had to go into overtime before winning 71-66.

Two days later a second undefeated team advanced to the Final Four when Rutgers eliminated VMI 91-75. After barely escaping the Princeton quicksand, Rutgers was now in full stride and toyed with the Keydets despite an early drought during which they failed to cash in a field goal for 7:47 of the first half. VMI took advantage to establish a slim lead but Rutgers surged back with a 22-7 binge and pulled away. Their quick breaking offense and a well executed trap defense combined to give them an edge that ballooned to 20 points. VMI's offense sputtered when their star, Ron Carter, picked up four personals in the first half. Ed Jordan and Mike Dabney each had 23 points.

Despite 16 points it was Phil Sellers' third straight sub par performance. In two previous contests the All American had been unable to find the basket. He had made only 25 percent of his shots (7 field goals in 28 attempts). Though his shooting improved against VMI, he allowed Will Bynum, his counterpart, 34 points.

Midwest:

The class of the Midwest regional was eighth ranked Notre Dame (22-5). The Irish's schedule was as uneven as a well-used comb. They played Indiana, Marquette and UCLA twice. The three were among the top five teams in the polls. They also played Kentucky, Maryland and Kansas, as tough a slate as any outside the ACC. For breathers they toyed with Valparaiso, Ball State, St. Joseph's of Indiana and Davidson, all of whom they socked by 30 points or more. The Irish feasted on weak teams and generally starved against the elite. Dantley's prodigious scoring helped his selection to an All American team again.

Washington (22-5), back for the first time since the days of Bob Houbregs 23 years earlier, finished only fourth in the Pac Eight. However they were picked because their overall record was better than Oregon and Oregon State ahead of them. They had won their first 14 games, including the Far West Classic, before running into a couple of conference heavies who muzzled the Huskies. They even trounced Seattle University, long the dominant basketball power in that city, 106-75.

Marv Harshman, Washington's coach, was making his first appearance in the tournament. This was surprising since he had nearly 500 victories to his credit, more than any other coach at a major school save Ray Meyer and Frank McGuire. He had also coached longer than anyone except Meyer.

Michigan (21-6), another also ran, featured 6′1″ Rickey Green who could outjump a kangaroo and outrace a roadrunner. He had led his Chicago high school team to a state championship, then had spent two years at a junior college where he had been an All American each time. He was supported by Phil Hubbard, the freshman center, only 6′7″ but solid as a pyramid, and Steve Grote, who not only resembled a Marine but was as tough as a drill instructor in bootcamp. Under likable Coach Johnny Orr, Michigan adopted a free wheeling style that was exciting to watch as fans learned to expect anything from the quick reacting Wolverines.

For only the second time in more than a decade neither Kansas nor Kansas State won the Big Eight. That honor went to Missouri (24-4), back in the tourney after 32 years in limbo. They slammed Kansas 99-69 in retaliation for many past injustices. A 96-60 outburst over Colorado, followed by another over Baylor 105-70, were mild compared to the 106-34 explosion against MacMurray. Missouri relied on Willie Smith for their scoring drives. The 6′2″ guard was the highest scorer in the history of the school. He and his brother Sam grew up in Las Vegas and dreamed of attending UNLV but neither had the grades for admission. Both attended Seminole Junior College but there their paths diverged. Sam was accepted at UNLV while Willie enrolled at Missouri, resentful perhaps that UNLV had not made him an offer.

Texas Tech (24-5) took the SWC postseason playoff, the first time it was held. They finished second to Texas A and M but defeated them in the playoff final. Under the SWC playoff setup the Aggies received a bye while the other eight schools produced a survivor to challenge the conference winner. The layoff might have been more detrimental than beneficial to the Aggies. The Red Raiders did not figure to be a factor in the regional since they had lost to Washington by 22 and to Notre Dame by 25 during the season.

Inconsistent was an apt description for Syracuse (20-8). After bowing to Austin Peay by ten in the season inaugural, they put together modest winning streaks interrupted by two 22 point defeats to West Virginia and UNLV. They ended their regular season by losing four in a row by a total of 48 points. Then in the ECAC playoff they regrouped once more and swept past

Niagara, who had clipped them just days earlier.

A new conference, the Metropolitan Collegiate Athletic Conference (shortened by the media to the Metro Six) had been formed just prior to the 1976 season. It was so new that a league schedule had not been worked out yet. Therefore a postseason tourney was held to determine a qualifier for the national championship. The winner was Cincinnati (25-5). Runner up Memphis State was also selected but sent to the West regional.

The Metro Six was composed of five former independents—Tulane, Georgia Tech, St. Louis, Cincinnati and Memphis State—and Louisville, a defector from the Missouri Valley Conference. They were all situated in major cities, hence the name.

The last four named schools had all played in the MVC at one time. The revolving door so characteristic of that conference had spewed out North Texas State and substituted Southern Illinois, probably the closest school to the Missouri River in that misnamed conglomeration. Wichita State (18-9) represented the MVC in the tournament in 1976.

Two very close first round games had the fans in an uproar. Cincinnati, ahead most of the way, relinquished its lead when Dantley's jumper put Notre Dame ahead 69-68 with a little less than four minutes to go. Hal Ward and Garry Yoder restored the Bearcats' advantage, but in the final minute Don Williams brought the Irish within a point. With eight seconds remaining Cincinnati lost the ball. It was an opportunity that Notre Dame did not waste. Time was almost out when Bill Paterno's desperation heave bounced away but right to Toby Knight who tipped in the rebound for a 79-78 win. The Bearcats were whistled for just 12 fouls but most seemed directed against Dantley, the only member of his team to go to the foul line where he holed seven of eight attempts.

Washington was also ahead most of the game partly because Smith, the number one scorer in the Big Eight, missed his first seven shots. But Missouri moved ahead early in the second period on Jim Kennedy's layup. A seesaw battle followed. The Huskies opened a little daylight 65-61 but Kennedy and Smith, who had now found the range, evened matters. Now the Huskies were struggling. They lost three players via fouls including 6′10″ forward Lars Hansen, while two others had four personals. This hurt because the Husky bench was weak. With 57 seconds to go Kennedy ran into James Edwards, Washington's center, who was called for blocking. It was his fifth personal and wiped out the Huskies' huge height advantage. To make matters worse, Kennedy made both his free throws. With four seconds to go and Missouri ahead 69-67, the Huskies blew their last chance when Clarence Ramsey's attempt hit the rim and bounced out. It was the fourth time in five tourneys that Washington had been eliminated by a team from the Big Eight. The Huskies finished ahead in every statistical department except foul shooting, not surprising for the team with the worst free throw percentage in the Pac Eight.

Texas Tech had little trouble eliminating Syracuse 69-56. The co-feature was much closer. Wichita State almost upset Michigan but eventually wasted opportunities caught up with them. Ahead at the break and still in front in the final minute they missed their opportunity to put the game away when Bob Elmore failed on the lead shot of a one-and-one. Again the Shockers got the ball back but this time turned it over to Michigan who did not let **their** opportunity slip. Rickey Green's baseline jumper at :06 made the score 74-73 for the Wolverines and that is how the game ended.

Of the four teams remaining in the regional only Michigan had a balanced, team strategy. The others all relied on a single star. Smith again needed time to warm up, sinking only one field goal in the first 12 minutes, but once primed he was deadly on 25 to 30 foot jumpers. With Texas Tech ahead 25-22 Smith cranked up and hit six long range mortar shots to give Missouri a 45-36 halftime lead. Rick Bullock, the Red Raiders chief offensive weapon, fouled out with nine minutes remaining after swishing 23 points. After that it was all Missouri as Smith performed his parabolic miracles to help the Tigers to an 86-75 win.

In the final analysis Dantley's 31 points for Notre Dame were not enough to sink Michigan's balanced attack. Despite an edge in rebounding and better shooting, the Irish committed too many turnovers in the second half to hope to win. Michigan dogged their opponents for a good part of the contest. Grote then bagged two charity throws with less than a half minute to go to give his side a seemingly safe 78-74 lead. The Irish had two more chances but flubbed them both allowing Michigan to advance 80-76.

A less than half capacity crowd of 8,378 attended the Louisville Convention Center to see Michigan and Missouri battle for a spot in the Final Four. This time it was Michigan which led for most of the game only to be caught in the latter stages by a hard driving, aggressive bunch of Tigers sparked, as usual, by Smith.

The Wolverines enjoyed a ten point spread in the first four minutes and were on top 41-23 at the 4:13 mark of the first half. An explosive counterattack by a determined Missouri team sliced the advantage into ever narrower decrements. It took them just eight minutes to tie the score 65-65 and their lead soon blossomed to five. Smith was firing on all cylinders now. His second half total of 29 points gave him 43 for the game. Despite control of the boards by Hubbard and Robinson, who took down 34 rebounds between them, Michigan seemed unable to reverse the tide.

But with six minutes left, Missouri's torrid pace began to ebb. The starters ran into foul trouble. Kennedy, eight for ten from the field, was disqualified. Smith, visibly tired, made several mistakes–a shot was blocked, a turnover, a charging foul. The exhausted Tigers missed eight of eleven free throws. Like a summer storm Missouri just blew itself out.

Two pairs of free throws by Robinson bracketed a Missouri foul shot to give the Wolverines a 79-78 lead. With their opponents luffing in the doldrums, Michigan put the game out of reach when Hubbard scored on a layup, Robinson on a tip in and Green completed a fast break with another lay in. Michigan was pulling away at the buzzer 95-88.

West:

Fourth ranked UNLV (28-1) was rated the favorite to take the West regional. The Running Rebels won their first 23 games, then fell to Pepperdine 93-91 before dousing their last five foes. In the process of establishing themselves as the best team west of the Mississippi, the Running Rebels shattered scoring records. Twenty times they pushed over the century mark including nine in a row, to set a new scoring record of 110 points per game climaxed by a 164-111 overindulgence against Hawaii-Hilo. They also wasted UC Irvine by 72 points. New Mexico pinched the Rebel score to 80 points, their lowest production of the year, but still they won. Their schedule was undemanding, yet they steamrollered all opposition with ridiculous ease.

UNLV was nicknamed the Running Rebels for obvious reasons. The second one of their players had control of the ball, the four others stripped their gears and headed downcourt like autumn leaves in a gale. Tarkanian's philosophy was for his players to shoot before their opponents could set up on defense. For that reason neither a man-to-man nor a zone worked well against them. The Rebels were all excellent shooters, so whoever had a reasonably open shot took the ball to the hoop. Speed and quickness rather than height and strength were the team's characteristics.

Despite appearances, UNLV's defense was the equal of their attack. They spent more time practicing their press than running their offensive patterns. The result was a great number of steals and pressure-induced turnovers which led to baskets and thus inflated scores.

Since there were so few outstanding high school ballplayers in Nevada—the Smith brothers, Sam and Willie, were an exception—Tarkanian was forced to look further afield for players. Eddie Owens, half-black, half-Japanese, was recruited in Houston. Jackie Robinson came from Los Angeles and Glen Gondrezick, the lone white starter, from Boulder, Colorado. Most of Tarkanian's men were junior college transfers without the needed grades, or too emotionally scarred fighting for survival in an urban ghetto, for admission to a four year college. Tarkanian was more than a coach to his players. He related especially well to black players, helping them with personal problems, always ready to listen and advise. For some he was more of a father than any they had ever had.

In some ways it was easy to recruit for Las Vegas. The school, only 21 years old, was situated close to the Strip, one of the most glamorous spots in America. Stars of screen, television and professional sports attended games which were completely sold out. A sympathetic coach, a glittering setting, the smell of money and success—the players could not wait to come aboard.

After more losses than any Bruin team in the past ten years and a few close escapes, UCLA (23-4) looked as if they had finally come to terms with their new coach Gene Bartow. Certainly the last three games—all victories by big margins on the road—had been a turnabout from a rocky season liftoff. And UCLA had won their tenth straight conference title. For anybody but the Bruins it would have been a very successful year.

The season had started catastrophically with that 20 point loss to Indiana. The Bruins then rattled off 11 wins in a row, all at home, including a pair of laughers over Seattle and Denver. Close games against Pac Eight opponents that former UCLA teams under Wooden would shrug off with ease, raised criticism of the new coach. Nothing but another national championship would do for the alumni.

"Clean" Gene Bartow was a natural successor to Wooden, at least superficially. He was a Midwesterner with the same sober demeanor and churchgoing habits as his predecessor. He did not smoke, rarely swore and was one of the most popular coaches to anchor a bench. But underneath Bartow was different.

First, he was much more low key, allowing his players freedom that Wooden would never have tolerated. Though his men were notably more relaxed as a result, they displayed a certain lack of discipline at times. It was all right to discuss strategy with the players, but some of them took advantage of the situation to pressure him into giving them more playing time.

Second, Bartow was lacking in the kind of intensity that had fired previous Bruin teams. Meyers was gone and with him the instinct for the jugular that characterized his play. Drollinger, the starting center (who after graduation joined the Christian organization Athletes in Action) was a mild-mannered player who showed none of the aggressive behavior expected of him. At times UCLA played more like teddy bears than the mean Bruins of the past. As a result Bartow began losing control of the team. His moves were tentative, then contradictory. He seemed unable to make decisions and stick with them. Under intense pressure from alumni and students and with scant cooperation from his team, Bartow lost 20 pounds, developed a chronic upset stomach and lost sleep when obscene phone calls woke him during the night. It had taken Wooden 15 years to win his first championship but the spoiled Bruin fans were unwilling to wait even for next year.

Towards the end of the season Bartow asserted himself. He replaced Drollinger with David Greenwood, a more aggressive player, stopped experimenting at guard and made Raymond Townsend and Andre McCarter his starting backcourt; and he got some excellent performances out of All American Richard Washington. It seemed as if the team was ready for another run for the title.

Bartow's old school Memphis State (21-8) was also in the regional. They had conquered Cincinnati during the season but were beaten by them in the final of the Metro Six playoff. Poor defense cost them their first four games, in which they allowed an average of 90 points.

Boise State (18-10), appearing for the first time, won the Big Sky. After taking the first two games the unimpressive Broncos dropped five of their next six. They righted themselves temporarily but swooned later, losing four of five. The problem was their inability to win away from home. They stumbled eight times in twelve tries on the road.

In the WAC, Arizona (22-8) qualified for their first tournament since 1951 with a couple of white knuckle decisions over New Mexico. A two pointer and another by one point gave the Wildcats the title that would otherwise have gone to New Mexico.

All six teams in the PCAC were bunched within two games. First place Long Beach State was still on probation. The conference playoff was captured by third place San Diego State (16-12), which had skidded to six losses in a row late in their schedule after leading the conference most of the season.

For years the best basket players from Washington, D.C.—Elgin Baylor, Dave Bing, Austin Carr, Adrian Dantley—had gone elsewhere to get an education and become All Americans. But that was before John Thompson took over the reins at Georgetown (21-6). The year before Thompson arrived, the Hoyas' record was 3-23. He quickly changed that and as Georgetown's record improved, the school began to get its share of local talent. His men looked up to Thompson in more ways than one: at 6′10″, Bill Russell's former understudy with the Boston Celtics was one of the tallest coaches in the country.

Pepperdine (21-5) rounded out the regional. Granted the Waves had a featherweight schedule which included only eight road games, still they pinned the only defeat on UNLV and tripped San Francisco twice. The second time was an 85-84 overtime thriller, the final, and deciding, game in the conference. The two best known players on Pepperdine were Marcos Leite, a 6′10″ center, who was the pivotman on the Brazilian Olympic team, and 6′6″ freshman forward Ollie Matson, son of the football Hall of Fame player of the same name.

In Tempe, Pepperdine avenged an earlier loss to Memphis State by swallowing the Tigers 87-77 as Leite funneled 34 points through the hoop. The host team, Arizona, felled Georgetown 83-76, using a conservative attack which capitalized on good shot selection. Georgetown meanwhile was taking 30 more shots with considerably less success. The Hoyas brought a large squad of 14 west with them and used every man.

San Diego State employed an effective 1-2-2 defense to hamper UCLA in the early action of another first rounder. But when Washington began his second half 19 point assault, the Aztecs had to abandon their zone. Unfazed, UCLA climbed over their opponents 74-64.

UNLV had even less difficulty subduing Boise State. Eddie Owens led a balanced attack with 24 points as the Rebels took 32 more shots, grabbed 23 more rebounds and scooted to a 103-78 victory.

Regional competition now moved to Pauley Pavilion in Los Angeles, an overwhelming advantage for UCLA who had accumulated an unprecedented 166-3 record on their home court over the past 11 years. The Bruins disposed of Pepperdine 70-61 as Greenwood and Drollinger held Leite in check.

The other contest was a wild and woolly shootout between two teams from sagebrush and cactus country, which the referees were barely able to control. A total of 63 fouls was whistled and four UNLV Rebels and three Arizona Wildcats fouled out. Jackie Robinson, UNLV's top rebounder against Boise State, hardly worked up a sweat before being disqualified, contributing just two points. Only one Rebel starter was left at the end of the game and he had four personals. There were allegations that the NCAA, who selected the referees, was making sure that a team coached by Tarkanian would never become a national champion. True or paranoia, the Rebels invariably picked up a lot of fouls (31 against Boise State) which could be attributed to their frenetic style rather than to any conspiracy.

Arizona led 51-47 at the intermission but UNLV pounded back. Outrebounded by a substantial margin because of foul induced attrition, the Rebels forced turnovers and hung tough, shooting like a string of Chinese firecrackers popping off in all directions. Only guard Herm "The Germ" Harris, who scored 15 of Arizona's last 27 points, and Jim Rappis, who eventually fouled out, kept the Wildcats in the game. Harris' free throw with 14 seconds left tied the score 103-103. Each of Arizona's 11 overtime points came from the line as Harris with four led a procession launched by the referee's repeated whistles. Despite three Rebels who scored more than 20 points, Arizona's 46 trips to the line were too much to overcome and they advanced to the regional final 114-109.

The Wildcats proved to be a stubborn foe in the regional final, though they sorely missed Rappis, their excellent playmaker who played sparingly on a sore heel. The Germ was once again the primary long-range threat as the Wildcats clawed their way back into a tie with UCLA at 11:45 of the second half. Bartow then signalled a time out and moved his men into a 2-1-2 zone, something unheard of under Wooden. The tactic worked. It disoriented Arizona enough to make them commit several turnovers, allowing UCLA to put together an old fashioned Bruin blast. The 12 unanswered points drove the Pauley patrons crazy. It was the beginning of the end as Arizona never threatened again. UCLA eventually triumphed 82-66, taking their twelfth regional championship in as many tries over the previous 13 years.

Final Four:

This was the year of the Bicentennial celebration and the NCAA had awarded the championship rounds to Philadelphia's Spectrum, just a long set shot from the Liberty Bell and Independence Hall. The tournament had achieved new heights of popularity. Television had annually showcased the spectacle and in the past three years the finals had become the highest rated basketball show on the tube, outdistancing the professional championship series in the ratings. Now in 1976 fans could watch two undefeated teams, the defending champion and an exciting dark horse reach for the top prize.

Rutgers, showing the strain of maintaining the longest winning streak in the country and playing in their first national semifinal, started poorly against Michigan and got progressively worse. By the end of the first 20 minutes the Wolverines had surged in front 46-29. Rutgers was misfiring at a 27.5 percent pace to that point and their All American Sellers, who had not enjoyed a single good game in the tournament to date, was floundering, shooting a frigid one for seven. He was being outplayed by Wayman Britt who was not considered in Sellers' class.

The second period saw no relief for the Knights from New Jersey. Not only were they outscored but outrebounded and outhustled, too. Michigan extended its lead to 23 points. The further behind Rutgers fell, the more disorganized they became. Each player felt he could turn the game around by himself and team cohesion evaporated. They missed uncontested shots, hurried their passes and ran around aimlessly. A livid coach did not help much. After Michigan's 86-70 knockout, Young blasted his players in the locker room. "We stunk the place out. To me it's a shame for Rutgers, a shame for Eastern basketball." The real shame was that Young should have been so intemperate as to chastise his players publicly after they had won 31 straight games and had come within two wins of an undefeated, championship season.

The focus of attention was now on Indiana and UCLA. After their humiliating defeat in St. Louis, the Bruins had improved considerably and were given an excellent chance to upset the Hoosiers.

Bobby Knight assigned Benson to guard Washington, but the Indiana center collected two personals in the first couple of minutes while Washington pumped in five points. Knight quickly switched Tom Abernethy to Washington. The effect was instant. Washington's output was shut off and he did not score for the next 25 minutes.

Using their strength to control the boards and dropping their iron curtain defense, the Hoosiers limited UCLA to 26 points in the first half. They outplayed the Bruins at every position but most glaringly at the guards. McCarter, who graduated from Philadelphia's Overbrook High School, had been looking forward to leading his team to victory before relatives and friends ever since the Final Four had been scheduled for Philadelphia several years ago. This was his senior year and he wanted to go out in glory. But his dream turned into a nightmare. While guard Bobby Wilkerson was hauling down an incredible 19 rebounds and Buckner was scoring 12 points, their counterparts in the UCLA backcourt were shooting a combined 4 for 19 while contributing just four points each. The ineffectiveness of the guards allowed the Hoosiers to fall back and clog the middle, putting additional pressure on UCLA's front line. Late in the first half Indiana struck for 15 points in five and a half minutes while UCLA floundered trying to mount an attack. Indiana's defense was almost impenetrable in the middle and their fluid offense was equally a testimony to brilliant coaching as they set screens, ran off picks and moved the ball well. For the first time that year Knight used just six players, sticking with his starters almost exclusively, very much the way Wooden had done in the 1975 final.

After shooting only 30 percent in the first half, the Bruins were due for an improvement. However, they were shut out in the first three minutes after intermission and continued hitting dry spells throughout the game. For the second time that season Indiana dominated UCLA, though the 65-51 final score was more respectable.

For the first time in the history of the tournament two schools from the same conference faced each other for the national title. Indiana and Michigan had played twice before that season and the Hoosiers won both. It seemed unfair to ask a team to face them for a third time. The fact that the Wolverines were the underdogs, reinforced by the difference in the personalities of the coaches, made them the sentimental choice. Had the title been decided on the basis of popularity, Orr's Wolverines would have won by acclamation.

It was an extremely physical contest. About two and a half minutes into the game Britt streaked downcourt pursued by Wilkerson. Britt went up for a layup a split second before the man guarding him. As he came down, he caught Wilkerson with his elbow on the chin and sent him sprawling. He lay there unconscious and was removed on a stretcher. Though obviously accidental, the contact was typical of the intensity of the game.

Indiana supporters were shocked when Wilkerson was felled. They remembered another key injury, to May the previous year, which may have cost the Hoosiers a title. Was fate about to toss Indiana another curve? After some experimentation Knight inserted Jim Wisman, the same player whom he had dragged off the court in an earlier game against Michigan. Though Wisman played well, it was Benson, May and Buckner who preempted the scoring. They accounted for 36 of Indiana's first 38 points. Still, it took Indiana some time to regroup and they left the court at the midway mark trailing by six. Michigan, hitting 61 percent of their shots, was peaking at the right time.

A grim Knight faced his players in the locker room and told them, "You've got to try harder." He doubted that Michigan could maintain their hot shooting and demanded even more defensive pressure from his players.

The fired-up Hoosiers came out roaring for the second half, like a torrent escaping a mountain gorge. They scattered Michigan like so much debris. The game began to resemble a battle zone. The fiercest combat was under the basket where senior Benson and freshman Hubbard tangled in a slam bang confrontation. Benson, who outweighed Hubbard by fifty pounds, won that battle and caused his less experienced opponent to foul out. In the final 20 minutes Indiana outscored Michigan 57-33 and claimed the crown easily 86-68. As the last seconds became history, Knight took his starters out one at a time to a series of standing ovations. May had scored 26 to lead the way and Benson had 25 as well as earning the MVP award. A triumphant Knight had found and claimed his Holy Grail. He was also the first man to have played on and coached a national championship basketball team.

1977

Al McGuire had always been a favorite with the press and the sportscasters of the electronic media. Aside from his intelligence and broad understanding of the sport, he was undoubtedly the most quotable man on or off the court. The New York Times once printed a selection of his choicest blurbs: "Winning is only important in war and surgery." "If you haven't broken your nose in basketball, you've only tokened it." "I don't know if I coach, I think I'm like the master of ceremonies. I create a party on the court and keep it going." The last was blatantly untrue. There was never any doubt that McGuire was always in total control, if not over himself then over his players and the game.

Raised in an Irish neighborhood in the borough of Queens, New York City, the scrappy street fighter learned how to fend for himself at an early age. Younger brother to Dick McGuire who had more basketball talent than Al, he had to fight for the recognition he felt he deserved. He learned a lot in the tavern his mother owned and operated—about people, confrontations, the street lore of communicating. A couple of years scrapping in professional ball (he once picked up eight fouls in one game—six personals and two technicals), followed by an assistant coaching position at Dartmouth and the head coaching job at Belmont Abbey, prepared McGuire for Marquette.

His first year was a losing one but it was followed by 12 winning seasons, including 11 consecutive years in which his Warriors posted more than 20 wins and six of seven consecutive years in which they recorded at least 25 victories. Eight NCAA tournaments, a NIT crown and a NIT runner-up spot were McGuire's credentials over the ten years preceding 1977.

McGuire built success by implementing the most consistent defense in the country. "Every coach coaches the way he played. I couldn't shoot, so I coach defense." McGuire had an almost uncanny way of relating to black players from city ghettos, though he spent little time recruiting. "I can't recruit a kid who has a front lawn. Give me a tenement and a sidewalk." He claimed he never watched a player whom he was interested in recruiting. His staff would make recommendations and then he would visit the prospect—once, just once, and he would not beg. When Butch Lee asked McGuire why he wanted him to come to Marquette since the coach had never seen him play, he answered, "Everyone knows you're the best guard in the Big Apple."

Though a tough disciplinarian on the court, he allowed his players almost complete freedom when the game was over. While other coaches imposed strict dress codes McGuire accomplished his objective "with flowers and beads and dignity." Dignity was not in evidence, though, when the players decided one year to pose for their team photograph in some flamboyant medieval costumes borrowed from a theatrical group. "The team should be an extension of a coach's personality. My team is arrogant and obnoxious." This was only partially true. In any case, it was only correct of the Warriors' off-court behavior. Once the game was underway the Warriors responded by playing the kind of disciplined ball that would have made a Wooden or a Knight envious. They played unselfishly as a team, passing to the open man, helping out at both ends of the court, executing the patterns their coach outlined in practice. Marquette never produced a high scorer under McGuire, yet many entered and remained in the professional ranks when others with superior statistics failed. "The most important thing in sports is that you play up to your capability."

Standing at courtside during practice McGuire would yell at his men (he claimed he never used a whistle) and they would just as often yell right back. The coach would drill the Warriors to play his style and he would not vary his strategy, regardless of the opponent. "You should never change anything once the season starts. Don't change the lineup or the system." He made adjustments in tactics during the game as the score, the home court, the time remaining and the severity of the referee's whistle dictated, but basically he expected his opponent to adjust to Marquette's style. And he always made his moves decisively and with confidence. "If you have indecision your players will act accordingly. It doesn't matter if you are on national TV with millions watching or in a small town gym with 200 watching; you do the same thing."

McGuire composed his team as rigidly as a Kabuki casting director. He recruited one blue chip player a year and rarely did a man in his sights escape. Brian Winters and Jim McMillian were the only two stars he wanted who did not enroll at Marquette. However, McGuire consoled himself by signing Maurice Lucas in place of Winters (whom he lost to Frank McGuire, Al's former coach). Aside from the blue chipper, McGuire acquired two or three "complimentary" (as he called them) players, a junior college transfer and transfer from a four year college. He also red shirted one of his players to maintain continuity. Using this system McGuire was able to avoid the trauma of losing several starters in the same year via graduation. Instead he spread talent over time and ended with teams that rarely dropped out of the top ten.

The blue chip player was guaranteed a showcase role in his senior year. It did not always work out that way. Some dropped out before graduation to turn professional and in 1977 Lee, a junior but a natural leader, stole much of the limelight from senior-star-in-residence, Bo Ellis, after a spectacular performance at the Olympic Games in Montreal.

McGuire was also an innovator without peer. At least he proposed ideas that seemed ahead of their time. After John Wooden retired he suggested that the ex-UCLA coach be appointed commissioner for all college basketball. He also urged the NBA to postpone their college draft until after the Olympics to allow senior stars to compete in the Games. Another suggested innovation which may still be adopted dealt with limiting the **total** height of players on the court at any time to 33 feet.

One idea McGuire was able to implement himself was designing a new Warrior uniform every year. He felt that brighter, more colorful, uninhibited uniforms would add even more interest and excitement to an already charged sport. He even changed the school colors to an electric blue and gold. Things were never dull at Marquette with Al around.*

Midwest:

The 1977 Marquette team was one of McGuire's weaker squads. They never really caught fire during a demanding season that included nine confrontations with schools that had been in the previous year's tourney. In December Al McGuire, aged 48, announced that after the current season he would quit Marquette and retire from coaching. If he thought this would spark the team he must have been disappointed. The Warriors dropped their next two games—at home. In all they lost five contests in an arena where in a previous season a single blot had been a catastrophic event. On closer scrutiny, the Warriors' 20-7 record was not as disappointing as it looked on the surface. They were nipped three times by one point, twice more by small margins, and three defeats had come against teams that would go to the 1977 tournament.

Maybe their finest game came against number one ranked Michigan at Ann Arbor in the final game of the season. By this time McGuire was wearing his lucky blue blazer to every game, hoping it would bring him an invitation to his last national tournament. At half time the long awaited invitation arrived and McGuire took off his blazer. His team came back on the court and blew the game to the Wolverines—but by only a point. Though he did not know it at the time, it was to be the last loss of McGuire's career—only his fiftieth in the last eleven years. However it was Marquette's seventh defeat of that year and no team had ever won a national championship with that many.

The invitation was to the Midwest regional, the one McGuire had spurned in 1969 when, in anger, he had taken his team to New York and the NIT. The NCAA had changed the tournament regulations since then to make it impossible for a coach to pull his team out of the competition. Such a thought never crossed McGuire's mind. He was delighted to play in the tournament. Any regional would do, though he must have noted that the Midwest was the weakest of the four.

---

*Despite his tendency to be the center of attraction, McGuire was the only coach among the first forty national championship teams not posing with his men for the official team photograph. It was his way of saying "The glory belongs to you."

Eighth ranked Arkansas (26-1) was the only school in the Midwest regional that had made it to the top ten—the first time in many years for a team from the SWC. Their only loss was to Memphis State. Consistency and accuracy were the prime characteristics of the Razorbacks.* Consistency is not a statistic compiled by the NCAA but field goal percentage is, and Arkansas had the best in the country. Not surprising considering Sidney Moncrief made 65 percent of his shots (slightly lower than the 67 percent he hit as a freshman) and Ron Brewer 61 percent. The third member of the trio of stars, known as the Triplets, was Marvin Delph who sank a mere 55 percent of his shots. The three were almost as similar as real triplets—all were 6′4″, black and native sons of Arkansas. (Coach Eddie Sutton was committed to recruiting within a 500 mile radius of the school's campus.)

Arkansas' one exploitable weakness was their vulnerability to the press. It was what kept them from an undefeated season. Ahead at the half against Memphis State, they subsequently folded when the Tigers hounded them all over the court. Arkansas overcame all other opponents and beat Houston in the conference playoff final, thus ensuring that the State of Texas would be unrepresented in the tourney for the first time in 20 years.

Kansas State (22-7) won the Big Eight and the conference playoff final over Missouri in overtime, after the latter blew a 17 point lead. Southern Illinois (21-6) tied with New Mexico State in the MVC but won the postseason playoff, thus assuring themselves of their first NCAA tournament appearance. The MVC with an uneven number of schools (the number varied from year to year as universities checked in and out like transients at a hotel) had concocted one of the most complicated playoff structures ever devised. The last four teams played each other, the winners played the second and third place teams in a semifinal round, and then the winners played each other for the right to challenge the conference leader.

Leading the Salukis was Mike Glenn, a true scholar-athlete. He had been president of his high school class and maintained a 3.5 average in college as a mathematics major. He passed up the 1976 Olympics to remain in summer school. Glenn was an extremely unselfish player who could undoubtedly have been one of the top ten scorers in the country if he had shot more often or from closer range. Considered by some as the best long range bombardier in college, his 61 percent average becomes even more amazing, given the distance the ball had to travel to its target.

The Metro Six had become the Metro Seven with the addition of Florida State. Louisville had the best conference record but Cincinnati (25-4) won the playoff. Coach Gale Catlett's modern, with-it personality was reflected in his splashy wardrobe—somewhat surprising for a man who had been an assistant to Adolph Rupp in his brown suit. An extrovert in other ways, too,

---

*On defense they had one five game string in which they allowed 60, 63, 65, 66 and 69 points and another when they gave up 58, 58, 59, 59 and 58 points. On offense a six game string produced scores of 81, 82, 76, 77, 78 and 79.

Catlett enjoyed talking—to the media, the fans, the players, anybody. He was a man who enlivened any group he joined and quickly became its center of attraction.

His was a success story. After several years as an independent, and not a particularly successful one at that, Cincinnati joined the Metro Six. Over the previous five years his team had averaged almost 22 wins and Bearcat fans were recalling the glory days of the early sixties. Much of that success was due to the team's invincibility at home, where it had not lost in four years through 1977.*

Two conference runners-up competed in the regional. Arizona (21-5) won their season opener over Arizona State on a last second shot, then turned to easier competition and executed their next two opponents by 55 and 60 points. Fred Snowden was one of the few black basketball coaches at a major university. He had come west from the University of Michigan where he had been an assistant and successful recruiter.

Wake Forest (20-7) lost their last four and five of their last seven, including a heartbreaker to last place Virginia in the opening round of the ACC playoff. None of their defeats were by more than six points and three of their last four were by a field goal or less.

Providence (24-4) pinned the first loss of the season on Michigan, rated number one at the time, in double overtime. Later the Friars were ambushed by Purdue, Louisville and Holy Cross. Then in the ECAC final, after surviving a 44-31 freezeout by Fairfield, they fell to Holy Cross for the second time.

Before more than ten thousand fans in the first postseason game to be played in Norman, Oklahoma, Arkansas established a comfortable 46-33 lead over Wake Forest. For the first 20 minutes the Deacons could not keep up with the faster and deadlier Razorbacks. Then, in the locker room, somebody must have remembered the Memphis State game because Wake Forest came out in the second half and set up a harrying press that compared favorably with a subway rush hour experience. Arkansas became flustered, lost their cohesion and more than that, lost the game 86-80. In effect the fans watched two separate contests, the second of which was won by Wake Forest 53-34. Rod Griffin's 26 points paced the winners while Jerry Schellenberg played an indispensible role. It is hard to accept defeat when one has shot 68 percent as Arkansas had; Moncrief, Brewer and Steve Schall potted an amazing 21 of 26 shots among them, but it still added up to Arkansas' second and last defeat of the season.

Kansas State also overcame a second half deficit to triumph over Providence. (This pattern of come-from-behind victories was established early

*There were some schools which played before such vocal, rabid fans that just the decibel level was worth at least ten points to the home team. Notre Dame, Cincinnati, Louisville and UCLA were four notorious sites where the audience was often balanced on the thin edge between bare control and spontaneous hysteria.

and continued through the finals, giving the fans an emotioal forty minute rollercoaster ride.) The lead changed 18 times and the score was even on nine other occasions before Kansas State posted an 87-80 victory. Curtis Redding, who scored 32 points, and Scott Langton were instrumental in the decision. Both fired from long range and found their target often. Joe Hassett, almost as deadly for the losers, had 26 points. Surprisingly, the Wildcats were able to pull down 50 percent more rebounds than Providence despite lacking a starter taller than 6′5″.

Meanwhile Marquette also came back in the final period after trailing Cincinnati at the half. Bob Miller with almost half his team's point production sparked the attack for the Bearcats. But McGuire was not about to fade out before a small gathering in Omaha. With Cincinnati on top 41-40, Jerome Whitehead and Bo Ellis went to work and combined for eleven points in a 13 point Warrior coup. McGuire's men activated their doomsday defense which shut off Cincinnati, allowing them only 20 points in the second half. The Bearcats managed just three field goals in the last six minutes and Marquette postponed their coach's departure by at least a week, winning 66-51.

Southern Illinois had their supporters worried late in the game after they blew an 11 point lead against Arizona. Herm Harris' basket tied the score 77-77 with two minutes to go but Southern Illinois' strategy to hold the ball for a last shot payed off when Gary Wilson's turnaround jumper found its way home with only three tics left. Mike Glenn then added a pair of free throws after the buzzer to make the final score 81-77. They were Glenn's thirty-fourth and thirty-fifth points.

The pattern established in the first round continued. Wake Forest, after being down at the midway mark to Southern Illinois, entered the last three minutes nursing a one point lead. The Deacons retreated into a shell and refused to put the ball up. Forced into taking a calculated risk, the Salukis gambled that their opponents would start missing from the line. The Deacons, though, continued to be deadly, netting 26 of 30 (including seven by Skip Brown late in the contest). Brown with 25 points, and Griffin and Schellenberg with 22 each, led the Wake Forest assault which rolled over Southern Illinois 86-81. The Salukis, who dominated the boards, the shooting and everything except the free throw line, had only Glenn's 30 points, a result of deadly long range firing, to cheer them.

Down by eight at the break, Marquette slipped even further behind Kansas State when the teams resumed hostilities. At one point McGuire went into his act, raised his hand to his throat and was slapped with a technical. But Oklahoma City did not seem an appropriate place to end McGuire's career either, so his players bore down to extend their coach's career one more game. As the second half matured the Warriors began to gain momentum with Butch Lee cementing the attack with 26 points. They were aided, too, when Larry Dassie, the Wildcats' leading scorer, ran into foul trouble. Kansas State's bench, which had contributed just two points in the first two rounds, had no adequate reserve for the task. A 15 foot jumper by Lee was the equalizer. Still, the Wildcats clawed their way into the lead again. It was time for Butch to take charge one more time. Seconds from oblivion, the mercurial guard drove in for the layup that gave Marquette a 67-66 victory.

Two days later, for the third time in as many games, Marquette trooped off the floor after 20 minutes at the light end of the score. Worse was to come. With 16 minutes left Whitehead, the Warriors' center, picked up his fourth personal and was replaced by Bernard Toone. The big man had been virtually invisible in the last two games, scoring just four points on abysmal 2-for-14 shooting.

Luckily for the Warriors, Wake Forest was not a good rebounding team. Toone immediately provided the spark that ignited the Warriors. He scored six straight points to give his team a lead they never relinquished. McGuire unveiled another defensive tactic in the second half—the triangle and two. Jim Boylan and Lee played man-to-man on Brown and Schellenberg, the Deacons' best scorers, while the other three set up in a triangular zone. It was extremely effective and Marquette pulled away to win 82-68. The Warriors had postponed McGuire's retirement once more and the team was off to Atlanta for a date with destiny.

East:

Fourth ranked North Carolina and sixth ranked Kentucky were the teams to beat in the East regional. The Tarheels (24-4) fell four times to ACC rivals—two one-point ledgehangers against Wake Forest, a two-pointer against North Carolina State and a 20 point knockout by Clemson, whom they had earlier stomped 91-63. (At the time Clemson had a 9-1 record and had beaten their opponents by an average of 35 points.) The ACC was still the toughest conference from top to bottom in the country. Only last place Virginia had a losing record overall and only they had lost more than twice outside the ACC.

North Carolina was flying high as the season closed, with 11 straight wins capped by two in the ACC playoff. The ACC final was a struggle. Virginia had fallen back to the basement but almost repeated their 1976 playoff upset. They were leading the Tarheels by eight points with eight minutes to go before suffering terminal collapse and losing the tournament bid. North Carolina was confident. They had lost only one starter from their superb team of a year ago, Mitch Kupchak. But Smith had moved LaGarde over to center and installed Mike O'Koren in his place. When healthy, the team was almost as strong as last year's edition. Unfortunately, at the time of the tournament LaGarde was on crutches and Walter Davis was recovering from a broken finger.

Smith had spent the previous summer as coach of the U.S. Olympic team, which included three of his players—Davis, LaGarde and Phil Ford—and had a gold medal to show for it. Actually several of the Tarheels sounded as if they had been recruited at the United Nations, if not the Olympics. Beside

O'Koren and LaGarde they included Rich Yonakor, Daves Colescott, Steve Krafcisin and Tom Zaliagiris, a melting pot that did not endear the Tarheels to the typesetters across the country.

The gold medal was just one more in a long list of honors Smith had won since graduating from Kansas where he had been a deep sub on Phog Allen's 1952 championship team. It included seven ACC conference crowns, six ACC playoff championships, four East regional titles, three NIT appearances, ten 20-game seasons, eight top ten year-end rankings and eleven straight postseason tourney appearances.

Although Smith's coaching philosophy was team oriented he had also developed nine All Americans including the current incumbent, Phil Ford, who conducted the famous four corners offense. Ford once scored 48 points in one half of a high school game and kept his considerable skills sharp by spending up to 12 hours a day on the basketball court. The rest of the team was not that dedicated. However, Smith's unique style of shuttling his players in and out, faster than a hustler promoting a shell game, ensured that everyone got some share of playing time and distributed the play load.

Smith was also the inventor of the four corners, a delay offense featuring a lot of passing and a little dribbling and trying to sucker the opposition into committing a mistake. The four corners was used mostly in the late stages of a game when the Tarheels had established a lead they wanted to protect down the stretch.

On December 11, 1976 Kentucky dedicated its brand new 23,000 seat Adolph Rupp Arena, the country's largest college basketball stadium and double the capacity of their old facility. The occasion was a game between the Wildcats and Kansas, Rupp's alma mater, matching the two winningest schools in college basketball history. The Baron who was sick and would be dead less than a year later was eulogized before the game and weakly acknowledged the cheers of the thousands of Wildcat fans gathered to honor him.

A lot was expected from Kentucky (24-3). Though they beat Kansas in the dedication game of the new Adolph Rupp Arena, they lost rather embarrassingly to Utah a few days later in their own invitational tournament. Joe Hall's suspension of Mike Phillips for a curfew violation may have been a contributing factor.

The Wildcats had won the NIT the previous year in their first trip to Madison Square Garden in 25 years. They were as aggressive, as tough, as dominant as they had been in upsetting Indiana two years before. To prove it they had clipped the Hoosiers' 35 game home and 56 game regular season string early in December. They followed that up by dismembering TCU 103-53. Their three losses—two of them to Tennessee—came by a total of eight points. Unfortunately, the Tennessee decisions, narrow though they were, cost the Wildcats the SEC crown and a spot in the Mideast regional.

Another conference runner up was Purdue (19-8) which finished third in the Big Ten. Second place Minnesota was on probation and thus ineligible.

Notre Dame (21-6) as usual played an uneven schedule against some of the toughest as well as some of the least formidable opponents around. They were stopped by Kentucky, Princeton, Marquette and UCLA, all tournament bound. But they also beat UCLA, in Pauley no less. In midseason the Irish went on a disastrous road trip losing five of six. A victory over Stonehill was sandwiched between defeats by Marquette and UCLA. But the Irish recovered and sped to 13 wins in their last 14 games, climaxed by a surprising 93-82 decision over top ranked San Francisco, undefeated in 29 games at the time.

The Irish had planned on putting a stronger squad on the court but Bill Laimbeer, their center, was declared ineligible and their All American, Dantley, defected to the pros, not the first time a star had given up another year of eligibility at South Bend.

Princeton (21-4) won their second Ivy title in a row. They also repeated as the stingiest team in the country, yielding an average of 51 points or eight fewer than runner-up Marquette. Princeton passed the ball so much the fans almost dozed off between shots. After scoring an atypical bucketful in an opening 95-48 drubbing of Colgate, Princeton returned to form and corked Navy 52-36. Three weeks later they captured the Kodak Classic, then celebrated the new year by upsetting second ranked Notre Dame by 14 points.

Organized in 1977 the Eastern Collegiate Basketball League, or Eastern Eight, was the country's newest conference. It was composed of eight former independents—Duquesne, George Washington, Massachusetts, Penn State, Pittsburgh, Rutgers, Villanova and West Virginia—all of whom had previously played in the tournament.

Duquesne (15-14) was an unlikely tourney participant. Their longest winning streak had been a modest three games. They had finished near the bottom of the standings with more defeats than victories. Still, it could have been worse; half their wins were by six points or fewer. Duquesne's condition before the Eastern Eight playoffs was much like a boat whose pumps were barely keeping ahead of the rising water. Given a second chance, they overcame Penn State, Massachusetts and Villanova (all of whom had beaten the Dukes during the regular season) in the league playoff to qualify for the tourney.

VMI (25-3) reeled off 19 consecutive wins, then beat Appalachian State in the Southern Conference playoff final. Hofstra (23-6) completed the field.

In first round action Princeton, outclassed by a taller, sturdier team, trailed Kentucky by just seven points at intermission. But their hopes were shattered when the Wildcats pumped in nine baskets in their first ten attempts to open the second half, on their way to a 72-58 rout. Kentucky netted 58 percent of their shots against the best defense in the country. Princeton, after shooting an anemic 28 percent in the first half, recovered their touch but were outmuscled off the boards where their leading rebounder grabbed just four ricochets.

Kentucky-Princeton was a skirmish compared to the full scale war that erupted between Hofstra and Notre Dame. The Irish were a physical team and punished Hofstra under the hoop. Control of the boards was at stake between the number one rebounding team and Hofstra's John Irving, the country's leading individual rebounder. The battle between Toby Knight of the Irish and Irving was a standoff as each grabbed a dozen boards. Each was also handed a technical foul as elbows dug into ribs, arms windmilled carelessly and shoulders rammed into unyielding flesh.

It was Notre Dame's guards who tilted the balance of power, especially on defense. Early in the second half the Irish opened a 17 point gap as Don "Duck" Williams poured it on to lead the offense with 25 points. They coasted the rest of the way to win 90-83. Rich Laurel's 35 points was wasted in a losing cause.

North Carolina struggled to a 69-66 victory over Purdue before a capacity turnout. Tom Zaliagiris scored the winner with 1:17 remaining and when Purdue subsequently turned the ball over, the Tarheels went into their four corners delay to perserve their advantage. Neither Davis nor LaGarde was in uniform but Ford invested 27 points in the Tarheel total.

Duquesne committed twice as many fouls as VMI and paid the price as three of their starters fouled out, including their sparkplug, Norm Nixon, with 27 points. VMI, with four times as many opportunities from the line, slipped past Duquesne 73-66.

In the regional semifinal Truman Claytor, a 5.8-point-a-game reserve, emerged from a phone booth to perform his Superman act by arcing 13 of 15 shots into the basket for Kentucky. But VMI proved to be a stubborn victim. With Kentucky ahead 14-4 and threatening to break things open early, the Keydets spun 12 unanswered points through the hoop. They were still ahead by five midway through the first period. Even when the Wildcats forged in front again, just before the break, VMI refused to die. Their range-finding outside shots kept them in the game and they tracked the Wildcats until they pulled even at 49. Then the roof fell in and despite Ron Carter's 28 points, Kentucky strung out a 93-78 decision. Claytor's performance gave him 29 points and a phenomenal 84 percent field goal average for the first two rounds.

The Irish were hoping some of the little people would help their big men bury the Tarheels this St. Patrick's Day. Indeed it seemed as if some leprechauns were sitting on the Notre Dame bench in the first half as they took a ten point lead into the locker room. Smith, constantly juggling his lineup, shunted 11 men in and out in the first 11 minutes. On the other side of the scorer's table Phelps was content to use just one sub. The Irish were shooting as if the hoop was barrel wide and twice primed 12-2 outbursts.

The Tarheels had developed a reputation as a second half team. Sure enough, less than five minutes after the second half tipoff they pulled even. A minute later Kuester's deep jumper put North Carolina ahead for the first time since the opening seconds. The sleepy leprechauns apparently woke in time to get busy with their magic again because Notre Dame streaked for the third time, dropping ten unanswered points into the basket. Ford, who finished with 29 points, then took charge and scored 15 of his side's last 23 points. Slowly slicing at their disadvantage, the Tarheels pulled to within four when Notre Dame went to their delay formation, a variant of the four corners. But turnovers by Rich Branning and Williams allowed North Carolina to even matters at 75 with 56 seconds to go. Reclaiming the ball once more, Ford was fouled and calmly sank both offers. A jump shot by Williams made it a new ball game. It was North Carolina's turn to go into a delay. Since Ford had the hot hand it was decided he should take the last shot. As the final seconds ticked away Ford aimed for the hoop, missed, but was fouled. With just two seconds remaining he converted both free throws —giving him a perfect 16 for 16 from the line in the first two tourney games and the Tarheels a 79-77 victory. The leprechauns were fast asleep by then. The Irish lost, despite torrid 67 percent shooting, when the fresher Tarheels took 25 more shots from the floor.

The two best teams in the regional faced each other on the following Saturday. For once the Tarheels were ahead at the half, leading Kentucky 53-41. Davis was back in the lineup and doing wonderful things for the Tarheels, his broken finger almost healed. They needed him because Ford was suffering through an atypically poor game. He picked up three personals while collecting just two points. Still, with the sick list down to just LaGarde it looked as if the Tarheels were about to break away. The fickle finger of fate, however, was not about to let North Carolina off the hook so easily. With 52 seconds gone in the second half Ford charged into Larry Johnson and was handed his fourth personal. Worse, he dropped to the hardwood writhing in paid and holding his reinjured elbow. Ford was finished for the game and Kuester came in to take his place. The Wildcats immediately took advantage of the situation and closed to within six. Alarmed, Smith moved the Tarheels into the four corners although there were still 15 minutes left in the game. The results were astounding. Three times the Tarheels found a man open for easy layins. The Wildcats decided to try another tactic. They fouled before North Carolina could set someone up for a shot. But this did not work either as the Tarheels made their last 14 points from the line, 12 of them in one-and-one situations. Kuester was the most deadly, hitting 13 of 14 while directing the offense. But it was Steve Krafcisin who plugged the game winner. With 36 seconds to go and North Carolina hanging on by a point, he approached the line for a pair. Kuester walked over to encourage him, "You can do it. You have the best follow through on the team." He did it, too, confidently making both. North Carolina expanded their lead to win 79-72. Once again the combination of an ACC conference and playoff crown had led to a regional title.

Smith's decision to go to the four corners so early was vindicated, because his team's foul shooting was absolutely phenomenal. In the second half they made 16 points from the line without missing once. They made 33 of 36 for the game and missed only 5 of 55 charity throws during the two games at College Park. For Kentucky, Jack Givens had his second straight 26 point game in a losing cause.

Mideast:

After its national runner-up season in 1976 Michigan had been ranked number one in preseason polls, a judgement that seemed well justified when they won their first five games by an average of 29 points. But the Wolverines did not live up to expectations and eventually dropped out of first place. At the end of the season they were number one again, primarily because San Francisco relinquished that spot after losing their final game. Michigan's 24-3 record was not as good as some other schools' but their tough schedule, especially in the Big Ten, gave them the benefit of any doubt. Losses to Indiana, Northwestern and in double overtime to Providence were the only blemishes on their record. With a first team All American, Rickey Green, at guard and a second team All American, Phil Hubbard, at center, Michigan had the kind of talent balance that could propel them to a national championship.

Another team with two All Americans was Tennessee (22-5) with the Bernie and Ernie Show back for another season on the boards. Both finished among the top 25 in point production. Twice the Volunteers tripped Kentucky, making it five times in a row they had caged the Wildcats.

The atmosphere in Knoxville was far from sublime though. Before the season curtain raiser King had jeopardized the star system at Tennessee by getting arrested three times for possession of marijuana, and drunk and reckless driving. It was enough to send Coach Mears to the hospital suffering from nervous exhaustion. King was suspended which had the effect of braking some of the cockiness on the team and making them bear down harder. When he was eventually reinstated, Tennessee lost two of their next three!

Tenth ranked Syracuse (25-3) barely squeezed by Old Dominion in the ECAC playoff to qualify for the tournament. Holy Cross (23-5) was another displaced eastern team in the Mideast regional. The Crusaders may have had the top freshman in the country in Ronnie Perry, son of the school's athletic director. The younger Perry, besides being a 90 percent free throw shooter, set a Massachusetts high school record for most career points. He also starred on his school's baseball and football teams but it was the indoor sport that claimed most of his attention. Perry's poise on the court was mentioned frequently, a result of the countless hours of coaching by his father.

Two other Michigan schools and another from Tennessee qualified for the regional. Central Michigan (18-9) tied with Miami of Ohio for the Mid American Conference crown but the Chippewas received the invitation because they had beaten the co-champion twice during the campaign. Detroit (24-3) received its first invitation since the days of Dave DeBusschere. After dropping their second game (to Minnesota by 24 points) the Titans fired off 21 wins before being shot down by a mediocre Duquesne squad. A powder puff schedule enabled Detroit to surpass 100 points eight times and post several victories by more than 40 and 50 points. The presence of 6′7″ guard Terry Tyler, who could jump, helped spring the fast break. The Titans' playing style reflected the personality of their coach, Dick Vitale, a dynamic, super-energetic cheerleader who vowed to "revitalize" the team.

Emerging victorious from the Ohio Valley playoff was runner up Middle Tennessee (20-8). Despite two losses to Austin Peay, the conferennce champs, the Blue Raiders turned the tables in the playoff final.

The only school making its tourney debut was University of North Carolina-Charlotte (25-3). Their schedule was even more minor league than Detroit's. Two victories over Baptist College—one by 49 points, the other by 33—improved their record, though it did less to enhance their stature than two point losses to Tennessee and Wake Forest.

The Forty Niners had come out of oblivion a year earlier to beat prestigious North Carolina State in the NIT semifinals at Madison Square Garden, and then almost upset Kentucky for the top prize before falling four points short. Sharpshooter Cedric "Cornbread" Maxwell had been named the NIT's MVP after swamping the nets and swishing 47 for 53 from the free throw line. During the current season Maxwell had sunk 64 percent of his floor shots.

UNCC was an offense minded team. Run, pass, shoot. Again and again. Twice in the seventies the school had fielded the top offensive team in the nation though the 1977 edition were only ninth in that category.

Four of the ten highest scoring teams appeared in the regional. (The Mideast had traditionally been the top point production quadrant of the tourney.) Detroit repeatedly accelerated downcourt like a quintet of drag racers on their way to the checkered flag in what turned out to be a 93-76 win over Middle Tennessee. Tyler claimed 15 boards and hurt the Raiders with 29 points.

An exciting match between Tennessee and Syracuse kept the fans on the edge of their seats from tipoff to final buzzer. An extraordinary number of fouls were committed considering both teams used zone defenses. King fouled out, as did 6′11″ Roosevelt Bouie and 6′8″ Louis Orr of the Orangemen. The latter, both freshmen, had been counted on to give their team some inside punch, but it was the guards who propelled Syracuse to a seven point lead with four and a half minutes to play. Larry Kelley and James Williams stayed out of foul trouble and their high trajectory winners over the zone were an important factor in Syracuse's 66 percent shooting in the second half. Tennessee sprinted down the stretch to tie the score at 78 on two free throws by Reggie Johnson with 24 seconds left.

In the overtime Syracuse pulled away quickly on medium range jumpers by Kelley, Ross Kindel and Bill Drew. Grunfeld's exit via fouls ended the Volunteers' hope for their first NCAA tournament victory. With their 93-88 win Syracuse became the only Northeast team to survive the first round.

Michigan may have underestimated Holy Cross before their first round contest. As the first half wound down Johnny Orr, his team up by seven points, decided to rest Rickey Green. As if on cue the Crusaders charged and sliced the lead to one during a furious two-minute burst. Green was quickly reinserted but Charlie Browne's layup just before the buzzer cost Michigan its lead at the intermmission. Playing without their star freshman and leading scorer, Ronnie Perry, whose season had ended three weeks before with an injury, the Crusaders refused to fold before the top ranked Wolverines. Even when leading scorer Michael Vincens was benched for seven minutes with four personals they continued to shadow their bigger opponents. With five minutes remaining, and Michigan nursing a tentative two point lead, Vincens fouled out. Michigan responded with eight points in a row to put the game out of reach. Green's 35 points were a considerable help in the 92-81 victory.

In the second half of the doubleheader UNCC came out blazing to establish a 49-46 lead over Central Michigan at the end of the first half. The Forty Niners cooled off after the break and fell behind by five but a 10-2 burst prepared the way to an 81-81 tie after forty minutes.

The Chippewas' Leonard Drake opened the overtime with a field goal. UNCC answered with five straight points but a Ben Poquette free throw and a Val Bracey layup knotted the score again. The Forty Niners' free throw sharpshooters now took charge. Lew Massey, Kevin King and Mel Watkins pumped in five one pointers in the last two minutes to give their team a 91-86 win. Both sides performed remarkably at the line—the Chippewas sinking 90 percent of their throws while UNCC connected on 84 percent of theirs.

The four regional survivors assembled in Lexington, Kentucky, where 22,286 fans turned out for the second round double header. High scoring action was expected since all winners had exceeded 90 points in the first round.

The games, played on St. Patricks Day, provided Irish-Americans with considerable satisfaction since UNCC, also known as the Mean Green, stopped the Orangemen 81-59 after leading by 16 at the break. The problem for Syracuse was at the guards where 6′0″ Kelley and 5′11″ Williams were overmatched by their 6′3″ and 6′4″ counterparts. The Orangemen's backcourt, which shot 2 for 15, was outscored 29 to 4. Faced with another zone, one much tougher than Tennessee's, Syracuse found themselves unable to penetrate, nor were they able to hit from outside. The Mean Green was red hot. Each member of the starting five buried at least half his shots while collectively shooting 68 percent. They also canned 80 percent of their free throws, led by Maxwell who had 11 chances without a miss.

The two Michigan survivors put on a much more exciting scrap in the nightcap. If not for Michigan's complete domination of the backboards, Detroit might have had a chance of pulling off the upset of the tournament. But a 51-33 rebounding advantage led by the Phil Hubbard's 26—the most in the tourney since Elvin Hayes pulled down 27 nine years before—was too much to overcome. As it was, Detroit outscored their opponents from the field but got only four free throw opportunities. For the second time in a row the nation's number one team barely survived against an opponent they should have buried. This time the score was 86-81.

UNCC was a frugal team, having learned that patient shot selection pays off. In their first two games the Mean Green had taken 23 fewer shots than their counterparts and still won. In the regional final UNCC took 21 fewer shots than Michigan.

The Wolverines began bombing the basket early but with little to show for it. They were also not getting their share of rebounds as Massey and Maxwell boxed out well and kept Hubbard from dominating the boards. And there was no easy way past the Forty Niner's disciplined doomsday defense. All this spelled trouble for Michigan. On offense UNCC used the unusual tactic of having their center bring the ball upcourt. With Maxwell and Massey playing decisive roles the Mean Green rolled up a 40-27 advantage at the half.

The Wolverines regrouped in the second period and with Green, who had had a poor game against Detroit after sinking 17 of 21 against Holy Cross, leading the way they moved ahead 49-48. It was then that UNCC showed poise and character by not folding under the Michigan onslaught. They switched to a spread formation and were able to get free for some easy layups. Eventually the Forty Niner's taller guards were also able to shut down Green. Before long the underdogs were in command again and Michigan, which had tottered in the first two rounds, finally fell 75-68.

West:

Three schools in the West regional were among the top five ranked teams in the country. Right behind Michigan in the rankings came UCLA (23-4). Though they had the same record as the 1976 Bruins they appeared to be not as strong as their predecessors. For one, they lost two games at home. For another, they twice were beaten by Oregon, the first time they had suffered such a double defeat in 11 years. They also suffered what was now becoming an almost ritual annual loss to Notre Dame*. Long a dominating team, UCLA was able to record only one blowout—a 107-60 pasting of Rice.

For the first time since Lew Alcindor put on a Bruin uniform UCLA was without a star center. Drollinger had graduated and Richard Washington had become the first Bruin to permit himself to be drafted by the pros with a year of eligibility left. That left Gig Sims and David Greenwood, who occasionally moved over from his forward position. Marques Johnson, the resident All American, held down the other forward position and Roy Hamilton, a teammate of Greenwood in high school, and Jim Spillane comprised the backcourt.

The number one team in the country most of the year was San Francisco

*The two losses to Oregon made it three in a row over a two year period. Strangely, Notre Dame and Oregon seemed to be the only schools able to contain UCLA consistently. There may have been a connection there since Coach Dick Harter of Oregon had once been an assistant to Digger Phelps of Notre Dame.

(29-1) which fell from the top spot on the last week of the season. It was almost like old times, a reincarnation of the champion Dons of the mid-fifties. Once again they featured a dominant center—7′0″, 270 lb. All American, Bill Cartwright (who had once scored 66 points in high school), and a brilliant guard, Winford Boynes. In two respects, though, the 1977 Dons were poles removed from their 1955-56 predecessors. The current squad emphasized offense at the expense of defense and they lacked the discipline of Bill Russell and his mates.

San Francisco ended the year third in the country in scoring and rebounding. Still they rarely faced top competition. Utah and Tennessee were the only formidable obstacles in an otherwise unchallenging schedule preceding San Francisco's finale against Notre Dame. The Dons carried off three major Christmas tournament trophies—the Rainbow Classic, the Utah Classic and the Cable Car Classic.

But the Dons were not a clutch team. Much of San Francisco's problem could be traced to three brilliant freshmen, Cartwright, Boynes and James Hardy, who entered school in 1976 and immediately displaced an equal number of starting seniors. The resulting friction between upper and lower classmen caused some players to threaten to transfer to other schools. Dissension continued throughout the year despite Coach Bob Gaillard's attempts to soothe ruffled egos. Matters came to a head in the playoff against Pepperdine when Hardy, the Dons' talented power forward and leading rebounder, refused to play in the second half. He claimed his teammates were acting selfishly by shooting too much and not passing off enough—presumably to him.

Trying to refine some of the raw talent on his team, Gaillard convinced Chubby Cox to transfer from Villanova before the 1977 season. The 6′2″ playmaker had a soothing effect on the turmoil that had rocked San Francisco. He directed the team and managed to impose some discipline, at least on the court. Rarely shooting himself, Cox set up his taller and more accurate teammates. Gaillard kept practice to a minimum, so as not to antagonize his men who hated the drills, and he also dispensed with a curfew.

Even though the coach's grip on the reins was extremely loose the Dons continued to complain and quarrel among themselves. Perhaps it was a sign of immaturity—they were still very young. Yet Gaillard, who had recruited tirelessly (he estimated it took 50 visits to land Boynes) to assemble a championship squad, felt betrayed. When he watched all those egos competing for the single ball, heard Hardy carping and saw the perpetual scowl stamped on his face, he must have known this squad would not hold together long enough to reach the Final Four, let alone the championship round.

If San Francisco stormed the baskets, then the University of Nevada at Las Vegas (25-2) created a virtual blizzard every time they played. Not quite as productive as in 1976, the Rebels nevertheless led the nation in scoring again, going over 100 points 20 times including 12 in a row. The deluge reached a crescendo in a 135-78 cloudburst against Idaho. Sometimes their opponents joined in the binge, too. The Rebels had to turn it on full to beat San Diego State 118-113 and Bradley 107-106. Not even Oregon, which had held UCLA to 60 and 55 points in their two meetings, was able to stop UNLV from scoring 78.

UNLV's schedule was not taxing. They split decisions between the only two teams in the top twenty that they faced, losing to Louisville and beating Utah. The only other blot on their record was a two pointer at Illinois State. Despite their nickname, UNLV was a well-disciplined team, certainly more so than San Francisco. The reason lay in the coach. Jerry Tarkanian had gained a lot of respect from his players over the years, taking mostly black kids and molding them into a functioning unit.

Tarkanian had been a winner during his entire coaching career. He took over at Riverside Junior College in 1963 and made them respectable. Four years later he moved to Pasadena City College, another junior college where the basketball team had won just 41 games in six years. In the two years he worked there his teams posted 35-1 seasons both times. He accepted the coaching job at Long Beach State in 1969, taking the entire Pasadena team with him. His record with the Forty Niners over five seasons was 23-3, 24-5, 24-5, 25-4 and 26-3. His teams won their conference each year and never lost a home game. When Long Beach State was put on probation for recruiting violations, he moved to Las Vegas, where in 1974 he recruited the Fabulous Five, four of whom were high school All Americans. In four years at UNLV his record had been 97-15. At the end of the 1977 season Tarkanian had the highest career winning percentage of any college coach living or dead—and that included some very famous people.

Popular he may have been with his players but what the NCAA thought of Tarkanian would have made hate mail sound like valentine cards. The NCAA tried to enforce its regulation, the so called "Tarkanian Rule." It stated that if a coach is found guilty of NCAA violations and his team is put on probation, should that coach move to another school, the new school loses its eligibility to play in a NCAA tournament for two years. The NCAA recommended that UNLV suspend its coach but when it tried to do so, Tarkanian went to court. He won his case. The federal judge who heard the case blasted the NCAA for carrying on a personal vendetta against Tarkanian. He allegedly was harrassed by investigators who vowed to destroy his career. His players and associates were questioned and in some cases allegedly threatened. In any case, the NCAA was unsuccessful in having Tarkanian removed from the college basketball scene.

It is hard to understand what provoked the NCAA to conduct such an expensive, time consuming, exhaustive investigation. Tarkanian, a pleasant man though somewhat sinister looking, resembled an underworld character in a Hollywood B film, hence the nickname Tark the Shark. He was also rather unconventional. When Denny Crum brought Louisville to Las Vegas to play the Rebels he took the opportunity to get married there. Naturally the players and coaches were invited. Everyone dressed for the occasion except Tarkanian who showed up in an electric blue, short sleeved sport shirt. Being unconventional, however, is not a violation of NCAA rules.

Louisville (21-6) won the Metro Seven conference but lost to Georgia Tech by a point in the playoff. The dunk shot had been reinstated for the 1977 season and nobody stuffed the ball as enthusiastically as the Cardinals. That uninhibited group called themselves the Doctors of Dunk and they operated frequently, causing hoops to vibrate and backboards to sway from New Orleans to Milwaukee. The dunk energized Louisville supporters, already among the most raucus in the country, to even greater heights of enthusiasm.

The highlight of Louisville's season was a trip to Las Vegas which was also the occasion for the previously mentioned wedding. Crum and Tarkanian were the two most successful coaches at the time. Over the years Tarkanian had won 86 percent of his games and Crum 81 percent. The game, a celebration of sorts, was basketball if not at its best, then certainly at its most entertaining. It resembled more than anything a playground game in Harlem or some other urban ghetto with fancy dribbling, virtuoso shooting, in-your-face rejections and seismic dunks. UNLV stopped the Cardinals when Gondrezick, the only white man on the court, bagged a pair of free throws to ice the 99-96 victory.

Louisville's four losses outside the Metro Seven were to tournament-bound teams, three of them in the top ten. The defeats came early and late but in midseason the Cardinals built a 15 game win streak enlivened by free spirited dunking to the delight of the fans.

Long Beach State (21-7) tied with San Diego State at the top of their conference but won the postseason playoff. Utah (21-6) seemed to be suffering from schizophrenia aggravated by poor defense. They split their first six games while giving up more than 90 points in half of them. They lost their own invitational tournament, then travelled to Lexington and claimed the Kentucky Invitational. A week later they grabbed the Reno Classic, too.

Idaho State (23-4) were schizophrenic to a degree, too, steamrollering several opponents but buckling by an average of 14 points in their four losses. St. Johns (22-8), far from home, was not expected to last.

Utah jumped to a 22-12 advantage over St. Johns in the opening round. The sharpshooting Utes maintained their lead until the Redmen rallied and led briefly 44-42 early in the second period. Utah urged on by their supporters who far outnumbered those of St. Johns and sparked by Greg Deane's 25 points, took the game 72-68.

Fate, or a poor draw, had matched two of the top five teams in the other first round contest. UNLV's kamikaze attack and a defense that would have made an octopus envious, shocked San Francisco into 19 first half turnovers and 32 over the full game. It was obvious early on that the Rebels had a team and that the Dons were five individuals thrashing around trying to keep their heads above water. Late in the first half UNLV shredded San Francisco's defense by firing off 28 points in seven and a half minutes. Nothing could have sounded more welcome to the Dons than the buzzer ending the half. The Rebels had run rampant in a 63-44 stampede and this was just the first half.

Things deteriorated even more for San Francisco after the intermission. Whatever cohesion had existed was destroyed under the slashing pressure of a poised UNLV quintet. The Dons became five frustrated, flustered individuals trying to turn the game around, a situation reminiscent of the Michigan-Rutgers semifinal a year earlier. After six minutes of the second period the Running Rebels were ahead 86-56 and still accelerating. When it was over and the dust had settled, they had tied the tournament record for most points scored and had beaten the team that two weeks before was undefeated and number one in the country. It could have been worse. Tarkanian brought in his substitutes when the game was out of reach, sparing the Dons further embarrassment. Nevertheless it was one of the major massacres in tournament history, a game that Gaillard and the immature Dons would have liked to forget but probably could not. The final score was a 121-95 embarrassment.

In the colder confines of Pocatello, Idaho, 7′0″ Steve Hayes and 6′10″ Jeff Cook picked the backboard clean to help hometown Idaho State to a 33-30 half time lead over Long Beach State. The gap would have been wider but for the effective way in which Long Beach State collapsed on Hayes. After a tactical adjustment he swished in eight points in the first five minutes of the second period. He added 15 more before the buzzer for a game high of 29 points as the offense got more and more into its flow. A 50 point Bengal second half helped eliminate Long Beach State 83-72.

Louisville had arrived in Pocatello by midweek, thereby breaking a NCAA rule forbidding a visiting team from practicing at the tourney site more than a day before the scheduled tipoff. But Crum wanted to acclimate his lowlanders to Pocatello's 5000 feet altitude and scorned any reprimand by the NCAA.

The extra practice appeared to have helped the Cardinals or maybe the lack of it hurt UCLA. The latter looked sluggish and unsure as they stood around and watched their opponents build a six point lead in the second period. Louisville used an effective zone that denied the Bruins the baseline. Unable to penetrate and trailing by four, Bartow inserted guard Brad Holland to deliver via long distance air strikes. Five minutes later Holland had 11 points and UCLA pulled ahead 66-65. The Cardinals retaliated and it was not until two crucial goaltending calls against them that UCLA pulled ahead for keeps. For the third time in four tournament appearances, Denny Crum was shown the exit by his former school, this time by 87-79.

Idaho State said goodbye regretfully to its friendly gym. Few gave them much of a chance against UCLA. The Bengals were confident they could do it. Cook's mother, who stopped in Las Vegas on the way to watch her son play, spurned the 16 points one gambler offered her and placed a modest bet on Idaho State, claiming she didn't need points and that UCLA would lose. The odds of that happening lengthened as the second half got underway with the Bruins leading by six and in control of the boards, normally Idaho State's long suit. But just as in their first round game, the Bengal front court made the correct adjustment, became more aggressive, boxed out better and Hayes and Cook took down the majority of the ricochets. In the second half Idaho State outrebounded UCLA 37-23. The Bengals' zone picketed Marques Johnson who had scored 19 points in the first half, allowing him just two free throws thereafter. Hayes, who was to wind up with 27 points, found the range and with four minutes remaining, the underdogs were ahead by one as their fans screamed their appreciation. A scoring flurry featuring a Hayes' hook and several free throws boosted the Bengals to a 71-63 edge with 2:08 to go. They tried to stall but the desperate Bruins roared back.

What saved Idaho State was their foul shooting. They missed only three times in 21 tries in the second half, converting 11 of their final dozen. Freshman guard Ernie Wheeler made four crucial points in the final 37 seconds. With his team ahead 72-69, he converted two free throws to ice the game apparently, but with nine seconds remaining and UCLA back to within a point, he had to do it all over again. Calmly he dropped in two more to clinch it. Two final points for UCLA were meaningless. Idaho State had pulled off the upset of the year 76-75.

Utah was upset minded, too, but its zone was more brittle than Idaho State's. The game was played at cyclonic speed. The tempo never withered as both sides ran, shot and burned rubber. The outcome was determined by UNLV's more stubborn defense as they confronted their opponents with a claustrophobic man-to-man. Meanwhile Utah had problems boxing out and preventing the Nevadans from muscling in for second and third shots, especially down the stretch. Larry Moffett, the Rebels' center, pulled down 17 rebounds that triggered several fast breaks. The country's leading offense was also able to hit on some long jumpers.

A one point lead with a little less than four minutes to play prompted Tarkanian to call a time out. He later claimed he wanted to switch to a zone but since the team had never practiced it he discarded the idea. "You can't just diagram it in a time out," he said. Instead Tarkanian ordered his men into a spread. The delay tactic was most unusual for this attack oriented team. The move worked as Reggie Theus was twice able to find Robert Smith unguarded under the net for easy layins to ensure an 88-83 Rebel win.

Fans had been looking forward to a classic confrontation in the regional final between UCLA and San Francisco, the number two and three teams in the country and the best in the west. San Francisco was long gone and now so was UCLA. Instead, what remained were UNLV and Idaho State, neither of whom had ever advanced this far. For the first 20 minutes it looked as if the Bengals had that extra desire that would land them in Atlanta. Only Moffett, who was holding Hayes in check despite a four inch height disadvantage, seemed to care. With the Bengals ahead 52-51, paternal Tarkanian tonguelashed his troops in the locker room, more severely than ever before.

Duly chastised, UNLV went back on the court and proceeded to raise the tempo of the game to full throttle. With increased intensity came increased pressure on defense. The keyed-up Rebels scored the first eight points of the second half. Moffett was charged with his fourth personal and had to be benched, allowing the Bengals to close to four. Two easy layups which would have tied the score were mishandled. It was their last gasp as UNLV made three jump shots in a row to pull away. At the final buzzer UNLV was on top 107-90, their second 100-point game of the tourney.

Moffett had another excellent game outrebounding the taller Hayes 16 to 13. For the third straight game UNLV claimed exactly 50 rebounds and outshot their opponents by a substantial margin.

Final Four:

Hardly anyone would have predicted the Final Four that met in Atlanta's Omni the following weekend. For the first time since 1966 UCLA was not present. Neither was there a representative from the Big Ten nor from the SEC. Instead there were two independents—rare birds by 1977—and the representative of the **Sunbelt** Conference. True, North Carolina and UNLV were ranked fourth and fifth respectively before the tournament, but the Rebels were suspect because of an undemanding schedule and the Tarheels had had a better squad in 1976. Marquette, represented by one of Al McGuire's weaker units, had been ranked sixteenth and UNCC, in their first NCAA tournament, were pegged no higher than eighteenth. Next to the venerable universities that had made the Final Four in previous years, two of the semifinalists had barely reached puberty. In 1957 when North Carolina had won their last national title, UNLV was one year old and UNCC was still a two-year college. While the titans of the court—Michigan, UCLA, San Francisco and Kentucky—were home watching on television, four upstarts were about to test each others' merits for the national championship. It promised to be a wide open battle.

The four semifinalists had several things in common. There were survivors; they shared the ability to come from behind; the accuracy of all four teams from the free throw line was formidable; and all four had demonstrated they could handle the pressure.

For the third time in four games North Carolina left the floor at the half faced with an uphill climb, trailing UNLV 49-43. They had only themselves to blame as 16 turnovers, seven by the normally steady Ford, threatened to sink the Tarheels. In a city sympathetic to the Southern cause the Rebels were as devastating as General Sherman had been more than a hundred years before. The fact that they were devastating the troops from North Carolina may have led to some divided loyalties in the Omni.

UNLV seemed to have the game under control until Moffett was accidentally punched in the nose and had to go to the bench. Without Moffett, control of the boards passed to the taller Tarheels. Incredibly the superb scoring machine ground to a stop and for almost five minutes not one Rebel was able to register. During one stretch North Carolina tallied 14 points to UNLV's two to assume a narrow lead which they protected by going to their four corners at 4:20. The move worked when the Tarheels were able to deliver from the line when fouled repeatedly. Kuester, who was running the formation in place of the injured Ford, alone popped five free throws in the final minute. The North Carolina advantage held up—barely—and they won 84-83.

The loss of Moffett was the turning point of the game. After snaring 150 rebounds in their last three games, the Rebels took only 29, a dozen fewer than North Carolina. Repeating a past pattern, they took 24 more shots than their opponents and with 51 percent accuracy outscored the Tarheels from the field, too. But the Rebels made only one free throw for the entire game in five tries while North Carolina stepped to the foul line 28 times. Tarkanian was livid, accusing the NCAA of loading the referees so his team, which was to go on probation after the tourney, would not win the championship and so become an embarrassment. Tarkanian had made similar insinuations after Arizona had beaten the Rebels in the West regional the previous year.

Whatever, North Carolina won because of superior shooting. The starting Tarheel frontcourt deadeyes claimed 26 field goals on 33 shots. Davis took seven shots from the floor without a miss while O'Koren was high man with 31 points. However, Phil Ford, only partly recovered from his hyperextended elbow, was effective only in spots.

Soon after he arrived in Atlanta, McGuire shot away on a borrowed motorcycle to relieve the tension that was building. Until now he had not thought Marquette stood a chance to take the title. By contrast, his players initially thought they could, and now, on the eve of their semifinal against UNCC, were convinced they would. McGuire too, was beginning to feel that the miracle might occur. Basketball fans around the country were hoping it would, and there was a feeling that even the referees subconsciously would give him the benefit of the doubt in a close call situation.

The abrasive McGuire, though far from humble had mellowed considerably since the day he was quoted as saying, "It's no secret that most people I play against grow to hate me," and on another occasion, "I don't care what the crowd thinks of our style. I'm not throwing a party." Now most of the fans and coaches were pulling for him.

While Marquette was cool under pressure, the team from the Sunbelt Conference, in their first tourney, was more nervous than a country bride on her wedding night. The Warriors stepped off to a 23-9 lead after 13 minutes, but then the team from Charlotte recovered dramatically to close to within three at the midway mark. Still, for the first time in the tournament, the Warriors were ahead at half time. Jerome Whitehead was having his best game after what McGuire called "three Edsel weeks." The Warriors' center had been in a horrible slump, having scored just one field goal in each of the last two games.

Marquette's lead did not last long. After two and a half minutes of the second period Lew Massey's jumper put the Mean Green on top for the first time. It was measure-for-measure the rest of the way. Both sides played cautiously, deliberately, realizing the consequences of a single mistake. When Mel Walkins dropped in two free throws to give UNCC a 47-44 advantage at 1:41, McGuire's career hung by a thin thread. But Lee gave the Warriors hope with a 22 foot jumper. The Mean Green tried stalling and Marquette was forced to foul. They fouled the wrong man though. Maxwell was shooting 80 percent from the line for the tournament and had made seven of eight in the game so far. But somebody up there must have been looking out for Al and his Warriors because Maxwell missed the front end of a one-and-one. Lee then put his team in control once more with another jump shot.

The Omni rocked as first one block of fans erupted, then the other, as the advantage swung from side to side. After each point, each referee's call, even after each shot, the faithful jumped to their feet and screamed, unleashing emotional waves which, in that enclosed space, fused into an almost continuous crescendo.

When Massey missed an 18 footer and Marquette controlled, it looked like curtains for UNCC. With 13 seconds remaining Gary Rosenberger, who had not scored until then, saw an opening and went in for a layup that would have been the clincher. He missed but was fouled. Rosenberger missed the first but made the second. The scoreboard read 49-47 Marquette, but UNCC had the ball and Maxwell drove straight down the middle for a layup to tie the game. There were still four seconds left.

McGuire immediately called a time out, then gathered his players around him at center court. This was a violation since huddles were restricted to the bench area and could have resulted in a technical. None was called though. The reason for the unusual location was twofold. McGuire was almost hoarse by now and the crowd was yelling so loudly that he wanted to make sure his players could hear him. A more important reason was for McGuire to check the height of the scoreboard which was suspended over the tipoff circle. The play he had outlined was for Lee to heave the ball the length of the floor to Whitehead—similar to a fly pattern in football—and the center would then lay it in or ram it home. There was no time for anything fancy. The play had to work perfectly or it would be overtime.

The players took their positions. Lee lobbed the ball in a high arc downcourt, just clearing the bottom of the scoreboard. Three pairs of hands reached for it. Ellis tipped it into Maxwell's hands but Whitehead wrestled it away from him and in the same motion whipped it into the net. The buzzer sounded before his feet touched the court. Pandemonium. Did the basket count? Neither official made a signal but instead headed for the timekeeper, with both coaches trailing behind, ready to explode. Twice the referee asked the timekeeper if the basket came before time had run out. Both times the answer was yes. McGuire hurried off the court one game away from the prize that had eluded him so often. He asked his men not to talk to anyone about the last shot. The reason is not clear but it might have been due to the extreme emotion McGuire was now enduring. He congratulated Whitehead for a superlative effort. "As long as you live," his coach said, "you will never play a better game." Aside from the winning basket the Warrior center had led his team in scoring and accounted for half its rebounds.

UNLV beat UNCC 106-94 in the consolation game. It was run-and-gun from tipoff to buzzer; a wild, uninhibited shootout in which three players scored 30 points or more—Maxwell and Chad Kinch for the Forty Niners, Owens for the Rebels. There were few surprises. UNLV took 95 shots—23 more than their opponents. Maxwell continued his magic touch at the free throw line, missing only once in 13 tries.

The final promised to be a classic confrontation not only between two fine teams but also between the two most successful coaches over the last decade. As as special bonus the fans would be treated to a *mano a mano* contest between Butch Lee and Phil Ford, considered to be the two best point guards in college basketball.

Lee may have felt some resentment toward Dean Smith for not selecting him to the Olympic team. He was not even invited to the tryout camp. Thus snubbed, he joined the Puerto Rican team. (He had been born on that island when his parents stopped there briefly on their way to New York from the Virgin Islands.) Then, almost single handedly, he came close to eliminating the USA in their toughest match in Montreal. In that game he outscored Ford 35-20. Though he did not say so, Lee might have welcomed the opportunity to beat Smith for not giving him the opportunity to win a gold medal.

There were more similarities than differences between McGuire and Smith. Both had excellent relations with their players. Both had developed athletes who, though not statistically potent, were always high draft choices for the pros and later justified this confidence by starring on their teams. McGuire had developed Chones, Lucas, Lackey, Lloyd Walton and now Ellis, Lee and Whitehead, while Smith had produced Scott, McAdoo, Bobby Jones, Kupchak with Ford, Davis and LaGarde in the current crop. Both coaches were dedicated to a team rather than a star system although McGuire stressed defense and Smith offense.

Smith had to make a major adjustment after his semifinal victory. Having just beaten the highest scoring team in the country, he had to take on the second stingiest defense. In the first few minutes both sides moved cautiously, sizing each other up. But then the Warriors, burning with confidence, blasted to a 12 point half time lead, creating their own opportunities by snapping pinpoint passes to teammates cutting for the basket, using the backdoor play several times.

For the first 20 minutes North Carolina allowed their opponents to dictate the tempo of the game. Now early in the second half the Tarheels began running and before Marquette could adjust, they took a 45-43 lead with more than half the period remaining. McGuire called time and spent most of the next 60 seconds indulging himself in an old fashioned, screaming, hand-waving tantrum. He bellowed at his players, kicked the scorer's table—he limped for some time after the game—and let off enough steam to fuel the

Omni heating system. Meanwhile his wife, who was sitting several rows away, was screaming at him to shut up.

When play resumed, the Tarheels went into their four corners—much too early according to some analysts. The tactic had worked well in the past but this time it had the effect of blunting the Tarheels' momentum. McGuire's tantrum had an instant effect on the Warriors. They adjusted to the four corners as if they had been playing against it for years. They did not give the Tarheels the opportunity of parading to the foul line nor did they give them any easy layups. Marquette refused to make any rash moves that would have allowed their opponents to pad their lead. Instead, they kept their big men, Whitehead and Ellis, close to the baseline to cut off that access lane. It was a marvel of discipline and a credit to a well-coached team.

These youths from the ethnic neighborhoods of Chicago, Jersey City and the Bronx were no strangers to conflict. As the inspired Warriors clawed and fought back momentum swung to them. They tied the score and when Ellis rejected Bruce Buckley's shot, the Warriors worked the ball patiently until Jim Boylan shook free to spin in a layup and give them a 47-45 lead. Then it was Marquette that went into a delay offense. The Tarheels were forced to foul and, now that the stakes were highest, the Warriors' excellent free throw shooting did not fail them. They turned 15 opportunities into 14 points and added three field goals for their last 20 points. Only Davis, who scored ten of his teams' last twelve, was a factor down the stretch. Still it was the closest finish since Loyola nipped Cincinnati in 1963. With 1:49 to play Marquette was barely on top 51-49 but a flurry of free throws sealed the verdict. The final score was Marquette 67, North Carolina 59.

At the buzzer Marquette players and fans erupted onto the court, hugging, pummeling and dancing around. Only their coach remained seated, his face in a towel blotting his brimming eyes. Asked later what he was thinking in this moment of greatest victory, the flamboyant coach answered with unusual humility, "Why me?"

He also remembered the road he had travelled over the years ending here in Atlanta, at the summit. He remembered the stations along that road, imprinted so well in his mind. The distance itself, the hundreds of thousands of miles from cold gyms in "East Cupcake" to superheated national tournaments in metropolitan centers. He remembered also the smelly jocks and socks, the west locker rooms, the fights, the half time and postgame dances on the court. And he also remembered a photograph taken in Eugene, Oregon, 1939. It showed the scene at the railroad station when the University of Oregon basketball team came home after winning the first NCAA tournament. It was a victory celebration with the students hanging from telegraph poles and from every available vantage point.

Al McGuire went home to Milwaukee to an even bigger victory celebration. Talking later about that scene in Eugene and the one in Milwaukee, he said with a little wonder still in his voice: "I always knew it could happen to me. I knew one time I'd come back and it would be bananas."

18

SOMETHING OLD SOMETHING NEW

1978-1979

1978

Mideast:

By 1978 the trend toward filling out rosters with star players became apparent. Until this development, coaches had built a team round one or two star quality players and filled out the roster with what was locally available. Now they did not consider their recruiting effort successful unless they had eight or nine men with blockbuster credentials on the squad, partly because more quality athletes were available. Such a team was Kentucky.

Before the 1978 season the Wildcats were picked the team most likely to win the national championship. No wonder. Four men who had played and lost to UCLA in the 1975 final were back as seniors. Two of them, Jack Givens and Rick Robey, were All Americans. In 1976 they had won the NIT; in 1977 they had lost in the regional final to North Carolina; and now they were burning to finally win it all. Coach Joe B. Hall was not given the credit he deserved as a super tactician because he had so much talent on his teams, his credentials appeared superfluous. He was to prove his worth on the bench before the tournament was over.

Hall had been a walk-on on the 1949 Kentucky national champion, not getting much playing time on the Fabulous Five that included Ralph Beard and Alex Groza. Apparently watching the action from the bench had given

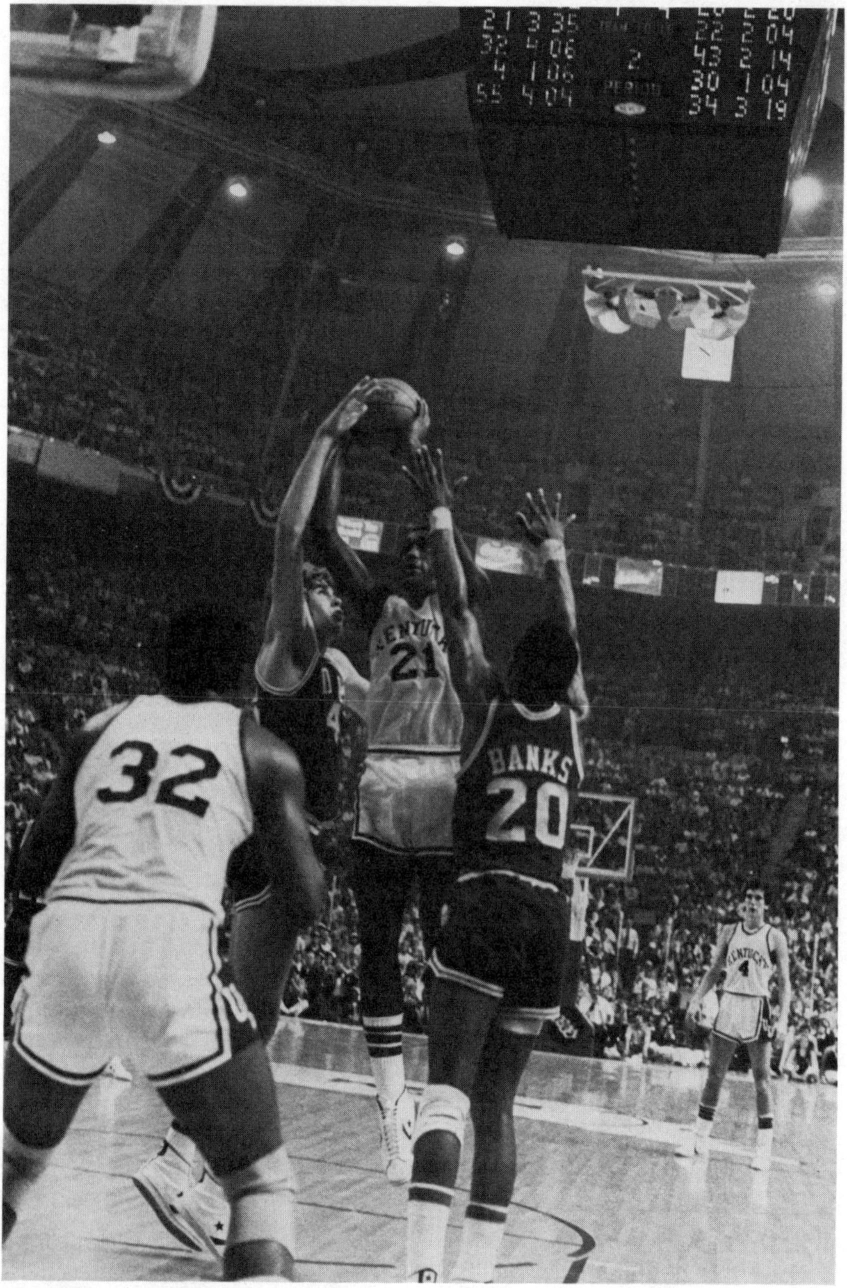

Jack Givens of Kentucky, the 1979 tournament's MVP, jumping over Duke's Mike Gminski while Eugene Banks reaches out to assist. The final was won by Kentucky 94-88.
(University of Kentucky photo)

him the kind of perspective that would later make him a great coach.* Despite his icy, aloof appearance Hall had a caustic wit and a mordant sense of humor. He had occasion to use it when, despite his impressive record, he came under extreme pressure from alumni to either produce a national champion or quit. The heir to Rupp was beginning to feel the heat. After all he was expected to fill the 23,000-seat Rupp Arena and this required an outstanding team. There was a feeling that 1978 was his best chance to go all the way before he was replaced. The Baron, who had wanted to live to see one more title for his Wildcats, passed away just as the season began.

Kentucky (25-2), ranked number one, had been singed by 16 points at Alabama and nosed out by one at LSU. The Wildcats had two new starting guards—Truman Claytor and Kyle Macy. Macy was a transfer student from Purdue who had sat out the previous season. He was the best foul shooter on the squad with an 89 percent completion average, a superb ball handler and the catalyst who most often ignited the team.

Third ranked Marquette (24-3), back in the Mideast regional, stood an outside chance of upsetting Kentucky. They had come away second best in encounters with Louisville, Notre Dame and Loyola of Illinois but had checked Minnesota, the runner up in the Big Ten, by 17 points in Minneapolis. Ellis had graduated and been replaced by Toone as a starter.

Hank Raymonds, Al McGuire's assistant, was now coach at Marquette and a sharper contrast in personal style between the new man and his mentor would be hard to find. Raymonds was a midwesterner, subdued, controlled and predictable, though every bit as knowledgeable as his predecessor. He had done much of the between-game coaching since McGuire often skipped practice to chase after other pursuits. In a way Raymonds had been McGuire's alter ego and they had performed well together. There were also differences in strategy. McGuire, for instance, was more rigid. He had used a set lineup and set tactics, whereas Raymonds was willing to experiment, allow his regulars more options and give the subs a chance to play more.

Still, most of the offense revolved around the Warriors' All American, Butch Lee. A very unselfish player, he took few shots, especially when well-guarded, preferring to shovel the ball off to an open man. Yet he controlled the game as surely as if he scored 30 points. "If I wanted stats, I'd be somewhere else," he remarked. "Marquette's tradition is low scoring, defense, unselfishness—and winning. We like to think we're the Celtics of college basketball."

Michigan State (23-4) had shot to the top of the Big Ten after a 10-17 season in 1977. The fifth ranked Spartans' revival was due to a pair of 6′8″ local

---

*The same is true of Dean Smith, Bobby Knight and Al McGuire, all of whom were marginal players on top level teams. Smith played for national titlist Kansas in 1952, Knight for the champion Ohio State Buckeyes in 1960 and McGuire on the St. John's team that went to the tournament in 1951. The exception to the belief that outstanding players do not make good coaches is, of course, John Wooden.

products from Lansing—Jay Vincent and Earvin "Magic" Johnson, who may have been the biggest guard in the country and was far from slow. Johnson had spearheaded his high school team to a state championship the year before. Though both Vincent and Johnson were only freshmen they showed unusual poise and maturity in the tough competition of the Big Ten.

Florida State (23-5) was the regular season winner in the Metro Seven but blew hot and cold outside their conference. They triumphed over Missouri 97-64 but were nailed by South Alabama, at home no less. The Seminoles were only tepid in the final of the Metro Seven playoff which they lost to Louisville after having beaten them twice earlier.

Almost all conferences were now holding postseason playoffs. (The exceptions were the Big Ten and Pac Eight, the WAC, and the SEC. The last would revive a playoff a year later.) For some reason the underdog seemed to be more successful in postseason games in 1978 than ever before. In several conferences teams that had been trampled twice turned on their oppressors in the playoffs and eliminated them.

Western Kentucky (15-13) finished third in their conference and had only a .500 record before entering their playoff but won the two games needed. Providence (24-7) was one team that lost their playoff match—to a team they had beaten earlier—but received an invitation to the tournament nonetheless. The Friars had waded through a difficult schedule which cost them six times against teams which earned tournament invitations themselves.

Most experts considered Syracuse (22-5) the strongest quintet in the Northeast. But they also lost in the ECAC playoff in a stunning upset. After torpedoing fourth ranked New Mexico and fifth ranked Michigan State and trampling four opponents by at least 40 points, Syracuse was not expected to have much trouble against St. Bonaventure, whom they had whipped in December 107-81. But the Bonnies won the rematch 70-69, assuring themselves a spot in the tournament. Miami of Ohio (18-8) rounded out the Mideast regional field.

Syracuse may still have been in a state of shock over their final loss when they took the court against Western Kentucky—a team even weaker than St. Bonaventure—in the first round at Knoxville, Tennessee. There seemed to be no other excuse for allowing the Hilltoppers to walk off with a first half tie. The local fans were hostile to Syracuse since the Orangemen had knocked their team out of the competition 12 months previously. Despite some singularly inept foul shooting, Western Kentucky trailed by only three points with two and a half minutes left in the game. Coach Jim Richards then signalled his men into a full court press which achieved its purpose when Syracuse lost the ball twice. The second resulted in Mike Reese funneling a 15 foot jumper into the hole to tie the score again 76-76.

The team that was responsible for more chewed fingernails in March had done it again. For the fourth time in as many years Syracuse was involved in a tournament overtime game. They had won the previous three but this time the Hilltoppers, helped by Darryl Turner's two free throws at :30, nipped the Orangemen 87-86. Marty Byrnes of the losers missed becoming a hero when the first of his one-and-one opportunity bounced away three seconds from the buzzer. The final curtain came down abruptly—two one-point losses to inferior teams in postseason action.

It looked for a time as if there would be an even bigger upset in the co-feature as Florida State ran away from the more ponderous Wildcats of Kentucky. Ahead by ten at one point, the Seminoles were satisfied with their 39-32 advantage at the half.

Seven points down and his team struggling, Joe Hall made a tactical move that few of his fellow coaches would have dared: he benched his two All Americans, Givens and Robey, along with Truman Claytor and started the second half with benchwarmers Dwane Casey, Lavon Williams and Freddie Cowan. It was a calculated risk designed to trade beef and rebounding for speed. The Seminole attack, which had blistered Kentucky with their fine transition play and subsequent fast break, was blunted by the fresh Wildcats who were able to get back on defense faster. However, FSU kept up a pressing defense and midway through the final frame the underdogs led 53-48. Some fine outside shooting by Macy and Phillips kept Kentucky in the game and when Robey and Givens came back, the team was ready to counterattack. For five minutes the Wildcats rolled over the Seminoles like an armored column over an outgunned outpost. When it was over, Kentucky had scored 14 unanswered points. The rest was a mopup operation culminating in an 85-76 victory. There was a measure of retribution in the decision. The last time the Seminoles played in the tournament they had shattered Rupp's final opportunity for a national title on their way to a runner-up finish in 1972.

Meanwhile a slam dunk by Michigan State's Greg Kelser opened the scoring against Providence. That overture set the tone for the one-sided contest. The Spartans took off to a 25-8 lead as they hit their first eight shots on the way to a 63 percent shooting performance. Kelser was deadly with nine of ten from the field and 23 points to head Michigan State's 77-63 win.

Marquette had met the Mid American winner eight times in previous tournaments and had advanced each time. Three times they had liquidated Miami of Ohio and in 1978 there was no expectation that they would not extend that string. For the greater part of the game Marquette looked as if it was in control of the situation. At 3:38 with the Warriors comfortably in front 68-58, Jerome Whitehead, the hero of Marquette's semifinal win the previous year, and John Shoemaker of Miami converged on the ball. The resulting tussle turned the game around. Whitehead wrestled the ball away from Shoemaker and in so doing conked him flush on the nose. The Redskin fell like a shaft of tall timber and lay there, decked, for two minutes while referee Peter Pavia threw Whitehead out of the game and hit Coach Raymonds with a technical foul for protesting the ejection too vehemently. It was his first of the year and could not have come at a worse time.

It was an unfortunate call. Most of the witnesses agreed that Whitehead's blow was not deliberate and, knowing the center's placid disposition, it would seem he was a victim of the circumstance. Once again, even without Al McGuire, Marquette found itself the center of controversy. It also kept their string of technical fouls in a tournament alive. Miami netted three of the four fouls they were awarded and scored a field goal after retaining possession, cutting their deficit in half. Without Whitehead's presence Miami began driving down the middle and scoring from point blank range. A Shoemaker layup with 20 seconds left gave Miami a 75-74 lead but he also fouled Jim Boylan after the shot. The Marquette guard made the first of a one-and-one but missed the second, sending the match into overtime.

The Warriors moved in front 81-79 with a minute left but Archie Aldridge completed a three point play to give Miami the lead. That was the ball game. The buzzer sounded the end of the scalping party as the Redskins danced off the court 84-81 to the good. The Mid American had finally penned the Warriors though it had taken a questionable call to accomplish it. Lee had 27 points in his last college game.

Kentucky and Michigan State completely outclassed the two upset perpetrators in almost identically lopsided games. The Wildcats ripped Miami 91-69. Phillips racked up 24 points on 11-for-13 shooting. Macy contributed just two points. "Kyle hasn't even showed up yet," announced his coach, a statement that two days later, was to prove how well Hall knew his talented guard. Michigan State trounced Western Kentucky 90-69. Magic Johnson had a cold shooting night making only 17 percent of his shots but passing for 14 assists.

The regional final was entirely different from the two semi-final blowouts. With Kelser banging the hoop for nine of Michigtan State's first 15 points, the Spartans moved ahead early. For the second time in three postseason games the Wildcats struggled through a chilling first half which ended with Michigan State on top 27-22.

The Wildcats just could not solve their opponent's 2-1-2 zone. At one point after moving the ball around for two and a half minutes, they took one shot which missed and they were back on defense again. It was another confrontation of finesse versus strength but though the quicker Spartans were able to check Kentucky initially, they paid a price which ultimately cost them the game.

Once more a critical adjustment by Hall saved the game. Ditching the man-to-man defense in favor of a 1-3-1 zone, Hall stacked his tall men in the middle so Michigan State was unable to penetrate. He also posted Robey at the top of the key to set picks for Macy. Both moves worked. The Spartans' offense, which was trying to slow the pace anyway, became almost moribund as they refused the long shot. Only Kelser seemed to be able to find the hole. Johnson, shackled by four personals, had to play cautiously and was held far below his average. Meanwhile Macy was snapping the cords at the other end of the floor and Kentucky's strength was wearing Michigan State down. With the score 35-33 James Lee stole the ball and tied the count on a rim rattling dunk. The teams traded baskets (the score was knotted at 33, 35, 37, 39 and 41) until Macy broke the final deadlock with a three point play.

Now with the Wildcat tide running against them, the exhausted Spartans fouled and fouled again. In the last seven minutes, all of Kentucky's points except for Macy's bucket came from the line. And the Wildcats, especially Macy who finished with 10 of 11 from the foul stripe, were deadly on free throws. Three times in the final three minutes with the game on the line, Macy calmly sank both ends of one-and-one opportunities, the last with eight seconds on the clock and his team ahead by a point. Before the clincher Michigan State called two time outs but Macy sank both shots to put Kentucky into the Final Four 52-49. It was the lowest point total of the year for the nation's number one team. They had made only 18 field goals but Macy's free throws pulled them through.

East:

Michigan State was not the only school that had risen from the ashes of the previous season. The East regional contained so many teams returned from obscurity they could have held their own revival meeting. One remarkable recovery was that of ninth ranked Duke (23-6). After four seasons in the cellar they had finished second behind North Carolina in the ACC and had beaten the Tarheels in the conference playoff final. As usual the ACC playoff had generated as much excitement as a Roman gladiator elimination. This was understandable since all the schools but Clemson had been in the top 20 at one time or another during the season.

The Blue Devils had been a national power in the mid-sixties. They lost to UCLA in the 1964 tournament final to give John Wooden his first national title. However, after Coach Dick Bubas resigned, Duke declined to the point where they were the doormat of the ACC and in 1974 they suffered their worst season in 30 years. A year before they had even offered the coaching post to Adolph Rupp. Improvement came slowly because their new coach, Bill Foster, like McGuire, recruited only one blue chip high school player a year. But in 1978 Foster's patience paid off.

Foster had been successful in reviving basketball programs at Rutgers and Utah. He worked tirelessly to promote the sport and spent much of his time on the road recruiting. Jim Spanarkel of Jersey City was his first success. The Northeast, which had always been such a fertile breeding ground for ACC teams, also provided him Mike Gminski and Eugene Banks. Foster refused to overload his team with stars, fearing it might lead to jealousy and squabbling. He therefore held out several scholarships a year.

It was a very young team—fast, explosive at times, and well-balanced. At center was 6′11″ sophomore Gminski with All American potential written all over him. At one guard, junior and team veteran, 6′5″ Jim Spanarkel directed the offense. At the other guard, sophomore John Harrell. The forwards were both freshmen, Eugene Banks and Kenny Dennard. Banks had gone to a high school in Philadelphia that won the city championship in each year that he played on its team.

The Blue Devils played at a fast pace from tipoff to buzzer with little perceptible letup. It was a tribute to Foster's conditioning program and to his highly respected motivational skills. The team owned the country's best free throw percentage—and by a wide margin. They lost only to USC outside their conference but were shocked by North Carolina State 74-50. They were, therefore, favored to take the East regional, considered the weakest of the four.

Pennsylvania (19-7), Villanova (21-8) and LaSalle (18-11) were all from Philadelphia. Villanova had tied Rutgers for first place in the Eastern Eight and had copped the playoff. LaSalle's chances were distinctly dim, despite the presence of Michael Brooks, their brilliant center. They had faced eight teams invited to the tournament—five of them in the East regional—and had been unable to salvage a single victory.

There was also Furman (19-10) which finished fourth in the Southern Conference but won that league's playoff. The victory had come as a surprise since the Paladins were skidding late in the season with five losses in their last seven games. Earlier, though, they had beaten North Carolina and North Carolina State in back-to-back games, bopping the Tarheels on their own court. A 61 point victory over Wofford in which they outscored their opponents by better than two-to-one had a cathartic effect on Furman.

Among the also-rans was Indiana (20-7) which had finished second in the Big Ten. After losing six of nine at midseason, including a trouncing at Michigan, the Hoosiers accelerated and won their last eight. In the Michigan debacle they gave up 92 points—unheard of for a team coached by Knight.

Another revival story was that of St. Bonaventure (21-7) which had succumbed to Syracuse 107-81 in their fourth game but had nipped them in the ECAC final when it counted more. A clutch team, they won their last four by three points or fewer. The Bonnies were among the top three free throw shooting teams in the country, all of whom were in the East regional. Duke and Furman were the others.

Another comeback was engineered by Rhode Island (24-6) which beat Providence in the ECAC New England final after they were pinched by the Friars by 20 points at midseason. The high point of their season was an upset over San Francisco on the West Coast; the low point a 92-64 thrashing by Michigan State.

Two local schools battled to survive the first round in Philadelphia. Neither Villanova nor LaSalle was able to build more than a four point lead in a very close first half. The players raced from end to end as if enacting a jail break, scoring almost at will. Defense had taken a holiday.

Down by three at the intermission, Coach Rollie Massimino of Villanova brought in Keith Herron. Though hampered by a sore knee, the 6′6″ senior forward responded by sparking the Wildcats to ten straight points in the first three minutes to unhinge the tight game. LaSalle was forced to abandon their zone which had not been very effective anyway. This allowed their opponents to exploit the middle and tally on layups and short jumpers. In the second half Villanova pumped 57 points through the hoop on 67 percent shooting as three Wildcat players finished with more than 20 points. At the buzzer it was Villanova 103, LaSalle 97.

Penn was able to overcome a tentative first half to halt St. Bonaventure 92-83. Kevin McDonald's 19 points kept the Quakers in the game during the initial 20 minutes when they looked totally disorganized. Their inability to react caused them to commit a rash of fouls which St. Bonaventure exploited with 22 trips to the foul line. A thorough briefing in the locker room led to the right adjustments and the Quakers came out and took charge early in the second half. In an almost carbon copy of the Villanova-LaSalle confrontation the Quakers pulled ahead with a burst. McDonald took charge again though he had considerably more help now. He finished with 37 points. The Quakers' 62 percent shooting in the second period also helped.

Surprising Rhode Island led Duke 31-30 at half time and refused to be shaken off down the stretch. At no time were the sides more than five points apart. With 33 seconds remaining Gminski hit the cords to create a 61-61 tie. Sixteen seconds later the Duke center had the ball again when Sylvester "Sly" Williams fouled him. His two free throws dropped through, assuring Duke an unexpectedly close 63-62 win. Williams' 27 points kept the Rams in the game. Had they been more accurate from the line, where they missed seven of eleven free throws, they might have won.

Indiana survived a similar scare from Furman. Ahead by 13 with as many minutes remaining, the Hoosiers appeared to be safe. Indiana was somewhat restricted because their offense was limited to Wayne Radford and Mike Woodson. The latter scored 12 of Indiana's first 18 points and appeared to be Knight's designated shooter as he lofted more than half the Hoosiers' shots.

Either Indiana became complacent, or Radford and Woodson burned out; whatever the reason, Furman spurted to within a point with two minutes to go. Tommy Baker's bucket after taking a pass underneath made it 58-55 at 1:32. A free throw by the Paladins was countered by a Hoosier layup giving them some breathing room. But Jonathan Moore cut the lead in half with a jump shot as the clock flashed 33 seconds. Three ticks later Indiana's Butch Carter was at the foul line for a pair. Radford had been the only Hoosier to connect from the stripe but Carter appeared to clinch the game when he sank three of four foul shots within two seconds. The opportunity came up when he made the first shot and hit the rim with his second. The ball bounced right back to him and he was fouled again as he tried for a short jumper. This time he hit the mesh both times.

Furman was not through though. Moore's stuff 15 seconds later, a missed Indiana free throw and a 26 foot prayer by Al Daniel that was answered made the score 63-62 Indiana with two seconds to go. When Wisman, confused by the screaming, predominantly Furman fans in the stands, was called for an inbounds violation, it looked as if a miracle was about to be bestowed on the Paladins. An inbounds pass by Furman, a 35 foot jump shot, a harmless ricochet, the sound of the buzzer. This time the prayer was ignored.

In its second round match against Villanova, Indiana was once again dominant in the first half. This time they were 12 points ahead with 15 minutes to go when the roof began to sway. Herron's 19 points had kept the Wildcats afloat in the opening frame while his teammates dozed. In the second half the Wildcats switched to a zone causing the Midwesterners to miss the target repeatedly. It might have helped if Indiana had spread the scoring load. Herron was getting more help from his teammates but on the other end of the court Radford and Woodson provided the whole offense. In the final 20 minutes they took all except two of Indiana's shots and finished with 38 of their side's 49 attempts. With 7:53 remaining Ray Tolbert was charged with his fifth personal and Indiana lost control of the boards. Alex Bradley took charge of the rebounds and was a major factor in the Wildcats' final drive, despite the fact that he was throwing bricks with one field goal in eleven tries.

Wisman gave Indiana its last lead at :35 with his only bucket of the game making the score 60-59. Indiana expected the ball to go to Herron on the inbounds play and covered him closely. The ball went to Rory Sparrow, normally a perimeter shooter, who took it to the left of the key and after imitating a corkscrew arched a short—for him—jumper into the net. Indiana's last threat was stymied when Herron batted a pass away preserving Villanova's 61-60 win. The Wildcats' unyielding zone allowed only 17 points in the second half. Radford and Woodson combined for the identical 46 points they had scored against Furman.

It looked for a while as if the regional final would be an all-Philadelphia affair as Penn led Duke 66-58 with eight minutes to go. But with Gminski sparkling on defense and Banks, a Philadelphian himself, on offense, Duke pulled out an 84-80 win. Gminski blocked three shots which led directly to Duke field goals, creating a potential swing of 12 points. McDonald, hampered by four personals for much of the second half, contributed only ten points. The Quakers lost the game, though, when they went into one of their patented swoons (which afflicted them sooner or later in almost every tournament) and managed only one field goal during one six minute stretch late in the game.

The regional final was decided almost before the players had a chance to work up a sweat. Villanova turned the ball over four times in their first seven trips downcourt as Duke, after establishing an 8-6 lead, accounted for the next 13 points, 11 by Spanarkel. Duke's fast break was moving with the efficiency of the Pony Express and that created some easy opportunities under the hoop. The Blue Devils shot 78 percent in the second half and 65 percent for the game as they trounced Villanova 90-72.

Midwest:

The Midwest regional also had its share of reborn Lazaruses, but none had come so far from the back of beyond than seventh ranked DePaul (25-2). A minor power until the mid-sixties, DePaul almost disappeared from the sports page for ten years until Coach Ray Meyer convinced Dave Corzine, a wide-shouldered center, to attend DePaul*. The reason Meyer was able to get Corzine, the first high school All American he had ever landed, was that he had finally obtained a recruiting budget but only after threatening to resign following an 8-17 record in 1971. Now, after a steady climb, Meyer had reached the top ten like the phoenix rising from its ashes.

Meyer was a man totally committed to—some would say obsessed with—basketball. He had been a sophomore on the 1936 Notre Dame team that was acclaimed the national champion. The captain of that squad was George Ireland who later coached DePaul's cross city rival Loyola. In 1938 Meyer had captained the Irish himself, even though the team included a pair of three-time concensus All Americas. It was almost inevitable that he met Marge, the woman he would later marry, on a basketball court. She played for a YWCA team which Meyer was coaching at the time. She, as well as their children, always called him "coach."

Meyer stayed at DePaul throughout his career, having the good fortune to arrive after George Mikan had already enrolled there. Meyer had taken DePaul to the NCAA semifinals in 1943 and won the NIT in 1945. More good teams followed and the Blue Demons played regularly in 17,000 seat Chicago Stadium. Then the Big Ten teams with their huge recruiting budgets began attracting the best Chicago basketball players who had previously attended DePaul. As the quality of the athletes declined, interest in the team waned and fewer games were scheduled in the large arena. The Blue Demons were forced to play their home games almost exclusively in their tiny gymnasium.

By 1978 they were performing before large audiences again. Attendance had tripled over the previous four years. Through the dry years Meyer never lost his intensity nor his love and enthusiasm for the sport. And the sport did not leave him behind. He stayed current, getting the most from the mediocre talent available. Now as DePaul prepared for its eighth NCAA tournament and fifteenth postseason appearance they were again getting topnotch players and were a powerhouse on the national scene once more. But he still recalled the days he had to clear the gym of tables left from the bingo games the previous evening and to stoke the furnace so his players did not freeze during practice.

---

*Corzine could be seen walking around the campus barefoot and was known to have flashed his middle finger at a referee. Given his strange habits and his exploding afro hairstyle, he became known as the Space Cadet. Meyer once remarked: "My greatest achievement was Corzine going out of here a man."

The Blue Demons had lost only to LSU by a point and to Marquette by six. On the plus side was a victory over Notre Dame at South Bend, a 100-52 blowout of Yale in the final of the Kodak Classic and a winning streak encompassing their final 12 games.

Meyer recalled that in the past he had been a "dictator" but he had mellowed considerably. Now at 63 with retirement pressures beginning to squeeze him, he had one burning desire. "I don't care if I win it. Just make the Final four. At least I'll know I've rubbed shoulders with the champions."

Tenth ranked Notre Dame's (20-6) schedule was an exercise in masochism. The first obstacle was UCLA and the Irish hurdled it 69-66 at Pauley Pavilion. But then they lost to Indiana 67-66 and to Kentucky and San Francisco. They took their second game from UCLA in front of a frenzied mob in South Bend, 75-73, but lost there to DePaul. In all, they toughed out ten games against tournament-bound teams, a formidable assignment, and achieved a 6-4 record.

The Irish were strong at all positions. Bruce Flowers and Bill Laimbeer alternated at center—a situation that pleased neither one of them. Laimbeer had dropped out of school because of poor grades but had returned after a year in junior college. Kelly Tripucka, a freshman forward with a Beatles haircut, was the son of a former All American Notre Dame quarterback. "Duck" Williams was the latest in a line of imports from the nation's capital where he attended Mackin High School, which had also sent them Austin Carr.

Texas and Arkansas, both highly ranked, finished in a tie at the head of the SWC but the Longhorns were awarded a bye until the finals of the conference playoff. Houston (25-7) had to play four games in the playoff to just one for Texas but beat the Longhorns 92-90 in the final after eliminating Arkansas 70-69. As a result Texas did not even get an invitation to the NCAA tourney—Arkansas was the selection committee's second conference choice— and went instead to the NIT which they won.

Houston posted six one hundred point games in a row. That string ended when they lost their next game to Arkansas by 19. Two losses to Texas followed but in March came the revival.

Last rites had been recited over Missouri (14-15) before the Big Eight postseason playoff and even their own fans had given up on what seemed a lifeless corpse. Their record at the time was 11-15 and they had lost seven of their last eight. But they were even worse than their record, which was buttressed by wins over powder puffs such as Midwestern of Texas, Butler, Valparaiso and California Poly at Pomona. They did not win once on the road. Quick elimination in the conference playoff to put players and fans out of their misery seemed the most merciful solution.

But the Tigers shocked everyone, including no doubt themselves, by winning three straight, something they had been unable to achieve in conference play all season, to win the playoff and the right to represent the Big Eight. Along the way there had been three heartstoppers won by two, three and three points respectively. They received a break when Kansas State upset eighth ranked Kansas in the semifinals. It would have taken heavenly intervention to produce a win over the Jayhawks who had destroyed Missouri earlier 96-49 in the worst defeat ever suffered by a Tiger team.

Utah (22-5) finished second in the WAC. Creighton (19-8) finished on top of the MVC and brushed by Indiana State in the postseason playoff final. St. Johns (21-6) qualified for the tournament by beating Army 65-63 in one ECAC regional final. It was the closest Army ever came to playing in the tournament.

Finally there was Louisville (22-6) who, in keeping with the trend, wrote their own comeback story. They started the season on the wrong sneaker by bowing to Providence, then lost their own Louisville Classic to an unimpressive Georgia squad.

The season had been a struggle for the Doctors of Dunk, who squeezed out seven wins by three points or less, but led by three local boys—Rick Wilson, Darrell Griffith and Bobby Turner—they had finished second in the Metro Seven. Florida State had topped them twice during the season and were close to doing it a third time in the conference playoff final. With nine seconds remaining Florida State had a 93-92 lead but the Cardinals had the ball. At that point Denny Crum inserted freshman Roger Burkman who had been held scoreless till then. Burkman took the inbounds pass and, as if programmed for the situation, dribbled the length of the court, jumped, pumped and hit a 15 foot shot with two seconds remaining to give the Cardinals a stirring comeback victory.

One spectacular play highlighted the opening period of first round action in Tulsa. Bernard Rencher of St. Johns took off downcourt with a Louisville defender plastered to his body and, without looking, flipped the ball over his shoulder to a trailing Reggie Carter for a layup. Louisville then broke open a close game early in the second half by going on a 14-0 tear to take a 55-38 lead. During that six minute span the Redmen missed an even dozen shots from the field. St. Johns closed to within four as George Johnson, who had been held scoreless in the first ten minutes led the resurgent Redmen. He finished with 24 points and 20 rebounds. But Griffith, who had rocked the arena with a 30 footer at the first half buzzer, sank a field goal and added six free throws to ice the game for the Cardinals 76-68.

St. Johns took 29 more shots than Louisville but their 33 percent success average was deplorable. "Now we have eight months to practice our shooting," philosophized Coach Lou Carneseca. It was their third defeat in the first round in as many years and their fourth straight since 1973. The game also completed a negative sweep for the five ECAC teams, none of which advanced beyond the first round.

Notre Dame trounced Houston 100-77 in another first round game. Missouri, trying for one more miracle, found their 63-55 lead with six minutes to go would not hold up. Utah's Danny Vranes came through with a three point play to tie the score at 64 at the end of regulation time. The sides were still tied at 70 at the end of the first overtime. In the second overtime Buster Matheney accounted for ten points to lift Utah to an 86-79 victory. He clinched the decision by tipping in a missed free throw with his team hanging on to a slim two point lead. Matheney's 36 points were a career high and overshadowed a very creditable 30 points by Clay Johnson of the losers.

In the final opening round encounter, two one-sided halves added up to a thrilling down-to-the-wire finish. There was no resemblance between the teams that answered the first and second half tipoffs though they wore the same uniforms throughout. In the first half Creighton converted 72 percent of their shots and rocketed to a 20 point lead. In the second half DePaul did slightly better and found the target 77 percent of the time. Despite DePaul's firehouse comeback and their torrid shooting, it was the poorest shooter on the court who sank the winning points. Bill Dise had been skunked all game—seven attempts, seven misses—when he stood at the line with 30 seconds to go and the score tied 78-78. But Dise delivered in the clutch, making both free throws to give DePaul a two point win. In the last half minute Rick Apke, the coach's brother, tried three shots for Creighton but missed each one.

Ten men on both teams were in double figures but only Gary Garland had as many as 20. Meyer rarely went to his bench, which in any case was weak, and Dise was in the game only because Curtis Watkins had fouled out.

Utah set the brakes and slowed the pace to a shuffle in their second round confrontation with Notre Dame. The Irish maintained a precarious lead until Earl Williams drove in for a layup at 6:04 of the second period to give Utah a 52-51 advantage. This shocked the Irish, who erupted for 11 straight points of which freshman Tripucka contributed five. Utah simply ran out of gas and failed to sink a basket in the last six minutes. Notre Dame took the checkered flag 69-56.

Louisville worked hard to overcome a big DePaul lead late in the game, but Corzine and Blue Demon free throw accuracy proved too much to overcome. Ahead by 11 with less than eight minutes remaining, DePaul was unable to stem a late Cardinal rally that knotted the score at 74 after 40 minutes. In the last two minutes Rick Wilson struck for three consecutive buckets to help Louisville's cause.

Both sides scored eight points in the first overtime and the second extra period was almost as close. The starters on both sides had played almost the entire game and energy reserves were approaching the red zone as exhaustion made each trip downcourt seem like the last mile. Once again it was Wilson who came to the rescue as he rattled in a base line jumper with 22 seconds to go to move the Cardinals ahead 89-88. DePaul worked the ball in to Corzine who swished a turnaround jump shot six seconds before the horn for a 90-89 reprieve. Though outshot and outscored from the field, the Blue Demons were brilliant from the line where they missed only three times in 25 tires.

It was the biggest night of Crozine's career, apart from the winning basket. Not only had he amassed a career-high 46 points on 18 field goals and ten for ten from the line, more than half DePaul's total, but he also broke Mikan's scoring record which had stood as a University mark for more than 30 years.

The regional final was more than just a crucial meeting, it was the most important game in the careers of both coaches. For Meyer that represented 36 years. Emotional overtones were superimposed on what was otherwise a confrontation between two midwestern Catholic schools with a long rivalry.

First, neither school had ever been in the Final Four though DePaul had made it to the national semifinals before there had been such an arrangement. For Meyer who was facing the possibility of retirement, this could well be his last chance. It was Notre Dame's fifteenth tournament; they had never gone beyond the regional and some of their fans wondered if they ever would. Second, Meyer had graduated from Notre Dame in the thirties and had been offered the Irish coaching position more than once but had turned it down each time. Third, there was the matter of revenge for DePauls' victory at South Bend. Fourth, there was the establishment factor. The game matched a small school's lean athletic budget against a large one that seemed to stretch its tentacles across the country and pluck whichever players it wanted. All but two of DePaul's starters were from Chicago—none of Notre Dame's came from Indiana.

Notre Dame's strategy was to wear an opponent down by substituting frequently. Such a move was ideal against a team with a weak bench like DePaul. But the continual shuffling of players in and out resulted in a lack of consistency and continuity so the Irish game progressed in fits and starts. Only 6′11″ Crozine matched up well physically with the Irish but he had dislocated his pinkie in practice the day before and was not 100 percent effective.

DePaul, playing a tight zone which Notre Dame was initially unable to penetrate, moved in front 29-21. When the Irish solved the zone, they took off on a 16-4 spree with short range baskets paving the way. The Blue Demons' counterbarrage exploded for 11 unanswered points to start the second half. But with DePaul in front 44-39, the balance tilted once more in Notre Dame's favor. Phelps alternated his two centers, Flowers and Laimbeer, on Corzine and they were willing to give up fouls to contain him. Tripucka also chimed in with crucial baskets at critical moments. Once ahead the Irish switched to a 1-3-1 zone and from that point matters deteriorated rapidly for DePaul. The Chicagoans gambled by shooting quickly before the zone had formed but that strategy did not work either. Finally it was 84-64 and Notre Dame was looking forward to their first appearance in the Final Four. They were to face Duke in the semifinal round. Had DePaul won, it would have matched the Blue Demons against the Blue Devils in what probably would have been a hell of a game.

West:

There was a decided imbalance in the four regionals. The West had the best teams primarily because several good ones—sixth ranked Arkansas (28-3), eighth ranked Kansas (24-4) and North Carolina (23-7) had lost their conference playoffs and had been dumped there by the NCAA selection committee. The best of the West was second ranked UCLA (24-2) who were playing under their third coach in four years. Gene Bartow had departed, unable to stand the pressure by fans and alumni. After Denny Crum had declined an offer, Dr. Gary Cunningham had become the Bruin coach. He had played on the 1960-1962 Bruin teams and been UCLA's freshman coach until 1975.

The only two losses suffered by the Bruins had been the two matches with Notre Dame and those by two and three points respectively. Other than that they were undefeated in the Pac Eight and had rolled over some respectable schools by astronomic margins. Their closest win was a 75-73 finger-crosser over BYU in the season opener.

San Francisco (22-5) lost three by a basket or less. One defeat was to Arizona State in the final of the Sun Bowl Classic. The schools met again in the final of the All College Tournament and this time the Dons repaid the favor.

The number one offense in the country belonged to fourth ranked New Mexico (24-3) which achieved triple figures 12 times. They opened the season with a 120-70 massacre of Idaho, then went on to average 110 points in their first eight games. Only twice was New Mexico held to fewer than 80 points but when UTEP handcuffed their sharpshooters, they still won 59-51. The Lobos shunned defense like the plague which resulted in some memorable shootouts. They perched on top of the WAC, losing only to Utah, USC and embarrassingly to Syracuse in the final of their own Lobo Classic.

There continued to be problems in the basketball program at New Mexico. Some of these would surface two years later and result in the dismissal, and subsequent trial on criminal charges, of Norm Ellenberger. The coach had always relied heavily on junior college transfers. Nine of them had moved to New Mexico in the past two years. But they brought trouble with them—with a capital T. One of them, Marvin Johnson, had either signed a letter or intent or enrolled at four different schools—Southwest Louisiana, Washington State, New Mexico State and Tulsa. The transient finally made up his mind to come to New Mexico but refused to dress for the first game because he was not ready to commit himself even then. When he finally did play he became their most outstanding athlete, setting a new Lobo record of 46 points in one game.

Ellenberger's reliance on JC transfers resulted from a desire for instant success which he felt was necessary to fill the school's 18,000-seat arena. In 1976 six black players left the school before the season finale, accusing Ellenberger of racism. A year later a petition containing 3,000 signatures was submitted, demanding the coach's resignation. Ellenberger stayed to babysit for his troubled squad. The free spirits on the team, immature, troubled youths, demanded more playing time and insisted on shooting whenever the mood impelled them regardless of the consequence to the team. Someone was always quitting or threatening to quit. So Ellenberger shuffled them in and out and let them run-and-gun to keep some semblance of peace, if not order. The talent was there, though in the rawest, most unrefined form.

Kansas won their first five contests, if they could be called that, by an average of 38 points. In the Big Eight they posted two victories over Kansas State, but in the postseason playoff their arch rivals turned the tables on the Jayhawks and sent them to the West regional to face much tougher competition. It was a considerable blow to the Jayhawks' aspirations to make the Final Four. The Midwest regional had been scheduled for Lawrence, on their home floor, but they would not be there.* Instead they would have to face UCLA in the first round. In the crunch Kansas went to their brilliant freshman guard Darnell Valentine and their hulking center Paul Mokeski who seemed to have awarded himself a permanent lease on the backboards. Mokeski was frequently in foul trouble, though, and had been disqualified in one-third of Kansas' games.

Arkansas had brought respectability to the SWC, for years a vast wasteland of college basketball. In total contrast to the Lobos, the Razorbacks under Eddie Sutton were disciplined. On their reversible warmups they wore the words DEDICATION on one side and DISCIPLINE on the other. The results showed. On offense they had the best shooting percentage in the country for the second year in a row. On defense they were number four.

The Razorbacks banked their first 14 games in the win column. Visits to Texas and Houston were unsuccessful but another to Memphis State resulted in a 95-70 bashing of the home team which boasted an impressive 11-2 record at the time. In the first round of the SWC playoff they terminated TCU 84-42 but lost to Houston in the semis.

It had been a disappointing season for Dean Smith. Despite finishing first in the ACC, North Carolina had lost to Duke in the playoff final and had to cross the country instead of playing the first round in friendly Charlotte. They had also dropped three games outside the ACC—to Furman, Providence and William and Mary, none of whom would have scared the Tarheels in years past. North Carolina's most memorable performance came in a game against Virginia, a good defensive team. The Tarheels, led by Mike O'Koren, the second best shooter in the country, canned 16 of 17 shots in the second half and finished with a 76.7 percent shooting average for the game, second best ever recorded by a NCAA team.

*Allen Fieldhouse in Lawrence had been renovated recently. The old court had been replaced and then broken up into four foot sections which were sold for $25 a piece.

The only two weak teams in the regional were Weber State (19-9), which had won only three of eleven road games, and California State at Fullerton (21-8). Both followed a pattern that became common in the current tournament —losing twice to the conference champs but upending them in the playoffs when it counted most.* Weber State had lopped Montana while Fullerton eliminated San Diego State, the PCAC titleholder, to reverse an earlier 25 point jolt. Unlike the ACC, SEC and MVC the weaker conferences could not expect more than one invitation so the first place team still had to win the playoff to be eligible for the tournament.

Fullerton was the only first time team in the tournament in 1978. Little was known about them or their coach. They played in a 3,000 seat mini arena and were called the Titans, a rather pretentious name for such an unprepossessing quintet. By the end of the regional, though, everyone agreed they had indeed been titanic.

Two of the top ten teams, UCLA and Kansas, met in the first round of the West regional. It was the blind luck of the draw that demanded one of them should be eliminated so early. The teams were evenly matched. Both featured quick guards and a big front court. Surprisingly, Kansas raced to a 13-3 lead; but the Bruins regrouped and caught up, only to drop behind again by three at the intermission. The Jayhawks leaped ahead 61-54 but found themselves in deep foul trouble. Mokeski, Donnie Von Moore and Ken Koenigs, their big boardmasters, all had four personals. A few minutes later Valentine was disqualified with his fifth. No sooner had he retired to the bench than John Douglas, the other guard, picked up foul number four, allowing UCLA to tie at 67. Kansas was getting charged with two fouls for every one committed by UCLA. Still the Bruins could not forge ahead until James Wilkes' one hander with six minutes remaining gave them a 71-70 advantage.

Koenigs and Clint Johnson also fouled out as the lead seesawed in the stretch. In the face of such a blizzard of infractions Kansas started losing their composure and forcing their shots while UCLA, with considerably more tourney experience, kept theirs. Their fast break, which had been effective in the first half, petered out. Still the Jayhawks were nursing a one point lead with two and a half minutes left and a chance to hand UCLA their first opening round loss since 1963.

At 2:19 Ray Townsend gave the Bruins a 77-76 lead when he flicked in two free throws. (UCLA was parading to the line and Kansas still was not in the one-and-one). When the Bruins regained possession, still in front, Cunningham directed them into a four corners delay. In the last 90 seconds Hamilton netted four free throws and added a field goal to nail the coffin shut. It had been a close call but UCLA prevailed 83-76. Kansas scored six more field goals than UCLA but the Bruins' ubiquitous presence at the line,

*Eight of eleven conference winners lost in postseason playoffs.

where they cashed in on 22 more opportunities than their opponents, made the difference.

Arkansas walloped Weber State 73-52 when the triplets—Brewer, Delph and Moncrief—scored three more points among them than the entire Wildcat team.

For the second year in a row North Carolina was hampered by an injury to their starting center. San Francisco had the early hot hands and enjoyed a 21-8 lead before the Tarheels accelerated to even matters after 20 minutes. Both sides continued to play cautiously. As a result the score was still tied 52-52 late in the game. But then Bill Cartwright swished a jump shot and his teammates chipped in with nine more points to put the game out of reach. A late Tarheel flurry narrowed the gap to two but San Francisco prevailed 68-64. Both Ford and O'Koren had poor shooting nights and no Tar Heel was able to bring down more than five rebounds. Thus neither of the previous year's finalists survived the first round.

New Mexico looked confidently beyond Fullerton to the regional that was to start the next week on their home court in Albuquerque. It was a foolish mistake. There were less than three minutes left when the Lobos pulled even with the surprising Titans on Michael Cooper's slam dunk. That made it 83-83 but Fullerton shrugged it off and sank seven of eight free throws the rest of the way to advance 90-85.

The Lobos were strictly spectators in Albuquerque and some might have included UCLA in that category too. Certainly there was little reason to suppose they had come to play as Arkansas sprang to a 16 point lead in the first half. Delph (who had 18 points on nine of eleven shooting) and Moncrief were torrid enough to have melted a medium-sized alp. Meanwhile the Bruin backcourt of Townsend and Hamilton, who scored 45 points against Kansas, was hibernating.

Back in the locker room Cunningham must have consulted the book on Arkansas because the Bruins started the second half with a full court press. The Razorbacks had been susceptible to this tactic for the last two years and they were still unable to handle it. They turned the ball over nine times in the first ten minutes of the second session. Hamilton's layup tied the score and when Kiki Vandeweghe stuffed the ball, the Bruins assumed a 60-58 lead, their first since the opening minute. However, Arkansas regained their poise and netted the next six points. They held off all subsequent challenges and won 74-70. This time the Triplets bagged 62 points. UCLA's two-for-eight from the foul line was unworthy of a ten-time national champion. Townsend's one-for-eleven from the court was even more disappointing.

The other regional semifinal looked as if it had been cribbed from the same script. San Francisco established a 15 point lead in the first half only to have Fullerton storm back using a pugnacious press that flustered the Dons into committing repeated mistakes. The Titans had been badly outrebounded by New Mexico, but they controlled the glass against the Dons even though Steve Shaw, their center, was four inches shorter than Cartwright. A 20 foot jump shot by Keith Anderson broke a 72-72 tie with four seconds left. The Dons called time out, not realizing they had used them all. The Titans sank the technical foul and were the victors in the second upset of the evening 75-72.

The experts had predicted a UCLA-San Francisco final as they had in 1977, but instead it was Arkansas and Fullerton in the spotlight. On one side of the arena Razorback fans with buttons proclaiming HOGS ARE BEAUTIFUL faced their counterparts on the other wearing more conventional red carnations.

Ron Brewer sizzled as he canned the first eight points for the Razorbacks and 12 of their initial 18. That made the score 18-8 in favor of Arkansas. By the intermission the Razorbacks were in front by 15. Phenomenal 65 percent shooting made the difference. Several of the Titans' missiles on the other hand were not even reaching their target as they were rejected by the springier Razorbacks.

By now Arkansas was expecting a full court press every time they held the lead and Fullerton did not disappoint them. For all the times they had been victimized by the tactic, they still did not know how to handle it. Twice they threw the ball away and gave their opponents opportunities to creep back into contention. They took their time—almost the entire second half—but when Mike Niles stole the ball at 2:47 and slammed it viciously through the hoop it cut the margin to one. Seventeen seconds later Brewer gave his team some breathing space with a jump shot.

Niles made both shots in a one-and-one situation to make it 57-56 as the clock swept past the two minute mark. The Titans got a break when Arkansas was called for a five-second violation and capitalized when Anderson's rainbow swished from the corner. With discipline, patience and determination they had whittled Arkansas' huge lead and now as they nudged in front the Titans' fans stood and amplified the blare into the mega-din range. The giant killers, it seemed, were about to bag another victim and advance to the Final Four in what would be the most improbable denouement in tournament history.

However, Brewer, who seemed to have taken charge of the Razorbacks' fortunes, lofted a twelve-foot jumper for the establishment to make it 59-58 and quiet the racket. Anderson then failed on two risks from the floor, the subsequent rebounds going to the Razorbacks' Jim Counce who had played an outstanding game on defense. Counce was fouled but missed his free throw. With 14 seconds to go the Titans had one more opportunity but lost it when Moncrief deflected a ball to Counce who scored on a layup just before the buzzer to make Arkansas the first SWC team in the Final Four in 22 years. Some of the fans were ecstatic, others depressed after Arkansas' 61-58 victory—but almost all were limp.

Final Four:

"Until a coach has been to the Final Four he has not got the monkey off his back," said Al McGuire. For many, making that select group is an end in itself so that there is a natural letdown in the semifinals and finals, if they get that far. Ray Meyer had expressed the feeling that just going to the Final Four was enough for him. Three of the four coaches in St. Louis seeking the national title had never gone beyond the regionals. "Just being here is a big accomplishment," acknowledged Lou Goetz, assistant coach at Duke. Only Joe Hall and his Wildcats had a larger goal firmly in mind. They had known a similar feeling of contentment after ousting Indiana in the 1975 Mideast regional and they felt that experience had robbed them of their intensity against UCLA.

Notre Dame got a basket from each of their starters to move ahead of Duke 10-6 in one semifinal. They had little trouble solving the Duke zone. With their quickness they were able to spring a man free under the basket for an easy layup. But the Blue Devils were just as quick and when Notre Dame's periodic substitutions interrupted the flow of their game, the men from Durham moved in front. Duke's zone closed off access to uptown baskets while they ran off ten straight points to take a commanding lead. Banks took charge of the rebounding, allowing Gminski to concentrate on plugging the middle. On offense, Gminski switched between high and low post, getting free of his confused Irish defenders on the transition. Repeatedly he received the ball under the basket for uncontested shots. Meanwhile, Banks patrolled the baseline and scored from the corners. Spanarkel's playmaking created movement which caught the Irish flat-footed. One spectacular play brought the curtain down on the first half. Spanarkel threw a half court pass to Banks who caught the ball with one hand while soaring to the basket and slammed it home before cartwheeling to the floor.

Duke maintained its 14 point half time advantage until four minutes remained. The Irish began applying pressure. As the seconds ticked away so did the Blue Devils' lead. Once the Irish stopped Duke from getting the ball across center line before the allotted ten seconds. A 10-2 spurt narrowed the margin to six. Time was the enemy more than an ineffectual offense and a sagging defense, but the seconds just were not being exhausted fast enough for Duke. "I was about to call a mechanic to check the clock," said Bill Foster after the game. The Blue Devils tried retreating into the four corners but that did not work either. Only the best free throw percentage in the country kept them in the game. They made their last ten points from the line without a miss.

At :20 Notre Dame bagged their fifth straight long jumper to make the score 88-86. On the subsequent inbounds play the Irish intercepted. With the fans standing and screaming themselves hoarse, they went for the equalizer. But when Williams' 23 footer was short, John Harrel retrieved the ball. He was immediately fouled and dropped in a pair to give Duke a 90-86 lead. That's the way it ended. Gminski's 29 points was a major factor in his team's move to the final as was its 32 for 37 free throw shooting. Notre Dame took 24 more shots and had seven more baskets, but they were stymied when their opponents went, swish, swish, swish, at the line.

Kentucky was another team willing to give up fouls in order to keep the pressure on. And the referees were not about to let the game get out of hand. They imposed a tight control, especially in the first half, naming some close calls fouls and quick whistling several three-second violations. The result was a lot of violations which hurt Arkansas more than Kentucky.

Steve Schall, the Razorbacks' only genuine big man, was charged with his fourth personal after only six minutes of play with Kentucky ahead 13-12. Ten minutes later, still in the first half, Jim Counce, the only other starter over 6′4″, also received his fourth. Arkansas was forced to switch to a zone, not as potent as their man-to-man. The exhausting period came to an end with Kentucky ahead 32-30.

James Lee, a leaper and dunk artist, was having his best game of the tournament for Kentucky. So was Givens who made 23 points and held Delph to 15. Macy, who had broken the Kentucky record for assists in a season, fed the bigger men. But it was Kentucky's defense that made the difference. They pushed the Razorbacks further away from the basket than they wanted to be so their efforts fell short.

It took Arkansas four minutes to score their first bucket of the second half. Nevertheless, they hung in and when they switched back to a man-to-man midway through the second half, they reversed the momentum. With three and a half minutes to play, Moncrief was at the line for two. He made the first but when he missed the second, Alan Zahn tapped in the errant ball to complete a three point play, narrowing Kentucky's lead to one. Five Wildcats had now been tagged with four personals. However, two foul shots by Lee, a Givens' layup off a long pass by Macy and another free throw offset one point by Zahn and the Wildcats were in the final 64-59.

The media accused the Wildcats of being standoffish and uncooperative before their national title contest with Duke. They were grim all right, since the four seniors—Givens, Robey, Phillips and Lee—remembered well their euphoria before their encounter with UCLA in the 1975 final. They vowed it would not happen again. They had come this far; they would not be denied. They wanted to be left alone and to prove on the court that they were indeed champions.

Some of the older Kentucky and Duke fans probably remembered when these two had last met as members of the Final Four. In the 1966 semifinal Kentucky had peaked too soon and had been flat against a scrappy UTEP squad in the final. But the Wildcats were up for this one. They outhulked the Blue Devils—someone claimed they were capable of winning the football championship, too—and pushed them all over the court.

Duke started in a zone but not a particularly effective one. They spread themselves a little thin by coming out and putting pressure on the Wildcat guards; but this created an opening near the top of the key which Givens exploited repeatedly (another example of Hall's tactical genius). Fed by his teammates, he shot line drive trajectories that wooshed through the net from 15 feet almost as consistently as chimes. Strangely, Gminski never came out of his slot under the basket to challenge him, not even when he scored Kentucky's last 16 points of the first half.

Duke was doing what they did best. They converted 20 of 21 free throw attempts but with only nine baskets it was not enough. Kentucky effectively hobbled their normally devastating fast break.

Givens continued to blaze in the second half and finished with 41 points. There was little disagreement when he was chosen the tournament's MVP. Robey, the other forward, had 20 points.

With 90 seconds to go, Kentucky had an eleven point lead and Hall took his starters out of the game so they could receive a well-earned ovation. But Duke was not dead yet. They stormed back to within four as the clock showed ten seconds remaining. Hall quickly reinserted his starters and the mini insurrection fell short. Kentucky held on to win 94-88. It was their seniors' one-hundred-second win in four years.

It was over and none of the many revivals, the second chance quintets, the comeback teams, had won the ultimate prize. But in a way Kentucky, too, was a story of resurgence from disappointment and approbation. Joe Hall and the four Kentucky seniors had indeed come back and vindicated themselves.

1979

Because of past poor performances by some conference champions, the NCAA tournament committee wanted to prevent them from receiving automatic tournament berths. This would have affected the Ivy League and some ECAC teams. But protests deterred them and instead they expanded the tourney to 40 schools. Even with 32 teams, the tournament had not found room in 1978 to accommodate schools with excellent records such as Temple (24-4), Detroit (24-4) and Illinois State (24-3).

The committee decided to make three changes for 1979. First, there would be ten teams in each regional but not more than two from any conference. Second, the teams would be seeded so the strongest teams would not meet until the later rounds, thus preventing another UCLA-Kansas first round confrontation which occurred in 1978. Six teams would get first round byes in each regional—a total of 16 teams would thus be competing in the first round. The return to a pre-1975 imbalance was something the committee decided they could live with. The conferences whose representatives would receive automatic first round byes were: ACC, Big Ten, Pac Ten, SEC, Sun Belt, Eastern Eight, Big Eight, SWC, Mid American, West Coast, Metro Seven, Southern, Pacific Coast, WAC, ECAC-New England and MVC. The decision was based on the conferences' performance in the tournament over the last five years. Third, if more than one team from a conference was selected, all would compete in the same regional, thereby preventing two teams from the same conference meeting in the final.

One other explanation for the tournament committee's decision to expand may be found in the revenue which the postseason television contract was bringing to the NCAA and its member schools. This had reached 4.69 million dollars by 1978.

Passing. Whatever happened to passing? Well, it had a rebirth of sorts in 1979. Passing, it seemed, had died when Walt Hazzard graduated from UCLA in 1964. But now two brilliant athletes revived that phase of the sport. One was a forward for Indiana State and the other a guard at Michigan State. Both were the flywheels that made their respective teams hum. In the words of their coaches, both controlled rather than dominated the game. Their schools catapulted from mediocrity to national prominence in one season as a result. Both athletes were named to everyone's All American team. It was almost as if they were destined to meet in some crucial, decisive encounter. But since the schools were not scheduled to play each other and their conferences were in opposite regional brackets, it could only happen in the game for the national championship.

Despite on-court similarities Larry Bird and Earvin "Magic" Johnson were completely dissimilar in their personalities and backgrounds. Bird was quiet, introverted and a rarity—a white player who, at 6′9″, was also big and dominating. He was the first white basketball superstar since Bill Walton but the press were not allowed to get close to him. He insisted on maintaining his privacy. One reason for his reluctance to talk to reporters was he felt they had invaded his privacy already by writing about his family. Another reason was that coming from French Lick, Indiana, population 2,059, he was genuinely overwhelmed by all the publicity he generated.

Bird originally entered Indiana University in 1974 but had returned to French Lick after a few days, unable to adjust to life on a campus with 31,000 students. He next enrolled at Northwood Institute, a small local college with 160 students, but lasted only a couple of months before returning home once more. He took a job with the local parks department driving a garbage truck and that is where Bill Hodges, assistant coach at Indiana State, found him when he came to French Lick to recruit his diamond in the rough. Hodges claimed it was not hard to spot Bird since there were few 6′9″ blond teenagers in French Lick and even fewer driving garbage trucks.

Hodges was able to talk Bird into enrolling at Indiana State. He was red shirted in 1976 but in 1977 he averaged 32.8 points per game, third best in the country, was among the top ten in rebounding and led the Sycamores to the NIT. The following year Bird's average dropped a couple of points but he again boosted his team to the NIT. Now in 1979 he was the nation's runner-up in scoring and fourth in rebounding. With his passing and assist production, he was the complete ballplayer. And very much a dedicated team player. When the Boston Celtics offered him a multimillion dollar pro contract if he gave up his last year of eligibility, he refused, returning instead to Indiana State in the hope he could lead them to a national championship. Because he had already quit two schools and had an offer pending to turn professional, his coaches were somewhat afraid of upsetting him and did their best to be accommodating—which meant keeping reporters at a distance.

Magic Johnson on the other hand was gregarious, extroverted, mischievious, happy. His jokes and good humor lifted the team. At 6′8″ he was one of the tallest guards in the country, and because of his size he was able to get a better perspective of the court. In addition, his natural court sense allowed him to see the play developing, enabling him to pass to teammates cutting for the basket. His favorite receiver was Greg Kelser who fattened his scoring average off Johnson assists. As a freshman he led the Big Ten in that department. "One passes and the other dunks," observed Terry Donnelly, the Spartans' other guard, succinctly.

Johnson had been high school All State for three years, an unprecedented achievement. The local hero from Lansing was urged, even begged, to remain at home and go to Michigan State. The whole town rejoiced when he agreed. However, Magic was not expected to return to school following his sophomore year because of the lure of a professional contract. So the Spartans had chosen him as one of their co-captains.

Midwest:

Until Bird came along, Indiana State was the forgotten university in a state that produced powerhouses like Notre Dame, Indiana and Purdue. Yet the Sycamores had a claim to fame, too. John Wooden started his college coaching career there in 1947 before moving to UCLA two years later.

Before the 1979 season Bob King, their coach, suffered a heart attack and soon thereafter had undergone brain surgery. Assistant coach Bill Hodges took over the reins. Except for Bird, the 1979 Sycamore starters were all new. Carl Nicks, their best guard, averaging just under 20 points, had spent the previous year at Gulf Coast Community College where he had been diverted by King to polish his playing skills. He got much more playing time there than if he had remained at Indiana State. Another player of note was super-sub Bob Heaton, a good man in the clutch. With a second to go and ISU trailing New Mexico State by two points, Heaton cranked up and banged a 50 foot shot off the glass into the net. The Sycamores went on to win in overtime despite losing Bird and two other players via fouls. It was the closest game Indiana State played all season, though they barely got past Illinois State by two points and Southern Illinois by one.

After 29 games they were still undefeated at the end of the season. Not until February, however, were they ranked number one because most analysts felt their schedule was too light to prove the Sycamores were the best.

Only All American Sidney Moncrief and a number of unknowns were left at Arkansas. This combination was good enough to lift the seventh ranked Razorbacks to a 23-4 record and a conference title. They shared the top spot with Texas at the end of the regular season after splitting their two matches. But they beat the Longhorns in the playoff final 39-38 when Jim Krivacs was hit with a technical 90 seconds from the end for protesting a referee's call too loudly. Moncrief converted for the margin of victory.

The Razorbacks won their first ten, then dropped three in a row. They bounced back by clobbering TCU 90-51, but suffered a relapse against Baylor before taking their last dozen games, including another shellacking of TCU 108-65. After leading the country in field goal percentage the previous year, Arkansas slipped slightly to the number three spot.

The other representative from the SWC was Texas (21-7). Abe Lemons, the sport's foremost wit, was in his third year as coach of the Longhorns. He had come from Pan American where he had stayed briefly after leaving Oklahoma City. Lemons was still a very offense-minded coach yet his defense, which he called "the Sieve," was adequate. Texas walloped an excellent BYU squad (which later won the WAC title) 96-57 and in a scoring orgy plastered Northern Montana 148-71.

Lemons had won his first game as pilot of the Longhorns before only 5,000 fans but attendance had risen dramatically. In keeping with the scale of things in the state, Texas had built a new arena called the Super Drum. It seated 17,000 spectators. In order to fill the Super Drum, Lemons had to step up his recruiting, not something he enjoyed. His comment on recruiting budgets: "Just give every coach the same amount of money and tell him he can keep what is left over."

The two representatives from the Metro Seven were Louisville (23-7) and Virginia Tech (21-8). Louisville, which had won their conference playoff in 1978 after finishing second, took first place this year but had the tables turned on them in the playoff by Tech. The inconsistent Cardinals won three by more than 40 points but were humiliated as often. In order to resolve this inconsistency, which Crum traced to a breakdown on defense, he sent Darrell Griffith, the team's star, to a hypnotist.

For a change Louisville was playing more of a team game, passing the ball around rather than freelancing one-on-one as often. Carlton "Scooter" McCray, a 6′8″ freshman, was their premier passer, fitting in well with the new ball movement trend. A good blend of enthusiastic freshmen and experienced juniors was another reason for Louisville's success.

Virginia Tech won their first nine and their last eight, but they slumped at midseason with a 4-8 mark, most of the setbacks coming against ACC teams. They swamped their first two victims by 86 points and later dismantled CCNY 113-51.

Jacksonville (19-10) finished fourth in the Sunbelt, losing to South Florida and South Alabama twice each during the season but knocking them both out in the postseason playoff. South Alabama (20-6) finished first and thus saved a tournament berth. Undefeated in the conference, they were tripped by lightweights such as Mississippi State, Alabama-Birmingham, North Carolina-Wilmington and Illinois State among others.

Weber State (24-8) played an exhausting schedule which started with four games in Alaska. They took the Big Sky title and then won two conference playoff games by 22 and 26 points. New Mexico State's (22-9) schedule was almost as long. The Aggies came closer than any other school to ruining Indiana State's undefeated season, losing to them in the final seconds the first time and in overtime the second.

The most surprising team in the Midwest regional was Oklahoma (20-9), known primarily as a football powerhouse, which won their first Big Eight championship since 1947. In that year they had gone to the NCAA finals in Madison Square Garden where they lost to Holy Cross and a then unknown freshman guard by the name of Bob Cousy. Only Kansas, Kansas State and Missouri had represented the Big Eight in the last 13 years.

The Sooners' coach was Dave Bliss, who had been an assistant at Army under Bobby Knight. His had been a far flung recruiting effort since he had been unable to flush out any local talent. Three players came from Indiana, one starter hailing from Knight's bailwick of Bloomington.

In a contest punctuated by mistakes perpetrated by both sides, Jacksonville took a 27-19 lead which Virginia Tech wiped out by half time. Led by freshman Dale Solomon's 18 second half points the Gobblers went on to win 70-53.

Weber State and New Mexico State took turns putting together short streaks. The Wildcats were ahead by nine after which the Aggies passed them to assume a 54-53 lead. Off went Weber State on another streak and forged ahead 63-56. New Mexico State responded by scoring 13 of the next 15 points. At that point David Johnson sank two baseline jumpers to send the game into overtime. A concerted effort in the extra period by Weber State brought them an 81-78 victory.

A surge led by Darrell Griffith early in the second half after the Jaguars had closed to within a point, helped Louisville ovecome South Alabama 69-66. In another second round match Oklahoma eliminated Texas 90-76. Sinking 16 of their first 22 shots from the floor helped, as did Ray Whitley's 25 points. The victory duplicated Oklahoma's last tournament win—a victory over Texas in 1947.

The first round winners confronted Arkansas and Indiana State. Larry Bird was wearing a bandage on a fractured thumb, fortunately on his non-shooting hand. That handicap plus the tension generated by ISU's first tournament appearance made the Sycamores nervous at first. Virginia Tech took an early 18-14 lead but were blanked for six and a half minutes from the midmark of the first half. Meanwhile Indiana State fattened their advantage with a 20 point explosion on their way to an easy 86-69 victory. Bird and Nicks divided 44 points evenly.

Arkansas shot better than 60 percent from the floor as Schall twisted free repeatedly under the basket for easy layins. Moncrief became the first Razorback to score more than 2,000 career points during the easy 74-63 win over Weber State.

The largest crowd ever to witness a basketball game in Ohio filed into Riverfront Coliseum in Cincinnati to watch Arkansas establish a 17 point half time lead over Louisville. The Cardinals made a blazing comeback with the tried and true anti-Arkansas press to lead 56-55. However, two free throws by Moncrief and a three point play by Ulysses S. Reed reestablished the Razorbacks' superiority. Whether Arkansas had finally learned to handle the press effectively or Louisville had dug themselves a hole too deep to escape from was still up for debate. Moncrief's 27 points were very real, though, in the 73-62 victory.

In the nightcap ISU, the country's fourth best rebounding team, took possession of the boards to blast Oklahoma's hopes 97-73. The Sycamores claimed 50 misses to 22 for the Sooners. Rarely has one team outrebounded the other by such a wide margin. Al Beal, the Oklahoma center, fouled out after playing only 17 minutes and there was nobody to prevent Bird from preying on the Sooners. He scored 29 points, took down 15 rebounds and his sparkling passes accounted for five additional baskets. But it was not until Beal was forced out of the game that Indiana State began to roll. The Sooners had their last lead, 33-32, when Bird stole the ball, and passed to Nicks who blew a layup. Leroy Staley, trailing the play, jammed the ball home to start the rout.

The regional final matched Indiana State and Arkansas. Since this was their first confrontation with a top ten team, those who had disparaged the Sycamores for playing an easy schedule expected them to be eliminated. Arkansas did lead through most of the contest. But late in the game the Sycamores pulled in front 55-53 on the way to a six point lead. The Razorbacks leapfrogged ahead 69-67 and two ensuing ties made the score 71-71 with just over a minute left to play.

Arkansas had the ball and decided to hold it for a last shot when Reed stumbled while dribbling and was called for steps. Now it was ISU's turn to hold the ball. With 18 seconds on the clock the Sycamores called for time. Hodges diagrammed a play and inserted his best shooters. Both benches and 17,166 fans expected Bird (who had 31 points already) to shoot, but when the ball came to him, he was so well-covered he passed it back to Heaton. The hero of the overtime game against New Mexico State delivered the ball to Nicks who forwarded it to Steve Reed. The final buzzer was imminent but Reed did not have a shot either. It looked as if ISU was not going to get the ball away before time ran out. Desperately Reed passed the ball to Heaton who immediately attracted a crowd. With players thicker than flies on a garbage can all around him, he switched the ball to his left, non-shooting, hand to get a better angle. The southpaw shot teetered on the rim, then dropped into the net as the horn sounded proclaiming Indiana State's 73-71 victory. Overcome emotionally, Heaton broke down and sobbed while the Indiana State fans swayed and chanted their victory hymn. Amen, Amen, Amen.

Mideast:

Michigan State (21-6) was expected to take the Big Ten title but the fourth ranked Spartans stumbled four times on the road in January and barely recovered to finish in a three-way first place tie with Iowa and Purdue. The midseason problem was resolved when Coach Heathcote, whose reserve strength was thin, moved Magic Johnson to forward and replaced him with Mike Brkovich. That made Ron Charles the sixth man, enabling Heathcote to generate some instant action off the bench.

The Spartans were much better than their record indicated. Five of their losses came by two points or fewer and only an inexplicable 18 point defeat to last place Northwestern caused some embarrassment. They beat a strong North Carolina squad, bested Indiana (the NIT champion to be) three times, trounced Washington State (where Heathcote had once been an assistant coach) 98-52, and claimed the West Coast Classic at Christmas time.

Most expected the Spartan's toughest challenge to come from fifth ranked Notre Dame (22-5). The Irish had been the top team in the polls for several weeks until they dropped one to UCLA at South Bend and were ousted from that perch by Indiana State. They also lost the final two of the season to DePaul, avenging the previous year's regional final, and to Michigan. The latter was played in the Silverdome in Pontiac, Michigan, before 37,283 fans, the second biggest crowd ever to watch a college basketball game.

However, all Notre Dame's losses had come in closely contested matches—none by more than five points. They registered a 44 point victory over Northwestern which later set back Michigan State. And they had socked UCLA at Pauley Pavilion for the third straight year. Nobody had ever done that to the Bruins before. UCLA's record at home while playing at Pauley was 204-7 and the Irish were responsible for three of those seven losses. Even worse was UCLA's overall record against Notre Dame over the last six years. In that span the Bruins had won 134 and lost 20. Yet against Notre Dame they were 4-7. Undoubtedly the Irish had UCLA's number.

The only other top ten team in the Mideast regional was ninth ranked LSU (22-5). The Tigers were participating in their first NCAA tournament since Bob Petit graduated in 1954. Theirs was an uphill struggle against adversity. They lost their brilliant star forward Durand "Rudy" Macklin after the second game of the season through injury. Then during the conference playoff DeWayne Scales, their other forward, was suspended because he allegedly changed his style of play on the advice of a pro scout in order to showcase his talents for the NBA. Since this conflicted with the role his coach had assigned him, disciplinary action was inevitable. Coach Dale Brown may have brought grief on himself since he was quite lenient in his handling of Scales. He noted, "DeWayne is like a bumblebee in a glass jar. If I restrict him too much, it would take away his effectiveness as a player."

In an unusual role reversal, LSU's best forward and best guard played counter to the norm. Scales, who was 6′9″, was Mr. Outside, popping in jump shots from 15 feet. Al Green, their 6′2″ guard, liked to weave inside for layups, earning the title of Mr. Inside. He also picked up a lot of fouls along his route. The combative guard had found a home at LSU after a year in junior college and two more at North Carolina State where his style conflicted with Norm Sloan's.

The SEC held a postseason playoff for the first time. Without Scales LSU lost to Kentucky in the first round—a team they had earlier beaten twice. Kentucky itself was knocked off in the final by Tennessee 63-59 in overtime, preventing the Wildcats from defending their national title. Tennessee's (20-11) record had been 12-11 at one time but they won eight in a row down the stretch. Now in their fourth tournament, they were still looking for their first win.

Few expected Iowa (20-7) to be among the tournament starters after the Hawkeyes' dreary getaway. They lost a pair to Drake and Colorado State by identical 72-69 scores, then barely edged Iowa State at home. Two games later Iowa repaid the compliment with a substantial dividend when they manhandled Drake 112-73. With renewed selfconfidence, they surged through the Big Ten schedule, blasting a very good Indiana team by 29 points along the way.

Appalachian State (22-5) won the Southern Conference and qualified for its first appearance. Similarly, Lamar (22-8), won the Southland Conference. The Cardinals displayed a strong offense which generated 100 points on eight occasions against second rate teams. Another entry with several easy opponents was Eastern Kentucky (21-7) with victories over Tiffin, Sewanee and Urbana. Detroit (21-5) received the invitation they felt they should have been extended in 1978.

Toledo (21-7) tied with Central Michigan for top spot in the Mid American, then won the playoff for the tourney bid. It was their first in 12 years though they had been near the top of their conference for some time. Over a seven year period from 1972 to 1978 Toledo had made the role of bridesmaid into a career. So thoroughly had they typecast themselves in the part that when they finally made it in 1979, it came almost as a shock. Their record over that span was 129-55 and they had finished as low as third only twice. The rest of the time they had either tied for first or finished second, not more than a game or two behind the leader. Only once in those years had they lost more than nine games yet a tournament invitation remained just out of reach.

Terry Crosby held high scoring James Tillman in check as Tennessee beat Eastern Kentucky 97-83 to win their first tournament game in friendly Murfreesboro, Tennessee. The Kentuckians were ahead by ten points in the first half but could not stem the Volunteer tide thereafter. In the other first round match Lamar eliminated Detroit 95-87 thanks in part to Clarence Kea's 33 points.

The Volunteers' joy lasted just two days. Carpetbagging Notre Dame arrived in town and after an even first half began pressing Tennessee all over the court. Using a zone trap in the backcourt, the Irish forced four turnovers in the first three minutes of the second half. The aggressive tactics resulted in a 10-2 Irish fling which in turn led to a 73-67 victory. Tripucka, with six-of-seven from the floor and nine-of-ten from the line, was particularly impressive. So was Michigan State in a 95-64 romp over Lamar. Kelser with 31 points and 14 rebounds was abetted by Johnson with 17 rebounds and 10 assists. The Sparans scored 16 more field goals than their opponents and hardly worked up a sweat.

LSU had almost as easy a time against Appalachian State. A Tiger spurt in the waning minutes of the first period and the inability of Appalachian State to budge Rick Mattick, LSU's seven foot, 270 pound, center from the lane, were the prime reasons for the 71-57 decision.

The other second round game was more of a contest, though the first half, which ended with Iowa ahead of Toledo 41-29, gave no indication of the sizzling finish to come. In the second stanza the Rockets' defense tightened and they held the Jayhawks for almost eight and a half minutes without a field goal. During one seven-minute stretch Toledo outscored their opponents, 19-4, a spree that included 11 unanswered points. They also shut down Richard Lester who had 18 first half points for the Jayhawks. The rally tied the score at 53 and the Rockets took off to a 69-66 lead before Bill Mayfield, who took up the clack left by Lester's dry spell, and Vincent Brookins tallied field goals to move Iowa ahead 70-69 with 43 seconds to go. A three point play by Jay Lehman gave the Rockets the lead again but this was wiped out by Brookins' basket with :11 on the clock. Finally Stan Joplin's 20 foot jump shot at the buzzer climaxed Toledo's dramatic 74-72 come-from-behind victory. The Rockets were aided by 41 opportunities at the foul line of which they converted 28.

For the fifth time that season Michigan State's underrated defense held an opponent to fewer than 20 first half points at the Spartans blew LSU out of the arena 87-71. Twice, early in the game, Kelser stole LSU passes and went in for uncontested dunks. Johnson received credit for 24 points though he shot a disappointing 30 percent from the floor. However, he converted 14 of 15 from the stripe when LSU, unable to control him, fouled repeatedly.

Once again Toledo faced an uphill grind when they fell ten points behind Notre Dame after 20 minutes. Despite a pressing counterattack sparked by Jim Swaney's 26 points, Toledo's rally fell short and Notre Dame prevailed 79-71. The luxury of a deep bench was illustrated when Orlando Woolridge was quickly replaced by Phelps after failing at one point to pass off to a teammate with an open shot and being stripped of the ball a few seconds later.

Notre Dame had been on national television five times during the season and had lost every time. The regional final against Michigan State was to be no exception. The tone of the game was set in the first five seconds when Kelser directed the ball to Johnson who fed Brkovich for a vicious slam dunk. The Spartans had their fast break humming thereafter and the bigger but slower Irish defenders were unable to react. After missing his initial six attempts and being shut out for the first ten minutes, Kelser netted 34 points, 12 of those coming on stuffs made possible by Johnson's passes. The Magic Man was credited with 13 assists for the game. The Irish were unable to penetrate Michigan State's opaque defense and made only 35 percent of their shots in the first half. It was a game in which Notre Dame never led and whose 80-68 final score did not reflect Michigan State's awesome dominance.

West:

For the second year in a row UCLA (23-4) was ranked number two in the polls. The Bruins also set a new season NCAA record for field goal accuracy with a mark of .555. The Pac Eight had expanded to include Arizona and Arizona State and was now called the Pac Ten. Regardless of the conference name UCLA won their thirteenth consecutive conference title despite narrow losses to Stanford, Washington and Arizona. But the Bruins came within eight points of a perfect season and they trounced Stanford and Arizona in rematches by 26 and 24 points respectively.

The upstate power, San Francisco (21-6), won their conference, too, and, like UCLA, fell to Notre Dame, but by 19 points. In a game reminiscent of their first round tournament encounter in 1977 the Dons were blown away by probation-encumbered UNLV. Several familiar faces were gone. Boynes and Hardy entered the professional ranks with a year of eligibility left. Gone too was Bob Gaillard, Coach of the Year in 1977. By the end of the 1978 season he had taken more than he could stand from this undisciplined crew who sometimes refused to enter a game when sent in by their coach. The fabulous rookies of 1976 whom many felt were destined to bring back the glory days and lead USF to another championship had disappointed everyone including themselves. Instead of a championship they had been eliminated in the first round in two tournaments and not survived the second round in a third. Only Cartwright was left. The big center, with a lot more character than his teammates, finished the season with the second best rebounding record in the country.

When Dave Corzine graduated, it looked as if DePaul (22-5) would slide back into mediocrity. But Ray Meyer, his recruiting mill now well-oiled, found a replacement in Mark Aguirre who became the leading freshman scorer in the country. A 6′7″, 235 lb. forward, he was deceptively quick despite his chunky appearance.

Meyer showed his versatility as a coach and his ability to be flexible when conditions changed. His strategy with the tall, slow Corzine in the lineup was to get the ball to his center. Without him, Meyer abandoned this patterned play and moved to a fast break offense which made best use of Aguirre's quickness and the speed of guards Gary Garland and Clyde Bradshaw.

DePaul lost their opener at UCLA 108-85 and their finale to Loyola (Ill), but victories over Marquette and Notre Dame contributed to an eighth place finish in the final poll. Aside from their trouncing by the Bruins the rest of the Blue Demons' losses were close affairs. Even that debacle had its bright side as Aguirre made a spectacular debut by exploding for 29 points.

All season long the team responded to their crafty coach and when it was over he was voted Coach of the Year. It was also announced that he would be inducted into the Basketball Hall of Fame, only the fourth active coach to be so honored. In 1979 he had more victories to his credit than any other active coach. Only one goal remained elusive—a place in the Final Four.

There were three Utah schools in the regional (four in the tournament counting Weber State in the Midwest regional). The national championship was to be decided in Salt Lake City and each of the Utah teams was hoping to be there. The one given the best chance was BYU (20-7).

The pride of the Cougars was 6′5″ guard Danny Ainge. He had been an outstanding all-round athlete at North High School in Eugene, Oregon, and had been picked to both football and basketball All American teams. (He had led his basketball squad to a 52-1 record over two years on their way to consecutive state championships). He also played shortstop during the summer for Syracuse of the International League, just a step below the majors.*

Completing the state contingent were Utah (20-9), which had lost to BYU twice by a total of 40 points, and Utah State (19-10). Also present were Marquette (21-6) and Pacific (18-11). The latter's season takeoff was far from auspicious. After barely winning their opener at home against Nebraska-Omaha, the Tigers encountered turbulence and fumbled their next six. There was improvement at midseason and then finally a happy landing with 11 wins in their last dozen games.

It looked for a time as if Pepperdine (21-9) would top its conference. But that was before they blew their last three games and finished second to San Francisco. Pepperdine's record was deceptive. They finessed two of their first three wins by a point and crashed by huge margins to North Carolina (28 points), Southwest Louisiana (29 points) and Oklahoma (26 points). USC (19-8), the Pac Ten runner up, completed the regional field.

The first round got off to a lively start with two clashes between California and Utah schools. The Californians had an advantage since the games were being played in Los Angeles. A jump shot by Utah's Scott Martin evened the score 75-75 and when, with two seconds remaining, he added two free throws it seemingly sealed the victory over Pepperdine. But Matson's inbounds pass was deflected by the Utes' Tom Chambers into the hands of Ted Scott who popped in the equalizer at the buzzer.

With one second gone in the overtime Chambers, Utah's center and leading scorer, fouled out after scoring 26 points. Tony Fuller converted to give Pepperdine a lead they never relinguished. Matson had been shackled in the first half but now scored eight in the extra period and Ricardo Brown added six, giving him 26 for the game. Their contributions accounted for the rest of Pepperdine's scoring. With Chambers on the bench Utah lacked a rallying point and succumbed 92-88.

USC's 86-67 win over Utah State gave the California schools a doubleheader sweep.

One half of the second round was also played at Pauley. The doubleheader featured three California schools and DePaul. UCLA, on its home court, was heavily favored against Pepperdine but found itself in a grim struggle with the Waves until well into the second half. Brown's shots, seemingly from the freeway, were dropping in with metronomic regularity. At 4:21 of the second half Greenwood's basket brought UCLA even at 48-48. Shortly thereafter Gary Colson, Pepperdine's coach, was branded with a two-shot technical foul. That doused his team's momentum and inspired UCLA. The Bruins responded by charging into a 62-52 lead which they nursed to a 76-71 victory. Brown's 27 points were wasted in a losing effort.

---

*With his days so completely taken up by sports, Ainge had little time for his studies. This resulted in his suspension from the team and ineligibility for the first half of the 1980 season.

With Aguirre and Curtis Watkins, DePaul's forwards, accounting for 52 points, the Blue Demons eliminated USC 89-78. It was close most of the way until the last three minutes when the Chicago school launched a mini rally that insured victory. The way in which they won illustrated the excellent condition and endurance of the Blue Demons. Despite the searing pace, they used no substitutes and still managed to rally late in the game.

In the other half of the second round both Marquette and San Francisco turned close games into routs by setting their own tempo after the intermission. Marquette applied their suffocating defense to stifle Pacific 73-48. San Francisco wore down BYU 86-63. A victory for the Cougars would have allowed them to advance to the next round which was scheduled for their home court in Provo. They had not lost at home all season. For a while it looked as if they might spring an upset. Cartwright was hobbled with three personals in the first period and scored only seven points. But in the second half the Dons played almost perfect basketball and ran away from the Cougars. BYU was the last of the four Utah teams to be eliminated; none got past the second round.

In 1956 San Francisco had beaten UCLA on its way to the NCAA championship. Since then the schools had met three times, each a regional final. UCLA had won all three. The schools were also favored to meet in the regional in 1977 and 1978 but upsets paved the way for other confrontations. Now the Bruins and Dons were meeting for the fifth time. No two teams had been matched as often in the tournament.

With 4:17 to go in the first half and San Francisco in control 37-28, the Bruins roused themselves to spurt to a 41-41 deadlock just before half time. Early in the second session the Dons were once again on top when UCLA went on another tear. This one, a 15-1 outburst, was even more damaging and one from which San Francisco was unable to recover. The Bruin guards, seniors Brad Holland and Roy Hamilton, put on quite a show in the second half. Holland was six of eight while Hamilton could not miss in nine tries. They wound up with 22 and 36 points respectively. As a team the Bruins made 73 percent of their shots in the final 20 minutes when they were building towards their 98-81 win. Cartwright was outstanding with 34 points in his farewell appearance as a Don.

The DePaul-Marquette contest was billed as a contrast in styles and whoever controlled the tempo would undoubtedly win the game. In the beginning it was Marquette that set a controlled pace, moving ahead 8-0 and 18-9. But then DePaul broke out and began scudding up and down court like a pack of coonhounds at a hunt. Only Bernard Toone's 16 first half points (of Marquette's 28) kept the Warriors in the contest. After a 20-4 binge the Blue Demons were in command until early in the second half. Then the tempo turned glacial once more as the Warriors moved the ball deliberately up court and hurried back on defense to greet their hard-charging opponents before they could spring a man free.

The second period was more than half over and Marquette held a 48-40 lead. But in the next two minutes DePaul broke loose again and arced eight straight points through the hoop. It was close for a time, but when Watkins layed the ball in with 1:41 to go, DePaul took a 54-53 lead which they expanded to 62-56 at the buzzer. This time Meyer made one substitution.

The victory had been DePaul's second over Marquette that season and their next game, against UCLA, would also be a second encounter. The first had been on UCLA hardwood where the Bruins were eclipsed about as often as the sun. This was to be on a neutral court, though, with a much more mature DePaul team just one victory away from fulfilling Ray Meyer's dream.

Surprisingly it was UCLA that lost its composure in the first half as DePaul used a pressing trap defense to force 14 turnovers. Running and shooting with confidence, the Blue Demons established a 51-34 lead at half time. The crowd was predominantly for the underdog, especially after the Bruin band alienated all but their own fans by greeting their players (returning to the court for the second half) with a loud fanfare while the half time entertainment was still in progress.

The Bruins came storming back in the second half and inexorably they closed the gap. A concerned Meyer told his men to waste a minute passing the ball around before attempting a shot everytime they brought the ball downcourt. The delaying tactic slowed the Bruin advance but DePaul had squandered all but five points of their lead with five minutes still to be played. With 29 seconds to go, Holland was fouled and made both free throws to bring his team within two, 93-91. UCLA should probably have fouled right away but the Demons were the fifth best free throw shooters in the country. The Bruins allowed them to work the ball to Garland who sank the clincher. Except for the final minute DePaul again relied exclusively on their starters. Meyer was ecstatic after the 95-91 victory. Said the beaming patriarch: "I don't care if we win anothe game, because all I ever said was that I wanted to make the Final Four in Salt Lake City."

East:

The ACC, long considered the toughest loop in college basketball, was still in ascendency in 1979. North Carolina and Duke had been tournament runners up the previous two years. Every one of the teams had a winning record against outside competition and the conference as a whole was 75-15 against non-conference opponents. They were also 8-5 against teams in the top twenty. Even Notre Dame, number one at the time, barely nipped last place North Carolina State. At the end of the season five of the seven schools were invited to either the NCAA or NIT tourneys.

North Carolina and Duke finished in a dead heat on top of the ACC (the teams split their four encounters) and both were ranked in the top ten—the Tarheels third and the Blue Devils sixth. In the postseason conference tournament where tickets, when available, ran up to $200 per seat, North Carolina outlasted Duke 71-63.

Before the start of the season, Duke (22-7) had been almost everyone's favorite to go all the way. In 1978 they had been the youngest team in more than 30 years to come so close to winning a championship and the starting team was back intact with the experience of high pressure tournament competition behind them. They were still ranked number one when they arrived in New York to play in the Holiday Festival. In the first game they blew a 17 point lead to Ohio State and in the consolation they frittered away a 19 point bulge against St. Johns and lost. Instead of winning as expected, they finished last.

Duke was never the same again. Whether it was a lack of desire or concentration or their confidence had been eroded, the fact remained the Blue Devils allowed too many big leads to slip away, either losing or hanging on to win by a narrow margin. And then in a late season game Clemson socked them 70-49.

North Carolina (23-5) was steadier, though they did lose to Furman and to Clemson after earlier flogging the latter by 22 points. But these were balanced by victories over Michigan State and five others which gained the tournament. Against Duke, in one of the strangest games ever played, Smith directed his players to stall for the whole first half. As a result the Blue Devils had a 7-0 lead at the intermission. The teams played a normal second half and the game went to Duke 47-40. It is difficult to understand what Dean Smith was trying to accomplish and he never explained his reasons for this strange strategy, for which he was severely criticized.

Smith made considerable use of his four corners, now being directed by Dave Colescott. He still favored a balanced attack with substantial output from center Yonakor and forwards O'Koren and Dudley Bradley, Baltimore's High School Player of the Year in 1975.

Tenth ranked Syracuse (25-3) was the only team given any chance against the two ACC powers. The Orangemen had lost twice in the Kentucky Invitational and then reeled off 19 straight victories before bowing to Georgetown in one ECAC final. They still received an invitation to the tournament. With Bouie and his wild Artis Gilmore type Afro in the middle, Syracuse finished the season among the top teams in rebounding, scoring and margin of victory. Nine times they scored at least 100 points, eight of those coming in neat pairs of back-to-back bombings. The Orangemen were invincible on their home court where they lengthened their winning streak to 40 games.

Georgetown (24-4) fell before Oral Roberts by a point, and to St. Josephs 37-36 when scoring fell to a pre-depression level.

Temple (25-3) was undefeated in its conference but bowed to Syracuse, Penn and Virginia. Rutgers (21-8) took the Holiday Festival by beating Ohio State in triple overtime. They claimed a tourney birth by taking the post conference playoff. Senior center James Bailey rattled the basket with his patented thunderdunk 116 times during the season and it never failed to bring a responding roar from the fans.

The Ivy League made freshmen eligible for the first time in 1979 but Penn

(21-5) relied on senior Tony Price, the league's Player of the Year, to lead them to victory. Connecticut (21-7) represented the New England area of the ECAC.

Jeff Ruland had been called by Dean Smith the best center to come out of high school since Bill Walton. In 1978 Ruland was number one in scoring, rebounding and field goal accuracy among the nation's freshmen. In 1979 the 6′10″ sophomore was the rebounding runner-up among all college players.

Jim Valvano, Ruland's coach at Iona, reminded some of Digger Phelps who had piloted Fordham from obsurity to national attention before moving to Notre Dame. Valvano had done the same at Iona, another metropolitan New York school, but he elected to stay, at least for the time being. The coach stressed a pressing, fast-paced game in which his players were expected to scramble and dig for every advantage. Valvano kept a stuffed rat on a skateboard on his desk, symbolizing the hustling game he expected from his players. An exceptional motivator, he was also very chummy with his men, a situation that had not worked out too well in the past at other schools. Iona (23-4) had won their first two by a margin of 79 points but had subsequently cooled off and squeezed by six opponents by a single field goal.

St. Johns (18-10) was two seconds away from an inglorious end to their season when Ron Plair swished a jump shot to send their semifinal ECAC contest against Wagner into overtime. They went on to win but lost to Iona in the ECAC final. They received an invitation anyway, the fortieth and last tendered by the selection committee. Nobody expected them to last very long.

Two New York and two Philadelphia teams travelled down to Raleigh, North Carolina, to play in the first round. Penn built a twelve point cushion in the first half against Iona but the Gaels chipped away to narrow the gap to one. Deadly free throw shooting—27 for 31—helped Iona. With 41 seconds left the Quakers were hanging on to a 71-69 lead when the Gaels put on a full court press causing the ball to pop loose. The ensuing scramble resulted in a jump ball. Ruland controlled and fed to Lester George who faked his defender out of position. Unfortunately for him, he also shuffled his feet and was called for travelling. Iona fouled immediately but the Quakers sank both free throws to make the final score 73-69.

Temple had beaten St. Johns during the season and were trying to make it two in a row. The Redmen had learned from that experience, though. They denied the Owls their fast break by slowing the pace. On offense they solved a pesky zone and were able to free 6′8″ center Wayne McKoy under the basket for layups. Towards the end, Temple had to abandon its zone but tried trapping the ball handler by deploying two or three men. This tactic often left a man free, enabling St. Johns to capitalize with some easy buckets. The 75-70 win broke St. Johns four-game losing streak in first round tournament competition.

The following day in Providence the largest crowd to fill the Civic Center watched Rutgers put away Georgetown when the Hoyas were unable to score on eight consecutive trips downcourt at a crucial point in the game. The score was tied 50-50 at 6:32 of the second period but for the next five minutes it was strictly Rutgers' show. Georgetown's rally came too late and served only to make the final score a respectable 64-58.

In the nightcap Syracuse got off to a fast start against Connecticut and their lead ballooned to 25 points after 18 minutes. The Huskies counter-attacked, sparked by Jeff Carr's rebounding, until, with 24 seconds to go, they were only four points down. It was then that Bouie's slam dunk clinched the 89-81 victory for Syracuse.

Duke and North Carolina, playing on their own turf in Raleigh, were prohibitive favories against St. Johns and Penn. No team from North Carolina had lost a tournament game in its state since 1961.

Duke was eager to reverse the loss against St. Johns in New York. Two starters, Bob Bender and Kenny Dennard, were both out with injuries but the Blue Devils were in front by five at the half and seemingly in control. McKoy picked up three personals in the first period and had to be benched which diluted the Redmen's board strength. They switched to a zone to neutralize All American Gminski's strength under the basket. But the Duke center made the same mistake he had against Kentucky in the 1978 final when he allowed Givens to patrol the foul circle. This time it was McKoy who hit consistently from the top of the key, normally beyond his effective range. St. Johns caught up and with the game on the line Reggie Carter flipped in a baseline jumper to upset Duke 80-78.

The shock waves had not subsided when North Carolina took the court against Penn. In a situation that mirrored the first contest, Price was charged with three fouls in the first half and had to be removed. He started the second half with O'Koren guarding him but when the Tarheel forward picked up his third personal early in the period, Smith switched defensive assignments. That unleashed Price who scored 15 second half points, including five straight, to give the Quakers a 55-50 advantage midway through the second period. It was a lead they never relinquished. The 72-71 Penn victory was the second seismic shock to hit Raleigh in two hours.* St. Johns and Penn were also the only tournament teams without a bye to survive the second round. A few days later in Greensboro, North Carolina, the tremors continued. Only 9,102 fans showed up to watch four Northeastern schools

---

*It was the end of the road for the two ACC teams but the three in the NIT fared no better and also did not survive the second round. Five Big Ten teams also made the major tournaments and had much better success. One made the Final Four while the three in the NIT—Purdue, Indiana and Ohio State—all gained the semifinals. Indiana beat Purdue in the final in an intra-state affair. Since Indiana State was still in the running for a NCAA crown, Hoosier fans were hoping for two champions from the state. It was a disastrous year for the ACC and the state of Utah but a super one for the Big Ten and the state of Indiana.

compete. Without a representative from the Tarheel state local interest was low and tickets that had been sold weeks ago were easy to come by.

Penn dominated Syracuse in the same way the Orangemen had mastered Connecticut in the previous round. The Quakers sprinted to a 17 point lead in the first 20 minutes and, despite a 52 percent shooting performance by their opponents, eliminated them 84-76.

The Redmen had to overcome a personal foul crisis against Rutgers in the co-attraction. Behind by ten in the first half, they caught up soon after the intermission. At that point key men began attracting the referee's whistle. First McKoy picked up his fourth personal. Half a minute later it was forward Frank Gilroy's turn and 33 seconds after that Plair, the other forward, came within one foul of disqualification. With a short team on the court, Lou Carneseca directed his men into a zone, a defense he did not particularly relish. The Knights refused to shoot over it. Their guards were also unable or disinclined to get the ball to Bailey. The ferocious center tallied just two points in the last 17 minutes.

With the score knotted 65-65, Carter forced Rutgers' Daryl Strickland into a five-second violation. The Knights controlled the tip but Strickland was fouled and when he missed the first of a one-and-one with 40 seconds on the clock, Gilroy cradled the rebound. St. Johns held until there were 17 seconds left, then called a time out. In the huddle Carneseca called for the same play that had wiped away Duke. This time Carter's jumper bounced off the rim—but McKoy's rebound bucket was equally decisive. St. Johns stepped into the regional final with a 67-65 victory.

Almost two thousand fewer fans showed up for the regional final, resulting in more empty than occupied seats. Once more fouls plagued both sides. Price retired to the sidelines for six minutes in the first half after collecting his third personal and St. Johns was forced into an ineffectual zone after Carter and McKoy were similarly hit. The Quakers grabbed a three point half time lead, later increasing it to eight. But a series of errors—a misplaced ball, a wild pass, two travelling calls and a three second violation—allowed the Redmen to pull even. A fourth infraction against Price encouraged St. Johns into a four point lead.

Tim Smith, one of Pennsylvania's poorer shooters, then surprised everyone by floating three shots from downtown to leapfrog the Quakers into a 53-52 advantage at 5:44. There were three more lead swings and as many ties before the final outcome. Carter fouled out with a little less than four minutes to go, giving the Quaker guards an advantage.

Penn was clinging to a 64-62 advantage but the ball belonged to St. Johns when Carneseca called time. Unfortunately, his clutch man was out of the game and so he directed his players to "take the first open shot," if the Quakers stayed in a zone, which they did. With the final seconds ticking away it was Tom Calabrese, shut out until then, who considered himself open enough to shoot for the equalizer from 20 feet. He missed. Gordon Thomas retrieved the ball and tried a ten footer that bounced away. Now it was Ron Plair's turn, but his attempted tipin also missed the mark. It was his first miss in ten attempts. When the ball stopped ricocheting, it was the Quakers who had possession. With two seconds to go, Price had the chance to ice the game. He failed on the front end of a one-and-one, giving the Redmen one last opportunity. However, a long downcourt pass was intercepted, assuring Penn a place in the Final Four.

Final Four:

It was an unusual quartet. Three had never made it this far before; the fourth, Michigan State, was returning after 22 years. There were enough Cinderellas to fill a small ballroom.

Indiana State was still undefeated even as the competition got tougher. DePaul was where their coach had always dreamed it would be. The folds in his lined face reflected the feelings of a man who was living the fantasies of a boy. Penn's fans were taking their team's success in stride but underneath was the question whether they belonged here, whether somebody had made some huge mistake. Michigan State seemed the most assured.

The long season and the tournament had taken their toll. Injuries abounded. Bird was still nursing a fractured thumb. Vincent, the Spartan center, was limping on a sore foot. And DePaul's Watkins was taped from mid-thigh to mid-calf to protect ligaments damaged in the win over UCLA. So far Penn had been able to avoid their patented swoon, where their shooters turned into bricklayers. Fans with good memories were waiting for the inevitable coming of the Quaker Ice Age. They didn't have long to wait. In the first semifinal in Salt Lake City, Michigan State devastated Penn so thoroughly in the first half that not only the Quaker fans, but the Spartans, too, were embarrassed. Rarely had an audience witnessed such a one-sided affair. When the Quakers scored their first basket dozens of red and blue streamers showered onto the court. It was their fans' first and last burst of enthusiasm. After falling behind 13-4, it took Penn another eight and a half minutes to light up the scoreboard again. It looked as if they had taken an early intermission, so lacking was their presence on the court. In the grandaddy of all Final Four droughts, they made only 16.7 percent of their shots in the first period while Michigan State soared to a 50-17 lead. The second half was almost even but the damage had been done. Magic's 29 points and Kelser's 28 paced the Spartans to a 101-67 win. As a team they shot better than 63 percent while Penn managed to hit only 29 percent of the time.

The second half of the twin bill was in sharp contrast to that debacle. The score was tied 15 times in the first 20 minutes and ended with Indiana State in front of DePaul 45-42.

Watkins had been guarding Bird but without much success, so Meyer switched center Jim Mitchum to cover the All American at the start of the second half. It made little difference. The Sycamores, with Bird playing as if he was conducting a clinic, moved in front by 11 after three and a half minutes. DePaul dug in and slowly narrowed the gap until Garland's set shot propelled his team into a 73-71 lead with a little less than five minutes to play. When the Blue Demons regained the ball with the score unchanged, they went into a freeze. The result was counterproductive. It stopped their momentum and gave the Sycamores time to regroup. A DePaul turnover resulted in a Heaton field goal. Garland's free throw reestablished DePaul's lead but only by one fragile point.

The teams entered the last minute with ISU on offense. Ten seconds later Carl Nicks drove down the lane and passed to Heaton, who always seemed coolest in crucial situations. The Sycamore sub again proved his worth in the clutch by threading the twine for a 75-74 lead. Maybe Meyer should have called a time out but he did not. The Blue Devils worked the ball to Aguirre for the last shot but his 18 foot attempt bounced off the rim. ISU added a meaningless free throw just before the buzzer as their fans went into their Amen chant.

Bird was a one man franchise. He controlled the ball in every aspect of the game. Despite 11 turnovers, he was responsible for 53 of the Sycamore's points—35 of his own, an amazing 16 for 19 shooting, and nine assists. To that he added 16 rebounds.

DePaul demonstrated their stamina once again. Against UCLA they had made their first substitution in the final minute but here Meyer was not taking any chances and his starters played the entire forty minutes. It was a cleanly contested game. The Blue Demons had only five opportunities from the stripe and hurt themselves by missing three of those despite their high season percentage mark.

Penn played their sixth game of the tourney in the consolation, the first team to play that many. After falling behind by 23 points the Quakers came back to tie at the end of regulation, thus restoring some measure of respect. Nevertheless, DePaul put them away in overtime 96-93.

The fans were about to get the treat they had been waiting for all year—the confrontation between the two most exciting players in college basketball. And the signs around the arena reflected the interest. Most were to be found on the Michigan State side, proclaiming such slogans as "Stuff the Bird," "Welcome to the Magic Kingdom." One fan moved about with a stuffed bird in a cage. The rivalry even extended to the size of the pyramid each side's cheerleaders could construct. There Michigan States' 20-foot human heap overshadowed Indiana State's more modest 15 foot effort.

MSU was favored primarily because they had blown out each of their four opponents to date. Still, Indiana State was the sentimental choice.

Because of his injury Bird was having trouble gripping the ball and this may have accounted for his worst game of the tournament. The Sycamore star had problems all evening, but most of them were caused by the Spartan defense which clogged the passing lanes. They played a zone and one with Donnelly on the point guard to prevent him from passing to Bird. Two men sandwiched Bird every time he received the ball—which was rarely. This so unnerved him that he became tentative. He finished the game with just two assists and made only one-third of his shorts. The Sycamores' nervousness was also evident at the foul line where they missed more often than not.

Jumping off from a 9-8 advantage, the Spartans moved in front by as many as 12 points in the first half. ISU had their opportunities, especially when Kelser and Johnson had to be benched with three personals each.

Magic played more carefully in the second half but Charles, starting in place of the injured Vincent, fouled out. Still, the Sycamores could not take advantage of the situation. The Spartan lead ballooned to 16 as they canned the first seven points of the second half. Their opponents countered by devising a zone press which brought them within six halfway through the second period. But Terry Donnelly, an infrequent shooter, stemmed the tide by sinking five long-range howitzer shots in as many tries. After that bombardment Michigan State was no longer in danger and won their first national championship 75-64.

It was a sore blow to the losers. They became the first team since Ohio State in 1961 to go to the finals undefeated and fall short in the ultimate game. Disappointment showed on every face; Larry Bird buried his in a towel.

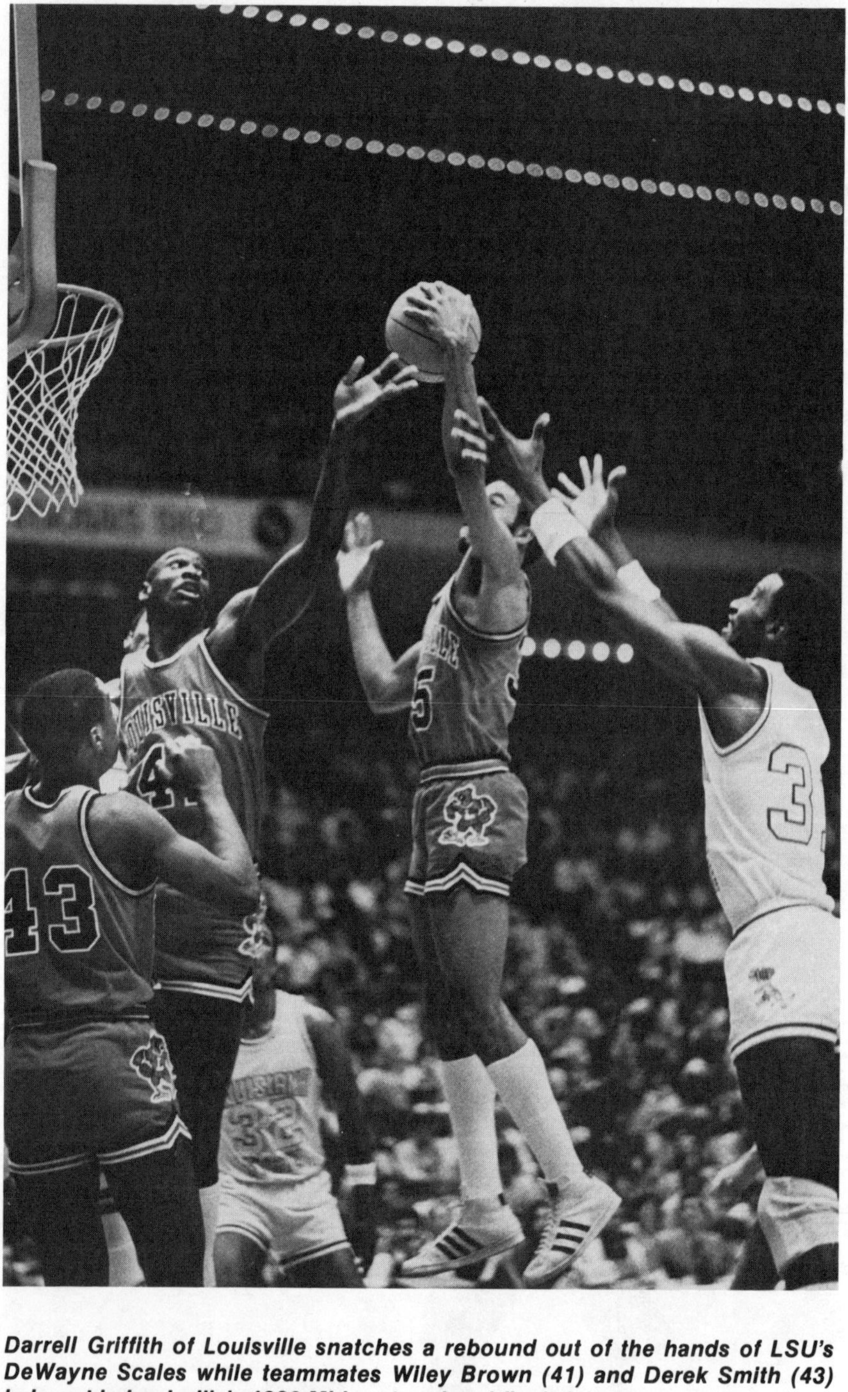

Darrell Griffith of Louisville snatches a rebound out of the hands of LSU's DeWayne Scales while teammates Wiley Brown (41) and Derek Smith (43) help out in Louisville's 1980 Midwest regional final victory. (Louisville University photo)

19

CINDERELLA, CINDERELLA 1980-1981

1980

Just as in political campaigns, the ability to peak at the proper time is crucial for a team with its eye on the national championship. In reality there is no such thing as a Cinderella team. What happens is that a group of players with unrealized potential jells, blossoms, gets their act together at the critical time and takes off in pursuit of the title. It takes a constellation of factors, some emanating from the players and their coach, some resulting from the luck of the draw—favorable matchups or proximity to the tournament site, for instance. Self-confidence and the ability of a coach to bring his team together by some magical psychological and emotional process are probably the most critical factors in making a Cinderella team perform to its potential and sometimes *beyond* it.

CCNY in 1950 is probably the best example of a Cinderella team. Four sophomores and a senior with tremendous talent, with a homogeneous background in New York City, put it all together during a two week span in March. They meshed perfectly. And they had the added advantage of not having to travel out of New York during the NIT and NCAA tournaments.

UTEP in 1966 is another example. This time it was five black kids from various ghetto backgrounds, grossly underrated until the end of the season. Marquette in 1977 was another Cinderella team with the added incentive of winning for its coach, who was about to retire. Then there were teams that came within one victory of the championship—St. Johns in 1952, Bradley in 1954, Seattle in 1958 and Florida State in 1972. Because they fell short in the final game made them no less Cinderella teams.

In the history of college basketball some coaches have been able to bring their teams to a peak of excellence at the most crucial time of the season. Forddy Anderson was such a coach. He took a 15-12 Bradley team that was a last-second desperation-choice to the tournament finals. The Braves were actually leading LaSalle at half time before being blown out in the last 20 minutes. He coached Michigan State, with a 14-8 record, to the national semifinals in 1957 and lost in triple overtime to undefeated North Carolina, the eventual champion.

Other coaches, sometimes with better material to work with, also showed great consistency in preparing their team for the national championship. When Dean Smith reached the Final Four in 1982 for the seventh time, critics pointed out that none of his teams had gone all the way. What they failed to mention was he had never lost a regional final in seven tries.* Despite the many All Americans whom Wooden coached from 1964 to 1974, his 38 straight victories in NCAA tournament competition is an achievement so incredible it is almost beyond belief and will undoubtedly never be matched.

Another great motivator entered the coaching ranks in 1972. After leaving UCLA where he had been an assistant to Wooden, Denny Crum moved to Louisville and took the Cardinals to the Final Four in his first year as head coach. He lost in the semifinals to UCLA.** In 1975 he again made the Final Four and once more lost to UCLA—by one point in overtime. Crum was an excellent recruiter and stocked his teams with flamboyant, free-spirited showmen who loved to dunk and exhibit their schoolyard skills with great exuberance. But when tournament time rolled around Crum demanded and invariably received a disciplied team effort very much in the style of Marquette.

Midwest:

The Cardinals were ranked fourth in 1980 with a 28-3 record. It was their thirty-sixth consecutive winning season, the longest such skein by any college in the country. During one stretch at midseason they had won seven games by an average margin of 20 points. They extended their winning streak to 18 before being ambushed 77-60 by an underrated Iona quintet.

Most of the Doctors of Dunk had gone on to other practices but the most

---

*In contrast, Lefty Driesell who recruited almost as many stars as Smith never won an ACC tournament or regional final and was able to steer nationally ranked Davidson past the finals of a weak Southern Conference only three times in nine years.

*Bill Walton, who led that team, was the last big center Crum recruited. Louisville's one weakness over the years was the lack of a big center.

awesome of them all, Dr. Dunkenstein, a.k.a. Darrell Griffith, their All American, was still in residence. He had led his high school team to a state title and on enrolling at Louisville, had brashly predicted he would help bring the Cardinals their first national title. Known for his 360 degree dunk and other spectacular variations of the genre, Griffith had once leaped completely over a defender—literally hurdling his body at the top of the lane—on his way to a rim-rattling stuff. Unaware of what he had wrought, he asked his teammates why the fans were reacting as if they had just witnessed a mirage.

In three of the previous four years Louisville had come unglued in the final weeks of the season—unusual for a Crum-coached quintet. The coach was criticized for holding the reins too loosely and for transmitting his cool, laid back style to his players. A more tangible problem surfaced in the third game of the season when center Scooter McCray was injured and lost for the year. His brother Rodney, still a freshman, was inserted in his place but this left Griffith as the only returning starter. Their inexperience helped to bring about a more dedicated attitude and a team cohesion that had not existed at Louisville for some time.

Alcorn State sported a fancy 27-1 record but was not ranked in the top ten. The Braves dropped their second game—to Mississippi State by three when Larry "Mr. Mean" Smith, the leading rebounder in Division I, was grounded—then ran off 26 wins in a row.

They were not only number one on offense, scoring margin and rebounding at the end of the season, but also shredded their opponents by an average of 23 points in the conference playoffs.

Bradley (23-9), also nicknamed the Braves, was back after a 25 year absence. They finished strongly, bagging 18 of their final 21. Two-thirds of their losses were by fewer than two baskets. The Braves had finished last in the MVC the previous year and were the first team in that conference to vault all the way to first place in one season.

Second ranked LSU (24-5) took the SEC playoff by upsetting Kentucky in a rubber match. The Tigers mirrored their volcanic coach, Dale Brown, who drilled his team in his fundamental 4Cs: "Control, Confidence, Class and Conquer." The fifth C was "Cookieman," center Greg Cook who liked wearing one of his collection of earrings. Also among the roster of colorful characters at LSU was Willie Sims, a member of two minorities being both black and Jewish, and dunk artist DeWayne Scales, easily the most disruptive player on the squad. This melange of individualists had had their share of trouble with the police, had moved from one campus to another like itinerant journeymen and dropped out and back in again several times. Together they clawed, snarled and intimidated their way from one victory to the next.

North Carolina (21-7) had bowed only to other ACC teams, twice to both Duke and Maryland. Arkansas (21-7) took their first six contests then ran into problems of, or rather *with*, State. In their next three, Louisiana State,

Memphis State and Kansas State stuck the Razorbacks. Missouri (23-5) set a new NCAA field goal percentage mark of 57.2. South Alabama (23-5) dropped their opener by a field goal at Louisville. Notre Dame (22-5) slammed UCLA twice and DePaul once. Kansas State (21-8) began to fade late in the season when they played a string of tight games decided by a field goal or less, culminating in a four-game losing streak. Wildcat games had a tendency to go to the wire so a 21 point victory over Kansas in the conference final came as a pleasant surprise and also restored some confidence.

San Jose State (17-11) gave their fans cause for cardiac arrest. Not until their eighth game was the margin of victory more than four points, and in over half of their matches the spread did not excede that. Texas A and M (23-7), on the other hand, left their fans yawning at one-sided outcomes. After absorbing a 26 point lashing by Iona in their opener, followed by a loss to Lamar, the schizophrenic Aggies won their next four by 40, 32, 24 and 43 points.

The NCAA had decided to add eight more teams to the tournament, bringing the total to 48. The four highest seeded schools in each regional received first round byes which became the subject of some controversy inasmuch as some coaches considered this to be a disadvantage. Naturally those who lost in the second round after sitting out the opening round were the biggest complainers. In the Midwest the four schools receiving a bye were Louisville, North Carolina, LSU and Notre Dame.

In the first round Kansas State held Scott Hastings, Arkansas' center and leading scorer, to zero points in the first half and rolled to an easy 71-53 victory. In the co-feature Missouri had to overcome a seven point half time deficit to eliminate San Jose 61-51. It was a tough night for starting centers. Missouri's Steve Stipanovich suffered from hyperventilation and managed only four points in the first 20 minutes. He sat out the whole second half but his replacement, 7′2″ Tom Dore, filled in very nicely, blocking five shots and contributing 11 points.

The next evening in Denton, Texas, South Alabama slowed the tempo to neutralize Alcorn State's high powered offense. The Braves, who had exploded for over 100 points eight times during the season, were held to 20 below their average but won their twenty-seventh in a row 70-62. Unable to shut down the offensive pyrotechnics, South Alabama was frequently whistled for fouls. In all Alcorn State went to the stripe 29 times, cashing in 20 points while the Jaguars had just five opportunities.

Texas A and M tied the count at 53 with 40 seconds to play against Bradley. The Braves' coach, flamboyant Dick Versace, dressed in black and looking very like a Mafia don, screamed at his men to hold for the last shot. But at :05 Dave Goff of the Aggies stole the ball and streaked in for a layup, which missed. He was fouled, though, and his two points made the final score 55-53 in favor of Texas A and M.

A pair of second round thrillers had the fans in an uproar, the players in a lather and the coaches in shock. Kansas State knotted the score 67-67 in their confrontation with Louisville when Rolando Blackman tipped in a ball with one second left in regulation time. Blackman again brought the Wildcats even at 69 on two free throws midway through the overtime. Louisville decided to hold the ball for the last shot. Griffith had fouled out and Crum was uncertain that his inexperienced team could handle the pressure. But Tony Branch, a deep reserve, who had taken only 29 shots all year, sank an off balance, last second, desperation jumper to lift Louisville into the next round 71-69.

Missouri's Stipanovich was breathing easier, and so were his teammates, when he broke a 74-all tie in the final minute with a layup against Notre Dame. But the crowd was brought to its feet again when Tripucka fed Woolridge for a last second bucket to tie matters at the end of regulation. Tracy Jackson, who was to finish with 27 points, almost won the game single-handedly for Notre Dame in overtime. Twice the Tigers went ahead by two, only to have Jackson tie the score. In all he tallied eight points in the five minute period. It was not enough. Missouri pulled ahead to stay and won 87-84. Mark Dressler had 32 points for the winners, mostly from close range.

In other second round action LSU wore down Alcorn State in a game of end-to-end action that resembled a horse race more than a basketball contest. Durand Macklin accounted for 31 points—21 in the second half—and brought down 19 rebounds. Right behind him was Sims with 30 points. Both LSU stars were red-hot throughout. At first the Braves gave Sims room to shoot but when they began crowding him, the hare-quick guard drove past his slower defenders. The 98-88 decision broke Alcorn State's long winning streak.

A Texas A and M blowout of North Carolina came with stunning swiftness. The Aggies fumbled away a 13 point lead, allowing the Tarheels to tie the game 53-53 after 40 minutes. Not a single point was scored in the first overtime. But the Aggie poured it on in the second extra session and won 78-61. It was one of the widest winning margins in an overtime game in the history of the sport. The reversal was totally unexpected. The Aggies suddenly discovered the solution to North Carolina's press while at the same time maintaining their own disciplined zone. After being blanked in the first overtime the teams scored 33 points in the last five minutes with the Aggies accounting for 25.

Louisville and Texas A and M, both survivors of overtime, squared off in Houston the following week. There was no indication in the early stages that it would be close. Griffith deflected the first Aggie pass of the game and slam dunked it home for a 2-0 Cardinal lead. He went on to score his team's first ten points. The Aggies were down 12-2 before they could get their bearings. The T on their jerseys could as easily have stood for "tentative" or "tall" because they were both of those. But good defense (and height) prevailed as they whacked a few balls back into some embarrassed Cardinal faces. The Aggies also checked Griffith by double teaming him, harrassing him whenever the other Cardinals got the ball to him. They crept back steadily to make a game of it.

By a strange quirk the scoreboard read the now familiar 53-53 when the teams headed into another overtime. But this time the Aggies were unable to solve their opponents' press and they were in turn blown out 66-55. Crum, a master of psychology, was thinking ahead when he told Branch to miss a free throw deliberately when the issue was no longer in doubt. Branch had made 16 in a row and Crum wanted to relieve the pressure should his young substitute be faced with a critical free throw in a later game.*

LSU played their normal physical game against Missouri, which meant a lot of contact with shoulders, elbows and knees. Most of the protuberances seemed to belong to Scales. Because Missouri was down to a nine-man roster, having lost several members via injury and academic ineligibility, they were particularly vulnerable to intimidation. When Stipanovich picked up his fourth personal with 15 minutes left in the game, LSU decided to try to protect its 55-52 lead by going into a shell. The tempo, hardly worthy of two teams proudly calling themselves Tigers, wound progressively down until in the final five minutes it was hard to detect much action at all. Like a toy with a run-down battery the attraction gave little satisfaction. But the tactic worked and LSU moved on to the regional final, 68-63.

Once again Griffith was the center of attention from the opening tipoff. However, this time the attention he attracted was not exactly to Crum's liking. He picked up his first personal after just two seconds of action and was charged with his third before the first half had become history. He retired to the bench with Louisville leading LSU 21-13. The Tigers reacted by scoring 16 unanswered points to take charge 29-21. The shocked Cardinals fought back. Using the devastating zone press which Crum had brought with him from UCLA, they looped in the last ten points of the half to take a slim lead at the intermission. An LSU field goal at the buzzer was disallowed, causing Dale Brown to erupt only slightly less violently than Mt. St. Helens.

Adversity brought out the best in Louisville. Their disciplined defense with its complicated switching assignments made up for the loss of their leader and star who spent most of the game on the bench, though he did contribute 17 points in 18 minutes on the court. The LSU band blared "Hold That Tiger" over and over, and a sea of purple and gold pompoms (strange colors for a team called Tigers) churned encouragement, but it was not enough. With eye-cheating quickness and an almost clinic-perfect transition game, Louisville flared to a huge lead. They limited their opponents to 39 percent from the floor while hitting 72 percent of their shots in the second half on their way to taming the Tigers 86-66.

---

*Crum had an excellent memory. No doubt he remembered Terry Howard's missed free throw after 28 successful attempts that almost surely cost his Cardinals the semifinal overtime game against UCLA in 1975.

East:

The class of the East regional was sixth ranked Syracuse (25-3). A prolific team, they had scored exactly 107 points three times and 99 four times. This made them second in scoring margin statistics. A one point loss to Old Dominion, a two pointer to Georgetown (which broke their 57 game winning streak at home) and another to Georgetown in the final of the Big East conference playoff were the only stains on their record. Syracuse featured the Louis (Orr) and (Roosevelt) Bouie Show. Orr, at 6′8″ and 190 lbs was a rail-thin guard while Bouie, a husky 6′11″, patrolled the pivot. He was ably backed by Danny Schayes, son of Dolph, the NBA Hall of Famer.

The Orangemen were accused of not having a killer instinct. They blew a 16 point lead to Georgetown and squandered a 13 point advantage against Old Dominion in the final four and a half minutes.

Tenth ranked Georgetown (24-5) was another team from the Big East (the conference was in its first year of operation and thus not eligible for an automatic tournament bid but received several at large invitations). When Georgetown broke Syracuse's long home winning streak, the Orangemen were held to 14 points fewer than in any game that season, a testimony to the Hoya's fine defense. After a mediocre start, Georgetown rode the crest of a 16 game winning streak into the tournament. Given their late season record and the two victories over Syracuse, Coach John Thompson was properly incensed when he discovered the NCAA committee had seeded his team third while giving the Orangemen the top seed.

Maryland (23-6) won the ACC regular season but was eliminated by Duke in the playoff final 73-72. It was just the latest of Driesell's failures in sudden death postseason competition. Lefty had scrapped all the fancy stuff—the three-guard offense, the double post and the rest of the showmanship—and returned to fundamentals. He was rewarded by a fine team effort that made the Terrapins number two in field goal accuracy. They were led by Albert King, younger brother of former Tennessee star Bernard. In addition to his scoring skills, he was a great leaper and excellent passer.

Iona (28-4) was moving to a major college schedule, beating Texas A and M by 26 points and Louisville by 17. In the latter game Ruland scored 30 points and grabbed 21 rebounds. However, he had secretly signed with an agent before the season, thereby jeopardizing his eligibility. Maybe Coach Jim Valvano had some inkling of his star's problem because his attitude towards his players changed noticeably. Or success may have made him take the sport more seriously. In any case basketball seemed a lot less fun than it had been earlier.

There were some who questioned Tennessee's (17-10) invitation to the tourney.. After dropping five in a row in February they bowed to Mississippi in the first round of the SEC playoff. North Carolina State (20-7) was a streaky team. After winning 11 in a row they came off second best in their next four before snapping out of whatever ailed them and chalking up seven more victories. All losses came in the tough ACC. Villanova (22-7) were led in scoring by freshman John Pinone but it was minuteman Rory Sparrow who bailed them out in the clutch. He won at least half a dozen games in the final seconds. Virginia Commonwealth (18-11) dropped five of six at midseason but finished strong with a 17 point victory in the conference playoff final against Alabama-Birmingham.

Furman (23-6) lost their opener but then reeled off 15 wins in the next 16 before coming a cropper in several contests against ACC teams. The Paladins were outclassed outside their conference. None of their losses were close, the average margin an astronomical 15 points. Holy Cross (19-10) had a similar failing, being dumped by an average of 12. Marquette (18-8) embarked on a roller coaster season which was completely atypical for the normally steady Warriors. They dropped four at home, were outbombed by Oral Roberts 102-101 and stopped by Stetson before upsetting Notre Dame at South Bend in the very next game.

The final team in the regional, Iowa (19-8), might have been better off showing up at an American Medical Association convention. Expenses for bandages, plaster, tape, drugs, shots and prescription pads undoubtedly set a NCAA record. The most critical injury was to star guard Ronnie Lester. With him in the lineup the Hawkeyes' record was 13-1, without him, they were losers. Kenny Arnold picked up part of the slack in Lester's absence but then he suffered a broken thumb. Among others who were hors-de-combat at one time or another were Mark Gannon with an injured knee, Kevin Boyle with a sprained ankle and a cut over his eye, and Vince Brookins with an assortment of bruises and mishaps. That Brookins was accident prone should have been evident to whomever offered him an athletic scholarship. Prior to enrolling at Iowa he had broken both legs, suffered a fractured shoulder, stunted his pinkie finger and been stabbed in the heart by a fellow student. While at Iowa he fractured his hand twice.

The Hawkeyes looked devastating in December. They smashed their first four opponents by 37 points and their first ten by 21. Then they lost Lester and hit the skids. When he returned at the end of February, they were back on the victory trail. Iowa's 9-0 record outside the conference was in sharp contrast to their fourth place 10-8 finish in the Big Ten. Their invitation to the tournament, therefore, came as a surprise.

In the first round Iowa had little trouble disposing of Virginia Commonwealth 86-62 and Tennessee, aided by Reggie Johnson's 28 points, had it almost as easy booting Furman 80-69. Villanova's match with Marquette was close for the first 25 minutes. With Marquette ahead 41-40 the Wildcats went on a rampage. Their lead ballooned to 22 points before they relaxed in the final two minutes to take a comfortable 77-59 decision.

The only close game in the initial round was Iona's 84-78 victory over Holy Cross. Ruland played in considerable pain with a bruised right hand and a chipped bone in his left. It was a wonder he could hold the ball at all. His hands were so swollen and red they looked as if he had been picking nettles. Yet he played 39 minutes and even slammed down a couple of spectacular dunks. Ron Perry of the Crusaders claimed 24 points to finish his career with 2524.

The fans in Greensboro, N.C., cheered second half surges that erased half time deficits in both games. Down by eight at the intermission, Maryland managed to draw even with Tennessee at 48. Several more ties ensued before Maryland exploded for 26 points in the last eight minutes to win 86-75. Greg Manning, Buck Williams and King accounted for 67 points for the Terrapins.

It was a fine evening for the Hawkeyes of Iowa but a miserable one for Hawkeye Whitney, North Carolina State's star, who fouled out after scoring only ten points. One factor helping Iowa was the number of free throw opportunities—they went to the line almost four times as often as the Wolfpack. Another was Brookins' reversal in the second period during which he swished 17 points, after being held scoreless in the first twenty minutes. Trailing by three at intermission, Iowa skipped ahead by 16 before taking the Wolfpack 77-64.

Syracuse eliminated Villanova 97-83. The outcome was due mainly to freshman Erich Santifer's season-high 29 points and an excellent fillin performance by Schayes who replaced Bouie after the brawny center was limited to ten minutes because of foul trouble.

Unlike the Midwest regional, the East seemed unable to produce more than one close contest in each round. The second round thriller matched Iona and Georgetown with two of the longest winning streaks in the country, 17 and 16 respectively, on the line. Ahead by three at the intermission, the Gaels jumped on the Hoyas with the first five points of the second stanza. At that point Thompson ordered his team into a full court press. This resulted in ten unanswered points—eight by Craig Shelton, who was to finish with 27. Though Iona lost their composure temporarily, they were still only a point down with 16 seconds left when Shelton missed a free throw. There was plenty of time for the winning shot but Glen Vickers forced a prayer from long range with :07 which Georgetown fielded. Shelton was fouled and this time he did not miss. The final score was Georgetown 74 Iona 71.

Valvano was livid, condemning the impatient Vickers. Iona had lost an almost identical contest the previous year when, in possession and holding for a last second shot against Penn, they had turned the ball over—with exactly seven seconds to go.

(It was a strange day in the tournament. The two longest winning streaks, Alcorn State's and Iona's, were snapped; Texas A and M recorded a blowout in double overtime; and UCLA and DePaul stirred the basketball world.)

The following Friday evening the two Big East teams went separate ways vindicating, in a way, Thompson's ire concerning Georgetown's seeding. The Orange were nursing a slim lead when a foul called on a Syracuse player propelled Coach Jim Boeheim off the bench with some choice non-compliments aimed at the referee. The ensuing technical plus two free throws gave Iowa the lead 58-57 and ball possession. Two minutes later the foul prone Bouie picked up his fifth personal and Syracuse played catchup the rest of the way. To no avail. Iowa made ten straight points from the line in the last two minutes to advance 88-77.

Only 15 miles apart, Georgetown and Maryland have established one of the hottest rivalries in college sports. With the Terrapins ahead at the half and Shelton on the bench with his fourth personal, picked up in the first minute of the second half, things looked grim for the team from Washington. But the Hoyas called on some reserve intensity and rallied to break the game open. Their defense stopped King with just two second half points. The 74-68 decision was another blow to Driesell, still looking for his first regional championship.

With momentum on its side, riding the crest of college's longest current winning streak, Georgetown was the favorite to become the first northeastern school to get to the national final in ten years. Between them and a berth in the Final Four stood Iowa, a decided underdog. After 69 seconds of the second half the Hoyas were coasting with a 14 point lead, their fans probably making plans for car pools and motel reservations in Indianapolis right after the victory celebration. That turned out to be a little premature.

Without panic or trying to digest the substantial lead in a single swallow, the Hawkeyes patiently and methodically climbed back into contention. With exquisite shooting (17 of 24 from the floor, 19 of 20 from the line, including 17 in a row) they pecked away at the Hoyas until at 4:48 they took their first lead 74-72. Lester directed the attack with nine assists. Having their star guard healthy again gave the Hawkeyes the confidence they needed to shoot over the Georgetown zone and connect. Even the substitutes caught the spirit. Steve Waite, a local boy from Iowa City, came in to replace Steve Krafcisin and banged in 13 points in the last 12 minutes. On the other side of the court Eric "Sleepy" Floyd accounted for 31 points on superb 11-for-14 shooting but was shut out in the last seven minutes.

An exchange of field goals culminated with a Shelton bucket off a feed from John Duren, tying the game at 78 with two minutes remaining. Lester and Boyle played catch for most of the final 120 seconds until Coach Lute Olson called time at the 14 second mark. Their strategy was to keep their options open and spring a man free for an uncontested shot. Boyle tried driving to the hoop and, finding his path blocked, passed to Waite who was standing just inside the baseline to the left of the net. His layup with five seconds to go and a free throw to complete a three point play promoted the Hawkeyes into the Final Four. Georgetown had no time outs left and Iowa, careful not to foul, allowed them a meaningless basket at the buzzer to make the score 81-80. It was Iowa's third straight upset victory, leaving John Thompson nothing more to say than, "This is the craziest season of basketball."

Mideast:

Third ranked Kentucky (between fellow SEC member Louisiana State and neighboring Louisville) was the team to beat in the Mideast regional. The 28-5 Wildcats opened and ended their season with losses. In between they tripped Iona in the final of the Great Alaska Shootout and swamped South Carolina 126-81. Directing the Kentucky offense was All American Kyle Macy, the third best free throw shooter in the country who missed only ten times from the line all year. Macy had intended to enroll at Indiana but had found Bobby Knight to be less than enthusiastic. Instead, he spent a year at Purdue before switching to Kentucky.

Duke (22-8) had beaten Kentucky in the Hall of Fame game to inaugurate the season, then had strung together 11 victories in a row, including three tournament crowns to rise to first place in the weekly polls. Seven defeats in the next dozen games had dropped the Blue Devils completely out of the top twenty. But in the postseason ACC tournament they reversed themselves once more and downed Maryland in the final. That defeat stung Driesell for another reason. Gminski, Duke's All American center, had attended Driesell's basketball camp as a high school star, with the intention of later enrolling at Maryland. But Terry Chili, a recent Duke graduate working at the camp, convinced Gminski to register at Duke and Driesell vowed never to hire a camp assistant from a rival ACC school again.

Indiana (20-7) was also ranked number one at one time during the season. The Hoosiers lost five times in the very competitive Big Ten and were also ambushed by Kentucky and North Carolina. But they did stop six teams that made it to the NCAA tournament and, despite an unspectacular record, were ranked seventh in the final poll and given a first round bye.

Indiana's five losses were still good enough for first place in the Big Ten which placed four teams in the NCAA tournament and three in the NIT. Negotiating the Big Ten schedule was like trying to swim through a tank full of barracuda. It was the cardiac conference of the year with 41 contests decided by five points or fewer. Bobby Knight found the experience so frustrating he wound up screaming at his own fans. The Hoosiers and Ohio State were tied for first place when they squared away in the finale for both teams. Still tied after regulation time, the Hoosiers eventually eked out a 76-73 win. (Beating OSU always gave Knight the greatest satisfaction. Not only had he graduated there but he was indignant at the way the school's administration had treated his coach, Fred Taylor.)

Three teams from the Northeast were included in the regional. All St. Johns' (24-4) defeats were at the hands of NCAA tournament participants, three of whom—Georgetown, Syracuse and Louisville—were good enough to get first round byes. After sinking 19 of their first 20 opponents they slumped as the season wound down. All the Redmen starters came from New York City including three—Bernard Rencher, Reggie Carter and Curtis Redding—who had transferred from out-of-town schools at which they had first enrolled. Redding had played for Kansas State where he had been voted All Big Eight. For many city kids the chance to get out of the ghetto environment was a dream to be fulfilled when presented the opportunity. Yet some came back when Coach Carneseca convinced them of the advantages of playing before their family and friends and the friendly New York media which provided national exposure.

Penn (16-11), after reaching the Final Four the previous year, was creamed in their first four encounters by an average margin of 17 points. After finishing in a tie with Princeton atop the Ivy League, they edged the Tigers in a playoff 50-49.

LaSalle (22-8) fell to Temple, Lafayette and St. Josephs but then turned the tables and beat all three in the East Coast Conference playoff to ensure a tournament berth. The Explorers featured two-time All American Michael Brooks who had scored 51 points against BYU during the season. Brooks had broken Tom Gola's career scoring record which had stood for 25 years. As a sophomore he had been the only player in the country to be among the top ten in scoring and rebounding.

Washington State (22-5) were making their first tournament appearance in 39 years when it had been the national runner-up. They dropped three close encounters—by a point twice and a field goal once—but destroyed Oregon State, the Pac Ten champion, 69-51. Virginia Tech (20-7) had romped over Cincinnati by 40 points during the season but had been jolted by the same team 65-51 in the first round of the Metro playoff. Florida State (21-8) played an inordinate number of close encounters; half their losses were by not more than a basket. Toledo (23-5), Western Kentucky (21-7) and Purdue (18-9) completed the regional field.

The Boilermakers had potentially the best center in the college ranks in 7′1″ All American Joe Barry Carroll. "Potentially," because Carroll lacked aggressiveness. Whether due to an absence of motivation or because it was a reflection of his off-court personality (which was discreet and unassuming) his tentativeness nevertheless became the target of considerable criticism. Maybe being ninth in the family had something to do with it. The fact was Carroll did not take charge the way he should have, and was well capable of, until his senior year.

In the first round game Carroll did take charge with 33 points as Purdue eliminated LaSalle 90-82. Brooks had 29 points but this one-man-team's effort was not enough.

In the co-feature the fans were surprised with the outcome of the first half between Pennsylvania and Washington State—a 27-27 deadlock. Penn fans were waiting for the Quaker swoon and when their team failed to score on nine of their first ten possessions after the break, they were ready to accept the inevitable. Rather than continue riding the crest of the wave that had swept the Cougars into a ten point lead, Coach George Raveling directed his men to begin a stall with 15 minutes left. His purpose was to make Penn come out of their zone since the Cougars loved to fast break and

Don Collins, their star, was an excellent one-on-one player. But the stall had the effect of cooling WSU down so that they managed only two points in the next five and a half minutes. Meanwhile Penn went on a 16-6 tear and tied matters at 49 on James Salter's layup. The Cougars were in deep trouble when Collins fouled out at 3:57, and Paul Little's five free throws in the final minute sealed the verdict—a 62-57 Penn upset.

Florida State outdueled Toledo in a firefight 94-91. Rodney Arnold, in only his second start, sparked the winners with 29 points while teammate Murray Brown's 26 also came in handy.

Virginia Tech, behind by 18 points at the intermission, woke from a deep snooze in time to rally and tie Western Kentucky, playing on their home court, 75-75 at the end of regulation. The Hilltoppers either became too complacent or the Gobblers were smarting from a locker room tongue lashing; for whatever reason, the visitors almost tore the net off the hoop in a 15-2 surge to open the second stanza. Their star, Dale Solomon, scoreless in the first period, tallied a point a minute in the final half and Dexter Reid knotted the score with twelve seconds remaining. Momentum carried them to an 89-85 overtime win.

Purdue had better luck playing at Mackey Arena, their home court. Not only did St. Johns have to contend with hostile fans but with an aroused Carroll who stood four inches taller than McKoy, the Redmen's center. On top of that the referees were not too kind, giving St. Johns just one trip to the free throw line in the first half. The visitors became rattled and midway through the game, went for six minutes without a point. When McKoy picked up personals two, three and four in the first four minutes of the second half, the handwriting was on the wall. The Boilermakers kept passing the ball to Carroll who responded with 36 points. After Purdue's lead had mushroomed to 18, St. Johns belatedly put together a 14-2 streak. But a momentum-breaking time out by the Boilermakers, followed by ten unanswered points, put an end to any Redmen hopes. At the buzzer it was Purdue 87 St. Johns 72.

Duke had almost as easy a time eliminating Penn, 52-42. Thus the two upstarts who made it to the regional final the year before were eliminated on the same card.

Kentucky toyed with Florida State, opening a 22 point bulge in the first half during which the Seminoles tallied just nine times from the floor. The latter's record from the line, where they canned barely half their shots, was not much better. But it was in the rebounding department that the Wildcats with a 34-13 edge completely dominated their opponents. Ten different Wildcats scored and five were in double figures as they coasted to a 97-78 decision.

Indiana had almost as easy a time against Virginia Tech. They swept ahead 26-12 but the Gobblers had the disconcerting habit of sweeping right back. Twice they got within two but were unable to tie or go in front. Indiana's superb defense clogged the middle, not allowing Tech to penetrate. Forced to foul, the Gobblers stood helplessly at the lane watching their opponents make their last ten points from the line to climax a 68-59 victory.

The third round at Lexington, Kentucky, matched a pair of Big Ten cross-state rivals from Hoosierland. Purdue and Indiana had split their regular season encounters and anything could be expected when these two clashed. But this time the confrontation proved anticlimatic as Purdue raced to a 19 point first half lead. The Boilermakers, who had finished last in field goal accuracy and ninth in free throw shooting in the Big Ten, were finding the target with much greater ease than usual. For once Indiana's defense broke down. Knight coached one of his poorest games and was charged with a technical in a crucial situation.

But the most critical blow may have been the loss of Mike Woodson with five personals. Woodson was the inspirational star of the Hoosiers. He had undergone surgery for a herniated disk in December, an operation that normally required a three-month recovery period. Woodson was back in uniform in six weeks and the Hoosiers won every game he played in for the rest of the season. Now, after fighting back to within six points, the spirit went out of the team when Woodson fouled out and they succumbed 76-69. Rookie Isiah Thomas chipped in 30 points but it was not enough.

Kentucky had beaten both Indiana and Purdue during the season but Duke, its third round opponent, had won the season opener between the two teams. Despite the usual capacity crowd of more than 22,000 cheering them on, Kentucky followed the pattern of earlier regional games by falling far behind. Down by 14 at the half, the Wildcats made a spirited comeback that primed their fans to bursts of booming encouragement. Aided by some truly terrible shooting by Duke, who managed only eight points in the first ten minutes of the second period, Kentucky triggered the biggest fan explosion of the evening when Fred Cowan hit a short jumper with 37 seconds to play. That tied the score at 54. It was also Cowan's twenty-sixth point. He had single handedly brought Kentucky back into contention by scoring the last 15 Wildcat points and holding Gminski to just four in the second half. Banks' single free throw 15 seconds later gave Duke the lead again. It was one of the few bright moments in an otherwise atrocious free throw shooting performance by the Blue Devils, who missed 13 of 24 from the line. After a Kentucky time out Macy missed the final shot of the game and the score remained 55-54 in favor of Duke. It was a rare accomplishment for the Blue Devils. Not only had they beaten Kentucky in Lexington, they had vanquished them twice in one season—their opener and their finale. It went a little way towards avenging their defeat by the Wildcats in the 1978 championship game.

The regional final was a disappointment for all except Coach Lee Rose and his Purdue Boilermakers. The fans, who had been expecting a showdown between their Wildcats and Indiana, which would have matched two top ten teams, had to settle instead for Duke, fifth in the ACC versus Purdue, third in the Big Ten. The game was unworthy of a regional final. Both sides played inconsistently and shot poorly. What the fans did get was a confrontation between the two best centers in the college ranks. Gminski, three inches shorter than Carroll and with less natural talent, nevertheless had the reputation for playing intelligently and certainly with greater consistency. Gminski had also never fouled out of a game at Duke.

Encouraged by the cheers of J-B-C, J-B-C, from the Purdue rooting section, Carroll enjoyed one of his better games and produced almost half Purdue's first half points. That still left them a basket behind Duke at the break. At 14:38 Arnette Hallman put Purdue ahead for the first, and the last, time with a rim-rattling stuff. But enthusiasm on the Boilermaker bench ebbed noticeably when J-B-C picked up his fourth personal with nine minutes remaining—understandable, since Carroll was getting little support from his teammates.

For the next 3:15 Purdue went into a stall. Duke eventually had to foul and the second-worst free throw shooters in the Big Ten responded well; Drake Morris even scored eight straight from the line. But it was J-B-C who was the difference, with 26 points (13 in each half) in the 68-60 victory.

As unexpected as Purdue's regional title appeared to be, it might have been forecast by the fortunes of Lee Rose. He had coached UNCC to the NIT final in 1976 just as he had Purdue in 1979 and now both of these accomplishments had been followed the next year with an appearance in the Final Four. In both cases Rose had won the Mideast regional in Lexington, which just happened to be where he grew up and where he later coached at Transylvania College. Welcome back, Lee Rose.

West:

DePaul was the number one ranked team in the country in 1980. With Coach Meyer's first Final Four under his belly-strained belt, an improving Freshman of the Year Mark Aguirre (now an All American), and two outstanding rookies—Terry Cummings and Teddy Grubbs—to lead the offense, the Blue Demons did not disappoint. They won their first 26 games, then succumbed to Notre Dame in the season finale, 76-74. In a way it was a relief not to take a long victory string into the tournament.

Yet there was cause for concern. The Blue Demons seemed to have more talent than was good for them and not enough class. When confronted by relatively weak teams, they loafed, barely edging Northern Illinois, Eastern Michigan, Lamar, and Dayton by a field goal and getting past Alabama-Birmingham by three points. But against tougher competition—LSU, UCLA and Missouri, for example—they won handily. They beat seven schools which were headed for the NCAA tournament. Still, there was no telling when they might let down. The Blue Demons were a team without a killer instinct, playing just well enough to win most of the time.

Aguirre set the tone for the team. Carrying 235 lbs. on a 6′7″ frame, his chubby appearance soon earned him a nickname, the Muffin Man. Overweight, with a lackadaisical attitude, he was hardly a good example to his teammates. Meyer's hardest expletive was "sonafabee" and "holy man."

Yet he could cut with the sharpest sarcasm and erupt in a towering rage, which he did frequently when confronted by one of Aguirre's frequent excuses. Once, when his star informed him in the middle of practice that he was sick, Meyer responded: "No wonder. The way these guys went around you, you probably caught pneumonia in the draft."

In the past promising prep school players had left Chicago to play in the Big Ten or at Notre Dame and Marquette. But now Meyer was able to skim the cream of the talent bank. Four of five DePaul starters were from the Windy City, including Skip Dillard who had graduated from the same high school as Aguirre. Yet the one Chicago product whom Meyer had coveted the most eluded him when Isiah Thomas enrolled at Indiana.

The amount of media coverage may have been one reason why the Blue Demons' heads became so big. For the first time in its history the school was ranked number one. All those stars and Meyer's jovial personality made excellent copy. Reporters and television commentators conducted interviews almost daily. "Where have you all been the last 30 years? I'm the same guy I was then," chided the surprised but gratified coach.

With its lofty ranking DePaul expected to play in a regional reasonably close to home; instead, they were sent to the West regional in Tempe, Arizona. Still, the teams there were weaker than the ones they would have had to face in the Mideast regional.

Fifth ranked Oregon State (26-3) was second seeded. The Beavers had five starters back and had little trouble winning the Pac Ten. Yet each one of their losses was a debacle—to UCLA 93-67, to Washington State 69-51 and to lowly Portland 94-86. They barely beat Hawaii by a point but shattered a respectable Idaho team 100-59. Stanford tried deep freeze tactics but were still chilled 18-16. A livelier rematch saw the Beavers on top 85-57. OSU had the third best field goal average in the country, attributable in part to center Steve Johnson's record-setting 71 percent average.

Ninth ranked Ohio State (20-7) suffered six defeats in the Big Ten. Strangely all but the last, against Indiana, came when they faced second division schools. Yet against teams headed for the tournament, they were 5-1. (The top three school in the regional seemed to be suffering from the same ailment—a lack of consistency and an inability to concentrate against weak opponents.) The balance in the Big Ten was reflected in the closeness of the Buckeyes' games. Two-thirds were decided by fewer than six points.

Another school that survived tough conference competition was Clemson (20-8) which was making its tournament debut. The Tigers were deprived of seven victories by their ACC opponents. Their eighth loss was to Oregon State, but that experience angered them enough to bounce back, creaming North Carolina by 17. Outside the ACC they were devastating, pummeling their first eight foes by an average of 25 points.

Weber State (26-2) stumbled out of the opening gate but lost only once thereafter. The Idaho schools gave them the toughest competition. A split with the University of Idaho and two overtime barnburners against an inferior Boise State quintet almost had the Wildcats ready to give up potatoes. Utah State (18-8) with four overtime victories was another contingent that played well in the clutch.

Lamar (20-10) fit the pattern of inconsistency characterizing the schools in the regional. They swung erratically from a 31 point bombing by Illinois State to coming within two points of upsetting DePaul; from 114-84 and 99-78 massacres of Portland State to giving up 100 points to West Georgia.

For most of the season Loyola-Marymount's (14-13) efforts seemed to swing in only one direction, namely the loss column. After a 7-12 start they racked up seven wins in their last eight to finish second to San Francisco in their conference. Lucky for them, San Francisco was on probation. Another example of an erratic team was BYU (24-4). In one eight-game stretch they smashed San Diego State by 32, squeezed past Hawaii by a point and won the next two by 34 and 25 point blowouts. Feast or rations!

Old Dominion (25-4) and Arizona State (21-6), with two victories over UCLA, were long shots.

Given almost no chance at all was UCLA (17-9), fourth in the Pac Ten and the last team to receive an invitation. Not since 1965 had the Bruins failed to win the Pac Ten (or Eight) title. Not since then had they dropped two consecutive non-conference games. They had lost just seven games in 14 years in Pauley Pavilion (against 221 wins) but in 1980 they went down to defeat four times. They fumbled one away to USC for the first time in 16 years. No wonder Curry Kirkpatrick wrote, "Now UCLA is just a team, Pauley Pavilion is just a building and the song girls are just cheerleaders. Gone are the awe, the mystique, the glamour. UCLA, R.I.P."* And Mark Aguirre added, "It's going to take them a while before they're UCLA again," after DePaul had tripped them at Pauley. That remark would come back to haunt him.

The Bruins had their fourth coach in less than six years. After Wooden came Gene Bartow, a small town, unsophisticated Missourian, lost in the pressure-packed atmosphere of the instant success demands of Los Angeles. After Bartow came Gary Cunningham who lost only eight of 66—none by more than four points—but could not satisfy the demands of the fans, alumni and local media for another national title.** Now came Larry Brown. He was as different in background and personality from his three predecessors as it is possible to imagine. He was Jewish, a native New Yorker and the product of North Carolina basketball, were his intensity had made up for a certain shortage of skill. A Jewish Al McGuire with saddle shoes!*** The offer of the prestigious position on the Westwood

---

**Sports Illustrated* 12/24/79.

**Wooden's assessment of him was that Cunningham "was not cut out for coaching." At the conclusion of the 1979 season he accepted the position of Athletic Director at Western Oregon State.

***In 1982 Brown went back to coaching in the NBA and was replaced by another totally different personality—quiet but authoritative Larry Farmer, a UCLA alumnus and the first black to coach at the school.

campus came as a surprise to Brown. He left his job with the Denver Nuggets (where he had made four times the salary he took home at UCLA) because the pressure of coaching in the NBA had been too much for him. Given the circumstances many doubted he would last very long.

Brown felt it would be best not to make waves or attempt some radical strategy. He reinstated the zone press and built the offense around the high post, two of Wooden's favorite tactics. He started his seniors at the expense of his underclassmen. To his credit Brown soon realized he had more young talent sitting on the bench than playing on the court. He therefore promoted 6′6″ Michael Sanders to starting center and made freshmen Rod Foster and Michael Holton his guards. He retained seniors James Wilkes and Kiki Vandeweghe at the forwards and he substituted less often. It created almost instant success. What the team lacked in height and size, they made up with quickness and speed.

The Bruins became known as Kiki and the Kids. Before benching his seniors at midseason Brown criticized them for a lack of leadership. This did not apply to Vandeweghe who had inherited leadership in his genes. Kiki's father, a dentist, had played for the New York Knicks, his uncle had been an All American at BYU, his mother had been a Miss America. Kiki had everything—brains, talent, looks and leadership.

Despite their mediocre record and close call with the tournament selection committee, the Bruins were confident they could at least win their regional—even more confident than their coach. It was not an uncommon situation. In 1957 Frank McGuire's Tarheels convinced their coach they would win the title and a doubting Al McGuire had been similarly reassured by his Warriors in 1977.

The winners of one first round double doubleheader both dissipated substantial second period leads but held on in the final seconds. Utah State wiped out a nine point deficit in as many minutes to tie Clemson at 71. But Fred Gilliam's two free throws at :42 and Bobby Conrad's solo effort clinched the 76-73 victory for Clemson. Dean Hunger, who scored 27 points, sparked the rally for Utah State.

Lamar almost blew an even bigger lead. Ahead by 22, they wallowed impotently as Weber State, playing in front of 11,505 hometown fans, closed the gap to a single point. The erratic Cardinals were playing to form. Yet much of their ineptitude late in the contest may have been due to exhaustion since they used only six players. Once again it was Mike Olliver (who had once scored 50 points during the season) who bailed them out. This time the Cardinal star contributed 37 in his team's 87-86 victory.

The other first round double header was a lot more lopsided. UCLA had little difficulty ousting Old Dominion 87-74 with Vandeweghe chalking up a career-high 34 points. Arizona State trounced Loyola-Marymount 99-71. After building a 51-29 half time lead, they extended their advantage to 68-33 and glided the rest of the way. It was just a light workout for the Sun Devils. Fifteen players participated but none had more than 13 points.

Two local schools had bitten the dust in the first round at Ogden, Utah. Now BYU became the third team from the state to join them as second round action continued.

This time it was Clemson which came from behind as BYU's 13 point lead evaporated in the steamy atmosphere of the Ogden arena. Seven times the score was tied in the last half but Billy Williams' bucket finally put Clemson ahead for good. Alan Taylor's 27 points could not make up for Danny Ainge's dry spell as BYU's star guard was held to two points in the second half. At the buzzer it was Clemson 71, BYU 66.

An upset of even more seismic proportions occurred when Lamar, playing their best game of the year, eliminated Oregon State 81-77. The Beavers may have underestimated their opponents because they found themselves 16 points down in the first half. They rallied to take a 46-45 lead on Mark Radford's three-point play, but the Cardinals, playing almost the entire game with their starters, pulled away again. Foul prone Steve Johnson, who scored 24 points and hauled down 18 rebounds, picked up his fifth personal with three minutes remaining and with him went the Beavers' last chance. Alvin Brooks' four free throws in the last 90 seconds preserved the victory for the winners who had 28 more opportunities from the line than Oregon State.

The following evening DePaul's small band of supporters showed up with buttons proclaiming "31-1"—the Blue Demon's season record after their expected national championship triumph. Coach Meyer did not share their confidence. The team's performance during recent practices had been poor and their momentum had been arrested by the loss to Notre Dame. Furthermore, given their attitude against weak teams and their win over UCLA earlier in the season at Pauley, as well as their triumph in last year's regional final, Meyer felt his squad, encouraged by the fans, was looking beyond the Bruins. This was a formula for disaster.

Right from the start it was obvious Aguirre was off his game. He was closely guarded by Wilkes and had to fight for every point. Unable to set up properly, he twisted his ankle at one point and became even more frustrated.

It almost seemed like the good old days when the Bruins would strike like lightning bolts in explosive bursts to put their opponents away. Behind by a point late in the first quarter UCLA struck for eight—evenly split between Sanders and Vandeweghe—in a span of 1:41 and never stopped rolling. Clemson did not aid their cause by scoring only once in their first nine trips downcourt in the second half. UCLA's advantage expanded to 18 and they won easily 85-74. Sanders and Vandeweghe each had 22 points while four rapidly maturing freshmen contributed 31.

Clemson was the last of the four ACC teams to be eliminated. Since the ACC prided itself in being the best conference this came as a blow to their prestige. But the Big Ten had two teams in the Final Four so they were apparently the better conference in 1980.*

*Virginia beat Minnesota in the NIT final restoring some honor to the ACC.

Both teams shot poorly at the start, but while DePaul became discouraged, UCLA gained confidence from their ability to stay close despite erratic shooting. Down by three early in the second half, the Bruins took charge with a 13-4 burst over the next six minutes. DePaul finally began to get into their rhythm but it was too late. They tied the score at 55 on a pair of Aguirre jumpers but though several more ties ensued they were never able to go ahead. The Bruins were playing with the confidence of the great teams that preceded them over the previous 16 years, as if the spirit of Hazzard and Goodrich, Alcindor and Walton, Johnson and Meyers rested on their shoulders, as if Wooden himself with his rolled-up program still patrolled the sideline. It was a total team effort. All participated yet nobody scored more than 20 points. In the final 90 seconds the two freshmen and the sophomore went to the line five times in a one-and-one situation and, like veterans, coolly converted each attempt. The victory was even more convincing than the 77-71 final score.

In the co-feature Herb Williams and Kelvin Ransey each tallied 25 points to power Ohio State over Arizona State 89-75. The home site had not been much of an advantage for the teams in the regional nor elsewhere in the tournament. Arizona State, Weber State, Kentucky and Western Kentucky had all lost on their home courts. Only Purdue survived at West Lafayette.

It was UCLA's quickness versus Ohio State's size in one regional semifinal and in the initial stages bulk prevailed. But Brown called a time out and his Bruins slowed the pace, overhauling their opponents before the break. Then outhustling their more ponderous opponents, the Bruins built a nine point advantage early in the second half, only to have the Buckeyes tie the count at 48-48. Significantly it was Ransey, the quickest of the Buckeye guards, who sprang loose for 13 of 15 Ohio State points in a five minute span. That burst included six baskets without a miss. Though they were scoring well from the floor, they were paying a price on defense where they were unable to halt the mercurial Bruins without fouling. In the end it was UCLA 72 Ohio State 68 despite Ransey's 29 points and a 31-22 Buckeye edge in field goals. The last team in the regional with a first round bye had been eliminated. Now there were only Cinderellas left at the ball.

The ever erratic Lamar Cardinals soared to a ten point second half lead but then turned the ball over four times in one minute. Offering almost no resistance and suffering total collapse, Lamar watched Clemson turn a dream into a nightmare with a 20-5 frolic during a four minute span. It was almost as if the ball had turned into a pumpkin for the Cardinals. Clemson advanced to the regional final on the strength of a 74-66 verdict.

Against Lamar it had taken Clemson more than a half to establish their inside game, featuring 6′10″ center Larry Nance. They were never able to do so against UCLA. The Bruins were again at a height disadvantage, facing a front court which averaged 6′10″. Yet they outrebounded the Tigers 40-34. With their quickness they were able to establish better position than their lumbering opponents.

Final Four:

Seldom had the Final Four included such an unlikely assembly of candidates for the national championship. They had 29 losses among them; three teams had at least eight each. Each regional top seed had been eliminated, three of them before even reaching the regional final. Indiana and Ohio State had been among the top five in the preseason poll and had finished 1-2 in the Big Ten. Yet it was Iowa and Purdue which landed in the Final Four. Louisville was not even listed in the top 20 at the start of the season. And UCLA. Well, UCLA had finished fourth in the Pac Ten and there were some who had accused the selection committee of including the Bruins on the basis of their past performance rather than their current merit.

All four schools at Indianapolis had some connection to that old Hoosier, Johnny Wooden. He had coached at UCLA, played at Purdue, been Navy athletic officer at Iowa during World War II and his former assistant Crum coached Louisville.

Beside the drama in Indianapolis, there were several comedic episodes, one involving Louisville's Wiley Brown. He left his prosthetic thumb on a restaurant table and when he discovered it missing, returned to find it gone. A search of the restaurant garbage cans uncovered the missing thumb.

Wooden was rooting for UCLA against his alma mater. This time they did not need the Wizard as they maintained control for most of the contest. The inconsistent Carroll had one of his poorer games and UCLA checked the Boilermakers 67-62 to advance to the final.

A duel of stellar guards piqued the fans in the opening minutes of the other semifinal between Louisville and Iowa. Griffith scored 16 of his team's first 18 points and Lester accounted for Iowa's first ten. But when Lester crashed into the stanchion supporting the basket and injured his knee and had to retire, the heart went out of the Hawkeyes.

Louisville was in its groove, fast break exploding downcourt, its zone press shutting off Iowa's bigger front court. Boyle was held scoreless and Brookins, who had kept Iowa in the game with 16 first half points in the regional final, sank only one-third his shots. Meanwhile Dr. Dunkenstein showed his versatility by blistering the hoop for 34 points on 67 percent shooting, all but one basket coming from the perimeter.

Iowa was behind by five at the intermission but was not overly concerned. They had been in a similar situation in three of their previous four games and had shot 70 percent in the second half. This time was different, though. The swarming Cardinal defense limited them to a 44 percent shooting effort, a crucial factor in the 80-72 decision favoring Louisville.

There was a profound similarity between the playing styles of the finalists. This was not surprising, given Crum's UCLA roots and Brown's revival of Wooden's tactics. Both teams were young (only three senior starters among them), quick, opportunistic, disciplined, intelligent and each had a devastating pressure defense. The opposing centers—6′6″ sophomore

Sanders and 6′7″ freshman McCray—were pygmies compared to those on the teams they had eliminated. But the similarities ended with the coaches themselves. Crum's laid back style contrasted sharply with that of the more intense Brown, who was often accused of overcoaching.

It was the second year in a row that a rookie coach had taken his team all the way to the final. UCLA had been there many times but never in the role of Cinderella, yet they seemed comfortable in the part. For Louisville it was their first time.

Both teams were tight or their defenses too strong. In either case both shot poorly in the first half which ended with UCLA ahead 28-26. In an atypical locker room outburst, Crum accused his players of choking. His teams had been eliminated by UCLA three times in the last eight years, twice in the Final Four, and he was not going to let that happen again if he could help it.

The dressing down in the dressing room had little effect at first. UCLA even increased their advantage until at 4:31 they led 54-50. It was then that Griffith took charge. With only minutes left to go in his career, he may have remembered his promise to bring a championship to Louisville before graduation. Rookie Michael Holton had done an excellent job containing the All American guard but he was tiring in an obviously demanding assignment. Twice Griffith drew the defense to himself before passing off to Jerry Eaves for baskets. The score was tied 54-54 when Vandeweghe raced in from the right sideline for a layup. Eaves cut him off and the resultant off-balance shot missed. It was the turning point of the game. McCray grabbed the rebound and Griffith's pop from the top of the key gave Louisville the lead. On the subsequent inbounds play the Bruins lost the ball under pressure and Louisville added three more points to make the final score 59-54. Midnight struck and Cinderella missed her coach. It was the closest final in 17 years.

Louisville's victory was attributable to their defense, which shut out the Bruins in the last four and a half minutes, and to Griffith's leadership. He was the only Cardinal in double figures and scored or assisted on the final, critical four baskets. He easily won the MVP award.

1981

It may not have been the best-played tournament but it certainly was one of the most exciting and the NCAA tournament committee wanted to maintain that level of intensity. To achieve that they came up with a new scheme in 1981 for assigning teams to regionals which would ensure a proper balance. (See Appendix 1.) The fact that half the teams receiving a first round bye had been ousted in a rash of upsets by the end of the second round confirmed the selection committee's judgement. Both previous year's finalists as well as the first and second ranked team in 1981 were among the victims. One theory to explain the high number of upsets in recent tournaments was given by Coach Pat Foster of Lamar who suggested that tournament pressure equalized the teams' performances.

The primary reason for more balance and closer scores was due to a more even distribution of talent. The rules permitted fewer scholarships so there was less stockpiling of players. Athletes stayed closer to home which helped the big city schools such as St. Johns, DePaul, Georgetown and Villanova. Freshmen wanted to play immediately and so picked less publicized schools for the opportunity. There were more black players in Southern schools thereby helping the programs of Alabama, LSU and Arkansas. There were more conferences with bigger arenas, especially in the Northeast, South and Southwest, bringing the sport to basketball-depressed areas. Television money dictated non-conference schedules because fans wanted to see the best playing the best on the home screen. In the Big Ten, parity had been achieved so well that Michigan and Minnesota had each played five overtime games during the season.

Another factor was the installation of multiple zone defenses which tended to keep scores low and therefore closer. Jud Heathcote had achieved considerable success and exposure with his 2-3 matchup zone (with pressure on the ball handler) during his championship season at Michigan State and many coaches were copying that tactic. Teams would switch between 2-3 and 3-2 and 2-1-2 and other variations to confuse their opponents.

The stakes were also rising. A team receiving a tournament bid in 1981 received $95,724 plus expenses and if it reached the Final Four that sum rose to $382,898. The comparable figures in 1982 would be $126,901 and $507,606. This put a lot more pressure on a team to win, using whatever tactic it felt necessary. It is not surprising that the incidence of the stall or slow down increased dramatically in crucial games and that a call for a shot clock was heard more frequently.

Still, the formula for success in the tournament was superior coaching and late season momentum. It is difficult to recall a single instance when an inferior or even an average coach has won a national championship. Rarely has a coach with other than impeccable credentials made it as far as the final game. On the other hand, superior coaches with inferior talent—

Anderson in 1954, Rupp in 1958 and Newell in 1959, for instance—sometimes manage to get there. (The last two mentioned went all the way.) As for momentum, a team can lose a few games early in the season and then streak to a championship; but one that loses down the stretch rarely does.

Mideast:

It was therefore not surprising that Indiana, despite an unspectacular 21-9 record, was ranked seventh in the final 1981 poll and seeded second in their regional. (To give an indication of how highly the pollsters regarded Indiana, the next school with as many as nine losses was ranked no higher than twentieth.) The ingredients for success were there. Bobby Knight is recognized as one of the top five coaches in the country; some would even say he is the best. The Hoosiers had dropped seven of their first seventeen but had lost only twice in the last thirteen, all against Big Ten schools.

Knight's biggest problem was his often uncontrollable temper. In the Pan America games in July, 1979 he was arrested for aggravated assault on a police officer in an altercation over practice time. He was tried in absentia in a Puerto Rican court and given a six month sentence which he never served. He has been described as churlish, profane, antagonizing and a bully.

It seemed that as long as he kept winning he could get away with such behavior. He had also been criticized for stubbornnes and insisting that his players adhere to assigned roles which had cost him crucial games. (His insistance that only Radford and Woodson shoot during the 1979 tourney games against Furman and Villanova is a good example.) However, when blessed with an outstanding player such as Isiah Thomas, he would loosen the reins and allow some freelancing.

He was also a careful recruiter, picking his men on the basis of personality—to determine how well they would cope under game pressure and that of his coaching—as well as the usual basketball skills. Strategically, he combined the defensive teachings of his former coach Fred Taylor (who had learned them from Pete Newell) with the passing theories of Henry Iba on offense.

But in an arena where accusations and revelations of cheating and exploitation of student-athletes were heard with greater frequency, Bobby Knight's integrity and dedication to the college sport provided a needed example to his peers.

After losing a pair of close ones to Kentucky and Notre Dame, the Hoosiers trounced California and Baylor by 36 points each. They were plagued by an early lack of concentration which infuriated Knight. Untypically, Indiana lost five of twelve outside the conference. And in the most embarrassing game of the year they were choked by Pan American 66-60 (the name seemed to haunt Knight's life). But at crunch time they finished on top of the Big Ten again, though dumped by Iowa twice.

The top seed in the regional and number one in the country was again DePaul (27-1). With their new, elevated status the Blue Demons began playing home games in the Rosemont Horizon, seating 17,000. It was there they blasted UCLA, ranked third at the time, 93-77, gaining a small measure of revenge for their defeat in the previous year's tournament. They also derailed six teams which later played in the tourney. The only blot on their record was a 63-62 squeaker against Old Dominion, but most of their victories were uninspired. DePaul doped through the season reading their statistics and press clippings while looking ahead to the tournament. Despite a weak schedule (Wagner, Illinois State, Gonzaga, Maine, Northwestern, St. Louis) and the best record in the country, they were only number five in margin of victory. They again lacked a killer instinct and played just well enough to win.

Aguirre, once more an All American and Player of the Year in some polls, had trimmed his weight and was as enthusiastic as ever, exchanging frequent high fives with teammates. But he was moody, too, and undisciplined, looking for challenges and showboating for attention. He wanted to play all the roles—scorer, playmaker, fancy dribbler—wanted to handle the ball all the time. In one game he scored 47 points which was nine more than the rest of his team. His need to be the center of attraction deterred his very talented teammates from contributing their potential.

Aguirre had been indulged by his coaches throughout his career and Meyer was no exception. One day in the gym the coach yelled at him for loafing. "If you don't want to practice, get out of here." When Aguirre headed for the exit Meyer called to him, "Mark, where are you going?"

Eighth ranked Kentucky (22-5) massacred Florida 102-48, recalling the days of the unmerciful Baron. But the consequences of an 80-48 blowout of Vanderbilt turned out less than satisfying when those same Commodores ousted their tormentors the following week in the first round of the SEC playoff.

Creighton (21-8) lost to Wichita State twice during the season before eliminating them in the MVC postseason tourney. Maryland (20-9), led by the 65 percent shooting of Buck Williams, trampled third ranked Virginia in the ACC playoff by 23 points. But in the final Driesell's troops once again failed to win the big one. For the second consecutive year they were downed in the final by a single point, this time by North Carolina. Another school with postseason playoff problems was Boston College (21-6) which finished first in the Big East despite the disclosure of a point-shaving scandal. They stomped last place Providence twice—by an average of 21 points—but were eliminated by the last place Friars in the first round of the conference playoff.

The postseason conference playoff upsets were just another indication of the current balance in college basketball. Not that one had to wait until the postseason to appreciate this. Alabama-Birmingham (21-8) finished in a three-way tie for first place in the seven-member Sunbelt. Tennessee-

Chattanooga (21-8) also was tied with two others atop the Southern. Seven of the nine schools in the conference finished within three games of each other. Most absurd of all was the Mid American race which ended in a five way tie.* It took some unraveling and the playoff structure was too complicated to describe. Ball State (20-9) survived as the conference representative.

Wake Forest (22-6) had a schizophrenic season. In the first half they were undefeated in 14 games. In the second they were 8-6. (In the last quarter they were 2-4. No momentum there.) Playing against schools honoring men named John brought out the best in the Deacons. They flayed Johns Hopkins and John Carroll by almost identical scores—111-58 and 110-59.

St. Josephs (22-7) and Western Kentucky (21-7) completed the regional field.

In first round action Maryland rallied from a two point half time deficit to dispose of Tennessee-Chattanooga 81-69. St. Joseph nailed Creighton 59-57 when freshman center Tony Costner sank a pair of free throws with three seconds remaining. Abysmal shooting by both sides marked a turgidly-paced first half. Still, it was the Hawks' first tournament victory in 15 years.

The next day the other hyphenated school fared better. Alabama-Birmingham, in its first tournament, raced to a 62-38 lead over Western Kentucky, then coasted to a 93-68 breather. In sharp contrast, Boston College had to struggle to sneak past Ball State 93-90. In the final minute Dwan Chandler and John Bagley of the Eagles each pumped in four points to more than offset Ray McCallum's three consecutive howitzer shots.

Dayton had been the stage for some memorable tournament games over the past decade. It was there that Adolph Rupp had coached his last game. It was also the setting for the adrenalin-pumping Kentucky upset of undefeated Indiana in 1975. But nothing matched the drama generated by the second round doubleheader.

The games were totally dissimilar. In one, Indiana mobilized like some Biblical scourge to lash Maryland into submission. The records of the teams were, after all, almost identical. Each played in a strong conference. So it was not the result but the measure of retribution that was so astonishing. Maryland scooted to an 8-0 lead, innocent of the force about to be unleashed. Suddenly the Hoosiers came to life and when it was over, they had crushed the Terrapins 99-64. Isiah Thomas, their All American and the best point guard in the country, drove Maryland crazy with 9 field goals on 11 shots and 14 assists. Ray Tolbert contributed 26 points and the rest of the team hit consistently enough to give Indiana a 65 percent shooting performance for the afternoon.

---

*Other conferences with tight finishes included the Big Eight (with half the schools separated by a game at the top) and the Big Sky (with three of eight separated by a game). Two teams tied for the Ivy League, the WAC, the WCAC and the Eastern Eight. And five of the seven teams in the Southwestern Athletic Conference were bunched within a game of each other.

The co-feature provided the fans with a totally different aspect of the game. Meyer was aware that DePaul was overconfident, knew that his players were looking beyond St. Josephs. Given their attitude against weak teams, there was reason for concern and Meyer had a premonition of defeat. Personality clashes had recently plagued the squad. Teddy Grubbs had been drained emotionally by mental problems and this had had its affect on the team.

St. Josephs knew their only chance was to set a slow pace, thereby neutralizing DePaul's fast break and freelance shooting. John Smith later admitted, "We thought if we kept the score in the low fifties and controlled the tempo, we could be there at the end." This is exactly what they did and the Demons did nothing to stop them.

Still, with six and a half minutes to go, DePaul enjoyed a 48-43 advantage. Smith's field goal 40 seconds later narrowed the gap to three. For the next five minutes the Demons were content to pass the ball around, secure in the knowledge that their opponents would have to come out of their shell. When they did, Costner, a poor choice at best, took a shot that missed. Fortunately Grubbs snatched the rebound but he was immediately tied up by Smith. Though Smith was three inches shorter, the Hawks were able to control the tap and when Bryan Warrick canned a 15 footer with 48 seconds left, panic set in. Twice DePaul had to call time out because they could not get the ball in bounds on time. Suddenly the ghosts of the past gathered with chilling immediacy. On everyone's mind was the defeat by UCLA exactly a year ago. "Oh God. It's going to happen again." The Demons were throwing the ball around as if it would explode. But then they got a break. Dillard, the team's best free throw shooter, was fouled with 12 seconds to go. Put them both away and Meyer could start preparing for the Indiana game. Dillard missed the first and never got a chance at the bonus.

What was left of team cohesion evaporated and mass confusion ensued. Warrick grabbed the rebound and headed downcourt. DePaul tried trapping him but he broke free, creating a five-on-three break. Smith, standing under the hoop, received the ball and spun it in for the winning points in the 49-48 victory. There was time only for an agonized Aguirre to cradle the ball to his chest and, as the buzzer heralded the upset of the year, he flung the ball toward the rafters and walked out of the arena.

Dillard and some of his teammates were crying. The coaching staff had to work to get the players off their emotional plateau. As for Aguirre, he refused to talk. After silently showering and changing, instead of taking the bus he grimly walked the two miles back to the hotel, shutting out the world with his walkman earplugs. Meyer, hiding deep disappointment, exhibited a fatalistic attitude. "Life goes on," he shrugged.

Some of the blame may have been Aguirre's. He took only two shots in the second half and had eight points for the game, his lowest at DePaul. But the rest of the team had to share the responsibility. They allowed the Hawks to lure them into a slow paced game, they had not scored a point in the last

6:28, and they disintegrated as a team in the final minute.

Upsets awaited two more teams in the other second round doubleheader. Wake Forest, whose momentum had run aground weeks ago, was eliminated by Boston College 67-64. Bagley's 15 foot jumper at 5:04 tied the score at 58, and he put the Eagles ahead for good 63-62 from the same spot just inside the final minute. Two Bagley free throws 34 seconds later and a steal by the junior guard sealed the victory.

Alabama-Birmingham, playing only its third season of basketball, held a seven point edge over Kentucky midway through the second half. However, Sam Bowie's two free throws at 4:40 evened matters at 52 apiece. This was followed by three more ties until Leon Morris put the Blazers ahead for good with a free throw. Their success from the stripe was the deciding factor in the 69-62 victory. Though they made only 19 field goals they flashed 31 free throws through the hoop. In the final 8:39 all but two of their 19 points came from the line.

Indiana continued their advance by ousting Alabama-Birmingham 87-72 on their home court in Bloomington. Thomas scored 12 straight points in the second half to break the game open. He totalled 27 points and eight assists.

St. Josephs determined the tempo in their confrontation with Boston College as they had against DePaul. The first half, which resembled the last lap of a dance marathon, ended with BC on top 22-18. Warrick, who had been an important factor in the previous round, played an even more key role now. He was the only Hawk in double figures and held Bagley to 11 points. At 14:05 of the second half he completed a rare four point play as he scored on a layup and added two free throws when the referee charged the defender with a flagrant foul. That gave the Hawks their first lead of the period. At 4:20 the Eagles went into their four corners to protect a three point lead. A minute later Warrick swiped the ball and streaked in for a layup. Then at 1:38 he stole the ball from Bagley again to bring his team within a point of the Eagles.

Either because their shooting was so cold (they made only 35 percent in the game) or the Hawks' defense so tough, BC held the ball for long stretches. This helped St. Josephs since their two tallest members were saddled with four personals during the final ten minutes.

Warrick again surfaced at a critical juncture when he calmly tallied a pair of free throws after BC had called two time outs to shake his concentration. (The second attempt homed in on the hoop after hitting the back of the rim, bouncing straight up and then rattling on the iron a couple more times before dropping through.) That made the score 42-41 in favor of the Hawks with 21 seconds to go. Bagley tried one from his favorite spot but missed. Another rebounded shot missed. Finally Smith got the ball and was immediately fouled. His miss gave BC a last chance. However, Chandler was forced back after crossing the center line and that final turnover ensured St. Josephs' victory. It was the lowest scoring tournament game in 32 years.

The outcome of the regional final was predictable. Indiana was playing on its home court and had built up a head of steam in two previous blowouts. Meanwhile, St. Josephs had won their three matches by a total of four points, all in the final seconds. There was no way that the well-coached Hoosiers would allow St. Josephs to let the air out of the ball. Coach Jim Lynam, who had played against Bobby Knight in the 1961 tournament semifinals, tried to ease the tension. Referring to Philadelphia, the site of the Final Four and also St. Joseph's home, he said, "We're going for sure. I don't know about them."

But the Hoosier juggernaut was rolling in earnest now. They asserted themselves early, building a 32-16 half time lead which blossomed to 40-17 early in the second period. Indiana combined a swarming, double teaming, trapping defense with an offense that seemingly could not miss. Their 69 percent shooting average set a new NCAA tournament record. Landon Turner hit seven of eight, Jim Thomas six of seven and Tolbert six of eight. It was the third straight blowout for Indiana, this time 78-46.

East:

Virginia (25-3) had had a taste of national attention when it won the 1980 NIT. Now it was preparing an assault on the NCAA title. Ralph "Stick" Sampson, a.k.a. Virginia Slim, and Jeff Lamp were both All Americans. There was ample reason for Sampson's nickname. He stood 7′4″ and weighed a skinny 221 lbs. He was slowly filling out but he sometimes lacked stamina and had to take himself out of the game. Lamp and teammate Lee Raker had both starred at Ballard High School in Louisville, leading their team to a state championship. Lamp had been voted the state's outstanding prep player with Raker the runner up. What Raker lacked in finesse he made up for in intensity and willingness to fight for every loose ball. He played with the abandon of a Marine taking a contested beach and the lacerations he suffered were the badges of his spirit.

After winning their first 23, which moved them to the top of the polls, the Cavaliers were shifted down to third place when they bowed to Notre Dame, Wake Forest and Maryland. Still, they finished ahead of the field in the ACC.

Villanova (19-10) had also been jolted by Notre Dame—by 31 points at home—one week after clobbering San Francisco (93-66) on the latter's floor. The hot and cold Wildcats had become the eighth member of the Big East but had fallen to Syracuse in the postseason playoff, probably from exhaustion. In the first round they raced to an 18-2 lead over Connecticut after 7:13. Like the hare in the fable, the Wildcats dozed off while their opponents pulled even by half time. A minute and a half into the second period Connecticut was in front 23-18. Villanova awoke after their 14 minute scoreless snooze and zapped 48 points through the twines in the next eighteen and a half minutes to win 65-54. The next day they outlasted Providence in overtime but failed to survive a triple overtime marathon against Syracuse. John Pinone played 43 minutes in the semifinal and 53 minutes in the final.

Houston (21-8) swung between extremes almost as wildly as Villanova. The Cougars were ambushed by a pair of lightweights, Biscayne and Alaska-Anchorage, but sailed through most of the SWC schedule unscathed. They hit a sinkhole, however, in the final two weeks and dropped four of the last five in the regular season. Just when it looked as if they had run out of momentum, the Cougars exploded for two SWC playoff victories by 20 and 25 points.

Ninth ranked Notre Dame duplicated their previous year's 22-5 record. Among their victims were Virginia, Kentucky and Indiana, all in the top ten. The Irish were a one-dimensional quintet with an exquisitely patterned offense that produced the second-best shooting statistics in the country, and little else. A fast-breaking opponent such as UCLA, to whom they lost twice, had the Irish at their mercy. Their attack also lacked continuity. Digger Phelps was notorious for overcoaching and his revolving door substitution policy frustrated his players and occasionally squelched an Irish rally. There were some who claimed he could not win in the clutch. Despite outstanding teams which featured several All Americans and were consistently in the top twenty, Notre Dame under Phelps had made the Final Four only once in eight consecutive years of tournament participation.

The current crop had excellent credentials which may have come to them through their genes. All American Kelly Tripucka with reputedly the best looking legs in college basketball (they won a beauty contest) was the son of Frank Tripucka, a former Notre Dame football quarterback. John Paxson was the brother of Jim Paxson, a former All American guard at Dayton. Orlando Woolridge, the third best shooter in the country, was a cousin of Willis Reed, a former pro star with the New York Knicks. Tracy Jackson, who had come via the well-travelled pipeline from Washington D.C. to South Bend, had no famous relatives.

Georgetown (20-11) never quite recovered from a pair of losses in the curtain-raising Great Alaska Shootout, although both schools which levelled the Hoyas eventually made it to the Final Four. Back from the edge of the tundra, Georgetown iced their next three opponents by an average of 36 points. Yet they never really jelled as they picked their way through a minefield of close encounters.

James Madison (20-8) was a very underrated team. Only once were they stopped by more than four points. Among the losses were two one-point heartbreakers against Virginia and Virginia Commonwealth. Princeton (18-9) tied for the Ivy crown with Penn but beat them in a playoff, 54-40. Despite the second best defense in the country their record outside their conference was only 5-8.

Another tie developed in the Sunbelt where Virginia Commonwealth (23-4) shared the top spot with two other schools but won a playoff by halting Alabama-Birmingham 62-61 in overtime. The Rams were frequently intimidated by their coach J.D. Barnett, a screamer who punctuated his diatribes by punching blackboards as a means of relieving tension and frustration.

(The conference had attracted its share of successful and controversial coaches. "Clean" Gene Bartow had emigrated to Alabama-Birmingham from UCLA, Lee Rose had taken up residence at South Florida after leaving Purdue, and Tates Locke was about to be sacked from Jacksonville after certain recruiting improprieties came to light.)

UCLA (20-6) was making its fifteenth consecutive NCAA tournament appearance. The Bruins had lost five Pac Ten games during a controversy-packed season. BYU (22-6) with All American guard Danny Ainge finished third in the WAC. If not for the tournament Ainge would have been at spring training playing second base for the Toronto Blue Jays. Tennessee (20-7) was an also-ran in the SEC.

The last team in the regional was Long Island University (18-10), making its first tournament appearance. Back in the forties when the Blackbirds were a power under the legendary Clair Bee, they could have had more than one NCAA tournament invitation but they always preferred playing in the NIT. After the 1951 scandal LIU dropped out of major college competition. Now they were back among the elite.

Danny Ainge's appearance in uniform during the warmup drill surprised quite a few BYU fans, especially his coach, who was aware that his star guard had been doubled over with back spasms just two hours earlier. He had been put to bed with hot packs and when the warmup produced no more discomfort Frank Arnold decided to start him. Ainge played the full 40 minutes and scored 21 points in a first round victory over Princeton. After permitting the Tigers to sink 65 percent of their shots in the first half, the Cougars switched to a zone and won 60-51.

James Madison was only in its fourth season of Division I competition but they played like veterans, eliminating Georgetown 61-55. The Hoyas had apparently never recovered from the previous year's regional final when they blew a 14 point lead to Iowa. That one point loss damaged their confidence and this was the culmination of a season long struggle.

The following evening the two most unpredictable teams in the regional squared off. Villanova was the more consistent and trounced Houston 90-72. Virginia Commonwealth had a temporary scare against LIU but won going away 85-69. Down by 17 points, the Blackbirds swarmed all over the Rams in one six-minute span and cut the deficit to one at 58-57. But an 11-2 spurt recharged the Virginians.

Saturday's East regional double header in Providence featured two teams from the West. The BYU star's back was still sore when he took the court against UCLA. It was hardly evident as Ainge executed one brilliant play after another, outscoring the entire Bruin team 23-22 in the first half. In all he played 39 minutes and poured in 37 points. The Cougars' front court was too tall for UCLA and an almost impenetrable defense kept the Bruins, who shot an anemic 34 percent, far down range. Steve Trumbo, Greg Kite and Fred Roberts held a lease on the backboards and their quick outlet passes triggered several fast breaks spearheaded by Ainge. In a runaway, the speedy Cougars handed UCLA their first opening game tournament loss since 1963 by the score of 78-55.

James Madison's strategy to slow the pace played right into Notre Dame's hands. The Irish were used to playing at half speed. Besides, Woolridge, their best rebounder, was limping with a bruised thigh. Guard Tracy Jackson took up the slack with a dozen boards in the 54-45 Notre Dame triumph.

The scoreboard showed 56-54 in favor of Tennessee when Virginia Commonwealth's Danny Kottack flipped in the tying points on a jumper from the left of the key at 2:24. The Vols held the ball until a last second shot was blocked by Kenny Stancell. The failure of that tactic did not impress the Rams who seemed content to pass the ball around for the entire overtime. Unfortunately, Kottack stepped on the line and now it was Tennessee's turn to go into a delay game. With the fans whistling impatiently and the tension building, the Vols worked the ball to Dale Ellis who sank the only shot in the overtime three seconds before the buzzer. Final score 58-56.

Virginia, the last surviving team from its state, faced an uphill battle when Villanova pushed to a seven point lead early in the second half. Sampson's two charity throws finally gave the Cavaliers their first lead of the period at 3:26. They were still clinging to a sliver thin 51-50 advantage when Pinone corkscrewed in for an off balance jump shot with 20 seconds to go. When he landed in traffic, he was given a charging foul which precipitated a loud, arm waving, foot stamping reaction. To no avail. Othell Wilson stepped to the line and sank a pair. Seconds later Virginia was on its way to the next round 54-50.

The Cavaliers had to come from behind again when they were down five points to Tennessee in the next round. But the Vols hit a dry spell for more than eight minutes and Virginia won easily 62-48. They got little scoring help from Sampson who managed only nine points in a cold shooting performance.

Notre Dame did an effective job neutralizing BYU's fast break. Using the deliberate offense which they executed so well, they led for almost the entire game. Paxson shrouded Ainge so well that the All American canned only two points in the first half. With a minute remaining he still had only ten points, though it was enough to give him is one hundred and eleventh straight game in double figures. At that point Greg Ballif's long jump shot moved the Cougars into their first lead, 49-48. The Irish ran the clock down until, with ten seconds to go, Tripucka hit the cords for the seeming game winner.

BYU called time. Their coach outlined a play but it never took place. The inbounds pass went to Ainge (naturally) and the speedy guard took the destiny of the Cougars into his own hands. Like a greased bullet he streaked past Paxson switching the ball to his other side in mid-dribble, slipped between Tripucka and Tom Sluby like a slalom racer, made a sharp left around Tim Andree like a switched locomotive and laid the ball in over Woolridge with the grace of a ballet dancer. There were two tics left but it was all over but the celebration.

With that 51-50 outcome BYU had advanced further than in any previous tournament. The regional final was close until after the break. For the third straight time Virginia had to play catchup in the second half. The turning point came when Sampson slam dunked a rebound off a shot by Lamp to wipe out a one point Cougar lead. Ainge insisted a little too vehemently that Sampson had hung from the rim which would have been an automatic technical. Instead, when Ainge continued chirping at the referee, it was he who got the technical. Lamp sank the free throw and Wilson's bucket off the subsequent possession gave the Cavaliers a 39-35 lead. The episode deflated the Cougars and Virginia went on to take the regional 74-60.

Midwest:

Seldom had a national champion nose dived quite as spectacularly as Louisville (21-8)—or recovered as dramatically. They lost six of their first seven and seven of nine. The Cardinals were an enigma to their coach and fans. After all, four starters were back as well as 6′9″ Scooter McCray. Only Griffith had graduated and though his spectacular performance was difficult to replace, it was his leadership that Louisville missed most. But following a 64-47 debacle at Kansas State they hammered 19 of their next 20 victims (none were close games) and entered the tournament with the longest winning streak in the country. Only Memphis State punctured the Cardinal's skein but that omission was avenged subsequently with a 96-65 thrashing. Another act of revenge was a 91-57 pasting of Iona. Crum had a good memory. And now he had momentum going for him again.

Yet it was fourth ranked LSU (28-3) that was top seeded in the regional. For the sixth consecutive year the Tigers improved their record. They had fallen to Arkansas in the Great Alaska Shootout, the second game of the season, but had then reeled off 26 straight victories before Kentucky bounced them in the season finale. In the SEC playoff the Tigers were victimized by Georgia in a semifinal test.

Dale Brown had lost none of his irascibility. In one game against Kentucky he charged the referee, pulled off his jacket and threw it on the court yelling, "You've taken away everything else. Take that."

Missouri (22-9) won most of their games handily and went down to defeat as easily. Stapanovich, the Tigers' 6′11″ center, was a bit of a flake who had been known to bounce a ball off an opponent's head for the novelty of it. He was not a particularly strong or dominating center yet he had led his high school team to two consecutive state championships and a 63-1 record in his junior and senior years. In December he had accidentally shot himself in the head with a pistol but had at first claimed that a burglar had entered the house and attacked him. Before he retracted that story he had become the center of some heavy security on the Missouri campus.

Also representing the Big Eight was Kansas (22-7) which bowed to

Kentucky by 16 points but then tamed their next ten opponents. Mississippi (16-13) lost seven of eight early in the season, the losing streak interrupted briefly by a 46-45 finessing of Auburn. They had never received a tournament invitation and their chances after finishing 8-10 in the SEC and 13-13 overall were microscopic. But a series of upsets brought an unlikely matchup of Ole Miss and Georgia (which had also never participated in the NCAA tournament) in the SEC playoff final. Ole Miss won. Mercer (18-11) was another school whose prospects were none too promising. The Bears had been unable to combine more than three victories in a row.

Arizona State (24-3) had won 16 of their last 17 including the final, which snapped Oregon State's long winning streak. Their lone loss during that kick was to UCLA by three. Lamar (24-4) finished first in the Southland but had been assaulted by Missouri 92-70. Arkansas (22-7) won the SWC and Iowa (21-6) was the runner up in the Big Ten. Southern - Baton Rouge (17-10) won ten times by fewer than five points. As a result the Jaguars gave up more points than they scored. The only consistency shown by Southern was when they scored 69 points in each of their last three games. That brought to twc the number of teams from Baton Rouge in the regional—the other being LSU.

Wichita State (23-6) captured their first eight by a margin of 28 points including a 105-46 drubbing of Hardin Simmons. This would be the school's last tournament for a while. The Shockers were headed for probation because certain irregularities, including the alleged payment for an abortion for a player's girlfriend by a member of the athletic department, had come to light. The team was also handicapped when its starting center was declared ineligible as a result of a falsified high school transcript. It could all be shrugged off as normal in the turbulant MVC. Coach Gene Smithson, as flamboyant as his counterpart Versace at Bradley whose curly perm he emulated, had the letters MTXE stitched to his players uniforms to remind them of "mental toughness extra effort."

Missouri hardly looked like the same team that had eclipsed Lamar by 22 points during the season when the two squared off in the opening round. Paced by Terry Long's 14 point second half effort and Mike Olliver's booming jump shots from the outer reaches, Lamar toughed it out 71-67. The final score in the co-feature was almost identical as Arkansas eliminated Mercer 73-67. The Razorbacks could have made it a lot easier for themselves had they been able to hit from the line. They threw 21 bricks in 40 tries, the worst culprit being Darrell Walker who canned just three of thirteen.

A pair of local schools found Wichita a friendly setting in other first round action. Southern forged a 20-14 lead but then their bubble burst as Wichita State shocked them 95-70. Kansas had a closer call. They were unable to stop Mississippi from grinding a 12 point deficit down to two. Elston Turner's field goal with 29 seconds to go brought Ole Miss within a bucket again and another with four seconds showing on the clock cut that margin in half. But a pair of clutch free throws by Tony Guy two seconds later preserved a 69-66 victory for Kansas.

The second round doubleheader in Austin, Texas, resembled the one in Wichita. In the runaway LSU socked Lamar 100-78. Hundred point games were becoming a rarity and this one was the result of board control—a 43 to 24 rebounding edge—and intimidation. After the game, Lamar's coach, Pat Foster, admitted, "LSU was the most physical team I've ever seen in my ten years of coaching." Macklin, with a season high 31 points, was LSU's leading offensive weapon.

The co-feature was considerably closer. With five seconds on the clock Derek Smith's fall away jumper gave Louisville a 73-72 lead and apparently sealed their sixteenth straight victory. But Arkansas' U.S. Reed cranked up and threw what Denny Crum later termed "a prayer shot" from beyond the midcourt line. The ball sailed 49 feet, straight and true and through the hoop as the buzzer sounded, signaling Arkansas' 74-73 win. Reed walked off the court past his jubilant teammates, straight into the locker room, shouting over his shoulder "How'd you like that?" He had made a similar shot against Texas and had been mobbed on that occasion and felt the locker room would be a safer place. So both 1980 finalists were gone early in the tournament.

The two teams from Kansas continued to enjoy Wichita's hospitality. In one matchup Kansas broke the game open, scoring the last ten points of the first half to take a 16 point lead on the way to an 88-71 upset of fifth ranked Arizona State. Guy sprayed 21 points through the hoop in the first half assault. He finished with 36 while Byron Scott had 32 for the losers.

Again a blowout was bracketed with a palm-sweating, down to the last tic, photo finish. Iowa, which had made up 14 points in the previous year's regional final, squandered as many and more. Ahead by 15 early in the second half they allowed Wichita to tie the score at 56-56. After a time out the Hawkeyes set up Boyle who missed with seven seconds to go. Antoine Carr swept the board and was immediately fouled. It was then that Lute Olsen committed what may well have been the most visible blunder of his career. The Iowa coach called for a time out, unaware that he had used his last one. Randy Smithson, the coach's son, made both technicals and though Carr missed the first of the one-and-one, Wichita retained the ball (because of the technical). Carr was immediately fouled and this time made both free throws to give Wichita a 60-56 lift to the next round.

It was now LSU's turn to enjoy friendly surroundings. Regional competition had moved to the Superdome in New Orleans where 34,036 fans, a tournament record, cheered them on. It was a rematch with Arkansas which had beaten the Tigers in the Great Alaska Shootout. Closer to home it was a different story.

The size of the crowd (considerably larger than in Anchorage) may have affected the players. They missed 16 of their first 18 shots which left the score 2-2 after five minutes. Eventually LSU drew inspiration from the partisan crowd but the Razorbacks remained flat. Building on a 34-18 half time advantage, LSU coasted to an easy 72-56 victory. In their first meeting Arkansas had outrebounded LSU 46-30 when Hastings, in the absense of the Cookieman, had ruled the board. Now with Cook in the lineup for LSU the outcome was reversed.

Once again the regional pattern of a close and a tight game held true. This time it was Wichita and Kansas which went down to the wire. It was their first meeting on a basketball court in 25 years. When the Jayhawks' Darnell Valentine stepped to the line for a pair at :56, with Kansas leading 65-62, he had an opportunity virtually to cinch the game. Instead he missed. Mike Jones, a 6′5″ reserve and normally a 43 percent shooter for Wichita, then assumed the role of instant star. While Kansas packed the zone against Carr and Cliff Levingston on the right side Jones took an uncontested shot from the left corner. It was somewhat beyond his range but it went in anyway. Trying to redeem himself, Valentine drove in for an easy layup that somehow would not go down. Once again Jones found himself with the ball, even deeper than before but with time running out. He shot from 25 feet with four seconds left and swish, it was 66-65 Wichita.

LSU looked even more aggressive than usual in the regional final against Wichita. Probably the huge crowd, almost solidly Tiger fans, had a lot to do with it. The players were also coming together as a team, integrating their talents into an awesome scoring machine. Gone was the disruptive Scales. Things were moving smoothly for LSU.

Wichita was ahead 12-11 when the Tigers punished them with 14 straight points. Late in the first period LSU was already out of sight, on the long side of a 42-21 score. Macklin, who had 17 first half points, had to sit down for twelve minutes with leg cramps and a dislocated finger but by then it did not matter. LSU rolled to a 96-85 shocker-resistant blastoff to the Final Four.

West:

They were known as the Orange Express and sometimes Clockwork Orange but whatever the name, they were a super team ranked number one until their last game when their perfect season ended with a shattering 87-67 defeat on their home court. Oregon State (26-1), though shaken by the margin of defeat, still felt some relief that the pressure of the long winning streak had been lifted. Coach Ralph Miller had performed a superlative job molding his lightly recruited quintet into a Pac Ten champion and had been voted Coach of the Year. Miller, who had played for the legendary Phog Allen at Kansas, insisted that there was nothing new in basketball since his college days in the early forties. And so he concentrated on the fundamentals—tight defense (which in 1981 averaged nine steals a game), teamwork, hitting the open man, back door play, setting picks, cuts to the hoop and good conditioning. By season's end Miller had 497 career victories, the third highest among active coaches.

The thing that distinguished Oregon State from other teams was its passing game. Once over the midcourt line the ball rarely touched the floor. The only sound on the court came from the ball smacking from one palm to the next and sneakers squeaking along the hardwood. Three of every four baskets scored by the Beavers came as a result of assists. In a game against Rhode Island 36 of 39 field goals were the product of a pass. In that game they had humiliated their opponents—a fine team that had beaten Oregon a week earlier—by a lopsided 103-55 score.

The offense started with the guards, Ray Blume and Mark Radford, a pair of native Oregonians who were constantly on the lookout for an open player. Often it ended with Steve Johnson, the center, who was almost unstoppable once he received the ball under the basket. Johnson set a NCAA record by making almost 75 percent of his shots. On defense he really clogged the middle. Known as the Big Behind for obvious reasons, it was said that in order to get around him one had to be careful not to step out of bounds. The problem with Johnson was he spent so much time on the bench. He managed to foul out of almost half the games during his career at Oregon State. Yet he was enthusiastic, coachable and loved the game so much he had run away from home while in high school because his parents refused to let him play. At one corner was freshman Charlie Sitton, a tough, brash enforcer. At the other Lester "The Molester" Conner, who though never a starter in high school had become the Beavers' best defensive player and the number one instigator of Operation Turnover.

There was some feeling that despite the NCAA selection committee's attempt at balance, the West regional was somewhat stronger than the others*.

Sixth ranked North Carolina (25-7) won the Great Alaska Shootout and despite finishing second in the ACC won the conference postseason playoff. Half their games had been against tournament bound teams and they had turned in a respectable 11-5 record against them, including a 65-56 victory over Indiana.

Utah (24-4) was the third school from the top ten in the regional. They had won 21 of their first 22. The almost perfect streak was interrupted by a one point loss to Drake. Wyoming (23-5) tied the Utes for first place in the WAC. Six times they had splintered their opponents by more than 30 points, though one of those, New Mexico, came back to beat them. The Cowboys were known for their smothering defense which kept their opponents from averaging more than 40 percent from the field. After appearing seven times in the tournament's first 15 years, Wyoming was returning after a 14 year absence.

---

*All but three tournament teams which finished in the top three positions in team statistics at the end of the year were in the West regional. Oregon State was first in field goal percentage and second in scoring margin. Wyoming was first in scoring margin and field goal percentage defense and second in rebounding. Fresno State was first in defense. Northeastern was first in rebounding and Idaho was third in field goal percent. In addition, San Francisco was the highest scoring team in the tournament and had the fifth best rebounding in the country.

Twelve times Fresno State (25-3) allowed fewer than 50 points, which made them the stingiest team in the country. In two successive contests their deliberate style had limited their opponents to 30 and 26 points bringing back memories of the twenties and thirties. They did step out of character, though, when they outscored Portland State 96-65. After taking their first ten, the Bulldogs encountered some stiff resistance at midseason but chased their final 13 opponents to finish on top of the Pacific Coast Athletic Association.

The Bulldog was a fitting symbol of the team. Coach Boyd Grant had installed a tenacious defense featuring several variations of the zone and man-to-man. Traps and pressure tactics on the ball handler, which produced many turnovers, added to their opponents' frustration. Grant had been reluctant to accept the position at Fresno but once there the success of his team had generated wild enthusiasm. Seland Arena had been sold out the previous two years and many of the raucus boosters showed up dressed completely in scarlet. One of their favorite pregame ploys was to form a human tunnel through which the players charged onto the court.

Kansas State (21-8) split their ten games with tournament-bound teams. They were ambushed by Arizona State by 23 points but socked Louisville 64-47 and claimed Arkansas and Fresno State among their victims, too. Illinois (20-7) beat Missouri by 18 but succumbed to Wisconsin, ninth in the Big Ten, at home 54-45. Idaho (25-3) started their season with eleven victories before tasting defeat.

Two-thirds of the way into their schedule Pittsburgh was only 9-9. They finished with an 18-11 record which was only good for fourth place in the Eastern Eight but went on to win the conference playoff. Howard (17-11) was even weaker. They failed their first three tests. Later in the season they repeated that losing streak twice. Howard suffered setbacks at the hands of North Carolina A and T, Campbell, Longwood, Florida A and M, Delaware State and South Carolina State, none of which would scare their regional competitors. San Francisco (24-6), which had once started a revolution that popularized defense when Bill Russell was in residence in the mid-fifties, appeared to be trying to start another trend, toward more scoring. In a throwback to the early seventies they beat Pepperdine 102-99. Finally there was Northeastern (23-5), far from home.*

In the first round Wyoming promoted a 16-13 lead over Howard into a 14 point spread in less than five minutes. Howard was nervous in their first tournament appearance and shot a sorry 21 percent in the first half. The second period was not much better and the Cowboys had little trouble lassoing the Bisons 78-43.

San Francisco's 12 point lead evaporated completely when Blackman's

---

*There were a record 12 schools making their tournament debut: Alabama-Birmingham, Ball State, Fresno State, Howard, Idaho, James Madison, LIU, Mercer, Mississippi, Northeastern, Southern and Tennessee-Chattanooga.

follow up shot put Kansas State ahead at 2:19 of the second period. Blackman had been held to four points until then, but he equalled that total in the last two minutes with another layup to clinch the 64-60 win.

The following evening the remaining two first round matches were decided in the last five seconds. There were still five minutes left when Fresno State evened the score at 53. Even with that much time remaining Northeastern decided to stall for the final shot and were rewarded for their patience when Chip Ruckers spun in a layup with four seconds showing.

After a long uphill struggle Pittsburgh's Dwayne Wallace tallied on a 15 foot jump shot to tie Idaho 61-61 in the final minutes. The lead changed hands several times before Ron Maben, Idaho's leading scorer, parlayed a pair of free throws into a 69-68 lead at the 17 second mark. Pittsburgh was facing a long flight home when the scales tipped one more time. Assuming the hero's role again Wallace kissed the ball off the glass for the winning basket with just three seconds left.

For those fans who like their games even closer, the second round doubleheader in Los Angeles was pure fulfillment. This time a total of five seconds separated the winning points from the final buzzer.

The score favored Wyoming 65-63 when Perry Range of Illinois found the hole with a 22 foot rainbow with 16 seconds left. When Bill Garnett missed one from the top of the key it enabled the Illini to take the last shot. Mark Smith was then fouled only three seconds before the buzzer and sank both attempts giving the Big Ten team a 67-65 decision.

It was now time for the **close** game, a beautifully coached contest between master tacticians Ralph Miller and Jack Hartman. Just as they had against San Francisco, Kansas State spent the whole game playing catchup basketball. Oregon State limited the Wildcats to 19 first half points but with the scoreboard showing 3:23 Ed Nealy, a husky 245 pound power forward, cashed a pair to bring KSU even at 48-48. Johnson committed his fifth personal on the play and fouled out of his fifty-first game since becoming a Beaver. Oregon State held the ball until Sitton was fouled. He missed the first of a one-and-one and now it was the Wildcats' turn to hold the ball. With two minutes to play Hartman called time out. The plan was to isolate Blackman on the baseline. This was a daring vote of confidence in a man who had already committed six turnovers and had had a mediocre tournament. But the play worked and once again Blackman delivered when it counted, swishing a 16 foot jumper just two seconds before the horn. It was Kansas State's first and only lead of the afternoon and presented them with a 50-48 upset.

Like DePaul, the Beavers had been among the top five in the polls the past two years but were eliminated in the opening game both times. (The following day Kansas beat Arizona State in a different regional. That gave two unranked Big Eight schools a 2-0 edge over a pair of highly favored Pac Ten teams who had lost just four times between them all year.)

There were no last second fireworks in second round action in El Paso. All

American Danny Vranes made 90 percent of his shots from the floor and scored 27 points to lead Utah in a 94-79 pounding of Northeastern. In the co-feature North Carolina survived some early uncertainty but eventually pulled away from Pittsburgh to triumph 74-57. When North Carolina was unable to dent the cords in the first five minutes while the Panthers shot into an 8-0, lead there was some concern among the Tarheel faithful. They no doubt remembered that their team had been eliminated in opening tournament matches the three previous years. However, with the score 19-16 in their favor, the Panthers ran dry for the next five minutes while the Tarheels flourished with 12 points. But life has never been easy for Dean Smith. Al Wood, the Tarheels' All American, picked up three quick personals and was forced to the bench for ten minutes in the opening period. By the time he fouled out, though, the issue was no longer in doubt. Besides, James Worthy and Sam Perkins each contributed 21 points to take up the slack.

The following week in Salt Lake City, Utah, playing at home where they had won all 15 games that season, were a slight favorite to unseat North Carolina. It was a classic confrontation of Division I's two best front courts. Facing Wood, Worthy and Perkins were Vranes, Tom Chambers and Karl Bankowski.

Once again the Tarheels' offense sputtered early, like a car on a January morning. But their zone bailed them out and stopped the Utes from establishing their inside game. Soon the home team began risking from long range with poor results. Eleven of 13 attempts went astray while North Carolina sped to a 25-13 advantage. Later Scott Martin's basket at the mid-mark capped a rally that moved Utah to within two points of the Tarheels. But Chambers picked up his fourth personal early in the second half and spent almost nine minutes on the bench. By this time the Tarheels' offense was at full throttle—they sank 70 percent of their shots in the final 20 minutes—and they claimed victory 61-56. North Carolina's front court each tallied 15 points while Vranes was a cold 5-for-14 and Bankowski was mired in a deep freeze with one field goal in nine attempts.

Illinois was icebound, too, when they missed ten of their first eleven tries against Kansas State. They never led though they outscored the Wildcats from the floor by five baskets. The difference came at the line where the Illini sank two of three while their opponents fattened their score with 17 free throws. Kansas State's only basket in the last 8:46 came with three seconds remaining. The rest of the time they trooped to the foul stripe on their way to a 57-52 triumph.

The Tarheels' defense had Kansas State totally confused in the regional final. They switched from one zone to the next, stymieing every Wildcat move. On the other end of the court they had little trouble solving their opponent's 3-2 zone with short passes that always seemed to find their way to Perkins underneath. In an effort to deny them the baseline, Hartman switched to a 2-3 zone. The Tarheels simply called long distance, hitting consistently from 15 to 20 feet. Dean Smith had never lost a regional final and this one was no exception as his team flattened Kansas State 82-68.

Final Four:

Philadelphia hosted the Final Four as it had in 1976. Two excellent matchups awaited the sellout crowd. In one a pair of ACC schools directed by coaches who held little love for each other promised an emotionally charged duel (Terry Holland's feeling for Dean Smith may be guessed when he named his dog after the Tarheel coach.) Indiana versus LSU promised to be just as exciting. Both teams had gathered a full head of steam in their previous three tournament games, wach having won the last two before an overwhelmingly partisan crowd. While both sides were well-trained in all phases of the sport, Indiana could shut down an opponent like a Central American curfew while LSU's offense could break open a game faster than a bull in a china shop. Each of the four teams had come this far because of their assertiveness and their ability to dicate the tempo.

Virginia had already beaten North Carolina twice but that did not mean much. So had Wake Forest but the Tarheels had swept them away in the ACC playoff when it counted most. In the two earlier games the Tarheels had blown 13 and 16 point leads. Nobody expected that to happen again.

Virginia's zone worked well enough in the first half, which ended in a 27-27 tie. But when North Carolina opened a narrow lead and threatened to go into a freeze, the Cavaliers were forced to switch to a man-to-man. That set up a mismatch which cost them the game. Jeff Jones at 6′4″ was unable to hold Al Wood, who was three inches taller. The All American went on a rampage; four superb jump shots and a free throw accounted for nine consecutive Tarheel points. During a 10:38 stretch, Wood exploded for 22 points, most of them on medium range driving jump shots. Virginia managed to knot the count at 37 but Jimmy Black's two points gave his team the lead again and they were never headed. The final score showed the Heels outdueling the Cavaliers 78-65. Woods had 39 points, accounting for one-half his side's output and a team-high ten rebounds. Sampson's presence was hardly felt with just three field goals and eleven points. Once again Smith had been able to turn the tables when it came to crunch time.

The Hoosiers looked fit and there was no question that Bobby Knight was in excellent form. He had deposited an LSU fan in a trash can after a taunting episode in a hotel corridor. The coach had scored the first basket for the Hoosiers, so to speak.

However, his players, aside from Isiah Thomas, were unable to locate the basket as easily as their coach in the first half. And a big problem was that Thomas, who had made six of eight shots, also had three personals. The Hoosiers were even shut out during the last 4:28 of the period. For the first time since the start of the tournament they were in touble.

Down by three at the half, their cause was given a revitalizing shot by four straight buckets, courtesy of Landon Turner. But the Hoosiers' fortunes seemed ready to take another plunge when Thomas picked up his fourth personal at 16:33. Knight sent in Jim Thomas to replace Isiah and though the namesake contributed just two points, he hauled down nine rebounds in 17 minutes against the much taller Tigers and blocked two shots.

LSU had gone into a delay during the last three minutes of the first half. This had effectively blunted their momentum and now they were unable to regain it. It took them more than five minutes to score their first point of the second half and they did not reach 40 until less than three minutes remained in the game. The aggressive Indiana defense was equally responsible for LSU's failure to score. Turner held Macklin to four first half points and shut him off completely in the second while scoring 20 himself.

In the face of such a disciplined opponent LSU's confidence disintegrated into an uncoordinated effort to rush back into contention. There was time for that but not in the purposeless attack the Tigers staged in the final 20 minutes. As a result, Indiana recorded its fourth consecutive blowout 67-49. It was the first time since 1949 that LSU had been held to fewer than 50 points.

In the last two weeks Indiana had won four games by an average of 25 points and even Knight could find little to complain about. The final was another rematch since the Tarheels had beaten the Hoosiers by nine earlier in the year. Few thought they could do it again. After all, this was Smith's sixth Final Four and third appearance in a title game without a championship.

Midway through the first half North Carolina enjoyed a 16-8 edge. At that point the Hoosiers' cloying man-to-man slowed the Tarheel attack to a crawl. Ten points in ten minutes was insufficient to ensure a half time lead when Randy Wittman plugged the hoop from the corner at the buzzer giving Indiana a 27-26 advantage. Isiah Thomas was shooting a glacial one for seven when his two steals, converted into baskets early in the second half, ignited his teammates. Jim Thomas again came off the bench—this time to replace Ted Kitchel, who had committed three very quick personals—to play a decisive role. He was assigned to guard Wood and though this created a mismatch similar to the one in the semifinal, Thomas held his taller opponent to less than half of what he had scored against Virginia.

Indiana's persistent defense was the deciding factor once again. They slowly pulled away to win the championship 63-50. Isiah Thomas was voted the MVP award, the second time in three years it had gone to a sophomore.

It was all quite familiar. Five years earlier Knight had won his first championship, also in Philadelphia, with the same disiplined tactics. Whatever criticisms may have been leveled against him, Knight had proven his coaching genius. Once more he stood at the pinnacle of college basketball supremacy. No other team had won a championship with as many regular season defeats. Yet no other team had so dominated its opponents—by 113 points—in the tournament.

20

FINALLY!

1982

1982

Two schools that had dominated the NCAA tournament over its more than 40 year history were UCLA—which made its fifteenth consecutive appearance in 1981—and Kentucky. They also dominated their conferences, creating something less than a healthy competitive environment. The same could be said to a lesser extent of Kansas and Kansas State in the Big Eight. This, however, was not true of the next two most successful schools, North Carolina and Indiana, which played in highly competitive conferences with at most two weak representatives.

Over the past 40 years the power centers of college basketball, aside from the isolated cases of UCLA and Kentucky, moved among the independents of the Northeast, the ACC, the Big Ten and the Missouri Valley Conference. (The Metro had in the past few years become recognized as a powerhouse, though mostly because of Louisville. This was also true of the SEC with the ascendency of Alabama, LSU and Tennessee which had begun to crowd Kentucky.) The Northeast independents, though very strong in the first decade and a half of the tournament—champions Holy Cross, CCNY, LaSalle—were, with the exception of an occasional success, not much of a factor in later years. It was the ACC, particularly the four North Carolina colleges, and the Big Ten that produced the heavy hitters.

But in 1980 Dave Gavitt conceived the idea of a new conference that would challenge the powers and reestablish Northeast basketball to the preeminence it had enjoyed in the thirties, forties and early fifties. With the help of Lou Carneseca, John Thompson and other area coaches he created

North Carolina's Jimmy Black (21) is closely guarded by Georgetown's Eric "Sleepy" Floyd in the NCAA championship contest. In the background from left to right are Pat Ewing (GU 33), Ed Springgs (GU 50), James Worthy (UNC 52), and Matt Doherty (UNC 44).
(W.C. Auth photo)

the Big East—an awesome name for a brilliant conception. Gavitt had been an average coach at Providence but he found his true niche as an organizer. He became the conference's first commissioner as well as serving on the NCAA's Division I tournament selection committee.

Performing a minor miracle, Gavitt and his associates had in a few months, organized seven schools in the most lucrative marketing areas of the Northeast. He had even sold the conference television rights in a very profitable package before the first whistle had been blown. Later he was to negotiate another million dollar deal with New York's Madison Square Garden for the conference playoffs which were to be held there from 1983 through 1985.

The Big East started competition in the 1980 season with seven teams. Three major cities in the Northeast corridor were represented by St. Johns of New York, Georgetown of Washington, D.C., and Boston College. There were also Providence, Syracuse, Connecticut and Seton Hall which had a large following in metropolitan New Jersey. A year later the last major city in the area, Philadelphia, was represented when Villanova joined. All but Seton Hall had played at least once in the NCAA tournament.*

Almost all had access to a large arena where they played before good crowds and even more substantial television audiences. Syracuse completed the largest auditorium designed specifically for college basketball—the Carrierdome, seating 25,000. The members were also blessed with excellent coaching. Rollie Massimino at Villanova and Lou Carneseca at St. Johns were two Italian-Americans who brought old world articulation and intensity to their sideline gyrations. Jim Boeheim at Syracuse was just as intense and John Thompson was an imposing figure pacing in front of Georgetown's bench, a white towel resting on his shoulder. Tom Davis at Boston College, a coach with a PhD, was one of the smartest tacticians to direct a team and Joe Mullaney at Providence and William Raftery at Seton Hall had more than 500 wins between them. It was no wonder that for the first time in decades the huge talent pool of the Northeast, which had been drained away by other conferences around the country, was now staying close to home and being absorbed by the Big East schools.

There was a natural rivalry between the ACC and the Big East schools that had existed long before the newer conference was organized: St. Johns versus North Carolina; Georgetown versus Maryland; Villanova versus Duke, which had recruited heavily in Philadelphia. In 1980 the new conference had produced enough good teams to make the likelihood of a confrontation between the two leagues in the NCAA finals a decided possibility. Unfortunately, neither placed a team in the Final Four. Instead it was a banner year for the Big Ten. Now in 1982 the expectation for such a showdown was again strong.

---

*Seton Hall with Walt Dukes had been in the top ten frequently during the early fifties but preferred playing in the NIT.

West:

They were known as the **Beat of the East,** the **Thunder Rolling Out of the East** and, slightly more flattering but equally intimidating, the **Stars Rising in the East.** They were the Hoyas of Georgetown (26-6). Despite their fine but unspectacular record—they did not even win their conference—the Hoyas were ranked sixth in the year-end polls, ahead of teams with better won-lost marks. At times they suffered from lapses of concentration. On other occasions though, they transcended their opponents so decisively, especially on defense, observers were convinced they were the best team in the country. The inconsistency was apparent in the two games against Seton Hall, both won by Georgetown, one by 40 points—the other by two. Despite the six losses, they were third in margin of victory in Division I. The NCAA selection committee recognized their superiority and seeded them number one in their regional. The Hoyas appreciated the honor but were not too happy that they had been moved to the West regional, with the first four rounds to be played in Utah.

Georgetown was either a slow starting quintet or else they did not acclimate to the cold very well. In any case they lost two in the Great Alaska Shootout in November just as they had the previous year. This was followed by a 13 game winning streak, amputated by three upsets in a row against second division Big East teams. With that out of their system, the Hoyas stumbled just once the rest of the schedule. They finished with a flourish, drubbing Villanova (which had finished ahead of them in the conference) by 18 points in the final of the Big East playoff.

The Hoyas were sparked by All American guard Eric "Sleepy" Floyd, who scored more than 2,000 career points, and seven foot center Pat Ewing, the Freshman of the Year. The supporting cast was made up of ordinary guys called Jones (Anthony), Smith (Eric) and Brown (Fred). Last year's starter Ed Spriggs had moved to backup center. Spriggs had never played basketball in high school. After graduation he had taken a job in the post office where he played in an amateur league for a few years until Thompson watched him one day and convinced him to enroll at Georgetown. That was why Spriggs was still in college at age 25.

But the prime reason for Georgetown's success was the coach. John Thompson had turned a limp basketball program—a 3-23 record the season before he arrived—into a powerhouse. He had done it not only by his vast knowledge of the game but also by his strength of character and dominant personality. "We are not running a democracy," he said. "The things I want on a court are discipline and order and consistency." The coach was also a clever scheduler. Aside from the Shootout, the Kodak Classic and conference away-dates, Georgetown played all their games at home.

Thompson's protective attitude toward his players did not endear him to the media. When he took his team to Utah, he moved them into a motel an hour's drive from the game site to keep the reporters away. Most of all he was protective of Ewing, his glowering, intense protege. Some of the early defeats were partly attributable to Ewing's inexperience and his tendency to pick up quick fouls. Still a little uncoordinated, the freshman was learning rapidly to add finesse to his power moves. Intimidation, on the other hand, was a characteristic that seemed to have been part of his breeding. He used his elbows unhesitatingly and seemed to get a great deal of satisfaction from in-your-face rejections. He took well to Thompson's coaching, as demonstrated by his greater concentration and fewer mistakes as the season progressed.

The size, the elbows, the intensity—all helped to intimidate opponents and make them tentative. Besides, Thompson's team played outstanding team defense. Not surprisingly, their foes, who were among the toughest in the country, were limited to 41.5 percent shooting efficiency. Constant pressure created steals and turnovers and tended to jog the other side out of its rhythm. As they prepared for the tournament there was an air of expectancy among those who followed the team, as if the Hoyas were about to take off and go into orbit, as if a thunderstorm was about to break.

Oregon State (23-4) was ranked fourth but had been seeded second behind Georgetown in the West regional. They dished out some painful punishment to Penn 102-64, Pittsburgh 88-58, Oregon 94-51, Stanford 81-38 and 111-81 and Arizona State and California by identical 74-43 scores. As a result they were number one in size of victory margin.* This was to have been a rebuilding year for Miller who had lost an All American center and the best backcourt in intercollegiate competition. But he surprised everyone, as he had in an identical situation at Iowa in 1970, by fashioning a conference champion.

Idaho (26-2) made the year end top ten for the first time in its history and was ranked eighth. The Vandals were more than halfway through the season, 16 games, when they suffered their first defeat. This streak included the Far West Classic, which they captured by an average margin of 20 points in the three game tournament. An indication of how far they had come in three years under coach Don Molson was a 71-49 drubbing of powerful Oregon State in the latter's own tournament. Only a pair of back to back two point losses—one in overtime at Notre Dame—marred their record. Most of their wins were blowouts making theirs the second best scoring differential mark. Even on the road Idaho managed to blast their opponents by 20 and 25 points.

Molson had arrived in Idaho in 1979. Prior to that he had been an assistant to Jud Heathcote at Michigan State, missing the Spartan's championship season by a year. He had incorporated his former boss' 2-3 matchup zone into the Idaho defense which effectively neutralized the team's lack of

*It was a reflection of the closeness of the contests played throughout the country that Oregon State's mark in this department was the lowest ever recorded.

height. All five starters averaged in double figures. So well-balanced was the attack that only five points separated the leading scorer from the least productive and most of that difference came from the foul line. Actually Ken Owens, the leading scorer, averaged only one basket more than Kelvin Smith. They were also equally matched in height, all starters aside from Owens standing either 6′5″ or 6′6″. The starting quintet accounted for 90 percent of Idaho's scoring and unless the game was theirs beyond any doubt Molson was loath to use his substitutes.

Tenth ranked Fresno State (26-2) had allowed the fewest points per game since Oklahoma A and M thirty years ago. Nineteen times they held the other side to 50 points or fewer, a feat they maintained for 14 consecutive games. They had bowed only to Southwest Louisiana in the latter's Bayou Classic and to Long Beach State in overtime. Only once, in a 73-61 victory over Utah State, had they given up more than 60 points.

Wyoming (22-6) won the WAC losing twice to UTEP in the process. The school finished high in several statistical departments, notably number one in rebounding and in field goal percentage allowed. The Cowboys' strong defense resulted in some anemic scores. A 27-25 victory over BYU was the result of stalling tactics but 29 points by Air Force and 31 by Colorado State were unsuccessful attempts to overcome a smothering defense in an otherwise normal game.

Pepperdine (21-6) split their first eight contests but finished strongly by whipping their last 14 challengers. A high scoring team, the Waves really lit up the scoreboard when they edged San Francisco 106-100—netting more than 68 percent of their shots—and Loyola-Marymount 105-104 in their final two appearances of the season. In all they exceeded 100 points five times. The Waves reacted well under pressure: they took each of their four overtime games, including a pair of double overtime marathons.

Gene Catlett, formerly assistant to Adolph Rupp and Lefty Driesell, and now head coach at West Virginia (26-3), had done an excellent job in directing his team to a first place finish in the Eastern Eight and to the tournament for the first time since 1967. The Mountaineers split their first two before taking off on a 23 game winning spree. Pittsburgh (20-9) burst West Virginia's bubble in the final of the conference playoff after enduring two losses at their hands earlier in the season.

Iowa (20-7) finished second in the Big Ten. The Hawkeyes cracked under the pressure of the stretch drive, losing five of seven, including their final three. The critical confrontation for the Big Ten title occurred against traditional rival Minnesota in Iowa City where the Hawkeyes had not lost all season. With thunder rolling down out of the packed tiers of fans, accompanied by lightning bursts of energy from the players, the game soon resembled a Wagnerian epic. When the action flowed into the third overtime, there was some question who would become exhausted first, the fans or the players. In any case Minnesota survived and Iowa lost their next two—an overtime game and a one pointer. The Hawkeyes were not exactly cresting at tournament time!

USC (19-8), Northeast Louisiana (20-9) and North Carolina A and T (19-8) completed the regional field. The selection committee had done an equitable job picking the best teams for the tournament but distributing them among the four regionals was another matter. Some schools were more privileged than others, it seemed. Kentucky, for instance, despite being ousted by Alabama played in its natural regional, the Mideast, while the Tide was sent to the East. Memphis State also was moved to the East whereas Louisville, which had finished behind them, played in its natural regional. Georgetown played in the West while Indiana and Kansas State with inferior records stayed close to home.

In 1982, as it had been for the past few years, the West regional was decidedly the strongest of the four. Two of the top six and four of the top ten in the country had been included in the field. The top three schools in margin of victory and field goal percentage allowed were there. Only DePaul had lost fewer games than Idaho and Fresno State. The best net rebounding team and the one allowing the fewest points per game were represented. The defenses of the top four seeds compared favorably with Corregidor.

In the opening round USC held a 57-52 advantage over Wyoming with 2:40 to play. It was then that Mark Wrapp, who had averaged five points per game during the season, stepped into a phone booth to emerge as Super-cowboy. Wrapp's three point play followed by his basket-a-minute later tied the score. USC nosed ahead 58-57 and with less than a minute left, Dwight Anderson was on the line in a bonus situation. He missed. In the scramble for the rebound Wrapp was fouled and converted both attempts. Then with four seconds on the clock he was fouled again and wrapped up the game with another pair, making the final score 61-58 for the Cowboys. The five-point-a-game journeyman had become a hero, scoring his team's last nine points in less than three minutes.

Nothing quite as exciting happened in West Virginia's 102-72 blowout of North Carolina A and T.

Despite the rugged defenses on site there were also teams that could fill the baskets. Pepperdine, leading almost all the way, enjoyed a scoring orgy, socking Pittsburgh 98-88. In the co-feature Iowa rebounded from a one point half time deficit to sack Northeast Louisiana 70-63. The teams were even at 53 when two baskets by the Hawkeyes' Bob Hansen eleven seconds apart and a pair of free throws by Kenny Arnold proved to be the turning point.

The higher seeded teams now joined the action and Fresno State's defense shackled the high flying West Virginians 50-46. The Mountaineers were held to 19 points in the second half compared to 58 in the same period of their first round contest.

The scoring chill was also evident in the second contest. Sleepy Floyd stole the ball twice early in the game and scored each time to give Georgetown a psychological edge over Wyoming almost from the start. Employing combinations of zones with a full court press, the Hoyas harrassed the normally patient and disciplined Cowboys. Mike Jackson, Wyoming's best ball handler, turned the ball over seven times trying to squirm his way out of the backcourt. When they were able to get across the midcourt line, they were most often confronted by a 1-3-1 zone with Ewing's enormous wingspan blocking any approach to the basket. The big freshman was easily identifiable from the gallery not only because of his size but because he wore a short sleeved tee shirt under his uniform. It was probably the first time such an outfit had been seen since the days of Bob Cousy.* By the end of the half Wyoming was down by only five but very much demoralized, partly because Wrapp had picked up four personals and Garnett, their ace, was saddled with three. There was no let up by the Hoyas in the second period and they advanced 51-43.

The following afternoon in Pullman, Washington, Oregon State accomplished something that had eluded them in the previous two tournaments: they won a game. And they did it with conviction, routing Pepperdine 70-51. For Pepperdine and West Virginia the pickings had been easy in the first round and they had flirted with the 100 point mark. But when they confronted teams with hard edged defenses and then allowed their opponents to slow the tempo, their scoring punch was cut literally in half.

Idaho pulled away to a quick 8-0 lead and were comfortably in front of Iowa at the intermission. But the persistent Hawkeyes caught up at 13:42 when Bob Hansen swished a ten footer. It was still tied at 57-57 with 31 seconds to go when Idaho decided to hold for the last shot. They waited a split second too long as Smith's short jumper flew through the hoop after the last note of the final buzzer.

With two minutes left in the overtime, the Hawkeyes were basking in the rays of a six point lead. The Vandals looked tired. Olsen had tried to wear them down by substituting liberally, knowing Idaho's bench was mostly window dressing. Four Hawkeyes fouled out but they could afford it. Meanwhile the Vandals played with only six men. But in the next 60 seconds two field goals and a pair of free throws evened matters and Brian Kellerman's fifteen foot jump shot with three seconds left, giving Idaho a 69-57 win, set off an ecstatic Vandal celebration. Since the Idaho campus is just across the state line from Pullman the revellers lost none of their intensity before they arrived home.

Georgetown crossed the country twice more to resurface the following week some 60 miles from the regional site in Provo, Utah. Not a single upset had marked the regional so far and the Hoyas made sure they would not become the first victim. Fresno State's 2-3 zone was no match against the blistering 63.6 percent shooting of Georgetown. The Bulldogs had nobody

*Ewing wore the tee shirt because he was vulnerable to colds.

big enough to guard Ewing, who accounted for 12 points in as many minutes in the second half. The one-sided outcome boosted Georgetown into the regional final 58-40.

Oregon State was highly motivated in the other semifinal against Idaho. The Vandals had humiliated them by 22 points in their own Christmas tournament and no parvenu was going to get away with that against the Brahmans of the Northwest. Molson displayed his 2-3 zone, using his starters almost throughout. Miller countered by spreading his men, who then snapped the ball around as if it had just come out of a baker's oven. This created a larger playing area and more opportunities to break into an uncontested space. The shuttle game often ended when a man maneuvered free at the baseline to take an open jump shot or received a pass as he cut for the basket for a layup. Both squads were equally disciplined but the Beavers had the advantage of a more experienced coach and of having faced tougher opponents during the season. Conner's 24 points, ten rebounds and four assists made Oregon State's task easier as did their 33 to 17 rebounding edge in the 60-42 trouncing—a swing of 40 points from their earlier meeting.

The West regional was still waiting for its first upset. Most observers felt an upset was impossible since Georgetown and Oregon State were so well-matched. Each had won its semifinal by 18 points. Some thought they were the two best teams in the entire tournament and felt this confrontation worthy of a national final.

The outcome was surprising only in the margin of victory. Everyone expected a close contest. Instead, the Hoyas put on a clinic. Just as they did in their win over Wyoming, they wasted little time in intimidating their opponents. The tone of the game was set early. The fans were still finding their seats when Ewing stole the ball and whipped it over his shoulder into the basket. A minute later he slammed another one home on the tag end of an alley oop pass. With 7:13 to play in the first half it was 30-13 in favor of Georgetown. By the intermission Oregon State was so rattled they had committed ten turnovers.

There was worse to come. The Hoyas sank their first ten attempts from the floor after the break. In all they connected 12 times on 13 shots in the second half—29 of 38 in the game for a tournament record of 76.3 percent. The shooting was so torrid that rebounds were scarce. Ewing grabbed only three though he was busy throughout attempting to establish position under the boards against Sitton. Elbows pumped like pistons drawing not only bruised flesh but also a cascade of fouls. Both men fouled out and Ewing spent only 22 minutes on the court.

With 12 minutes to go, Georgetown was in orbit with a 60-33 tailwind speeding them on. Predictably, they hit a short calm and the Beavers put together a modest 8-3 surge. The Hoyas were still ahead by 22 with less than eight minutes remaining but Thompson directed his players to go into a shell. It was an unnecessary tactic and the crowd responded with some lusty booing. There was no way the Beavers could recover. Yet Thompson was nervous. He remembered his team had blown a 14 point lead in 1980 against Iowa. He also had a lot of respect for Ralph Miller. So he played it safe and won 69-45.

East:

The weakest regional field was the one in the East. One bracket was scheduled for Charlotte and the final two rounds for Raleigh, both sites a puddle jump from the North Carolina campus. It looked as if the selection committee and the schedulers had given Smith's Tarheels a clear road to the Final Four. Number one North Carolina (27-2) was ready for its most serious run at the national championship. Six times Smith had vied for a regional title and six times he had won, the last time in 1981. But each time he had been denied the biggest prize.

The loss to Indiana in the final the previous year had been a bitter disappointment for Smith. But though Al Wood had graduated he could console himself with the realization that this year's squad was even better. Sam Perkins and James Worthy, both 6′9″, were matched All Americans. They were joined in the frontcourt by 6′8″ Matt Doherty. Freshman Michael Jordan and point guard Jimmy Black rounded out the quintet. Worthy had missed most of his freshman year with a broken ankle and had still been tentative at times as a sophomore. But now he was at the top of his game following in the footsteps of Bob McAdoo, Mitch Kupchak and Tom LaGarde.

Until recently Smith had been known for his frequent substitutions to the point that it was suggested he install a revolving door on the sideline. Now he mostly stayed with his starters, an indication of the thinness of the Tarheel bench. It was an excellently coached and well-disciplined team. Each man knew his assignment, was aware of his limitations, was directed to follow the same ritual when he stepped to the line—one he had developed himself and was expected to adhere to. It was the kind of attention to detail that made the Tarheels the only school consistently in the top 20 for the last seven years. It also accounted for the fact that Smith had established the third best record among active coaches, despite playing in the country's toughest conference. He understood the factors in the game, how well they balanced each other and how they could be manipulated to his benefit. As a tactician he had few peers.

Twice, against Kentucky and Virginia, the number one Tarheels encountered challengers ranked second and both times beat back the challenge. They outsmarted Virginia in a controversial contest in the ACC playoff final 47-45. With the score 44-43 in favor of North Carolina and 7:43 to play in the game, Smith waved his men into the four corners. Virginia chose not to go after the Tarheels who did not take a shot for seven minutes. This interlude in a well-played, tightly contested game drew a torrent of boos from the fans. They had paid a considerable tariff for tickets and looked forward to a white knuckle finish in what everyone south of the Mason-Dixon Line saw as the game of the year. The stall tactics were also strongly criticized in the press. "The primary reason for college basketball's prosperity is exuberant play," wrote George Will in **Newsweek**, "but increasingly that is being suffocated by stalling tactics."

The only team given a chance to derail North Carolina before the Final Four was Memphis State (23-4). The Tigers had made the biggest improvement over the previous year of any Division I school. After three consecutive losing years they had stormed to ninth place in the polls at the end of the season. They dropped two of their first three but then concocted 18 wins in their next 19 games—only an overtime loss to Tulane interrupted that streak—to take the Metro title away from Louisville.

Only two starters returned from a mediocre 1981 squad. The big difference was center Keith Lee, considered the country's second best freshman behind Ewing. The 6′10″ pivotman was nicknamed Air Traffic Controller for his shot-blocking ability. It was a young squad with one freshman, three sophomores and a senior among the starters.

Ohio State (23-7) finished third in the Big Ten. Games were as tight as ever in the conference. During one span of eight games the Buckeyes were tied at the end of regulation six times. The fans were getting their money's worth; having paid for forty minutes of action they were often getting 45 or 50 minutes.

The Big East also had its share of barn burners. In a six game stretch Villanova (22-7) strained their coach's adrenalin supply with six one point decisions and a pair of two pointers. That streak ended with a 35 point massacre of LaSalle followed by a 20 point scalping of St. Josephs (just to show who was top dog, or cat, in Philadelphia). Despite three losses to Georgetown, the Wildcats finished in first place in the Big East. Assisting John Pinone, Villanova's star the previous two seasons, was 6′9″ freshman Ed Pinckney who finished with a 65 percent shooting average, third best in the country.

Alabama (23-6) lost to Kentucky twice during the regular season but upset them in the SEC playoff final, in Lexington no less, 48-46, breaking their host's 30 game winning streak at Rupp Arena. Old Dominion (18-11) was in the tournament because it beat James Madison in the ECAC South playoff. The Monarchs skidded during a pair of four game losing streaks. Pennsylvania's nine game losing streak was more like a free fall from 10,000 feet. Yet the 17-9 Quakers got it all out of their system in one burst. Part of the problem may have been due to jet lag. Early in the season they spent more time in airplanes than on the court, flying from Philadelphia to California, back to Philadelphia, to Tokyo, Japan, to Albuquerque, New Mexico, and back to Philadelphia again.

James Madison (23-5) finished first in the ECAC South but were checked in the playoffs despite their best shooting performance of the season. They canned two-thirds of their shots in a 58-57 loss to Old Dominion. Against Virginia they performed better than North Carolina, losing by eight while the Tarheels got hammered by 16 points.

The only other team to beat North Carolina was Wake Forest (20-8). St. Josephs (25-4) brought back memories of their ganglia-tingling upset of DePaul the previous March. Once again the Hawks forced their opponents to accept a slow tempo. But this time the Blue Demons survived an overtime ordeal 46-44. St. Johns (20-8) crumbled three times against Georgetown, by a total of 62 points. They also swooned twice against Villanova but managed to beat them in the Holiday Festival. Northeastern (22-6) lacked height and a challenging schedule.

With ten minutes left in its first round match with James Madison, Ohio State was ahead 42-34 and seemingly in control. But the Dukes rallied for 14 unanswered points, a streak that was interrupted when their center Dan Ruland accidentally tipped the ball through the Buckeyes' hoop. Then the Dukes added three more, giving them in effect 19 straight points. The final score was 55-48 in favor of James Madison. The little-known school, which was playing in only its second NCAA tournament, had claimed Georgetown and Ohio State as first round victims in the past two years. Coach Eldon Miller of the Buckeyes was disgusted. "The second half was as bad a half of basketball as we've had in a long time," he explained. If patterns hold true the result should not have been unexpected. The Buckeyes had lost back-to-back games three times during the season. Since they also lost their finale, this one made a natural pair.

Ahead 60-52 against Old Dominion, Wake Forest swished ten points in a row to dethrone the Monarchs 74-57.

Penn reverted to its annual postseason chill, shooting 35 percent in a lackluster 66-56 loss to St. Johns.

The co-feature was a contrast in execution and level of intensity. St. Josephs was back to its old tricks, this time against Northeastern. Ahead 36-35 at the break they were enjoying a balmy—for them—58-52 lead when Northeastern struck for nine straight points, six off the hot hand of Perry Moss. The shorter Huskies were outrebounding their opponents by a wide margin. They had almost been crippled before the first minute of the game had elapsed, though. Moss, the eighth highest scorer in the country, who averaged more than twice as many points as the next best scorer on the Huskies, had picked up two personals in the first 51 seconds. The prospect of losing his ace threw Coach James Calhoun into a fit.

A short pop by Tony Costner at 3:51 sliced Northeastern's lead to one. The Huskies went into a semistall spread and did not take a shot for the next two minutes. When they did, Moss' jumper missed but so did Bryan Warrick's of the Hawks. A pair of free throws restored Northeastern's three point edge. Warrick missed again with 24 seconds to go but connected 12 seconds later with a 15 footer. St. Josephs got one last opportunity when their alert, swarming defense frustrated Erick Jefferson, who was unable to put the ball in play in the allotted time. A last second shot by Warrick went wide and Northeasterm advanced 63-62. Moss had 24 points, his season's average, as did Lonnie McFarlan of St. Josephs.

All four second round contests went down to the final buzzer—three were decided by a total of four points and the fourth went into a third overtime. The fans in Charlotte and Uniondale, N.Y., were delighted as were the top seeds—all four of whom survived, but barely.

James Madison, an extremely disciplined squad rapidly acquiring a reputation as a giant killer, refused to panic when North Carolina pulled into a 37-30 lead three and a half minutes into the second half. The Dukes had enjoyed a five point lead but that had long since evaporated. Now they marshalled their forces and with 1:38 remaining they had rallied to within a point of the Tarheels. Smith decided to use discretion and went to his tried-and-true four corners. Black noticed Worthy cutting back door and hit him with a perfect pass which the All American converted into a three point play. Seconds later Charles Fisher drove for the hoop and collided with Worthy who had arrived a split second earlier to establish position. The offensive foul gave Worthy two tries from the line and he converted both. There were only 34 seconds left but the six point lead was barely enough. James Madison added four more points to make the final score 52-50. Worthy expressed the respect of his teammates for the Dukes when he said after the game, "It's tougher playing a team that's disciplined than a team that has a lot of talent." James Madison outrebounded and outshot the top seeded Tarheels from the floor and from the line. For once Smith was unable to count on a single point from his bench.

Keith Lee hardly seemed to be present in the early going against Wake Forest. The Memphis State rookie had attempted only three shots in the first period. Not until the Deacons pulled ahead by seven did the Tigers come alive. Then with Lee spearheading the attack, they tied the count at 47 midway through the second half. Two minutes later the score was still deadlocked at 51-51 when Memphis State went into a delay offense—a very popular tactic among coaches that year but extremely frustrating to fans who voiced their anger vociferously. Halfway to the buzzer the Tigers risked a shot and Lee rebounded home a two pointer. Another Lee bucket and a free throw gave Memphis State a five point edge. Wake Forest came within a point but Danny Young's 35 footer clanged off the rim at the buzzer, preserving Memphis State's 56-55 victory.

Sunday afternoon Alabama corked St. Johns 69-68. Mike Davis of the winners missed a free throw with 15 seconds to go and his team ahead by a point, giving St. Johns a final chance. The Redmen, who had squandered their last time out, were forced to improvise. First Billy Goodwin missed an 18 foot baseline jumper. Controlling the rebound, Kevin Williams zeroed in from the lane in a futile attempt to beat the buzzer.

Even closer was the Villanova-Northeastern encounter. It was a remake of Northeastern's epic struggle in the first round. Once again it was a confrontation between a Philadelphia and a Boston school taking place in New York. (Given their success against Beantowners—they had beaten Boston College three times during the season—prospects looked good for Villanova.) Again Northeastern outrebounded their taller adversaries, this time by a huge 45-30 margin. Once more Moss played on the sliver edge of disqualification when he collected his fourth personal with nine minutes left in the game. And then, too, the Huskies were faced with coming back from a halftime deficit just as they had against St. Josephs. This one, though, was considerably more difficult, coming against a team that had finished first in the Big East. Besides, the Wildcats seemed to be benefiting from the referee's calls. They went to the line 23 times after intermission while the Huskies made only three appearances. When Moss picked up his fourth foul they trailed by eight and it looked like the curtain was about to fall on their season. But, in a well executed comeback, Northeastern's mustang-quickness neutralized Villanova's plowhorse strength and height.

With 16 seconds left in regulation Jefferson's medium range jumper finally brought Northeastern even at 56-56. The clock wound down to double zero without a change in the score. In the first overtime the Huskies had a chance to win the biggest game in their history when Dave Leitao penetrated to within six feet of the basket at the five second mark but missed. His follow up tipin likewise bounced away. That left the teams tied at 58. Now it was the second overtime. With Villanova ahead 64-61 Ed Pinckney stepped to the line with a chance to clinch the game. He made the first but missed the second. Still there were only 23 seconds to go and the lights were beginning to dim for Northeastern. But the Huskies had come too far to roll over. They still had Moss and one more miracle to invoke. The senior guard drove in for a layup at :09 to bring his team within two. They wasted no time fouling Pickney two seconds later. The freshman, with another chance to put the game away, blew his first attempt from the line. Whippet quick, Moss flew downcourt but his last second shot fell off the target. Luckily Jefferson was in the right place and tipped in the rebound at the horn.

Later Jefferson described the jubilation in the Huskies' huddle before the start of the third overtime. "We thought destiny was in our hands, or fate, or whatever. We had it." They did for another couple of minutes but then the bubble burst; the impossible dream became just that, and power and reason elbowed aside daring and hope. Midway through the third overtime Pinckney, frustrated by missed free throws, stuffed a rebound off an errant shot to give Villanova a 71-70 lead. Shortly thereafter the longest tournament game since UCLA beat Dayton in 1974 came to an end with Villanova on top 76-72. Moss finished his career with a 31 point performance, 12 of those coming after he picked up his fourth personal.

The action moved to Raleigh which North Carolina found just as friendly as Charlotte. Alabama was in foul trouble almost from the start, trying to contain the powerful Tarheel front court. Both of the Crimson Tide's forwards and their center fouled out. Although Alabama never led, they were within a basket with 12 minutes remaining when six points by Worthy and four by Perkins triggered a 10-2 surge to move North Carolina out of danger. The 74-69 final score made the game seem closer than it was. Once again Smith stayed with his starters through most of the game. The substitutes contributed just two points.

Pinckney and Lee, a pair of well-matched freshman centers, were the focus of attention as Villanova and Memphis State squared off in the other regional semifinal. Though Lee had received more press recognition, Pinckney had no trouble holding his own, especially on defense. He blocked six shots, stole the ball twice and checked in with some crucial points. Lee, on the other hand, was victimized by the referee's whistle. He spent the major part of the second half on the bench, the first time after picking up his fourth personal and the second after fouling out. While he was playing he held the Tiger offense together. Lee returned for the last time at 7:31 with Villanova nursing a 54-53 lead. He scored the next two Tiger baskets but fouled out on a play that a more experienced player might have avoided. Pinone drove for the hoop with Lee in front of him like a human cowcatcher. Arriving under the basket Lee leaped a split second before Pinone, leaning into him and so drawing his fifth personal.

Still the Tigers' prospects looked good when Bobby Parks arced two free throws through the net to give them a 61-58 advantage with a little more than a minute left in the game. Pinckney's field goal narrowed the gap but Otis Jackson's first of a one-and-one made the score 62-60 at the 47 second mark. Eighteen seconds later Pinone barreled down the lane and scored when Derrick Phillips, fearing a foul, allowed him an uncontested shot. The Tigers called time out to set up a play for Phillips. But the 6′9″ sophomore became disoriented and failed to pick out the clock in the confusion of lights of an unfamiliar arena. Thinking that the buzzer was about to sound he threw up a wild 30 footer that rattled around the rim and bounced out.

Memphis State was feeling the pressure. Relatively inexperienced with only one senior starter, with their star out of the game, with three dismal seasons before the present one fresh in their memory, they were unprepared for the stress generated by the tournament. They had survived against Wake Forest but Villanova had also survived an even greater test against Northeastern. Now as the Wildcats moved into their second extra period game of the tournament the veteran Pinone took charge with four of his teams eight overtime points. In the end the Wildcats prevailed 70-66. It was their fourth overtime victory of the season against no losses.

The regional final was anticlimatic. Villanova led briefly at the start but it was all North Carolina the rest of the way. The Tarheels were ahead 12-9 when the Wildcats dug their own grave by scoring just one point on their next eight excursions downcourt. In the second half the Tarheels singed the nets with 75 percent shooting, including ten field goals without a miss. It was

Dean Smith's seventh regional victory without a loss. He was still waiting for the grand prize.

Mideast:

Had third ranked Virginia (20-3) not been in the ACC they would probably have finished the season as the number one team in the country. They gained 27 victories in their first 28 games—a five point slip at Chapel Hill was the spoiler—before falling to Maryland in overtime. Then in the ACC final they dropped the rubber match in their set with North Carolina, in the highly criticized, foreshortened delay game. But the Cavaliers were nowhere near as dominant in the last third of the season as they had been earlier. In nine of their final ten games their winning margin had been less than six points. Though Jeff Lamp had graduated, they still had Ralph Sampson, not only an All American but also the Player of the Year.

Seventh ranked Minnesota (22-5) had won the Big Ten, clinching the title in their final game against Ohio State. The Gophers, with 7′3″ Randy Breuer at center, had sunk almost 70 percent of their shots in that encounter.

Indiana (18-9) and Kentucky (22-7), perennial Mideast regional powerhouses, were crippled by the loss of two stars who had been expected to lead them in their assault on another national championship. In a tragic accident Landon Turner, Indiana's hope now that Isiah Thomas had elected to turn professional, was left paralyzed and confined to a wheelchair, never to play basketball again. Without a senior on the squad Knight still fielded a veteran team with national championship experience. The Hoosiers lost only one game at home but suffered a slump in late December when they dropped both contests in the Holiday Festival and then fell to feeble Michigan State and Northwestern following that collapse.

Kentucky's loss was less permanent. Center Sam Bowie was at first thought to be out of action for a few weeks but he sat out the whole season, forcing Joe Hall to make a lot of adjustments. The Wildcats bowed to North Carolina and to six different SEC teams. In their final regular season game they committed 33 turnovers and were squelched 94-78. But against Notre Dame they survived the delay tactics of Digger Phelps to triumph 34-28 in overtime when they holed 13 of their 17 shots. The Wildcats, playing their home games in Rupp Arena, were used to performing before large audiences. It was the small ones they had problems with, losing all three games played before fewer than 10,000 spectators.

There were three teams from Tennessee in the regional. Tennessee (19-9) tied Kentucky for first place in the SEC despite losing three of their last four. Dale Ellis with a 65 percent average was the second best shooter in the country. Middle Tennessee (21-7) was a team which had learned to endure under pressure. They had prevailed in all five overtime games in which they were involved. In the Ohio Valley playoff they had survived the semifinal and final by two points in each instance. Tennessee-Chattanooga (26-3) had won the Southern by a mile—or the equivalent, which in this case happened to be four games.

Southwestern Louisiana (24-7) beat Georgetown in their season opener 70-61, then went on to take the Great Alaska Shootout. This was their first tournament appearance since 1973 when they played under the notorious Beryl Shipley. So heinous were his recruiting crimes that the NCAA saw fit to bar the school from all competition for two season. It all but expunged every mention of the colorful Ragin Cajuns from the NCAA record book.

Alabama-Birmingham (23-5) ran away with 15 of their last 16 games to take first place in the Sunbelt Conference. The lone setback came against DePaul. This was UAB's fourth season of competition and the seniors on the team, most of whom were locally recruited, became part of the university's first graduating class. Oliver Robinson had been the first player to sign a letter of intent in 1978. He figured he could make the team since nobody was ahead of him.

Robert Morris (17-12) not only did not beat any major school, they got hit by some punching bags losing to Stetson, Baltimore and Towson State twice. LIU belted them 112-87 but they picked themselves up and returned the favor in the ECAC playoff. North Carolina State (22-9) was an also ran in the ACC.

Louisville (20-9) had a typical season for the Cardinals, which meant schizophrenic. Most of the time they were a tight, well-disciplined team which, since it had no stars, fed the man with the hot hand. On those occasions they flattened opponents such as Florida State 97-73, Duke 99-61 and St. Louis whom they trounced three times by an average of 29 points. But then the Cardinals suffered their inevitable slump. This time it came at midseason when they dropped five of six. It included a four game losing streak, their longest since 1965. Still, six of the losses came against teams in the top ten and as usual Crum had his team rolling at the end of the season when it mattered most. They captured eight of their last nine.

Indiana continued where it had left off the previous year by trouncing Robert Morris 94-62 in the first round. The Hoosiers were actually more merciful than the score indicated. Ahead 48-24 at the half they were up 83-38 before clearing the bench and allowing the Colonials to make the score respectable.

A jittery Middle Tennessee watched Kentucky charge in front 8-0 after three minutes. Five turnovers and a blocked shot had the fans anticipating another blowout, but the Blue Raiders settled down and caught the Wildcats at 16-16. Three minutes before half time, Jerry Becks' three point play gave Middle Tennessee a 28-26 advantage. They never trailed again. With twelve and a half minutes left in the game and nursing a 44-40 edge, the Raiders opted for what was becoming increasingly popular—a delay. The score remained unchanged for the next seven minutes until a Kentucky basket cut the difference in half. But that was it for the Wildcats as they went down to defeat 50-44. The Raider defense was superb, only seven personals were charged to them. Meanwhile not a single Kentucky player reached double figures.

Two more schools from the Volunteer State advanced the following night. After a close first period during which the lead changed hands seven times and the score was tied a dozen times, Tennessee pulled out a close one over Southwestern Louisiana 61-57. The Volunteers assured themselves of victory when Michael Brooks sank six straight free throws in the final minute.

North Carolina State scored more points in the last seven minutes of their game with Tennessee-Chattanooga than they did in the first 33. The Wolfpack missed their first six shots and did not get on the scoreboard until almost five minutes had elapsed. By half time they had managed a total of 13 points on frigid 32 percent shooting. With a little more than seven minutes left in the game the Wolfpack were still icebound on the trailing end of a 44-24 score. They thawed rapidly thereafter but it was too late as the Moccasins claimed a 58-51 decision. The victors' final 14 points came from the line.

Almost everyone had been looking forward to a Louisville—Kentucky clash in the second round but that was before Middle Tennessee had dumped Kentucky two days earlier. It would have been their first meeting since 1959. Instead the spectators watched a rather dull contest which the Cardinals won in a landslide 81-56. The Blue Raiders were drained emotionally after their upset of Kentucky. They did not seem to have their minds on the game and committed 26 turnovers.

By contrast Alabama-Birmingham was concentrating very well on the task at hand, namely beating Indiana. The senior-dominated squad was out to revenge last year's defeat and they showed little mercy. Storming into a 26-7 lead, UAB maintained a 20 point advantage almost throughout the first half. A late Indiana rally made the score UAB 80, Indiana 70.

Early in the season Virginia had been unstoppable. Now they were struggling in every game. Against Tennessee they were down by seven as they lined up to start the second half. Sampson's stuff had evened the score at 14 early in the contest. But then the Volunteers ran off ten points in a row in a two and a half minute span.

The opening minutes of the second half gave no relief to the Cavaliers. Tennessee forged ahead by ten and looked firmly in control. But then the Volunteer offense ground to a halt. For the next eight minutes all they were able to generate were two free throws while their opponents leapfrogged into a 43-40 lead. (In an identical situation the previous year, Tennessee had hit a second half scoring drought against Virginia which had lasted a little more than eight minutes and cost them the lead and the game.) The Volunteers regrouped and forged in front once more 51-47, but Virginia drew even on a pair of buckets by Sampson. There were two minutes left. Tennessee, with the ball, tried to draw a foul without shooting. Twice they went to the line but Brooks and Dan Federman both missed the first of one-and-one opportunities. Later Coach Don DeVoe uncharitably claimed his players had "choked at the line." If true, they were not the only ones. The Cavaliers had missed 13 of 18 from the line when Ricky Stokes stepped up with 15 seconds left and sank a pair to give Virginia a 54-51 victory. Both sides were tight in free throw situations—only 15 of 39 attempts went through the hoop.

Tennessee-Chattanooga also enjoyed a half time lead against Minnesota but it, too, evaporated in the final seconds. The Moccasins' Willie White was superb in the first 20 minutes with 18 points. He missed only two shots. Meanwhile, at the other end, Randy Breuer did not see very much of the ball. "The four guys playing with him forgot he was there," complained Jim Dutcher. The Gopher coach rectified that situation in the locker room and his teammates began running plays for their center in the second half. Dutcher also adjusted defensive assignments so White was able to take only two shots after the intermission. Still, he finished with 22 points on 11 for 13 shooting.

Breuer's layup off a missed tip just inside the one minute mark gave Minnesota a 62-61 lead. The Moccasins held for the final shot but Russ Schoene blew an easy layup with four seconds to go. They fouled immediately and were rewarded with a last chance when Gary Holmes missed the first in a bonus situation. But Holmes quickly redeemed himself when he intercepted UTC's subsequent inbounds pass.

As a result of the doubleheader, the last two Tennessee schools were eliminated. Both teams were faced with the almost impossible task of containing overpowering centers—and both almost pulled it off. Willie Burton of Tennessee gave away nine inches to Sampson and fouled out without scoring a point. Stanley Lawrence of UTC gave away seven inches to Breuer and also fouled out, with two points to his credit.

The following week the two tallest centers in the major college basketball ranks had considerably less success. Louisville neutralized Breuer while Lancaster Gordon, who had averaged ten points a game in the regular season, went on a rampage scoring 17 in the second half. The score was tied 48-48 when two baskets by Gordon propelled the Cardinals into the lead they never lost on the way to a 67-61 triumph over Minnesota.

For once it was Virginia's opponent that had to rally in the second half. But UAB stayed close and overhauled the Cavaliers midway through the second period when Robinson's three point play tied the score at 50-50 and his next rainbow gave the Blazers the lead. When Donnie Speers' three point play moved UAB in front, 55-52, they went into the ever popular delay. Virginia was forced to foul, giving their opponents 18 attempts from the stripe in the last seven minutes. The Blazers made their final 14 via free throws.

The Cavaliers' downfall was a result of their inability to get the ball to Sampson. UAB defended so well that Virginia's repeated attempts at passing to their center backfired, causing 18 turnovers. The final score favored the Blazers 68-66.

The regional final pitted two excellent coaches, Bartow and Crum, both with UCLA connections. It was an extremely physical game with the Blazers trying to wear down the quicker Cardinals. Elbows slashed, shoulders bashed and bodies clashed, yet Louisville refused to be intimidated. Derek Smith, who had to have six stitches after the Minnesota game, was hit in the jaw while attempting to block a shot. He went to the bench rather groggily, but a few minutes later he returned only to be felled with another blow to the mouth in a scramble for a loose ball. In the end it was UAB that ran out of steam. They played with essentially a six-man squad while Louisville's bench was much stronger. Statistically Louisville's reserves outscored their equivalents 31 to 6. Besides, they had experience on their side, too. Four starters had been on the team that had won the national championship in 1980.

With 3:28 left in the first half, UAB was nursing a one point lead when Louisville erupted for 11 straight points, including six by Smith. The fresher Cardinals, with one of the finest transition games in the sport, were streaking downcourt on every change of possession. UAB without a tall center was an ideal opponent for them. Still the Blazers regained the lead in the second half and were ahead 54-52 when Charles Jones layed one in off the glass to equalize. This was followed by a pair of dunks, one by Rodney McCray, the second by Jones. The exhausted Blazers were through. Louisville scored their last ten from the line to advance to the Final Four 75-68.

Midwest:

Although DePaul (26-1) had the best record in the country they were only ranked number two in the season's final poll, the first time in three years the Blue Demons had dropped out of the top spot. The reason for the demotion was their lackadaisical play against weak opponents. It was an old story. DePaul played to the level of their opponents. The schedule was not all that demanding which might have been the problem. When challenged they played well, otherwise they lost interest. They barely overcame Marquette, Evansville, Furman, all one point victories. They allowed St. Josephs, against whom they certainly had strong incentive, to dictate the tempo as they had in the first round the previous year, before beating them in overtime. However, DePaul's only setback had been against UCLA in their fifth game and they had won their last 22.

Mark Aguirre, picked number one in the draft, had left to join the Dallas Mavericks. The team leadership fell to All American Terry Cummings, who some felt should have received the Player of the Year award rather than Sampson. Cummings, a serious, born-again-Christian, was a natural leader. But these qualities had been hidden during the two years he played in the shadow of the flamboyant Aguirre.

Fifth ranked Missouri (26-3) was the first school in 48 years to win a Big Eight championship three years in a row. After winning their first 20 they had been badly deflated at home by Nebraska in a 16 point paddling. Then, with the season almost over, they had stumbled twice more, against Georgetown and Kansas State. All the Tigers' starters were excellent sharpshooters from the line and Ricky Frazier had once sunk 16 straight free throws against Louisville.

Tulsa (24-5) had finished second in the MVC after winning the NIT the previous year. Their record was deceptive. Two losses had been by a point and one had come in overtime to Bradley, the winner of the conference. Even more impressive was a game at Chapel Hill in which they had extended number one North Carolina to the limit. In all they had hosted 19 victims, increasing their home court winning streak to 35.

The Hurricane starters were a close knit group and for good reason. When Nolan Richardson III had been offered the coaching job in 1980, he brought with him four players who had helped him win the National Junior College championship at Western Texas J.C. that year. A fifth juco transfer had joined him from the runner-up team in that tournament. The MVC had always been known for its hospitality to junior college transfers. But it had never experienced a whole team instantly created by jucos as happened at Tulsa. Even the women's basketball team had been revitalized since the players brought their girl friends with them. The results were immediate. The Hurricanes had been decaying for years, winning only 35 percent of their games over the last five years, but within two weeks they had beaten national champion Louisville.

Richardson was an all-round athlete. He had played basketball for the Dallas Chaparrals and football for the San Diego Chargers and was also sought by the Houston Astros for his baseball skills. His coaching style was strongly influenced by Don Haskins, for whom he had played at UTEP. Emphasis was placed on quickness and tough defense which triggered the offense. The Hurricanes pressed constantly, thereby creating turnovers which in turn led to fast-paced, high-scoring games. Richardson had the ideal player to make his team click in Paul Pressey, who may have been the quickest forward in college in 1982. Pressey was also a great defensive player, able to guard centers as well as men in the front and backcourt in man-to-man situations. He was used on the point in Richardson's 1-3-1 zone.

But Pressey also had an excellent supporting cast. In their first nine games the Hurricanes produced seven different high scorers. It was a well-balanced team which included five men who averaged double digit scoring. Richardson was looking forward to a third straight national tournament title for himself and his men.

If Kansas State (21-7) had not had to play against teams from Oklahoma they would have had a much better record. They dropped their four games against Oklahoma and Oklahoma State but split a pair of white knucklers with first place Missouri, winning 57-56 on the road and losing by an almost identical score, 59-58, at home.

Houston (21-7) travelled to Seton Hall early in the season where they were shocked by the lowly Pirates. That experience produced three consecutive 100 point games which the Cougars won by an average 45 points. Included in that rampage was a 145-78 massacre of Texas Lutheran during which the winners fattened their statistics by sinking 64 of 94 shots! The Cougars finally cooled off at the midseason when they hibernated during a six game stretch, losing five times. Four starters were from the Houston area. However, the most colorful athlete on the squad was a seven foot reserve center from Nigeria by the name of Akeem Abdul Olajuwon, nicknamed Jellybean.

Veteran coaches like Jack Hartman of Kansas State, Guy Lewis of Houston and Norm Stewart of Missouri were wily schedulers who rarely played on an opponent's court if it could be avoided. Of course conference schedules had to be accommodated and there were Christmas tournaments, normally played on a neutral court. But schools with a marketable team rarely played more than one or two non-conference games in a hostile arena. This helped them considerably to post superior records.

Arkansas (23-5) pummeled their first eight victims, none of any stature, by an average of 21 points before dropping their SWC opener. Later the games got much tighter. The Razorbacks were involved in five one-point decisions and three overtime contests. Three of their losses were by a total of four points. They split a pair with Houston but won the rubber match in the conference playoff final, decisively.

Marquette (22-8) played three consecutive overtime games, losing two by identical 68-65 scores. All their losses were to tournament-bound teams. Evansville (23-5) won the Midwestern City Conference, a remarkable comeback for a school whose entire team and staff had been wiped out in a 1977 airplane disaster. Alcorn State (22-7) played only one team in the top ten, losing to Missouri 82-51. Boston College (19-9) finished fourth in the Big East. There were some, including Dick Versace of Bradley, who felt BC should not have been selected for the tourney. (Versace's Braves had finished first in the MVC but lost to Tulsa in the conference final and were left out.) He hinted that Dave Gavitt, head of the NCAA tournament selection committee, may have been prejudiced since he was also executive director of the Big East. But the Big East was so strong that even a fourth place finish gave the Eagles a respectable record. However, they had lost five in a row at the turn of the year, sinking to a 5-6 record. But they snagged 14 of their next 16 before succumbing to Villanova by three points.

The team with the worst record in the tournament was Northern Illinois (16-13). Before the Mid American conference playoffs they had done no better than split their regular season games. The Huskies played on the thin edge of disaster all season. Half their games were decided by three points or fewer. Their total production for the season was 45 points fewer than their opponents' and they were never able to put together more than three victories in a row. They were also handicapped by an inequitable schedule, playing only two of their first 13 at home. But the Huskies also had a certain stubborn, never quit, streak about them. They won those games they needed to win including four of five overtime contests. The most crucial of these came in the conference playoff. In the first round they eliminated Ohio University 70-68 in overtime. (The Huskies had played OU to a standoff all season. This was the second time they had beaten them 70-68. They had also been edged by Ohio 69-67. Three games with almost identical scores decided by two points.) Next Northern Illinois ousted Bowling Green 67-66 and survived another overtime in the playoff final against Ball State. By then Husky fans had gnawed their fingernails down to the wrist.

The twelfth team in the Midwest regional was San Francisco (25-5). The Dons' biggest problem was keeping their minds on basketball. Often they seemed far removed from the action on the court. They were socked by Notre Dame and Rice, both comparatively frail, and barely edged New Orleans and Colgate on their own court. St. Marys posed a challenge though they should not have. The Dons licked them in double overtime and again by a point. However, they did bear down at crunch time, winning four of five extra period contests including two in double OT. San Francisco's two clashes with Pepperdine harked back to the wild shootouts of yesteryear. It seemed that whenever these two trigger happy teams met, at least one of them scored 100 points. This had happened the last four times and their last meeting was a 106-100 extravaganza.

All American Quintin Dailey, the fifth highest scorer in the country with better than a 25 point average, sparked the Dons' attack. Another attack almost landed him in jail. He was charged with the sexual assault of a woman in a campus dormitory, pleaded guilty to one felony count and received a suspended sentence.*

In the first round Houston bounced Alcorn State 94-84 while Marquette had a somewhat tougher time subduing Evansville 67-62. The Purple Aces, obviously nervous in their first tournament appearance, shot a limp 27 per-

---

*After the conclusion of the season President John LoSchiavo announced that the university was dropping intercollegiate basketball. The sports world was shocked at the expiration of this colorful, exciting and successful (two national titles and a NIT championship program.) The warning signs had been there for years. In 1979 Bob Gaillard had resigned in frustration, unable to cope with the likes of Boynes and Hardy. He had been replaced with Dan Belluomini and the Dons had been put on a year's probation in 1980. Another year's probation was tacked on in 1981 for additional recruiting violations. Belluomini was fired at the end of that season but the school was again under investigation in 1982. The sexual assault charge against Dailey was a criminal matter but not so the accusation, later admitted, that Dailey had accepted $1000 a month from an alumnus for work he did not perform, in other words a violation of NCAA rules. In the final analysis all the chicanery did not bring San Francisco closer to a championship. The players that were recruited by misguided coaches and alumni were marginal students, selfish and demanding on the court as well as off. None of them, except Bill Cartwright the only team player the Dons produced in their last four years, succeeded in the pros. Had they used Phil Woolpert and his 1955 and 1956 championship quintet, the model of an unselfish team, as an example, they would have saved themselves a lot of grief.

cent in the first half. Brad Leaf, their star, had a terrible time locating the hoop and made only one basket in 12 tries. Meanwhile Marquette soared to a 47-34 advantage as Dean Marquardt contributed eight points in the first ten minutes of the second period. But Leaf began to find the range and Evansville closed to within two just inside the five minute mark. That was as close as they got though.

The following evening Kansas State pared North Illinois 77-68 and Boston College trimmed San Francisco 70-66. John Bagley, BC's quarterback, picked up his third personal after only 2:10 of the first period. His coach became so enraged at the referee that he was hit with a technical. The shock energized the Eagles who chased San Francisco off the court in the first 20 minutes though Bagley was never a factor in the game. Quintin Dailey was held to eight first half points but responded with 20 in the second. It was too little, too late. It was also too late for the San Francisco basketball program.

The top four seeded teams survived their initial game in the East, West and Mideast regionals. Not a single upset was recorded. Not so the Midwest regional where some heavyweight teams were about to be deposed.

It was an ideal program for tiger fanciers. Not only were the Tigers of Missouri featured, but both Marquette and Tulsa sported some of the fanciest duds ever seen on a basketball court, with tiger stripes rippling down the sides of their uniforms.

Missouri entered the game with a considerable handicap. Stepanovich was hobbled with a sprained ankle while teammate Marvin McCrary was still recovering from a concussion received less than two weeks earlier in a court collision. Still, the Tigers overcame 18 first half turnovers to establish a modest lead. Marquette pulled to within a point in the second half which prompted Missouri to go into a delay. As a result the Tigers were blanked from the floor in the last eight minutes but sank 13 of 16 from the line. Marquette scored six more baskets than their opponents but committed twice as many fouls trying to separate the ball from the Tigers' paws. The rather tedious contest went to Missouri 73-69.

Tulsa, playing on its home court, was trailing Houston by 14 points after six minutes of the second half. A Hurricane blitz caused the Cougars to run for shelter. Stalling tactics slowed down the force of the rally, but only Rob Williams' eleven straight points at the height of the Tulsa comeback gave the Cougars the impetus to triumph 78-74.

The next afternoon Ed Nealy's five steals helped Kansas State open up a ten point gap over Arkansas midway through the second half. A belated Razorback spurt set the stage for a dramatic finish. With twelve seconds to go the Wildcats were on top 65-64 when reserve guard Ed Galvao stepped to the line with a chance to become a hero. Instead he missed the first of the bonus, giving the Razorbacks a chance to make the biggest steal of the evening. Hastings became Arkansas' last hope as he tossed the ball toward the hoop with only three seconds remaining. "It felt fine," he said later. Unfortunately, when it arrived at its target, it was less than that, bouncing off the rim to the sound of the buzzer.

For the second year in a row DePaul allowed their opponents to set the tempo and suffered the consequences. Against St. Josephs DePaul had been unable to take the initiative from the deliberate Hawks. This year they seemed unprepared for a team that was ready to run with the Blue Demons, a style that should have been much more to their liking. Five DePaul players fouled out including three starters. Cummings managed to stay the distance but he picked up his fourth personal with almost 14 minutes remaining. With so many of his players in foul trouble, Ray Meyer had to rely on unfamiliar combinations which contributed to the 20 turnovers perpetrated by the Blue Demons. Then, too, Boston College's full and three-quarter court pressure harrassed them through most of the game so they were never able to get into their flow.

The Eagles were just too quick for the sluggish Demons. The two shortest men on the court—6′0″ John Bagley and 5′10″ Michael Adams—were able to penetrate consistently, picking up free throw opportunities along the way. Had it not been for their atrocious foul shooting the Eagles would have put the game out of reach much sooner. They made only 7 of 16 in the first half and 24 of 42 for the game. Bagley finished with 26 points while Adams, a freshman reserve who had averaged five points during the regular season, chimed in with 21.

"We didn't deserve to win," said a bitterly disappointed Meyer. "We had to play their tempo." For three years his teams had been seeded number one in their regional and they had not a single victory to show for it. From 1980 to 1982 they had been 79-3 during the regular season but 0-3 in the tournament. Whether it was a lack of character among the players, or fate, or bad matchups, there was something inevitable about this third straight tournament debacle.

In St. Louis the following Friday evening both Big Eight teams were favored to advance to the regional final. But Houston and Boston College had other plans. Normally an excellent free throw shooting team, Missouri could not deliver from the line against Houston. Late in the match the Cougars were ahead 69-57 when they went into a tailspin for the second time in as many games. With victory in sight they started getting fancy, overpassing to each other or taking ill-advised shots. As a result of a squall of turnovers, Missouri crept to within six at 4:25 on two straight Ricky Frazier jump shots. Less than two minutes later Stipanovich's ten footer made the score 73-69 with the Cougars desperately trying to hold on to their shrinking lead. But time was the Tigers' bigger enemy. With six seconds left Frazier reduced the gap to three and his tipin just before the buzzer was too little and too late as Houston celebrated their 79-78 victory. If not for Frazier's 29 points, 22 in the second half, the score would not have been as close. The last of the top four seeds in the regional had been eliminated.

Boston College got considerable mileage from its reserves again in the other regional semifinal. John Garris, with an eight point average, kept the Eagles close with 16 first half points while pesky Michael Adams seemed unable to miss. Still, Kansas State held a five point lead when they walked off the court at the intermission.

However, BC's three-quarter court press began to have its effect as the game wore on. It ground the Wildcats down while the Eagles' quickness and Bagley's potential explosiveness made them wary and tentative. Sensing their opponent's vulnerability, Boston College went to a spread offense with six minutes to go using three quick guards. The turning point occurred at 1:45 when the Eagles, protecting a 61-59 lead, turned the ball over but got it right back when Adams deflected the Kansas State inbounds pass to a teammate. They converted their final eight opportunities from the line to win 69-65. Adams collected 20 points on seven-for-eight shooting.

Both Big Eight schools had been favored but both went down to defeat. The maligned Eagles, considered too weak to be picked for the tournament, were still alive. Of the final eight surviving teams, three were from the Big East, the only conference with more than one team represented.

The regional final was a treat. There was no stalling, no delay tactics. It was just end-to-end offensive basketball, a throwback to the exciting days of the sixties and seventies when teams were less cautious and attacked with speed and daring.

Houston played almost errorless ball for the first 20 minutes, committing just three turnovers. They showed a lot more poise than they had against Tulsa and Missouri. To combat Boston College's press they stationed two men at midcourt to help the dribbler bring the ball across the midline. But though their frontcourt was taller than their opponents' by several inches, they were unable to prevent the Eagles from penetrating with some consistency. Garris again came off the bench to spark the Eagles. This time he scored 19 points, one more than his total against Kansas State.

The tempo did not let up in the second half. At 8:11 of the period the Cougars brought in their own supersub. John Gettys had averaged only seven minutes a game and in the previous 31 contests had made a total of eight free throws in ten attempts. Over the next eight minutes he stepped to the line ten times and snapped the cords each time, more than doubling his free throw production for the year. At 1:35 Adams drove in for a basket that made the score 90-88 in favor of Houston. It was still anybody's ballgame. But when Rich Shrigley missed two free throws and Adams' layup attempt was in and out, the Eagles were done. Houston made their last nine points from the line to advance to the Final Four 99-92. Williams had 25 points for the winners, the fourth time he had reached that total in the tournament.

Final Four:

Unlike the previous two tournaments there had been few surprises aside from the Midwest regional. The four teams gathered in New Orleans had the advantage of experienced and highly respected coaches. Smith was making his seventh appearance in the Final Four in 21 years; Crum his fourth in 11 years; Lewis his third in 26 years. Besides both Smith and Crum had taken teams to the national championship finals in the last two years and many of the players that had performed were still on the teams. John Thompson had never gone this far but his team was at the top of its game. Georgetown had momentum going for it and like Indiana the previous year, had blown away its two most recent opponents.

The largest crowd ever to witness a basketball game in the United States greeted the semifinalists in the Superdome in New Orleans. A total of 61,612 fans cheered two closely contested matches in which the defenses predominated.

Georgetown's defense stifled the Louisville fast break and kept the Cardinals out of their rhythm so they were unable to execute their devastating transition game. So tenacious were the Hoyas, they held their opponents to less than 40 percent shooting from the floor for the twenty-first time in 36 games. But Georgetown was not very active offensively either. They made only six baskets in the second half and none in the final 10:15. After the seven minutes mark they stopped shooting altogether but made 11 free throws the rest of the way. Louisville held a couple of brief leads but mostly it was the Hoyas who were ahead. With 5:50 to go Georgetown enjoyed a nine point advantage. Twice their opponents crept to within three but at the end Thompson's men prevailed 50-46.

Guy Lewis was looking for his five hundredth coaching victory in the other semifinal. His prospect seemed grim for a time. North Carolina, looking as if they might blow Houston right back across the Gulf of Mexico, rushed into a 14-0 lead. Houston took seven shots, all misses, and did not snag a single offensive rebound. Meanwhile the Tarheels swished seven of their first nine shots. But the Cougars regrouped and finally drew even at 29-29 on Larry Micheaux's shot with one and a half minutes left in the first half. The Tarheels tallied the final two points of the period. As they walked off the court they knew it was not going to be easy to trap the Cougars.

It might have been disastrous for North Carolina if Rob Williams had played anywhere near as well as he had in his previous four games. But the junior guard, who was under tight surveillance by Jimmy Black, just could not find the basket. He seemed to be playing on his own personal patch of permafrost and after missing a few times he simply stopped shooting, even though his coach encouraged him to. He became tentative and his whole game disintegrated. He finished the contest with two points and no field goals. William's problem may have been connected to the Superdome. He had played two other poor games there during the Sugar Bowl tournament and had shot a frigid 8-for-33. Bad vibrations.

With seven and a half minutes left the Tarheels were nursing a 52-48 lead when their coach directed them to go to their patented four corners delay. This was greeted by lusty disapproval especially from the Houston cheering section. However unpopular, the tactic was successful and North Carolina expedited the Cougars 68-63. The starters did it all again; the Tarheels got no scoring help from the bench. Though some blamed Houston's defeat on Williams' poor performance, the strain of coming back from a 14 point deficit was an equally valid reason for the outcome.

The final was a classic in almost every sense of the word, one of the most exciting games ever seen anywhere and the closest national championship contest in almost 20 years. It was a dream matchup: the ACC versus the Big East; the two most powerful conferences of the year and liable to be so for some years to come; the establishment versus the new organization built on the vision of a rebirth of basketball in the cradle of the city game.

And the coaches. A contrast and yet a reinforcement of all that was good and right and refreshing about the sport. On one side 5′10″ Dean Smith in his fourth championship game, a quiet but intense genius who kept his deep emotions hidden behind a benign appearance. On the other side John Thompson, a foot taller, in his first championship game, sitting in the middle of the bench with his players on either side of him, outspoken, proud, domineering. These two shared a great respect and friendship for each other and often consulted during the offseason. And they always kept their responsibilities in perspective. Almost everyone who had played for Smith had an academic degree to show for it. He had even discontinued the practice of accepting junior college transfers to Chapel Hill. Thompson's integrity and dedication to learning was equally strong. He had hired an academic counsellor to help his players with their classes. As a result only one of his players during his tenure at Georgetown failed to graduate.

From the first second the game had the intensity usually found in the last minute of overtime. Ewing made his presence felt early. He was called for goaltending five times in the first half—the first four in the opening minutes accounting for North Carolina's initial eight points. Not until more than eight minutes had elapsed did they score points resulting from their own effort. Ewing's intensity was so palpable that when he stood at the line for a free throw, stroking the ball in his massive hands and glaring at the net before firing, it almost seemed as if he was directing it through the hoop by sheer will power.

The Hoyas led by a point at the break despite being outrebounded by the shorter Tarheels, led by Worthy, who had 16 of his side's first 22 points.* The

*It was the first time in the tournament that one of the Tarheels had taken charge. In the first four games the scoring had been evenly distributed. Smith, who in previous years played his whole squad, stuck to his starters and his bench contributed just seven points in the five tournament games.

sides then battled on even terms for most of the second half. Ewing and Floyd divided the first 17 points of the period for Georgetown. Ahead 57-56 with 5:50 to go Smith went to his four corners, a move that was again vociferously booed by most of the more than 61,000 fans in the arena. Smith had used the same tactic in the 1977 final against Marquette and the move had backfired. It almost cost him the championship again. Many of the Tarheel supporters were apprehensive but coaches are anything if not consistent. Coaching in their comfort zone they call it.

Ewing picked up his fourth personal at 5:32 and Black's two free throws made it 59-56. Georgetown moved back to within a point but two more minutes had run off the clock when Jordan's driving basket gave North Carolina a 61-58 lead. A minute later Ewing's twelve foot jumper closed the gap once more. It was his twenty-third point, equalling his season's high score. The Tarheels continued in their four corners, trying to protect their precarious lead. With 1:19 to go Floyd stole the ball but fouled Doherty in the process. However, the Tarheel forward flubbed his chance at the line and Ewing grabbed the rebound. There were 57 seconds remaining when Floyd floated a twelve footer through the hoop to give his team a 62-61 edge.

The Tarheels looked for an opening and not finding one, called for a time out. Back on the court they passed the ball around until Jordan holed a 16 foot jump shot to make it 63-62. There were 15 seconds showing on the clock. The Hoyas inbounded the ball, trying to beat their opponents downcourt, hoping to catch them before they set their defense. And indeed Worthy was far out of position trailing the play. Fred Brown, dribbling in the backcourt and challenged by a Tarheel, saw from the corner of his eye what he thought was Floyd running alongside with a clear track down the sideline. He passed the ball and no sooner did it leave his hand than he wished he could have it back. It was a moment that would haunt him for years. He had thrown the ball right at Worthy, who was trailing the play. The All American took off in the opposite direction to drop in the clincher. He missed but was fouled in the act of shooting. As if there had not been excitement enough, Worthy prolonged the tension by missing both free throws. But there was not enough time for Georgetown to score and Dean Smith finally had his first national championship.

Despite missing the last two free throws, Worthy scored 28 points on 13-for-17 shooting. He was voted the tournament's MVP. When asked where they were going after the game, one of the Tarheels shouted "Crazy!" The players cut the net down in the traditional ceremony, reserving one or two strands for their coach. The boisterous Tarheel fans streamed out of the Superdome waving their blue and white pompoms ready to celebrate from one end of Bourbon Street to the other.

Another NCAA basketball tournament was over. It had come a long way since 1939 when Oregon whipped Ohio State in a small gymnasium in Evanston before a sparse crowd of enthusiasts. (Total attendance at all sites over the first **four** years of the tournament were about equal to the numbers at the Superdome.) Yet a sure chain linked this latest championship to all those that preceded it. Along that chain were strung the winners—the Cinderella teams and the Walton Gang, the Fabulous Five and the Fiddlin' Five, the Miracle Miners and the Deadeye Buckeyes. For so many players to be crowned national champions was the greatest moment of their lives. Because as long as they lived they would know that for that one glorious night **They Were Number One**.

APPENDIX

Setting the National Championship Bracket

Before the NCAA Division I Men's Basketball Committee began its seeding and placement process, it established several guidelines it would attempt to follow in creating an equitable bracket with four balanced regions. The following principles were used:

1. The committee established 12 levels that ran across each of the four regions. This permitted the group to evaluate four teams simultaneously on the same level, establishing four institutions to be considered as numerical seeds on an equal level rather than predetermining from the true seed format the No. 1 seed would be in one region, the No. 2 in another, etc. The committee determined the four highest seeds would be DePaul (26-1), Louisiana State (28-3), Oregon State (26-1) and Virginia (25-3). None of these institutions was considered the top seed in the tournament.
2. The committee divided each region into three section with four levels in each. This step permitted the committee to evaluate three different tiers within each region against the complementing tiers in every other region in its attempt to create balance.
3. The committee was not interested in replaying conference schedules or tournaments. It determined a conference could have only one repre-

sentative in each of the three sections within a region. For example, the Southeastern Conference could not have a team seeded No. 2, No. 3 or No. 4 in the same region with LSU, the No. 1 seed, but it could have a representative seeded No. 5 in it.

4. After the preceding points had been addressed, the committee considered the geographic relationship alignments which arbitrarily placed conference champions in a designated region. When a team was moved from its natural region, however, the committee would make every attempt to place it in the next closest region. Utilizing LSU again as the example, the Southeastern Conference champion traditionally has been placed in the Mideast region. But the committee placed the Tigers in the Midwest region for two reasons. First, the travel distance to Austin, Texas, was shorter than to the nearest Mideast site, and secondly, New Orleans was the site of that regional championship.
5. The committee also elected to permit institutions hosting tournament competition to play at home if the preceding principles were not compromised.

With these thoughts in mind, let's review the seeding and placement of teams for a portion of the 1981 tournament bracket.

As indicated in Principle No. 1, DePaul, LSU, Oregon State and Virginia were placed on level one. Each of these institutions could easily be placed in the four regions. Virginia and Oregon State were obvious for the east and west regions respectively, LSU was placed in the midwest, and DePaul was left in the mideast.

	East	Mideast	Midwest	West
1.	Virginia	DePaul	LSU	Oregon State

Level No. 2 included Arizona State, Kentucky, Notre Dame and North Carolina. Arizona State and North Carolina were excluded from their natural regions because Principle No. 3 prevented placing a second Pac-10 team and ACC team in a designated section within a region with another team from these conferences. Oregon State and Virginia, you will recall, were Level No. 1 teams in the West and East respectively. Kentucky was placed in the Mideast, its natural region. Arizona State could not stay in the West; the next closest region was the Midwest. North Carolina could not be placed in the East (Virginia), Mideast (Kentucky) or the Midwest (Arizona State). The only place available, therefore, was the West region. This left Level No. 2 in the East region for Notre Dame.

	East	Mideast	Midwest	West
1.	Virginia	DePaul	LSU	Oregon State
2.	Notre Dame	Kentucky	Arizona State	North Carolina

Teams placed on Level No. 3 were Indiana, Iowa, UCLA and Utah. The Midwest and West regions were scheduled at Indiana and Utah respectively. Since no other Big 10 or WAC teams were placed on Levels No. 1 or No. 2 in either of these regions, Indiana and Utah were granted the opportunity to play at home if they survived first- and second-round competition. The West (Oregon State), Midwest (Arizona State) and Mideast (Indiana) were not available to UCLA, and although the Bruins were hosting competition, the only berth available on Level No. 3 was in the East region. Iowa was placed in the remaining Midwest berth.

	East	Mideast	Midwest	West
1.	Virginia	DePaul	LSU	Oregon State
2.	Notre Dame	Kentucky	Arizona State	North Carolina
3.	UCLA	Indiana	Iowa	Utah

The final level in the upper tier of each region was completed by the selection of Illinois, Louisville, Tennessee and Wake Forest. Illinois could not be placed in the Mideast (Indiana) or Midwest (Iowa). Tennessee could not be placed in the Mideast (Kentucky) or Midwest (LSU). Wake Forest could not be placed in the East (Virginia) or West (North Carolina). The committee, therefore, placed Tennessee in the East and Wake Forest in the Mideast; each was moved only one region and geographically close to competition sites. Louisville was placed in the Midwest, the natural region for the Metro-7 Conference, and the only berth available for Illinois was the West.

	East	Mideast	Midwest	West
1.	Virginia	DePaul	LSU	Oregon State
2.	Notre Dame	Kentucky	Arizona State	North Carolina
3.	UCLA	Indiana	Iowa	Utah
4.	Tennessee	Wake Forest	Louisville	Illinois

With the first section of four levels in each region completed, the committee approached the second section of four by following the same principles. Wyoming was a Level No. 5 team, and it could be placed in the West since Utah, a WAC representative, was in the first section of four. A third conference team could not be placed in the middle section of four levels in the West, and Brigham Young, placed on the sixth level, was moved to the East region.

After the second section for four levels was completed, the committee began seeding and placing teams in the final section of four. Here is the complete bracket for the 1981 tournament:

East

1. Virginia
2. Notre Dame
3. UCLA
4. Tennessee

5. *Virginia Commonwealth
6. Brigham Young
7. Georgetown
8. Houston

9. Villanova
10. *James Madison
11. *Pennsylvania
12. *Long Island

Mideast

1. DePaul
2. Kentucky
3. *Indiana
4. Wake Forest

5. Boston College
6. Maryland
7. Alabama-Birmingham
8. *Creighton

9. *St. Joseph's
10. *Western Kentucky
11. *Tennessee-Chattanooga
12. *Ball State

Midwest

1. Louisiana State
2. Arizona State
3. Iowa
4. *Louisville

5. *Arkansas
6. Wichita State
7. *Kansas
8. *Lamar

9. Missouri
10. *Mississippi
11. *Southern-Baton Rouge
12. *Mercer

West

1. *Oregon State
2. *North Carolina
3. *Utah
4. Illinois

5. Wyoming
6. *Fresno State
7. *Idaho
8. Kansas State

9. *San Francisco
10. *Pittsburgh
11. *Northeastern
12. *Howard

*Automatic Qualifier

As indicated the committee could keep equity and balance continually in focus by dividing each region into levels and sections and adhering to the principles it had established. Once these principles are understood, it is obvious why teams were placed in specific regions. The seeding and placement of teams was not an unorganized dart-throwing process.

ACKNOWLEDGEMENTS

I am very grateful to the many people who helped me to complete this book. I would like to thank Jim Van Valkenburg of the NCAA who provided me with all the statistics and background material I could possibly use; Helen Kerlin who typed the manuscript; Nancy Welts who set up many interviews; Rudy and Denise Fernandez who were gracious hosts when I attended the Final Four; Steve Wacker who helped me with the research; and all the coaches and players who gave of their time to provide first hand recollection of their tournament experience. In particular I would like to thank Tessa Kendall who provided the love and encouragement which made this book possible.